MW01621141

STATES OF CULTIVATION

STANFORD **OTTOMAN WORLD** SERIES

STATES *of* CULTIVATION

IMPERIAL TRANSITION AND SCIENTIFIC AGRICULTURE IN THE EASTERN MEDITERRANEAN

Elizabeth R. Williams

STANFORD UNIVERSITY PRESS
Stanford, California

Stanford University Press
Stanford, California

Printed in the United States of America on acid-free, archival-quality paper
Library of Congress Cataloging-in-Publication Data
Names: Williams, Elizabeth R. (Elizabeth Rachel), author.
Title: States of cultivation : imperial transition and scientific agriculture in the eastern Mediterranean / Elizabeth R. Williams.
Other titles: Stanford Ottoman world series.
Description: Stanford, California : Stanford University Press, 2023. | Series: Stanford Ottoman world series | Includes bibliographical references and index.
Identifiers: LCCN 2022043708 (print) | LCCN 2022043709 (ebook) | ISBN 9781503634688 (cloth) | ISBN 9781503635937 (ebook)
Subjects: LCSH: Agriculture and state—Syria—History—20th century. | Agriculture and state—Lebanon—History—20th century. | Agricultural innovations—Syria—History—20th century. | Agricultural innovations—Lebanon—History—20th century. | Imperialism and science—Syria—History—20th century. | Imperialism and science—Lebanon—History—20th century. | Syria—History—French occupation, 1918-1946. | Lebanon—History—French occupation, 1918-1946.
Classification: LCC HD2057.5.Z8 W54 2023 (print) | LCC HD2057.5.Z8 (ebook) | DDC 338.1/85691—dc23/eng/20230327
LC record available at https://lccn.loc.gov/2022043708
LC ebook record available at https://lccn.loc.gov/2022043709

Cover design: Michele Wetherbee
Cover image: *The Botanical Regions of Syria*, from George Post, *Nabāt Sūrīyah wa-Filasṭīn wa-al-quṭr al-Miṣrī wa-bawādīhā* (Beirut, 1884). Source: Hathitrust.
Typeset by Charles Elliott Beard and Newgen in Gentium Book Plus Regular 10/14.25

To my parents, Alan and Blanche Williams

CONTENTS

List of Illustrations ix

Note on Transliteration xi

Maps xii

Introduction 1

1 **Provincial Legibility and Ecologies of Extraction** 22
Agrarian Networks and the Making of
Late Ottoman Rural State Space

2 **"Agriculture from a Book"** 74
"Scientific" Agriculture in the Ottoman Eastern Mediterranean

3 **The Trials and Tribulations of Tractors** 117
From Ottoman Provinces to French Mandate States

4 **The Politics of Agricultural Expertise and Education** 162
Exerting Rural Influence Under the French Mandate

5 **Of Mice, Sunn Bugs, Drought, and Taxation** 207
The Pests of Mandate Rural Administration
and the Crisis of the 1930s

Epilogue 264

Acknowledgments 279

Notes 283

Bibliography 379

Index 407

ILLUSTRATIONS

Figures

1 Aleppo Province, c. 1890s xii

2 District of Zor, c. 1890s xiii

3 Provinces of Syria and Beirut and the districts of Mount Lebanon and Jerusalem in 1896 xiv

4 Detail from a chart of agricultural statistics with accompanying map compiled by the Agriculture and Commerce Ministry, c. 1913–1914 xv

5 The mandate states of Syria and Lebanon, c. 1936 xvi

6 An 1884 rendering of "The Botanical Regions of Syria" 10

7 "Double waterwheel" on the ʿAsi River in Hama 11

8 Ottoman agricultural statistics with map compiled by the Agriculture and Commerce Ministry, c. 1913–1914 64

9 "Bee-hive homes" with threshing sledge in Muslimiya 85

10 Halkalı Agricultural School, Istanbul 88

11 "Derʿâh Getreidedreschen mit dem Dreschschittlitten, 1906" (Derʿa [in the Hawran] grain threshing with threshing sledge, 1906) 100

12 Established and planned agricultural institutions in the Ottoman Empire, c. 1911 103

13 The machinery of scientific agriculture 109

14 "Camels loaded with sheaves near Baʿalbak [in the Biqaʿ Valley]" 113

15 "Map of Syria: Syria within its natural boundaries," as envisioned by Faysal's government 133
16 French map from the 1860–1861 Syria Expedition 137
17 "La Syrie intégrale," as envisioned by supporters of French expansion into the eastern Mediterranean 141
18 Students from the Salamiya agricultural school in a cotton field, c. 1920s 180
19 Centre Agricole de Bouka, 1929 195
20 "Threshing floor in Syria" 214
21 A farmer feeds his crops to a ravenous dog representing "taxes and the tithe" 225
22 An aerial view of the village of Kusayr and surrounding farmland 227
23 Map of Sunn bug spread from 1924 to 1926 sent to the League of Nations 229
24 A baby lamb labeled "Syrian Agriculture" confronts a ferocious lion labeled "Usurers [interest]." 232
25 Petition from Hama cultivators protesting tax collection, 1935 256

Table

1 Statistics for Agricultural High Schools and Practical Schools in the Ottoman Empire, 1913/1914 76

NOTE ON TRANSLITERATION

This book draws from sources in multiple languages, some of which require transliteration, namely, Arabic and Ottoman Turkish. Deciding how to transliterate terms that appear in multiple languages over the course of the book while also ensuring some kind of continuity for the reader has proven a challenge. In general, for words that have common spellings in English, I have used those. Occasionally, I have opted to transliterate a less commonly used word based on the primary origin of the source material for a particular section. Thus in the chapters covering the Ottoman period, the name of the agricultural school in Syria appears as Selimiye, which is transliterated from Ottoman Turkish into modern Turkish. In later chapters dealing with the mandate, I render it Salamiya, reflecting its transliteration from Arabic. Transliterations from Ottoman use the convention of modern Turkish and transliterations from Arabic follow the style of the *International Journal of Middle East Studies* without diacritics.

Most Ottoman documents include dates in two forms, *Hicri*, based on the Islamic lunar calendar, and *Rumi*, based on the Ottoman solar calendar. Throughout the manuscript I have included the *Rumi* date along with the Gregorian (*Miladi*) date in brackets. The only exceptions are when a document included only a *Hicri* date or when the *Rumi* date was illegible; in those cases I have converted from the *Hicri* date. Until 1918, the *Rumi* year started in March and ended in February. When a document's date is the *Rumi* year (e.g., 1329), I include the two Gregorian years covered by that year (e.g., from mid-March 1913 to mid-March 1914) separated by a dash, e.g., 1329 [1913/1914]. For the conversion of dates, I used https://www.ttk.gov.tr/tarih-cevirme-kilavuzu/.

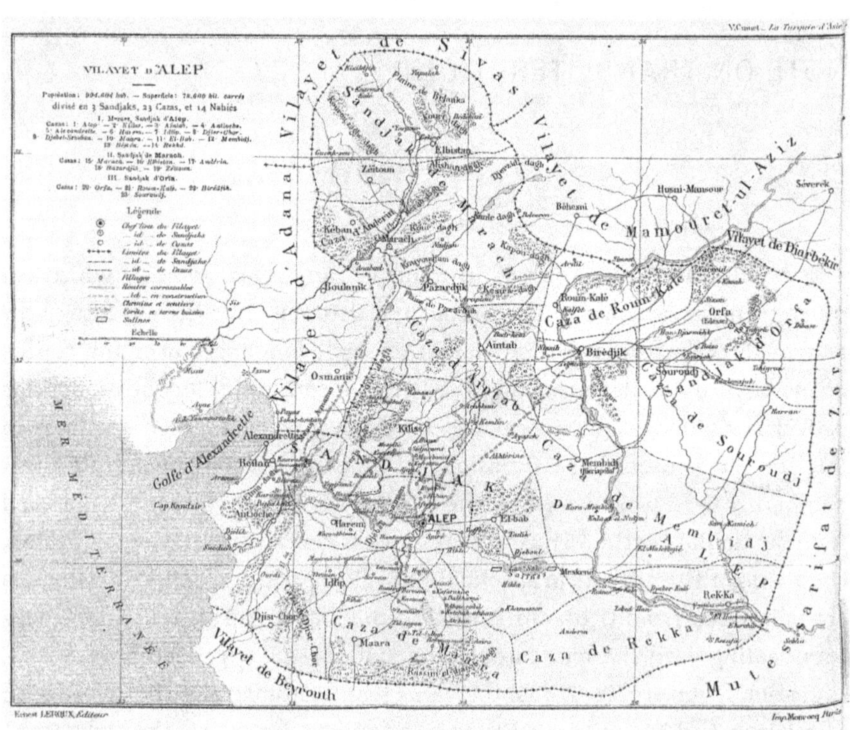

FIGURE 1. Map of Aleppo Province, c. 1890s, from Vital Cuinet, *La Turquie d'Asie, géographie administrative: statistique, descriptive et raisonnée de chaque province de l'Asie Mineure*, vol. 2 (Paris: E. Leroux, 1891–1894). Source: Wikimedia Commons.

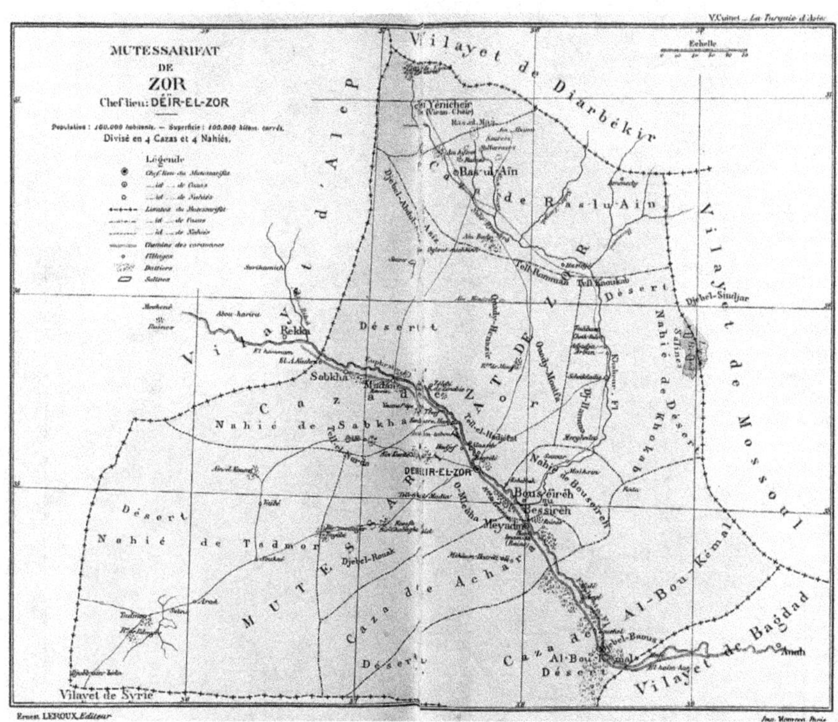

FIGURE 2. Map of the District of Zor, c. 1890s, from Vital Cuinet, *La Turquie d'Asie, géographie administrative: statistique, descriptive et raisonnée de chaque province de l'Asie Mineure*, vol. 2 (Paris: E. Leroux, 1891–1894). Source: Wikimedia Commons.

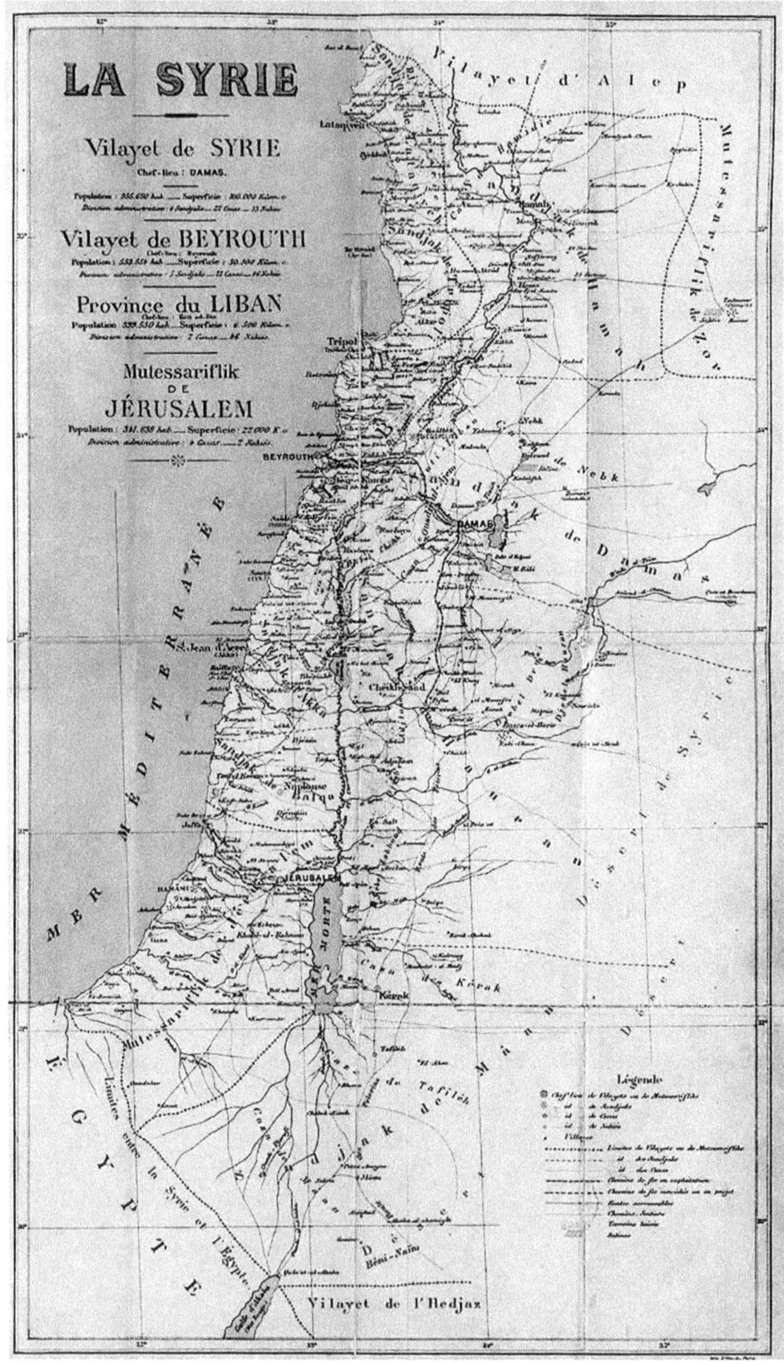

FIGURE 3. Map of the provinces of Syria and Beirut and the districts of Mount Lebanon and Jerusalem in 1896, from Vital Cuinet, *Syrie, Liban et Palestine, géographie administrative: statistique, descriptive et raisonnée* (Paris: E. Leroux, 1896). Source: Wikimedia Commons.

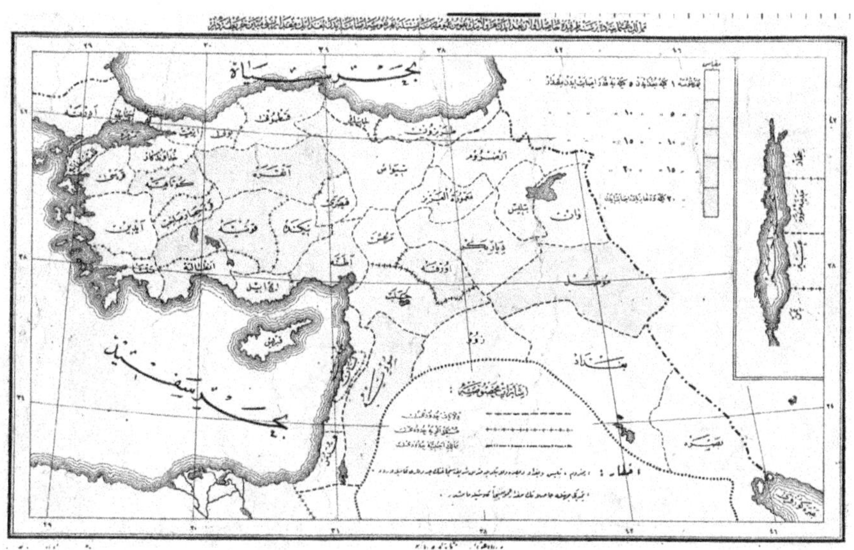

FIGURE 4. Detail from a chart of agricultural statistics with accompanying map compiled by the Agriculture and Commerce Ministry, c. 1913/1914. Reproduced with permission of Atatürk Library, Hrt_000219.

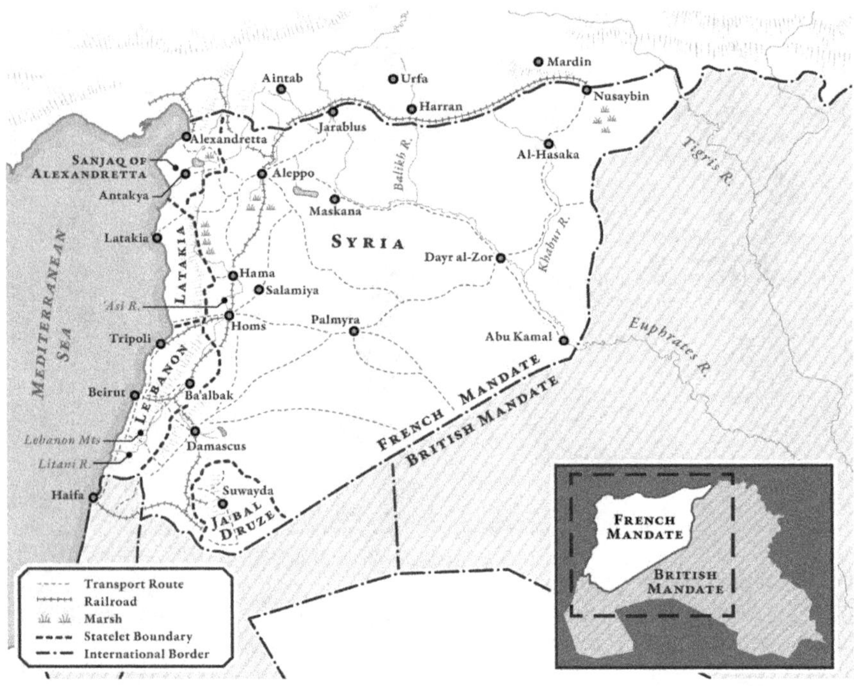

FIGURE 5. The mandate states of Syria and Lebanon, c. 1936.

STATES OF CULTIVATION

INTRODUCTION

During the final years of World War I, Ottoman bureaucrats in the eastern Mediterranean who wanted an expert opinion on developing the region's agriculture turned to one man: Hüseyin Kâzım. Privileged and wealthy, Kâzım was the son of the governor of Trabzon and pursued studies at the Soğukçeşme military school, the Mülkiye (Civil Service) School, the English Commerce School in İzmir, and the École Agronome de Paris.[1] Later, having given up a plan to travel to New Zealand with his friend Tevfik Fikret, Kâzım decided to work on a small farm on land bought by his father in Manisa not too far from Izmir. According to his memoirs, during this period he read about scientific and mechanical agriculture and "tested the most practically applicable theories and did not abstain from investigating the region's agricultural qualities and conditions."[2] Following the Ottoman Empire's Second Constitutional Revolution in 1908, Kâzım joined forces with Tevfik Fikret and Hüseyin Cahid to start *Tanin*, the Istanbul-based daily paper of the Committee of Union and Progress (CUP), an influential mouthpiece in the post-1908 moment.[3] Among his copious publications were seven books about agriculture, including two distributed by the Society for National Defense (Müdafaa-i Milliye Cemiyeti) for use in village schools and a French agricultural textbook translated into Ottoman.[4] By the time he fell out with the CUP and moved to Beirut, where he lived in self-imposed exile during the war, his reputation as an expert on matters of scientific agriculture was well-established.[5]

Thus in 1917, when Rafiq Tamimi, the Beirut commerce school's director, and Mehmet Behcet, the Sultani school's assistant director, compiled a two-volume report on the province of Beirut at the behest of its Ottoman governor, ʿAzmi Bey, they invited Kâzım to contribute the section on "Agricultural Matters."[6] Soon after, the governor of Mount Lebanon, Ismaʿil Haqqi Bey, also solicited Kâzım to write about agriculture for his two-volume set on Mount Lebanon.[7] Both compendiums aimed to provide a "scientific" (*ʿilmi*) perspective on, or guide to, the regions they described, and, as Kâzım explained in his introduction to the Mount Lebanon series, to ensure "that the government knows its essence and defines itself."[8] As such, they represented the culmination of decades-long efforts undertaken by successive Ottoman bureaucracies to extract and compile knowledge about the empire's provincial hinterlands.

In the final years of the war, Kâzım's contributions aimed to offer a blueprint for the region's postwar economic development. His essay in the Beirut volume, "A Few Words Concerning Syria's Agriculture," took a comprehensive approach to assessing the eastern Mediterranean's potential.[9] According to Kâzım, the region had a soil and climate that were eminently suitable to agricultural production, even with basic methods, and made the area even more fertile than other provinces. He acknowledged the region's illustrious history as a source of agricultural bounty for the Phoenicians and Romans but blamed environmental changes for what he considered its underdeveloped potential in the early twentieth century—in his assessment there were fewer forests, more silted-up riverbeds and swamps, and decreased soil fertility than in the past.[10] But "by science and industry humankind found ways to enable domination [*tahakküm*] of nature and land and searched for remedies to weather and climatic events."[11] New industrial and mineral substances promised alternative means to replenish the soil.[12] The province of Beirut already produced a variety of crops, including wheat, barley, beans, millet, and lentils, but with improved rotational methods, it could expand the cultivation of potatoes, beets, and carrots, providing additional nutrition for both humans and animals.[13] Fruit tree and vegetable cultivation, forestry, vineyards, silk production, poultry raising, and dairy-related industry all held promise.[14] By applying science and industry, planting forests and pastures, draining marshes, and improving irrigation and seeds, Syria would quickly rank among "the most progressive agricultural regions in the world."[15] Before shifting to more productive rotations and intensive cultivation, however, the region first needed educational infrastructure and institutions to encourage investment.[16] In Mount Lebanon Kâzım suggested prioritizing reforestation, expanding pasture lands, and increasing fruit and vegetable cultivation.[17] With careful technocratic planning, he envisioned myriad possibilities for making the region's agriculture an even richer source of revenue for the state.

At the same moment that Kâzım was formulating his vision for the region's agriculture, another group in the south of France was eyeing the eastern Mediterranean's agricultural lands' "richness" with a different goal in mind. Undertaking a campaign to shore up political support for French control of the eastern Mediterranean in the war's aftermath, they emphasized the "possibilities" that the region's agricultural resources offered the French empire. The campaigners, many of whom had commercial interests in the region and were connected to the Colonial Party, expressed confidence that the expertise of French foresters and agronomists could be applied to reforestation and hydraulic projects to ensure extraction of the region's "economic value."[18] The area's value was not just of importance to domestic and internal imperial economic interests but also to France's ability to compete with its imperial rivals. The same year that *Beyrut Vilayeti* appeared, another book in France, *La Syrie et la France*, urged the campaign's opponents to consider the imperative of expanding France's access to resources in the face of imperial competition from Britain and Germany. The anticipated agricultural riches that French rule promised would secure not only a steady stream of raw materials for French industries but also France's influence in the eastern Mediterranean.[19]

These two assessments of the region's agricultural potential came at a pivotal moment for agriculture globally. The late nineteenth and early twentieth centuries marked a moment of rapid innovation in agricultural technologies that ignited the imaginations of bureaucrats, large landowners, and well-off farmers alike. These new technologies promised lucrative and transformative results if officials created supportive institutions and enacted administrative policies, technologies in their own right, to facilitate their spread. They represented the fruits of new developments in chemistry, mechanization, and the use of fossil fuels. If properly applied and tested, so the thinking went, farmers would no longer be primarily bound by careful husbanding of the soil to maintain its fertility, nor would they be at the mercy of inadequate rainfall or pests that wreaked havoc. On the contrary, they would be able to "dominate" nature, intensifying existing output or expanding into regions that had remained uncultivated because of insufficient labor or lack of water resources. In the early twentieth century the full ramifications of these technologies and their interactions with the environments they purported to dominate had yet to unfold. The devastation of the 1930s Dust Bowl in the United States and massive expansion in crop production as well as the "violence" of the Green Revolution were still years, if not decades, away.[20]

Nonetheless, technocratic elites were already experimenting with new measures to facilitate access to these capital-intensive technologies and assess their effectiveness in relation to existing methods. In the eastern Mediterranean matters were no different; however, these two assessments represented two different imperial frameworks within which this experimentation would unfold in the region. One was an Ottoman framework whose days were numbered even as Kâzım made his proposals, and the other was a French colonial framework, which, due in large part to these campaigners' lobbying, imposed itself on the region in the war's aftermath. *States of Cultivation* explores the ramifications of the contrasts and continuities between these two empires' approaches to "dominating" nature in this moment of possibility.

At the Intersection of Environment and Capital: Agriculture, State Building, and Imperial Politics

As bureaucrats around the globe mustered their administrative capacities to facilitate the flow of more capital resources into agricultural production and produce expertise to assess the effects of untried technologies, the region at the center of this story underwent a fundamental reconfiguration of its economic and political space.[21] This book focuses primarily on the territory that comprises what are today the nation-states of Syria and Lebanon. But in the nineteenth and early twentieth centuries these discrete nation-states did not exist; rather, the region contained provinces of a reforming Ottoman Empire whose contours looked quite different from the region's current borders.[22] Following World War I, a short-lived Arab government ruled from Damascus before British and French officials divided the region into mandates sanctioned by the League of Nations and incorporated them into their respective imperial spheres, a state of colonial rule that lasted through World War II. Post-independence developments are beyond the scope of this book, but as discussed in the epilogue, the legacy of the technocratic ideas that circulated during both the Ottoman and mandate periods continued to live on even as the policies and rhetoric of the mandate period facilitated a representation of the region as agriculturally behind and in need of "development."

World War I has typically functioned as a periodization break in the literature, with most historians focusing either on the Ottoman period or the mandate that followed it. A small body of work has recently started to explore elements of continuity from the late Ottoman period through the mandate.[23] This study builds on these analyses by tracing institutional developments and demonstrating intellectual and practical continuities and divergences related to the region's agricultural administration across this transition.[24] It also aims to place regional developments in their imperial and global contexts.[25] Broadening the historical and geographic scales for assessing regional developments underscores shared technocratic ideals and projects and clarifies how regional particularities shaped divergent trajectories.[26]

Juxtaposing the parallels and contrasts across these historical and geographic scales offers an alternative to the view that Ottoman approaches to governance in certain more distant provinces, such as those in the eastern Mediterranean, were akin to colonialism.[27] First, this alternative approach demonstrates how Ottoman technologies of rule that aimed to produce a more comprehensive corpus of knowledge about its territory and create more homogenized infrastructure across its provinces paralleled efforts undertaken by other nineteenth-century states. The eastern Mediterranean provinces were integral to these projects, in contrast to other regions where certain forms of institution building were not extended to the same degree and where scholars have argued that administrative strategies were more invested in delineating difference.[28] This is not to deny that these efforts at homogenization often played out differently as imperial officials responded to and frequently integrated local particularities.[29]

Second, this *longue durée* perspective enables a study in contrasts between Ottoman strategies of governance and those deployed by French mandate officials after World War I, when the empire's eastern Mediterranean provinces were divided into mandates and incorporated into French and British imperial peripheries in what was clearly a colonial endeavor.

The mandate system's thinly disguised pretext for this colonial rule insisted on the region's inhabitants' need for "tutelage" from France and Britain to prepare them for self-governance.[30] Implicit in the idea of the mandate was that the mandated regions would one day become independent states. Hence from the beginning of French rule, as efforts to intensify capital investment in agricultural production and grapple with emerging technologies to increase revenue continued, Syrian and Lebanese officials propounded and pursued their economic priorities within the framework of national development. Their vision predated French colonialism and drew on efforts, which largely continued Ottoman practices, from the brief period of Arab government rule following Ottoman withdrawal from the region; it also challenged French priorities, creating a clash between another state-centered plan for development and a colonial plan and the state building it denied.

Central to the plans of all these actors was a version of how they aimed to "dominate," in Kâzım's words, or administer nature to achieve their desired ends. Their plans were contingent on and shaped in part by their (mis)conceptions of the environments before them but also by political, economic, and technocratic considerations.[31] Yet despite aspirations of profitable environmental management and transformation, at times buttressed by visions of a more prosperous distant past, these efforts often had unintended consequences. A common theme in histories of the environment is how the natures created by such projects often involve unanticipated ecological responses: Canals silt up, undesirable species thrive, lakes dry out.[32] Explanations of such phenomena can focus primarily on the features of dirt or water flows, but widening the lens brings other factors into play—namely, the social, political, and economic arrangements that facilitated a particular "way of organizing nature"[33]—that is, not just how certain aspects of nature thwarted or reconfigured these designs but how flows of capital and nature were coproduced at the interstices of these multiple factors.

Drawing inspiration from this literature and that of political ecology, which aims to "unravel the political forces at work in environmental access, management, and transformation," this book traces Ottoman and French mandate efforts to exert greater control over the management of agricultural resources and the capacity to extract from them in the eastern Mediterranean.[34] In so doing, it interrogates how the trajectories of imperial rule and state building affected the dynamic intersection of environmental management, capital formation and accumulation, and expertise production, contributing to a growing literature that has addressed aspects of these impacts in neighboring regions, such as Egypt, Iraq, and Adana.[35]

In the eastern Mediterranean, despite shared technocratic ideals that animated imperial policies during both the Ottoman and French mandate periods, divergent motives on the part of Ottoman, Syrian, Lebanese and French actors led to different approaches to commodifying the region's land and implementing projects aimed at increasing the value extracted from it. As the region transitioned from integrated Ottoman provinces to a colonial periphery of the French empire, new infrastructures and relations between imperial center and local institutions and actors led to intensified extraction, less protection from the inroads of foreign capital, increased tensions between technocratic officials, and decreased attention to ecological constraints. Ottoman, Lebanese, and Syrian actors emphasized sovereignty in operations of capital accumulation, embraced local expertise, and promoted technocratic governance. In contrast, French officials viewed the region as a repository for surplus French capital, privileged French expertise, and expressed disdain for local technocratic approaches and those who advocated them, if French officials acknowledged them at all. The transition from Ottoman state-building strategies to the colonial ones of French mandate officials yielded increasingly fragmented spaces and natures that reflected the conflicts between these contrasting priorities and their intersection with regional environmental limits.

At the center of this analysis are the myriad human actors whose activities not only involved circulation in global networks of expertise production but also movement between urban and rural spaces at the regional and local levels. Detailing the motives driving these interventions in rural communities, whether by Ottoman bureaucrats, local technocrats, nationalist elites, French colonial officials, or other foreign interests, demonstrates the significance of rural areas to state, nationalist, and colonial projects of environmental management and resource extraction, expanding on a perspective that is largely lacking in the region's urban-dominated historiography.[36] It also reveals the mutually constitutive nature of urban and rural developments.

Different as their goals might have been, all parties emphasized the capacity of scientific practice and technology to facilitate their control over the environment.[37] Although not a new phenomenon, the scale on which these changes could be carried out had increased substantially by the late nineteenth and early twentieth centuries—a shift in scale made possible by new advances in chemistry and the increasing use of fossil fuels.[38] The ever more compressed global space-time that this new scale facilitated created increasing disparities and unevenness.[39] Colonial powers' extraction and exploitation of environmental resources in spaces characterized by vast power disparities between metropole and colony were a crucial part of this process.[40] Policies that sought to transform agricultural production, making it more amenable to metropole needs and training the land's productive capacity on the raw materials its industry desired, were central to imperial projects of "development" at the expense of local subsistence. Not infrequently these policies also led to dispossession.[41] In the eastern Mediterranean, French colonial rule sought to reorient the region's agricultural productivity and processes of extraction at a pivotal moment of innovation in agricultural technologies. Foregrounding local dynamics with reference to this global context highlights how this transition exacerbated unevenness as a result of shifting political, economic, and spatial dynamics.

Ottoman strategies for implementing "scientific" agriculture—what Burbank and Cooper identify as imperial "repertoires of power"—provide an instructive counterpoint to French repertoires.[42] The comparison enabled by a perspective of over a century juxtaposes Ottoman efforts to thwart elite capital accumulation and direct more revenue into the imperial treasury, and French policies aimed at channeling surplus capital into the countryside and intensifying extraction. It contrasts the gradual construction of an interconnected network of "scientific" agricultural infrastructure during the Ottoman Empire's final decades with the piecemeal, desultory, and even destructive approach to such institutions under the mandate. Juxtaposing these two approaches provides fresh insight into the mandate's impact. The shifting of imperial space after the war not only constrained aspirations for national economic development but also realigned the circulation of capital and expertise within a new imperial sphere. The demands of this new imperial framework exacerbated the effects of environmental variation and limitations, laying the groundwork for resistance driven not only by political but also by economic and ecological grievances in which the political was intimately bound up.

The Eastern Mediterranean

The landscape onto which Kâzım projected his plans for agricultural development was one bursting with ecological and agricultural diversity. In other regions, such as Egypt, a single river (or its watershed) might provide the seasonal rhythms and lifeblood for most agricultural production as well as a unifying lens for colonial officials and nationalists alike in their plans for economic development and for historians in their analysis of those plans and their consequences. For example, in Egypt during the nineteenth-century, cotton monoculture replaced large areas of subsistence crops as Egypt's well-watered fields supplied British textile mills.[43] In contrast, Syrian agriculture remained more diverse and subsistence oriented, with wheat and barley the predominant staples, especially in the rain-fed plains. These were supplemented by vineyards, olives, and a variety of fruit crops.[44] Mulberry trees, which provided silkworm sustenance, flourished on the hillsides of Mount Lebanon.[45] The eastern Mediterranean offered a multiplicity of ecological zones with their respective advantages and challenges for technocratic planning.[46]

In broad strokes the region's geography consists of a narrow fertile coastal plain that rises to a series of mountains dominated by the often snow-covered peaks of Mount Lebanon with lower mountain ranges and hills to the south and north. Because of a system of faults created by the boundaries of two tectonic plates meeting along the region's western edge, these peaks drop dramatically to the depths of the Jordan Valley and the Dead Sea in the south and somewhat less dramatically to the fertile but formerly marshy Biqaᶜ, Ghab, and Amik Valleys in the north.[47] More arid hills to the east of these valleys give way to the rain-fed plains of the interior, which eventually become eastern grasslands extending into semi-arid desert crisscrossed by the cultivated banks of the Euphrates River and its tributaries. The region boasts a rich variety of agricultural production. Like Kâzım, nineteenth- and early-twentieth-century local agronomists and technocrats saw all manner of potential in these diverse ecologies, but the approaches, like the ecologies themselves, would have to be diffuse and place-specific.

Managing the region's water resources was key to this planning because unreliable access to dependable irrigation was a primary concern. Most of the region's rivers, such as the ᶜAsi, Kuwayk, Barada, Euphrates, Litani,

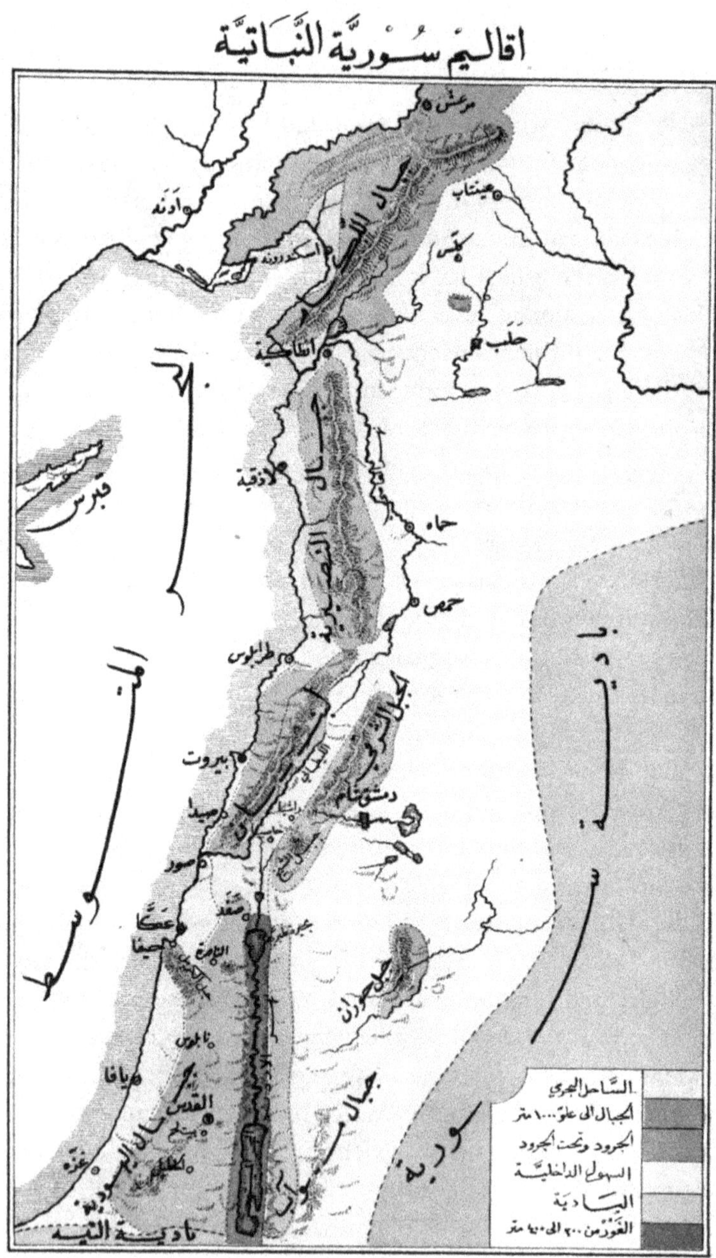

FIGURE 6. An 1884 rendering of "The Botanical Regions of Syria." A color-coded key distinguishes between the coastal plain, mountains up to 1000 meters, the high mountains and those below them, interior plains, the desert, and the Jordan Valley. From George Post, *Nabat Suriya wa-Filastin wa-al-qutr al-Misri wa-bawadiha* (Beirut, 1884), 411. Source: Hathitrust.

Yarmuk, and Jordan, and their tributaries were already used for small-scale irrigation. Some promised additional possibilities in limited areas and even hydroelectric power. However, challenges were rife. For example, the ʿAsi River, though one of the most extensive rivers after the Euphrates, was prone to swampy breeding grounds of malaria that made year-round habitation not just undesirable but potentially deadly.[48] The lack of a gradient along much of its course required creative techniques, such as the waterwheels (*nuria*) of Hama, which raised the ʿAsi's waters to channels connected to irrigation networks. Other rivers were not reliable as year-round sources of water. Notably, following the division of the former province of Aleppo between Syria and Turkey, the Quwayq River, which started north of the border and flowed south through the city of Aleppo, ran dry in the city during summers.[49] Meanwhile, vast expanses of fertile rain-fed land, located far from the reaches of these rivers, required other strategies to ensure adequate moisture.[50] The summer months were dry with rainfall starting in mid-fall, signaling the beginning of soil preparation for

FIGURE 7. "Double waterwheel" on the ʿAsi River in Hama. Source: G. Eric and Edith Matson Photography Collection, Library of Congress, https://www.loc.gov/item/2019698855/.

planting, and continuing through the spring. Not just the amount but also the timing of rainfall was crucial for a successful harvest.

Ottoman, Syrian, and Lebanese technocrats pursued a variety of strategies to address what they regarded as one of the most pressing obstacles to agriculture's development, prioritizing dry-farming studies alongside plans for dam building or drainage projects.[51] Exploring multiple options suited their goal of encouraging a diverse array of crops. In contrast, French officials fixated on irrigation schemes, which were most conducive to ensuring water for their preferred crops, such as cotton, although they ultimately focused more on the planning and studying than on actual execution. Only one small project to raise the dam on the lake near Homs was under way by the late 1930s, despite multiple studies.[52]

Fluctuation in water levels was one of the primary variables that determined the relative bounty of the agricultural season from year to year, but other factors also posed challenges. The perennial threats of locusts and field mice were joined by Sunn bugs soon after the mandate's arrival in the region. Winds, untimely frost, or hail were also matters of concern. Humid winds bringing moisture from the west were beneficial, but northern winds were cold, and dry winds from the south, east, and southeast, which appeared at the end of spring and could blow into the fall, were hot and could be devastating, particularly at certain points in the season when they scorched crops and led to losses.[53] Although some of these factors proved more challenging to resolve than others, all were in play as technocrats assessed their options for the region's agricultural development.[54]

Networks and the Production of Knowledge

Knowledge about agricultural technologies and the administrative tools developed to facilitate their use circulated in networks at the global, imperial, and local levels. Goals such as increasing the legibility of provincial hinterlands, incorporating rural production more fully into state or empire-centered infrastructures of capital accumulation, and making production itself more lucrative through either more intensive or extensive methods drove these circulations. The "imperial intersections" between competing empires facilitated exchanges and encouraged innovation.[55] An increasingly robust scholarship on networks has documented the transnational and coproduced nature of the knowledge that networks have generated, but it also has demonstrated how this knowledge is contingent on uneven power relations and local particularities.[56] Technocrats and administrators trained in Ottoman or French imperial contexts brought their experiences to the new colonial context of the mandate, where, despite speaking a common technocratic language derived from these networks, they advocated divergent approaches to translating ideas into local policies derived from conflicting interests and the particularities of their backgrounds.

By tracing the circulation of Ottoman, Syrian, Lebanese, and French technocrats in these common networks, this book provides a counterpoint to the historiography that, to the extent it has examined the factors influencing approaches to governance, has focused on colonial officials. For example, scholars have explored the backgrounds of French officials and how their experiences in other regions of the French empire, such as Morocco, influenced their approach to mandate rule in Syria and Lebanon.[57] The backgrounds of their Syrian and Lebanese counterparts have received less attention, particularly regarding their circulation in Ottoman and international networks and the impact on their ideas about economy and governance.[58] Despite noting the participation of some of the most elite among them in Ottoman institutions, scholars have yet to examine the full ramifications of these actors' education and participation in these institutions.[59] Situating local and French technocrats in common global networks of expertise circulation not only adds to our understanding of how French policymakers' *formation* and colonial experiences informed their rule in mandate Syria but also illustrates the parallels that characterized the experiences of local and French technocrats, making the divergences in their practice resulting from different end goals and prior points of reference all the more stark.

An emphasis on these individual actors facilitates a narrative that operates on multiple scales and across shifting arrangements of space, underscoring their unique contributions.[60] Just as mandate policies reflected French officials' attempts to apply techniques developed in other areas of the French empire to the idiosyncratic nature of colonial mandate rule, local officials drew on the Ottoman legacy and their training in that milieu to formulate counterproposals. Constrained by the uneven power relations of colonial rule, these proposals largely went unfulfilled and have remained unaddressed in the literature. However, just because local technocrats were unable to implement their vision of economic planning does not mean that their proposals are undeserving of attention.[61] On the contrary, not only do their ideas suggest paths not taken as a result of colonial interventions into the environments and economies of the eastern Mediterranean, but they also provide long-term context for programs of rural development and agricultural self-sufficiency whose emergence scholars date to the aftermath of World War II.[62] Recently, scholars examining the political-economic perspectives of "men of capital" in mandate Palestine and nationalists in British-occupied Egypt have demonstrated the diversity and complexity of their ideas.[63] By detailing the perspectives of Ottoman, Syrian, and Lebanese technocrats, this book provides not just further evidence that ideas circulating in the region were far from mere pale imitations of European models but also demonstrates their roots in and the inspiration they derived from long-term developments in local institutions and practice.[64]

The term *technocrat* used throughout the book refers to a group of administrators or midlevel bureaucrats, some agronomists among them, who insisted on technical or "scientific" knowledge (*ʿilm*) and a more managerial approach as the basis of administration, particularly when dealing with economic questions.[65] Typically occupying positions less prestigious than provincial governors, government ministers, or nationalist notables, their central role in formulating and implementing policies of governance has long been overlooked.[66] Whether of local origin or assigned to an area from farther afield, over the course of the nineteenth century the Ottoman government increasingly relied on these officials with their "scientific" training to carry out administrative policies.[67] Sidelined during the mandate, they made their displeasure known.

State, Empire, and the Politics of Rural Space

The institutional continuities that characterized local technocratic proposals for expanding infrastructures of state space in rural areas challenged French plans for those localities; French officials considered the exploitation of these areas an essential component of their efforts to incorporate the region into their imperial sphere. State space refers to the product of an array of institutions and technologies designed to organize and manage the creation of a seemingly homogeneous but hierarchical space that facilitates surveillance, control, and the reproduction of power.[68] *Colonial* state space works to reinforce those hierarchies between the metropole and the colony while incorporating the colony into a globe-spanning imperial sphere in which those elements of exerting power are deployed in the service of imperial competition and expanding the imperial economy. As Manu Goswami argues about colonial India, "The colonial state space was inseparably part of a broader imperial *scale*-making project, one that sought to secure and maintain a Britain-centered and globe-spanning imperial economy."[69] In a similar vein, French officials pursued the production of a colonial state space in Syria and Lebanon through an array of technologies that sought to realign the space between the local and the global sphere and serve the expansion of their own imperial economic interests.

Contrasting the tension between Ottoman, French, Syrian, and Lebanese visions for the respective state spaces they worked to produce (or in the case of Syrian and Lebanese nationalists, aimed to produce) illustrates stark differences. From the efforts, albeit gradual and incomplete, to create increasingly homogenized institutions and hierarchical provincial administration of the Ottoman period, mandate rule fragmented the region, and each statelet's administration developed its own peculiar structure. The attempts of urban-based administrators to implement in the rural countryside policies developed through global and imperial networks often stoked controversy and resistance. Tracing the implementation of, resistance to, and reformulation of technologies of land reform, taxation, agrarian credit provision, and education underscores the negotiations involved in establishing boundaries that characterized the maintenance of the Ottoman and mandate states' "social and political order."[70]

As technocratic elites implemented these technologies at the regional and local levels, they sought to establish new forms of relationships with rural areas.[71] But the framework in which they understood the significance of their work was not just local; it was global as well. As Goswami observes, "Colonial practices of spatial and political-economic restructuring were indissolubly tied to broader processes of global restructuring whose pervasive if uneven effects were articulated on multiple spatial scales."[72] The same can be said of state practices in the metropole. In the late nineteenth and early twentieth centuries, "governments . . . turned increasingly to scientific expertise to deal with the problems of capitalist production, resource management, and social order."[73] Ottoman, Syrian, Lebanese, and French technocrats were well aware of the economic competition they faced as technocrats the world over assessed the latest innovations and experimented with strategies to restructure their institutions to accommodate them.

A number of scholars have dealt in turn with Ottoman efforts to reorder the empire's state space and the place of rural communities within it, whether redefining their rights to land, streamlining processes of extraction, or intervening in local relationships of debt and obligation.[74] This book traces how these various reforms intertwined and built on each other. Their consequences, intended and unintended, reshaped the relationships between urban and rural actors and the impact of these policies continued to resonate in local technocratic proposals during the mandate. These proposals also foreshadowed the projects purportedly aimed at rural development and peasant enlightenment in the 1940s and 1950s, demonstrating their deep roots in local rural administration.[75]

Modernity, Science, and Expertise

The Ottoman and French mandate political-economic projects transformed local rural spaces and the region's relation to the global economy and networks of expertise. The region's encounter with the technological changes and shifts in circulation of capital that characterized this historical moment produced increasing unevenness. But intimately bound up in these projects was a representation of the region's rural spaces, environments, and communities that was productive in its own right. By and large, as we saw at the beginning of this introduction, these discourses represented the region as previously flourishing but later, for various reasons, unable to fulfill its potential. These perceived shortcomings necessitated an intervention. This intervention and those who considered themselves capable of successfully carrying it out used modifiers such as *scientific* and *modern* to define the kinds of expertise they claimed to possess and the methods they insisted would allow them to "dominate" nature and recover that flourishing past.

Technocrats' and officials' claims to "scientific" or modern" expertise constituted a performance as well as a means of asserting a sense of belonging to an elite group of globe-trotting technocrats.[76] The representation of their expertise as scientific constituted a form of "*boundary-work*," distinguishing their knowledge from that of local farmers and identifying it with the knowledge of their similarly trained counterparts.[77] Their claims to modernity also involved a performative element; as Mitchell argues, "The modern occurs only by performing the distinction between the modern and the non-modern."[78] Fully understanding the productive work achieved by a term such as *modernity* means teasing out the multiple registers asserted by its use as "a claim-making device."[79] Similar to what Michael Gasper has detailed with respect to "scientific" agriculture in Egypt, elites' enthusiasm for this "science" and more broadly the package of technologies that would make rural spaces more legible to and exploitable by state institutions in the eastern Mediterranean derived in part from the ability it gave them to claim a role mediating between the state's administration and rural communities.[80]

The neat binaries produced by these discourses belied the more complex realities that characterized the production and application of these forms of knowledge. Despite visions of dominating nature, nature is not so easily cowed. New technologies encountering the idiosyncrasies of different environments did not always produce the results anticipated. In such instances, as Mitchell has argued, "the projects themselves formed the science."[81] That is, knowledge deemed scientific emerged from a process of trial and error that often involved the input of local forms of knowledge that represented what "scientific" knowledge defined itself against. These processes constituted an aspect of the "translation" necessary "to render models of modernity intelligible."[82] The knowledge produced was indebted to local expertise but through boundary-work elided its contributions.[83]

A recent group of works on the history of science and technology in the region has examined topics as diverse as the history of astronomy and the social sciences in nineteenth- and early-twentieth-century Egypt and the eastern Mediterranean,[84] science and subjectivity among Ottoman elites in Istanbul,[85] and the building of the power grid in mandate Palestine.[86] These works offer in-depth analyses of the contingent nature of developments and showcase the debates, translations, subjectivities, boundary-work, and infrastructures they produced. The literally dirt-bound debates and contestations over "scientific" or "modern" approaches to taxation, land reform, agrarian finance, and agricultural practice may seem far removed from the ivory towers and government offices where many of these other debates and contestations played out. Yet, as this book demonstrates, the productive power of their claims did not just identify the farmer as a particular kind of subject or the technocrat as a privileged mediator; it generated practices and created material realities on the ground in rural areas that continually shaped and reshaped rural communities' relationship to Ottoman and then French mandate state space.

This rhetoric also had lasting legacies on a more global scale. Not only were representations and manifestations of boundary-work integral to the outcomes of imperial and state-building projects, serving to justify and buttress them, but they often also had ramifications well beyond the colonial state's demise. Scholars of environmental and agricultural management in French North Africa have demonstrated the productive nature of colonial misrepresentations of the local environment. In Morocco and Algeria declensionist narratives deployed by French colonial officials represented the region as a former granary of Rome that was being neglected by its current inhabitants. Such representations justified policies of dispossession that persisted post-independence and continue to manifest in knowledge production by NGOs and the United Nations.[87]

As Ottoman, nationalist, and colonial technocrats surveyed the eastern Mediterranean and envisioned a prosperity that they insisted once had been and could be again, they shared common notions of the "scientific" and "modern" approaches they considered necessary for that revival, but the claims staked in those terms had contrasting meanings and were put to different ends. Contextualizing those claims within the global, imperial, and local networks through which they circulated and the practices they engendered highlights the intricacies and multivalent nature of these representations. In the eastern Mediterranean, as in North Africa, the final iterations of these practices and the representations they inspired, forged at the intersection of colonial state policies and nationalist resistance, had ongoing resonance and productive power post-independence. Not only did they justify intervention framed as "development," but they also completely elided the long history of "scientific" and "modern" claim making that had characterized Ottoman, Syrian, and Lebanese expertise production.

Methodology and Sources

Agriculture is a particularly fruitful lens and the context of the late Ottoman Empire and French mandate is an instructive moment for exploring a series of questions positioned at the intersection of environmental history, histories of political economy, and science and technology studies. Agriculture was a central component of the state's budgets throughout this period, a primary source of financial obligations between urban and rural actors, and, of course, an essential element of rural communities' basic sustenance and the region's provisioning more generally. Despite the topic's importance, the literature on agriculture in the late Ottoman eastern Mediterranean and under the French mandate has not fully addressed the consequences of many of these dynamics.[88] In particular, understanding how local technocrats in the eastern Mediterranean went about managing the productive intersection of environment and capital through their approach to agricultural policy making remains largely unexplored. *States of Cultivation* focuses on this intersection and its consequences, shedding new light on the region's agrarian history. It does so by examining these technocrats' interactions with urban landowners anxious to invest in and apply the latest technologies to their lands, peasants eager to demonstrate their expertise but resistant to policies that might imperil their subsistence, economic interests, or claims to land, and colonial officials whose technocratic ideals they often shared but whose imperial designs they challenged.

Chapters 1 and 2 focus on developments during the Ottoman period. Chapter 1 traces the myriad reforms passed following the initiation of the Tanzimat to make the empire's provincial countryside more legible and therefore increasingly more lucrative for the Ottoman state. With a focus on the eastern Mediterranean, these developments are positioned in a global context of political-economic restructuring and the technocrats increasingly tasked with carrying them out in the global networks of expertise that informed their projects. Chapter 2 examines how Ottoman administrators translated global expertise into the establishment and expansion of institutions promoting "scientific" agricultural practice throughout the empire. Representations of the knowledge produced in these institutions tended to obscure the incorporation of local expertise, even though they were reliant on it, insisting instead on a "scientific" knowledge that was distinct from these contributions. Chapter 3 explores the consequence of the region's shift from integral provinces of the Ottoman Empire to a colonial periphery within a French imperial sphere at the end of World War I. It demonstrates how this shift in imperial space led to multiple incompatible visions for developing the region's agriculture and the contestations these provoked.

Chapters 4 and 5 examine developments in expertise production and administrative strategies parallel to those in chapters 2 and 1, respectively, but in the context of the mandate, underscoring the continuities and divergences from the Ottoman period. Chapter 4 contrasts the competing narratives of nationalist technocrats and French officials as they promoted their respective plans for agricultural education and experimentation in the region. Although local technocrats called for expanding infrastructure as part of cultivating a national state space, mandate officials eschewed any such comprehensive plan, favoring instead a piecemeal approach that was more intent on spreading French influence, rewarding local clients, or supplying French industries. Chapter 5 follows rising discontent with mandate agricultural policies that refused to acknowledge the ecological limits of extraction, provoking multiple episodes of resistance that escalated into increasingly organized political protest by the 1930s. The crisis enabled Syrian nationalist elites, many of whom had investments in agriculture and were therefore not immune to these adverse effects, to promote themselves as mediators intervening with mandate authorities on behalf of cultivators. Finally, the epilogue contrasts local technocratic efforts to grapple with the mandate's legacy and representations of the region in the post–World War II development literature. It underscores the extent to which characterizations of the region as "behind" in this literature can be traced to colonial rhetoric and a lack of acknowledgment of local technocratic expertise and its *longue durée* contributions to agricultural change in the region.

Tracing the networks of technocratic expertise that spanned the late Ottoman and French mandate periods has involved quite a journey, literally and figuratively. Piecing together the stories of the myriad actors whose voices fill these pages entailed work in archives and libraries in Turkey, France, Lebanon, the United Kingdom, Italy, Switzerland, Syria, and the United States. This book draws on a wide variety of published and unpublished sources, many of them previously unexplored, including official correspondence, investigation transcripts, petitions, government reports, statistics compilations, journals, meeting minutes, pamphlets, parliamentary debates, telegrams, textbooks, theses, newspaper articles, consular reports, cartoons, photographs, maps, and personnel files. Composed primarily in Ottoman Turkish, Arabic, French, and, occasionally, English, these materials provide intimate insight into the perspectives and decision-making processes of Ottoman, Syrian, Lebanese, and French officials and technocrats, many trained agronomists among them, as well as nationalist activists and rural communities. Although rural communities' individual voices are at times mediated or obscured by the pen of the transcriber, a colonial translator,[89] a technocrat's account of their exchange, or petitions signed by many, reading these sources against the grain when necessary enables insight into how farming communities responded to technocratic attempts to intervene in their land-tenure arrangements, lending relationships, tax collection methods, and agricultural practices. Exploring the vitality but also the precariousness of life in the countryside as it intersected with the idiosyncrasies and enthusiasm (albeit at times rather misguided) of technocratic planning has been quite a fascinating adventure. As we embark, may the reader find it just as compelling.

ONE

PROVINCIAL LEGIBILITY *and* ECOLOGIES *of* EXTRACTION

Agrarian Networks and the Making of Late Ottoman Rural State Space

In 1893 Ahmet Reşid Bey, the Ottoman agricultural inspector for the provinces of Syria and Beirut, left his post without permission and hopped a ship bound for New York to attend the World's Columbian Exposition in Chicago.[1] Despite failing to obtain permission for the excursion, he apparently decided that the experience gained through such an adventure would compensate for his absence without leave. His gamble was not misplaced. Initially following his departure, government officials expressed consternation at his audacity, and they started to look for a suitable replacement.[2] However, amid reports from the Chicago exhibition's Ottoman commissioner, Hakkı Pasha, who vouched for Reşid Bey's well-spent time, officials relented from such punitive measures.[3] Ultimately, Reşid Bey was allowed to keep his position. The knowledge gained from his experience with international networks of agricultural expertise and its application for increasing agricultural output overcame the qualms of administrators who wanted to punish him for insubordination.[4]

That same year, 1893, also saw the Ottoman government form the Ministry of Forest, Mines, and Agriculture, the culmination of fifty-five years of experiments with different ways of organizing the government's agricultural administration.[5] These efforts to achieve a suitable organization of the empire's agricultural infrastructure paralleled the reforms of the Tanzimat era and its aftermath. In part, these reforms aimed to produce knowledge about evolving Ottoman state space and to make rural communities, their land, and its production more legible to central administrators and provincial officials. Lawmakers also designed them with an eye to disrupting the power exercised by local elites in rural areas by incorporating these elites into the administration and legislating greater control over their activities.[6] Reforms ranged from the 1858 Land Code to the reorganization of provincial administration to new tax collection strategies. Each of these reforms played a role in ensuring that the cash-strapped empire could more effectively extract from its agricultural production, which was still its main source of revenue. By the latter decades of the nineteenth century, officials also increasingly focused on making the land itself more productive, either by expanding cultivated areas or by experimenting with new intensive methods and technologies. Reşid Bey's Chicago adventure exemplified Ottoman agronomists' enthusiasm for participating in international networks devoted to "scientific agriculture" (*fenn-i ziraat*), an approach to agricultural practice deemed new and distinct from existing methods.

Ottoman officials were not alone in facing the quandary of extracting more from agricultural production to meet the demands of nineteenth-century finance. Technocrats around the globe confronted challenges as they too grappled with how to increase agricultural productivity. At times Ottoman officials, like their counterparts in France, Russia, England, Germany, and elsewhere, drew ideas and inspiration from foreign experiments. Nonetheless, Ottoman responses to these demands reflected not wholesale adoption of reforms from foreign models but rather a distinct Ottoman approach driven by internal dynamics that built on existing contexts, practices, and networks while also being shaped by "inter-imperial interaction."[7] In fact, many of these reforms could not have been adopted fully fledged from Europe precisely because many European countries themselves had not yet wholly instituted comparable reforms. They were also struggling to juggle competing interests in rural areas with technocratic intervention. Sometimes, they even looked to the Ottoman Empire for possible strategies when grappling with their own administrative dilemmas.

The evolution of these Ottoman reforms reflected a process of constant renegotiation, as administrators, lawmakers, and other officials responded both to external pressures and internal resistance to and manipulation of the statutes' intents. Externally, the need to boost revenue became increasingly urgent because of the debts racked up during the 1853–1856 Crimean War, the worldwide economic depression of the 1870s, the Ottoman default of 1875, and the subsequent creation of the European-controlled Public Debt Administration in 1881. Internally, frequent revisions to the statutes issued hint at local strategies to circumvent or exploit the institutions and instruments created by these reforms and their aims. In particular, a number of local elites used them to accumulate substantial assets and power, reshaping state space to suit their interests. For many these assets involved the acquisition of rights to land use, spurring interest among them as well for "scientific agriculture" and the expanded capacity for exploitation it promised.

This chapter focuses on the development of these dynamics in the eastern Mediterranean and places them in a broader global economic and geopolitical context. It demonstrates how the reforms built on each other and reflected targeted responses to the increasing fiscal and political challenges that the empire confronted as well as the internal resistance and manipulation they encountered. The eastern Mediterranean was an integral part of these Ottoman state-space-making processes, and the co-optation and contestation that these measures provoked from local elites and rural communities in this region exemplify the tensions and contradictions they embodied. These responses also establish a contrast with the reaction to these reforms' ongoing legacies under the French mandate, discussed in chapter 5.

In the fin de siècle eastern Mediterranean, elites with interests in agriculture grew increasingly impatient with what they considered insufficient state support for more capital-intensive endeavors. Meanwhile, officials grappling with the fallout of elite maneuvering continued to hone the laws in an effort to encourage investment, infuse more capital into production, and make agriculture more lucrative, ostensibly in ways that favored small cultivators. Although these efforts grew out of Tanzimat initiatives and intensified under the Hamidian regime, they gained even more momentum after 1908, as technocrats, frustrated with what they considered inadequate attention to rural areas and their needs and the failure to rein in these elites' power grabs, rose to prominent positions in the new CUP (Committee of Union and Progress) government. At the same time, the reinstatement of

Parliament meant that some of these very elites became provincial representatives. In Aleppo these conflicting interests led to a particularly spectacular clash, creating a showdown between provincial elites, including a member of Parliament, and the recently appointed CUP governor to Aleppo, Hüseyin Kâzım, examined in the final section of this chapter.

The Land Law, Provincial Regulations, and Tax Farming Reform: Setting the Stage During the Tanzimat

The proclamation of the Edict of Gülhane on 3 November 1839 marked the official beginning of the Tanzimat, an era of reform characterized by efforts to homogenize institutions and legislate increasingly greater degrees of supervision over their operations across the empire. The Tanzimat project built on earlier efforts at reform even as it responded to new exigencies of the nineteenth century.[8] Struggling to maintain fiscal solvency in the face of encroachments primarily from France and England and their expanding colonial empires, one of the primary foci of these efforts was agriculture, which continued to be the empire's primary source of revenue.[9] How agriculture was taxed, financed, and practiced and how its products reached markets were primary concerns. Given agriculture's intersection with various discrete divisions in the bureaucracy, the administration struggled with how best to position an entity dedicated to these concerns. Before the proclamation of the Edict of Gülhane, the administration created an agriculture and industry council in 1838 under the auspices of the Foreign Ministry.[10] Shortly afterward, it was renamed the Council of Public Works and incorporated into the Commerce Ministry in 1839.[11]

The Gülhane decree targeted taxation of agricultural production through tax farming (*iltizam*) as one of three primary areas for reform because it resulted in "submitting to the discretion of one man the financial matters and political interests of a country and perhaps to the violence of subjugation and force, for if he is not in essence a good man, he will look after his own selfish interest and all his actions will consist of injustice and cruelty."[12] A dishonest tax farmer was likely to not only squeeze taxpayers but also fleece the treasury. In place of this practice, the edict proposed appointing a tax (*vergi*) according to each individual's "property and capacity"—an elusive goal that administrators were still pursuing well into the mandate period, as discussed in chapters 3 and 5.[13]

In 1840 an initial effort to implement this reform, which consisted of appointing government-salaried *muhassıls* to collect the taxes in lieu of tax farmers, was short-lived, but the challenges it exposed proved instructive for shaping future reforms. At the heart of the issue was the question of risk and who bore it. Agricultural yields could fluctuate substantially from year to year because of any number of factors, such as drought or locusts. Tax farming enabled the government to transfer the risk of a deficient harvest to the tax farmer, who bid in ascending-price auctions, ostensibly ensuring that the government received a set revenue from these bids no matter the eventual state of agricultural yields.[14] The *muhassıl* system essentially transformed these rental contracts to wage contracts, thereby transferring the risks to the government. The government's exposure was exacerbated by the fact that it could not rely on advances from moneylenders, whose power it sought to curb. Instead, it insisted on collecting a portion of the tax from taxpayers early, provoking revolt.[15]

The appointment of *muhassıls* was an initial attempt by the government to make inroads into local administration and perhaps to create conduits for synthesizing information about the countryside. However, the system was prone to inefficiencies; for instance, places to store the crop collected in kind for taxes were lacking.[16] The *muhassıls* also defrauded the government in cahoots with local council members or harassed villagers.[17] Resistance from villagers and other influential groups mounted and tax revenues fell, leading the government to eliminate the *muhassıl* system in 1842.[18] It was replaced in 1843 with auctions based on a fixed price derived from an average of previous years' revenue. Only if no bidders could be found would the government resort to collecting the tax with its own agents (*emaneten idare*).[19]

Following this turn of events, the government shifted gears and focused its attention on an array of preliminary experiments that aimed to collect and synthesize knowledge about rural areas and agricultural production, respond to cultivators' concerns, explore possibilities for agricultural education, and create an administrative unit dedicated to agriculture. These efforts represented a more holistic approach to assessing the countryside's needs and creating channels for investment in rural infrastructure and the agrarian economy. In 1843 a new agriculture council was formed under the aegis of the Finance Ministry.[20] That same year the Supreme Council of Judicial Ordinances (Meclis-i Vala-yı Ahkam-ı Adliye) prepared an economic development program for the Agriculture Council to implement.[21] Surveys sent out to the provinces sought to gather information about the crops grown in each region, the kinds of assistance farmers needed, how to improve lands that remained uncultivated, and transport options, among other concerns. A major issue was the high rates of interest farmers faced.[22] In an initial attempt to respond to this issue, between 1843 and 1846 the government gave provincial governors more than 12.5 million gurush to distribute to farmers interest-free from a public works treasury (Hazine-i Nafia).[23] The timing of Ottoman experiments to address the issue of agrarian credit closely paralleled similar early attempts in other countries.[24]

Alongside these efforts to collect detailed data about rural areas, the administration also created regional councils that gave local elites a more structured role in the oversight of provincial activities, such as tax collection.[25] In anticipation of ensuring that knowledgeable local officials were in place specifically to grapple with implementing the Agriculture Council's program, in July 1844 an ordinance was issued for appointing agricultural directors at the provincial and subprovincial levels and deputy agriculture directors in districts, subdistricts, and large villages. These officials were posted throughout the countryside, especially in small towns.[26] The directors and deputy directors, who were chosen by the local populace (*ahali*) and the community councils (*mahalli meclisleri*), had to be local (*yerli*). They were unsalaried and were expected to advise the Agriculture Council on the best ways to improve agriculture, industry, and commerce in their area. The goal was to encourage not just wheat and barley cultivation but a diversity of animal and plant production. Their responsibilities included identifying those in need of assistance, to whom the state would lend money with low interest by means of chain guarantees (*teselsülen tekeffül*). Should a farmer or artisan be on the verge of losing the tools needed to ensure his or her living because of debt, the director or deputy director was to prevent the sale to reduce disruption to the government's revenue. Litigation was not to proceed without the official's presence.[27] Along with finance officials, they were expected to monitor tax farmers.[28]

To obtain more information on provincial needs from a local perspective, a *firman* issued in February 1845 invited two notables from each province to Istanbul, where they formed a commission to offer recommendations.[29] To carry out their proposals, the government created ten improvement council commissions (*meclis-i imar komisyonu*), which were tasked with detailing, in addition to matters affecting merchants and artisans, what crops farmers grew, how they transported them to the nearest port, the condition of the land, and whether any fertile land was empty and, if so, what facilities of capital were necessary to cultivate it.[30] In 1846 the government used funds collected from the credits distributed between 1843 and 1846 to establish a public works capital, which had approximately 10 million gurush for building and repairing roads and bridges as well as for additional credit lending.[31]

Shortly afterward, in 1847, the administration opened a farm school on the outskirts of Istanbul with the specific goal of improving local cotton varieties under the direction of "an American agriculture expert." Translators at the school were to translate foreign textbooks to send to the appropriate regions.[32] One foreign observer, in assessing the effects of Tanzimat policies, hailed the school as "one of the best institutions flowing from the reforms of Turkey."[33] Notably, experiments with grain crop cultivation do not appear to have been a priority, despite grains being a major source of tithe revenue and despite their cultivation methods being a frequent object of derision, particularly from outside commentators.[34] Ottoman administrators seemed less concerned about such matters and more intent on increasing the production of a cash crop, namely, cotton, whose role in Egypt's recent economic and industrial boom they had no doubt noted. However, the school closed in 1851, and the administration did not pursue plans to establish additional institutions for agricultural experimentation and education again until the 1880s, a development that is addressed more fully in chapter 2.[35]

Instead, officials spent the next several decades honing their administrative technologies, including approaches to rural taxation, instruments for land registration, and provincial organization. This shift in emphasis suggests that administrators calculated that they would not be able to sufficiently tap investments in increasing agricultural output if provincial infrastructure was not in place that would support local investment in these new methods and ensure the streamlining of procedures for extraction (i.e., taxation). Hence, in the same year that the administration established the school, it also promulgated the 1847 Title Deed Regulation (*tapu nizamnamesi*), the first in a series of decrees that would fundamentally change land claims' legibility to government officials and how those claims could operate as objects of value. In the following decades, lawmakers promulgated a series of laws that aimed to amass a record of these claims and their value and to create a system for lending against them. Ultimately, such records could potentially serve as the basis of a land tax that could supplant the tithe.

Before instituting these reforms, *selem* contracts were one of the most pervasive forms of provincial borrowing available to farmers, and these kinds of contracts continued to thrive even as reforms took hold. Rooted in Islamic law, *selem* contracts were essentially advance purchase contracts by a moneylender for a farmer's crops. The farmer repaid the borrowed money with a pre-agreed amount of the crop after the harvest. The agreed-on price per unit was substantially less than what the moneylending investor would have paid at market price, ensuring a good profit that functioned as hidden interest. Because the contracting parties made these agreements outside the purview of any government institution, the central government had no control over them and certainly did not see any direct financial gain from them.[36] Such a system involved a level of flexibility that could prove beneficial to both the moneylender and the borrower.[37] On the other hand, in instances where power relations were more uneven, tax demands more pressing, and climatic conditions less favorable, the system could lead to spiraling debt. If an underwhelming harvest did not yield the requisite amount of pledged crop, the borrower would have to repay the debt in subsequent years with much larger quantities.[38]

When lawmakers started formulating their own program for direct lending to farmers, they did not seem to have considered an option along the lines of a *selem* contract. Aside from the local knowledge regarding crops and market prices that such loans relied on, the contracts also necessitated having a place to store the harvested crops until the moneylender could sell them or use them in manufacturing.[39] If the government lacked storage facilities for crops collected as taxes, it presumably also lacked them for crops collected as surety against loans.[40] Instead of using crops as guarantees, lawmakers seem to have initially settled on using chain guarantees in the lending instructions they laid out for agricultural directors.[41] But these too were rooted in local relationships of obligation and power. Not content with this system, the government increasingly directed its efforts at creating instruments whereby government officials could gain greater oversight and control over transactions involving land, particularly usufruct rights held by cultivators in *miri*, or state, land. Through new forms of documentation and registration procedures, these instruments gradually increased *miri* land's legibility to state officials.[42] Because *miri* land constituted most of the land under cultivation, especially in grain-growing regions, providing a means by which it could be used to secure loans under government oversight had the potential to greatly expand avenues for investing in agricultural production.

This transformation began in the 1840s with a series of decrees formalized in the 1847 *tapu* regulation and the 1849 Ahkam-i Meriye (Laws in Force). The *tapu* regulation explicitly intended to "protect cultivatable land from idleness."[43] Among the most consequential changes instituted by these laws were the inheritance rights granted to women. Although women had the right to inherit in Islamic law at half the share of male offspring, males tended to inherit land.[44] The laws of the 1840s dictated that daughters could inherit land and that mothers could bequeath their land on equal footing with sons and fathers. A sultanic decree explained this change by underscoring how women contributed to agricultural prosperity: "Even if women were not from the masters of agriculture [*erbab-i ziraat*] in deed," they could create a family that would develop the lands transferred to them.[45] Inheritors could partition their rights over land, and there were no restraints on renting out land held by *tapu* (title deed).[46] Evidence from Saida province (*eyalet*) suggests a potentially robust response to these new measures, as more and more women appeared in the Nablus Islamic Court to defend their claims to land starting in the mid-nineteenth century.[47] Rewards were offered for those who brought to light uncultivated or abandoned (*mahlul*) land. Anyone who reported such land would receive 5% of the sale price (*bedel-i muaccel*), and the agriculture directors would receive a fifth or half a fifth if the deputy director reported it (the deputy director received the other half).[48]

The timing of these reforms coincided with an 1849 administrative restructuring that created provincial councils to oversee aspects of their implementation.[49] In addition to imposing responsibility for ensuring the smooth operation of tax farming auctions, the new regulations enjoined the councils to concern themselves with new borrowing initiatives, the activities of the agricultural directors, the registration of lands by *tapu*, and, particularly, the delegation of "escheated and empty" lands.[50] Further revisions to tax policies aimed to bypass powerful regional elites by having villages themselves collectively farm their tithes at a fixed price. Although this enabled the treasury to continue offloading the risk, most villagers did not have the resources to carry this risk themselves and pay the fixed amounts, empowering more affluent villagers to assume the role of tax farmer.[51] In one petition sent to the governor of Jerusalem in the autumn of 1851, the villagers accused the village shaykhs of "forcing them to sign" a *selem* contract with a local merchant for payment of taxes on the olive harvest. Drawn up without the villagers' knowledge, they understood its goal to be the shaykhs' "own personal aggrandizement."[52] Even though collective village-level apportionment of taxation was not new, this accusation suggested that village elites may have used newfound leverage enabled by provincial reorganization to enrich themselves or at least amass greater authority as intermediaries.[53] This tax initiative might also explain the preponderance of court cases involving "collective [village] debt brokered by village shaykhs" in the region of Hama in the early 1850s, the substantial amount of debt some community leaders owed as guarantors (sing. *kafil*), and the great interest shown by the district governor and advisory council in at least one of these cases.[54] Ultimately, the policy was short-lived, and the government resorted to a fixed price based on an average of the previous five years' tithes (*tahmis*) but permitted its farming by villages, tax farmers, or local government administrators.[55]

In response to the fiscal exigencies of the 1853–1856 Crimean War, the 1850s saw a rapid succession of developments that would have far-reaching ramifications for the government's financial sovereignty and reform efforts. First, during the war, the government decided to once again take on the risk of taxation and largely reverted to wage contracts, although they did continue to allow fixed-price rental contracts in more distant areas. In a significant shift from the *muhassıl* era, wage contracts were predominantly held by government employees.[56] In the final months of the war, during which international borrowing became easier and reliance on Istanbul moneylenders decreased, the government resumed ascending-price auctions and individual villages became the tax farming unit.[57]

In February 1856 the Islahat Fermanı (Reform Edict) reaffirmed the empire's commitment to eliminating tax farming but sought to limit the participation of government officials until this could be effected, forbidding them and council members from leasing these contracts or having financial interest in their execution.[58] This decree also specifically called for removing any impediments to the improvement of agriculture and the establishment of banks to provide the funds necessary for increasing the empire's "material wealth."[59] In May 1856, within months of the decree's promulgation, the modest, primarily British-backed Ottoman Bank was incorporated in Istanbul and promptly began doling out advances to the government to assist in covering expenses.[60] Although these resources might have buoyed the government, the bank's policy not to lend against unharvested crops and strict rules regarding loans against produce likely hindered its capacity to serve as a credit institution for cultivators.[61]

Even though the bank provided a source of external funds to help the empire meet its mounting financial obligations in the aftermath of the war, Ottoman administrators were also keen to create or increase access to additional internal sources of revenue. By 1858 the ripple effects from the 1857 panic in the United States that had subsequently spread to Europe reached the empire, where the value of *kaime*, Ottoman paper money, fell considerably.[62] In the eastern Mediterranean these European financial troubles ended a boom in the export of raw materials, particularly grain whose export had thrived as a result of the Crimean War; credit markets constricted, and, combined with a disappointing 1858 harvest, local purchasing capacity decreased.[63]

It was against this backdrop that Ottoman officials promulgated one of the most consequential reforms of the nineteenth century, the 1858 Land Code. Designed to create a foundation from which the empire could extract more value from one of its primary resources, this reform centered on making the most pervasive form of agricultural land, *miri* land, more legible to state officials as an object of investment and extraction. To this end, in 1858 officials established the Ministry of the Cadastre (Tahrir-i Emlak Nezareti) and promulgated this Land Code.[64] Huri İslamoğlu situates these developments in a nineteenth-century "age of property," during which Ottoman administrators closely tracked contestations in France resulting from efforts to impose "individual and absolute ownership" in the wake of the revolution.[65] Despite attempts to draw up a rural code in the early nineteenth century, French officials found themselves incapable of implementing it until 1881 because of elite attempts to appropriate its measures in support of their own interests.[66] In contrast, İslamoğlu assert that the 1858 Land Code demonstrated "the Ottoman government's ability to establish its claims to mediate among different interests."[67]

In great detail, the Land Code instituted a process for the commodification of *miri* land that involved oversight by state officials at every step. Notably, the law did not create a way to wholesale transform *miri* land into freehold private property, or *mülk*, but it did codify a roadmap whereby the usufruct rights to *miri* land could be inherited (*intikal*) and partitioned as well as sold or transferred (*ferağ*). With regards to transfer, although the law did not allow for pledging the property as security, it did provide a mechanism (*ferağ bil-vefa*) whereby a holder's usufruct rights could be transferred, but with right of resumption, once the debt was paid.[68] This right could thus be used like a security, enabling a form of mortgage on *miri* land overseen by a government official specifically appointed for this purpose. The law recognized this official, in his capacity to permit and grant use rights, as the successor to the positions of tax farmer and *muhassıl*, which, at least in the case of the tax farmer, it aspirationally characterized as abolished.[69]

Although some scholars have criticized the Land Code for not being truly aimed at delegating rights to individual cultivators, Article 8, which opened the law's first chapter and was fundamental to the regulation's overall logic, stipulated that the entirety of a village or town's lands could not be granted to the village as a whole or to one, two, or three of its inhabitants, even if they had been chosen. Rather, individual pieces of land were to be given to each person along with a title deed (*tapu*) indicating their possession.[70] Research into the law's local implementation in the province of Syria has indeed demonstrated the meticulousness with which officials recorded land claims on the basis of individual plots or shares in *miri* land.[71]

Further details concerning the mechanics of issuing these *tapu* deeds followed in the 1859 *tapu* regulation. Building on the fundamentals laid out in the Land Code, the 1859 regulation specified that local finance officials, by which it meant the provincial treasurers (*defterdar*), the finance directors (*mal müdirleri*), and the district directors (*kaza müdirleri*), were *sahib-i arz* in matters of tendering (*ihale*) and delegating (*tefviz*) land.[72] Literally, *sahib-i arz* means "possessor of the land," but as underscored by Mundy and Saumarez Smith, the intent was that these officials embodied "the legal *persona* . . . assigned the 'estate of administration' in land."[73] As such, they were responsible for carrying out the multitude of oversight functions assigned to the "land official" who featured so prominently throughout the Land Code.

Notably, whereas the earlier *tapu* regulation outlined a role for agriculture directors and deputy directors in finding and selling empty land, the new regulation explicitly denied them any part in the transfer, inheritance, and granting of land, noting that they were merely members of the council with no special authority.[74] Such a distinction suggested an emerging effort to clearly delineate between those responsible for improving agricultural production and those entrusted with ensuring that the land from which the products grew was duly delegated and registered.

Immediately after the promulgation of these rules implementing a process of registering land from the bottom up, the administration passed yet another regulation in 1860 establishing a process for registering land and property values by property commissions that would travel to communities and compile registers of all plots of land, what was planted in or built on them, and the jobs and incomes of the individuals associated with them.[75] According to İslamoğlu, the 1860 regulation "suggests that . . . [initial attempts at registration in the late 1850s were] not entirely to the satisfaction of the central government."[76] In particular, the new regulation singled out for critique the role of the headman (*muhtar*) as one held by "the lowest from the people," adding "people of integrity and notables reject . . . this work." The commissions were to "immediately dismiss the headmen and elect [another one] from the notables and . . . people of honor" who would "give confidence to the local community [*ahali*] and to the state."[77] This insistence on replacing local headmen with notables elected under the supervision of the commissions underscored the importance that this role was coming to occupy in administrators' plans for liaising with communities, foreshadowing its essential functions in the 1864 provincial regulation.

In addition, although scholars have often argued, based on dubious evidence, that the Land Code resulted in villagers refusing to register their land because of fear of conscription or other consequences of increased legibility to state officials, this new regulation suggested that the government was in fact finding the opposite to be true.[78] The regulation declared that various notables had been "daring to conceal people and wealth" to avoid conscription of their children and pay less in taxes, even going so far as to help others do the same to maintain their silence. To combat this evasion, it stipulated a punishment of three years' "hard labor in chains" for such concealment and laid out stringent new measures for a census to curb offenses.[79] The juxtaposition of these two articles suggests that, even as state institutions depended on local notables as intermediaries, they also regarded them as the most likely actors to subvert the intent of their new policies.

With such regulations in place, registration continued apace. Ostensibly, because the gradual acquisition of *tapu* deeds and compilation of the commissions' surveys increased the legibility of land values and landholdings to government officials, the values could then serve as the basis for a new land tax. First instituted in 1861 at a rate of 0.4%, the new tax was yet another means of extracting revenue from these newly assessed and registered properties.[80] However, the new values were a source of local discontent; in Syria the General Council accused the land office of overvaluing properties and demanded a process for appealing their estimations.[81] In some areas the refusal to address these inflated land values would snowball into a major cause of farmer dispossession in the decades to come, as discussed later.

Officials were not unaware of the dangers. Almost immediately following the issuing of these new regulations, concerns appear to have arisen about the likelihood that this new legislation would lead to farmer dispossession, in particular, loss of their homes and sustenance in contravention of the "old law" (*nizam-i ʿatik*). Subsequent imperial decrees and laws therefore exempted from seizure for debt the cultivator's smallest house and the *miri* land necessary to provide sustenance for that household. According to an 1862 decree, sale of usufruct rights to *miri* land for debt had been prohibited by the Land Code, but this provision applied only if the the debt was between private individuals. Usufruct rights in *miri* land could be sold to pay for debt owed to the government directly.[82] This prompt effort to prevent complete dispossession perhaps indicated that creditors had been quick to seize on the lack of such a provision in the initial laws. Nonetheless, even as the law reaffirmed cultivators' rights to shelter and subsistence, it established a mechanism whereby *miri* land could indeed be sold for debt under government oversight—what Mundy and Saumarez Smith have referred to as the law's "Janus-faced character."[83]

As the Land Code started to take effect, the Ottoman government once again adjusted its approach to tithe collection. Balancing the interests of an insatiable treasury and peasants grappling with the vagaries of nature proved an ongoing dilemma. Learning from previous experience, in the early 1860s officials instituted fixed-price farms at the village level but allocated them collectively to village communities (*ahali*) as "legal personalities" to prevent powerful villagers and tax farmers from monopolizing the process.[84] In some areas the high values set for the fixed-price farms provoked an outcry, leading the government to readjust and allow for tax farmers even as it continued to encourage the new approach in other regions.[85] One report from the districts of Saida and Sur in the province of Syria indicated that the civil servant responsible for collecting tax arrears, appalled by the coercion visited on villagers by powerful urban tax farmers, had instituted this system in 1869. Villagers hastened to take advantage of the scheme, which also included adjusting tithe amounts when necessary to account for losses resulting from locusts and damaging winds and restricted urban dwellers' involvement in the transactions. According to the account, villagers received "this just system" enthusiastically and the collection was done in two weeks.[86] Elsewhere, urban speculators were not so easily foiled. In the Biqaʿ Valley and around Baʿalbak, foreign merchants continued to use "*selem* contracts that are forbidden by the state" (*devletçe memnu olan selem*) and "corrupt" tax farming arrangements to profit from village lands in contravention of the *tapu* regulation, despite notifications from the government.[87]

In June 1861 Sultan Abdulmecid I died and was succeeded by his brother, Abdulaziz, who immediately dismissed the grand vizier and installed Fuad Pasha, signaling a desire to vigorously pursue fiscal reform and balance the budget.[88] With the tithe system still not producing yields as hoped and needing funds to cover mounting expenses and government debt that had resulted from the ongoing effects of the 1857 financial crisis, the empire turned again to Britain and France for a loan.[89] A rather optimistic 1861 assessment of the empire's finances by Lord Hobart, representing the Board of Trade, and Morgan Hugh Foster, from the British Treasury, led to the granting of an £8 million loan in 1862.[90] Fuad Pasha drew up a new budget that promised a 98 million piastres surplus for the 1862/1863 fiscal year.[91] In late 1862 the Ottoman Bank merged its organization with a French group headed by Crédit Mobilier to form the Imperial Ottoman Bank.[92]

The bank's resources enabled the government to refinance and address the empire's immediate fiscal situation; however, being indebted to a foreign-funded institution with the potential to exercise such oversight power was not ideal for Ottoman financial sovereignty. Officials thus continued to focus on refining the administrative technologies that were crucial to revenue extraction. Given the resistance to their most recent attempt at tax reform, in the ensuing years the government shifted its focus to a complete overhaul of its administrative apparatus, refined through a series of regulations governing provincial organization, the most significant of which were issued in 1864 and 1871. They aimed to incorporate local councils and elites into a hierarchy of a state-centered bureaucracy with meticulous instructions regarding their selection and the distribution of responsibilities among them.[93]

Responsibilities related to the development of agriculture were a priority in this administration. At the provincial level the 1864 regulation provided for an official chosen by the Commerce and Agriculture Ministry who would compile written reports about provincial production as well as imports and exports.[94] A general council composed of members elected from the *sanjaks*, the largest subdivision after the province, would meet annually to discuss matters related to infrastructure, security, agriculture, commerce, and taxes.[95] Provincial yearbooks (*vilayet salnameleri*) began to appear following the reform—notably, the provinces of Aleppo and Syria were among the first for which they were compiled—and often included scrupulous records of the crops grown at the district (*kaza*) and sometimes subdistrict (*nahiye*) level.[96]

The duties allocated to the various councils at each level sought to ensure a direct line of communally assessed concerns regarding agriculture from the village level through to the provincial governor. At the provincial, subprovincial, and district levels, administrative councils and, at the village level, a council of elders would deliberate agricultural affairs.[97] Although the councils of elders were responsible for issues affecting their particular group within the community (*sınıf-ı ahali*), such as tax distribution, with regard to agriculture the law enjoined them to work together. District-level council members reported to the General Council issues pinpointed for discussion, which were then reported to the provincial governor.[98] The law also outlined specific duties for the mukhtars elected as leaders at the village level; notably, it designated them as the government agents responsible for tax collection.[99] By identifying elected village mukhtars as the assessors and collectors of taxes, the law aimed to establish a position that was within both the local community and the bureaucratic hierarchy for this role, whose desired reform had thus far eluded the government.

In tandem with this provincial reorganization and bottom-up process of gathering and collating information from the empire's villages, reformers renewed their efforts to find a solution to the agrarian credit question. Despite the Imperial Ottoman Bank's interest in financing commerce and public works projects, it would not invest in loans against land until the years immediately before World War I.[100] In 1863 Midhat Pasha, in his capacity as governor of the Danube Province and with the approval of the central government, introduced a regional fund (*memleket sandığı*) as a source of credit for farmers.[101] With capital derived from monies obtained by selling extra crops set aside for this purpose, loans could be made against a guarantee (*kefalet*) or against a mortgage or pledge (*rehin*) on land or a valuable object. A borrower could also do some combination of the two.[102] The fund was successful enough that in 1867 the government promulgated a law making their establishment obligatory in other provinces.[103] More than 300 funds, which could be used as much for public works as for more explicitly agricultural concerns, were created throughout the empire and administered by four-person committees elected by towns and villages.[104]

Establishing a means by which farmers, particularly small farmers, could access greater capital resources had become a preoccupation of numerous government officials in the mid-nineteenth century. Farmers required different terms than most borrowers. They needed a repayment cycle that was amenable to the seasonal rhythms of crop production, low interest rates, and flexibility given the uncertainties inherent in agricultural production. The regional funds were some of the first to try to address this challenge, emerging around the same time as early experiments in the German states and France. Between 1862 and 1871, the year of German unification, the number of local reciprocal Raiffeisen funds in the German states increased from four to seventy-five.[105] In Russia the first agricultural cooperative, inspired by another German model, the Schulze-Delitzsch funds, opened in 1866.[106] In both cases local elites tended to co-opt these funds and exploit their operations to consolidate their influence.[107]

In France, following the establishment of the Crédit Foncier in 1852, which was intended to provide substantial long-term loans for major undertakings and thus primarily targeted large landowners, the government facilitated the formation of a precarious Crédit Agricole in 1860.[108] However, it faced strenuous resistance from elites, including members of the Society of Farmers of France, established in 1868, who rejected the intervention of the state in what they considered "a private industry."[109] The hypercentralization of the Crédit Agricole also meant that it lacked the flexibility and knowledge to respond to local conditions.[110] Ultimately, it became ensnared in the fallout from the 1870s financial crisis in Egypt, collapsed in 1876, and was incorporated into the Crédit Foncier.[111] Clearly, such efforts had to contend not only with the challenges posed by nature but also with the power wielded in rural areas by elites whose interests they either threatened or unwittingly reinforced.

As the regional funds expanded throughout the empire, so did efforts by the Ministry of the Cadastre to create new property registers for towns and villages—at least ten towns in the eastern Mediterranean were registered by 1867 and work was ongoing.[112] An 1866 addendum to the original regulation specified that for rural areas property commissions were to be established for each district and subprovince (*sancak*).[113] Like clockwork, that same year instructions arrived in Syria detailing how to form these commissions, and work began in Aleppo.[114] Provincial elite cooperation was integral to these operations—in Aleppo, Raghib al-Jabri, a member of one of the city's two most powerful families, headed the *tapu* office and remained in the position until he died.[115]

With a new provincial organization in place, cadastral teams at work, and an experimental attempt to provide agrarian credit under way, the late 1860s saw yet another effort to reorganize the agrarian bureaucracy with the reinstatement of the Commerce and Agriculture Ministry.[116] In the eastern Mediterranean this renewed focus on a ministry devoted to agricultural concerns came in the wake of a period of increasing demand for raw material exports, first because of the Crimean War and then because of the American Civil War, and high prices for agricultural products.[117] It also coincided with efforts to expand the amount of land under cultivation. Starting in the 1850s, policies that offered favorable conditions, such as tax breaks, exemption from conscription, and free land, had encouraged farming communities to move into areas closer to the desert line or Bedouin to start or increase their involvement in agriculture.[118] During the late 1860s, Reşid Pasha, the governor of Syria from 1866 to 1871, sold large tracts of *miri* land in the Hawran and the Biqaʿ Valley to wealthy Damascene entrepreneurs. The immediate goal was to raise funds for the provincial treasury, then to expand tax assessment and extraction by the provincial government into the region, and ultimately to facilitate "agricultural development." The sales raised substantial sums, but they met stiff resistance from Bedouin of the Bani Sakhr, who had prior claims to the lands and did not want to be relegated to lesser pastures or denied access to the agricultural surplus.[119]

Recommendations debated and formalized in a report (*mazbata*) sent to Istanbul by Syria's new General Council suggested their stance on the potential benefits of these sales and their elite view of desirable agricultural reform projects in the province. They advocated the formation of agricultural councils at the district and special district (*mutasarrifiya*) levels to distribute government-provided seeds to encourage both farmers to expand the land they cultivated and Bedouin to try growing crops around deserted villages. Perhaps seeking to capitalize on the increasing legibility of *miri* land as surety and the perceived mounting credit requirements of agricultural development, they proposed allowing wealthy locals to start banks lending at 12% interest or less. They also suggested planting trees and gardens around villages in the Hawran and ensuring the implementation of the Land Code throughout the province.[120]

The General Council members were not the only ones interested in the Land Code's effects. English and French officials also followed the repercussions of Ottoman land-related reform efforts attentively. In 1869, as England contemplated strategies for land reform in Ireland following the devastating midcentury famine (the Landlord and Tenant Act in Ireland was passed in 1870), the Foreign Office requested information about land-tenure arrangements from countries throughout Europe, including multiple reports from officials in the Ottoman Empire.[121] The perspectives they offered on the Land Code's impact were diverse if not always particularly acute.[122] For instance, the British consul in Trabzon, W. Gifford Palgrave, submitted a report for "eastern Turkey" that painted areas as diverse as "Anatolia, Koordistan, Irak, and Syria" with the same vague disparaging brush as he insisted that the law had led to general impoverishment and a depreciation in land values.[123] Underlying his analysis seems to have been a particular disdain for small property ownership—England, notably, was a country that appeared in no rush to break up large property—and a discomfort with the usufruct-based rights of the Land Code. He contrasted his disdain for small property ownership with the view held by his counterparts across the Channel, noting that the empire's dismantling of large estates had "received much praise from a certain school of European writers, French in particular."[124] As for the Land Code's usufruct-based rights, he critiqued the code for "giving a legal preference to the contingencies of doubt and transfer over those of possession and permanence."[125]

The recent investors in the land sold by Syria's governor did not appear to share these misgivings, nor did Ottoman officials, who continued to focus their efforts on modifying provincial organization, passing an 1871 regulation that reflected a desire for bottom-up assessments of concerns regarding agriculture, taxation, and cadastral operations, albeit with additional layers of oversight. In particular, the regulation added an intermediate administrative unit between the district and the village, a subdistrict, to be headed by a *müdir*.[126] Notably, the law entrusted this official with informing the district administration of escheat *(mahlulat)* or hidden *(mektûmât)* lands that came to his attention—presumably through headmen who were enjoined to transmit this information to the subdistrict level—and any complaints from members of the community against headmen or elder councils concerning tax collection.[127] It also created directors of the *defterhane*, positions for employees involved in property registration, and a director of agriculture and commerce who would propose reforms that were "practically and scientifically necessary with regards to agricultural matters" based on the "geographic situation and natural suitability of each area [*mahal*]."[128] Each director was expected to submit annual reports to the governor.[129]

By the end of 1871, efforts to register the empire's lands with *tapu* deeds were proceeding, although half still lacked them.[130] In response, the government also started roll-call *(yoklama)* registration, whereby the *tapu* scribe, working presumably from lists of the village inhabitants and property records from the tax office, would register still undeclared or abandoned land based on the report of a council composed of village officials. In southern Syria *yoklama* registration had started by the late 1870s.[131] Court records demonstrate the rapid incorporation of *tapu* deeds into judicial processes to verify claims to land. In one sampling from Damascus the percentage of cases referencing *tapu* deeds increased from 12% in 1878–1879 to 100% in 1887–1889.[132]

In addition to new measures concerning land registration, following the promulgation of the 1871 provincial regulation, officials again tackled the issue of tax collection. Additional laws passed in 1871 and 1872 limited the extent of a tax farm to one village, made auctions more local (holding them at the district level), and forbade tax farmers from combining leases from multiple villages.[133] The 1870s were risky years for tax collection in the eastern Mediterranean. From an excellent harvest in 1866, lack of rain devastated harvests in Syria in 1870, doubling grain prices and forcing people to make bread from corn instead of wheat. Drought continued for much of the following decade.[134] From 1872 on, harvests in Anatolia were not much better, leading to massive animal deaths in 1873–1874.[135] The 1878–1879 winter in Aleppo was particularly severe and, combined with food shortages caused by the Russo-Ottoman War, led to looting in the town's central market.[136] A drought in 1879 in eastern Anatolia led to devastated crops and widespread animal mortality.[137]

Although state officials had technically transferred the financial risks associated with drought, deficient harvests still depressed revenue.[138] Meanwhile, as other countries increased tariffs to shelter their industry and markets from the expanding production, falling prices, and intensifying competition that precipitated a global financial depression starting in 1873, foreign powers thwarted Ottoman efforts to rebalance the budget, or at least reduce the deficit, and pay off foreign debt through alternative revenue sources, such as increased customs duties.[139] In France, for example, such policies had facilitated a reduction in the tax burden on rural communities.[140] According to one assessment, foreign ambassadors were far more "concerned with maintaining the tax immunities enjoyed by their nationals in Turkey [*sic*] than with protecting the very large class of holders of securities."[141] Reduced revenues combined with the depression, which would last until 1896, made it increasingly difficult for the empire to pay off its high-interest (12%) loans, which were attractive to investors but onerous to repay. In February 1875, much to the chagrin of many Ottoman officials (and Russia), the government granted the British- and French-capitalized Imperial Ottoman Bank the capacity to collect state revenues, from which it would service the empire's debt, essentially making it imperial treasurer.[142]

Then, on 6 October 1875, the government declared that for the next five years it would pay half of its loan payments in bonds instead of cash, essentially declaring bankruptcy.[143] Such bankruptcies were not an uncommon occurrence in the nineteenth century. A number of countries had defaulted multiple times even before the 1870s financial crisis. During the 1870s the

Ottoman Empire was joined by Spain, twelve southern US states, Egypt, and a number of countries in Latin America.[144] With agriculture still the empire's major source of revenue, the productive capacity of the land that could be brought under cultivation and the technologies deployed to enhance extraction from it remained inadequate to the task of sustaining the revenues necessary to service the debt enabled by new financial arrangements and fed by mounting expenditures, creating dire financial straits.

In the midst of this crisis, the government renewed efforts to implement programs aimed at making agriculture more remunerative. Reaffirming the centrality of agriculture to the mission of the Commerce Ministry, it added "agriculture" back to its official name and established the Commerce and Agriculture Council under its purview in 1876.[145] A 6 April 1876 memorandum spelled out the processes for creating a hierarchy of agriculture and commerce societies at the provincial level with four members at the district level, eight at the subprovince level, and twelve in the provincial center. There would also be a 24-person commerce and agriculture society with honorary membership in Istanbul.[146] These societies were to provide information to the central ministry on local agricultural conditions and suggest ways to increase production.[147]

During the brief three-month reign of Murad V, who was notably sympathetic to the reformist contingent in the government—a contrast to the reformers' contentious relationship with Sultan Abdulaziz, whom they deposed in May 1876, followed by his death shortly thereafter—the government issued a detailed decree laying out the council's duties.[148] It outlined an ambitious comprehensive program under its oversight that aimed to increase the empire's agricultural output through a variety of measures that in many ways reflected a resumption of previous projects. Key components included administering the public works funds (*menafi sandıkları*), assessing the improvement of "dead" lands, creating a bureau to collect agricultural statistics, establishing schools in the imperial center and model fields in the provinces, studying needs for old and new agricultural implements as well as storage facilities, encouraging publications about new "scientific" techniques, and ensuring that farmers had good seeds and necessary tools. It also proposed collaborations with the Public Works Ministry to clean up areas that were inhospitable for cultivator settlement and with the Finance Ministry to address taxes that were an impediment to agriculture, commerce, and industry.[149]

The ascent of Sultan Abdulhamid II in August and his agreement to the promulgation of a constitution in December 1876 perhaps gave reformers hope that the realization of such programs would follow in short order. Parliament met in March 1877 and tried once more to abolish tax farms in an April decree.[150] In their stead, a newly created Office of Tithe and Livestock Tax was to oversee the implementation of a land tax.[151] After a second session in December 1877, Abdulhamid II "temporarily prorogued" the Parliament in February 1878 in the midst of the 1877–1878 Russo-Ottoman War.[152] Russian forces marched on Istanbul, eventually forcing the Ottoman government to sign a treaty that included relinquishing some of its most agriculturally productive provinces. In the aftermath of this foreign aggression, Abdulhamid II did not recall Parliament, and it was suspended until after the 1908 revolution, meaning that the following decades of tax, land, and agrarian finance reform were largely driven by the new sultan's priorities.

Hamidian Priorities, an Expanding Bureaucracy, and Elite Critiques

The final decades of the nineteenth century and the early part of the twentieth century witnessed a general flourishing in agricultural production throughout the Ottoman Empire.[153] In eastern areas of the provinces of Aleppo and Syria, more land came under cultivation as extensive but not necessarily more intensive agriculture increased.[154] But the empire faced a conundrum: Even as production increased, the 1873–1896 depression caused the prices of agricultural products to drop, making it difficult to meet its budget obligations.[155] In part, this was due to the influx of cheap grain, especially from North America, into domestic markets. Local grain could not compete at remunerative prices and, because the empire could not raise tariffs like various other states, domestic production lacked protection. In response, officials proposed improving transport networks to reduce costs, intensifying cash crop production, increasing assistance to farmers, and shifting taxation to alternative forms that were not so dependent on a volatile agricultural commodity market.[156]

Nonetheless, during the empire's final decades, it remained largely reliant on revenue from agricultural sources to meet its annual budget. Thus the 1880s and 1890s saw intensified efforts to make agricultural tax collection more efficient, finally realize many of the agricultural projects that had been proposed but postponed in the preceding decades, and continue expanding cultivation into the empire's "empty lands."[157] It was in this context that Reşid Bey's unauthorized excursion to the Chicago World's Columbian Exposition, even though it ruffled feathers, came to be regarded as beneficial for the insight it provided into the latest developments in international, and especially American, agriculture.

Experiments with taxation struggled to strike a balance between consistent revenue for the treasury and maintaining farmers on their land. Shortly after suspending Parliament, in 1879 Abdulhamid II ordered an empire-wide survey of tax methods. He preferred a land tax, but this required a depth of local knowledge that still largely eluded Ottoman officials, so tax farming continued to dominate. In tacit acknowledgment of the challenges involved in eradicating what the survey's committee considered an intrinsically "fair and equitable" tax, the committee proposed collection in kind by government agents where administratively possible, collection in kind by tax farmers in largely pastoralist regions (e.g., areas of Aleppo province), and collection through a cash land tax by government employees where requisite information was available.[158] Notably, unlike the early-twentieth-century technocrats discussed in chapter 5, the committee did not view the varying degrees of investment required for production in different areas to be a major point of concern.[159]

In accordance with the recommendations of this committee, the new Office of Tithe and Livestock Tax, which finally took shape in 1880, tried to definitively shift tax collection to a wage-based approach (*emaneten idare*).[160] In theory, government officials, unaccompanied by gendarmes, would carry out collection.[161] In practice, the office lacked the requisite staff and employed tax collectors who were not only primarily ex-gendarmes but also not authorized to collect the tithe, leaving it in the hands of village elites.[162]

In the midst of these experiments, the governor of Syria, Hamdi Paşa, attempted to apply the *tahmis* to the harvest of 1884. Calculated by averaging the tithes from the last five years, which had been good, the preestablished sum aimed to both provide the treasury with a set amount for budgetary planning and relieve farmers from the coercion of tax farmers and gendarmes. However, the *tahmis* caused an uproar because its elevated rate, which was based on previous good harvests, did not make allowances for the current year's lower yields, not to mention the timing of collection meant that peasants had to borrow from moneylenders and the rate's fixed nature decreased opportunities for evasion.[163] One group of taxpayers, identified by the provincial governor as people from Beirut and Haifa who had grown accustomed to benefiting from possessing lands (Beirut) and tax farming lands (Haifa) in the Biqaʿ Valley, Baʿalbak, and ʿAkka, sent a telegram declaring that, to the treasury's detriment, they would "leave cultivation of the lands" if the tithe was replaced by the *tahmis*.[164] Mounting discontent led to the abolition of the *tahmis* the following year and, by 1887, under a newly constituted Tithe Auction Directorate, most areas reverted to tax farming. Increased supervision and control exposed tax farmers to greater risks, and their bankruptcy rates rose.[165]

These rapid shifts in agricultural tax collection paralleled another major development in the empire's financial fortunes that in part explains officials' mounting desperation to secure more lucrative extraction. In late 1881, six years after its initial 1875 default, the empire allowed key revenues to be subjected to the exactions of the Public Debt Administration (PDA). With limited options available to pay off its debt and pressure from its creditors following the Russo-Ottoman War, imperial officials agreed to the PDA after lengthy negotiations.[166] The PDA facilitated the empire's access to international capital but also gained control over revenues from a number of profitable sources, including the silk tithes, fish, stamp, and spirit taxes, and the monopolies on salt and tobacco, creating tension between the central government and the local elites who had previously collected these revenues.[167] The PDA also acquired tithe-derived kilometric guarantees to ensure profits for its railway concessions, including the Hama-Damascus line.[168]

With so many sources of revenue diverted to service the empire's debt, officials turned once more to the tithe as a way to raise additional funds for public works, education, and agriculture. In 1883 they increased oversight of the regional funds network and renamed them public works funds (*menafi sandıkları*).[169] To provide a more secure source of capital, in March 1887 the government decided to increase the 10% tithe on the harvest to 11.5% with 1% (the share to assist public works [*menafi hisse-i ianesi*]) going to the funds and the remaining 0.5% (the share to assist education [*maarif hisse-i ianesi*]) levied to support local educational institutions.[170] But these adjustments did not satisfactorily address the issues—illegally high interest rates, co-optation of funds by elites, and loans to insolvent debtors—that prevented the funds from meeting expectations.[171]

To provide yet more oversight, in 1888 the government established the locally capitalized Agricultural Bank, whose operations offered a stark contrast to those of the primarily foreign-capitalized Imperial Ottoman Bank.[172] On paper the Agricultural Bank aimed to ensure a stable source of lower interest loans that were more responsive to the financial and ecological challenges that farmers faced than the loans offered by local moneylenders.[173] Interest started at 6%, considerably below the rates of private moneylenders, for a one-year loan, but each additional year incurred a further 3% interest, meaning a borrower paid back the maximum ten-year loan with 33% interest, much closer to or exceeding private rates.[174] Loaning to anyone but farmers was forbidden, and debtors who could prove catastrophic circumstances could delay repayment.[175] Later adjustments to the bank's statutes expanded the repayment period for acute suffering, stipulated that a borrower or their guarantor had to mortgage property, and enacted a cross-referencing procedure with the land and cadastre tax (*tahrir vergi*) offices to ensure that the property mortgaged was not already encumbered.[176] The documentation necessary for cross-referencing and holding guarantors accountable was a direct result of instruments instituted by the Land Code and *tapu* regulations passed decades earlier—knowledge officials were able to draw on to address these issues.

The Agricultural Bank ostensibly provided a conduit for officials working within the institutions of Ottoman state space to intervene more directly in rural finance. But despite lofty goals of assisting small farmers, the composition of the local branches' boards suggested that local elites had plenty of opportunities to exercise their influence, if not outright corruption, through the bank's administration.[177] In Damascus, for example, the leadership of the Chamber of Agriculture and the Agricultural Bank drew heavily from members of large landowning families, some of whose acquisitions had occurred quite recently.[178]

Furthermore, despite the Agricultural Bank's emphasis on loaning exclusively to cultivators, the scope of its activities extended considerably beyond this. As officials struggled to find funds not already encumbered by foreign obligations, they turned to the bank's resources, leading it to acquire a rather wide remit that made it in essence an aspiring rival to the Imperial Ottoman Bank.[179] Although not explicit among its original duties, the Agricultural Bank administered and/or provided funds for education, the military, refugee resettlement (including provision of agricultural implements), forestry programs, road and railway construction, public works projects, and the estates of the sultan's privy purse. Its resources helped defray the costs of the Russian war indemnity and a loan from Deutsche Bank in addition to guaranteeing several international loans. Viewed narrowly, these various projects might appear to have "nonagricultural functions," but, as discussed earlier and later, officials considered many of these activities just as essential, if not more so, than the implementation of exclusively scientific agriculture projects:[180] Better roads meant lower costs for crop transport; increased security expanded the areas available for more extensive agriculture; refugee resettlement provided additional agricultural labor; and schools increasingly incorporated classes in scientific agriculture.

Some cultivators also quickly took advantage of the new bank, whereas others were more wary. In 1890 in Aleppo, the British consul noted that, since the creation of the Agricultural Bank, the bank had loaned 200 pounds out of its 5,000 pound capital and that cultivators' loans ranged from 3 to 10 pounds based on their land values.[181] Aviv Derri's work on loan registers from Nazareth, Haifa, and Safad demonstrates that a number of villagers took out loans from the bank often for just under the ten-year limit (in order to benefit from the nine-year interest rate). The amounts and loan periods varied depending on region, and not everyone who applied for a loan was granted one, but Derri's analysis makes clear that villagers of varying means, not just elites, were availing themselves of the Agricultural Bank's services.[182] Nonetheless, other sources suggest that some villagers remained cautious about the operations and obligations involved in accepting the bank's capital. The formalities involved could be costly.[183] Furthermore, the bank's insistence, at least initially, on land as collateral raised the specter of the cultivator's source of livelihood being promptly seized and auctioned off if they defaulted. Borrowing from private moneylenders offered more flexibility, because they accepted crops or valuables as collateral, let debtors wrack up higher levels of interest, and allowed payment in kind.[184] Not long after the bank's formation, the Istanbul Chamber of Commerce proposed that it accept alternative forms of collateral, such as tools or crops, as this would be more amenable for smaller farmers and sharecroppers who did not own or possess rights to land, but these suggestions were not immediately implemented.[185]

The progression of property registration also began to bear fruit in the struggle to ensure better yields from tax farming even as it created new difficulties for cultivators. Officials still grappled with how best to handle the effects of drought in regions such as Syria, where one year's tax farming amounts could be less than a half or even a third of the previous year's, property values needed regular reassessment, and cultivators had to borrow at high interest rates to pay the sums demanded—a situation that officials urged addressing with "special measures."[186] Meanwhile, new tithe regulations in 1887 and 1889 required tax farmers to secure their bids with registered property or a material surety, such as cash, and provided clear instructions as to who in the now well-established provincial administration was responsible for auctioning them.[187] In providing mortgage-based security for the tithe, including the additional 1% that constituted part of the Agricultural Bank's capital, these tax farmers became key agents for ensuring the empire's liquidity, albeit with far more mechanisms to ensure their compliance than earlier in the century because of the legibility provided by processes put in place by the Land Code and *tapu* regulations.[188]

These increasingly fine-tuned efforts to streamline extraction and increase investment paralleled more aggressive measures to expand the empire's agricultural administration. In 1878 Kevork Efendi, who in 1875 had served as the agricultural official among the senior commerce clerks, acquired the title of agricultural director on the Commerce and Agriculture Council, where he was joined by Amasyan Efendi, a graduate of the Grignon Agricultural School in France, and Agop Efendi.[189] To lay the groundwork for the empire's agricultural reform program by assessing conditions in the provinces and making recommendations about local agricultural reform needs, one of the first new posts created in this agricultural administration was that of agricultural inspector.

Shortly after the appointment of Amasyan Efendi as agriculture director and the creation of two general agriculture inspector posts in 1879, which were held by Aram Efendi and Kevork Efendi, also a Grignon graduate, more students were sent abroad to study in France in 1880/1881 and Germany in 1884/1885. Upon their return, the students who had studied in France were appointed as inspectors in Aydın, Adana, Syria, Sivas, Bursa, and Salonica, and the students returning from Germany were appointed to Aleppo, Monastir, and Erzurum.[190] Their dispersion among these provinces suggests an attention not only to particularly fertile regions of the empire but also to those regions with lands considered ripe for extending cultivated areas. Thus in the eastern Mediterranean by 1885 the province of Syria had its own agricultural inspector, Qalavas Efendi, and by 1890 Manuk Efendi was serving as inspector in the province of Aleppo.[191] As provincial inspectors, the local knowledge they gained helped provide direction to the central administration for future projects, a role examined in greater detail in the next chapter. In 1892 the Halkalı Agricultural School (Halkalı Ziraat Mektebi) in Istanbul accepted its first class of students to be trained locally by some of these returned graduates.[192] For much of this time agricultural affairs came under the purview of the Commerce and Public Works Ministry until finally in February 1893 the administration established an independent Forest, Mines, and Agriculture Ministry.[193]

In the midst of this rapidly expanding administration, Ahmet Reşid Bey made his impromptu trip to Chicago the same year the new ministry was founded. Educated in the Mekteb-i Sultani and France, he had been appointed inspector for the provinces of Beirut and Syria only the previous year.[194] A French friend wrote to congratulate him on his new position, noting his immense suitability to the post in a "significant region" with its crops of wheat, cotton, olives, and grapes.[195] In bustling Beirut, which just five years earlier had become the center of its own new province, the governor also recognized Reşid Bey's "scientific knowledge, capacity, and ability" and proposed raising his salary and promoting him to public works director to meet the provinces' pressing need for such expertise.[196]

But Reşid Bey had a more ambitious scheme in mind. In March 1893 he wrote for permission to accompany a group of Beirut merchants bound for New York with a cargo of Syrian crops in order to study American agriculture.[197] When permission was not forthcoming, he departed anyway, sending a telegram from Port Said to confirm his whereabouts.[198] Consternation at his departure swiftly turned into efforts to find and confirm a replacement. Meanwhile, Reşid Bey made his way to New York, passed through Canada, and, according to diplomatic correspondence, was already looking for another job.[199]

Reşid Bey had studied agriculture in Paris, where he attended the 1889 Exposition Universelle, and he justified his decision to attend the Chicago exhibition by noting the insights it offered into the latest developments, particularly American ones, in a rapidly evolving market.[200] The Chicago exhibition's Ottoman commissioner, Hakkı Pasha, lent his support, suggesting that Reşid Bey be given a partial stipend to enable him to extend his stay because his own funds were running low.[201] Although concern was rife that such a move might be seen as pardoning his "impertinent" (*münasebetsiz*) behavior and encouraging repeat offenses, ultimately some funds were authorized from the exhibition's appropriations.[202]

In a long elaborate report submitted about his experience, which probably was key to mollifying official opinion back in Istanbul and Beirut, Reşid Bey described the agricultural, horticultural, forest, and minerals displays, including a list detailing each foreign government's contributions.[203] He discussed new tools and implements and observations about American approaches to cultivating potatoes, cotton, tobacco, and forage crops. The report concluded with statistics for each American state's production of wheat and corn for 1859, 1879, and 1887. Clearly aware of the challenges posed by the expense of new technologies, Reşid Bey expressed hope that "with a little bit of encouragement" the factories producing farm equipment in each large American city might be able to supply the empire with machines at "very cheap prices," which made them more competitive than European ones for Ottoman farmers.[204]

Reşid Bey also recommended inviting American manufacturers to participate in the Ottoman Agricultural and Industrial Exhibition being planned for Istanbul, the goal of which was in part to demonstrate to Ottoman cultivators methods from which they might choose to "enlarge their ideas of their own work and enable them to improve it."[205] Despite the exhibit being primarily about showcasing Ottoman goods, Ottoman officials, apparently impressed with the information provided, decided to invite American manufacturers to participate, albeit informally and as an exception.[206] The exhibition was canceled because of an earthquake, but this concession indicated the value attributed to Reşid Bey's knowledge and experience.[207]

Although the new minister of agriculture, Selim Melhamé Bey, himself a Beirut native appointed to the position when the ministry was created in 1893, threatened to deprive Reşid Bey of one to two months of work upon his return or even to replace him with the agricultural inspector from Edirne, he was ultimately allowed to resume his post.[208] The consideration given to Reşid Bey's report, despite his insubordination, illustrated the importance placed on these exchanges. According to the Chicago exhibition's promoters, the sultan had taken a personal interest in the event because it was a chance to demonstrate "Turkish [*sic*] progress in science and education."[209] The exhibition offered the empire an opportunity to project itself as a "modern civilized member" of the world's major powers on a global stage.[210] It was also a key nexus for international exchange and consumption of knowledge about new technologies. Through his observations, Reşid Bey made the argument that the French- and German-based training of the empire's current coterie of agricultural experts was insufficient and could benefit from experiences further afield.

Having made the case for his unauthorized (*mezuniyetsiz*) departure, Reşid Bey thus returned to carry on his duties as the agricultural inspector of Beirut and Syria, issuing reports about maintaining the competitiveness of grape-based products or the positive impacts of a government-sponsored medical school given the existence of American- and French-directed ones.[211] He was also likely the agricultural inspector for Syria and Beirut who observed corruption in the region's Agricultural Bank branches, leading the bank to appoint special inspectors to investigate in 1894.[212] However, he was not in the post for long. By 1896 the province had a new agriculture inspector, and Reşid Bey was apparently living in Egypt, where he started to publish a journal that was banned in the empire.[213] Perhaps indicative of why it was banned, among those whose work he published was Ahmet Rıza, a fellow student of agriculture, an increasingly vociferous critic of the Hamidian regime, and an acquaintance of Reşid Bey's from years earlier.[214] In October 1895—the same year that Rıza formed the Parisian branch of the İttihad-ı Osmanni or, as he renamed it, İttihat ve Terakki Cemiyeti (Committee of Union and Progress [CUP])—issue 7 of the journal featured the introduction to the first of Rıza's "Six Memorandums," a series of texts offering advice to the sultan that were also published in London that year.[215]

Rıza, better known for his embrace of positivism while living in France and its influence on his critique of the Ottoman state, also had a background in networks of scientific agriculture, which shaped the material and practical aspects of his proposals for the economic well-being of the state.[216] In fact, this is where his advice to the sultan started. In his opening paragraphs, Rıza positioned his critique as a response to the "miserable" plight of the empire's peasants, which during his youth he had observed while traveling around Anatolia. Clearly unimpressed with the results of reform policies thus far, his solution lay in improving cultivators' agricultural methods, but he acknowledged that they lacked the capacity to make the necessary investments on their own.[217] Thinking a degree in agronomy would enable him to do something about these conditions, he studied at the Grignon Agricultural School, but was disillusioned upon his return to find no work in agriculture-related positions, leading him to temporarily turn his attention to education.[218]

As disaffected would-be reforming elites critiqued imperial policies from abroad, within the empire officials continued to refine the administrative processes established over the preceding decades, albeit with mixed results and inconsistent application. In 1891, after years of avoiding the risks associated with tax farming by means of wage contracts while extracting as much as possible through alternating experiments with fixed- and ascending-price auctions, government officials reverted back to ascending-price auctions. Nadir Özbek argues that this time it was with greater success, noting the substantial increases in revenues achieved. By outsourcing the risks, he claims, decades of reform had effectively limited the wealth and power one tax farmer could amass because of the tougher oversight measures.[219]

Still, the application of ascending-price auctions was not necessarily universal, as provincial officials negotiated local conditions. In late 1896 in the Hawran, a brief attempt to institute the *tahmis* provoked such resistance in the midst of an already violent conflict between the provincial authorities and Druze rebels that authorities quickly withdrew it by 1898.[220] Until 1897 Syria's provincial yearbooks differentiated between the tithe collected through fixed-price auction (*maktuan ihale*) and that collected by means of government agents (*emaneten idare*). In general, the amount collected by government agents was only approximately 10% of the total. Fixed-price auctions continued to dominate.[221] Meanwhile, foreign powers, insisting on the capitulations and PDA agreement, thwarted Ottoman efforts to supplement this revenue through an increase in customs fees from 8% to 11% in March 1900.[222]

Efforts continued to extend land registration into areas where it had not yet been applied or to update registers. In the Hawran registration enforcement started in 1892 and was reported to be complete in 1893, despite resistance from villagers, Druze shaykhs, and Bedouin.[223] Registration was also carried out in western areas of the province of Syria around Zabadani and Baʿalbak in 1898–1899 in what seems to have been an expansion of *yoklama*-esque procedures.[224] Supposedly, a new cadastral project had been proposed in 1895, so it is unclear whether these registers represent a new approach to registration or a continuation of previous practices, the new project having failed to materialize.[225]

As these reforms increasingly made rural areas more legible, they also imposed additional burdens on rural communities. Multiple reports from the eastern Mediterranean suggested that officials tended to register properties at values higher than their actual worth, meaning the land tax amounted to more than the official 0.4%.[226] Tax farmers (and state officials) also faced challenges collecting the surtax on the tithe for the Agricultural Bank.[227] For some villages the surtax remained unpaid for years.[228] Ongoing adjustments to the Agricultural Bank's procedures for handling property offered as collateral for defaulted loans suggest that its terms remained contentious.[229] Although the bank did make concessions to allow for the use of chain guarantees (*kefalet-i müteselsile*) starting in 1895, with further adjustments in 1898 and 1901, the overwhelming number of loans made by the bank were against property.[230]

A brisk market in agricultural land emerged as imperial officials, landowners, and cultivators struggled with the fallout from the 1870s financial crisis, increasing competition from foreign crops, a customs regime that left little defense against this competition, and agricultural production that primarily increased only by more extensive rather than intensive cultivation.[231] "People of capital" parked surplus wealth in land using recently established instruments—such as *tapu* deeds and land tax payments—to ensure the legal verification of their claims and thwart challenges.[232] Sometimes, this process involved manipulating these instruments to reshape the emerging state space to serve their own interests more fully, at times contravening lawmakers' intent.

When some influential locals found that the import of these laws hindered their interests, they did not hesitate to ignore them or reinterpret them according to their own purposes. Officials who were considering extending the *tahmis* taxation method to areas of Syria discovered another "tahmis" method in play. This one involved an elaborate scheme in which wealthy locals joined forces with provincial government employees, namely, those working for the Agricultural Bank, to confiscate village lands and form "companies" (*kumpanyalar*). Having farmed the tax revenue and made loans to the villagers, these "masters of monopoly" (*erbab-ı ihtikâr*) would secure a pretext by which they would pay the village's land tax (*vergi*) in exchange for a fifth of the harvest. Using "deceptions" and unlawful contracts, they would acquire the village's "right of chairmanship" (*hakk-ı riyaset*) and force the farmers to turn over all their grain as payment for this fifth, eventually causing farmers to transfer their rights to these wealthy elites (*muhammesler*) and migrate to other areas.[233]

The Council of State expressed consternation, declaring that such chicanery contravened the spirit and letter of multiple laws passed in the past half-century of reforms. In particular, these contracts were contrary to Articles 8 and 113 of the Land Code. Article 8 stipulated that village lands could not be granted as a whole to the villagers, nor to one, two, or three among them, and Article 113 strictly prohibited the transfer of land under duress. Furthermore, the tithe regulation specified that, unless there was an acceptable excuse, it was forbidden to tender en masse the tithes of several villages or districts to one tax farmer, especially for two or three years all at once. To counter such predations and ensure legal means for preserving the rights of the local community (*ahali*), state officials insisted that cultivators should use their Agricultural Bank branches (after first ensuring they were staffed by scrupulous officials who would not aid the monopolists), noting that four new branches had recently opened and that eight more were on the verge of doing so. Meanwhile, local judicial, *tapu*, and *defter-i hakani* officials were urged to carry out investigations to ensure compliance with the law and were reminded not to sanction such illegal transfers.[234] From the Council of State's perspective, these elites' manipulations had thwarted the intent of provisions in the Land Code and Agricultural Bank statutes that sought to defend small cultivators' claims and provide official alternatives to private moneylenders. Realizing this intent involved holding accountable local elites who had worked the system to their advantage.

Despite such admonitions, in 1905 a petition from Hama indicated that out of ninety-nine villages in the subprovince (*sancak*) that had been in the hands of farming communities who were also *sahib-i arz* (i.e., who presumably had titles to the lands), eighty-six had fallen into the hands of the region's wealthy and the other thirteen were in the process of doing so. A similar phenomenon was under way in the nearby districts of Selimiye and Hamidiye. As a result, most of the villagers had left for the desert, and those who stayed "remained sheltered under the protection and patronage of the property and land owner [*emlak ve arazi sahibi*]."[235] The documents do not specify the names of the wealthy individuals involved; however, it is worth noting that in the ensuing decades, when scholars discussed the issue of large landownership in Hama, where the practice was considered particularly pernicious compared with other regions,[236] the number of villages described as belonging to large landowners was in the nineties.[237] The correlation between these numbers and those in the 1905 petition suggests that the phenomenon of large landholding in the region was relatively recent and that the consolidation of land in the hands of these regional elites did indeed happen as a result of the processes set in motion by the 1858 Land Code, but not for the reasons commonly cited in the literature, such as villagers refusing to register their lands.[238]

Villagers had registered their lands and had tried to hold on to them, but their inability to do so resulted from the way in which the Land Code had created new revenue streams in marginal environments. Debt was indeed at the heart of how they lost these lands, but the debts incurred, at least in the case discussed here, were debts created by "the workings of the land code" and the processes of land registration and valuation it generated.[239] According to the documents, the villagers had been forced into this situation because of land value registrations "at the time of the *tahrir*" at ten to fifteen times the land's real value. Over the course of twenty years the heaviness of the land tax (*vergi*) based on these inflated values coupled with years of drought forced the villagers to seek loans.[240] When they could not acquire them from the Agricultural Bank, they turned to mortgaging or transferring their lands to the wealthy of the district.[241] Overestimated land values in a region prone to drought had created an impossible situation for those who lacked the capital necessary to pay the assessed rates. Years of debt accrued from unpaid land taxes led to consolidation, as those with capital to spare profited from the villagers' misfortune.

Ottoman officials were dismayed by this turn of events because they considered farmer-owned villages more beneficial to the treasury. Large landowners were likely to use various "wiles" and "ruses" in their tithe farming (*iltizam*) operations to avoid paying even a tenth of the tithe due on their shares. The frustration was palpable; despite the government's having established Agricultural Bank branches throughout the region as an alternative to villagers' borrowing from local elites, the branches did not fulfill this purpose, even though villagers had turned to these banks first in their time of need.[242]

As some powerful elites manipulated the instruments of Ottoman state space to facilitate their acquisition of landed wealth, a younger generation of these elites, many of whom came from landowning families, became increasingly invested in the promises of "scientific agriculture" and by extension agricultural policy making. Like Rıza Bey, they were willing to foot the bill to travel abroad, participate in international networks of knowledge production, and study scientific agriculture with the intent of applying their learning through local experimentation.[243] They were alarmed by trends—for example, the expanding grain production in places such as the United States, Canada, and Australia—that made it increasingly difficult for Ottoman farmers to obtain a remunerative price for their crops, barring protection by higher tariffs.[244] Critical of insufficient government support for risk-mitigating infrastructure and frustrated with the precarity of the empire's financial circumstances, they were nonetheless optimistic enough about future possibilities to deem the expense worthwhile.[245]

Among the young men who studied abroad at the turn of the century from the eastern Mediterranean, at least three, Wadi Médawar, Edouard Saadé, and Toufik Saadé, attended the Institut Agricole de Beauvais, an agricultural school located just northwest of Paris.[246] Hailing from wealthy families, they represented themselves as go-betweens who, with their newly acquired knowledge, possessed the expertise to elaborate plans and proposals for how "the state" should handle its approach to agricultural reform in the region.[247] Edouard Saadé, son of Jibraʾil Saadé, one of the "avant-garde of the economic men" in Latakia, explained that he had chosen to study at Beauvais for three years because reform projects must "emanate from the initiative of . . . fellow citizens," and thus he hoped his training would be "useful for the recovery of agriculture in my dear country."[248] On the one hand, the students' concerns echoed those that had bedeviled Ottoman lawmakers for decades; on the other, their proposals sought to carve out a particular role for educated local agronomists such as themselves whose aspirations and efforts they insisted should be the focus of government support.

Streamlining taxation had enabled the extraction of more revenue, but ultimately there was a limit to how much the land could produce. Like Abdulhamid II's officials, these agronomists agreed that a tax taken in proportion to the harvest was well suited to the region's economic needs.[249] Recent efforts to impose a fixed tax, though driven by the treasury's need for more revenue, had made the collection process less lucrative for tax farmers and more onerous for cultivators; a fixed tax in cash needed to wait until more consistent harvests could be assured.[250] They lamented the use of force should a tax farmer have difficulty collecting the tithe and the delays in selling or storing the harvest while cultivators waited for the tax farmer to collect the government's portion. As alternatives, they proposed allowing village shaykhs or large landowners to farm the taxes to avoid delay—a tactic that some large landowners had pursued by making the final bid on a tax farm's set value but that required resources beyond the means of those less affluent.[251] The root of the problem was that the treasury's demands compelled government officials to extract more than their predecessors from land that was not producing more. Their solution? Focus less on extraction and more on increasing production.[252]

In principle, these agronomists agreed that the Agricultural Bank should be a boon to small farmers and agricultural development, but they urged the government to lower its interest rates, simplify its procedures, and ease its "draconian conditions" in the event of default. With fees the bank's interest rate could reach 8–9% (or more, as discussed earlier); loans were small, given the substantial guarantees required; and the bank moved too swiftly to auction the pledged property in the event of a default. They insisted that villagers still preferred private lenders, despite their higher rates, because moneylenders tended to just add interest to the original loan instead of immediately seizing a cultivator's land.[253] This state of affairs could lead to a situation in which the debtor lost the land to repay a loan that was not even half the value of the property, the other half being composed of the unpaid interest.[254]

"The State," according to Wady Médawar, had demonstrated good intentions toward agriculture through establishment of the Agricultural Bank, importation of duty-free implements and fertilizers, and its customs regime. But its emphasis on helping the small cultivator meant that it not only had not helped either the cultivator or itself but had also bypassed those who could benefit most from its support and in turn truly increase production, namely, hesitant "capitalists" and aspiring agronomists like themselves.[255] In the eastern Mediterranean, these agronomists suggested expanding access to agricultural education by building an agricultural school like that in the western part of the empire for the many young men who desired to study but could not afford to go abroad; in addition, they suggested awarding bonuses to encourage agricultural innovation and facilitating the formation of societies, companies, and associations.[256]

Given the state's limited resources for investment, "capitalists" should form associations to pursue initiatives such as irrigation expansion, transportation, and "agricultural speculations"—undertakings too daunting for an individual.[257] With state support, these associations could mediate between the state and the cultivator while pooling capital resources and distributing risk, but they needed sufficient capitalization.[258] Drawing on the experience of comparable endeavors in other countries, Médawar declared that "one of the biggest economic errors that had generated in the beginning the most catastrophes consisted precisely in wanting to lead enterprises of intensive high culture with insufficient capital."[259] Big landowners supported the current state of affairs because "they know perfectly well that this train advances at the rate of a camel, but they count on the government to harness more modern engines."[260] That is, they were unwilling to take upon themselves the risk of investment unless the government provided more fuel for possible initiatives, although the government's financial straits made this proposition more aspirational than concretely achievable. Nonetheless, these agronomists argued, the government could at least throw its influence more firmly behind such projects and attribute the same value and prestige to the contributions of rural areas as it did to those associated with urban areas such as commerce and industry.[261] Meanwhile, the authority conveyed by a group of landowners working in association would make the state's cooperation easier to achieve.[262] Their activities would be mutually reinforcing.

As these elites made their case for how the government could support them, lawmakers continued to focus on such matters as refining tax procedures. A new tithe regulation issued in 1905 provided increasingly detailed instructions regarding collection schedules based on the harvest cycles of various crops. Among other adjustments, it based the payment of tithe installments on when crops matured, varying the collection schedule from place to place depending on the time of the harvest.[263] This approach likely aimed to reduce cultivators' need to take out substantial loans in advance of the harvest.[264]

As Ottoman lawmakers worked to bring the cycles of taxation more in line with the cycles of diverse harvests, imperial officials became increasingly involved in agriculture-focused international organizations, which provided forums of exchange between an array of elites with agricultural interests. The first iteration of these organizations, the International Congresses of Agriculture, started in the 1870s as states sought protectionist measures to counter foreign imports amid falling grain prices. The congresses were dominated by French influence. The former (and future) French minister of agriculture Jules Méline, known for his protectionist policies, was the president of the Commission Internationale d'Agriculture, established in 1891 to ensure the congresses' longevity. The congresses provided a forum in which elite representatives from multiple countries discussed common issues while advocating for national interests.[265] The significance of Ottoman participation in such forums found expression in the *Ottoman Agriculture and Commerce Journal*, which started publication in the spring of 1907 with the aim of bringing readers insights about new methods and tools as well as the latest news from these gatherings. Reporting on Ottoman participation in the 1903 Rome and 1907 Vienna meetings, the journal published an excerpt from a speech by Méline, considering his perspective helpful to readers in their common cause of advancing agriculture. Méline urged protections for agriculture similar to those for industry and hailed agricultural "science" for how it promised to raise poor farmers' standard of living and general prosperity.[266]

In June 1905 an Ottoman delegation participated in the initial meeting in Rome to establish the International Institute of Agriculture, precursor to the Food and Agriculture Organization of the United Nations.[267] Attended by representatives from China, Japan, Iran, Egypt, the United States, and many European and South American countries, one of the institute's main goals was to collect and distribute official agricultural statistics on production each year.[268] It also aspired to provide a forum for exchanging information on a multitude of common concerns, from plant diseases to agricultural credit, insurance, cooperatives, and protecting farmers' common interests.[269] Within the empire this participation led to the compilation of crop production statistics for dissemination. In the summer of 1906 the Interior Ministry sent out requests to each province for the information desired by the institute to contribute to these forms of international knowledge production and consumption.[270] Participation in these organizations provided avenues for both performing technocratic expertise and sharing mutual frustrations about the subordinate stature of agricultural development to industrial production.[271]

Starting in 1908, the second constitutional period saw efforts to intensify many of these Hamidian-era projects of agrarian reform. A number of influential members in the CUP—the organization of reformers that rose to power after the revolution—had studied agriculture before 1908 and saw the second constitutional period as an opportunity to finally realize their ambitions.[272] Hüseyin Kâzım Kadri Bey and Ahmet Rıza Bey were two exemplary figures in this regard. Ahmet Rıza Bey, former agricultural inspector Reşid Bey's aforementioned colleague from the late 1800s, and, postrevolution, the president of the Chamber of Deputies, finally found himself with the influence to pursue the reforms he had found lacking under the Hamidian regime. Hüseyin Kâzım, as described in the introduction, was one of the editors of *Tanin*, the CUP's daily journal, and a passionate proponent of scientific agriculture.[273] Under the CUP-led government, Ahmet Rıza Bey was elected the honorary head of the newly formed Ottoman Agricultural Society. Hüseyin Kâzım became one of its vice chairmen. The organization, one of three agricultural societies formed during this period, first met on 22 August 1908 in the Veterinary School in Istanbul.[274]

The elite group of Ottoman technocrats who composed the Ottoman Agricultural Society capitalized on the sentiments circulating both internationally and among local elites, proclaiming a mission that aimed to reduce rural to urban migration and increase agriculture's prestige. In line with the suggestions of the Beauvais graduates discussed earlier, their goals included ramping up publications dedicated to agricultural improvement, helping to secure government assistance, holding competitions, writing agricultural books, and informing agriculturalists of the agricultural needs of each area.[275] Such objectives clearly suggested that their primary targets were elite landowners or aspiring gentlemen farmers rather than poor or middling villagers. Kâzım, writing in the first issue of the society's journal, declared that "in no matter what country, agriculture and agricultural industries' desired degree of maturation is dependent on the amount of energy and effort that the government expends."[276] The society's founders established it with the express intent of working to ensure that the government served the agricultural sector and to secure a basic livelihood for cultivators by negotiating better trade covenants, installing a protectionist regime, expanding transportation networks, and establishing agricultural banks.[277] As their mouthpiece, the journal would report on the "agricultural needs of the country" and highlight the causes behind the difficulties facing farmers, all as part of its work "for this respected nation's economic and social progress."[278]

As one of the Ottoman Agricultural Society's activities, a delegation from the Society along with the agricultural journalist Yusuf Sadiq Bey proposed to tour the Anatolian countryside accompanied by a mobile printing press to demonstrate new techniques and print and distribute booklets to "enlighten" rural communities. The press would allow them to print their observations after investigating local agricultural information and conditions, tailoring to the region the recommendations they left behind in pamphlets "that everyone will be able to understand." Their adventure would also contribute to the Ottoman administration's long-standing project of collecting knowledge on rural areas, as they planned to bring back crops, products, and even local clothing for a public exhibition in Istanbul.[279]

Reports sent to the Interior Ministry from the eastern Mediterranean in 1910 underscored how provincial developments were complementing the Ottoman Agricultural Society's goals despite multiple obstacles. In Syria the provincial council decided to establish bank branches in Tafila and Maan, continuing the steady southward expansion of the Agricultural Bank. However, *mushaʿ*—that is, land held in shares and worked according to collective rotational arrangements—posed a challenge. The province's agriculture office reported that these lands constituted a grave impediment to "agriculture's progress" (*ziraatın terakkisi*) and insisted that they needed to be partitioned (*ifraz*) in the Hawran, Karak, and Hama subprovinces. It suggested giving stakeholders usufruct deeds (*senedat-ı tasarrufiye*) in exchange for establishing the exact areas that they would work.[280]

Lawmakers continued to grapple with the challenge of collecting the tithe and creating a cadastre that could serve as the foundation of an alternative taxation system.[281] Despite official enthusiasm, efforts to complete a cadastral survey of agricultural lands, which was supposed to replace the existing base for fixed-price auctions (*maktuan ihalesi*), proved contentious, and lack of local knowledge posed obstacles. In Syria the governor complained that "cadastre methods" (*kadastro usulü*) were expensive and causing disputes. Debates had arisen over which crops were subject to the tithe, and because tax farmers refused to tender some villages, the extent of their crops and fields were unknown for auction. Nonetheless, the governor assured the Interior Ministry that the administrative council was investigating crop rates and estimates and would use local precedents—namely, the methods of transferred property (*emlak-i müdevvere*), that is, the former lands of the sultan that were transferred to the state after the revolution—to assess them. He further insisted that everyone—the local community, the treasury, and the tax farmers—would have their rights preserved and that the province would continue to use auction tenders until these matters could be sorted out.[282] In Beirut province the governor praised the cadastre as an antidote to discord among the local community and problems caused by tax farmers.[283] Nonetheless, these reports underscored the extent to which centralized knowledge collection about the provinces and the implementation of reforms remained an incomplete process.

Efforts to consolidate knowledge about rural production and make it accessible continued with the publication of empire-wide statistics, including the 1907/1908 agricultural statistics for Ottoman Europe and the 1909/1910 agricultural statistics for Ottoman Asia and Africa.[284] The Commerce and Agriculture Ministry created a map of the empire's provinces in 1913/1914 color-coded according to capacity for wheat production and encircled by bar charts to visually represent in a succinct colorful display key statistics on production for each province.[285] Not only did such collections, despite their shortcomings, make this information more easily accessible, but they also displayed and asserted a scientific approach characterized by systematic and comparable quantification.[286]

In Parliament lively debates ensued about how best to allocate resources for the agricultural budget.[287] The pace of borrowing also picked up substantially as the government sought to finance increasing expenses, especially for the military.[288] The increased need for revenue likely figured into the decision to pass a series of laws intended to facilitate access to additional capital resources. This legislation responded not only to mounting pressure from those local elites waiting for the state "to harness more modern engines" but also to the clamoring of foreign investors seeking more outlets for their surplus capital.[289] Temporary legislation outlining guidelines for a cadastral survey passed in February 1913, leaving little time for implementation before World War I. Another temporary law passed later that month sought to enable a mechanism whereby a piece of land to which multiple parties had claims could be used to take out multiple loans. It also expanded the institutions from which mortgages could be obtained, including the Agricultural Bank, the Administration of Vakifs, and authorized banks and Ottoman societies, although notably this last category could not possess the properties offered as guarantees through an "absolute transfer."[290] This stipulation enabled access to more sources of capital, but limited the extent to which Ottoman territory could be alienated.

*Musha*ᶜ lands continued to frustrate officials, as they considered them incompatible with the Agricultural Bank's lending practices. As in the

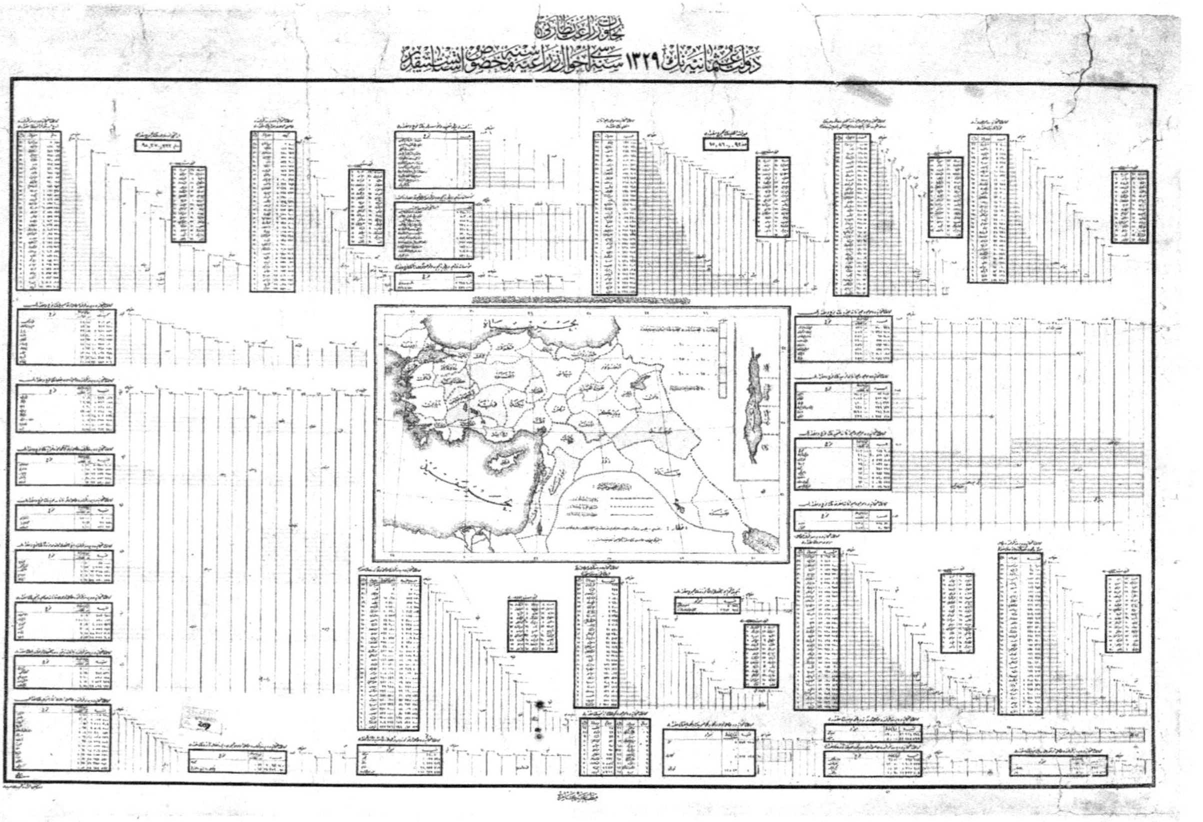

FIGURE 8. Ottoman agricultural statistics with map compiled by the Agriculture and Commerce Ministry, c. 1913–1914. Reproduced with permission of Atatürk Library, Hrt_000219.

agriculture office in Syria, the bank's general director identified this practice as particularly prevalent in Syria and an obstacle to the land "improvement" (*imar*)—a problem for the treasury and the Agricultural Bank.[291] When Ottoman administrators embarked on registering the empire's lands in the second half of the nineteenth century, they dutifully recorded parcels held in *musha*ᶜ arrangements—arrangements that helped distribute risk and protect against land loss.[292] Ironically, as elites argued for greater cooperation to ensure that farmers and capitalists were less exposed to the risks of more capital-intensive undertakings, officials debated ways to register these collective landholding arrangements along lines that threatened the security they provided.

The Agricultural Bank's issue with these lands was that they could not be used as security for bank loans. In April 1912 the Council of State responded to the province's general council's decision to subdivide lands worked in *musha*ᶜ. It stressed the need to settle in court disputes between shareholders who were willing to subdivide and those who were not.[293] Two years later, both the governor of Syria and the general director of the Agricultural Bank wrote to the Interior Ministry in support of dividing *musha*ᶜ land and assigning parcels individually to facilitate borrowing from the bank.[294] If they did not, the governor warned it would have an "exceptionally negative impact" on the "land's improvement and agriculture's progress."[295] The issue was particularly acute in Selimiye and Deraᶜa.[296] Mukhtars would be brought in to determine a way to partition these lands "in accordance with [their] method and order."[297] The tensions evident in this correspondence underscore rural communities' resistance to these attempts at interference in their risk management strategies as well as officials' efforts to enlist local knowledge in response to this resistance.

Decades of reform had created an Ottoman state space that was increasingly more homogeneous in its institutional frameworks and administrative technologies as well as hierarchical in its provincial organization than it had been in the 1840s. However, the particular shape that these reforms took at the provincial level reflected how local dynamics and power relations had influenced their implementation. This state of affairs underscored the process of negotiation that had characterized the realization of these reforms as they encountered uncooperative environments, shrewd elites, and harried cultivators, leading to often distinct and incomplete configurations of that state space at the local level. Far from disrupting the influence and power of local elites, maintaining this state space's "social and political order" had entrenched their interests in the institutions of reform even as they had at times thwarted its purposes.[298] Some CUP reformers were furious at how powerful provincial elites had dominated this new provincial infrastructure, subverting the reformers' intent. None was perhaps more vocal and passionate in his quest to break their grip than Hüseyin Kâzım, who in 1910 was appointed governor of Aleppo province, where a monopoly of elite interests was seen as particularly well ingrained in the fabric of provincial institutions. Both an agronomist and an ardent technocrat, Kâzım's approach focused on exposing the ills these elites had perpetrated by, to his mind, sabotaging the institutions meant to facilitate agricultural development and, by extension, imperial prosperity. With an eye to the global competition facing the empire, he was determined to break their hold on the provincial administration, clearly hopeful that the change in political regime in Istanbul would aid his cause. He was to be disappointed.

Hüseyin Kâzım and the Limits of Reform in Aleppo

Toward the end of January 1911, during the onset of the coldest winter in living memory in Aleppo province, Hüseyin Kâzım compiled a report that he hoped would spur the new constitutional administration in Istanbul into action. Livid with what he portrayed as flagrant disregard for his authority as governor and upholder of the CUP ideals of freedom (*hürriyet*), equality (*müsavat*), and justice (*adalet*), or as he put it "the most comprehensive political and civil law in the world," he demanded that the central government demonstrate that it could administratively enact what it claimed to ideologically represent.[299] In particular, his outrage centered on the corrupt state of land registration practices in the province. Kâzım presented himself as a reforming intermediary with purportedly special powers granted from the center, excellent connections, relevant technocratic expertise, and a passion and commitment to the ideals of the revolution. However, his technocratic expertise and powerful connections to the new government would be no match for the local elites of the city who not only had managed to consolidate their power by gaining control of much of the local administrative machinery created by decades of reforms but also had one of their own in the newly reconstituted Parliament.

Explanations of Kâzım's story have represented him as exemplary of Ottoman "modernity" and reform or as a rabble-rousing governor who confronted the "landlords" in Aleppo in a move "anticipating the Baʿthist reformers of the 1950s."[300] But Kâzım was not an isolated case. As the arc of this book demonstrates, the plans of the "Baʿthist reformers" had deep roots in Ottoman ideas of technocratic governance covered in this chapter, of which Kâzım was a prominent proponent.

Kâzım's emphasis on land as one of the most contentious issues reflected a common issue following the reinstitution of the constitutional monarchy.[301] Over the course of the late nineteenth and early twentieth centuries, the implementation of the 1858 Land Code had "gradually transform[ed] use rights on land into exclusionary land rights."[302] Furthermore, despite state officials' insistence that this legal framework was meant to protect the rights of small cultivators, as illustrated by the situation in Hama from earlier in the century, powerful elites, by using a number of processes and practices, had gained control of land, seizing it as payment for taxes or unpaid loans, through fraud, or by other "tricks," to use Kâzım's word, although such was not always the case or necessarily the norm.[303] Sometimes these means acquired legal status, and sometimes they did not, but Aleppan villagers' attempts to seek redress for their grievances seem to have been particularly frustrated by a provincial administration whose resources had been wrangled to benefit local power holders.[304]

Kâzım's experience underscores how, in Aleppo, local elites co-opted or appropriated administrators' efforts at reform and increased local oversight to maintain, if not increase, their influence. As discussed in the following chapter, by 1910 the expansion of institutions dedicated to scientific agricultural expertise was proceeding apace in line with these elites' priorities, but concerns about security of tenure and the conditions involved in accessing capital resources limited the scope of those willing to take the risk. Although the 1908 revolution spurred efforts to address these obstacles by sending out officials, like Kâzım, who were passionate about these reforms, Kâzım faced stiff resistance from local elites who had negotiated them to create a local "social and political order" that furthered their interests and limited the reforms' ideal goal of creating industrious smallholders thriving on Agricultural Bank capital.[305]

For Kâzım, defending villagers' rights to their land and "accurate" registration of land ownership and value was not merely about ensuring that local rural communities were able to secure those rights. More fundamentally, Kâzım aimed to wrest the domination of state space from these local elites and remold it, especially in rural areas, according to the ideals of Ottoman lawmakers—from land registration to tax collection—articulated through the prism of agricultural development.[306] Following on the heels of an apparently productive stint as the governor (*mutasarrıf*) of Siroz, Kâzım arrived in Aleppo on a mission, considering the tenure of his time as governor even more temporary than most. He had come to Aleppo, so he informed the British consul, invested with "special powers," in particular, over the judiciary. Once he had used the "ax . . . to clear the way for his successor," he would leave.[307] His influential position in the Istanbul affairs of the CUP was not lost on the British or French consuls, the latter of which noted that Kâzım was "an important figure and very well-liked of the Committee."[308] Kâzım's arrival followed the recall of the previous governor, Fakhri Pasha, over an affair of press freedoms, although dissatisfaction with Fakhri Pasha's rule had run deeper.[309] In the words of the French consul, "He [Fakhri Pasha] was a *débonnaire* man with excellent intentions, but of a nature very easy to get around. He quickly became an instrument in the hand of the large landowners who, under a *libéral étiquette*, continue to use the worst processes from the past."[310]

The target of Kâzım's reforming zeal confirmed the import of the consul's observation. Having arrived in the city on Friday, 7 October 1910, Kâzım immediately set to work, publishing an announcement in the local newspaper *al-Taqaddum* on 1 November 1910 excoriating the "oppressive notables" or rather the "notable oppressors."[311] The statement opened by generally criticizing the notables for stealing the assets of orphans and unfortunates and assuring them that he and those government officials true to the fundamentals of the "constitutional administration" had the power to deal with their "tyranny." The heart of the matter, though, was that "the government employees complain about you, saying that you steal the tithes that are the sacred right of the treasury [*'Beyt al-Mal'*] or rather the property of all the nation, that you deny the legality of the rights of those who dare to buy the tithes of your villages."[312] The essence of the issue was much as it had been since the beginning of the Tanzimat: the notables' use of tax farming to enrich themselves at the government's and cultivators' expense, despite the intervening reforms that had sought to curb this practice.

The accused notables were unimpressed. Kâzım's primary nemesis in the province, Nafiᶜ Pasha, was no stranger to constitutional parliamentary government. In fact, he was the Aleppo delegate to the 1908 Parliament after having already served in the 1877 Parliament (at the age of 29)—the only delegate to attend both.[313] However, reports of his activities on the local level belied any notion that his presence involved representing the interests of the province's general population. In a 1908 report, two years before Kâzım arrived on the scene, the British consul noted Nafiᶜ Pasha's overwhelming influence with respect to every aspect of the province's administration, asserting that "he and members of his family have practically invaded the government house and are fast usurping the powers of the various departments." Among the departments infiltrated by their influence he listed the Correspondence Department, the Dragomanate, the Civil Court of Appeal, the Examining Court, and the Public Prosecutor's office.[314] Kâzım's reports back to Istanbul confirmed the degree of Nafiᶜ Pasha's iron grip on the provincial bureaucracy, although he was actually one of three particularly egregious offenders cited by Kâzım. The other two, Mudarris Zade Zeki Paşa and Birket Zade Rifat Ağa, had died by the time of Kâzım's arrival, although this did not exempt them from his wrath, as he declared that he was sure they were "now, in the afterlife, busy with giving an account of the places they took from the poor."[315]

Kâzım seems to have been particularly affected by a ten-day trip he made through the province, probably around mid-December 1910. Intent on examining local conditions for himself, he traveled to İskenderun, Antakya, Belan, Kilis, and Aintab, areas to the province's north and west. Upon his return, the French consul noted that for at least three days he did not emerge from his house, prompting rumors that he was about to resign in the face of stiff opposition from the "landed aristocracy."[316] It seems instead that he was quite busy. By 8 January 1911 he had composed a lengthy report to the Interior Ministry describing the state of and his proposals for improving the province's ports, railroads, roads, marshes, schools, gendarmes, and taxes along with his vision for a hydroelectric power project.[317] Then in late January, as the worst winter in local memory descended on the region, with temperatures falling to 18 degrees below zero Celsius, the city of Aleppo cut off from the outside, and people and animals dying from the cold, he coordinated a large-scale relief effort.[318] At the same time, Kâzım compiled a set of documents and accompanying reports detailing what he perceived to be some of the most egregious examples of abuse in the province.

The heart of the injustices inflicted by Nafiᶜ Pasha and his extended family related to their manipulation of landownership and land value to their benefit. Referencing the various tricks (*hile*) used by them, Kâzım described how they would buy a few fields in a village and then take over the whole village by bribing the deed registrar (*tapu katibi*) with a few gurush. The Agricultural Bank was also a target. Kâzım insisted that instead of benefiting cultivators, it led to their ruin. Not only were loan terms harsh, but also any failure to pay interest became an immediate excuse to auction off the land used as security, which the "notable oppressors" purchased cheaply. On the other hand, when villagers improved their land, they faced difficulties registering its increased value. Kâzım compared the system unfavorably with that of the United States, where, he claimed, a farmer had twenty years to pay back borrowed money with interest. He concluded, with typical exaggeration, that such terms would be infeasible in the province for twenty or perhaps even a hundred years.[319]

Kâzım illustrated his assertions with anecdotes from his encounters with local farmers. Some villagers near Aintab explained that they had improved their land by planting olive trees, vineyards, and orchards, thereby increasing the land's value from 5–10 gurush twenty years ago to at least 50 lira per *dönüm* according to the bank's estimation. They claimed they were happy to pay higher taxes but could not get the increased value registered. If their lands were to be auctioned, they worried that the local *agha* would be able to acquire them quite cheaply. In another village a father, with the consent of his sons, bequeathed a portion of his property to one of his sons whom Kâzım described as "paralyzed and possessed of holy folly" (*menzûl ve meczub*), in order to provide for him. Nafiᶜ Pasha desired this man's land and colluded with one of the man's brothers to make it look like the disabled brother had signed a contract, and then when he could not pay the "debt," Nafiᶜ Pasha used it as a pretext to take his land. In another case a man was paying off a debt from the Agricultural Bank on some land in Bab district when one of the administrative officials, contrary to what was written in papers from the bank, which indicated that the land should not be sold at auction, decided he would sell it to a captain (*yüzbaşı*). Thus 660 *dönüms* of land registered for 66,000 gurush were sold to this captain for some 1,000 gurush, ostensibly to pay off the remainder of the unpaid debt.

Only when Kâzım learned of the situation and intervened did the administrative official cancel the transaction. As evidence for his claims, Kâzım included copies of petitions (*arzuhals*), administrative council decisions, and other relevant documents, including a photograph of the wronged disabled man.[320] Kâzım's critique highlighted the insecurity inherent in such malpractice, which if it did not deprive people of their land, reduced their incentive to invest. More fundamentally, it underscored the limits imposed by local elites on initiatives from center-based administrators to mediate property registration, credit relations, and tax collection.

Despite these efforts, what Kâzım referred to with rhetorical flourish as remnants of the Celali brigands (*Celalilerin bakıyetüssüyuf*) stymied exertion of his authority.[321] He requested support from the Interior Ministry in Istanbul, appealing to it to demonstrate the new government's "justice and equality" as the petitioners demanded. For Kâzım personally it was a matter of "honor and self-respect."[322] The incorporation of local elites into provincial institutions had enabled ongoing abuses, allowing these elites to retain power and influence. Istanbul needed to take drastic action to address the situation. Kâzım threatened his resignation but also offered another judicial solution: that the right of jurisdiction be given to the administrative councils or that people be given the right to appeal decisions handed down from the court of first instance, which would give them recourse to judicial facilities less beholden to the control of a few notables and enable them to finally see "a little justice."[323] Matters only escalated in the aftermath of the harsh winter—a war of telegrams ensued[324]—prompting Kâzım to travel to Istanbul in April to explain the situation and, he hoped, obtain greater powers to achieve his aims. At the end of May he returned with renewed confidence that he could achieve his goals and was greeted with great acclaim at the train station. Even the British consul thought it likely that the war between Kâzım and the notables could "end in the Notables coming in, one by one, and tendering their submission."[325] Despite his popularity, such a surrender did not materialize, and Kâzım returned to Istanbul for good in July. Despite overwhelming local support for the governor, Nafiᶜ Pasha, or the "respected representative" (*mebus-u muhteremi*), as Kâzım liked to sarcastically refer to him, prevailed.[326]

The incorporation of these local elites into provincial administrative offices meant that their interests largely determined the contours of provincial state space, limiting other state officials' capacity to act. The tension is apparent in the "government employees" who complained about the local notables' actions but were incapable of overruling them. Furthermore, the new Parliament, far from being "representative" of the province's interests more generally, was, like the provincial administration, just one more institution through which local elites continued to pursue their interests. Even an uncompromising technocratic governor with a flair for the theatrical found his "energy, integrity, and capacity," extensive local support, and even seemingly strong backing from the center thwarted by the well-entrenched interests of Aleppo's landed gentry and parliamentary representative.[327]

Conclusion

As the financial demands of the nineteenth century mounted, the Ottoman government, facing limited options for increasing revenue, became increasingly strategic in its efforts to extract more for a budget that was still largely funded by the products of the empire's soil. Streamlining tax collection methods was just one step in this process. Officials also sought to extract value from the land itself, both through a tax on its assessed value and by creating the infrastructure to make it a legible commodity for the purposes of state-centered capital accumulation. Despite efforts to channel revenue from tax collection and land commodification through state-directed institutions, whether by means of state-appointed tax collectors or through the Agricultural Bank, local intermediaries continued to play central roles in these financial operations. As a result, Ottoman officials demonstrated agility in frequently refining imperial policies in an effort to constantly renegotiate the empire's state space at the provincial level and at least partly diffuse the power that local elites sought to amass and exert through their manipulation of these new technologies of rule.

They were not alone in trying to enact these kinds of reforms and disrupt the influence of local elites in rural areas. Technocrats around the globe were grappling with similar concerns and experimenting with their own particular solutions. The Ottoman administration's efforts were not entirely in vain. As Nadir Özbek has pointed out, Ottoman officials managed to more than quintuple tax revenue between the early nineteenth century and the early twentieth century, a rate that was greater than France's and Britain's for the same period.[328] By the second half of the nineteenth century, new technologies raised the possibilities of not just streamlining extraction but also augmenting what could be extracted, either through intensive or extensive means, and global technocratic networks became places of exchange about the promising potential of this new "scientific" agriculture.

Accompanying and complementing these extraction efforts were projects to collect and compile knowledge about the empire's rural areas. Given variation from year to year as a result of environmental factors or farmers' choices, agricultural production proved elusive to fully "know." Yet center-based elites considered such knowledge essential in strategizing agricultural policies and ultimately acquiring the information necessary to produce a cadastre.

In the eastern Mediterranean elites were instrumental to implementing central administrators' programs, even as they challenged their full realization and turned new institutions to their advantage. Nonetheless, critical of what they considered insufficient investment, they advocated initiatives to support their desire to pursue greater risk taking. They were also becoming acutely aware of their own ignorance about agricultural practice, even as many of them acquired substantial holdings of agricultural land. E. Saadé suggested that large proprietors, who relied on intermediaries to manage their farms, "imagine themselves humiliated when they engage in the culture of the soil," insisting "agriculture is a science that, to prosper, necessitates serious studies."[329] Spurred by enthusiasm for the promises of scientific agriculture, he and his fellow enthusiasts urged the government to prioritize institutions that offered agricultural education. State officials agreed, even as state funding did not always accommodate their aspirations. The next chapter looks more specifically at the fruits of these aspirations: a network of agricultural schools, model farms, and model fields and their role in the production of scientific agricultural expertise.

TWO

"AGRICULTURE *from a* BOOK"

"Scientific" Agriculture in the Ottoman Eastern Mediterranean

In May 1910 the Ottoman agricultural inspector for the provinces of Beirut, Syria, and Aleppo returned from a 22-day trip dealing with locusts in Urfa, several hundred kilometers away, only to confront an unfolding uproar in the province of Syria. In particular, attempts to establish an agricultural school in the town of Selimiye had aroused considerable controversy. According to the inspector's office, the controversy pitted the local governor (*mutasarrıf*), Nazim Bey, characterized as a valiant reformer intent on "diffusing education and expanding and improving agriculture," against the "corrupt works of the usurpers and enemies of progress" and their "intentions of devilishness" who sought to thwart the governor's efforts.[1] In language that grew increasingly exasperated, the inspector explained how, upon his return, he had finished compiling the estimation report for the project of building the agricultural school. Attracting interested parties proved challenging—having circulated the report widely in Beirut, Aleppo, Damascus, and Hama for bids, he received no takers as of 7 June. After extending the deadline to 3 July, he finally received bids from Hama and Beirut and decided to proceed with the architect from Beirut, Nafliyan Kaspar Bey.

But securing a bid from a regional contractor was only one difficulty posed by the project. In Selimiye itself other troubles were brewing. First, the people of Selimiye had promised to provide a certain amount of building materials—namely, stone, lime, and gravel—the costs for which had not been included in the estimation of the original bid. However, when the builders required these materials to continue, they were withheld, forcing the workers to return to Beirut. Second, to compound matters, Nazim Bey was incapable of dealing with the situation because he was occupied with a mob that attacked the government's district office and plundered the seed storehouses in the market.

The need to complete the school so that classes could start in the fall made finding a solution urgent. In an effort to move matters along, the inspector and Nazim Bey set off for Damascus to consult the province and Hicaz railroad's head engineers with a view to adding the lacking materials into the existing contract. After some back and forth over the proposal between the governor of Syria and the local administrative council, they finally reached an agreement. With wagons of supplies the contractor and his men set out again for Selimiye, only to have Nazim Bey derailed by a competing proposal from the town purporting to be able to do the job for less. Kaspar Bey and his men returned to Beirut, and the wagons of supplies were sent to Aleppo. The offer did not turn out to be serious; however, it delayed the project yet again.[2]

The reasons behind this resistance to the school's establishment were complex and seem to have consisted of multiple grievances.[3] One of the most salient complaints involved a disagreement over how some of the school's funding had been allocated, dividing the local community between the "owners of wealth and property" (*ashab al-tharwa wa al-amlak*), who favored the school, and those who lacked such resources and did not support it.[4] Meanwhile, the negotiations and decision making being carried out at the highest levels of the provincial administration to ensure that construction proceeded underscored state officials' determination, despite this resistance, to expand the empire's network of institutions that offered training in "scientific agriculture." The Selimiye school was eventually completed. It was not the first agricultural school established in the empire, nor was it even the first regional institution for agricultural experimentation. However, by 1913/1914 the empire's agricultural statistics identified the school as one of the empire's four practical agricultural schools providing hands-on agricultural training, and it was surpassed in level only by the Halkalı Agricultural High School (Halkalı Ziraat Mektebi) in Istanbul (see Table 1). As such, the Selimiye school marked the regional culmination of a decades-long effort to build and expand a network of infrastructure for agricultural education and training throughout the empire.

These institutions offered technocrats in the central administration and provincial elites avenues for experimenting with new agricultural methods and technologies. Their common interest derived from the increases in production that they anticipated emerging technologies would provide by facilitating more intensive methods and expanded areas of cultivation. But at what cost? If developments in administrative technologies provided new means by which officials expanded Ottoman state space into rural areas, as discussed in chapter 1, emerging agricultural technologies

TABLE 1. Statistics for Agricultural High Schools and Practical Schools in the Ottoman Empire, 1913/1914

School	Current Number of Students	Diplomas Granted	Number of Employees	Annual Salaries and Expenses[a]
Halkalı Agricultural High School[b]	131	41	0	1,139,823
Hüdavendigar Practical Agricultural School	117	21	13	527,382
Ankara Practical Agricultural School	57	0	1	43,090
Selimiye Practical Agricultural School[c]	40	9	8	191,375
Adana Practical Agricultural School[d]	0	0	0	0

Source: Ticaret ve Ziraat Nezareti, *Memalik-i Osmaniye'nin 1329 senesine mahsus ziraat istatistiğidir*, n.p.

a. No denomination is given for the monetary units.
b. It is unclear why the Halkalı school is listed as having no employees.
c. The Selimiye school continues to provide agricultural training today as a college of agriculture and architectural engineering.
d. Information not available.

constituted untried interventions into regional ecologies and local agricultural practices. Early experiments in the eastern Mediterranean suggested some of the challenges. A combine harvester worked well for landowners in the Biqaᶜ Valley but proved unusable in mountainous regions such as the Hawran.[5] In some irrigated areas dikes made from boards posed obstacles to machine use. Machines also frightened horses unused to their noise, required repair facilities, and needed spare parts that were difficult to find.[6] How chemical fertilizers would affect plant growth in the soils of Syria and how new plows and harvesters would perform given rainfall patterns or the constraints of plot size remained open questions.

Risk was not just a function of these technologies' ecological suitability. It also derived from the major capital investment they entailed. In fact, many of those most enthusiastic about experimenting with these methods were not skilled farmers themselves. Contrary to claims that elites were generally disinterested in these technologies, a broadly shared enthusiasm for these projects characterized the reaction among certain groups in the eastern Mediterranean with the capital and land to spare for the risks they entailed.[7] Like the Beauvais graduates in chapter 1, some even developed a keen interest in learning about agriculture and sought to pursue training in these new methods themselves. The *Levant Trade Review*, a publication directed at American commercial concerns, even remarked on the trend, explaining to readers that "while, some years ago, the rural population of Turkey [*sic*] began to quit the native soil, being attracted towards the town by the vision of luxury and welfare, an opposite current of ideas is manifesting itself among the well to do classes. Young men of wealth look towards the farm finding a brighter future in the agricultural line and especially in the dairy farming industry, than in commerce."[8]

For its part, the Agriculture Ministry, beginning in the late nineteenth century, undertook various projects to assess these risks. Paralleling similar initiatives in countries such as France, Germany, the United States, and Russia, it built model farms and fields, established agricultural schools and classes, and stocked depots with the latest equipment.[9] As with the bureaucratic technologies discussed in chapter 1, the form these projects took in the eastern Mediterranean was as much a product of local circumstances as it was of central government initiatives. Local actors at times resisted, at times exploited, and at times went beyond the government's proposals to pursue and advocate for their own interests regarding this infrastructure. Thus the implementation of this infrastructure reflected a combination of local dynamics and state officials' prerogatives, shaped in turn by obstacles in the bureaucratic, fiscal, village, and natural worlds.

Despite these challenges, by the end of the first decade of the twentieth century—that is, around the time controversy erupted over the Selimiye school—this infrastructure was becomingly increasingly systematized. A diverse empire-wide network of agriculture-related institutions had been established, and others were planned or in process.[10] The recent ascent to power of the Committee of Union and Progress (CUP) and the influential positions held in its administration by those with an interest in new agricultural methods and the "development" of rural areas had further accelerated efforts to expand this infrastructure. The eastern Mediterranean had been an integral part of this planning from the beginning, and by 1910 the region boasted model farms and fields, agriculture classes in local schools, and the Selimiye school, which was devoted solely to agricultural education and experimentation.

However, as the case of the Selimiye school demonstrates, not everyone was enthusiastic about this new infrastructure. Distinctions in access to wealth and property between different members of rural communities were at the core of these divergent responses. Although official rhetoric claimed that peasant enfranchisement and enlightenment were part of the scientific agricultural project, in practice wealthier landowners were its beneficiaries. These landowners, including those of relatively recent origin who had profited from the new financial instruments discussed in chapter 1, were, according to one local agronomist, "animated by a belief . . . in the promises of the Science Fairy."[11]

The Science Fairy's spell had a wide reach. Official discourse was replete with representations of the knowledge produced in model farms and fields as *fenn-i ziraat*, the "science of agriculture," portraying it as distinct from the practices of unlettered farmers.[12] Officials attributed this "scientific" or "modern" knowledge to those who learned from books in government or foreign schools and gained official recognition of it through institutional certification. Yet even as they frequently denigrated existing techniques, in practice and sometimes even in rhetoric, they recognized them as integral to the successful implementation of "scientific agriculture" and fundamental to the functioning of its institutions. Their rhetoric consisted of a form of boundary-work, emphasizing the novelty and break from the past represented by scientific agriculture while eliding its reliance on the forms of knowledge that this discourse simultaneously deemed antiquated.[13]

A close look at practice, however, demonstrates how contingent this "modern" and "scientific" expertise was on prior knowledge cultivated in the field. In the Ottoman context, as in others, local knowledge was not destroyed and replaced "by standardized formulas legible only from the center" but rather integrated into the production of what came to be considered the "science of agriculture."[14] Translating administrative enthusiasm for new machines and technologies into actual practice required the input of local farmers and demonstrations of the feasibility of new crops and methods that transpired over months, if not years. This integrated approach also manifested in imperial decisions regarding planning for agricultural developments. Their realization relied on existing local specializations, whether in terms of livestock, crops, or methods, and local expertise to determine the best programs and projects to implement in accordance with a region's ecological profile.

During the last three decades of the Ottoman Empire, these dynamics were all part of the expansion of scientific agriculture in the provinces of Syria, Aleppo, and Beirut, a region that officials came to consider integrated in terms of its agricultural infrastructure. In the years immediately preceding World War I, these provinces shared an agricultural inspector. Documents regarding the construction of regional agricultural institutions suggest that local officials considered them to be at the service of interested parties throughout the three provinces.[15] At the same time, these regional institutions were integrated into broader imperial networks of scientific agriculture, which enabled employees, animals, new plant varieties, and recently produced expertise to circulate, catering to the region's ecological particularities while also developing its diverse agricultural possibilities.

The concept of co-production examines how "scientific knowledge . . . both embeds and is embedded in social practices, identities, norms, conventions, discourses, instruments, and institutions."[16] Tracing the co-production of this "scientific" infrastructure and the social differentiation it heightened in rural communities demonstrates not only the distinct roles played by provincial elites, technocratic officials, and cultivators in shaping the local implementation of these projects but also how these projects contributed to new distinctions in rural society based on who could afford the risk and expense they entailed and who could not. This "science" was accessible only to those with means. Provincial schools such as Selimiye catered to the elite. Poorer cultivators who lacked the capacity to invest or undertake such gambles on their basic subsistence recognized this bias and expressed it through their frustration over the appropriation of resources for such an institution. Their critiques of this infrastructure and the knowledge it privileged underscore how economic, social, and environmental factors mediated involvement in its activities.

Imperial Networks and Local Implementation: Hamidian-Era Developments

As discussed in chapter 1, Ottoman interest in institutions for agricultural education can be traced back to at least the 1840s, when a short-lived agricultural school was established in 1847 in the western environs of Istanbul; it closed only a few years later in 1851 because of unsuitable land, harsh winter weather, and insufficient books and tools.[17] Additional efforts would largely be put on hold until the 1880s, when the government drew up plans for establishing a network of institutions throughout the empire and for training the civil servants who would staff them. The process of creating these institutions did not always go according to plan. Sometimes there were ecological constraints; often there were financial and even bureaucratic ones. Despite these obstacles, a clear set of priorities motivated the proposals of those technocrats entrusted with the development of the empire's agricultural sector. They envisioned a well-distributed network of institutions among productive agricultural regions of the empire that would capitalize on local knowledge and specialties while also sending students abroad to observe and study new methods in regions that were ecologically comparable to the areas of the empire in which they were destined to be employed.

From the early years of these developments, insights derived from observations of local provincial conditions were valued. Despite the elite training that Amasyan Efendi, the empire's agricultural director, shared with a growing coterie of foreign-trained Ottoman agronomists, in 1893

Aram Efendi, head of the recently established Scientific Agriculture Committee, suggested that it was Amasyan Efendi's failure to adequately respond to the concerns of provincial agricultural inspectors, based on their observations and experiences, that led to his resignation.[18] The newly appointed inspectors wrote a number of reports to the ministry explaining their various perspectives on agricultural reform, but, in the assessment of Aram Efendi, they found their time wasted because their concerns did not receive adequate consideration. To address the issue, they gathered in Istanbul to discuss the problems they faced and eventually issued a memorandum about what they considered necessary for reform. Shortly thereafter, in 1888/1889, Amasyan Efendi was dismissed and replaced by Nuri Bey Efendi, the French-educated student who had been originally posted to Aydın province as an inspector and who would remain in the position of agricultural director until the post itself was eliminated in 1892/1893.[19] Such a transition in leadership suggested a preference for someone with firsthand experience and local knowledge based on working in the provinces.

In the aftermath of Amasyan's departure and in keeping with an approach that prioritized provincial specificities over abstract central planning, Ottoman administrators undertook to expand this initial cadre of foreign-trained civil servants by sending another group of students abroad to schools located in regions with diverse ecological and climatic conditions that approximated those of different Ottoman provinces. In 1890 Nuri Bey Efendi proposed sending twenty-three students to French and Algerian schools based on the Ottoman province where they would work upon their return. Training Ottoman agronomists was preferable to bringing in foreign ones because of the expense involved and the language barrier.[20] According to the proposal, six students would study hot-climate agriculture at the Rouïba school in Algeria, and in France nine students would specialize in irrigation at the school in Avignon, five in cold-climate agriculture at the school in Merchines, and three in cheese making and viticulture at Marmirolle. Two additional students were to be sent to tool factories in France and Belgium to prepare them for employment in a similar factory at the Halkalı Agricultural School in Istanbul.[21] Nuri Bey Efendi insisted that the primary intent of the project was to train capable farmers versed in science, and thus, as much as possible, the students should be the children of farm owners. However, the immediate need to staff a nascent network of model and experimental fields and agricultural schools so as not to overburden the current inspectors with these tasks took precedence.[22]

For budgetary reasons the commerce and public works minister amended this plan to include only ten students—still with the aim of matching ecologies and specialties. However, for unclear reasons after the proposal reached the prime minister's office, the decision was made to send five students to France and the other five to Germany.[23] It is possible that political considerations trumped ecological ones, as the decision came not long after Kaiser Wilhelm's first visit to Istanbul in October 1889, signaling the beginning of closer German-Ottoman cooperation.[24] Shortly afterward, the French embassy, perhaps in an effort to maintain its edge, offered to waive the fees for four additional students to attend French agricultural schools, ultimately increasing those sent abroad to fourteen.[25] As part of the students' training, the administration prioritized the acquisition of practical knowledge, requesting in 1892 that five students who had attended the Avignon and La Brosse agricultural schools be given permission to continue their studies at Grand Jouan and Montpellier, two of the three national schools of agriculture in France (the third being Grignon), to ensure they had sufficient practical knowledge.[26]

Although gaining this knowledge and having it certified with a diploma clearly was a priority for Ottoman officials, it was just the first step. Despite efforts to choose sites that would be ecologically comparable to different Ottoman provinces, officials recognized that the knowledge acquired in these distant schools would not in itself be sufficient to ensure successful new cultivation practices or to convince Ottoman farmers of their effectiveness. How were these French- and German-trained agronomists supposed to assess the applicability of their knowledge to the soils, climatic conditions, and other ecological exigencies of the Ottoman domains, and, once their applicability was determined, how were they to convey this to farmers? A network of model fields throughout the empire would target particularly fertile regions along with those ripe for the expansion of extensive agriculture, and in them these recently returned graduates could ostensibly assess the applicability of their knowledge and communicate the results to farmers and landowners in their local languages.

In October 1888, just over a year and a half after the 1887 Hatch Act established agricultural experimental stations in the United States, the Ottoman Council of Ministers issued a decision that targeted the provinces of Syria, Aleppo, Adana, Konya, Ankara, Sivas, Monastir, and Yanya as well as Izmit *sancak* for model and experimental fields because of their "importance agriculturally."[27] These fields would serve as places not only where new techniques, seeds, and implements could be tested but also where agricultural models could be demonstrated to local residents (*ahali*).[28] They were also places where knowledge of new implements and methods would be applied alongside local knowledge; therefore Ottoman officials were attentive to regional specializations in deciding how to staff and operate a field in a given area. For example, in Aleppo the model field complex was slated to contain a model stable that would be used "to improve the cattle species for which the region is famous" and would be dedicated to the production of butter and cheese. Therefore a director with particular knowledge of these matters was chosen for the field.[29] Officials in Istanbul based the field's raison d'être on existing local expertise and resources. Such considerations suggest that these projects relied first and foremost on this knowledge and not on that acquired in foreign schools. The application of local knowledge to new methods and tools would determine which ones might be suitable for more widespread dissemination.[30]

Although initiated just before Amasyan's dismissal, the program would primarily unfold under the auspices of the newly constituted Forest, Mines, and Agriculture Ministry and its new minister, Selim Malhamé Bey, a Maronite from Beirut and a favorite of the sultan who was appointed in February 1893.[31] The process of establishing the model fields faced a number of obstacles. Finding a decent-size piece of good land with adequate water resources close enough to a critical mass of the local community who were supposed to benefit from its demonstrations was easier to authorize than to achieve in practice. In Aleppo, field operations were under way by February 1893, but Vahan Efendi, the agricultural inspector assigned to the province when the field was established, had located the field in an "inappropriate and faraway place," which proved to be an ongoing source of frustration.[32] On the other hand, in the province of Syria land was purchased and construction work on the field's buildings commenced, but the lands procured for the field were discovered to be unsuitable.[33] In particular, finding land with adequate water resources proved difficult: In Syria the land lacked a basic water source, and a well dug to remedy the matter also failed to yield sufficiently.[34] Similar issues affected other fields as well.[35]

Start-up and operational expenses also had a tendency to run over budget. Outfitting a model field was costly: Not only did it require new buildings, but also wells had to be dug and pumps, seeds, feed, and animals purchased and transported. Shortfalls in the Aleppo field's budget meant that the central government had to seek additional funds from other government institutions and offices for the completion of the field's buildings or the purchase and transport of a European-made pump.[36] Citing the importance of reform to increasing harvests, the Council of State allotted additional funding to the Commerce and Public Works Ministry for the pump.[37] In late 1895 the minister of agriculture insisted on another substantial sum from the Commerce and Public Works Ministry for the model field's dairy and director's office, including funds for installing windows in the granary and stable and for establishing a shady reservoir near the stable.[38]

Selim Bey often turned to the Agricultural Bank as a source of financing; the bank's bylaws included a provision that reserved one-third of its profits for funding scientific agricultural projects.[39] In September 1894 Selim Bey ordered the bank to provide an additional 3,000 gurush each to the Aleppo model field and to fields in Konya, Erzurum, and Sivas along with the Hüdavendigar model farm to buy the necessary instruments for recording temperature and tracking changing weather conditions.[40] When the model field in Aleppo could not produce enough barley and edible vetch to feed its animals, the agricultural minister requested that the Agricultural Bank hand over 2,500 gurush for both animal feed and seeds.[41] In Aleppo the bank's 1312 [1896/1897] budget contained a credit of 34,200 gurush 10 para for the province's agriculture school and model field, most of which was spent.[42] In 1898 the Damascus and Aleppo model fields' bank allotment amounted to 15,635 piastres and 23,870 piastres, respectively.[43]

The government also took steps to reduce mounting expenses. The reproductive capacities of the living resources of one agricultural school or model farm could supply others. In January 1895 the practical agricultural school in Hüdavendigar sent one bull each to the Aleppo and Konya model fields with the reserve agriculture budget instructed to cover the transfer costs.[44] Exempting materials, such as pumps and tools ordered from Europe, from custom dues eased costs and underscored the government's commitment to these projects.[45]

By the summer of 1896 the Aleppo model field was humming with activities, both agricultural and potentially illicit. A major investigation into alleged misdeeds by the field's director, Melkon Efendi, provided a detailed glimpse into the field's operations.[46] The head farmer, Ahmet, age 47, came from the nearby village of Tal Jabin, located north of the city of Aleppo and just slightly northwest of the field's site in Muslimiya. He first worked in the field for two months for a 150 gurush salary and, after receiving permission to continue, by January 1897 had worked for another three years at an 8 mecidiye (152 gurush) salary.[47] Although, based on his salary, his knowledge was not valued at the same level as the diploma-certified students who were promised no less than 800 gurush a month, his contributions to the field's experiments were essential. Referred to as "Farmer Ahmet," he was the one, almost exclusively, who worked the foreign plow (*Frank saban*) often morning and evening.[48]

FIGURE 9. "Bee-hive homes" with threshing sledge in Muslimiya, site of the Aleppo model field and the Aleppo stop on the Baghdad Railway, between 1898 and 1946. Source: G. Eric and Edith Matson Photograph Collection, Library of Congress, https://www.loc.gov/item/2019698585/.

Fellow field laborers, such as Hamud, age 30, also came from Aleppo province, and Serkis, age 28, hailed from Harput. They were among a number of field workers, sometimes referred to as *yanaşma*, or hired labor, who did not appear to have any particular institutionally acquired expertise.[49] The field staff also included an ironsmith (Agop, age 36, from Urfa) who was responsible for repairing the field's tools; a veterinarian (Faris, age 55, from Aleppo), whose primary work seems to have consisted of keeping the field's animals, which included a pair of oxen and workhorses, well-shod; and a servant for Melkon.[50] Aside from Melkon Efendi and the field's guard, Mardirus Ağa, none of these workers appeared in the empire's official yearbooks; their labor was virtually invisible save for the fact that the field's operations became the subject of a court case.[51] Nonetheless, these insights into the field's staff and their activities underscore the central contribution of local expertise to the "scientific" knowledge produced in the field.

Despite their lack of training in foreign agricultural schools, their facility in local agricultural practice, especially that of Farmer Ahmet, made them indispensable to the field's work.[52] The field's crops were diverse, and an array of equally diverse activities focused on assessing how new implements and plants fared alongside those currently used and grown in the province. Among the plants cultivated by the field's staff were barley, wheat (including a wheat specifically designated as local [*yerli hınta*]), "Hungarian" provender (*macar alefi*), Egyptian corn (*mısır darısı*), flax, potatoes, "bird" provender (*kuş alefi*), and chamomile. In addition to experimenting with these crops, the staff planted and diligently watered poplars and mulberry trees and dug wells.[53] The field's daily work log systematically recorded the instruments used and the amounts of a plowed but fallow field (*felhan tarlası*) versus a field of unbroken ground (*bor tarlası*) they were able to work in a morning, evening, or both. Their experiments included the use of local plows (*yerli saban*) alongside foreign plows (*Frank saban*) as well as a reaping machine (*orak makinesi*). The log often included key points of reference, such as the high and low temperatures for each day. These methodical recording practices indicated that a systematic process of experimentation, calculation, and observation had been established for monitoring the field's activities, turning local knowledge into the knowledge of scientific agriculture. It was this knowledge that would provide the ultimate continuity in the field's work: By 1897, following the investigation, Melkon Efendi would be replaced by Şevki Efendi, whereas Farmer Ahmet would continue working in the field up until at least just before World War I.[54]

Although Farmer Ahmed's expertise and those of his fellow day laborers underpinned the operations of the Aleppo model field, the architects of the empire's scientific agriculture programs were focused on cultivating another kind of expert: those trained in schools of agronomy, their knowledge certified with a diploma. To this end, in parallel with the implementation of the model field program in the 1890s, Ottoman officials also encouraged the expansion of homegrown opportunities for agricultural education, such as local initiatives to establish new agricultural schools or coursework in existing high schools. Practical agricultural schools opened in Salonica and Bursa in 1890 and 1891, respectively.[55] In Bursa locals drove the initiative, from the administrative council seeking official permission to a local committee choosing the necessary land.[56] The Halkalı Agricultural School in Istanbul accepted its first group of students in 1892, some eight years after the issuing of its initial charter in 1884. The number of applications indicated substantial interest; from 700 applicants, the school accepted 30 for its first class. The stipulations that enabled these students to be nominated in the first place underscored that the school catered to elites. Students had to be "from farm, vineyard, and orchard owners or farmer children" and had to demonstrate their knowledge of reading, arithmetic, geography, and the tithe system.[57] In addition to similar requirements for entering the Bursa school, potential students had to agree, in the event that they did not complete the program, to pay the state 16 gold liras per year attended.[58] Obviously, facility in such a range of subjects indicated access to at least some level of basic education in the empire's *rüşdiye* or *idadiye* schools, and such financial guarantees could be offered only by the well-to-do.[59] Nonetheless, the large number of applications suggests that many aspiring agronomists reciprocated this interest.

The Halkalı Agricultural School drew its instructors from those who had studied abroad, including some who had already served a number of years as provincial inspectors. Eventually, as the school started graduating students, some of them joined the faculty as well.[60] Its graduates started at the fourth rank and could reach the first rank in the Ottoman bureaucracy and had the potential to earn a monthly salary of 3,000 piastres as agricultural inspectors. In contrast, their compatriots in the Bursa school, after starting at the fifth rank, could reach only the third rank, which corresponded

FIGURE 10. Halkalı Agricultural School, Istanbul. Reproduced with permission of Nadir Eserler Kütüphanesi, Istanbul University.

to 1,500 piastres per month and a post as an agriculture teacher.[61] Nonetheless, all the schools' graduates constituted an elite coterie of agricultural experts who were more primed for (and indeed obligated to) government service than they were for returning to work the land.[62]

Despite the substantial sums expended on the model field program and the expansion of institutions of agricultural education, by the summer of 1898 the Council of State expressed dissatisfaction with the lack of results from these initiatives. There is some ambiguity as to whether the critique of the agricultural ministry's programs was fully justified or whether it actually reflected a more personal conflict between powerful figures in the central administration.[63] Nonetheless, the criticisms leveled at the model field program illustrate the challenges it faced and how the government reassessed the effects of its agricultural priorities in the fin de siècle empire.

The difficulties encountered by the institutions that were part of these networks in the eastern Mediterranean are illustrative. In the province of Syria the attempt to sell the model field's land had been unsuccessful and led to it being abandoned for a considerable time, during which the "fragmentary traces" of initial construction work fell into disrepair. Despite containing a nursery, the Council of State insisted, based on a report received from the province, that "even if new tools were used in the model field and a 500-tree nursery planted," the field would not accomplish its anticipated benefits because the people competent in agriculture (*erbab-i ziraat*) in the area lacked wealth and thus the field would fail to attract them.[64] Such an assessment underscores the skepticism that many farmers exhibited toward the more capital-intensive and therefore unaffordable methods that the model fields demonstrated as well as the council's recognition that some degree of wealth was a precondition for access. Nonetheless, it did not dismiss their skepticism as evidence of ignorance but understood it as a reaction to economic infeasibility.

In the province of Aleppo the Council of State did not express the same concerns. Despite some initial bumps, its model field was operational, although its distance from the city remained a concern for the province's administrative council because it limited its usefulness as a model for the local community.[65] Thus farmers' economic capacity was not the main issue; rather, the primary concern was the field's inaccessibility to those who would have the necessary economic resources. In addition to being more accessible to urban landowners, farmers passing through town could more easily visit a model field closer to the city.

The provinces of Aleppo and Syria were not alone in falling short of the expectations that had been set for the model field program. In general, the Council of State report found fault with virtually all the model fields in the empire, despite "quite a lot of time having passed since their establishment."[66] Of course, in 1898 all the fields had been around for less than a decade and at least part of that time had been spent finding sites, ensuring adequate water resources, and building each field's infrastructure—each of which had often posed its own particular challenges. Given that assessing the outcomes and effectiveness of new agricultural techniques could take years, only after which farmers might be convinced to adopt them—if they had the resources—the council's assessment comes across as hasty. Lamenting the lack of agricultural journals and access to basic education, the council blamed these factors for preventing local communities from fully appreciating the model fields' work—not to mention that if the techniques used in the fields were not successful or yielded less than farmers' current methods, that would likely chill enthusiasm even more.

Agricultural developments, the Council of State argued, needed an approach more in accord with the "disposition [*mizaç*] of the community [*ahali*]." To this end, the council suggested a focus on agricultural education, particularly in a form that would take the demonstration to the cultivator and would not expect the cultivator to seek out the model field. Students from the practical agricultural schools would be distributed among villages in rotation, and new tools would be given to districts. They would be tasked with showing the community how to use new implements, making note of and planting crops best suited to a particular region, teaching scientific methods for cheese, honey, and vineyard production, and swapping out "old and useless seeds" for "good and healthy seeds."[67] Instead of continuing to spend lavishly on the model fields and an elaborate school like Halkalı, what funds were available would be spent on practical agricultural schools along the lines of the Bursa and Salonica model. These schools would not only cost less, the council maintained, but also, because the graduates of the agricultural schools would be spending most of their time in villages, their salaries would be lower—300–400 gurush for the first three years, after which they might be appointed as an agricultural inspector and could receive a salary of 500–600 gurush if they worked for ten years. Finally, these posts would not follow a path in the administration and, to facilitate this intent, would draw their students from farm children and local communities.[68]

As the nineteenth century drew to a close, a shift in the administration's priorities seemed imminent. In many ways its proposal reflected the priorities from a decade earlier, as elaborated in the rationale for sending additional students to study in Europe. Yet a fundamental tension continued to exist between the desire to train and certify a group of agronomists in scientific agriculture and the desire to see these agronomists take up a life centered around the farm. Their training initiated them into networks of agronomistic expertise at the international and imperial levels, and it was in these networks that their knowledge was recognized as valuable. Their knowledge of new methods and machines would be valuable at the local level only if such methods and machines could be proven effective through the application of a local knowledge unavailable in their elite, at times foreign, institutions. This dilemma would continue to plague technocratic elites globally in the decades to come. In contrast to other sectors of the economy, the production of a science of agriculture remained grounded, literally, in a depth of knowledge about local elements. Intimate knowledge of the soil, local weather conditions, pests, and so on remained indispensable no matter how much book knowledge one acquired.[69]

Ottoman practice clearly demonstrated reliance on this local knowledge, even as the language of scientific agriculture worked to distinguish the knowledge emerging from the empire's model farms and fields as a break from this locally grounded expertise.

"Agriculture from a Book": Elite Education and the Nature of Expertise

A 1907–1908 academic year report card from the Idlib high (*rüşdiye*) school in Aleppo province included among the coursework for the second- and third-year students a class called Agricultural Information from a Book (*malumat-ı ziraiye kitabından*).[70] The inclusion of such a course in the school curriculum of Idlib (a major town in Aleppo province but not the provincial center) reflected increased efforts to incorporate agricultural education into provincial schools during the early years of the twentieth century. Despite the Council of State's recommendations, the model field program was not completely shut down; however, emphasis shifted to incorporating basic agricultural education in provincial schools, presumably to reach the children of cultivators more directly.

In Aleppo, for instance, the model farm continued its operations, but an initiative from the Education Ministry to include agricultural classes in the Aleppo preparatory (*idadi*) school spurred efforts to span the irksome distance between the model field and the city. In Syria local officials also advocated for the inclusion of agricultural education in the provincial high schools. Although there was clearly imperial support for such measures, a closer look at provincial developments underscores the local initiative and enthusiasm that ensured their realization. It also highlights the increasingly hierarchical nature of agricultural expertise embraced by the central administration. Despite the Council of State's expressed preference for the expertise produced in practical agricultural schools such as those in Bursa and Salonica, ultimately the knowledge produced in the Halkalı school remained the highest achievement and the most desirable qualification, including for local teachers of "agriculture from a book."

In September 1900, when the Education Ministry announced a plan to open an agriculture branch in the Aleppo preparatory school, the Aleppo education directorship found itself unable to secure specialists (*erbabı ihtisas*) from the Istanbul school.[71] To ensure that the plan could proceed, Ahmet Hamdi, the Aleppo agricultural inspector and deputy assistant director of the model farm, agreed to take on the task of designing and teaching the program.[72] He had graduated from the Salonica agricultural school and, in 1899, had been appointed as the assistant to the Aleppo model field's director, Şevki, whose duties he had essentially taken over by 1900.[73] However, the demands of his multiple positions meant that he could not teach the ambitious array of agricultural classes by himself. As a result, a group of six different teachers, including Hamdi Efendi, were assigned to teach the fourteen different agriculture classes. The appointed teachers had all attended or graduated from Ottoman high schools, and some had practical local experience in agricultural matters. In addition to Hamdi Efendi and his training at the Salonica school, Shakib, Cevdet, and Abdullah Efendis were graduates of the Mekteb-i Mülkiye, Kemal Efendi had studied at the state veterinarian school and was currently serving as the province's veterinary inspector, and Nasih Efendi had worked in agriculture since his graduation from the Aleppo preparatory school.[74] Their qualifications reflected a combination of elite schooling and local knowledge but little institutionally derived agricultural training.

These qualifications were apparently considered inadequate, and by 1903 efforts were under way in Istanbul to exert greater control over the program and to staff it with teachers trained at the Halkalı school. This plan seems to have come as a bit of a shock to Hamdi Efendi. After teaching for two academic years and despite fulfilling his duties with aplomb, according to both his and the governor of Aleppo's assessment, he was dismayed when he was not invited back to teach for the 1902/1903 academic year. This would have been the third year of the agriculture program, but instead no agriculture classes were offered. Meanwhile, the Istanbul newspapers, which Hamdi Efendi had been following, were full of stories about the "reorganization and instruction of agricultural classes" in the preparatory school.[75] Hamdi Efendi appeared concerned by these developments, sensing that this buzz in the newspapers was indicative of excitement for the kind of work he had been performing but also that it potentially spelled the end of his teaching services. Before deciding to request graduates of the Halkalı school for the new program, Hamdi Efendi's local expertise and devotion to the program led to a discussion about his suitability for teaching the revised curriculum.[76] However, after some debate, multiple parties agreed that he was not qualified, and the preparatory school's administration urged the Agriculture Ministry to send two Halkalı graduates immediately.[77]

Hamdi Efendi's fears were confirmed, and he launched petitions to both the Education Ministry and the Aleppo Education Directorship emphasizing his local knowledge and his commitment to the program. Citing his eight to nine years' experience conducting experiments in the Aleppo model field, he insisted that this experience made him the most specialized for the task of teaching in the local school. He also stressed the initiative and expense he had put forth to ensure the success of the program. Because the school did not have the ability to procure the necessary implements, he had brought them as well as various seeds from the model field to demonstrate seasonally in the classroom.[78] He had even invested his own personal financial resources in the program, taking out loans above and beyond his promised salary, which had not been paid for nearly three years, to cover the costs of traveling the distance between the model field and the school.[79] He was particularly incensed that the new teachers were likely to be appointed at the third rank with corresponding salaries when, as of 3 February 1903, his own salary for teaching during the current semester had not been confirmed.[80]

In the end, Hamdi Efendi's protests were to no avail. Two graduates of the Halkalı Agricultural School, Abdussettar Efendi and Nureddin Efendi, were in due course appointed to teach the entire load of forty-three hours at a salary of 780 gurush each.[81] Thus by 1904, in line with an Education Ministry reform that same year to increase provincial courses not only in agriculture but also in industry and commerce to encourage students to pursue work in those areas and not just positions in the civil service, an entirely different slate of instructors staffed the agricultural branch with Abdussettar as the principal teacher.[82] Abdussettar's records from the Beirut preparatory school, where he had excelled in agriculture, jurisprudence (*fiqh*), the knowledge of ethics (*ʿilm al-ahlaq*), and trigonometry, and his 1902 diploma from the Halkalı Agricultural School carefully documented his achievements within the empire's expanding networks of agrarian expertise.[83] This institutionally certified knowledge at the highest levels ultimately trumped Hamdi Efendi's local knowledge.[84] Furthering this program was a hot-off-the-press book titled *Agricultural Information* (*Malumat-ı ziraiye*). Written by none other than Satiʿ al-Husri—the latter-day Arab nationalist educator but in 1904 a teacher in the Yanya secondary school and later director of the Istanbul Teachers' Training College—the book was to serve as the basis for instruction in the second and third years of high school.[85]

The Education Ministry clearly valued Abdussettar and Nureddin's certified expertise from the Halkalı school over the local, hands-on experience that the existing group of teachers, with their respective duties as the assistant director of the province's model field or its veterinary inspector, might have provided.[86] Official insistence on providing diplomas for the first crop of graduates from the three-year program at the Aleppo preparatory school further underscored the changing ways in which the central ministry sought to certify and institutionalize the acquisition of agricultural expertise.[87] Nonetheless, despite enthusiasm and support for these developments, finding adequate funding for continuing these programs was an issue. In the fall of 1904 Abdussettar complained about the failure to extend his post for a year.[88] By 1905 the elaborate program disappeared from the province's yearbook and only one teacher was listed as teaching a class called Agricultural Information in the preparatory school.[89]

In the province of Syria, as the global financial depression stretched into its third decade, the governor, supported by the Sublime Education Council (Meclis-i Kebir-i Maarif), wrote to Istanbul and insisted on more targeted educational facilities, namely, preparatory schools specializing in agriculture, commerce, and industry, to increase imperial competitiveness with respect to foreign products.[90] The Syria education director added his support, stressing the fertility of the region and the involvement of a large proportion of the population in agriculture-related work.[91] Noting that students who did not go into government posts or military schools from the local preparatory schools were most likely going to work in agriculture, he suggested that their grade school agricultural training should be sufficient for those who might seek entrance into the Halkalı school in Istanbul.[92]

Just as with the Halkalı, Bursa, and Salonica schools, these provincial institutions prioritized elite access. Although the rhetoric used to urge the establishment of such educational resources referred to those who would "work in agriculture," the schools targeted were much more likely to cater to the children of large landowners than to the children of small farmers, not to mention tenant farmers or others involved in agricultural labor. In 1902 a reorganization of classroom instruction in the preparatory schools of Hama and Damascus called for the inclusion of a class called Agricultural and Health Information, which would replace the Maintaining Health class in the old system.[93] Initially envisioned as a class taught by the headmaster of each school, it was eventually proposed that an agricultural school graduate employed by the province of Syria be hired to teach the class in the Damascus school.[94] The school in question was none other than Maktab ʿAnbar, an educational establishment renowned for its elite graduates, many of whom would go on to occupy positions in the local government and eventually the post-Ottoman mandate administration.[95]

Eventually, the provincial agriculture inspector Melkon Efendi was chosen to teach the classes, although a delay in his confirmation meant that the education director was not able to pay his salary, set at 200 gurush for six hours, in full.[96] Furthermore Melkon's inspector responsibilities, which involved working in the garden of the hospital and the local model field, especially during the winter and spring, meant that he was unavailable to teach in 1904. Nonetheless, the education director petitioned the Education Ministry to have Melkon's appointment reconfirmed for the fall of 1904, underscoring how irreplaceable the director considered his expertise as well as the dearth of people he held to be properly qualified.[97] Indicative of the ambitions that the administration had for the school, in August 1904—the same year of Abdussettar's appointment to the agricultural branch in the Aleppo preparatory school and the empire-wide Education Ministry reform program—an imperial order allotted 55,724 gurush (and change) to build seven classrooms, one model salon, and a shed as an extension of the Maktab ʿAnbar complex in an effort to incorporate lessons in agriculture, commerce, and industry.[98] These plans, like similar ones in the province of Beirut, were canceled for unclear reasons—budgetary concerns seem a likely explanation—but the fact that they were so meticulously laid out, including the drawing up of a blueprint for the proposed addition, demonstrates the thwarted aspirations involved.[99]

Despite the lack of an elaborate facility or the challenges involved in securing personnel with the desired training, Maktab ʿAnbar's curriculum in the early twentieth century did include agricultural classes. Furthermore, at least some of the school's students considered them a stepping-stone not only to higher education within the Ottoman domains at Halkalı, Bursa, or Salonica, but also, if they had the resources like the students discussed in chapter 1, education abroad. Fakhri al-Barudi was another such student.

Al-Barudi hailed from a landowning Damascene family with substantial holdings around the city, and his father "preferred to lead the life of a country squire in Duma" rather than hold posts in the administration.[100] Although al-Barudi was ultimately unsuccessful in literally translating his Maktab ʿAnbar knowledge into agricultural educational opportunities abroad, his experience provides insight into the nature of his interest in foreign schools, the increasingly dense networks of Ottoman students from the eastern Mediterranean who were in the process of attending them, and the importance of certified expertise to entering the system.

Al-Barudi, having studied agricultural methods at Maktab ʿAnbar, which he attended from 1902 to 1908, traveled to France after the completion of his studies with the intent of continuing his agricultural education.[101] In March 1911, upon arriving in Montpellier, site of one of the most prestigious French agricultural schools, he was met by Subhi Bey al-Hasibi, a Damascene from another major landowning family who was already studying at the school.[102] On the third day after his arrival he spoke with the school's director, who told him that he would need to improve his French before he enrolled and suggested that he consider applying to the Farm School (École Ferme) in Lyon.[103] Al-Barudi dutifully headed to Lyon, where he observed the school, which he described as "an intermediate school teaching students practical agriculture with a simple element of theoretical sciences," but encountered difficulties in enrolling because his Maktab ʿAnbar diploma was not translated into French.[104] Unable to have his diploma properly translated and certified in Lyon, he contacted Ahmad Qadari, a fellow Damascene living in Paris, to see if he could do it. Qadari in turn invited al-Barudi to Paris, suggesting that he could enroll in the Grignon Agricultural School, which had a similar farm school program.[105]

Al-Barudi set off for Paris but stopped along the way in Chalon-sur-Saône, where he met up with three members of a Syrian student delegation—al-Amir Mustafa al-Shihabi, Izzeldin ʿIlm al-Din, and ʿAbd al-Ghani al-Shabandar—who had been chosen by a Damascene committee and sent to France in 1910 to pursue higher education. Two out of the three—al-Shihabi and ʿIlm al-Din—were there to study agriculture.[106] Al-Shihabi, after a year in Chalon-sur-Saône, where there was a practical school of agriculture and vine growing, would take up his studies at the Grignon Agricultural School, and both he and al-Hasibi would go on to become agricultural engineers (*muhandis zira'i*), holding key positions overseeing state lands and agricultural policy in Syria during the mandate period.[107]

Upon his arrival in Paris, al-Barudi did try to enter the Grignon Agricultural School, but concerns over how he would fund his studies eventually led him to abandon his quest and return to Damascus after a bit of sightseeing.[108] Although al-Barudi may not have been successful in his quest for higher education in agriculture, his detailed descriptions of the schools he visited and agriculture's prominence among the subjects studied by his colleagues, especially those sent as part of the Damascus student delegation, underscored the priority its study held in elite circles. Their interactions illustrate the nature of the networks cultivated among those who had identified scientific agriculture as key not only to exploiting their own wealth and property but also to establishing priorities for reform from the late Ottoman period through the mandate. As discussed in later chapters, al-Barudi would become a prominent nationalist leader during the years of the French mandate, and his critiques of its administration reflected these interests.

Despite administrators claiming to prefer that institutions of scientific agricultural education prioritize the children of cultivators, they mainly seem to have reached the children of elite landowning families. The Beauvais students discussed in chapter 1 emphasized the need for state support for agricultural education, specifically a school that would train *agronomes* to travel the countryside, or, if that was too expensive, agriculture classes in existing schools or free agricultural conferences.[109] They aimed for agriculture to be recognized as a career with "incontestable advantages" and a "science" requiring "serious studies," like medicine.[110] Although unlikely to work the land themselves, they gained authority from these "scientific" studies that justified a role situated between the rural sphere where their economic interests lay and the urban space of their social and political circles. For those whose families had acquired substantial swaths of land through the state's new instruments, scientific agriculture had an as yet uncompromised allure. In the eastern Mediterranean the implementation of proposals along these lines had proceeded in fits and starts during the Hamidian period, but after July 1908 these ambitions for agricultural educational infrastructure led to even more aggressive efforts at expansion.

Agricultural Change Under the CUP

Al-Barudi's travels coincided with the aftermath of the July 1908 revolution and the rise to power of the CUP, heralding a renewed burst of activity aimed at expanding the empire's networks of scientific agriculture institutions. The agricultural minister, Selim Bey, after a long and checkered time in the position, would flee the country in the revolution's aftermath, when his closeness to the sultan and his penchant for alienating such powerful figures as the grand vizier had become a clear liability.[111] As discussed in the previous chapter, a number of the new administration's members were fervent proponents of scientific agriculture. In contrast to the tensions that had previously existed between different administrative offices, under the CUP there was considerably less ambivalence about the benefits of the model field program and the agricultural schools. The Halkalı school was slated to receive a substantial influx of funds, modifications to its program, and a duplication machine requested by the students for their various texts. Meanwhile, interested parties in the provinces found their proposals for scientific agricultural infrastructure responded to with greater alacrity.[112]

Pressure from these parties had been building in the months immediately before the revolution. The Aleppo model field had stayed operational; by the spring of 1907 it was experimenting with American cotton varieties. However, although the province of Syria had hosted exhibitions of new European-made threshing, reaping, and agriculture (*ziraat ve felahat*) instruments alongside local ones, administrators lamented its defunct model field.[113] The 70 "old dönüms" procured for the field and tree nursery were one hour's distance from Damascus and consisted of rocky soil that was difficult to irrigate and was of "second-degree fertility."[114] Still abandoned years after its acquisition, only a ring of poplar trees around the edge forlornly marked the site.[115] Early in the summer of 1908 the Interior Ministry wrote to the Forest, Mines, and Agriculture Ministry to suggest that a site in the Ghuta, the fertile oasis around Damascus, would be ideal for a new model field if more land could be acquired. This process would involve either gaining the consent of local landowners or purchasing land through an operation in accordance with eminent domain law (*istimlak kanunu*).[116] In making a request for the appropriations necessary to establish the field, the Interior Ministry stressed its public benefits (*istifade-i umumiye*). The rich agricultural potential of Syria had been neglected, and thus the province had a special need for establishments of public utility (*müessesat-ı nafia*) to ensure that the local population could benefit from demonstrations in scientific agriculture.[117]

Meanwhile, in Zor, the largely desert region located east of the province of Syria and crisscrossed by the Euphrates and its tributary, the Khabur, the governor and a number of other local officials seized the initiative to demand their piece of the scientific agricultural pie. They asked the state to provide them with a model field as well as a scientific employee with a 1,000 gurush monthly salary to demonstrate how to apply new methods and equipment.[118] Identifying more than 4,700 fertile fields that remained unexploited, they suggested that the necessary funds could be taken from the tithe and small, local contributions. Claiming a "lack of experts" but urging the tax value of the region if the benefits of the fertile land and irrigation from the Euphrates and the Khabur were realized, they explained how a group of four to five farmers had already gathered during two seasons to plant wheat, millet, and sesame with various implements.[119] The Council of State responded favorably to their request but insisted that it was inappropriate for the local community to pay; the council maintained that the funds for the field and technical expert had to come from the agriculture appropriations.[120]

Following the 1908 revolution, the administration responded to such demands with new urgency. By August 1910 plans were under way to establish a model field in Zor and the Commerce and Agriculture Ministry was making arrangements to include funds for an implement depot, an iron foundry, and useful seeds in the 1327 (1911/1912) budget.[121] In Beirut the members of the General Council outlined their proposals for a practical agricultural boarding school, which, along with mobile agricultural agents for each district, was to be funded with capital from the Agricultural Bank.[122] The agriculture minister also indicated that there would be funds in the following year's budget for a special silk facility, given the industry's importance in the region.[123] The governor proposed ensuring adequate capital for the agriculture chamber to buy new machines that could be operated with a fee, establish an agricultural school, and hire an agriculture employee in every subprovince and a veterinary employee and mobile agricultural teacher in every district.[124] In Aleppo planning included selling the distant model field and opening a closer one, establishing a repair shop with the latest machines and a capable master, which would be followed by the creation of a tool depot, appointing an agriculture director exclusively for the province, building a silk school in Aintab, and intensifying the fight against locusts.[125]

In Syria wealthy locals were eager to form partnerships that would facilitate irrigating 100,000 *dönüms* of gardens and vineyards in Jordan Valley land in the Salt district; saplings and seeds were being acquired for a new model field in Karak, plans were under way to bring in a specialist to dig wells in the Hawran, and the Chamber of Commerce council had decided to plan an exhibit to promote the province's production.[126] The administration also heeded calls to establish a practical agricultural school in the Hawran. Despite being a key breadbasket region, the Hawran had been excluded from central planning initiatives regarding agricultural education because of its distinct administrative status. Nonetheless, by 1913 the administration had appointed two officials and established an agricultural implements depot staffed with another employee who had been traveling the countryside for over a year and a half demonstrating the "progress of agriculture" to both the "local government and all classes of the

FIGURE 11. "Derʿâh Getreidedreschen mit dem Dreschschittlitten, 1906" (Derʿa [in the Hawran] grain threshing with threshing sledge, 1906). Bernhard Moritz, photographer. Berlin: Dietrich Riemer, 1916. Source: Library of Congress, https://www.loc.gov/item/2014648726/.

community." He had also established schools in Jabal al-Druze, Ajlun, and the Hawran.[127]

As for Syria's model field, the governor's office urged the Interior Ministry to establish one that was "complete and proper," as opposed to just a model nursery, in the center of the province.[128] Despite the local population's "capacity and predisposition" for agriculture, they used "old tools and implements with ancient methods," which, the governor's representative felt, limited the benefits that might be gained from their labors. The governor's office also recommended the establishment of an agricultural school either within the field or nearby to ensure both practical and theoretical applications.[129] Such an assessment indicated an appreciation for local farmers' knowledge coupled with a desire to ostensibly enhance it through access to education in new methods. To pay for the project, funds could come from the 372,715 gurush that represented two-thirds of the 1323 (1907/1908) fiscal year dividends (*temettü hissesi*) held by the Agricultural Bank.[130] A school in the area would also help to balance the preponderance of such institutions in more westerly regions of the empire.

By June 1909 momentum was building for the establishment of a theoretical and practical agriculture school in the province of Syria, but budget constraints remained a problem. The budget did not contain appropriations for such a school, so the agriculture minister urged the Interior Ministry to take it into careful consideration in the coming year.[131] Within a year, construction on an agricultural school would be under way in the province, albeit in the town of Selimiye, about 200 kilometers northeast of Damascus and just southeast of Hama.[132] Although this does not necessarily seem to have been the preferred location for the school, the focus on its construction in the agricultural inspector's 1910 report for Syria, filed alongside a collection of similar reports from around the empire, suggests that this was where the plan came to fruition.[133] Whether because of the failure to allocate a budget for these initiatives or not, some local administrators appear to have taken matters into their own hands and contrived a creative solution for their funding problem. At least a portion of the funds used to build the Selimiye agricultural school had been obtained under controversial circumstances. The resulting conflict offers a glimpse into the differential effects created by projects of scientific agriculture and how different groups in this rural community perceived the unequal access integral to these projects.

If some urban landowners and members of rural communities who had achieved a certain level of wealth and property found common cause over such institutions, for other members of those communities the appeal (or lack thereof) of scientific agriculture could not have been more different. The relatively significant sums of capital it required, its untried compatibility with local environments, and its lack of suitability to local land-tenure arrangements, to name just a few examples, all posed challenges. The risk on multiple levels was just too great.

The Selimiye Agricultural School and Rural Reaction

As demonstrated by the vignette that opened this chapter, the genesis of the Selimiye agricultural school was a contentious affair. For central government planners and some local administrators, the area around Selimiye, though lacking the irrigation possibilities and proximity to Damascus of the Ghuta, held other advantages. Selimiye and surrounding towns were located in a plain of fertile land that received just under 350 millimeters (13.8 inches) of rainfall annually. This level of rainfall placed the area on the margins of rain-fed cultivatable land. Over time, largely because of this environment, occupation predominantly by pastoralists or semi-pastoralists had alternated with settlement by those involved primarily in cultivation. Since the mid-nineteenth century, the proportion of cultivators had increased as a result of an influx of Ismaili communities from areas west of Hama; the government had encouraged their move to east of the city with such policies as exemption from conscription and taxation.[134]

The region also had a topography conducive to a distinct and long-practiced method of irrigation. Surrounded by hills to the east and southeast, the slopes of these ranges provided an ideal gradient for building tunnels, or *qanat*s, that channeled groundwater into the plain, where it could be distributed for irrigation.[135] A number of *qanat*s, some likely dating back to the Roman period, had been built and/or restored by the plain's inhabitants over the centuries. By the nineteenth century many had fallen into a state of disrepair because of a lack of permanent settlement in the region for several centuries.[136] When the government encouraged eastward settlement, the Ismailis initially chose Selimiye as their base in part because it was surrounded by these tunnels, which, after some preliminary repair work and with regular maintenance, could be made operational again.[137] The provincial governor noted that the community would be encouraged to organize partnerships (*şirketler*) to facilitate the formation of neighborhood quarters (*hara*) and artificial forests (*sınai ormanlar*) in the 40,000 hilly *dönüms* of escheated *miri* land (*mahlul miri*) surrounding the site of the school.[138]

The district of Selimiye was also adjacent to the Homs and Hama regions, areas dominated by large landowners—scientific agricultural institutions' target audience.[139] Thus, from the government's perspective, Selimiye had a number of advantages as a site for an agricultural school: Not only was it close to a region where a critical mass of people had the necessary land and capital to risk experimenting with new technologies, but it also had an arid ecology that provided a striking contrast to other places in the empire with agricultural schools, such as Istanbul, Bursa, Ankara, Adana, and Salonica.

According to the governor, the agriculture inspector's office had chosen land for the school with the consent of the Ismaili community, which had donated 6,000 lira to the project.[140] Increasing the appeal of the site, several local landowners were prepared to donate land as well. However, although

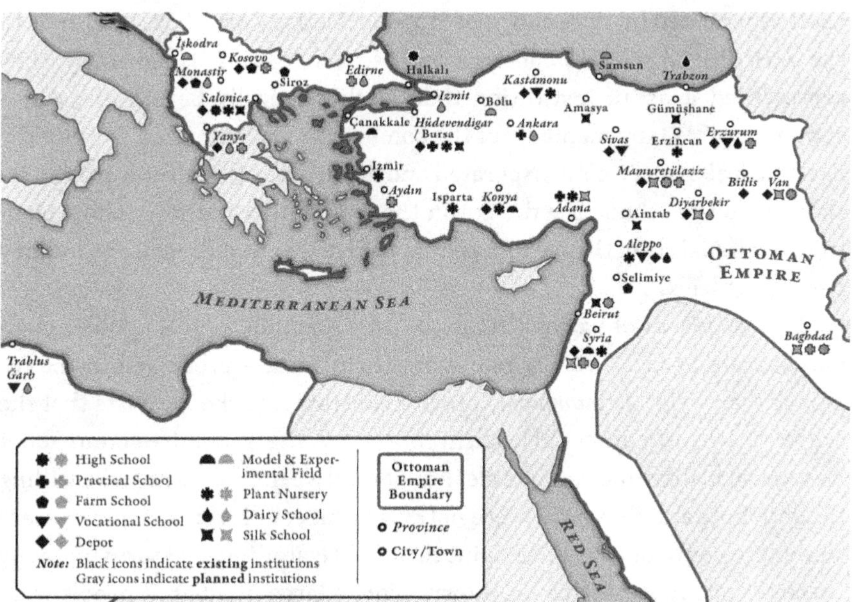

FIGURE 12. Established and planned agricultural institutions in the Ottoman Empire, c. 1911. Locations based on the Ottoman *Forest, Mines, Agriculture, and Veterinarian Review*, 13 March 1911.

some in the local community were eager to support the school, most of the cultivators considered it immaterial to their interests. The reactions that its construction provoked illustrate the range of perspectives on the "general utility" of scientific agriculture, for despite the agricultural inspector's insistence that the school was about "diffusing education and expanding and improving agriculture," most local cultivators found themselves unwilling contributors to a project from which they expected little benefit.[141]

It is unclear to what extent, if any, the funding for the school came from the Agricultural Bank, as the governor's office had suggested, but at least a portion of the funds came from 10,000 lira (9,000 in cash and 1,000 in jewelry) that the governor of Hama and the *kaimmakam* of Selimiye had confiscated from Ismaili communities in the region. The funds had originally been collected as *zakat* to be sent to the Ağa Khan, who was based in British-colonized Bombay and who the Ismailis had recognized as their spiritual head, but the government would not allow such a sum to leave the Ottoman domains.[142] The government claimed it was unable to return the donated funds because the amounts given by individuals had not been carefully recorded. As an alternative, local experts (*erbab-ı vukuf*) and outside investigators supported by the Council of State decided to contribute the funds to the agricultural school's construction because, at least rhetorically, they represented it as an institution that would generally benefit the whole community.[143] Many members of the community did not agree. Despite the agricultural inspector's exasperated and dismissive attitude toward the resistance to the school, the dissent in the community reached such a pitch that an official from the civil inspector's office was sent to make an inquiry and report back.

The responses of various actors in the community—from government bureaucrats to local leaders and a small cultivator—preserved in the inquiry's transcript (*istintakname*) provide insights into the interests that the school served on a practical level, in contrast to the discursive claims about its general utility, and reveal a clear divide between those who were willing to contribute and those who were not.[144] A number of local landowners were content to contribute—at one point the investigator insisted to an unhappy witness that, according to his information, a large number of people were in favor of spending money on the school—but poorer residents of the Selimiye region refused.[145] Among the witnesses 18-year-old Muhammad bin ʿAli, who identified himself as not having any "lands to work with rent," and Muhammad bin Ahmet, who introduced himself as working in agriculture (*ziraat ve felahat*) and running a small shop, refused categorically to consent to their contributions being used for the school.[146]

According to the headman of the east and west neighborhoods (*mahalle*), about 100 people out of 2,000 men and women supported the use of their donations for the school. He clarified that these were the owners of land and wealth and that those who opposed the school tended to be tenant or migrant farmers (*serseriye*) lacking in land, property, and work.[147] Two other headmen also bore witness that in their neighborhoods similar objections applied: In the Qabile neighborhood 200 out of 4,000 people wanted to contribute, and in the eastern neighborhood some 100 out of 2,000 were willing.[148] Those who were willing were once again identified as the "owners of wealth and property" (*ashab al-tharwa wa al-amlak*).[149]

Despite recognizing the economic interests involved, one headman nonetheless referred to those who desired to donate their money to the school as the "enlightened ones" (*mutanawwirin*).[150] The clear logic of economic imperatives could not save those who opposed the administration's appropriation of a small portion of what little wealth they owned from being relegated to the "enemies of progress." The local civil inspector further affirmed this characterization when he wrote to the Interior Ministry that certain members of the local community wanted to ensure their children's enlightenment and education by establishing this agricultural school, despite the "pesterings" of some in the community who were against it.[151] The inquiry underscored a clear solidarity among those with a certain level of "wealth and property" who saw the scientific agricultural education the school would offer as furthering their interests. In addition to experiments and training in new techniques that might enable them to more profitably exploit their lands, they likely also saw the school as offering their children alternative paths to higher education and maybe even a government post.

Even as the agriculture inspector relayed information about the school's contested origins in March 1911, instruction in the school was under way with eighteen students. Several local landowners had donated 374 *dönüms* of land for the school's experimental field.[152] The governor of Syria was also enthusiastic, claiming that the school demonstrated the value of scientific agriculture and "what that means" to the local community. Complaining that the agriculture officials appointed to the province were ineffective, he insisted that the Selimiye agricultural school and the province's model farm were the best investments for agricultural resources.[153]

If the fertile soil and irrigation resources around Selimiye made it a suitable region for agricultural experimentation, its location close to the intersection of the provinces of Syria, Aleppo, and Beirut made it a plausible destination for students throughout the eastern Mediterranean. But as its detractors were well aware, not everyone was welcome. Based on a report about the school's activities and prerogatives, poorer farmers were justifiably skeptical about the benefits it would offer them. Despite official promises of the school's enlightening role for all, the school's main beneficiaries were to be limited to those with means. The school's new director exemplified the elite networks circulating the latest book-derived scientific agricultural knowledge. In fact, he was none other than Abdussettar, a Beirut native and one of the Halkalı Agricultural School graduates appointed to replace Ahmet Hamdi in the Aleppo preparatory school several years earlier. He had since become a teacher and assistant director at the Beirut preparatory school before being appointed director of the Selimiye school sometime in early November 1910.[154]

The scope of the school's in-progress and anticipated activities was wide ranging.[155] By March 1912 it was on the verge of demonstrating to villagers the application of new methods in the planting and harvesting of certain staple crops such as wheat, barley, Egyptian millet, cumin, and common vetch, which were currently planted in the region by biennial rotation (one year of fallow, one year sown). Experiments conducted by the head of the municipality (*belediye reisi*), who had successfully grown crops unfamiliar to the region, namely, three varieties of Egyptian cotton and Marseille and Cyprus potatoes, in an irrigated field also gave the school direction. The cotton yield was impressive—300 *okka* of cotton pods from 1 *okka* (2.83 pounds) of cotton seeds. Only after his success did the school decide that these crops presented an attractive prospect for experimentation. Given such auspicious results and these crops' importance to commerce, Abdussettar noted that they would plant a larger quantity the following year. The school would also plant other crops new to the region, including sesame, Egyptian and Adana local cotton, and melons. The school's director appears to have been rather conservative in his approach, prioritizing crops that were familiar to the local population and more willing to branch out when the possibility of success with new crops had already been demonstrated.[156]

In his discussion of the crops planted and methods used, Abdussettar's meticulous report demonstrated not only the attempt to draw distinctions between "scientific" and existing means of agricultural production but also the obstacles that hindered the production of this distinction, as the school's experiments faced ecological and climatic challenges to the use of new methods and implements. Emphasizing measurement, quantification, and control of nature, Abdussettar described his use of itsy-bitsy (*ufak tefek*) instruments, in the absence of the astronomical observatory that had not yet been built, to determine that temperatures had averaged between 13 and 14 degrees Celsius, rainfall was good, and the weather in general moderate. But quantifying aspects of nature did not mean wresting it to one's will. Lingering snow cover from a harsh winter led to disappointing wheat and barley yields, and the pulling capacity of the school's current animal stock determined which machines were feasible. One of the oxen had already died from a "pain in the bowels." Furthermore, although it had rained during the usual season, the amount was not enough, which meant that the harvest had to be collected with "normal reaping" (*adi orak*). New Wood and Deering reaping machines stood at the ready and, Abdussettar noted, "the local community was keenly waiting to see their good qualities," but the harvest-ready crops' height of only 20 centimeters and their closeness rendered these machines impractical.[157]

Not only did environmental conditions and natural limits pose obstacles to implementing scientific methods, but local agricultural practices also created challenges. Before partitioning the land (*ifrazdan evvel*), a process whose completion would quiet the unrest according to the previously discussed inquiry, cultivators had always used normal local plows (*adi yerli kara sabanlar*) and a system of biennial rotation. Only after partitioning would cultivators be able to undertake the initial plowing that would fallow and prepare the fields for seeding (*nadas usulü*), deploy the school's new implements, and undertake "agriculture that is carried out within the bounds of science."[158] Furthermore, "because the community's agriculture is sown according to the strip method, harvesting machines could not be used."[159] Essential components of local practice that aimed to distribute risk more evenly presented challenges to new machines and practices.

Although the school's capacity to demonstrate scientific agriculture to the local community as envisioned by Syria's governor was a fraught process, the students targeted by the school's educational program were from the start those envisioned by the locals who had demanded their money back. Abdussettar, in addition to discussing the progress of the school's various experiments and operations, also clarified who the school sought to attract as students. The school, in his assessment, needed to improve its curriculum, including the array of courses it offered, and appoint two additional teachers to appeal to the children of large landowners. Competition loomed large from the empire's older institutions of scientific agricultural education. Three-fourths of the land in the provinces of Syria, Beirut, and Aleppo was in the hands of "distinguished men" (*mütehayyiz adamlar*), he explained, but their children were likely to go to more established schools in Salonica and Istanbul if his suggestions were ignored. The school, he insisted, should not become an almshouse (*darülaceze*) for landless children whose lack of land would mean that they could not translate the school's training into more expansive experiments in scientific agriculture. Students should come from families who owned large amounts of land where they could experiment with the techniques taught. Science was a prerogative of the wealthy and landed, its universal benefits not quite so universal.[160]

In the years to come, the Selimiye school would continue to cater to the children of local elites.[161] Despite claims about its "general utility," the school's ongoing activities underscored the extent to which it was instrumental in the co-production of "scientific" knowledge alongside heightened distinctions between those in rural society who could access this knowledge and the profit they anticipated from it and those who could not. This cooperation between local elites and the proponents of scientific agriculture in the Ottoman administration would continue to define the implementation of projects in the empire's final years.

At the Intersection of Imperial Networks and Private Initiatives

In the years leading up to World War I, the number of publications in Ottoman and Arabic dedicated to scientific agriculture increased substantially. Articles such as those published in the journal *Cultivator* (*Ekinci*) hailed agriculture as the base of a thriving economy, proclaiming, "Before everything, agriculture is necessary." So long as agriculture was "underdeveloped," industry could not flourish.[162] Whereas in the late nineteenth century the

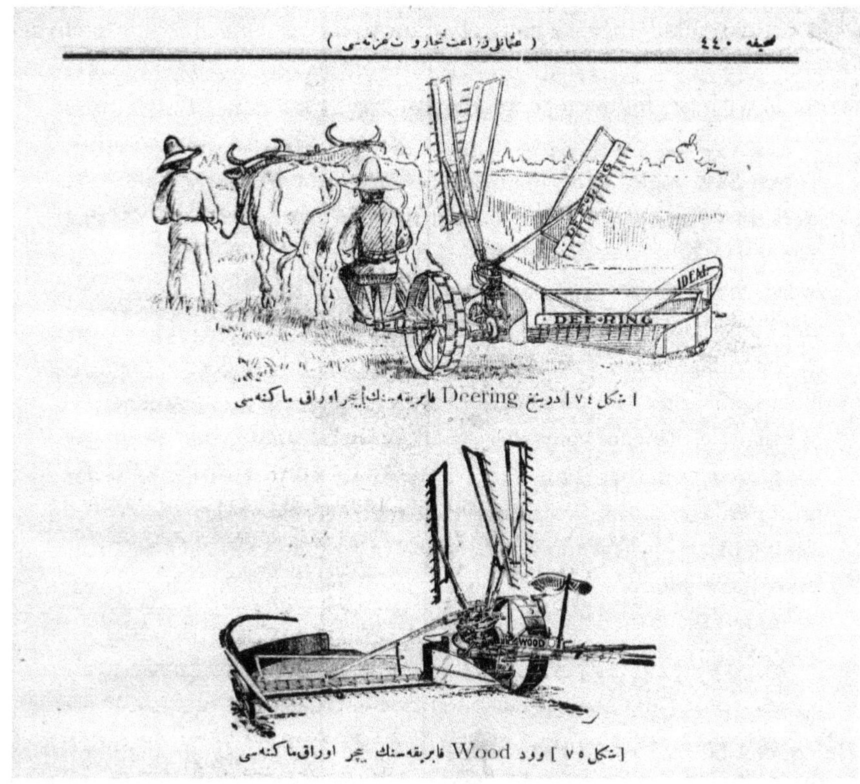

FIGURE 13. The machinery of scientific agriculture. Source: *Ottoman Agriculture and Commerce Gazette*, 21 April 1910, Milli Kütüphanesi.

Council of State had lamented the lack of journals circulating with information about agricultural advancements, in the early twentieth century and especially following the CUP's rise to power, the Commerce and Agriculture Ministry increasingly published and disseminated reports from the empire's scientific agricultural institutions, detailing results from their latest experiments. They offered assessments of machines that worked, others that did not, new plants that demonstrated promising results, others that failed. The institutions' employees made recommendations, based on results from the experimental fields, regarding the crops they thought had the potential to be generalized in a particular area or the machines that seemed most promising for broader use.[163]

A primary challenge, though, was how to convey this information in accessible language. One exasperated reader of the agricultural journal *Ekinci* wrote in with the following complaint:

> Let me be straight with you—until now I have not seen any benefit in the agriculture books that have passed through my hands. Because those who know how to read and write a little like us farmers even with the words written would not be able to understand. Now then, those who do not know how to read and write, our village brothers, even if you read it to the village imam from those words no one would understand. If these books are written for farmers like us, please write so we can understand. If you are writing for yourselves, that's something else.
>
> Moreover in these books are written quite difficult things to be done in our villages, in our fields. Since the first issue of your *Ekinci*, I have been taking [it]. From "Farmer Conversation" [a regular feature of the magazine] I saw a lot of benefit because you are writing things that are easy to undertake, beneficial, and simple. However, because these words are piece by piece in the journal, they are forgotten, they go away.[164]

He concluded by urging the editors to write an equally simple book. Not only were existing books difficult to understand, but they also described methods that were incompatible with local practices. His letter does indicate that the journal's editors were attempting to present more accessible advice, but its serialized nature made it difficult to follow.

The editors took his complaint seriously, replying that they had thought long and hard while reading it and had decided to write a book. However, although they had traveled around the provinces some time before, their previous information was "quite lacking." Acknowledging both the rapid changes in agricultural production and the importance of local expertise, they envisioned the book as a joint project. Appealing to their readers, the journal's editors requested provincial agricultural inspectors and teachers to send in their knowledge about agricultural conditions, crop types and species, and observations about agricultural improvements. They also asked local farmers to provide details about the agricultural methods of particular villages and towns, such as what kinds of products were grown and what transport options were available.[165] Hüseyin Kâzım was already working to address the issue. The same year as this exchange, the Society for National Defense (Müdafaa-i Milliye Cemiyeti) paid for the printing of hundreds of copies of two books authored by Kâzım: *Farmer Child* (*Çiftçi Çocuğu*) and *Farmer Advice* (*Çiftçi Öğüdü*). The booklets were to be distributed to provinces that requested them. Concise and with a relatively simple vocabulary and ample illustrations, the free copies were quickly depleted.[166]

Meanwhile, both private entrepreneurs and state institutions ramped up their efforts to facilitate access to new implements with a view to ensuring that farmers could observe, assess, and even spend considerable time working with machines that interested them in order to be convinced of their suitability. P. J. Louisides, writing in the *Levant Trade Review*, urged the American Chamber of Commerce to establish a permanent exhibition of American-made implements and machinery, noting that this would "enable agriculturalists to decide for themselves, by actual trial, which machines and implements are best suited to their requirements."[167] Acknowledging the importance of taking into consideration local knowledge in pursuing such an enterprise, he added that "European agents and travelers," who, he claimed, were "well acquainted with the tastes and wants of the farmers, . . . may be found purchasing implements manufactured locally in a primitive way which they send home to imitate and improve."[168] In 1911 the Agricultural Bank in Aleppo organized a demonstration for local farmers of "several mowers, drills, ploughs, harrows, etc.," and in October 1911 "a small steam power threshing machine (of English make) with view [*sic*] of introducing them to the farmers."[169] In Beirut the offices of the journal *al-Iqtisad*, an enthusiastic advocate for agricultural "progress," moved their administration to a space near the Ottoman post office, where they explained that people could view agriculture implements from the most famous English and American makes.[170]

Such efforts bore fruit, as various large landowners in Syria and Aleppo, convinced of the wealth-generating potential of these new methods and technologies, seized the initiative and sought to invest in applying them to their lands. Drawing insight from local experiments and demonstrations, some in turn reached out to global networks of experts to assist them in assessing and applying the most appropriate implements. In 1913 Fuad Mudarris Zade, a major landowner in Aleppo and one of Hüseyin Kâzım's nemeses, asked the American consul in Aleppo, Jesse B. Jackson, to make inquiries on his behalf for an American specialist who would help him develop part of his land. He directed these inquiries to specialists in the southwest or western United States, likely seeking someone with knowledge of techniques for more arid lands.[171] Meanwhile, in Damascus, toward the end of World War I, the wealthy landowner Abd al-Rahman Pasha al-Yusuf would turn to German specialists for assistance. He had lands that were deemed ripe for the application of dry farming.[172]

According to Jackson, Mudarris Zade owned 20,000 acres of land located an hour and half by train from Aleppo between the city and the Euphrates.[173] He had initially planned to develop 7,000 acres of it with a rumored investment of $10,000–$13,000 but had since readjusted this proposal to 2,500–3,000 acres, or about 10,000 *dönüms*. The area was upland with red clay soil, of which about 1,500 *dönüms* were stony, although a motor plow could work it "without hindrance." Mudarris Zade claimed that the soil was good for growing grain and cotton and had been worked for 40–50 years, albeit with relatively shallow plowing—only 3–5 inches deep—and in rotation. He planned to order the equipment from England, with an initial expenditure of £2,000, and wanted an agent who could recommend what was needed in the way of "a steam, or fuel oil burning motor gang plow, harrows, threshers, and perhaps rollers." Mowers and binders were not necessary, however, as they "cut the grain too short to utilize it afterwards for feed in this country."[174]

Such an observation suggested that Mudarris Zade had perhaps learned from the Aleppo farm school's experiments. According to a report from the school's director published in June 1912, Aleppo's hot, dry climate stunted grain height and led to shorter stalks than in Anatolia and Rumeli. As a result, straw was expensive and farmers, in order to ensure that they benefited from every last centimeter of it, harvested it by plucking it from the surface of the ground. The new machines struggled to replicate this method. The field's activities had demonstrated the economic pitfalls of these machines, and Mudarris Zade's stipulation suggested that he was aware of this fact.[175] The knowledge produced in the fields was circulating, at least among a certain class.

To assist Mudarris Zade in his quest, Jackson wrote to Stanley Morse, at the University of Arizona Agricultural Experimental Station. Although Jackson's initial proposal to Morse received a negative reply, Morse forwarded the proposition to several colleagues, including George W. Shaw, a "consulting agriculturalist and land expert" from San Francisco; John Widtsoe, president of the Agricultural College of Utah and author of a recently published (1911) book on dry farming; and B. Youngblood, director of the Texas Agricultural Experiment Station.[176] Shaw was interested in pursuing additional correspondence with Mudarris Zade, and Widtsoe and Youngblood were each confident they could find men who would be suitable for the post, provided the compensation was adequate.[177]

Mudarris Zade, however, was not interested in a salary-based form of compensation. Agreeable to a contract of five to potentially ten years, he was prepared to reinvest all his profits made "over and above the first four *shumbuls* for the one." However, he refused to pay for the agent's travel expenses and would only compensate the agent in shares equivalent to half of what remained after the tithe and the first four *shumbuls* (i.e., four camel loads) were subtracted from the total harvest.[178] His offer resembled the *murabiʿan* contract in which the landowner supplied all the necessary capital for exploitation and the cultivator provided labor in exchange for a fourth

FIGURE 14. "Camels loaded with sheaves near Baʿalbak [in the Biqaʿ Valley]." Source: John D. Whiting, photographer, *Diary in Photos*, vol. IV, 1938, Library of Congress, https://www.loc.gov/resource/ppmsca.17416/?sp=31.

or fifth of the harvest after the tithe was exacted.[179] However, Mudarris Zade recognized the agent's anticipated expertise and apparently was willing to offer a somewhat more generous share.[180] Likely he felt the need to stipulate these terms because of the region's unpredictable yields: Taxes were taken in proportion, so why should not compensation be paid in a similar manner? In the end, however, this form of payment was not sufficiently attractive; all of those who expressed an interest in the project were only willing to work for a salary.[181] Nonetheless, the story illustrates the lengths to which some large landowners with connections were willing to go to pursue these new forms of agricultural practice, but it also demonstrates the obstacles they faced as they remained sensitive to nature's whims.

Meanwhile, in Damascus, Abd al-Rahman Pasha al-Yusuf sought out the assistance of foreign expertise to exploit his vast landholdings. Controlling approximately 100,000 hectares, he had 7,500 hectares of irrigated orchards and other crops near Damascus; another holding, irrigated by canals and planted with grain and maize, near the desert east of the city; and a third portion consisting of forty villages in the Jawlan. The land near the desert in particular had areas ripe for dry farming. Although cultivators worked much of the land and received one-third of the crop, some hectares remained fallow because of the absence of tenants. For Abd al-Rahman, a key attraction of these new technologies was their utility in areas where he lacked access to sufficient labor. In the years immediately before World War I, he entered into discussions with a French-Belgian company about farming the land; however, the start of the war scuttled the plans.[182]

Demand from some (usually quite wealthy) landowners for new technologies coexisted with even greater demand for plows made according to local designs but with improved features. In April 1914, T. R. Varbedian, the assistant director of the Aleppo agricultural school, expressed interest in placing an order with an American manufacturer for steel and iron plows based on local designs. The American consul suggested that the order could be for as many as 200,000 plows, the annual market for plows in the region.[183] Meanwhile, another local entrepreneur, Mr. Demirjian, sought to become the exclusive agent in Aleppo for the Walter A. Wood company, an American reaper and mower manufacturer whose machines were among those demonstrated at the Selimiye agricultural school.[184] Such evidence suggests a prevailing confidence in the prospects for agricultural expansion and "improvement" in the region. The emphasis on plows of local design, even coming from the assistant director of the Aleppo agricultural school, indicates that existing approaches to agricultural practice continued to thrive alongside optimism about the prospects of newer technologies. A number of local farmers were clearly interested in taking advantage of new features they hoped would be beneficial, even if they were not yet convinced of the efficacy and reliability of the more expensive machines championed by the advocates of scientific agriculture.

In the years following the 1908 revolution and immediately preceding World War I, the empire generally and the eastern Mediterranean in particular saw the expansion of the empire's network of model farms and fields as well as agricultural schools catering to various specialties and levels. In addition, interested locals who wanted to learn more about new machinery could visit a number of depots established by the government or showrooms such as those advertised in *al-Iqtisad*. However, interest in these new technologies and methods remained largely divided along class lines. Despite rhetoric that stressed the general benefits of these programs and investment in crops and tools that had the potential to be of broad utility, the enthusiasm in the local and imperial press reflected a narrow set of elite interests. Ultimately, the capacity to take the risk of applying these new methods was rather unevenly distributed.

Conclusion

In the years immediately preceding the outbreak of World War I, agricultural experimentation was proceeding apace, even if the expanded application of new methods was limited to a privileged few. Nonetheless, efforts to increase yields bore fruit, most likely derived primarily from existing methods. Yields were good compared with what they would be after the war. One estimate placed wheat production in Syria at 727,700 tons and barley at 450,000 tons—a level that would still not be matched by the early 1930s.[185] Initiatives from technocratic administrators often supported by local elites ensured that institutionally a network of model farms and fields, agricultural schools and classes, and depots to showcase implements provided opportunities for various interested locals to examine and become acquainted with the latest technology.

Examining the implementation of these projects underscores the local initiative and knowledge to which they were beholden, even as shifting notions of agricultural expertise in official rhetoric questioned or denigrated existing methods. Midlevel local officials appear to have exercised a high degree of autonomy in pursuing scientific agriculture experimentation. Often local persistence and agency ensured the implementation of proposed programs in the face of funding shortages or administrative wrangling. Individual prerogatives were also instrumental in determining projects' particular shape. Meanwhile, the increasing emphasis placed on certified, institutionally acquired expertise elided the debt that the production of scientific agricultural knowledge owed to local expertise and practice. Although this knowledge was clearly valued, as evidenced by efforts to focus on local specialties and hire local farmers, the discourse of scientific agriculture denoted its sphere of praxis as separate and distinct.

Finally, despite rhetoric that emphasized scientific agriculture's capacity to "dominate" nature and overcome various ecological and climatic limitations, scientific agriculture was in fact very much a product of those limits. Environmental obstacles and social and economic practices, many derived from responses to those environmental constraints, would challenge and shape the forms that scientific agriculture could take. Those who could afford to experiment were those with enough "land and wealth" to undertake the risks entailed by these obstacles. The result was ongoing tension between the program's stated beneficiaries—Ottoman cultivators writ large—and its actual ones—wealthy landowners with capital and land to spare. This was a tension that continued to characterize the implementation of agricultural reform projects well into the postwar period, albeit within a different political context that would present its own distinct challenges.

THREE

THE TRIALS *and* TRIBULATIONS *of* TRACTORS

From Ottoman Provinces to French Mandate States

[Money] is the tongue to whom wants eloquence and
it is the weapon to whom wants combat.
—*Arabic poetry*

Asceticism cannot be relied on.
—*Ibn ʿArabi*[1]

In the summer of 1922, Depolla, the Fordson tractor dealer in Aleppo, was angling to score a major coup: outfox the other dealer in town and sell a new tractor to Aleppo's governor. After holding some local demonstrations, he suggested that the governor purchase one. Following much "hemming and hawing," the governor offered to buy one for 150 gold livres, substantially below the going rate. If his price was not met, he threatened to not only buy an Avery tractor but also to "invite all the *agriculteurs* of the state of Aleppo to imitate me," certain that his influence would determine which tractors could be sold in the vicinity.[2] Clearly, the governor held a high opinion of his influence; Depolla concurred, but was mystified as to how his competition could afford to undersell him.[3]

Depolla learned how shortly thereafter. While walking down a road, he happened on an Avery tractor on a truck—the governor had apparently carried out his threat. Insinuating himself among the "gawking onlookers,"

Depolla examined the machine and discovered rounded hinges that should have been angular and a missing piece of metal. The next day, he pretended to run into the governor's aide-de-camp as the latter was passing by his shop and casually suggested that maybe the governor's "new" Avery tractor was not in fact new. This suggestion swiftly reached the governor, who then asked to meet with Depolla. After putting the governor off several times, Depolla finally met with him and agreed to examine "as a friend" the as-yet-undemonstrated Avery tractor. Closer examination revealed more signs of "already advanced usage" as well as a tag indicating that the machine "had come from the factory in November 1920 destined for Egypt"! The governor, at Depolla's suggestion, assembled a "commission of expertise," which determined that in fact the tractor had already been used for 350 hours.

The governor insisted on a refund and found himself tractorless with only two months to go until his untilled fields would need to be sown. To the rescue, Depolla assured him that only a Fordson tractor could do the job in a month and a half. Reluctantly, because the governor blamed Depolla for his hurt pride, he finally agreed to buy a Fordson tractor for 200 gold livres. This price was still "sacrificial," but Depolla agreed because it would prevent a competing company from gaining such a high-profile client and would boost future sales as other large landowners sought to imitate the governor.[4] As anticipated, in short order, Depolla had more requests than he had tractors to sell; interested inquiries came in not only from Aleppo itself but also from surrounding areas such as Antakya and Hama.[5]

Advances in the technology of scientific agriculture were proceeding rapidly in the early twentieth century. In particular, World War I had seen major innovations in agricultural machinery. This competition between two American tractor makers in postwar Aleppo exemplifies the advantages these manufacturers had over their European rivals, primarily as a result of rapid expansion in tractor buying and use by American farmers during the war as they responded to demands for increased food exports to war-torn Europe and the income these exports ensured.[6] Sales of the Fordson tractor had started in 1917 as part of this trend.[7]

But tractors were only as effective as the surrounding infrastructure that facilitated their use, including but not limited to credit options, fuel access, repair facilities, and property size. Tractors embodied much of what made new agricultural technologies inaccessible to most cultivators. They were expensive and affordable only for those with substantial resources. The swath they cut as they tilled a field worked best on expansive areas of land, not the small narrow plots that characterized many villagers' land-tenure practices. Their inner workings were highly complex and consisted of many parts susceptible to breakage, thus necessitating the assistance of a specialized repair expert to ensure that they stayed in working condition. Finally, skepticism reigned as to just how well they would work. The relatively rapid expansion of tractor use in the United States would lead some farmers to face their own reckoning with unintended consequences in the Dust Bowl of the 1930s.[8]

In contrast to their popularity in some regions of the United States, tractors did not enter widespread use in much of the world, including France, until after World War II, although the interwar years did see them feature in the discourse and planning of technocrats eager to facilitate their eventual spread.[9] For those who had adequate financial resources and did not have to be too concerned about the ecological and subsistence consequences if experimentation failed, the work that these machines could accomplish was impressive, leaving large landowners "under the spell of admiration."[10] In the eastern Mediterranean local technocrats encouraged those with resources to consider investing in a tractor, viewing the machines as a component of the modern agricultural methods necessary to stay competitive in global markets.[11] For influential French mandate officials, "motoculture" (not to be confused with monoculture) featured prominently in their plans for the region's *mise en valeur* (development) and bolstered their justifications for occupying it.

The same period that saw tractors emerge as a technological marvel with revolutionary potential was also the period in which the region that would become the nation-states of Syria and Lebanon would undergo a fundamental political and economic transformation. World War I heralded an abrupt shift in orientation for the eastern Mediterranean. This region, which had been an integral part of the Ottoman Empire, found itself in the wake of the war divided along lines roughly derived from the secret wartime Sykes-Picot Agreement, which served British and French imperial economic and strategic interests. Because the mandates disrupted regional flows of capital and goods, areas that had once been economically integrated were forced to compete against each other in the service of these interests.

As with the Ottoman administration, agriculture was at the core of French, Lebanese, and Syrian administrators' plans for the region's economic development, with all three groups making a case for the "natural" boundaries encompassing the space they claimed should be theirs to exploit and develop. Whereas Ottoman government planners and civil servants had approached developments in the region with an eye to its integrated place within the empire's provincial administration, French officials treated it as a colonial periphery, with a corresponding view of its development. Ottoman technocrats cultivated the eastern Mediterranean as a region that could contribute agriculturally in myriad ways to the "national economy." In contrast, French proponents of the mandate who were influential in metropole politics from late 1918 to 1919 emphasized the cultivation of raw materials required by metropole industries or necessary for imperial self-sufficiency in foodstuffs, particularly grain. They also underscored the region's value as a market for French products and a repository for surplus French capital.

But the mandates of Syria and Lebanon were not technically colonies; the mandate system promised the eventual independence of the mandate states. Thus French officials found their colonial goal of deepening the region's dependence on capital and commodity flows within a French imperial sphere in constant tension with the program of nationalist technocrats, whose evolving projects aimed for self-sufficiency and economic prosperity within an eventually independent national space.[12] Local technocrats were keen to exploit the variety of agricultural possibilities that Syria's environment offered with an eye to promising cash crops and other raw materials to support the growth of local industry—goals thwarted by mandate officials whose primary objective involved shaping the region's economy and agriculture to serve French capital, commercial, and industrial interests.[13] Their respective approaches to tractors exemplified this divide. Whereas local technocrats championed the infrastructure that would make tractors a viable option for some farmers, once French officials realized the expense involved and that French tractors were unlikely to be most people's first choice, their interest largely waned. For local technocrats such disinterest stymied their efforts to expand or even maintain the infrastructure on which tractors, not to mention other technologies and plans for economic development, relied. The inability to build this infrastructure meant thwarted plans for economic growth. Ultimately, the stakes were existential: So long as the mandated regions lacked political independence, they remained economically vulnerable and exposed.

The Space of Ottoman Scientific Agriculture Before and During World War I

On the eve of World War I the Ottoman administration had made substantial investments in the empire's scientific agricultural infrastructure while simultaneously bolstering its methods of extraction from agricultural production.[14] It had also taken measures to make various aspects of agrarian administration more conducive to capital-intensive investment and legible to officials in Istanbul. Provincial branches of the Agricultural Bank were distributed throughout the region and were well integrated into rural financial matters.[15] More surveillance in taxation had led to a threefold increase in revenue as a proportion of gross domestic product between 1850 and 1914, a revenue predominantly raised on agricultural products.[16] In 1913 the central government passed one decree to undertake a new cadastral survey and another to regulate mortgages that sought to grapple with how best to manage agrarian credit, given the preponderance of land held in shares, or *musha*ʿ.[17] The infrastructure for scientific agricultural education was considerable; agricultural schools and model farm and field networks expanded alongside a number of depots constructed to house a variety of implements for local demonstrations and experimentation.

The state of agricultural infrastructure in the province of Aleppo illustrates the fruits of this expansion by the early twentieth century. Central administrators prioritized the province for agricultural institution building because it was a rich agricultural region and a key transit point for goods coming from southern Syria or the ports of Beirut and Alexandretta bound for Anatolia.[18] By 1910 Aleppo had a robust roster of eight salaried civil servants and nine wage laborers employed in the agricultural administration of the province.[19] Six were dedicated to general agricultural administration, two worked in the Aleppo depot, two staffed the Aintab silk school (*darülharir*), and seven were employed by the province's model field.[20] All but one of the salaried civil servants were graduates from either the Halkalı Agricultural School (four) or the Salonica practical agricultural school (three).[21] The highest paid wage laborer was the depot's ironsmith, who had completed his studies at the Adana Industrial School and was likely kept busy with inevitable machine repairs.[22] Although it is unclear how many cultivators these schools were turning out, they were certainly providing a ready pipeline of civil servants to staff positions in the empire's scientific agricultural institutions.

The division of labor among the province's agricultural employees indicates an ongoing reliance on local knowledge for practical agricultural activities, especially in the model field, under the supervision of "scientifically" trained employees who hailed from farther afield and circulated in the empire's networks of expertise. Aleppo's agricultural director in 1910, Emin Zihni Efendi, was a graduate of the Salonica school and hailed from Leskofça in the Balkans. Previously, he had served as director of the Adana model field. The other salaried posts were held by men from Istanbul, Denizli, and Antalya.[23] However the farmers and gardeners in the province's model field primarily came from Aleppo and its surrounding villages.[24] While these employees toiled in the fields, the agricultural director compiled statistics for Istanbul on the mean prices per kilogram for the province's crops in a chart highlighting the province's agricultural diversity.[25]

Despite the distant hometowns of the scientifically trained employees, prior experience in the region was valued. Emin Zihni Efendi had previously worked in the Adana field, and Agop Oscan, the employee who replaced him as agricultural director in 1911, had served a multiple-year stint working in Aleppo province's model farm from 1904 to 1909. Originally from Istanbul and an 1896 graduate of the Halkalı school, his resume reflected the circulation of its graduates within the empire. He had worked with the agricultural inspector in Edirne, as a technical agricultural employee in Chios, on a "special mission" to deal with orange and olive tree diseases in Trablus Gharb, as assistant director and then director of the model farm, as a technical agricultural employee in Aleppo, and as director of agriculture in Diyarbekir. He returned to Aleppo as the director of agriculture in September 1911 and served until November 1915, when he was fired during the Armenian genocide because he was Armenian.[26] The charts he compiled and his frequent correspondence as director suggest an industrious and detail-oriented administrator.

The contents of implement depots in Aleppo, Damascus, Homs, and the Hawran and their operations demonstrate the Ottoman administration's commitment to encouraging farmers and landowners to experiment with new tools.[27] By October 1914 the Aleppo depot had sold 36 out of 126 machines for a total of 11,894 gurush 10 para.[28] Out of twenty different kinds of purchased items, the most expensive was a Deering Ideal reaper, but the most common purchases were the Izmir, Eckert, and Rud. Sack plows. The sale of two Alfa Viola cream separators underscored the importance of the dairy industry in the region.[29]

The sums handled by these depots indicate expanding interest and investment. In Aleppo funds taken in from implement sales were deposited in the local Agricultural Bank branch, and periodically portions were sent to the central administration.[30] In 1913/1914 (1329), the Aleppo depot imported over 35,000 gurush worth of equipment financed by the Agricultural Bank (20,935.10 gurush) and the Finance Ministry (14,712.35 gurush) and exported 13,967.25 gurush worth.[31] Both the Beirut and Damascus depots imported substantial stock in the years immediately before World War I. Their numbers suggest brisk sales. For example, in Damascus between 1910/1911 (1326) and 1913/1914 (1329) the depot imported 179 implements valued at 58,109.70 gurush, and by the beginning of 1914/1915 (1330) it had in stock 93 implements valued at 26,188.25 gurush, suggesting that at least 86 implements with a value of 31,921.45 gurush had been sold.[32]

Implements that were well suited to local environmental conditions, such as the hillsides of the Hawran, saw rising demand after their introduction in that region's depot. The Hawran was known for its productive grain fields, and its depot took in 66 implements worth 26,668.10 gurush in 1911/1912 (1327) and acquired 686 implements worth 67,653.35 gurush in 1912/1913 (1328).[33] Among the most popular implements were a series of plows from the American Syracuse Chilled Plow Company. An initial stock of three each of the Syracuse 0 and 00 plows rose to thirty each the following year, suggesting that these plows were finding favor with local farmers.[34] Syracuse designed these plows specifically for tilling hillsides, and they had been among the models displayed at the 1893 World's Columbian Exposition attended by the former agricultural inspector Reşid Bey, as discussed in chapter 1, and listed among their models for export.[35] The slopes of the Hawran often posed challenges to new implements, but these plows clearly appealed because of their suitability to the challenging topography.[36] They were made with "chilled wearing parts," which were produced through a casting process that made the outside more durable and the inside stronger.[37] By 1913/1914 (1329), the depot was beginning to increase its stock of Ottoman-produced implements, adding five Izmir plows to its offerings.[38]

Depot inventories tended to be dominated by German manufacturers such as Rudolph Sack and Eckert and American companies such as Deering and Syracuse, but they also included some French and Ottoman products. In 1329 the Homs depot was stocked with 119 implements (32 different kinds), 3 of which—a German Eckert plow for light soils, an American Deering harvester, and a French Marot grain sorter—had been sold by the beginning of 1914/1915 (1330).[39] These numbers did not suggest a buying frenzy for these implements. Given their costs, the buyers were likely well-off farmers or landowners; however, it is possible that buyers may have intended to rent them out as well. Nonetheless, the diversity of implements stocked by these depots suggests that offering farmers a number of options sourced from various countries with an emphasis on the machines' suitability to provincial environmental particularities and economic exigencies was a priority of the Ottoman administration.

But distributing this new equipment was not without its challenges. Agop Efendi expressed particular concern about ensuring the effectiveness of the Aleppo depot to house, handle, and supply new farm implements arriving from Beirut. On multiple occasions he wrote to express his frustration at the state in which certain tools arrived. Implements without contracts or guarantees were arriving in a broken or deficient state, and this was posing a quandary.[40] Proper guarantees were necessary to cover the tools' journey by rail from Beyrut to Aleppo just as they were key to transferring them to more distant internal provinces, such as Urfa, Zor, Baghdad, Mosul, and Diyarbekir. Without such guarantees, funds were needed to cover repairs.[41] His multiple requests to deal with the issue underlined the additional demands these tools placed on local infrastructure and the priority given by the local administration, as represented by Agop Efendi, to ensuring that these implements were properly maintained and distributed.

Reports churned out by the region's model fields underscored the array of sources, both from within the empire and outside it, that the Ottoman administration turned to in an effort to improve crops varieties and assess the possibilities of generalizing them in new locales. Field employees experimented with local crops alongside those brought in from various areas of the empire, such as Istanbul, Bursa, Salonica, Izmir, Samsun, Trabzon, and Adana. Plants such as potatoes, wheat, barley, and sainfoin were procured from France alongside Egyptian and American cotton (the latter brought by way of Adana) and wheat and potatoes from Cyprus.[42]

The reports detailed results over the season and made recommendations about which crops were suitable for more general distribution in a given area. In Aleppo, for instance, the director of the farm school noted that a soft awnless wheat originally from France produced puny stalks and parched grains and was thus not recommended, but he encouraged the planting of a red hard Cyprus wheat, which reached maturity before the locusts appeared.[43] On the other hand, in Syria, in addition to urging the more widespread distribution of Chevalier and spring barleys and Iskenderiye clover from France, the province's 1910/1911 (1326) report noted that red pepper from Vodena and Spanish pepper and white sugar beet from France had proven particularly well adapted to Syria's soil and climate and should be encouraged based on the results obtained in the model field.[44] Circulated in the empire's Commerce and Agriculture Ministry yearbooks, the results of these experiments were accessible to interested parties throughout the empire.

These institutions also sought to assess and respond to local concerns and expand the reach of their experiments. When farmers in Jabal Samaan, near Aleppo, insisted that planting chickpeas was not worth it because of an insect problem, the farm school set aside 1 *dönüm* of land in its field to apply "scientific investigations and studies" and, according to the school's director, managed to raise a crop without pest interference.[45] To overcome the limited ecological footprint of the model field, the agricultural civil servant in Syria sent seeds to farmers to assess in their localities around the province. One wheat brought from Baʿalbak was planted in the model field of Syria and in the plots of various *efendi*s in Duma and Wadi al-ʿAjam and of another farmer in Zabadani. The seeds planted in Duma and Zabadani thrived. In fact, those in Duma did so well that it was decided not to sell the crop but to save it and replant the next year. In contrast, a harsh winter overwhelmed the seeds sown in the model field and those sent to Wadi al-ʿAjam.[46] In another instance, the official gave corn seed to a village in Duma, and when the results were promising, he enjoined the whole village to plant it the following year, an order accepted by the village's owner.[47] Such arrangements indicate the ongoing collaboration with elites and incorporation of local knowledge into the production of scientific agriculture, but they also suggest impositions on local villagers whose lands were designated for these experiments.

The reports indicate more widespread planting of cash crops such as cotton, which had not been planted widely in the region in recent years, and new crops such as potatoes, which were also desirable, but they also imply that further experimentation and encouragement were necessary. In Aleppo, American cotton varieties were preferable to Adana and Aleppo local varieties. Egyptian cotton, meanwhile, could be fruitfully planted along the Euphrates, where the environment more closely resembled the Nile. In Syria, the report observed, the rich black volcanic soils of Salt, the Jordan Valley, the Hawran, Ajlun, Hama, and Homs were suitable for cotton, whereas the white chalky soils of the Ghuta and Nebk were not. Encouraging potato planting, on the other hand, proved challenging, because potatoes reached maturity at the same time as a number of other vegetables and people did not consider them particularly delicious.[48]

The Ottoman Empire entered World War I in the fall of 1914 with a substantial and active array of scientific agricultural institutions, even if their reach was limited. Well-stocked depots located not only in provincial centers such as Aleppo, Damascus, and Beirut but also in productive agricultural regions such as Homs and the Hawran provided a breadth of options to local farmers who could afford their products. Agricultural schools and model farms conducted experiments and exchanged information. Meanwhile, the Committee of Union and Progress (CUP), in accordance with its "national economy" program, took various steps to protect local production, such as canceling the capitulations in September 1914 and introducing higher customs tariffs in the fall of 1914 and the spring of 1915.[49]

The war, however, devastated the region's agriculture. In addition to a breakdown in provisioning capacity, inflation, "disruption of security" in eastern areas, and lack of labor and transportation, an array of environmental challenges also confounded efforts to maintain the region's agricultural output.[50] Field mice spread from western Syria in the war's early days only to be followed by birds who ate the freshly sown seed, forcing farmers to sow again. The following year, locusts descended and devastated everything, even the "onions in the belly of the earth." During the fourth year, drought in the east and southeast forced farmers from villages in Raqqa, Jabal Samaan, and Maara to abandon their fields and seek refuge in the western marsh of al-Amik, near Antakya, where they could access water for themselves and their animals. The government attempted to respond but struggled to keep on top of the compounding factors.[51]

Despite these difficulties, efforts to maintain and expand scientific agricultural infrastructure continued over the course of the war. In Syria the governor sought to make up for a shortfall in the funds needed to establish an agricultural school in Damascus; 30,000 gurush had been allotted, but an additional 25,000 was necessary.[52] Labor and transportation shortages in the eastern Mediterranean posed obstacles. The Allied blockade of the coast and the restriction of the railroad to military necessities made importing implements and "useful plants" from the United States or Europe impossible.[53] Despite funds allotted to continue to pay for the salaries of agriculture teachers and employees of agricultural implement depots, qualified individuals were unavailable to replace conscripted agriculture teachers from Salt, Baᶜalbak, al-Biqaᶜ, Hama, Quneitra, and Nebek. The depot in Homs remained staffed, and a director and a teacher were engaged to replace the conscripted employees from the Damascus and Deraᶜa (Hawran) depots, respectively.[54] Funding was also allotted for "an agricultural boarding school" in Syria. However, labor shortages combined with the existence of the applied agriculture school in Selimiye and the agricultural industry school in Taanayel led the commerce and agriculture minister to suggest to the Interior Ministry that a third school was unnecessary.[55] Ultimately, the school in Syria was not established for "some reasons," but the funds allotted for it were transferred to Taanayel, where a school was opened on 7 November 1916 with sixty students and where, as of April 1917, lessons and experiments were ongoing.[56]

If a new school was deemed too extravagant, Syria's model field was in full swing with 5 *dönüm*s of vineyards and gardens and another 5 of fruit trees, as well as various kinds of wheat and barley in addition to flax and corn, the latter of which soldiers ate fresh.[57] Meanwhile, in Dayr al-Zor, located on the banks of the Euphrates in the heart of pastoralist countryside and surrounded by desert beyond the reach of the river's waters, lands were being delimited and taken as eminent domain for the establishment of a model field in 1917 and 1918. Eight of the town's elite, or as Zor's governor referred to them, "those who desire the region's progress," had brought items from Aleppo to donate to the school.[58] Although there also appears to have been contestation over the delimitation of lands for this model field, the cooperation of local elites with government authorities regarding strategies for agricultural and industrial development continued even as the final years of the war raged and the ravages of famine gripped much of the eastern Mediterranean.[59] The war strained agricultural infrastructure, but the government and local elites were committed to maintaining what they could.[60]

Ottoman officials were also looking to the future. In 1917 Hüseyin Kâzım gave his official assessment of Syrian agriculture, urging that it was important to incorporate agricultural classes into preparatory schools and teachers' colleges, produce "classic" simple agricultural texts, and establish institutions that would lend against crops with better terms and experimental cooperative companies.[61] His recommendations largely reiterated those that had driven Ottoman policymakers' and local elites' proposals for decades, underscoring the still limited scope of these projects in reaching most cultivators and the desire to find ways to make them more accessible. In the midst of war, famine, and general devastation, Ottoman technocrats continued planning for how best to expand the infrastructure of Ottoman state space among rural communities in the eastern Mediterranean. Little did they realize that the next year they would be packing their bags.

Competing Visions of Agricultural Self-Sufficiency and National Space in the Postwar Eastern Mediterranean

In the fall of 1918 the army of the Arab Revolt, backed by British forces, occupied Damascus. As they did so, Ottoman administrative personnel met in Aleppo to start the process of withdrawing themselves as well as significant records and monetary resources to the north.[62] Among the monetary resources taken were 447,000 Ottoman gold pounds from the region's Agricultural Bank branches' capital and 396,000 Ottoman gold pounds of their deposits.[63] Meanwhile, French and British forces occupied the west coast of Syria in October 1918 and started distributing grain and other forms of sustenance to a population whose suffering had intensified throughout the war as a result of their coastal blockade.[64] Then, in the fall of 1919, the British withdrew, allowing the French alone to occupy Cilicia and areas along the coast and leaving Faysal, who had helped lead the Arab Revolt and had become head of the Arab government in Damascus, on his own in the interior.[65] In Damascus the Faysal government, to the extent that it could in the midst of these shifting dynamics of power and spaces of sovereignty, not to mention various financial constraints, began to pursue its own agricultural policies. It prioritized an agricultural program that was largely continuous with that pursued under Ottoman rule. The main difference was that instead of contributing to a national economy based on the agricultural resources in the ecological space of the Ottoman Empire, policymakers worked to reimagine an agriculture-based national economy in only the eastern Mediterranean's ecological space.

Despite the brevity of this moment before the French invasion, the myriad initiatives announced and to some extent undertaken during the Arab government's brief reign demonstrates the alacrity with which it went about setting up the trappings of a new state. The new government drew on local agronomists and those who had served in the Ottoman administration to craft and oversee its agricultural policy. Yusuf al-Hakim, a graduate of the American School in Latakia and the Sultani school who had served in various administrative capacities in Mount Lebanon until 1918, was appointed the minister of public works, commerce, and agriculture.[66] Mustafa al-Shihabi, a member of the student delegation whom Fakhri al-Barudi met with in France (see chapter 2) and a graduate of the Grignon Agricultural School and an *ingénieur agricole*, or agricultural engineer, was appointed director of the agricultural division.[67] On 20 February 1919 the Parliament (Majlis al-Shura) issued a decree creating a seven-member agriculture committee composed of "landowners that have expertise in modern agricultural methods and complete practical knowledge of the agricultural needs of this country and it is preferred that among them are graduates of the agricultural schools."[68]

The Parliament tasked the committee with an array of responsibilities and enjoined it to work with local communities to determine best practices for increasing output. After consulting each region's community and assessing the best crops for their area, it would acquire "the requisite seeds and seedlings," import agricultural equipment suitable to different regions, and sell it at "fair prices" or in installments. Measures of support for farmers using new machines and methods included opening repair facilities, providing free training and instructions for applying new fertilizers, and encouraging the use of purified seeds. Crucially, to ensure that the state saw increased economic benefits from these efforts, the committee would create charts detailing the land's natural conditions and degrees of soil fertility, which would serve as the basis for a new tax once the tithe was annulled. It would also produce "detailed maps" of districts and villages to be deposited with *tapu* offices for settling future disputes.[69] These initiatives essentially continued those under way during the Ottoman period.

Faysal's government encouraged other forms of investment as well. In April 1919 the official paper announced the formation of the Aleppan

Agricultural Company, which was capitalized with 100,000 Egyptian pounds and had a mandate to undertake "agricultural projects" using "the methods of modern science."[70] The government also established a system of chambers of agriculture that would meet weekly, assess local needs, and provide an annual report regarding their activities and local agricultural conditions.[71] The agricultural banks throughout the region reopened after a painstaking reproduction of their Ottoman-era accounts based on the documentation that remained in local branches.[72]

Expanding or building new institutions for agricultural education continued to be a priority. Al-Barudi asserted his interest in and support for agricultural developments, penning a front-page article in the official paper urging the establishment of a school for cultivators and another for merchants. He suggested that the beneficiaries themselves should contribute to avoid too much dependency on the government.[73] Perhaps his position was in part due to the financial struggles the government faced. Despite these challenges, the government briefly established an agricultural school southwest of Damascus in the western Ghuta, the fertile oasis surrounding the city, where students carried out various studies between 1918 and 1919.[74] The school lasted only one year before being converted to a model field and consolidated with the Salamiya school, but its brief existence indicated an effort to follow up on World War I–era Ottoman plans.[75] Similarly, a proposal to transform a barracks in Deraʿa (a town in the Hawran) into an agricultural school, for which the government considered it necessary to allot 500 pounds, also echoed Ottoman plans for the region.[76] Meanwhile, the Parliament passed a decision to reopen the Muslimiya agricultural school with a plan to charge 30 pounds per year for room and board, although the education itself would be free. To ensure that this education would also be accessible to at least some students who could not afford such fees, 20% of all boarding students could attend for free.[77]

In Salamiya the Ottoman-era school was to become the region's primary agricultural high school because it already had 2,000 *donums* dedicated to it by *tapu*, good sources of water, a variety of implements that had been bought by the Ottoman government, and thousands of trees and vines already planted. Such resources promised an income of at least 1,000 lira per year, plus there was concern that, if the school were closed, it would "leave the large buildings playing in the hands of the saboteurs." Based on these considerations, the Parliament agreed to allot 1,500 lira for the school's restoration.[78] The school would accept both domestic and foreign students with the intent to allow fifty students, particularly the sons of farmers and poor villagers, to attend free of charge.[79] Its strategic position at the center of "the four sides of the country of Syria" meant that students arrived from "northern Aleppo to southern Gaza and from the sea coast to the eastern Homs and Hama." There were high expectations for the school eventually becoming among the "finest ranks of agricultural schools" with "graduates spread in the country's plains and mountains and filling its east and west as promoters for science."[80]

The new government sought to demonstrate that it was capable of seeking out, assessing, and applying the technical assistance it required without the colonial interference implied by a proposed mandate and its "technical assistance." One journalist compared its efforts to those undertaken by Japan, which was "eastern like us." Just as Japan had sent out scientific missions to gather information from the "west," Syria was sending its students to schools in Europe to learn. Their insights would ensure that the country benefited from its land just "as the Americans, French, English, and Swiss benefit. . . . Dirt must be turned into gold nuggets and desert into fertile soil."[81]

A month earlier, an agriculture teacher from Eskişehir's teacher's college and a member of the Farmers Association (Çiftçiler Derneği) wrote about how tractors could be the key to doing just that if approached with care. Based on observations from a tractor competition in Algeria in 1913, he conveyed in meticulous detail his impressions to the association's membership, which included men from Aleppo, Damascus, Beirut, and Hama.[82] He explained how long each tractor ran per day, how deep it plowed, how much fuel it used, and how much ground it covered, but he was most concerned with how each tractor broke up the soil. If it packed the earth or did not break the dirt into fine enough clumps, it was unlikely to be suitable for use in areas with the long, dry summers typical of the eastern Mediterranean.[83] Without well-crumbled soil, the roots would not be able to grow deep enough for the plants' survival during the summer.[84] Although motorized plows were impressive, the teacher's observations underscored the concerns involved in bringing new technologies to local ecologies: Any adoption of scientific agricultural practice was dependent on ensuring its suitability to local environmental exigencies.

Perhaps inspired by such concerns, officials in the government further asserted their capacity to stay abreast of the latest developments by making a public spectacle of efforts to bring new technologies to Syria for experimentation. In the spring of 1920 the Syrian government "decided to buy some agricultural machines, especially tractors," and hold a competition in Damascus during which various companies would exhibit and then demonstrate their machines. The government extended an invitation to French manufacturers and requested information about their availability so that it could schedule the competition at a time that would allow them to attend.[85] Such overtures conveyed the Faysal government's willingness to work with French officials but also their refusal to grant them exclusivity in the Syrian market.

In terms of agricultural planning, the fruits of the government's efforts were evident in al-Shihabi's *al-Zira^ca al-^cAmaliya al-Haditha* (*Modern Practical Agriculture*), published in 1922. Drawing from experiments in the Ghuta school, the 604-page book reflected the administration's efforts to take stock of the region's agricultural resources, assess the challenges they faced, and propose a comprehensive roadmap for developing them, because "agriculture is from the greatest means of producing and growing wealth" and no one could deny its "importance in our country Syria."[86] Al-Shihabi hoped that Syria's "masters of agriculture" (*irbab al-zira^ca*) would "find the desired benefits from its observations." He expected his book to provide assistance to students, such as those from Salamiya, for whom it contained "all that they need from this science" and to function as a helpful summary of "general and specialized agriculture" studies for students who had attended a school like Halkalı.[87] The chapters covered the gamut of scientific agricultural concerns from the basic fundamentals of soil composition, weather conditions, geology, and pests to emerging "modern" knowledge about fertilizers, agricultural methods, and irrigation techniques. The book also included chapters on each of Syria's diverse crops, from those of extensive culture, such as wheat and barley, to industrial cash crops, such as cotton, and everything in between.[88]

Written and published before the full repercussions of the postwar division of the region between British and French mandate rule had become clear, al-Shihabi's proposals assumed administrative jurisdiction over a region essentially contiguous with "Syria within its natural boundaries," the construct that dominated discursive imaginaries of national space

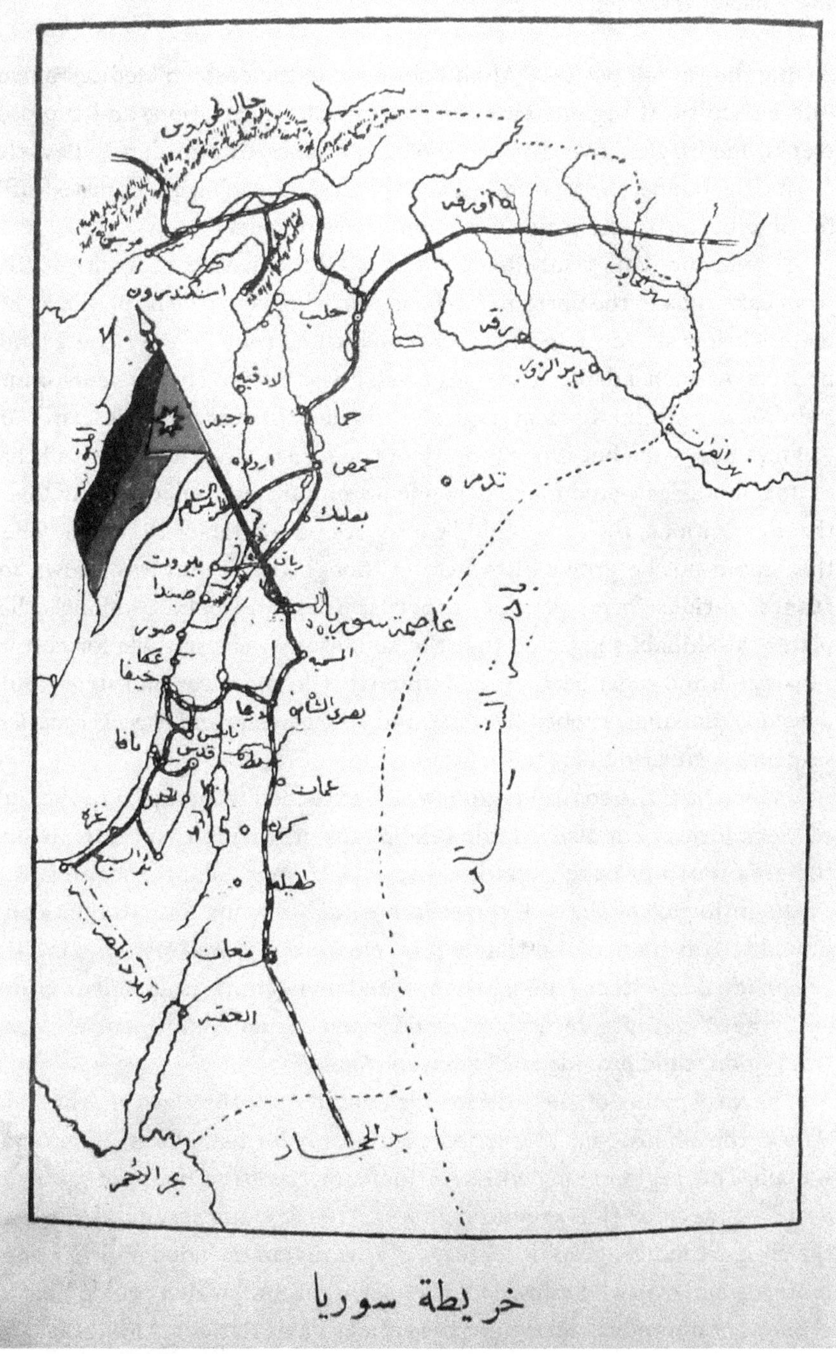

FIGURE 15. "Map of Syria," "Syria within its natural boundaries," as envisioned by Faysal's government. Source: *Dhikra Istiqlal Suriya fī 17 Jumada al-Thaniya sanat 1338 al-muwafiq 8 Adhar (Mars) sanat 1920* (Miṣr: Matbaʿat Taha Ibrahim wa-Yusuf Barladi, 1920).

during the Faysali period.[89] Al-Shihabi divided the eastern Mediterranean into agricultural regions based on temperature, elevation, and types of plants, identifying five distinct ecological zones (the Jordan Valley, the coasts, the plains, the mountains, and the desert), each with a role to fulfill in contributing to the region's economic development.[90]

The Jordan Valley (al-Ghor), which al-Shihabi defined as stretching from Lake Hula in the north to the Dead Sea, whose surface he placed at 300 meters below sea level, in the south, constituted some of the richest lands in Syria. At such a depth below sea level, it was extremely hot year-round. Rainfall was minimal—on average al-Shihabi estimated no more than 250–350 mm per year—but improved use of the Jordan River's waters and that of its tributaries would make dependence on rainfall unnecessary.[91] Given these conditions, the area could be a source of vegetables in winter, when they could not be grown elsewhere. Although the region was known for rushes, various forms of cane, papyrus, lilies, and palms, among other plants, al-Shihabi suggested that the conditions were suitable for cotton, sugarcane, and sugar beet, around which textile and sugar industries could develop.[92] Bananas, rubber, bamboo, and *Washingtonia* and *Phoenix canariensis* palms were also likely to thrive.[93]

In contrast, the coastal region, which extended from Aqaba to the Gulf of Alexandretta but also included the plains of Marj Ibn ʿAmir, Jenin, and the area north of Lake Hula, was cooler with more abundant rains. Due to the influence of the sea, temperatures did not fluctuate dramatically, humidity was higher, and clouds protected crops from frost, making the region ideal for citrus fruits, bananas, and pomegranates as well as grains and vines.[94] Because vegetables would ripen earlier than in colder areas, this region could provide an off-season supply.[95]

The vast plains of the interior included Karak, the Hawran, the Biqaʿ Valley, the Ghuta, and the raised plains of Palestine, Homs, Hama, and Aleppo. This region along with the Ghor was the "storehouse of grains in Syria"—the region that produced its wheat, barley, and sorghum. However, the climate and geographic features of this region included multiple wind patterns and overwhelming dependence on rainfall, which could inject an element of unpredictability into the farmer's calculations.[96] Al-Shihabi insisted that mulberry and almond trees and vineyards could be grown in these rain-fed lands so long as the soil was worked well in the spring to prevent moisture evaporation.[97] Fruit trees and vegetables were also possible but would be limited to irrigated areas, such as the Ghuta, Baᶜalbak, and Homs.[98]

The mountains, which included Karak, Salt, Ajlun, Qalamun, Jabal al-Shaykh, and Mount Lebanon, were rainier and colder and would support "rain-fed olive, vine, fig, almond, pine nut, cypress, wild pistachio, sugarberry, and grains" cultivation as well as a variety of fruit trees cropped in irrigated lands.[99] Finally, the hotter and drier desert regions were generally not suitable for cultivation, although al-Shihabi noted that the area between Palmyra, Sukhna, and Salamiya had the potential to be productive with dry-farming techniques in years with enough rain. Nonetheless, these lands constituted a key component in his economic agenda, as they produced grasses in winter and early spring that were crucial for grazing pastoralists' flocks.[100]

Al-Shihabi's description reveled in the diversity of crops that already grew in each region and the possibilities for future diversification. His proposal for the region's varied ecologies not only underscored its potential to produce the crops of both tropical and more temperate zones but also outlined a space of virtual self-sufficiency, including an extended season for fresh vegetables, as crops in geographically close areas would ripen at different times and could then be redistributed.[101] Al-Shihabi also included initial suggestions for what agriculture-based industries might be profitably developed. Approaching the region as an integrated whole, his proposals reflected technocratic planning for how its agricultural resources could be best exploited for both local consumption and revenue-generating export from the state's perspective.

Al-Shihabi was not the only one taking stock of the region's resources and assessing the viability of a national space based on its agricultural potential in the post–World War I moment. With a project that was fundamentally at odds with al-Shihabi's, in Beirut another group of elite technocrats and businessmen promoted a space of agricultural self-sufficiency as justification for extending the borders of an independent "Greater" Lebanon. Their position reflected that advocated by proponents of Lebanese independence who were living abroad and, by mid-1919, that of the Mount Lebanon administrative council. In early 1919 representatives of the council had initially traveled to the Paris Peace Conference to present their demand for "autonomy" within a Greater Syria under French mandate, but by May 1919 this demand had shifted to a call for the "political independence of

Lebanon in its geographical and historical frontiers."[102] In line with this shift, a number of contributors to *La Revue Phénicienne*, a publication coordinated by the Beirut businessman Charles Corm, urged a technocratic perspective for carving out space for a Lebanese state from sufficient territory that would ensure both political and economic independence.[103] Between July and December 1919, they made their case with pointed appeals to French authorities for their support.[104]

Fundamental to these authors' plan was redrawing the boundaries of Ottoman "administrative Lebanon" to encompass "natural Lebanon."[105] Since the 1860s, the Mutasarrifate of Mount Lebanon, or "administrative Lebanon," had consisted of the mountain range of Mount Lebanon and the coasts immediately south and north of Beirut from Saida to south of Tripoli. From their perspective, these borders represented an injustice perpetrated by the Ottoman administration in the aftermath of 1860 because they aimed "to confine the Lebanese in a rocky and unproductive territory" with "830 inhabitants per square kilometer of cultivable land," thereby destroying their "economic equilibrium."[106] With an agricultural output dominated by silk, "administrative" Lebanon had to rely on remittances from America, free silkworm importation from France and Italy as well as silk exportation to France, and "the freedom to receive from the interior the necessary cereals for the subsistence of men and animals."[107]

"Natural" Lebanon, or Greater Lebanon, which Albert Naccache juxtaposed with "East Syria," constituted a space that would be economically independent based primarily on its capacity for greater agricultural self-sufficiency.[108] Composed of "a political and economic entity that permitted it to live, to suffice for its needs and to freely develop itself," "natural" Lebanon would include Beirut, the Biqa^c Valley, lands around Saida and Tyre to the south, and the ʿAkkar plain north of Tripoli.[109] During the Ottoman period, all these lands except for the Biqaʿ Valley, which constituted the western edge of the province of Syria, belonged to the province of Beirut.[110] Adding Beirut would ensure a major port, and the areas to the south produced substantial grains, olives, and other foodstuffs. The agriculture in the northern region, although less abundant, included cereals and citrus crops in addition to a well-developed silk industry. Industry, such as soap making and silk and cotton spinning, was generally better developed in this region. The fertile Biqaʿ Valley was rich in wheat, second only to the Hawran, and was the premier region for vineyards. Finally, the addition of

FIGURE 16. French map from the 1860–1861 Syria Expedition used as a point of reference by proponents of "natural Lebanon" (C. Hakim, *Origins*, 220, 242). Source: Library of Congress, https://www.loc.gov/item/2021668659/.

the Anti-Lebanon mountain range would ensure control over the hydraulic basins of the ʿAsi and Litani Rivers, allowing for the region's reforestation, an increase in hydropower, and the development of irrigation networks for the ʿAkkar and Biqaʿ plains as well as lands farther south.[111] The improved exploitation of these areas through industrializing production, establishing model farms such as the one at Taanayel, and developing existing and new industries based on this production would undergird a space of economic and, by extension, political independence.[112] Al-Shihabi and the contributors to *La Revue Phénicienne* conveyed irreconcilable visions of regional self-sufficiency and national space: Both "natural Lebanon" and "Syria within its natural boundaries" could not coexist. Yet central to each construction of a nationalist space was a diverse agriculture that would ensure internal provisioning, profitable exports, and industrial expansion as the basis of a national economy.

The developments of late 1919 and early 1920 meant that the ambitious annexation scheme of "natural" Lebanon's promoters accorded more and more with French priorities. The need to shore up the support of local allies became paramount after negotiations with Faysal, which were initiated under French prime minister Georges Clemenceau, faltered under Clemenceau's successor, Alexandre Millerand, and the French struck a deal with the British at the San Remo conference in April 1920 for splitting control of the region under the mandate system.[113] Millerand reassured the president of the Lebanese delegation in Paris that "France would recognize to the Lebanese the rights that they have to the independence and to the natural borders that they require."[114] On 1 September 1920, shortly after the French victory at the Battle of Maysalun in July secured French control over Damascus and the fall of Faysal's government, the French declared the formation of the state of Greater Lebanon.[115] Although it did not encompass all the territory desired by some contributors to *La Revue Phénicienne*—in particular, the new borders split the plain of ʿAkkar between the mandates of Syria and Greater Lebanon, leaving the town of Safita, which some had viewed as a key center for "natural" Lebanon's silk production, on the Syrian side—it did ensure that the grain-rich Biqaʿ Valley fell within Lebanon's borders.[116] The technocratic vision for a space in which Lebanon's agricultural self-sufficiency would be possible was largely realized.[117] In contrast, al-Shihabi's scheme faced a different fate. Between 1920 and 1923 additional borders representing divisions between British and French mandatory regions, between the French mandate and the Turkish nation-state, and between the different statelets of Damascus (or Syria), Aleppo, the ʿAlawite State, Jabal al-Druze, and the *sanjak* of Alexandretta—statelets that French officials devised to divide up the mandate of Syria—were formalized. These borders created administrative, political, and economic distinctions and realities that ensured that al-Shihabi's vision for the comprehensive agricultural exploitation of "Syria within its natural boundaries" would never be possible in practice.

Envisioning Agricultural Exploitation in an Imperial Space: The Mandate and the Politics of Empire

As technocratic elites in Beirut and Damascus formulated their proposals for the region's agricultural development based on spaces deemed conducive to national prosperity and self-sufficiency, a group of French politicians, businessmen, professors, and agronomists eyed the region's soil with a different set of prerogatives. Composed primarily of commercial interests based in Lyon and Marseille with long-standing ties to the eastern Mediterranean, in the postwar moment this group lobbied to incorporate this territory into a French imperial space.[118] French ties to the region already included multiple investments in Ottoman infrastructure, such as roads, railroads, ports, docks, tramways, and water and gas utilities, as well as commercial ties with merchants in coastal cities such as Beirut and communities in Mount Lebanon based around such industries as silk production.[119] No other European country had a railroad in the region.[120]

Despite these ties, in the years immediately before World War I, France was only the third largest importer to the region and exports to France were much higher than its imports. This disparity was a major contrast to the region's other main trading partners, the United Kingdom and Austro-Hungary, whose imports to the region were decidedly higher than their exports.[121] Even given the low customs tariffs on which France and the Ottoman Empire's other major trading partners insisted, French parties with invested interests in the region saw this trade imbalance as detrimental, especially in the aftermath of the war. Having acquired a massive war debt from disproportionate imports coupled with a wartime decrease in exports,

France needed somewhere to "drain" the output of its new industries and a source of raw materials for its factories to further boost exports. If France could extend its control over Syria, then the eastern Mediterranean would be capable of providing both a drain and a source while also serving as a repository for surplus French capital. Bringing France's imports to the region more in line with its exports would be an added advantage.[122] However, exerting this control over the region was likely to be costly. To counter objections to this expense, those with vested interests in occupying the region, intent on making their case for why it would indeed be remunerative, justified their proposals with an emphasis on the region's potential for economic development.[123]

Efforts to build a broad base of consensus and support for this perspective were under way from the first year of the war. By the spring of 1915 the Comité de l'Asie Française and other interested parties started seeking support for a stance in which France would lay claim to "la Syrie intégrale" from the Taurus to Egypt if the Ottoman Empire were eventually to be partitioned. Citing public opinion, they argued that this region was "the natural part of France in the eventual division of Turkey [*sic*]."[124]

Their campaign was spurred by what they perceived as efforts being waged counter to their interests, the essence of which was questioning the region's value to France. In particular, Victor Bérard, a "rather famous journalist," was insisting that "Syria had no value, that it was a desert."[125] In response, advocates of French occupation insisted that under French guidance the region's agricultural production had immense potential. Henri Terrail, a Lyonnaise silk merchant and the ex-vice-president of the Lyon Chamber of Commerce, insisted that "there is no doubt that this country after the second or third year of our occupation will flourish marvelously. All of the region of Haifa, the Hawran, and the valley of the Litani and the region of Homs are of an astonishing fertility, that the harvests will triple in value."[126]

The Chamber of Commerce of Marseille took up the challenge, adopting after deliberations in July 1915 a statement in the form of a letter addressed to the minister of foreign affairs on the "question of Syria" followed by "A Note on the Economic Value of Integral Syria."[127] After establishing France's historic ties to the region, their letter highlighted Marseille and Lyon's economic links and the "possibilities" for future development based primarily on its agricultural potential.

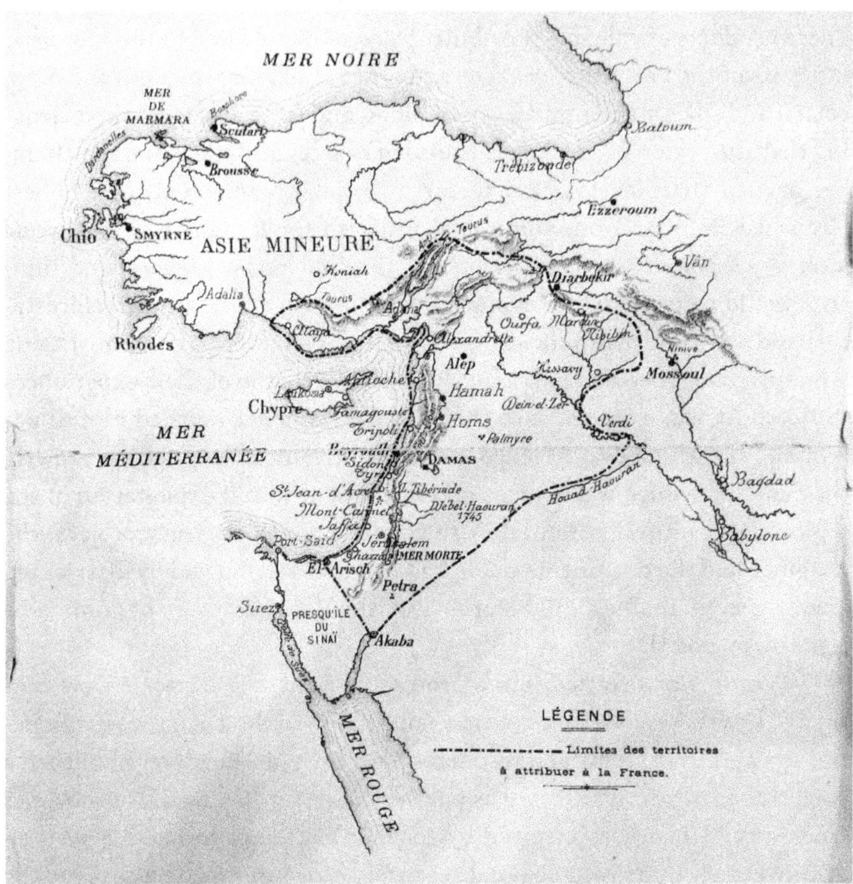

FIGURE 17. "La Syrie intégrale," as envisioned by supporters of French expansion into the eastern Mediterranean. Reproduced with permission of the Chambre de Commerce de Marseille Archives, MQ.5.4/35.

> France occupies *first rank* as European client of Syria and, after Great Britain, the second rank in the overall commerce of this part of the Ottoman Empire. Marseille is, with Lyon, the almost exclusive outlet of the raw silks of Lebanon; and our purchases of fruit, cotton, wools, hides, etc., . . . could increase, with the inevitable response of sales on our part, for our sugar . . . and manufactured products. . . .
>
> But that which the attached note especially shows, these are the incontestable "possibilities" of development of Syria, keeping in mind the richness of some of its lands and the role that our foresters and agricultural engineers could play there.[128]

These products of valuable possibility were all closely tied to the economic interests of the two cities: oranges and other fruits for the confit industry, cotton and silk for their mills, wools, hides, and even licorice. Acknowledging that the region's "irregular" rains led to irregular harvests, the chamber argued that development under a "regular, competent, and honest [French] administration, admirably prepared for its task (*and this would seem very important*) by its experience in the *Arab* lands of Algeria and Tunisia," would counter this irregularity with, among other things, reforestation and scientific hydraulic projects.[129] French foresters, agronomists, and administrators, deemed particularly expert by virtue of their experiences in North Africa, would ensure that this development reached its full potential. "French medical science" would contribute to population growth, the dearth of which was seen as an impediment to full exploitation of the region's agricultural potential.[130] To garner support for their project, the chamber had the documents published in a booklet and widely distributed among potential allies.[131] By March 1916 the Paris Chamber of Commerce was also on board.[132]

As World War I settled into a protracted fight, these efforts were buttressed by others who placed Syria's value in the context of a postwar imperial struggle over access and resources.[133] In 1917 Carl Roederer published a book titled *La Syrie et La France* as part of the series "Les Grands Problèmes Coloniaux," which was inspired by England's attempt to make a systematic inventory of its own colonial resources. Roederer made a case for the region's economic and strategic significance based on the writings of his deceased brother, Paul.[134] Paul, who died during the war, had been a Beirut-based industrialist, secretary-general of the Society of Economic Initiative in Syria, and a council member of the Bank of Lebanon.[135] His intent, particularly with the society, had been to make French commerce more competitive in relation to other foreign concerns by facilitating communication between producers and clients.[136] Based on Paul's writings, Carl made the case for a French protectorate in the region that would ensure France's "equity" and "equilibrium" with its imperial rival England and declared that "to the disciplined and active associations of Germany we will counter with French groups of commercial expansion also active and disciplined."[137] In reply to critics of his plan who deemed the French empire "sufficiently sprawling," Roederer insisted that the Mediterranean must stay "a French sea."[138] French dominance in Syria was key to this strategic goal.

Justifying why this imperial vision made sense focused on the richness of Syria's agricultural resources. In response to "timorous polemicists" who questioned the wisdom of capital outlay from France's budget to fund projects ranging from swamp drainage to road building, Roederer insisted that Syria was worth it because its receipts from agriculture would triple or quadruple after these improvements had been completed.[139] According to his calculations, based on official 1914 statistics, the provinces of Aleppo, Syria, and Beirut and the mutasarrifates of Jerusalem, Zor, and Mount Lebanon had a total revenue of 75 million and expenses of only 38 million, thus running a surplus of 37 million. Instead of characterizing this surplus as indicative of responsible fiscal management, however, he criticized the "corrupt practices" of Ottoman officials and "all the embezzling inherent to the Turkish [*sic*] administration," certain that "in the hands of scrupulous administration, the results would surpass the most audacious projections."[140] A three- to four-week mission to the region to study the market would provide additional support for his case.[141] The mandate's proponents used France's vulnerabilities laid bare by the war, in particular, its reliance on industry and its requisite raw materials, to justify incorporating the eastern Mediterranean into the empire as a supplier of these materials, thereby decreasing the "financial sacrifices" France would have to make in the future.[142]

In the aftermath of the war, with a French victory secured but support for the Colonial Party's Syria scheme still unsure, the Chamber of Commerce of Marseille once again rallied their allies, convening a three-day conference in January 1919 to discuss French interests in the region and present resolutions for their maintenance.[143] At this point, their hopes for maintaining a colonial claim to the entirety of *la Syrie Intégrale* had been dashed by the Sykes-Picot Agreement, in which the British and French governments had agreed to split the region into zones of influence and control, but they still intended to assert their prerogative in northern Syria, including Cilicia. To make their case to Parliament, they sent a mission headed by Paul Huvelin, a professor in the Faculty of Law in Lyon and secretary general of the Lyonnais Committee of French Interests in Syria, to the region to assess and report back with eyewitness data on Syria's "value."[144]

The resulting mission would be an early attempt among many to produce forms of knowledge about Syria's resources that aimed to facilitate France's colonial control and make the region increasingly legible as a space of exploitation for French industry and capital.[145] From the spring of 1919 through the summer, a team of twelve scholars and technical experts in various fields traveled the region they hoped to bring under French control. The two men entrusted with assessing the region's agricultural potential were Edouard Achard and Paul Parmentier. Achard was an *ingénieur agronome* originally from Marseille who had obtained his diploma from the Institut national agronomique in Versailles; he would become the agricultural counselor under the mandate.[146] Before his stint in Syria, he had worked as an agricultural inspector in Indochina (1899–1908) and Argentina (1908–1915).[147] Parmentier, who came from a family of farmers and had received his doctorate in natural sciences from Lyon, had been a professor of agricultural botany since 1898 in the Faculty of Sciences in Besançon.[148]

Their inquiries in the region were limited by the impacts of physical malady and the predilections of personal interests. Parmentier, waylaid by a grave illness, was unable to visit northern Syria and had to confine his inquiries to Mount Lebanon, the Biqaʿ Valley, the Damascus area, and Palestine, the last of which would ultimately not come under French control. Based on observations in these regions, his primary contribution to the mission's conclusions was that mulberry trees, vines, and olives would do well in Mount Lebanon and fruit trees in Jaffa but that all would need better irrigation.[149] Achard, a "specialist of large colonial crops," focused his attention primarily on Cilicia, which would also not be included in the French mandate, observing with particular interest local cultivation of cereals and cotton. Based on a visit to the Aleppo region after his Cilician travels, he suggested that sparsely cultivated plains between Aleppo and the Euphrates could also be fertile ground for extending cotton and grain cultivation. He concluded his journey with a jaunt to Palestine before heading to Antioch and Alexandretta for "personal studies."[150] In stark contrast to al-Shihabi's assessment, these initial observations reduced the complexity of the region's productive capacity to a few crops notable for their value to metropole provisioning and industry.

Once Millerand, a more ardent nationalist and imperialist, succeeded Clemenceau in January 1920, the influence of the Comité de l'Asie Française and its allies in the Quai d'Orsay who staunchly supported France's imperial expansion gained more traction.[151] The first high commissioner of the mandate, Henri Gouraud, and his handpicked secretary general, Robert de

Caix, belonged to this group. Millerand would also appoint another member of the Comité, Philippe Berthelot, as his secretary general in Paris.[152] Syria, they insisted, was of utmost strategic importance, because it lay between the "African and Asian worlds" with all the "wealth that, from this exact location, can flow for the region."[153]

The Colonial Party continued to fend off critics' objections that Syria would not pay for the "political, military, and financial effort of France," and eyewitness testimony from the mission served to bolster their claims.[154] Achard could confirm that a map being used to assess the state of agriculture in the province of Aleppo, which "shows extended 'white areas,'" suggesting that the desert started immediately east of the Aleppo-Hama railway line, was in fact "an error." Rather, "a recent exploration"—presumably his 1919 travels in the region—had disclosed wheat and barley cultivation as far as Maskana, neighboring the Euphrates.[155] Areas of cultivation that had been expanded under the Ottoman administration since the mid- to late nineteenth century thus came to French attention.[156] Despite lower levels of rainfall, Achard was impressed by how the "Arab" with "primitive instruments and rudimentary methods of working can draw from the soil a product remunerating his effort." He promised that "European agriculture, having the materials and perfected methods of 'dry farming,'" would make it even more productive and that introducing cultivation done by "mechanical traction will compensate . . . for the poverty of the population" by increasing their capacity for export.[157]

This agronomist-certified information was crucial to Berthelot's case for the occupation, which emphasized that cotton and cereals were "the two essential elements of Syria's prosperity . . . that is to say, the two raw materials of primordial necessity which France lacks and which the abundant production of would permit on the one hand to liberate one of our principal industries from foreign markets and on the other hand supplement its own production in conditions much less onerous than present conditions."[158] In short, France's raw material needs defined Syria's prosperity. Optimism reigned about cultivation possibilities in northern Syria, particularly along the banks of the Orontes (ʿAsi) and Euphrates Rivers. These areas, Berthelot noted, "give the same facilities of culture as the atmospheric condensations of Cilicia."[159] Meanwhile, grain production, even with current "rudimentary" methods, far surpassed local consumption, but with "dry-farming" the future held "unknown" possibilities.[160]

Nonetheless, the ambitions of the Colonial Party faced vociferous opposition in the Sénat. One opponent cited the demands of the Syrian Parliament, noting that they had declared, "Send us technical experts, professors, intellectuals, send us engineers, but we do not want armed expeditions against us."[161] With no regard for such declarations, in April 1920 delegates to the San Remo conference agreed to a French mandate over Syria and a British one over Palestine and Mesopotamia. Established under Article 22 of the Covenant of the League of Nations, the mandate system "provisionally recognized" Syria's "existence as [an] independent nation . . . subject to the rendering of administrative advice and assistance by a Mandatory until such time as [it is] able to stand alone."[162] After this formal division of French and British claims in the region, debate heated up, leading to repeated clashes over the coming months as the expenses necessary for a French military invasion and occupation spiraled and additional budget appropriations had to be approved.[163] Meanwhile, Syrians throughout the region resisted the French invasion on multiple fronts. Even after the defeat of the largely volunteer force of several thousand led by the minister of war, Yusuf al-ʿAzma, at Maysalun on 24 July 1920, which enabled the French to take Damascus and oust Faysal, pockets of resistance continued to oppose French rule in the ʿAlawite region and around Aleppo until the fall of 1921.[164] At the same time, in Parliament delegates spoke of the ongoing need for funds to ensure "pacification."[165]

While Syrians fought the mandate's threat to their independence and sovereignty, some senators strenuously objected to the expense of the military occupation it entailed and the investments required to make it reimburse their trouble. The Colonial Party's old nemesis, Bérard, who was elected to the Sénat from the Jura in 1920, continued to be a thorn in their side, even wielding the lackluster results of their own mission to make his case.[166] Despite the mission members' "devotion" and "tenderness" for the Syrian project, their own assessment was quite pessimistic: In Bérard's summation, no mineral riches were to be found and, though agriculture was possible, it would yield only after spending "three to four billion" on irrigation works.[167]

In response, the Colonial Party doubled down, insisting that France needed this territory to ensure imperial self-sufficiency and access to supplies for the metropole. Unexploited cotton-growing lands were available in France's colonies in Cambodia and Indochina, but these regions were far away and could be difficult to access. In contrast, Syria was "at the door of Marseille" and would "complete in a marvelous way [France's] Mediterranean possessions."[168] Gouraud insisted that the region's "future was, for the moment, only agricultural, but it is magnificent," and he cited Achard, who estimated that the region's productive capacity was "3 million tons of cereals and 100,000 tons of cotton."[169] Huvelin, with grand optimism based on precious little specificity, argued that if 46% of Syria's arable land were planted in wheat with a yield of 1,400 kilograms/hectare, two-thirds, or "at least two million tons," could be exported, which he noted, conveniently, was exactly France's domestic wheat deficit for the 1920–1921 harvest season.[170] As for cotton, although Cilicia could have provided two-thirds of France's needs, he noted regretfully, cobbling together the yields of various regions in Syria that seemed promising for cotton cultivation would still supply about a third of them.[171] In the end the joint efforts of the mandate's proponents won the day, Parliament funded the occupation, and the mandate became a reality for Syria for the next twenty-six years.[172]

Mandate Exploitations: French Frustrations and the Value of Land

Designed by the victors in the wake of the war to extend a form of colonial rule over former German colonies and Ottoman provinces, the mandate attempted to legitimize these territorial grabs by designating that these mandate states would eventually be independent once they had reached "maturity."[173] Although the mandate sanctioned French control over Syria, to satisfy the demands of other League of Nations members who did not want their economic interests in the region prejudiced, it also placed constraints on French action that frustrated mandate administrators. Mandate authorities were supposed to abide by an open-door economic policy whereby they could not favor their own national economic interests over those of other League of Nations members.[174] French settlers were not allowed.[175] Mandate officials chafed at these constraints and attempted to find ways to circumvent them in order to draw the region into an exclusively French imperial sphere. Meanwhile, local government officials found themselves subjected to a dual administration in which each Syrian minister had a French "counselor" counterpart who effectively dictated policy.[176]

The Colonial Party's justifications for how Syria would pay for the mandate were largely based on increasing the region's agricultural output and revenue. Thus all these factors that characterized the peculiar nature of the mandate regime would manifest in agricultural policy making, enmeshing the region in a mandate state space that contrasted with the state space of its Ottoman past. Despite the restrictions that the League of Nations imposed on mandate powers, French officials used their control of the region as an opportunity to privilege French products and increase the region's institutional and financial dependence on France. They were dismissive of projects undertaken by Faysal's government, which one French intelligence report claimed "had completely disorganized the services of agriculture" because it "seem[ed] not to realize that this country pulls from agriculture the major part of its resources."[177]

Gouraud and de Caix were particularly obsessed with mechanized agriculture (motoculture), which was all the rage in France as well, and envisioned thousands of additional hectares under the plow and a valuable agricultural machinery market dominated by French products.[178] The Foire-Exhibition organized by Gouraud in the spring of 1921—less than a year after occupying Damascus and just a year after Faysal's government organized a similar effort—was indicative. In line with mandate proponents' aim to secure the region for French commerce, the trade fair showcased French products. Berthelot noted, however, that no obstacles could be placed in the way of foreign companies exhibiting, because of American objections at the San Remo conference, which aimed to prevent mandatory powers from using the system to pursue exclusive economic policies.[179] Nonetheless, in the final catalogue of exhibitors, the number of French businesses far surpassed the number of their foreign competitors.[180] Gouraud made special mention of the fair's motoculture exhibit in his remarks at the opening ceremony. Syria had been "one of [Rome's] richest granaries" and, although devastated by war, he insisted, France had a more "powerful weapon" than Rome for the region's development: motoculture.[181] However, in contrast to the diversity of farm equipment that had been available for exhibition and demonstration in the late Ottoman period, only Case tractors from the United States and a number of French agricultural companies participated.[182]

Despite these efforts to privilege French manufacturers, they were reluctant to get involved. De Caix urged the minister of foreign affairs to encourage French companies to participate. He claimed that landowners in the north were willing to give their lands over to a company to cultivate and raised the specter of English competition if French ones did not take advantage.[183] Others echoed his concerns. In February 1921 the economic bulletin of the French commercial office in Beirut warned that the American manufacturer Case was planning to establish agents in Aleppo, Damascus, and Tripoli and later in Homs and Hama, giving them an advantage over a "good French company" in the "commercial struggle."[184] Meanwhile, the director of the French School for Engineers in Beirut worried that foreign educational institutions would encourage young farmers-in-training to prefer equipment from non-French manufacturers and expressed consternation at the competition posed by a new American professional primary school in Saida, Lebanon. Among its ten buildings, he noted "a garage for automobiles, a workshop for mechanical repairs indicating clearly the orientation of the education and the pursued goal: American machines, American tools, all for favoring American exportation: in five or six years there will be two or three hundred adults familiar with American machines," including tractors and agricultural machines. The loss in income to French concerns, he literally underlined, would be enormous.[185]

Still, French companies made little effort to establish the infrastructure necessary to inspire buyer confidence.[186] Whereas Case prepared to establish an "active agent equipped with a repair shop, a fitter, an array of spare parts, [and] to hold demonstration sessions and to maintain or at least keep an eye on the tractors sold," no French company made such arrangements. If a spare part was needed, it had to be requested from France.[187] Mandate officials tried to forestall the effects of foreign encroachments by halting the importation of any non-French equipment until its French equivalent had already arrived.[188] The government itself even imported machines and "loaned [them] to the land owners for experimental purposes."[189] But given the equipment's high prices and the lack of infrastructure, local landowners remained skeptical, demanding a number of demonstrations over the course of the agricultural cycle to establish that mechanical methods could indeed accomplish tasks from seeding to harvesting to threshing.[190] That one machine got stuck in the mud during a demonstration in Aleppo likely did little to assuage doubts.[191]

The spatial dimension of mandate rule, with the base of the High Commission in Beirut, also hindered French aspirations. For instance, arranging accessible and accurate motoculture demonstrations for the trade fair proved challenging, because prospective buyers needed to see the machines in action. Nowhere in the immediate vicinity of Beirut, the location of the fair, was suitable. The Biqaʿ Valley across the mountains to the east or the ʿAkkar plain north of Tripoli were the closest areas where such demonstrations might be feasible, but each location required special transportation arrangements. Furthermore, the main market for tractors was in Aleppo, and neither the Biqaʿ Valley nor the ʿAkkar plain was an ecological match for the Aleppan hinterland.[192] The locus of French rule in Beirut meant that the areas where officials had anticipated achieving their agricultural ambitions were not the ones over which they exercised the greatest control, especially in the early years of the mandate.[193] In Aleppo at least, by 1924 French merchants had begun to lose interest, because their machines "did not prove satisfactory in operation." In response, mandate authorities, anxious not to lose the revenue they foresaw generated by these new technologies, had "a complete change in . . . attitude" and began to encourage imports from elsewhere. As of 1924 there were just sixteen tractors in the Aleppo district, but all were of American make.[194]

If French motoculture was not going to take the region by storm, Achard and Parmentier had other suggestions for how to make its agriculture serve French interests. Parmentier proposed expanding agricultural education opportunities, creating a cadastre, protecting forests and "rationally" managing water resources, building infrastructure for crops and products prioritized by France, such as wine and tobacco, and improving and expanding transportation networks.[195] He also compiled an agricultural manual in French for Syrian cultivators and schoolchildren.[196] Achard, despite initially hailing mechanical implements as key to increasing production and reducing poverty, abruptly reconsidered, insisting that the simple plow already in use was the best implement for the stony ground common in Syria. He noted that

> it can pass anywhere; if it encounters a stone of slight weight, it throws it to the side; if it encounters a more resistant rock, it moves and continues its furrow. . . . What would our plows with large and sharp plowshare, moldboard, low central support beam, headstock do in these stony soils? . . . If we thus envision the use of our modern agricultural material, the cultivatable surface area of Syria is much less than that which rudimentary local materials permit to cultivate.[197]

Achard's on-the-ground observation of local equipment, albeit brief, had clearly demonstrated to him its advantages.

Achard acknowledged that various writers pinned the "progress of Syrian agriculture" on extending irrigation networks, establishing agricultural schools, experimental stations, banks, and agricultural cooperatives, and reforming the land tax. But he insisted that all such efforts were beside the point until the achievement of one essential reform that would make Syria's land legible to French capital.[198] According to Achard:

> Rare, very rare in fact, are the authors, who have envisioned as the base of Syria's agricultural progress the reorganization of the Ottoman land legislation, the revision of the cadastre, and the replacement of the tithe with a land tax. . . . Agricultural Syria . . . suffers from a chronic *mal*: the regime of too large property. . . . It is necessary to give to these farmers some interest in the exploitation of the soil, before envisioning the realization of a program of reform which, without that, would have the greatest chances of not giving any interest.[199]

In particular, Achard claimed that big landowners "do not interest themselves technically in cultivation" and "are ignorant of the extent of their lands," citing the example of a "young Syrian agricultural engineer, receiver of a diploma in Constantinople" who evaluated the extent of his family's lands based on the time it took to ride a horse across them.[200] He insisted that an institution such as the Agricultural Bank served only to perpetuate this system of negligent landowners because it merely provided another source of cheap capital for their lending, perpetuating peasant indebtedness.[201] Revising the Ottoman cadastre in order to institute a land tax to replace the tithe would allow the state to create attentive small property owners.[202]

"The easy formation of small property" was a mere side note to the most important potential consequence of reorganizing Ottoman land legislation. Of far greater import was that it would enable French administrators to "rid Turkish [*sic*] law of all the pitfalls that, in fact, make property inaccessible to the foreigner," responding to the demands of those with surplus capital in the French imperial sphere who were seeking additional repositories.[203] That is, not only did mandate officials aim to use Syria's land to supply France's postwar needs in raw materials, but also the foremost goal of "agricultural reform" was to make that land legible and accessible to circulations of French capital within the empire.

Efforts toward these ends had been under way since before the end of the war. In August 1917, N. Moussalli, a Beirut merchant based in Geneva who represented the "Syrian Syndicat" wrote to the French consul at Lausanne to urge the establishment of a Syrian *crédit foncier* after the war. He envisioned a national but also joint French-Syrian enterprise in which "French capitalists will have the upper hand in direction and control" while Syrians would also contribute capital and, with their intimate local knowledge, collaborate in directing matters to avoid "fumbling."[204] French banks were uninterested in such a collaboration, as they made clear in the war's aftermath when they immediately undertook moves to consolidate their presence in the region.[205] The Crédit Foncier d'Algérie et de Tunisie (CFAT) in particular positioned itself to dominate the property credit market.[206] By 19 January 1921 CFAT had acquired the Crédit Foncier de Syrie, which put 50 million francs at its disposal to be used for mortgage transactions in Syria, the Ottoman Empire, Salonica, and Izmir.[207] A convention between CFAT and the Crédit Foncier of France essentially gave CFAT the responsibility of developing mortgage credit in Syria.[208]

Despite this eagerness to take advantage of the Syrian mortgage market, CFAT had one major concern. The Ottoman law of 1913 (25 Şubat 1328 [10 March 1913]), which still governed mortgages in Syria, specified that "assets, real estate can be given as mortgage to societies or banks authorized by the government to consent advances on built property or lands, but these societies and banks cannot possess the said real estate *à titre definitive*." That is, Ottoman law prevented them from fully possessing these properties. CFAT and the Crédit Foncier de Syrie demanded clarification of what this clause in particular meant, suggesting that instead "it could be stipulated that assets put up for sale in case of nonpayment could be acquired by the two societies or by one of them."[209] With the Ottoman government out of the way, the mandate government stood poised to redraft this legislation to grant surplus French capital unfettered access to Syria's land.

From the perspective of these French parties, the incorporation of Syria into France's imperial sphere provided an opportunity to create a mandate state space calibrated to exploit Syria's land to serve the interests of French capital and industry. On the one hand, these parties considered Syria's land a source of close, easily accessible raw materials that would lessen any vulnerabilities they had experienced during the war. On the other, it was virgin territory for the investment of foreign, particularly French, surplus capital. Although the mandate system did not give France exclusive rights to the region's economic space, it gave them a framework within which they could use their control to ensure that their interests were prioritized not only over foreign competitors but also over the interests of local merchants, technocrats, cultivators, and landowners.

Reform Negotiations: Syrian Technocrats and the Mandate's Early Years

As French officials debated how the mandate could best serve particular financial and commercial interests in the metropole, Syrian and Lebanese technocrats, merchants, and agronomists reassessed the political landscape and their options for moving forward with their own agendas. Those who had served in or supported Faysal's government found themselves formulating an agriculture-based national economic policy in a much more truncated space. New customs barriers required additional protection for agricultural production and industries, which constituted 90% of its exports, from international competition, both from the usual suspects and from neighbors who, just a few years before, had belonged to the same provincial state space.[210] Furthermore, local technocrats had to contend with the fact that mandate officials, in a classic colonial divide-and-rule maneuver, had created a number of smaller statelets within the mandate of Syria whose administrations were entirely separate and uncoordinated. For mandate officials these statelets aimed to facilitate the cultivation of pro-French sentiment among certain "minorities," such as the Druze in Jabal al-Druze or the ʿAlawites in the ʿAlawite State, to counter nationalist activity, which they considered more intense in cities such as Aleppo and Damascus.[211] For local technocrats these statelets posed a challenge to coordinating a unified national economy.

Initially, during the first five years of the mandate, local technocrats and agronomists demonstrated a willingness to work with French officials, approaching the collaboration as one of debate and information exchange between a community of elite equals. Their educational trajectories and careers reflected their participation in networks of technocratic expertise dating from the late Ottoman period; thus many had received comparable training, and some even more prestigious training, than their French counterparts. Despite their approach to agricultural reform having clear political implications, their language stressed the scientific and modern nature of their proposals. Such terms accomplished a form of boundary-work that operated not only to mask the political intent of their reforms but also to assert their authority as comparable to that of their French counterparts.[212] They thus framed their efforts as analogous to what their colleagues elsewhere had enacted to accommodate the modern and scientific methods that agriculture required.

A widely distributed journal, *al-Zira*ʿ*a al-Haditha* (*Modern Agriculture*), published in Hama by a local technocrat, ʿUmar Tarmanini, who was associated with the Salamiya agricultural school, often included reports in Arabic by Parmentier, Achard, now the *conseiller agronome* for the Syrian government, and Ivan Wilhelm, the Syrian government's inspector of public works.[213] Issues from 1924 and 1925, for example, carried a series of articles by Parmentier titled "Agriculture in Syria" that the journal translated from articles published between February and May 1922 in *Revue de botanique appliquée et d'agriculture colonial*.[214] Such articles, sometimes with strategic edits or additions in translation, were interspersed with others detailing observations from experiments conducted by local farmers and agronomists as well as excerpts from a variety of international publications.[215] Tarmanini said that he started the journal—the only one of its kind in Syria and Iraq—because there was a need for agricultural publications and he had found an eager audience among cultivators in Arab countries, "indicating some readiness and attention for the ideas" he presented.[216]

Meanwhile, the Chamber of Commerce in Marseille exchanged pleasantries and economic bulletins (or promises thereof) with its counterparts in several cities crucial to developing its commercial interests. After sending a mission to visit the chambers of commerce in Damascus, Tripoli, and Aleppo, the Marseille chamber encouraged a similar Syrian mission to visit France. Although the Marseille chamber flattered the different chambers and promised them that they could expect a "beautiful economic future" under the mandate, the Syrian chambers were more measured in their responses.[217] The Damascus chamber urged that "a close collaboration between our two countries, giving us common and immediate advantages, will permit us to envision the future with calm and assurance of success," whereas Salim Janbart, president of the Aleppo chamber, went a step further, noting that the relations between French and Aleppan establishments "can be sensibly bettered if the French merchants would interest themselves a bit more to stay exactly up to date on the needs of our country," especially regarding the products they requested.[218]

Perhaps to assist such an effort, in 1925 the Aleppo Chambers of Commerce and Agriculture patronized the publication of *La Revue Économique*. Among pages studded with advertisements for Avery tractors, potassium and nitrogen nitrate fertilizers, and the Banque Française de Syrie, the journal's authors offered their assessment regarding what would define the agriculture of the future.[219] Noting that even as rural populations were moving to urban areas, "educated, energetic youth" of more privileged classes were returning to the land, spurred in part by a decrease in available commercial opportunities in the city.[220] "Science and association [*ʿilm wa tasharuk*]" defined the agricultural future that these youths represented. Agriculture had acquired "a purely scientific form," and the additional costs this involved required agricultural syndicates that would ensure "mutuality" (*taʿadud*) and "solidarity" (*tadamun*).[221]

In an effort to make their views accessible to both local and French readers, the journal's format consisted of side-by-side columns of French and Arabic. More than half its articles were devoted to specific agricultural concerns, such as locusts, new machines, especially tractors, and fertilizers. Both local agricultural engineers and French officials such as Charles Pavie, the economic and agricultural counselor and then agricultural inspector for Aleppo, contributed to the journal.[222] The prestige of Pavie's qualifications, however, paled in comparison to many of his Syrian counterparts, even when considered within a French educational sphere. His suitability for the position was based on two years (1905–1906 and 1906–1907) of courses at the practical agricultural school in La Brosse (Yonne, France), a stint at the agricultural school of Mikveh Israel near Jaffa, and just over a year (July 1910–August 1911) working as the inspector for the Société Anonyme agricole et industrielle d'Egypte on the estate of Maʿsarat Duda in Fayyum.[223]

As illustrated by the exploits of Aleppo's Fordson dealer that opened this chapter, some local technocrats, merchants, and landowners were intrigued by the possibilities of motoculture. Most local technocrats and agronomists agreed that expanding the use of these machines was crucial to successfully competing in global markets—tractors promised a potentially "revolutionary" solution to leaving land uncultivated because of the scarcity and high cost of labor or the expense of animals.[224] However, interest was tempered by a number of practical considerations, none of which concerned whether the machines were produced by a French company or not. Demand differed from region to region depending on whether farmers and landowners considered their land suitable. As in other countries, tractors were most attractive to those with land in flat plains and capital to spare, hence the heightened interest in Aleppo, where large plains lay fallow, but the relative disinterest in the hilly Hawran.[225]

The skepticism that French officials observed reflected internal debates among local technocrats about the relative benefits of these new machines as they responded to cultivators' concerns. As one technocrat admitted, most cultivators viewed them "like the ghoul," considering them difficult to work, prone to breakdowns, and hard to repair. Hence a key role of the Salamiya school was to teach cultivators how to use the machines and demonstrate their cost-effectiveness.[226] In May 1921 experiments carried out with a Fordson tractor at the school ostensibly confirmed that the cost of plowing with a tractor (65 gurush/*donum*) was more economical than that of a "normal plow" and mules (79.79 gurush/*donum*).[227] Recognizing that many cultivators still found this unaffordable, al-Shihabi suggested forming companies that could rent out the tractors.[228]

The fear of being unable to repair a broken part also constrained sales.[229] The wealthy landowning al-Barudi family had established their own private repair station to overcome such shortcomings, although such a solution was beyond the resources of most.[230] The reluctance to invest in French machines contrasted with the interest shown in American models sold by energetic agents with the infrastructure to back them up. Eight days after the Fordson dealer sold his first tractor in Aleppo, it broke down.[231] The dealer, anxious to demonstrate to potential buyers that his service was capable and had the necessary organization to respond to such emergencies, wrote with haste to the Beirut office requesting the necessary spare parts. The buyers, he claimed, were "enchanted" with their repaired tractor and were inviting others to check it out.[232] Shortly thereafter he managed to make the sale to the governor.

Finally, the machines' interaction with local environments and fueling costs were a concern. Potential buyers demanded trials in the specific tract of land where they planned to use the tractor.[233] Was it easy to use? Did it operate with sufficient traction, but not too much pressure that it would compress the soil to the point of sterility? How much fuel did it consume?[234] Around Aleppo customers were anxious to assess how effectively a tractor would rip up tough grasses known as *injil* in previously unworked land.[235] *La Revue Économique* encouraged its readership to consider a tractor and offered free guidance.[236] Al-Shihabi recommended that only those with more than 500 hectares of land, insufficient supplies of manual labor, and adequate capital consider such a purchase. Once they had determined it was economically sound, they needed to ensure that their agent was honest, have the tractor tested by a specialist, inform themselves of all its specifications, procure a good driver, and assess the available repair options.[237] Ecological and infrastructural factors were just as crucial to farmers' decisions as cost concerns.

Encouraging the use of the latest technologies was central to Syrian technocrats' and agronomists' plans for agricultural development, but it was just the tip of the iceberg. A coterie of elite, largely foreign-educated technocrats and agronomists, some of whom were also landowners of means, joined al-Shihabi, who transitioned from director of agriculture and forests to director of state lands in 1923, and Tarmanini in expounding on a comprehensive vision for the nation's economic development.[238] Among them was Tawfiq al-Ahdab, an agricultural engineer and frequent contributor to *al-Zira*ʿ*a al-Haditha* who had studied in the Hama *ʿidadi* school and the Laique school in Beirut before continuing his studies in Paris, where he earned a diploma from the Grignon Agricultural School in 1919. After additional training in Belgium, he returned to "his private farm and property in Hama" but was forced to flee to the ʿAlawite mountains in 1923 "due to his lack of agreement with [French] policies."[239] He eventually returned to Hama to become director of the Salamiya agricultural school before moving to Aleppo to take up the post of "general inspector for agriculture of the northern area" until 1946.[240] Yusuf ʿAtallah, another agricultural engineer, completed his secondary education at Aintoura in Mount Lebanon, studied agriculture at Grand Jouan and Grignon in France, and specialized in finance, administration, and economic science at the University of Paris. He had been in charge of administering the agricultural cooperative society in Toulouse from 1917 to 1919, after which he returned to Syria, where he was appointed inspector general for agriculture in 1921 before becoming director of economic affairs in Damascus.[241] Finally, al-Amir Muhammad ʿAli ʿAbd al-ʿAziz al-Jazaʾiri had a doctorate in political economy and had graduated from the agricultural high school in Berlin, a more theoretically oriented school that trained students for administrative positions.[242]

These technocrats countered French officials' metropole-centered reform priorities with detailed proposals of their own for "the fundamental reforms that the agricultural *nahda* requires," the core of which was a state-implemented economic plan for a unified Syria.[243] Their vision, though drawing inspiration from an international array of examples, emphasized the need to develop an approach that would be in accordance with Syria's own distinct practices and exigencies just as, in ʿAtallah's words, every one of the "advanced" peoples had enacted "an economic political plan designating agricultural policy" according to "its traditions, needs, ills, and deficiencies."[244] Critical of the economic exploitation inherent to colonial control, their suggested reforms emphasized local self-sufficiency and responsible spending and investment that, they argued, did not primarily exploit. Underpinning this program was a reliance on technocratic solutions and the expertise they offered.[245]

These technocrats viewed the threat as existential. According to al-Ahdab, since the onset of the mandate, "many farmers lost large amounts of money due to the massive drop in prices of grains and animals."[246] Proposals focused on shielding farmers from this brave new postwar world. Agriculture was becoming increasingly capital intensive, and cultivators who did not have adequate support faced steep obstacles from international competitors who did, facilitating their use of "modern implements" and methods. Syria's lack of comparable encouragements and support systems was not only a "danger to [its] agriculture, commerce, and industry" but also a danger to its "national existence."[247] To counter this threat, they proposed reforming taxation, consolidating collectively-held (*mushaʿ*) and "scattered" forms of land tenure, establishing cooperative societies, unions, or agricultural associations, renegotiating trade agreements, forming well-funded agricultural chambers to support research, holding exhibitions, improving transport infrastructure, protecting small cultivators, especially with regards to holding onto their land if they fell into financial difficulty, and educating them in modern methods.[248]

As the challenges posed by mandate policies to implementing this comprehensive economic plan and protecting the nation's agriculture and industry became clear, especially following the 1925–1927 Syrian Revolt, as discussed in chapter 5, al-Shihabi made an impassioned plea for a rejection of dependency and a focus on self-sufficiency, albeit within a more constricted space than he had envisioned in *Modern Practical Agriculture.*[249] Between 1920 and 1925 the ratio of exports to imports had improved but still lagged behind prewar levels, when imports were only two times exports.[250] He urged boosting domestic production of sugar, potatoes, and wheat, and products made from wool, leather, or fruits from the Ghuta. Revising his earlier proposals, he calculated that substantial tracts of land in the Ghuta were well suited to sugar beet cultivation, requiring only sugar factories to process them.[251]

Processing raw materials locally would moderate the damage caused by the mandate's customs regime, which made only slight concessions to local producers, aiming primarily to benefit French products without too overtly contravening the mandate's open-door economic policy.[252] Thus, for example, reliance on French industry for dying silk hurt national industry even in regional markets where trade was already substantially below prewar levels.[253] Because pure Lebanese silks were sent to Lyon to be dyed before they were exported to Palestine, the mandate government assessed customs dues as though they were primarily foreign-produced goods, although only the dye was foreign. As a result, al-Shihabi calculated that local silk factories lost 14,400–14,600 gold lira.[254] A local dye factory would cost only 20,000–30,000 gold lira, eliminating the need to pay 10,000 lira to the factory in Lyon each year and enabling silk producers to realize a greater profit from their "national products."[255] Such a proposal, of course, ran directly counter to the interests of some of the mandate's most ardent supporters.[256]

Ultimately, economic independence was tied to political independence.[257] Colonial policies, al-Shihabi explained, had two goals: "restrict the products of the colonized country to the merchants of the imperialist country [and] the debts of the colonized country to the products of the imperialist countries," creating a closed circuit of trade within the imperial sphere of the colonizer and preventing the occupied country from trading with others.[258] So long as the region remained under mandate rule, then, the plans and projects of this technocratic elite, despite agreeing with mandate officials on the basic components of a reform program, constituted an ongoing challenge to mandate priorities. For Syrian technocrats, these reforms were essential components of a competitive, wealth-producing national economy that they were well positioned to direct. For mandate officials, they represented a means to increase the region's dependency on institutions, capital flows, and markets within a French imperial sphere.

This tension is reflected in the fact that publicly Tarmanini and al-Ahdab each received the Ordre du Mérite agricole, a French honor given to those who had made significant contributions to agriculture, while privately, as of 1925, both were under surveillance for "directing propaganda hostile to the mandate."[259] Al-Shihabi was awarded a "medal of agricultural merit . . . and a medal of the French Academy," although internal mandate correspondence characterized him as a "Francophobe."[260] ʿAtallah also received the "French agricultural medal," but he would find himself in a heated critique of mandate policy by the early 1930s, likely doing little to endear himself to mandate officials.[261]

Firmly enmeshed in networks of agricultural expertise predating the mandate, these technocrats espoused a vision of reform that had its antecedents in processes set in motion in the late Ottoman period: revising tax policies, implementing land reform intent on breaking up collectively held lands, facilitating access to sources of capital, expanding agricultural educational opportunities, and forming cooperative societies. Overall their proposals represented continuity with those offered by Hüseyin Kâzım in his contribution to the *Beyrut Vilayeti* volume just seven years earlier. Meanwhile, French officials' approaches reflected their experiences both in French colonies, particularly North Africa, and in the metropole. Although they espoused many of the same priorities, except for the cooperative societies, the exact form they wanted these reforms to take differed, because they saw them primarily as a means to draw the region more firmly into a sphere of French influence and cultivate it as a repository for surplus French capital and a source of raw materials for metropole industries. For Syrian technocrats, government investment in and extraction from agriculture were two sides of the same coin: Increasing extraction was not possible without also increasing investment. In contrast, as with other aspects of mandate rule, French officials were loath to invest in a region that was ostensibly en route to independence, and thus their approach focused far more on maximizing extraction.[262]

Conclusion

Al-Shihabi's critique of the colonial power's impact on the colonized economy, coming in the wake of the aftermath of the Syrian Revolt, marked a shift in tone from earlier reform proposals with its frank assessment of the mandate's effects. In the decade following World War I, the establishment of mandates in the region imposed borders that crisscrossed and disrupted the integrated Ottoman state space of the eastern Mediterranean. The mandates shattered the brief attempt to maintain some truncated semblance of this state space under Faysal's Arab government. Except for the special province of Mount Lebanon, all the region's other provincial centers were severed from at least some portion of their former hinterland. To facilitate the incorporation of the mandates into a French imperial sphere, French policies produced a colonial state space that aimed to align the region's infrastructure with metropole interests along lines that exacerbated hierarchical relations between the imperial center and the colonial periphery.

Meanwhile, local technocrats, stymied in their effort to maintain the region's independence and pursue policies geared toward the production of a self-sufficient national state space, initially attempted to work with French officials, emphasizing a shared language of science or modernity in their approaches to technocratic governance. But ultimately, their contradictory aims for what this governance should achieve—a colonial state space versus a national one—led to increasing division, tension, and resistance. French prerogatives prevailed, leading to a region that internally found itself becoming more fractured and fragmented by colonial policies that thrived on divide and rule, whereas externally it contended with growing unevenness in its economic and political relations with an increasingly interconnected global sphere.

Over the course of the mandate, French officials systematically dismantled or restructured the institutions of Ottoman-era state space from courts to banking to draw the region inexorably into a French imperial sphere.[263] A crucial part of this restructuring involved mandate policies related to agriculture. From agrarian credit relations to tax collection and land tenure to agricultural education and experimentation, French officials persisted in their effort to extract the value the mandate's proponents had assured the French Parliament it could produce. In addition, their policies aimed to establish ties of institutional dependency, hinder the development of an independent industrial sector, and secure lasting inroads for French capital into rural land. Despite these efforts, Ottoman-era institutions and the local technocrats steeped in them would prove remarkably resilient.[264]

FOUR

THE POLITICS *of* AGRICULTURAL EXPERTISE *and* EDUCATION

Exerting Rural Influence Under the French Mandate

In the September-October 1927 issue of *al-Zira*ʿ*a al-Haditha*, Ahmad Wasfi Zakariya, a 1912 graduate of the Halkalı Agricultural School in Istanbul, a former teacher and headmaster at the Salamiya agricultural school, and an inspector of state lands, recounted the grim anecdote of a friend and former army officer who, seeking a new means of livelihood after the mandate occupation, turned his hand to farming.[1] Convinced that farming with the latest technologies was a remunerative proposition and the "management of cultivators easier than leading battalions," he rented a farm of "moderate fertility," bought "modern implements," and "worked . . . his partners [*murabi*ʿ] like he had worked his soldiers."[2] He plowed and planted "as his conceptions and observations in European books inspired him."[3] Despite these efforts, the result was a disaster. The ex-officer's machines broke down, his animals became emaciated, he lost his anticipated crop, and he ended up saddled with a massive loan. According to the seasoned agronomist Zakariya, most of the information contained in these European books "could not be applied literally in our territories and soil."[4] His friend had learned the hard way.

Aside from demonstrating that a martial labor pace was not conducive to the rhythms of nature, Zakariya intended for his anecdote to illustrate the pitfalls of book-derived agricultural knowledge, especially that produced in different ecologies. Such knowledge was insufficient, especially for someone who had lived all his life in the city and could not "distinguish wheat from barley and mules from donkeys."[5] The challenges that agriculture presented could be complex and discouraging. As a result, amateur urban enthusiasts inspired by a "return to the land" zeitgeist found themselves reassessing their priorities and opting for the relative comfort and prestige of work as civil servants, usually in some position at least tangentially related to agricultural concerns, rather than as actual cultivators.[6] Success in farming, Zakariya insisted, required a different kind of temperament from that demanded by industry or commerce; a successful farmer needed "patience for hardship" and "imperturbability."[7] As his example implied, success also necessitated a cautious approach to new methods and technologies, with cultivators adopting them only after careful assessment of their suitability to particular environments.

Debates about the pursuit, production, and application of *ʿilm*, or knowledge, in agricultural practice proliferated during the interwar period. In particular, as the technologies available expanded to include not just mechanization but also motorization, with its decreased reliance on the reproductive cycles of agriculture's biotic resources, the stakes (and risks) increased.[8] Aware of these costs, "conservative" cultivators reasonably demanded adequate facilities to assess their impacts.[9] The model farms and fields and the agricultural schools of the late Ottoman Empire had provided at least some space in which this experimentation could take place. Under the mandate these kinds of experimental spaces decreased and study abroad became the only option for advanced agricultural training.

Local technocrats' interest in new technologies combined with their reliance on local knowledge manifested in a tension between privileging forms of institutionally derived agricultural knowledge while also acknowledging cultivators' expertise. Even as urban elites urged planning for agricultural education in multiple forms, including model fields, upper-level agricultural schools, and primary schools in rural areas, the reluctance of many landowners to adopt new methods implied a tacit admission of the reliability of local cultivator knowledge.[10]

These priorities and perspectives reflected continuity with the Ottoman era, but, under the mandate, the space in which local technocrats had room to maneuver was constrained and defined by the priorities of mandate authorities, which contrasted sharply with their own. As local technocrats advocated policies aimed at building a national economy and the infrastructure to support it, French officials used their control of the mandate's administration to implement policies that tied the region economically and infrastructurally to France and its empire. Institutions devoted to developing and propagating agricultural knowledge were an integral part of this process. The political and economic dynamics of the mandate permeated the relationships between cultivators, local technocrats, and mandate officials, producing a more fractious and fragmented state space than that of the late Ottoman period.

These dynamics restricted local technocrats and agronomists primarily to a French sphere of exchange and collaboration where, despite their often substantial qualifications, they tended to be regarded as insufficiently trained and educated. Under the mandate, local engagement with international networks of knowledge production that Ottoman policies had encouraged and facilitated became a source of suspicion, as French officials emphasized ties of expertise with the metropole above all else and closely monitored access to these networks. New borders compounded the issue. Local technocrats followed the latest developments in the Turkish Republic to the north or the British mandates to the south and east as well as internationally, but they were frustrated by their inability to enact comparable policies in Syria.[11]

Agricultural education increasingly became a pretext for establishing politically charged ties with rural areas. Thus mandate agricultural education policies aimed not only to increase dependency on French infrastructure but also to exert influence in the countryside. Such motives clashed with those of local technocrats, for whom the institutions of rural education worked to integrate rural cultivators into a national state space and encourage them to be more industrious and adopt more "modern" methods, ostensibly making them more productive and thus contributing to the national economy.

The 1920s and 1930s saw increased attention to the question of agricultural education and its political repercussions on a global scale. Recently formed international organizations, such as the International Institute of Agriculture, the Commission Internationale d'Agriculture, and the International Labor Organization, also debated the purpose and form of agricultural education.[12] Who was it for, and what kind of farmer did it aim to produce? Was it better to pursue a more practical course of study or a more theoretical one? These concerns echoed those that had beleaguered Ottoman (and other) officials for decades. However, in the interwar era these debates increasingly involved the intervention of international actors in spaces like those of the mandate. Representatives of some of the countries that composed these international organizations increasingly looked to agricultural education—often repackaged more narrowly to elites as "technical assistance" or more broadly for rural communities as "rural development"—as a pretext for spreading their influence abroad, especially in countries deemed to be "developing."[13] Such efforts prefigured neocolonial post–World War II development initiatives. Mandate officials, intent on securing French influence, were vigilant about the possibility that other countries might try to use rural education or agricultural programs to intervene and undermine French prerogatives. In contrast to the exclusive control exerted in French colonies, under the League of Nation's mandate system, French officials could not outright prevent other "nations" from importing their technologies or offering their expertise, thereby threatening French interests.

Internationally shared discourses about the importance of scientific or modern agricultural training were thus deployed by different actors to elaborate conflicting visions of economic development for the region. Local technocrats advocated state intervention, French officials touted imperial tutelage, and other foreign actors championed "philanthropic" aid. Juxtaposing developments under the mandate with those of the late Ottoman period discussed in chapter 2 demonstrates how references to the expansion of agricultural production during the mandate, to the extent that it happened, elide the highly politicized nature of this expansion.[14] The mandate disrupted Ottoman infrastructural networks and largely frustrated elite initiatives related to scientific agricultural development. As during the Ottoman period, officials privileged certain forms of agricultural expertise over others as representative of progress and rationality and used scientific agricultural infrastructure to forge connections between urban and rural areas. However, within the context of the mandate and its distinct framework of governance, these policies had additional repercussions. Privileged "scientific" expertise became a means of reinforcing hierarchies of knowledge between the metropole and the mandate and reinscribing them institutionally.

Syrian and Lebanese agronomists' conception of who possessed agricultural expertise and how it circulated differed from their French counterparts. These perspectives supported divergent visions of economic development for the mandate versus the metropole, fundamentally affecting institutional developments within the mandate's unique space. Local experts, themselves participants in international networks of expertise, found their perspectives marginalized by the hierarchical structure of mandate rule and the institutional arrangements that privileged mandate officials' priorities over those of local technocrats. Meanwhile, French officials posited a unidirectional transmission of expertise that obscured what local technocrats insisted was its multidirectional circulation.

Imperial Interests and Hierarchies of Expertise: Disseminating and Defining Agricultural *ʿIlm*

In the mandate's early days, Edouard Achard, the agricultural counselor and therefore the most influential figure in formulating agricultural policy, insisted in his public reports that there was little demand in Syria for agricultural education.[15] In contrast to this dismissive attitude, a published French report noted that the Salamiya school "attracted students from diverse parts of Syria as well as Palestine."[16] French intelligence reports expounded on this interest, noting that in Aleppo

> it is also an agricultural school that the population demands. The agriculture classes of the high school do not give, it must be confessed, but mediocre results. It could not be otherwise. It's a simple theoretical initiation with practical works a little ridiculous in the courtyard of the high school. The young people desiring to learn agriculture for real, with the aim of cooperating in the modernization of the crops, principal source of the richness of their land, are obliged to go live abroad and to go at great expense either to Algeria or to France. . . . That which seems most immediately useful, this would be a school for training some agricultural supervisors, some foremen of cultivation. An experimental station would be the natural complement.[17]

Notably, this report did not suggest the establishment of a school like the one in Salamiya, which is likely what Aleppans had in mind; rather, it proposed a more limited kind of institution, focused on training supervisors, accompanied by an experimental station. This solution served French prerogatives, even if it did not meet Aleppans' demands.

Indeed, experimental stations were mandate officials' preferred institution for assessing the suitability of new plants, equipment, or methods in the mandate's statelets. Shortly after consolidating their control, they had established stations in the ʿAkkar plain north of Tripoli, in Muslimiya north of Aleppo, at the Salamiya school in the statelet of Damascus, and near Latakia in the ʿAlawite territory.[18] In colonial settings such stations were intended primarily for the production of knowledge for European consumption.[19] Under the French mandate, their operations aimed primarily to assess the viability of crops deemed a priority by French officials and predominantly sourced from within a French imperial sphere. This strategy served French business interests, but it narrowed the options available to local agronomists.

In addition to cotton and grain, French priorities focused on tree cultivation, particularly mulberry trees as the basis for silk production, olives, and a variety of fruit trees.[20] Officials encouraged the cultivation of crops they preferred, often based on results obtained at the stations, through seed and sapling distribution. However, French officials' divide-and-rule approach meant that each statelet operated stations with varying degrees of sophistication, continuity, and encouragement to generalize. Furthermore, coordination between statelets was mostly lacking. In general, state(let)s regarded by French officials as allies to be cultivated, namely, Latakia and Greater Lebanon, received more attention and funding, whereas Aleppo and Damascus were sidelined despite local demand.

The ʿAlawite State (renamed the Government of Latakia in 1930) saw perhaps the most sustained and extensive efforts to promote French-oriented agricultural development under mandate auspices.[21] French officials fostered this statelet as a bulwark against what they perceived as the more strident antimandate sentiment of Aleppo and Damascus, and the statelet's proximity to mandate headquarters in Beirut and its ecological potential for expanded cotton and silk production likely contributed to these efforts.[22] In 1922 the governor of the ʿAlawite State, General Billotte, started construction on an experimental and agricultural studies center at Bouka on the outskirts of Latakia. The center combined an experimental station with a practical agricultural school and an agricultural orphanage, which would be outfitted with "a sizable order [of materials] . . . made in France."[23]

Another station in Tartus soon confirmed, among other experimental results, that North African wheat fared better than French varieties in the fertile coastal plain.[24]

The work of these stations was bolstered through various strategies. Latakia was the primary target of seed distribution "to the population" in the mandate's first years.[25] By 1924 a subsidy enabled the establishment of forty plant nurseries throughout the state, which distributed seedlings free of charge to "the most deserving *agriculteurs*."[26] Several more nurseries, centrally located in Latakia and Tartus on the coast, increased supply.[27] Mulberry trees were on offer, and the state also constructed a model silkworm farm.[28] Motoculture stations in Latakia and Tartus opened in November 1923, introducing the French Renault tractor to the region, and repair stations were under construction.[29] In 1929 these tractors plowed 600 *donums* for individuals and 500 *donums* for the state at Bouka, Jabla, and a government farm at Sukas.[30] Although the equipment bought by state enterprises favored French manufacturers, mandate officials kept scrupulous tabs on their competition, because private individuals were more likely to purchase American Fordson or Avery tractors.[31] In addition to loaning out the stations' machines to individuals for plowing under stubble and threshing, the state also undertook cultivation trials by contracts or "in association" with local producers for crops such as cotton, rye, wheat, barley, and potatoes.[32]

The state of Greater Lebanon saw a similar flurry of activity. Within the first few years of the mandate, officials had established a nursery and an experimental field specializing in garden crops north of Beirut at the mouth of the River Kelb. They also had plans for a 92-hectare experimental center for cotton and grains in the ʿAkkar plain north of Tripoli and an accompanying experimental farm where interns from the "landowners of the country" would learn "practical agronomy."[33] Tractor use expanded. In the Biqaʿ Valley alone by 1926 there were fifteen tractors, including both Fordson and Renault makes.[34] However, the mandate administration scrapped plans for an agricultural school in the Biqaʿ Valley, opting instead to establish three more experimental centers—deemed a more economical alternative to "expensive and limited model fields"—in the Biqaʿ Valley, Tripoli, and Tyre.[35] Each 30-hectare center would specialize in a crop of particular importance to that region—cotton in the ʿAkkar near Tripoli, flax and spring wheat in the Biqaʿ, and fruit trees in Tyre—and would recruit twenty-five interns on scholarships "from among the agricultural class" to complete a two-year course of study.[36] The first center was established on state lands at Ras al-ʿAyn southeast of Tyre in 1927.[37] The following year saw a nursery and experimental center erected on 5 hectares in the Beirut suburb of Furn al-Showbak, where "numerous *agriculteurs* passing through Beirut gather all the time."[38]

As in Latakia, the state distributed seeds and saplings of preferred crops for free or at low cost, including Yerli and Idlib cotton suitable for dry farming, mulberry trees from the Biqaʿ experimental field, American vines from the Tyre field, and Italian olive trees.[39] French plow demonstrations in Ras al-ʿAyn were well attended, and future trials aimed to convince farmers that heavier moldboard plows were suitable for widespread use.[40] The state had not only a model silkworm farm but also a silk station with "modern refrigeration" and a French technician as director.[41] Conferences in Beirut, Saida, and Tripoli and accompanying brochures offered "practical advice relative to the adoption of modern techniques" on topics ranging from machines and fertilizers to new crops.[42] Stations for selling and repairing improved agriculture tools were slated to open following consultations with the main *maisons* of France.[43] The state bought 260 tons of chemical fertilizers to distribute and, by the end of 1930, had made twenty-five tractor and eight plow repairs at the first such station to open at Chtaura in the Biqaʿ Valley.[44] In 1932 the government subsidized an Arabic publication by the Order of Agricultural Engineers of Lebanon titled *The Agricultural Life* to the tune of 3,000 francs.[45]

Such developments contrasted starkly with those in Damascus and Aleppo, viewed by French officials as strongholds of nationalist resistance. Officials such as Achard still emphasized experimental stations as the main vehicle of agricultural development, but their efforts were more piecemeal and uneven. The Ghuta agricultural school in Blass near Damascus became an experimental station for potatoes and cotton and offered free beech trees for marshy areas and sales of ornamental and fruit trees.[46] The Salamiye school housed another station. To consolidate resources, mandate officials designated Salamiye the sole agricultural school for Syria with a plan to focus on dry farming.[47] However, despite some initial efforts to expand its buildings and resources, by 1926 mandate officials claimed the region was "not benefiting enough from it," and by 1928 it still had not achieved "desirable ameliorations."[48] By the early 1930s, the Salamiye school was shuttered.[49]

In Homs, a region dominated by large landowners, officials initially outlined a program that included elementary agricultural education, brochure distribution, a model farm, agricultural syndicates, mineral fertilizers, and advanced machinery. The idea was that this program would contribute to the "emancipation of the peasant" and encourage peasant support for the mandate.[50] Some early cotton experiments in a garden in Homs were promising, and tax exemptions aimed to encourage cultivators, although it is unclear to what extent those who had the resources to take advantage were the "peasants" of the earlier report.[51] In contrast to the Latakia government, the Syrian government did not start distributing cotton seeds and building ginning facilities in Homs and Hama until 1931.[52] Unlike Lebanon's *Agricultural Life*, the Hama-based agricultural journal, *al-Zira*ʿ*a al-Haditha*, does not appear to have received a government subsidy.[53]

In Aleppo, where mandate officials had pinned their hopes on expanding cotton cultivation, an initial wide-ranging program for agricultural education bore little fruit.[54] The Muslimiya school acquired an experimental station for training drivers, especially for tractors, and transformed into the Foch orphanage with an emphasis on agricultural education.[55] Mention of its activities quickly faded from official mandate reports.[56] Various piecemeal efforts ensued while officials worked on securing another experimental station. Once they realized that the Rud. Sack plows found in the town's Ottoman-era depot and belonging to the Agricultural Bank sold well, they decided to repair the remaining ninety plows and sell them at "minimum prices for propaganda."[57] The government also distributed seeds to "good" "serious" farmers and fruit and nonfruit trees among the region's districts. Seeds for individuals were ordered from the French seed company Vilmortin.[58] A successful trial led officials to sell Texas cotton seeds at the price of the Idlib variety.[59]

Finally, in October 1928 operations started at a nursery and experimental center in the northeastern Maydan quarter after the city encountered a number of obstacles in acquiring the land. One of the center's primary goals was to teach peasants "a rational rotation" in which successive crops were planted "without diminishing the [land's] productive force."[60] Aside from the fact that peasants already had a well-established rotation, the acknowledgment that, despite "sufficient buildings and a complete staff," the center's soil proved "insubstantial" and "mediocre in areas" suggested that its experiments may not have been as effective as desired.[61]

Meanwhile, peripheral towns such as Harim, west of Aleppo, gained a nursery and model garden, and Dayr al-Zor, on the Euphrates River in the desert to the southeast, had an experimental station by 1928, which was destroyed by a flood in 1929.[62] In Alexandretta plans to drain the Amik marsh prompted officials to create a 50-hectare experimental station at Soğuk Su, which started operations in October 1934, specifically to study the kinds of plants that could be grown in lands exposed by the drainage.[63] Officials insisted that the station offered a "more rational" approach to trials, which had, until then, been carried out by private individuals. The *sanjak* also benefited from official nurseries and demonstrations of machines, disease treatment, grafting, and seed disinfection by itinerant employees.[64] In the state of Jabal al-Druze "little educational nurseries" were created from which people "gladly" bought, according to French reports.[65]

The attention, effort, and expense devoted to each statelet's institutions of agricultural knowledge production reflected a combination of the statelet's ecological capacity to satisfy French industry's raw material needs, its geographic proximity to areas of French influence, and the political dynamics that determined the extent to which local elites and French officials were willing to collaborate in each region. Notably, the statelets of the littoral zone (Greater Lebanon, the ʿAlawite State, and the *sanjak* of Alexandretta) were the areas where French officials were most directly active.

The agricultural knowledge produced and disseminated by this infrastructure served to "socialize" Syrians and Lebanese to the priorities of French commerce and industry while largely denying more ambitious local aspirations.[66] None of the additional institutional planning envisioned for the region in the late Ottoman period or Faysali era came to fruition. The practical school in Aleppo, the farm school in Salamiya, and the model and experimental field in Damascus were decoupled from their broader Ottoman network and diminished in their objectives or eventually eliminated. Meanwhile, officials abandoned planned additions, such as an agricultural high school in Beirut comparable to the Halkalı Agricultural School in Istanbul.[67]

In their reports to the League of Nations in Geneva, French officials explained their approach by denigrating local expertise and denying local concerns, stating "in all circumstances, the mandate administration is employed to make the local administrations understand the necessity of substituting modern exploitation methods for ancient processes of *mise en valeur*."[68] According to this framing, only French officials truly understood the value of "modern" methods. In on-the-ground policy making this distinction translated into a narrative that contrasted French "rationality" with local "tradition" in order to justify a French-centered program of agricultural development, which like much of the material content of experimental centers, would make the region institutionally dependent on France.

The mandate's blueprint for agricultural knowledge production within the rubric of technical education was largely the brainchild of Monsieur Bériel, the mandate's counselor for technical education and Greater Lebanon's counselor for professional education.[69] His program reflected not local demands for agricultural education but rather his prior experience in Tunisia, where his approach involved training teachers to educate rural children, apprenticeships, and evening classes for adults. The education of these rural children, who were all sons of landowners, had taken place at a farm school on a prosperous settler-owned establishment; the school paid for itself from the farm's profits and served as the site for teacher training.[70]

Under the mandate the administration did not have settler-owned establishments to turn to, nor was it willing to invest large sums of money. New technologies were expensive, as were the spaces necessary for experimenting with them. As discussed in chapter 3, initially mandate officials were eager to promote new French technologies in pursuit of market expansion, but they quickly realized that local farmers found these technologies underwhelming, largely dashing these officials' ambitions and their main motivation for investment. This realization could help explain the rapid shift, exemplified in Bériel's plan, from an emphasis on capital-intensive methods to a focus on "good, practical training" for young Syrians with land who would return to work it, "practicing the same cultures as before but in a more rational [and remunerative] manner."[71]

Whereas Ottoman administrators had distinguished between science and existing practice in decades prior, Bériel's conception of this distinction had an added element: Rationality and science came from the Occident, especially France. In Syria, according to Bériel, local peasants were "about as ignorant as the times of the Bible" and the population largely lacked "scientific notions"; thus the goal was not "to buy a tractor for each Bedouin" but to get local farmers to "better know [their] land" and "to improve [their] traditional methods of cultivation."[72] In fact, the "spirit" in which the training was done—that is, "in an experimental and scientific sense"—was even more important that the content itself.[73] However, there was a caveat. In "marching resolutely toward progress," one must know how "to manage the traditions and not wreak havoc on the established social order under the pretext of making Occidental science penetrate."[74] The benefits of purveying "scientific notions" needed to be weighed against the potential disruption to the social order they could create. "Science" was Occidental and therefore inherently at odds with this order, defined by "traditions."[75]

In articulating the distinction between science and tradition in these terms, Bériel refused to acknowledge the explicitly "scientific" conceptualization of Ottoman-era agricultural infrastructure. The postwar reincarnations of these institutions were objects of his contempt, mentioned merely to highlight their incapacity to live up to their purported counterparts in metropole France. According to Bériel, the Salamiye school "pretends" to be a scientific establishment teaching agronomy, but its "facility is far from perfect," and he doubted Lebanese students would "willingly" (*de bon coeur*) attend it because it was so far away.[76] Meanwhile, "the stations of Muslimiya (Aleppo) and ʿAkkar (Lebanon) would be, if they had succeeded," experimental stations.[77] Not only were these institutions insufficient, but, in Bériel's telling, local agronomists were incapable of successfully applying scientific methods on their own. Rather, they required expensive "superior [French] personnel" who would cultivate "disciples" and whose Occident-derived "scientific" and "rational" approach would enable them to claim expertise, even over an unfamiliar environment.[78]

To further drive home this point, Bériel claimed that Arabic was incapable of expressing scientific concepts, characterizing it as "an instrument of very imperfect knowledge because it does not possess modern vocabulary, . . . lacks precision and . . . its logic is not very rigorous."[79] To be properly trained in "the rudiments of science," students had to become proficient in French.[80] Textbooks needed to be imported from France or North Africa, adapted to the country, and as required translated into Arabic for adults.[81] Bériel seemed unaware of Arabic texts recently produced or about to be published by authors whose goal was to make scientific agricultural knowledge more accessible and who had no reservations about the capacity of Arabic to convey it.[82]

Not only did Bériel's project not recognize locally produced knowledge as comparably scientific and rational to that possessed by French experts, but he could not conceive that this knowledge had mediated between global networks of expertise and local practices and ecologies. Rather, he premised his project on delineating a fundamental difference between local experts and French ones to justify bringing expertise from France, whether in the form of people or books. This course of reasoning sought to establish a transfer of knowledge conceived of as unidirectional and hierarchical. As a result, Bériel's plan furthered the linkage of the region to the metropole through an institutionalized hierarchy of knowledge production. Notably, a local place for training agricultural engineers with advanced degrees was absent from his program except as some distant prospect. Instead, the mandate would prioritize sending young people to the "grandes écoles" and technical schools of France.[83] Eventually, *agronome*-training scientific establishments, experimental stations, and farm schools would be established; however, the mandate administration's immediate priority was only farm schools.[84]

Bériel's plan for technical education in Greater Lebanon reflected this emphasis on institutional dependency. In the immediate future he suggested sending children to a facility that the Benedictines were proposing to establish in Baᶜalbak, which, while an "inconvenience" and "eccentric," would require only a subsidy and would avoid the full cost of a "complete facility."[85] Until this school was operational, inspectors or engineers from the agriculture department or even young French-educated Lebanese could give agricultural lectures to older students.[86] Lessons would focus on materials that could be "distributed in French," because French was "the only means of establishing a link with subsequent technical education, which must also be given in French."[87] Rural schools would prepare students for an agricultural school to be "created as early as possible," but "a higher order of education would be instituted later, if the necessity were felt, by the sending to France, whether in the schools of arts and métiers or the schools of agriculture, the subjects of the elite, thus trained and the cycle would be complete."[88] The high commissioner supported these stages: adding classes to primary village and town schools to prepare students for professional education, then creating professional schools of agriculture based on region, and finally establishing an agronomy school for superior technical education.[89]

French materials and French-educated instructors ensured that students who continued to higher levels of education would be predisposed to pursue their training in French institutions, especially if they lacked local institutions of higher education.[90] In the metropole itself, such a limited program—that is, one that prioritized agricultural education only for those who would return to work their own land—had long been deemed inadequate. Farm schools were part of the French system, but so were schools whose primary goal was to create a bureaucracy of those trained in scientific agriculture to teach, inspect, and fulfill other administrative positions related to technical education in the metropole.[91] Under the mandate, however, officials claimed that a lack of economic development justified minimizing technical education. From the mandate's inception, a perceived lack of technicians and "young people likely to fruitfully pursue technical studies of an advanced level," instead of spurring the expansion of technical education, justified minimizing its institutional presence.[92] By the early 1930s Syria's assistant counselor for public instruction still insisted "in every country, the development of technical education followed and favored, and did not precede and create, economic development."[93]

For mandate officials the mandate's economic development was inextricably linked with France's economic interests, whether maintained through dependence on French products and institutions or through resource extraction for French industry. As Bériel concluded, instituting the plan he proposed was urgent "if we want to lead them to sufficient production to assure themselves their needs and to permit us, after enriching them, to involve our business and industry in their profits."[94] In this vision the mandates were static, rife with ossified traditions that mandate authorities were to disturb only insomuch as necessary to produce the profits France sought. More drastic, expensive innovations were unnecessary. They were superfluous not only for the kind of economic development but also for the mandate bureaucracy that French officials planned. The institutional diversity of the late Ottoman period's agricultural infrastructure produced a network of certified experts who circulated around the empire as teachers, inspectors, model field directors, agriculture directors, and more. Under the mandate, not only were many comparable positions reserved for French officials, but also a bureaucracy maintained at strategically anemic levels meant fewer local officials who might propagate nationalist ideas in rural areas.[95]

Bériel's insistence on an exclusively French-derived "rational," "scientific" practice failed to acknowledge the legacy and agency of local technocratic initiatives that had been grappling with the dilemmas of scientific agriculture since the nineteenth century. One of the main representatives of that legacy, Mustafa al-Shihabi, the director of agriculture and forestry and then of state lands under the mandate, offered a rather different perspective on the circulation of knowledge that had culminated in "modern" agricultural expertise.[96] Al-Shihabi's *Modern Practical Agriculture*, published in the immediate aftermath of the Arab government's brief rule in Damascus and a year before Bériel submitted his report, opened by delineating Arab contributions to the development of scientific agricultural expertise in Europe.[97] For al-Shihabi, Ibn Wahshiyya's ninth-century translation of the *Book of Nabatean Agriculture* was indicative of Arabs' "exerting a major impact in attention to agriculture"—even contemporary French experts had praised the work.[98] Al-Shihabi pointed out that the French agronomist Max Ringelmann had identified the book as the first to record agricultural experiments in "a character of science [*sibghat fann*]" and that it was "a treasure of beautiful agricultural sciences."[99] Ringelmann had also acclaimed the work of al-ʿAwwam, an agriculturalist living near Seville in twelfth-century al-Andalus who had written a book based on a combination of his own experiments and other sources such as Ibn Wahshiyya.[100] Al-Shihabi noted that Ringelmann considered it "a collection of the best agricultural research written about by the Nabateans, Greeks, and Romans with that which was followed in al-Andalus."[101]

According to al-Shihabi, only 400 years after al-ʿAwwam would "Europe," which he claimed had "stayed ignorant of agricultural matters," start to study agriculture—a process he pinpointed as beginning with Olivier de Serres's book *The Theatre of Agriculture and the Administration of Fields*, originally published in 1600.[102] As evidenced by Ringelmann's praise, this did not mean that these earlier works were disregarded. In fact, to contribute to the development of agricultural expertise in the nineteenth century, the knowledge contained in al-ʿAwwam's lengthy work (over 1,000 pages) was translated into both Spanish (1802) and French (1864).[103] Al-Shihabi noted that copies could be found in Paris, Leiden, the Escorial in Spain, and the British Library.[104] Al-Shihabi's account of the longevity and influence of an Arab legacy of scientific agricultural practice reflected the Arab nationalist rhetoric of the Faysal period—a history of knowledge circulation that Bériel's Occident-derived science could not admit.

Having established Arab authors' bona fides in the production of agricultural knowledge historically, al-Shihabi then turned to the production of knowledge in the present. *Modern Practical Agriculture* was a compendium of the knowledge produced by applying the latest scientific methods in Syria, and it concluded with a special section devoted to "dry-farming [*zira*ʿ*at al-*ʿ*ard al-yabisa*]" techniques, because they were of particular relevance to most of Syria's arable rain-fed lands.[105] Observing that dry farming was not necessary in Europe because of "frequent and well-distributed" rains—an observation suggesting that those trained in metropole-based schools would lack relevant experience—al-Shihabi instead sought insights from a book published in 1912 by John A. Widtsoe, the president of the Agricultural College of Utah, titled *Dry-Farming: A System of Agriculture for Countries Under a Low Rainfall*.[106] However, al-Shihabi also underscored that aspects of this knowledge were already well known among cultivators of the region, noting, "Our *fallah* are not ignorant of some of the rules of this science and the Arabs previously followed it as is evidenced from the public reading [*tilawa*] of the Book of Agriculture [*kitab al-falaha*] that Yahya bin Muhammad bin al-ʿAwwam al-Ishbili composed."[107]

If, for al-Shihabi, al-ʿAwwam's book demonstrated the science of agriculture that the Arab *fallah* had followed for centuries, the Spanish and French translations in the nineteenth century suggested its broader appeal. The Spanish translator aimed to make al-ʿAwwam's ideas accessible to Spanish readers, but the translator of the 1864 French version, J. J. Clément-Mullet, explicitly linked his incentive to the French colonial project in North Africa.[108] Clément-Mullet explained that, though he was translating for both French and foreign scholars, the recent conquest of Algeria and efforts to undertake "useful work" in the region had made this kind of agricultural knowledge particularly valuable.[109]

> In order to use in all of its extent its soil so fertile in cereals and which makes [one] to conceive of such lovely hope for the culture of cotton, it cannot be but very advantageous to aim to popularize the precepts taught by the Arabs. Written for the south of Spain and for Syria, in their greater part, they can thus be advantageously applied to Algeria, which has so many connections, for the climatology, with these two regions.[110]

He thus aimed to facilitate the integration of "scientific" agricultural knowledge produced in Syria and al-Andalus into the development of

French agricultural expertise in North Africa. From Syria to al-Andalus to Algeria and from Utah to Syria, such circulations of agricultural knowledge belied the notion of a simple unidirectional process of knowledge transmission and the binary suggested by Bériel to justify French intervention in Syria's agricultural sphere. In fact, taking such circulations into account suggests that Bériel himself, with his experience in Tunisia, had likely benefited from what al-Shihabi characterized as the Arab legacy of scientific agricultural knowledge.

Elite Expertise and Rural Education: The Local Politics of Agricultural Knowledge Production

As French administrators privileged their experimental stations, nurseries, and basic practical agricultural training, local technocrats and agronomists advocated for a more comprehensive approach.[111] They argued that a variety of agricultural institutions, including schools of all levels with accompanying experimental fields, were necessary to produce the knowledge that would undergird a thriving national economy and spread it among both cultivators and landowners.[112] In addition, employees—likely graduates of the upper-level schools—could travel the countryside visiting agricultural centers and giving lectures with "cinema machines" to explain "scientific agricultural works."[113] These institutions and activities would facilitate connections between urban government administrators and rural communities, ensuring the fledgling administration's capacity to exercise increasing influence in rural areas. Their vision espoused many of the same principles that had shaped late Ottoman agricultural planning.

Citing the example of countries in Europe where agricultural schools and societies had proliferated, such as France, Denmark, Belgium, and Germany, the editors of *al-Ziraʿa al-Haditha* insisted that this abundance of institutions producing and sharing knowledge indicated how these countries maintained their economic strength and the high quality of their "economic life."[114] Syria needed 82 schools and 3,387 students to reach a level comparable to that of Germany and 95 schools with 10,000 students, not to mention 130 centers of seasonal agriculture lessons with 11,000 attendees, to compete with Denmark. That Syria had only two schools and one of them, Bouka, was foreign was a sign that "this country, delayed in agriculture, is behind in other branches of economic life."[115]

The nonforeign government-run Salamiya school, where the mandate had consolidated agricultural education resources, became an important locus for the gathering and distribution of information about the latest agricultural developments as well as a hotbed of protest against the mandate government's refusal to pursue an agricultural policy more accommodating to their demands.[116] Its administrators and students, who hailed from throughout the region, were frequent critics of the mandate regime and vocal advocates for their vision of agricultural development.[117] Their critiques along with the activities of the school were frequently featured in the pages of *al-Ziraʿa al-Haditha*, which ʿUmar Tarmanini and his brother Saʿid published out of Hama, the city closest to Salamiya.[118]

The school's resources were substantial. It had a 1,000-*donum* farm, an orchard, a vineyard, a vegetable garden, artificial meadows, a nursery, and fields for experimentation with an additional 2,000 *donums* of cultivable land and permanent meadows.[119] Primarily French-educated teachers provided practical training to prepare students to run a rural farm or serve in the mandate's agricultural services.[120] Similar to the division of labor in the Ottoman model field, they worked alongside wage-earning employees who did much of the field labor.[121] Among other initiatives, the school spent 4,800 francs to clean one of the canals that channeled groundwater from the surrounding hills into the plain around Salamiya, providing a source of water for irrigated cultivation in a region where crops were otherwise rainfed. The repaired canal provided 66 liters of water per hour.[122]

Students and local technocrats viewed this education as a step toward a degree on par with that of an *ingénieur agricole*.[123] The school's director, Tawfiq al-Ahdab, maintained that its main goal was to produce qualified "agronomist managers" to oversee large farming operations.[124] Many of the school's students also considered its degree a gateway to posts as civil servants in the state's agricultural administration, whether serving as teachers, agricultural employees, or directors (*mudirs*) in the administration of local subdistricts, much as such training had functioned during the Ottoman period.[125] This perspective was particularly prevalent among students who came from more modest backgrounds and saw the education as a means for social advancement.[126] In contrast, mandate authorities insisted that the school's main goal was to produce *agriculteurs*; because only 12% of the students returned to farming, they contended that the school was not "attaining the goal for which it was founded."[127] However, one local

FIGURE 18. Students from the Salamiya agricultural school in a cotton field, c. 1920s. Source: Haut-Commissariat de la République Française en Syrie et au Liban, *La Syrie et le Liban sous l'Occupation et le Mandat Français, 1919–1927* (Nancy: Berger-Levrault, 1929), n.p.

technocrat suggested that, if officials' main goal was to produce cultivators versed in the latest techniques, then that was the purpose of experimental or model fields, since they were "equivalent to practical agricultural schools" for cultivators (*fallahin*).[128] In contrast, pursuing agricultural education at Salamiya was not just about producing enlightened cultivators but involved multiple goals, depending on one's social position and aspirations.

During the summer of 1928 the school's graduates implored the High Commission to set the value of their diplomas from a "scientific perspective" and find them jobs in the state domains or give them preference for posts associated with the Ministry of Agriculture, such as in the agricultural banks, in the service of the cadastre, or in the state's veterinary service.[129] The deputy delegate of the High Commission supported their request, writing to the high commissioner that the Salamiya degree was supposed to be equivalent to that of a practical agricultural school in France and the Syrian government wanted to find positions for its graduates in the administration. He added that six students currently served in the state domains and gave "full satisfaction."[130] Alternatively, recent graduates proposed that the government rent them state land in various subdistricts with the promise to eventually sell it to them. However, this suggestion was, as one writer in *al-Zira^ca al-Haditha* put it, "like a scream in a valley," despite a decree in May 1926 that made it the preferred process for achieving *mise en valeur* and small property ownership.[131] *Al-Ziraᶜa al-Haditha* also rejected claims that the students were uninterested in farming, insisting that "a number of the graduates welcome agricultural work no matter how tedious or tiring."[132]

The students' ambitions stymied, the relationship between the school and the mandate state became increasingly acrimonious. On 9 November 1929, while ᶜUmar Tarmanini, the school's director, was away in France, the students went on strike, demanding the firing of one of their supervisors who had tried to suppress the chanting of "obscene and biased" songs.[133] The instigators were the son of Nawras al-Kaylani, an antimandate Hama notable, albeit one unaligned with the National Bloc; Nazim, son of Arif Kaylani; and Khadir, son of Abdul Rahman Shishakli and brother of Tawfiq Shishakli, a rising nationalist star in Hama.[134] The Directorate of Agriculture closed the school temporarily on 13 November, and officials recommended that the strike instigators not be allowed to return, given the school's reputation as "a center of advanced nationalism."[135] Six students were suspended for a year.[136] Less than a year later, in September 1930 the Ismaili *qa^ʾimmaqam* of Salamiya, Amir Mirza, accused Tarmanini and other professors of undertaking a nationalist campaign among the Ismailis, whom French officials viewed as allies. The students were charged with "caring especially for politics and very little for their agricultural studies . . . manifested many times by their disorders and strikes."[137]

In the midst of this fracas, mandate authorities proposed to "reform" the school by converting it from a practical agricultural school into a farm school—a demotion in the educational hierarchies of scientific agricultural expertise that the students and nationalist press fiercely protested.[138] This change compromised the status of the students' expertise and their capacity to circulate in the local and global networks where this certification conveyed prestige.[139] Meanwhile, the nationalist newspaper *al-Qabas* lamented that one of the main reasons given for changing the school's status was to economize on expenses, querying why such an institution was expected to pay for itself. Rather, it claimed "that science/knowledge [*al-ᶜilm*] has never been a means to bring profit" and "that economy is not allowed to be in the role of education"—if the government truly wanted agriculture to flourish, it actually needed to expand the school.[140] Nonetheless, such a "reform" reflected Bériel's priorities, as did one of the main obstacles identified by French officials to granting the desired degree: The students did not study enough French. In fact, French had not even been offered at the school for the 1930–1931 school year.[141] Tarmanini, who published the *al-Ziraʿa al-Haditha* in Arabic, including numerous articles translated from French, clearly did not consider French necessary for "modern" agricultural training.[142] However, Bériel ultimately called the shots and insisted that "there is no assimilation possible between the *bac* [high school diploma] and a diploma of Salamiya." At most, the education at Salamiya was equivalent to the first part of the *bac*.[143] The denial of a *bac* equivalency meant that the students, who understood their diploma to be equivalent to one of secondary instruction, lacked the certification necessary to continue their studies.[144] Lapsed French instruction antagonized mandate administrators because it denied them a key means through which they aimed to ensure the mandate's institutional dependency on the metropole. Meanwhile, the school's students not only found the degree they aspired to denied but also lacked local options for continuing their studies.[145]

Al-Ziraʿa al-Haditha also rejected mandate officials' emphasis on a primarily French-derived agricultural knowledge, regularly reprinting translated excerpts of agricultural advice and expertise from locales as diverse as Brazil, Queensland, California, South Africa, and Scotland.[146] The editor traveled to Germany, and each year the students would take field trips to observe agricultural practices in different environments.[147] In addition to disseminating expertise from around the globe to its literate subscribers, the journal also encouraged efforts to engage with local cultivators' knowledge. In the spirit of this goal it published a series of articles titled "Hadith al-Fallah" that chronicled the visits of an *effendi* agronomist to villages in order to talk with local cultivators (*fallahin*). Ostensibly his visits aimed to convey to them the benefits of scientific agriculture, but in illuminating peasant conceptions of expertise for the journals' readers, the articles underscored how, even as the *effendi* interlocutor sought to distinguish his "scientific" agricultural expertise from their "nonscientific" knowledge, he simultaneously affirmed it.

The inclusion of the articles suggested that the journal's elite readers were intrigued by these insights into village life, which confirmed through their presentation of peasant knowledge the "scientific" expertise that the journal's readers valued.[148] The author acknowledged that peasants had a treasured agricultural knowledge passed down from father to son through proverbs that were "almost . . . their agricultural rules and regulations, and their fathers and grandfathers have honed them so among them [that these proverbs] have the sanctity of the glorious past and the holiness of the venerated law."[149] As recounted by Zakariya in the beginning of this chapter, book learning could not easily supplant such knowledge.

Indeed, some evidence suggests that a degree of skepticism characterized landowners' regard for knowledge acquired in institutions, especially foreign ones. Enthusiasm for new techniques notwithstanding, opportunities for young foreign-trained agronomists were limited despite supporters' insistence that their expertise could extract ten times their fee.[150] The reluctance of wealthy landowners to hire them, instead of indicating primarily a refusal to invest, could in fact be interpreted as a preference for the reliable knowledge of the *fallahin* over the untried scientific expertise of these youths, especially given the financial insecurities of the mandate period.[151] For example, the Aleppo Chamber of Agriculture, which continued to be controlled by urban landowning elites, in requesting the establishment of agricultural chambers in each district, specified that they should be "composed of farmers, not very educated, it is true, but having experience," as that would be "much more effective than guidance emanating from young people for whom experience is almost totally absent."[152] Without solid knowledge of local environments and practices, notions acquired in foreign institutions led to "highly impracticable" ideas and even the "ruin" of some families whose sons studied abroad.[153] Insights gained from talking with cultivators (*fallahin*) provided a valuable local sounding board to reassess these notions.

In narrating his interactions, the author of "Hadith al-Fallah," who signed his articles "*fallah*," or "cultivator," emphasized his efforts to spend time with peasant farming communities—going to their councils, attending their nightly gatherings, and listening to their economic woes—as well as the tendency of his presence in a village to always cause a stir because he wore European (*ifranji*) clothes but also claimed familiarity with (*waqafa ʿala*) agriculture![154] During a visit to a village of more than 100 houses west of Aleppo, the *fallahin*, in disbelief that the visitor was "from those who plowed the earth with their own hands," gathered to quiz him on his agricultural knowledge.[155] They asked him questions about wheat and barley and lamented the lack of rain, wondering whether Europeans (*al-ifranj*) could bring down "water of the sky" when they chose.[156] There ensued a rich exchange in which the author, intent on proving his knowledge to the peasants, discussed various topics with them. He would note, for example, the need to sow seed with care, to which the peasants responded with proverbs that conveyed similar ideas. In particular, they cited "the fallow is a flute" (*al-bur tunbur*) and "the splitting is adornment and the second is a mirror" (*al-shiqaq zawaq wa al-tanay maray*), both of which conveyed the sense that failure to properly prepare the soil for sowing resulted in poor returns.[157]

The author requested more proverbs and described how a peasant elder sitting in a corner "listening to our conversation like a venerable shaykh to his young grandsons" responded with the "serious wisdom" and "precious advice" from his grandfather, who had lived to be 120 years old and had insisted on "conquering the earth with work." The shaykh explained that one should not be content with merely two plowings; rather, "the third is stabilization and the fourth opens the pit and sale and the fifth goes in the bag, and the sixth builds upon it the row, so plow the earth many times and mark into it many rows for to each row there is a season and to each peasant a harvest."[158] In response, the *effendi* played his scientific agricultural trump card, explaining that European plows had the capacity to reach in one or two plowings the depth achieved by local plows after five or six (and they were cheap, or so he insisted). According to his account, most of the peasants responded, "If only the government gave us these types of implements and taught us how to use them."[159] Mediated by the author's reporting, the tone of the response is not easy to judge. It suggests that the villagers did not reject the possible usefulness of this technology out of hand but stressed the need for infrastructure and government support to make it a feasible option—clearly a position very much in line with *Modern Agriculture*'s own.

An exchange during another visit further elucidated the distinctions between the peasants' and the agronomist's perspectives about the essence of productivity. The *effendi* author insisted that productivity was tied to more work and not just swearing by the ways of their forefathers. In particular, he urged the peasants that "blessing is in movement" (*al-baraka fi al-haraka*) and that new approaches to *feddans* and plowed rows were the issue, which could be fixed by learning the "science" of agriculture in schools.[160]

The farmers, in response, rejected *feddans* and plowed rows as the key to improved agricultural production, insisting that what the earth brought forth was a factor of "blessings [*baraka*] from God."[161] Productivity for them was largely tied to elements beyond their control, such as rain. When the author extolled the Salamiya agricultural school's benefits, he was surprised when an elder responded,

> *Walla ya effendi*, one of those that you mentioned [i.e., a student of the agricultural school] passed by and informed us of many benefits about how to cultivate vines and prepare the soil, and he said that he obtained this good information in the agricultural school in Salamiya, and ideally if we were rich and our children could read and write, we'd send them to the agricultural school to learn agriculture [*falaha*] from the agricultural teacher.[162]

Again, though not completely dismissive of the agricultural school, the peasant elder emphasized the economic and social differences that mediated access to this privileged scientific expertise, exposing the slippage between the *effendi*'s assessment of the peasants' problems and the peasants' assessment.

Some local technocrats were well aware of these concerns. Improving and expanding rural infrastructure, particularly along lines that would strengthen urban-rural connections, was essential to their plans for economic development.[163] As Halim Najjar, a teacher of animal science at the American University of Beirut, observed, the main needs of farmers were not large combine harvesters or even schools but rather "improving markets for distribution" and ensuring that they received a good price for their products. "How," he queried "can we ask [the *fallah*] . . . to use modern agricultural tools and implements if the harvest does not increase his income?"[164] The agricultural expertise privileged by local elites, the mandate authorities, or international organizations would have little value without basic infrastructure facilitating market access or policies ensuring decent crop prices. Until then, farmers' own more-cost-effective expertise would remain the most economically viable.

In any event, although local technocrats might suggest that the *fallahin* could learn from the Salamiya school's students, as during the Ottoman period, peasant children were not the students for whom its programming was intended. Rather, local technocrats emphasized that increasing literacy and providing elementary practical agricultural training in village schools was also a fundamental component of their economic development plans.[165] They tended to agree with French officials on the purpose of this training—it was not about social mobility. According to one French report, Syria needed to "modify the programs of village school with regards to reading, writing, agriculture, and economic principles. The students will study the sciences which their milieu needs like industry, agriculture, and commerce."[166] They were to be trained as workers or farmers instilled with "a taste for manual professions."[167] Similarly, *al-Ziraʿa al-Haditha*, in proposing the opening of one school for each district and large subdistrict, underscored that they should teach basic agricultural principles and industries, but the level of food or dress should not exceed the life conditions of the students' rural families.[168] The Committee of Economic Recovery of Beirut urged "much less literature and much more agricultural and botanical knowledge, less ambition and pretention and a bit more of that practical simplicity that assures to a man a happy and peaceful life."[169] The technocratic consensus was that agricultural education in villages should remain basic so as not to encourage children to leave their communities and aspire to higher levels of study. In towns it might even inspire them to move to rural areas.

French reports to the League of Nations scrupulously documented increases in rural primary schools. By one count, in 1929 the statelets under mandate had 1,612 rural schools, 510 of which were official.[170] Such numbers aimed to illustrate the fruits of mandate policies to the League, but local critiques suggested that lack of oversight, training options, and attention to particular areas' needs limited their effectiveness. The inhabitants of Dayr al-Zor complained of neglect, insisting that during the Ottoman period there were 15,000 residents and four primary schools, but under the mandate they only had one primary school and as a result had to raise 50 Syrian liras to create another class to accommodate one that had grown to over eighty students.[171] *Al-Ziraʿa al-Haditha* also criticized poorly distributed teacher resources as well as a failure to carry out inspections.[172] It claimed that one district had three schools with only four to twenty students between them. In another, during a tour, the education minister discovered a school that had two teachers (each of whom received a monthly salary of 25 gold French lira) but only twenty students, resulting in one teacher always being absent and the other busy "writing amulets." In response, the minister ordered the absent teacher to teach in a city of not less than 50,000 inhabitants, while the other teacher remained.[173]

The journal also highlighted projects undertaken by the Near East Foundation, such as funding an agricultural school in the Biqaʿ Valley and experiments in subdistricts throughout Syria in cooperation with the American University of Beirut, as well as a three-branch program at the Kadoorie school in Tulkarim, Palestine, to provide agricultural secondary education, basic instruction for *fallahin* children, and teacher training. It urged the Syrian Education and Agricultural Ministries to consider a similar program.[174] In a bid to create ever more productive peasants, it also urged the formation of industrial agricultural schools, both stationary and mobile, that could teach peasants, especially girls, crafts that they could pursue in their free time.[175] If peasants were ignorant, the editor insisted, the government bore responsibility and the peasant had every right to complain about this negligence.[176]

According to *al-Ziraʿa al-Haditha*, lack of administrative oversight and technical expertise not only among teachers but also among those in rural administration contrasted starkly with administrative practice during the Ottoman period. The Ottoman Civil Service School (Madrasa al-Mulkiya) had "graduated for the country what it needed from administrative authorities and they would gradually advance along the ladder of progress rung by rung starting from the counties [*mudiriyat*] of the subdistricts. Then God willed to separate Syria from this wide empire and we do not know—would we say that this separation was from its misfortune or good fortune?"[177] Having "boldly" posed this question, the journal went on to claim that "the governments of Syria have appointed people [to the directorates] that are not connected to the corps of administration or knowledge [*ʿilm*] at all [*bi-sila min al-silat*]." In fact, their qualifications for these posts remained unclear, as there was no longer a school like the Ottoman Civil Service School to train civil servants for basic administrative positions.[178] The editor alleged that if questioned about their accomplishments after years in these positions, directors (*mudirs*) would have no answer and had likely "not seen an inspector the entire time . . . in the job."[179] The absence of government oversight meant that incompetence went unchecked.[180]

Insufficient oversight and the lack of institutions such as the Ottoman Civil Service School to provide institutional training and qualifications gave a school like Salamiya, according to its advocates, even more importance in terms of what it could contribute not only to agricultural change but also to rural administration.[181] *Al-Zira'a al-Haditha* insisted that not only were Salamiya graduates eager to fill posts in rural areas as directors, officials, or teachers in subdistricts but also, because of their agricultural training, they were better positioned to understand the "maladies and pains" of those who practiced agriculture.[182] Because directors were posted among farmers and *fallah*, it argued, the graduates were ideally suited for these positions and could serve as an example to farmers and a link between the village and the government.[183] That is, the goal of training these technocrats involved not merely encouraging new agricultural practices but producing administrators who could serve in rural areas, creating stronger linkages with state institutions and oversight of rural communities.

Syrian technocrats may have agreed with French officials about the level and limits of instruction in village schools, but for them this aspect of agricultural education constituted only one part of a more comprehensive institutional program geared toward the production of a national state space. National economic development required training not only cultivators to increase or expand their production but also government employees who had the scientific agricultural expertise to oversee farming enterprises, serve as civil servants, or even teach agriculture in village schools.[184] Establishing local higher-level institutions could not wait until some indeterminate later date.

The students and administrators of Salamiya challenged mandate priorities on multiple levels. By engaging international networks of agricultural expertise, they defied French efforts to maintain the primacy of knowledge circulating within a French imperial sphere. Their potential role in the production of national state space by representing the state and building connections on its behalf with rural communities was also a threat. French officials carried out their divide-and-rule policy not only through dividing the region into statelets but also by pitting the rural areas, where they sought to attract allies, against the urban areas, where they considered resistance to the mandate strongest.[185] Allowing Salamiya students to obtain influential posts in rural areas would hinder French efforts to spread their own propaganda and influence in the countryside, hindering the production of colonial state space. Mandate officials were particularly wary of international or nationalist influence infiltrating rural areas and regarded agriculture-related projects as a key means by which this might happen.

Finally, as an upper-level educational institution run by local specialists, the Salamiya school represented resistance to French efforts to build institutional dependency within its imperial sphere by restricting access to such institutions within the mandate.

Following a protracted series of elections whose manipulation by French officials sparked a flurry of protests to the League of Nations, including one from the students of the Salamiya school as a bloc, a government led by moderate National Bloc candidates with their policy of "honorable cooperation" came to power.[186] In 1932 the new agricultural minister, Jamil Mardam Bey, announced the closure of the school that summer.[187] The reasons cited were that the students wanted to go into government service rather than actually work the land themselves and that the school's closure was economically necessary.[188] The former reason was in line with graduate expectations of such institutions in the Ottoman period. As for the latter, *al-Zira*ʿ*a al-Haditha* exclaimed, "When did economy necessitate closing a scientific establishment in a country thirsty for knowledge?"[189] *Al-Qabas* insisted that the alternative of sending students to study in Europe was even more expensive, and, besides, if students were to be sent abroad, it was better for them to study medicine than agriculture.[190] The outcry from some nationalist sources suggested that they viewed the move as acquiescence to French pressure. For some National Bloc members the decision was potentially a form of retaliation against non–National Block nationalists in Hama, for example, al-Kaylani. In any event, the decision infuriated local technocrats. *Al-Zira*ʿ*a al-Haditha* published the ministry's decision as a "service to history," lambasting the lack of expertise of those in the Agriculture Ministry and in the report submitted by the Agriculture Committee to the Economic Conference in Damascus.[191] The report proposed closure of the school and in its place the establishment of an experimental center to "improve agriculture," a decision precisely in line with mandate officials' priorities but decried by *al-Zira*ʿ*a al-Haditha* as constituting "corruption" (*fasad*).[192] In perhaps a gesture of reconciliation, the journal concluded by urging these nonexperts to cooperate with the experts, who were "no doubt known to the responsible powers" and to at least do more for elementary agricultural education.[193]

Elementary agricultural education was indeed where the new government decided to concentrate its resources in line with the policies Bériel had outlined almost a decade before. In July 1933 a law established a plan for incorporating agricultural education into elementary and primary education and complementary professional education classes.[194] In this program elementary education of four years was specifically designed "to furnish to a large part of the population an education exactly adapted to its needs and more in harmony with the degree of social evolution and the kind of life of our countryside." Although not "ideal," this "modest" program would be sufficient to provide students with some basic notions "without which the state does not have citizens."[195] Instead of training civil servants eager to facilitate connections between urban and rural areas and the spread of nationalist influence that this might entail, the program emphasized disciplining rural children into citizens through basic education.[196]

The program did include calls for superior schools of agriculture, which would create technically trained supervisors for large agricultural undertakings, but these continued to be a mirage.[197] A year later, Bériel outlined some plans along these lines that proposed establishing professional rural schools oriented toward agriculture, a farm school in Aleppo, and ways to popularize "modern" methods among adults, but there is no evidence that any of this materialized.[198] Instead, beginning in 1935, "elementary schools of rural type" were to incorporate basic agricultural education, but, despite a dozen being established, "apathy" led to the disappearance of all but two around Homs. Still this was the model that the French education counselor continued to push, which he conceded, after substantial development, might be augmented by slightly more advanced practical schools attached to the experimental centers. As for a school comparable to the national agricultural schools of France, such an institution, he insisted as late as 1941, was "completely inappropriate."[199] By 1938–1939 four schools of arts and métiers (two in Damascus—one for boys and one for girls; one in Aleppo; and one in Beirut) and two for commerce offered technical education.[200] But the only upper-level agricultural training was the Farm Management Course at the American University's International College, which had moved from Izmir to Beirut in 1936.[201] The agricultural educational infrastructure of colonial state space was decidedly basic.

Meanwhile, in Salamiya, intrigue surrounded the school and its lands. Initially relegated to an agricultural station, in 1935 the school hosted teacher training courses, although, according to Gabriel Bounoure, the High Commission's counselor for public instruction, this proved unsatisfactory, and, after three years, the classes were moved to the agricultural station in

Aleppo.[202] Meanwhile, the school's lands and nurseries were farmed out to individuals, leading to more tension.[203] Pierre Berthelot, the assistant delegate for Homs and Hama, passed along intelligence that a Homs "nationalist leader," Yahya Khankan, and the brother of Hama deputy Tawfiq Shishakli had formed a *syndicat*, and their friends had already rented lands adjoining those of the school, as they had been promised access to the school's "fruitful, well-watered, well-planted" lands for a good price. Not only would they gain a "financial advantage," but the move "doubled as a political action" because Salamiya's Ismaili community had remained largely resistant to the National Bloc's advances. In his opinion, the school, which he characterized as a "French-Ismaili creation" and thus paradoxically, given the shenanigans he described, not well-loved by the "nationalists," belonged to the Ismaili community. Emir Suleiman, the Ismaili deputy, had expressed his displeasure to the Syrian government over the school's closing and the plan to lease its lands.[204] Certainly members of the Ismaili community had provided funds and land for the school during the Ottoman period, but this characterization of the school's purpose was its own political action. Not only did this characterization dismiss the school's original and ongoing role as a state institution, albeit one with contentious origins, but it viewed the school primarily as a pawn for maintaining allegiance in a colonial politics of divide and rule.

In 1939 Berthelot continued his targeted campaign for reopening the school as an instrument for "economic development of the region and our propaganda." The Ismaili leader Mirza Mustapha suggested Monsieur Bonniot de Fleurac for director, transparently appealing to mandate officials' preferences for French supervisors. Despite de Fleurac's familiarity with the region and providing "all proof of agricultural capacity," Bounoure refused, citing the *mal chronique* that led to the school's closure and the necessity to ensure that any manager of an agricultural school possessed "great technical competence and a deep experience."[205] The closed school became a political palimpsest on which different factions projected their respective interests: on the one hand, derided as too expensive, ineffective, and rambunctious and, on the other, promoted as instrumental to the region's or the state's economic development, French influence, or "nationalist" ambitions.

The school's students remained active. Following the school's closure, they wrote articles critiquing mandate policies in publications such as *Les Échos* and the National Bloc–aligned newspaper *al-Qabas*. In particular, they attacked the mandate's agricultural counselor, Achard, for influencing the rejection of an agricultural reform and reorganization project proposed by the director of agriculture and economic services, Yusuf ʿAtallah, in the midst of a severe drought.[206] One *Al-Qabas* writer opined that the failure of the plan to pass the agricultural commission "affected the population in a way even more grievous than closing the Salamiya school," which symbolized the mandate's failure to promote the expertise necessary to realize Syria's economic and agricultural potential.[207] The newspaper queried whether the project's "meager budget" was beyond the means of the treasury.[208] The school's derelict condition came to symbolize the degradation of institutions under mandate rule considered essential to Syria's economic development.

In 1933 five of the school's former students obtained 250 hectares of state land 13 kilometers east of Saraqib in Tal Tuqan through Aleppo's agricultural inspector.[209] After a year of work they had plowed 80 hectares with a tractor, planted various European wheats, and were on the verge of building a house with a garden. Bériel, happening upon the fruits of their efforts in his rounds, described it as "an extremely interesting experiment" that, if they "persevered," would achieve "a work of colonization analogous to those of North Africa and Palestine, of which there have not been until now any model in the territories under mandate."[210] Tellingly, Bériel's frame of reference for understanding an enterprise of such scale could associate it only with the "work of colonization," despite it being carried out by local elites. The experiment, he suggested, could be repeated on other state lands, which merely contained pastoralists' routes or small local property. The contestation that might arise from disrupting these routes or infringing on these properties seemed of little concern. Such a plan "completed the program of education and popularization started by the reform of primary education and followed by the creation of a farm school" because it would provide local farmers with practical demonstrations, which a school of agriculture by itself could not provide. In Bériel's scenario, a Syrian school of superior agriculture was unnecessary, as was increasing the number of students sent to study agronomy in France, because Syria only needed good agricultural workers, not more agricultural engineers.[211] His assessment failed to acknowledge that those whose initiative he commended were the aspiring agricultural engineers of a defunct school he found superfluous.

Aspirations to undertake a similar enterprise in Syria's south motivated in part an effort to acquire private lands in al-Btayha in 1934. The fervor for purchasing the Btayha lands, located on the eastern shores of Lake Tiberias and owned by the Damascene al-Yusuf family, was initially prompted by fears that the family would sell them to the Jewish National Fund.[212] Although the High Commission passed decrees blocking such land sales in March 1934, concerns lingered, accompanied by a growing enthusiasm for the possibilities that these lands offered local investors.[213] Not only were the al-Yusufs heavily indebted and looking to sell, but also much of the land was located in the hotter, humid Jordan Valley, or Ghor—a prime location for cultivating garden and fruit crops that matured earlier or later than in other areas of Syria, thus fetching higher prices in the off season.[214] The size of the land also meant that its exploitation would suit the latest technologies—tractors, foreign plows, and so on.

To promote the plan and attract investors, by June 1934 a "scientific committee" that included Zakariya and other members known for their "specialization in agricultural matters from their scientific and practical aspects" compiled a report about the project.[215] Then on 16 August 1934 the Syrian president passed a decree endorsing the establishment of the Syrian Agricultural Stock Company, which was officially established on 26 August. However, its capital of 150,000 Turkish pounds, divided into three 50,000 Turkish pound shares, proved too steep. The fallout from the early 1930s drought and economic crisis hit landowners and farmers particularly hard as a result of mandate taxation and agricultural bank policies, as discussed in chapter 5. Because these were the individuals most likely to be willing and interested in investing, their financial straits meant that the company was unable to find the necessary starting capital and was disbanded a year later.[216]

For local technocrats, national economic development required a comprehensive approach to agricultural education. Although they agreed with French officials about the importance of basic rural education that would keep children of cultivators in their villages, they also insisted on the simultaneous need for advanced institutions to train a qualified rural bureaucracy and to provide instruction to those with the lands and means to experiment with more capital-intensive techniques. They considered a trained bureaucracy key to staffing the institutions of national space state and those with the means to experiment essential to the nation's economic prosperity and competitiveness. Relegating upper-level agricultural education only to the metropole meant not only that access to it was mediated by various political and economic considerations but also that the training obtained lacked any connection to local knowledge and conditions, rendering it ineffective. In recognizing the importance of familiarity with the region's ecologies, local technocrats tacitly acknowledged the expertise of the *fallah*, even if they still distinguished it from their own "scientific" version.

Influence in the Countryside: The Politics of Educating the *Fallah*

As local technocrats and agronomists struggled to implement their projects for agricultural and rural education, mandate authorities forged ahead with the activities of nurseries and experimental centers, especially those in Greater Lebanon, Latakia, and Alexandretta, which continued to serve as sites of distribution and assessment primarily for French crops, despite lackluster results. Meanwhile, contestation over the other scattered efforts at agricultural education and rural development projects beyond those discussed so far underscored the ongoing importance of this sphere to attempts at exerting influence, whether by French, other foreign, or local interests—a preview of what would become de rigueur with postwar development schemes.

Despite initial enthusiasm for nurseries, the assessment in both Syria and Lebanon was that, in general, they had been a major disappointment. The Committee of Economic Recovery of Beirut, headed by ʿUmar Daʿuq, a nationalist Beiruti politician and merchant who had been willing to work with French authorities, in contrast to other more "radical" nationalists, highlighted the issue in a 1935 report to the high commissioner.[217] Although the committee agreed that encouraging the cultivation of plums, peaches, nuts, pears, apples, and cherries was worthwhile, they criticized the mandate for distributing such plants to cultivators accustomed to tending mulberries, figs, olives, and vineyards. Because fruit cultivation of this nature required care unfamiliar to the cultivators and soils different from those in which they planted the new saplings, their results were meager. Despite the distribution of theoretical pamphlets by the Agriculture Directorate, what the peasants really needed, they insisted, was a "practitioner gardener with a diploma" attached to each nursery and paid for by the state who would counsel peasants on the saplings best suited to their lands, monitor their crops, and provide instruction and products to help them protect their trees from insects and disease.[218]

Hikmat al-Hakim, a deputy to the Syrian Parliament from Idlib, echoed similar concerns, noting that the nurseries had proved a disappointing and wasteful expense because of negligence and the lack of basic instruction from agricultural employees about planting, grafting, and dealing with pests. He claimed that many of the transplanted saplings had thus "lost their vitality."[219] Attempts to abruptly encourage a shift toward new production without adequate support infrastructure clearly proved troubling, although the main issue was not the new plants themselves but the failure to deploy certified expertise to facilitate their broader adoption.

The nurseries were not the only project that provoked controversy. In contrast to the drama surrounding the Salamiya school, the Bouka school in Latakia became the poster child of mandate agricultural education. Officials submitted a photo of the school to the League of Nations' 1929 Exposition de la Paix to exemplify the agricultural institution building accomplished under the mandate.[220] In line with mandate priorities, the school focused on elementary education with a student body that grew from twenty-four in 1927 to forty-two in 1928.[221] The school paid for its costs from the sale of its produce and recruited students from among the sons of proprietors who wanted to develop their own lands, although it gained a

FIGURE 19. Centre Agricole de Bouka, 1929. Reproduced with permission of the Centre des Archives Diplomatiques de Nantes, Syrie-Liban/2, 67, "Exposition de la paix et de la Société de Nations."

cheap source of additional labor when the Latakia orphanage for boys was transformed into an "agricultural orphanage" and moved to its premises.[222] In 1930 the ʿAlawite State's mandate administrators arranged a contract to transfer the center to a Benedictine congregation, which already had a cheese making operation in Baʿalbak.[223]

Despite the relatively collaborative relationship between mandate officials and Latakia's Representative Council, several of the council members raised questions about the school's privileged status and the financial favors this conveyed.[224] In particular, the sale of the center without interest in a series of twenty-five annual installments caused concern. One member suggested that in buying the domain from the state, the congregation should pay some annual interest, and another stated that "from a purely commercial point of view," he did not consider the project "compatible with the interests of the State." In response, the state's governor, Ernest Schoeffler, insisted that the sale would not only save the state 10,000 livres syriennes annually but would also bring to the region "experienced farmers" who would "introduce new methods of culture" and "use modern farming instruments."[225] An agreement was reached and, in addition to the center's subsidy from the ʿAlawite State, it received one from the Oeuvres Françaises, which, in the 1931–1932 budget, amounted to 5,000 francs.[226]

Bouka's project of expertise dissemination increasingly came under fire as politicized. Student numbers fell following the sell-off to the Benedictines; an enrollment of forty-two in 1928 dropped to twenty-three in 1931 and, after a high point of thirty-five in 1934, was down to eleven by 1938. Demand for entry exceeded this.[227] Tensions flared between the center and local authorities as the Representative Council debated whether funding demands for the orphans' upkeep were inflated.[228] The more overtly critical "Executive Committee of the Economic Agricultural Congress" from Tartus denounced the center as among the various "unnecessary" and "useless" projects that had received lavish state funding.[229] Although this politicization likely contributed to the center's ineffectiveness, the problem was even more fundamental. The clay-limestone soil that made up the center's lands was not very fertile—a fact local *agriculteurs* tried to convey to unheeding mandate administrators before the center's establishment.[230]

The preferential treatment accorded the Bouka establishment incensed Tarmanini in Salamiya. While Bériel complained of Salamiya's distance "from any center," Syrian officials emphasized its excellent terrain—a "second Ghuta"—for various kinds of experiments, especially the dry-farming ones deemed a priority.[231] French reports agreed, noting that the region consisted of a "vast plain of sandy-clay, fertile soil and enjoy[ed] a temperate climate."[232] Despite a more favorable ecological setting, the school struggled to expand on its Ottoman-era infrastructure. In requesting additional funds, Tarmanini insisted that he aspired merely to bring the Salamiya school to the level of Bouka, which "the government of that area commenced building following the occupation and completed upon the most modern standard before three years."[233] His critique underscored the political nature of its support.

After the 1936 Franco-Syrian Treaty of Independence administratively attached Latakia to Syria and expanded the National Bloc's governing powers, the political nature of the Bouka establishment became more explicit.[234] The center's director, Peyrton, concerned about the direction events were taking, wrote to ask about amending the center's covenant with the government. He suggested that the center could start accepting students from Syria, Lebanon, and Jabal al-Druze, as this would provide a way of ensuring agricultural agents "who will have a particular influence in rural milieus . . . receive a French training rather than a nationalist training, in the bad sense of the word." This policy would enable French influence to penetrate the "peasant population with which the mandate has had virtually no contact."[235] He also wanted to ensure the center's "normal development" by putting it perpetually under the High Commission, where it would be "free from any control of local authorities."[236]

The new minister of education in 1937, Abdul Rahman al-Kayali, visited the school and declared that any decision about its status would be left to the local government, adding that he could not foresee allocating funds for the center "because [the Ministry] possesses in its services the necessary schools to train in professions and agriculture."[237] Given the lack of agricultural schools in Syria, lamented by Mustafa al-Shihabi during his brief tenure as minister of education in 1936, al-Kayali's stance suggested a calculated critique of the school's political nature and ecological unsuitability as well as his government's refusal to support institutions seeking to advocate foreign influence more than agricultural knowledge.[238]

The attempt to turn the Ottoman-era Muslimiya model field into an instrument of French influence as the Foch Orphanage also floundered, prospering only when French authorities reluctantly relinquished it to local control. As the model field for Aleppo, Ottoman officials had chosen a 40-hectare site of excellent soil watered by the Quwayq River about 20 kilometers north of the city. After converting it into an Armenian orphanage in 1921, mandate authorities started heavily subsidizing it in August 1925 to the tune of 105,000 francs per year.[239] Operating as a farm school, this subsidy continued until 1928, when constraints on the French budget reduced it to 50,000 francs and the suggestion was made to ask the state of Syria for help. The mandate's Damascus delegate deplored this possibility, explaining, "I must expose to you how much it seems to me dangerous to alienate thus the independence of a purely French oeuvre, which counts among those that has contributed the most to maintaining our influence especially in Aleppo."[240] When additional French funds were not forthcoming, Delhumeau, the director of the orphanage, decided to resign. The Damascus delegate saw this development as a "considerable loss," because "[Delhumeau] made of the orphanage an oeuvre essentially French consecrated to young disinherited Muslims [*sic*]," despite leaving with one month's unauthorized salary when he resigned.[241]

Unable to find a French director to replace Delhumeau, much to the regret of the delegate of Damascus, the assistant delegate in Aleppo proposed for the post none other than the agricultural engineer Agop Oscan, former agricultural director of Aleppo from 1911 to 1915 and employee of the Muslimiya model field from 1904 to 1909.[242] Despite official misgivings about his physical rigor for the job, Oscan appears to have proven himself an adroit manager.[243] By December 1930, even with the reduced credits at his disposal, he had managed to balance the orphanage's budget, settle his predecessor's 9,732 franc debt, and achieve a 24,000 franc balance, which he intended to use for further construction.[244]

Several years later, even Bériel commented on the orphanage's flourishing state since a visit three years earlier. He noted that "the crops looked good, a vegetable and fruit garden had been created, the hen house and stable were clean, the orphans themselves, always in tatters, appeared in a good physical state and resembled little peasants."[245] Despite its distance from the city, it had even cultivated a rather large clientele that would come from Aleppo to buy its poultry and garden products.[246] Bériel attributed this "satisfactory" state of affairs to the cutting of subsidies and the ensuing need for the orphanage to support itself from its own resources.[247] He made no mention of the change in management shortly after the subsidy cut that had brought in a director with local knowledge and previous experience managing the same model field during the Ottoman period.[248] The contributions of local expertise did not figure into his assessment. Mandate officials lost an instrument of French influence, but the ties between Aleppo and its model farm continued.

Another local initiative that sought and failed to obtain a government subsidy underscored the politicization of these institutions. In 1934 the Greek Catholic abbots Gariador and de Lajudie wrote to French authorities to request assistance in creating a "modern" agricultural establishment on the domains of the Convent of ʿAyn al-Juza near Saghbin in the Biqaʿ Valley. Parts of the plan were already in progress. Supported by Risqallah Nour, an *ingénieur agronome* from the French school of Fribourg, the community had established a dairy and also had plans for a school of agriculture, which they suggested could either be built at the dairy or on a more sizable piece of land in ʿAnjar. Antoine Issa Obeid, a student of the Institute Agronomique in France, had already studied this possibility in a report submitted to both the French and Lebanese governments.[249]

Despite aiming to create the intermediate-level farm school preferred by the mandate administration, relying on expertise derived from French institutions, and demonstrating local support, Bounoure and Lagarde demurred.[250] After consulting a large proprietor in the Biqaʿ Valley who was also a Zahle deputy and Greek Orthodox, Bounoure refused to support the farm school, insisting that the convent's location in a well-watered but narrow area surrounded by steep hillsides was unsuitable to a school of agriculture. His primary concern, however, was the abbots' desire to operate the school on the principle of "Direction par des indigènes, contrôlée par des français" (management by locals, inspected by French [officials]), an arrangement that Gariador insisted would have "genuine advantages" but that Bounoure considered a "rather contestable" approach "inspiring a certain defiance."[251] Citing Peyrton's management of Bouka as exemplary of the will and experience necessary to run a farm school, Bounoure claimed that Peyrton had succeeded only because "he concentrates between his hands all the authority," despite overseeing a project that had its own share of contestable results.[252] Partnering with two French-trained Lebanese agricultural experts was insufficient. Local management, even if inspected by French officials, was unworthy of support.

Bounoure's response to another project located in Bsharri, a village perched in the Qadisha valley, further underscored the political nature of these institutions. If support meant furthering the interests of a valuable ally, then Bounoure was happy to oblige. In Bsharri, Rashid, the brother of the Maronite patriarch ʿArida, had paid for a building intended to house an agricultural and technical school. Although the project had been constructed in accordance with plans drawn up by the Lebanese government, three years had passed and, as of 1938, the school still was not being used. ʿArida thought Bounoure's intervention might help and asked him to pressure the Lebanese government to open the school by October. Aware of mandate priorities, he suggested that the director of the School of Arts and Métiers in Beirut could oversee it, but he provided no details about the school's animal, plant, or land resources.[253] Despite ʿArida's at times confrontational stance toward French policies, Bounoure responded with alacrity to his request, characterizing the school as "so useful."[254]

Bsharri's inhabitants, however, raised doubts about the school's usefulness shortly after it began operations. Initially supportive, they found its activities rather different from what they had anticipated. Much to their consternation, they reported that it had become a school of "European dance." Its director was a relative of the patriarch and, despite being a student of the Bouka school, was, they claimed, almost illiterate and had received the post only through clerical intervention. Only ten students had been at the school during the inspector of public instruction's last visit, and they had been specifically brought there for the occasion. If the government was going to spend 3,000 Syrian-Lebanese pounds on such a project, the villagers demanded that it "be entrusted, in the interests of our children, . . . to experienced individuals, secular or clerical."[255] Not only did their complaint highlight concerns about Bouka's inefficacy, but also it affirmed their interest in agricultural training directed by qualified individuals, even if their concept of qualification differed from that privileged under the mandate.

Mandate officials regarded agricultural education not only as a source of French or nationalist propaganda but also as a means for other League of Nations' members to exert their own agendas in rural areas through the guise of agricultural training. In 1930 a group of professors from the American University of Beirut visited the mandate's delegate in Latakia to present their plans for the Institute of Rural Life under the auspices of the

US-based Near East Foundation. The delegate immediately expressed his concerns to the high commissioner about "allowing the interference of a foreign association in the conduct of the government."[256] Bayard Dodge, the president of the university, seemingly aware of the mandate government's suspicions, aimed to reassure the high commissioner. He insisted that the philanthropic project would be modest and "in no way wished to impose purely American ideas." On the contrary, the institute desired to collaborate with the mandate governments.[257] The purpose of the institute was merely "to inspire landowners and tillers of the soil to cooperate in the use of scientific knowledge for the improvement of rural life."[258] In another instance of boundary-work, the language of science became a way to deflect any suggestion of a more political project.[259]

A committee of five professors from the American University of Beirut as well as a director, J. Forrest Crawford, and an assistant agriculture director, Halim Najjar, would run the institute. Dodge stressed their local connections and their US- and French-based training. Crawford had been born and raised in Lebanon and was working on a doctorate in agriculture from the University of California. Najjar had a bachelor's degree from the American University of Beirut and had studied agriculture for two years at the University of California and six months in Montpellier. Echoing Najjar's concerns in the article excerpt republished in *al-Zira*ʿ*a al-Haditha*, Dodge claimed that the project responded to an assessment that "the areas where the work of reconstruction remains the most urgent were agriculture, the sale and dispersal of products of the soil, handicrafts, and the development of public hygiene in the countryside."[260] To this end, they were open to participating in all manner of activities, from starting model farms, experimental fields, and nurseries to helping local governments fight diseases or demonstrating modern methods. "Véritables techniciens," not amateurs, would conduct the work and politics was strictly forbidden.[261]

The competition and implicit critique that this project posed to French interests and governance was a palpable concern among mandate administrators, who took umbrage at the suggestion that the region was still suffering from wartime conditions and was in need of "reconstruction" more than a decade after the war's end.[262] From a political and juridical point of view under the League of Nations, they acknowledged that they could not refuse the operations of a foreign organization so long as it did not engage in "political or religious propaganda." Nonetheless, they queried whether the proposed activities of the Institute of Rural Life could perhaps raise "from a political perspective, a rather grave objection."[263] As its goal seemed to be to "guide, counsel, and assist the populations or the already existing agricultural organizations, . . . it could be indeed inopportune that to the inspection and control of agricultural matters by official bodies of the High Commission and the States [i.e., the mandate statelets], is added a similar activity of a private organization of nationality and foreign tendencies."[264] Bounoure and another French official Reclus concluded that, although a practical farm school was desirable, the Institute of Rural Life as envisioned was "inadmissible."[265]

To counter its potential influence, Bounoure suggested that the technical personnel of the institute should include a French *ingénieur agronome*, the High Commission and States should be regularly consulted, and copies of the reports dispatched to New York should be sent to the High Commission. Dodge had already agreed to the first two conditions. Finally, Bériel was to be consulted on how to guide the institute.[266] Despite Dodge's reassurances and use of the language of science to depoliticize the project's impacts, mandate officials clearly considered it a source of potential foreign influence in rural areas, necessitating careful monitoring and control.

Initially the Institute of Rural Life rented a 72-hectare farm in the Biqaʿ Valley at Talabaya, where, under the direction of Crawford and Najjar, cereals, vegetables, forage crops, and fruit trees were planted and ten cows, two bulls, and four oxen acquired. A young Frenchman named Gabert was appointed head of cultivation, presumably in response to the stipulation to employ a French *ingénieur agronome*. To prevent students from aspiring to improve their social position, the farm focused on educating the children of small property owners with short-term courses (4–6 months) as a way to ensure that they would not seek administrative posts, remaining content with "the simple life of the village." The farm school hosted nine students in 1932 and ten in 1933, and, after the students returned home, the institute continued with extension work in their villages.[267]

By 1934 the farm school had added summer courses intended for primary school teachers in Lebanon, although only fourteen teachers from Transjordan and twenty from Lebanon, of whom only eight were in public instruction, attended. Bounoure suggested boosting these numbers by offering bonuses for taking the courses and applying the material learned. He also commended the school's "concrete and lively instruction, capable of producing very useful results in the rather underdeveloped rural milieu where the farm school recruits its students."[268] Apparently French concerns had been mollified by the application of their conditions.

Although the farm school closed in 1937 because of a lack of funds, a conference held on its premises led to the creation of the Village Welfare Service in 1933. The service aimed to provide an alternative to "political fomentation" for "educated youth" by instilling in them a sense of public service through work with "neglected" rural communities, or, as French reports characterized the venture, they sent "propagandists" to villages in the Biqaᶜ Valley to offer practical agricultural and hygiene advice.[269] Initial summer camps in the Biqaᶜ Valley and ᶜAkkar inspired more camps in Damascus in 1937 and Aleppo in 1938, which received support from the Syrian government, although one report suggested that certain landowners in Aleppo were suspicious of the program as being "not far from communism."[270] American University of Beirut students in Palestine organized a similar effort, and students from Transjordan started negotiations with their government for a camp after visiting the Biqaᶜ Valley.[271] Articles chronicling the activities of the Village Welfare Service appeared in the local press, although the agricultural component of the program proved challenging to realize—agriculture's seasonal cycle was not that of the university (i.e., summer was not the best time for this work), nor was it "sufficiently under the supervision of experts."[272] The students' lack of the necessary expertise led to a revamping focused on lecturing them about the benefits of "rural reconstruction."[273]

Given the unpromising results of conveying new agricultural techniques through a university summer camp, efforts shifted to focus more on year-round extension work. The Farm Management Course offered by the International College at the American University of Beirut sought to train promising students as extension workers. Expressly intended to educate the sons of wealthy landowners who would return to their family estates to conduct practical experiments, the course aimed to provide an alternative to the "impractical" ideas acquired from study abroad that were not conducive to students' "home environment."[274] Meanwhile, the installation of an extension agent who was "well known" in the Damascus area and checked in with farmers throughout the year led to "unprecedented" success for the 1939 summer camp: 2,000 men came to the opening night and 100 illiterate peasants attended the evening classes.[275] Fledging cooperatives in ᶜAbadiya and Damascus grew in popularity. The Institute of Rural Life produced and mailed out thousands of circulars in Arabic on a variety of topics and started offering short courses during the winter to farmers who could pay for them.[276] In January 1940, sixty-four farmers, including men and women from forty-one villages—some having traveled 250 kilometers—attended the institute's fourth annual fruit-growing course. Small farmers rubbed shoulders with Shukri al-Quwwatli, the former finance minister in Damascus and future first president of independent Syria, and Nazik al-ʿAbid Bayhum, cousin of the former president of Syria, both of whom hailed from families with major landholdings in the fertile Ghuta around Damascus.[277] Despite French misgivings about foreign influence, officials seem to have resigned themselves to the institute's activities. Given mandate rules, technically they could not prohibit them. Ultimately, the program's declared intent to emphasize practical training and maintain students as farmers accorded well with mandate officials' stated goals for agricultural education and did not threaten their efforts to discourage more advanced instruction locally.

Despite the dissemination of "scientific" and "modern" agricultural expertise being a frequently proclaimed essential component of imperial and nationalist development plans, under the mandate such projects found little support unless they were French-run or could support themselves from their own, or heavily surveilled foreign, resources. Political considerations carried far more weight than the environmental suitability of a particular area, local demand, or effectiveness.

Conclusion

Increasing the use of new agricultural technologies was a priority for countries seeking to rebuild and/or expand their economies after World War I. Meanwhile, in colonized areas of the world, as demands for independence mounted, such technologies and the training associated with them increasingly represented an alternative means for imperial powers to maintain their influence beyond the end of colonial rule. Yet despite emphasis on agricultural education in programs of imperial and national development, in mandate Syria and Lebanon such projects remained largely absent. In 1933 Valentine Dannevig of the League of Nations asked Robert de Caix, France's delegate to the Permanent Mandates Commission in Geneva, about the state of agricultural education in the region. She noted that "there exist few agricultural schools in this country, which is essentially agricultural."[278] De Caix responded that there was an aversion to "manual labor," which inhibited technical education, to which Dannevig replied that she hoped "it will be possible to bring the population to better understand the importance of agricultural education as a means of improving the economic situation of the country."[279]

As demonstrated in this chapter, in contrast to this patronizing view of matters, there was widespread concern about the state of agricultural education in Syria and Lebanon, especially among a certain class, which was attested to not only by local actors' words and actions but also by mandate authorities themselves. Local technocrats and aspiring agronomists were adamant and vocal about the importance of multiple levels of agricultural education to their plan for the nation's economic development. At the elementary level they agreed with French officials that this education should not encourage villagers to leave their land; however, they also insisted on more advanced levels for those planning to pursue government posts, supervisory positions, or experimentation with new technologies on their own or government-supplied land. This training not only conveyed a certified expertise, providing a means for some to improve their economic and social status and assert their legitimacy as experts in international networks, but also prepared them for positions in the institutions of national state space. Mandate officials disagreed. Seeking to produce a colonial state space and to embed hierarchies of knowledge and dependency between the mandate and the metropole, they tried to limit access to advanced levels of education in scientific agricultural knowledge to the metropole.

Agricultural knowledge and practice were fundamentally products of local environments and conditions. Convincing farmers that changes to them were worth the risks required applying this knowledge to new methods or tools in these environments and demonstrating that they could be effective. Even more so than other forms of technical education, agricultural training based on expertise developed in other contexts or environments was particularly susceptible to misapplication or shortcomings. As a result, French officials' insistence on reinforcing a hierarchy of expertise between the mandate and the metropole, whether through privileging French experts or relying on students sent abroad for advanced study, did little to satisfy local demands for agricultural education. Meanwhile, because agricultural instruction provided new forms of connection between rural and urban spaces, French officials viewed with suspicion other efforts to respond to these demands. Ultimately, this opposition to building local infrastructure for agricultural education and experimentation under the mandate meant that as its days waned, the region's lack of this infrastructure became a pretext for further intervention framed in the discourse of development.

FIVE

OF MICE, SUNN BUGS, DROUGHT, *and* TAXATION

The Pests of Mandate Rural Administration and the Crisis of the 1930s

In the late 1930s, during a session of Syria's Parliament, Hikmat al-Hakim, a doctor and deputy from Idlib, had something to get off his chest about the state of the country's agricultural infrastructure. The Parliament, recently reconstituted after the 1936 treaty negotiations between France's government and the National Bloc, was discussing whether to grant the Agriculture Ministry additional funds to carry out its work. As the debate raged, al-Hakim recounted how some years earlier in Idlib, the Sunn bug pest had been particularly devastating, devouring all the wheat that had otherwise promised an excellent harvest. A technical civil servant had been dispatched to the region to deal with the pest, so al-Hakim decided he would go discuss the matter with him, assuring the civil servant that, as a doctor, he could easily understand the scientific complexities revealed by experiments into the pest's nature.

Much to al-Hakim's astonishment, instead of showing him to "a special, scientific lab containing the necessary tools and implements to study this pest," the civil servant led him to a room empty save for one chair. Taking a cigarette case off the shelf—al-Hakim assured him he did not smoke—the civil servant opened it to reveal some of the Sunn bugs, noting that this was the pest al-Hakim had asked about. Exasperated, al-Hakim said, "I saw them in the field so where is your lab to study this pest from a scientific perspective?" The civil servant replied, "This is all I've got." For al-Hakim this example summed up the state of the Agriculture Department: It was "a name without a body." Before agreeing to additional funding, he wanted to ensure that the ministry had a "comprehensive scientific program" prepared—a program he strongly desired—so that employees had the tools they needed to "revive Syrian agriculture."[1]

Responding to his objections, the minister of national economy, Faʾiz Khuri, made an impassioned plea for the extra funds. Noting that agriculture provided almost half the country's revenue but received only 2% of spending, he agreed that the Agriculture Ministry was weak from years of neglect, which made it difficult to defend, but he insisted that its employees did not deserve the blame. He urged the deputies to "give them a weapon if you want real productive work from them." Following this debate and the minister's rousing speech, the Parliament agreed to the additional credits.[2]

This discussion represented the culmination of a debate that had raged since the beginning of the mandate almost two decades earlier. At its heart was the fact that agricultural taxation was a primary source of state revenue. However, over the course of the mandate, production had fluctuated wildly as a result of various environmental factors. There were the usual culprits, such as drought, locusts, and field mice, but, starting in the mid-1920s, the Sunn bug had emerged to join their ranks, resulting in the destruction of vast swaths of crops. Strategies for mitigating its effects proved elusive, as did investments in measures that local technocrats maintained were necessary to preserve and ultimately bolster agriculture-derived treasury revenue in the face of such fluctuations. These measures included expanded access to irrigation, experiments with new methods and technologies, and "scientific" pest control. However, if aspiring agronomists had found their ambitions thwarted, as discussed in chapter 4, local technocrats' demands for investments that corresponded to agriculture's importance as a source of revenue and the adoption of scientific expertise as the foundation of its administration also went unfulfilled. Not only did the colonial state reject such demands, but despite the decreased production available to tax, it was unrelenting in its insistence on maintaining a set level of revenue for the treasury incommensurate with the diminished returns. By the mid-1930s this insistence led to a full-blown crisis for many farmers and landowners, which in turn provided a key impetus for political mobilization to challenge the colonial state. The anxieties that had driven that resistance continued to simmer beneath this parliamentary debate.

As discussed in chapter 3, a national program to encourage technical and scientific innovation in agricultural administration and practice that would boost production and related industries had been a priority for local technocrats from the earliest days of the postwar Faysal government, representing continuity with technocratic aims in the late Ottoman period. Like Ottoman officials, local technocrats were intent on streamlining revenue extraction from agricultural production and ensuring a stable annual revenue for the treasury, despite the cyclical challenges of drought, bugs, and other pests that led to highly variable annual yields. However, in recognition of the rising costs involved in implementing new agricultural technologies and the methods that they aspired to generalize, their proposals urged further innovations in tax assessment, agrarian finance, and land reform to accommodate these developments and the additional capital they required. These goals went hand in hand: Streamlined extraction and stable revenue depended on state financial support, policies that encouraged investment, and reliance on technical expertise to guide administrative strategies.

French officials also advocated streamlined extraction and a stable treasury revenue, but they were less keen on investment and state support. As demonstrated in chapter 4, their willingness to invest in agricultural infrastructure was largely lacking unless it directly benefited French interests. In agreement with local technocrats, French officials considered an overhaul to the land registration process and the institution of amended taxation policies to be key to achieving these goals. Where feasible, new irrigation projects would reduce the impact of variable rainfall. For local technocrats such measures were the essential foundations of a prosperous national economy. For French officials they were a means to facilitate inflows of surplus metropole capital, meet the exigencies of bloated mandate budgets, and support the prerogatives of a colonial economy. Contrasting proposals for how to achieve these reforms reflected these divergent ends. Whereas local technocrats emphasized cost-effective methods that did not overtax farmers', landowners', and the state's resources, especially given the government's parsimonious approach to investment, such constraints were of less concern to French officials, who focused more on ensuring the legibility of local institutions and practices to French capital and commerce.

As mandate policies designed to draw the region into a French imperial space intersected with and exacerbated existing and new environmental challenges, they produced increasing "unevenness," not only between the space of the mandate and that of the global sphere but also among communities at the local level. Structured to benefit the metropole, mandate policies produced a colonial state space that exacerbated power inequities and created increasingly hierarchical relations between the metropole and the mandate.[3] The linking of the Syrian pound to the French franc, which experienced major fluctuations at critical junctures, had devastating consequences.[4] Insufficient tariff barriers left the mandate states exposed to the "dumping" of agricultural products, especially grain from countries such as the United States and Australia. When harvests were decent, farmers often faced the dilemma of being forced to sell at low market prices, and mandate policies did little to ease their predicament. Meanwhile, when harvests were bad, due to a number of environmental crises from pests to drought, farmers faced escalating tax demands, which left them increasingly indebted and compounded the adverse effects of other policies.[5] Rising tensions erupted in the 1930s as a drought- and pest-stricken countryside also struggled to cope with the global economic crisis of the early 1930s. The mandate regime's inflexibility in the face of these mounting crises provoked an outcry from peasants and landowners alike, creating political opportunity and bolstering nationalist mobilization.

Despite the unevenness produced by these policies, mandate officials justified and promoted them as rational, orderly, just, equitable, and progressive, frequently drawing contrasts with the prior Ottoman administration, which they characterized as unjust, disordered, irrational, antiquated, and inefficient. Those who suffered their consequences, from peasants to elite nationalists, underscored the hypocrisy of these claims, citing the injustices and lack of logic inherent in mandate policies and exposing the incoherence between mandate discourse and practice. Mandate officials and scholars largely dismissed these contestations. To explain away their resistance, they characterized local peasants as backward and accustomed to violence and oppression by unscrupulous landowners.[6] Meanwhile, landowners' losses were the just deserts of a "crumbling social class" whose predicament was "in the natural order of things."[7] Mandate administrators were merely objective arbiters attempting to intervene in this enduring struggle.[8] Such a stark portrayal of difference between mandate and local practice extending back to the Ottoman administration obscured not only the many similarities between French programs of reform and those of local technocrats but also the continuities in technocratic ideals promoted during the mandate and late Ottoman periods. On the other hand, divergent approaches to implementation and the different ends these reforms sought to produce led to disparities in the kinds of resistance these reforms provoked during the mandate versus the Ottoman period.

The mandate's impacts on rural areas led to the consolidation of land into larger holdings, increases in rural to urban migration, and unrest stemming from rural areas, most notably in the 1925–1927 Syrian Revolt, belying a "pro-peasant strategy."[9] As discussed in chapter 4, mandate officials took a "pro-peasant" stance only insofar as they considered it a means to cultivate loyalty to the mandate and away from local powerholders and elites—most proposed projects rarely found realization. On the contrary, these trends suggest that the countryside experienced some of the harsher effects of mandate policies. Scholars who have primarily focused on urban areas have attributed this state of rural and agricultural affairs to "failed" plans "to bolster agricultural income in Syria," low crop yields compared with prewar levels, and environmental conditions that contributed to unrest with little to no explanation of how mandate agricultural policy, particularly its interplay with environmental factors, actively encouraged these developments (or lack thereof).[10]

A closer look at the effects of mandate rule on rural areas suggests that this rural agitation and the increasingly dire straits in which farmers found themselves and the state of agricultural production was a direct consequence of mandate administrative strategies that resisted accounting for the unpredictability of the agricultural cycle and the local environmental, social, and economic conditions. Instead of dismissing such policies as failed, James Ferguson's argument about the "'development' apparatus" provides instructive insights.[11] That is, examining *what* mandate policies produced and *how* they produced it underscores that mandate officials aimed to exploit Syria's soil primarily by making it legible to French capital investment and attempting to stabilize the revenue intake from its production.[12] Given this focus, French administrators resisted adjusting their policies to respond to the exigencies of local conditions or dynamics, perpetuating or creating further inequality.[13] When attempts to extract more revenue elicited resistance or farmers defaulted on their loans, French officials blamed a backward peasantry and oppressive politics-playing notables, not the politics of French empire, to explain why they could not achieve the goals they discursively claimed—a convenient discourse adopted by those seeking to cast agriculture in the region as an object of development during the waning days of the mandate and the aftermath of independence.[14]

Land Reform and "Rationalizing" Taxation: Ottoman Precedents, Mandate Practice, and Local Proposals

From the early years of the mandate, both local technocrats and French officials prioritized land reform as fundamental to ensuring agricultural development and prosperity. Not only did they consider land reform essential to facilitating capital investment in rural land, but they also viewed it as providing the basis for a new taxation system that would account for the more capital-intensive demands of recent agricultural technologies. Despite agreeing on the importance of land reform, they offered contrasting perspectives on its primary aims and the most suitable approach to implementing it. Discussions of the ideology of land reform under the mandate have focused on French officials and their ideas.[15] Such historiographic narratives are silent on the role played by local technocrats in shaping this reform and do not fully account for the degree to which it represented continuity with Ottoman projects.[16]

Mandate officials realized early on that the region was unlikely to become a major market for French agricultural equipment, but the investment possibilities for surplus French capital seemed more promising. French banks were already eager in the late Ottoman period to gain greater access to land investment opportunities in the region. With French officials in charge under the mandate, they finally hoped to rid Ottoman laws of some of the provisions that had favored borrowers while shoring up the Ottoman state's sovereignty over its territory.[17] Land reform also aimed to make tax collection more lucrative; early French estimations suggested a potential windfall in revenue, tripling the intake of the early 1920s.[18] For French officials, streamlining extraction and ensuring the legibility of local landholding arrangements to French banks took priority over creating an environment where cultivators felt secure pursuing more capital-intensive methods.

In contrast, local technocrats, in line with their vision of state economic planning discussed in chapter 3, were more concerned with ensuring that reforms were cost-effective and that they provided a framework supportive of more capital investment in agriculture. Given the greater costs involved in the new technologies and methods they considered fundamental to increasing revenues, they insisted that cultivators needed infrastructure that would support their preliminary investments, including lighter taxes initially until the anticipated increase in production took effect.[19] In addition to financial prudence and government support, their proposals stressed the need to be sensitive to local dynamics, underscoring continuities between their plans and practices of the Ottoman past that stretched back to the Tanzimat era.

For the first years of the mandate the state continued to tax agricultural production using the tithe that had been in effect during the Ottoman period, technically assessed at 12.5% of the gross harvest.[20] Like Ottoman bureaucrats before them, French officials and local technocrats criticized this system. It could mean leaving harvested crops exposed on the threshing floor to theft, fire, or adverse weather. Threshing could be delayed if tithe collectors arrived late, slowing the crops' arrival at market and the chance to sell them at higher prices.[21] Whether collected by government officials or by tax farming, one French report claimed that "the methods of estimation and collection" incurred "abuses and odious vexations for the farmer."[22] Mustafa al-Shihabi, the director of state lands, also acknowledged "mistakes" made by estimation committees and noted that the system could lead to onerous assessments during a drought, which made higher market prices, the basis for estimating the tax, more likely. As a result, peasants could be assessed more tax in a drought year despite lower yields.[23] Furthermore, villages owned by peasants tended to bear a disproportionate tax burden compared with those owned by large influential landlords, and even in peasant-owned villages there were disparities in how the tithe was divided between poorer and wealthier members of the community.[24]

Although local technocrats agreed that the tithe collection process posed issues, according to al-Shihabi, they considered the "greatest vexation to agriculture and biggest challenge to its development" to be the tithe's assessment on gross yields, which failed to accommodate the investments required by scientific agriculture.[25] This method discouraged investments because it took a greater percentage of the net profits of those

FIGURE 20. "Threshing floor in Syria," between 1898 and 1946. Source: G. Eric and Edith Matson Photograph Collection, Library of Congress, https://www.loc.gov/item/2019698573/.

cultivators who chose to invest in "modern tools," better animal stock, and fertilizer than of those who continued to use their current tools and methods. "It is no surprise then," he concluded, "if the masters of agriculture [*irbab al-ziraʿa*] prefer to follow the old ways in exploiting their land and say that the tithe [*aʿshar*] is among the greatest reasons that prevent the progress of agriculture and its improvement in our country."[26] ʿUmar Tarmanini, editor of *al-Ziraʿa al-Haditha* and a teacher at the Salamiya agricultural school, agreed, even citing precedent in Islamic law (*al-sharʿ al-sharif*), which he claimed differentiated between the tithe on rain-fed lands, assessed at 10%, and that on lands requiring additional effort and expense, assessed at 5%. Because "agriculture today is not possible to do right without implements . . . and expenses," the government should proceed in this "spirit" and "[save] the cultivators from hardship."[27] He suggested a land tax based on rent or a tax on net yields that did not exceed 15%. If farmers had annual revenues that were less than 15 Ottoman gold liras, they should not be taxed or, barring that, their seeds and 20–30% of their yields should be exempted to allow for their expenses.[28] One of the main benefits of a land tax (*al-dariba al-ᶜaqariya*) was its basis in rent, or net revenue, which ensured that the cultivator would retain invested capital.[29]

At the same time, local technocrats tempered their criticisms with concerns about environmental factors and the general heaviness of the tax burden on a sector that was becoming more capital intensive across the globe and needed government encouragement to stay competitive. Yusuf ᶜAtallah, director of economic affairs in Damascus, emphasized flexibility, insisting that, given agricultural yields' susceptibility to natural factors, taxes could not be assessed and collected in one standard way. Instead of roundly condemning the current system's injustice and inequality, he insisted that estimation committees tried to adjudicate a just tithe each year. Although it might be inconvenient for the treasury, expecting the tithe to increase each year exposed the cultivator to "injustice and mistreatment."[30] Tax policies needed to be sensitive to these environmental constraints.

Despite such concerns, French officials were eager, until a land tax could be implemented, to find an alternative to the tithe that would establish a fixed annual revenue for the treasury. Drawing on French experience in Morocco, early reports proposed the *tertib*, a tax on revenue, but eventually officials settled on a version of the tithe, dubbed the *terbiᶜ*.[31] Established in May 1925, this fixed tax was an average of the tithes for the years 1921–1924.[32] The law stated that the *terbiᶜ* expounded on the Ottoman law of 22 June 1905, responded to "cultivator complaints," represented an adjustment based on "modern methods" that preserved "the rights of the treasury and cultivators," protected cultivators from "oppression and dishonesty," and made collection more efficient. It also referred to an "important modification" that was under study but would not be achievable for at least a year—a gross underestimation, as will be discussed later.[33]

Local agronomists were skeptical of the *terbiᶜ*. As discussed in chapter 1, the Ottoman government had tried on several occasions to impose a fixed tax but had quickly rescinded it in each instance because of the resistance it provoked. Muhammad ᶜAli al-Jazaʾiri, inspector for the Agriculture Ministry, reminded *al-Ziraᶜa al-Haditha*'s readers of the unsuccessful attempt by the governor of Syria, Hamdi Pasha, to apply the *tahmis*, a fixed tax based on an average of the previous five years, in 1885.[34] Al-Shihabi was more scathing, calling the *terbiᶜ* unjust when regions received less rain and "corrupt" (*fasid*) because it maintained the exaction on gross returns and replicated the existing inequalities in the previous system—that is, villages protected by powerful landowners retained their privilege over other villages. It was "shameful" (*min al-ʿar*), he maintained, to continue using a system based on the tithe when "all civilized governments" had renounced it.[35]

Other technocrats willing to contemplate the possibility of a set *terbiʿ* had suggestions for moderating its effects. Tawfiq al-Ahdab, director of the Salamiya agricultural school, initially proposed decreasing it to 10% on gross harvests but revised this, suggesting the base should be, like the Ottoman-era *tahmis*, an average of five years that excluded the war years (i.e., 1911, 1912, 1913, 1920, and 1921). The revised tax would replace both the tithe and the property tax and remain in effect for only ten years, primarily to reduce expense.[36] Until the government ensured security, access to plenty of agrarian credit, and "effective measures to prevent the cultivator from selling his land . . . when he ends up in extreme financial distress," the "new tithe regime" was unrealistic.[37] Ultimately, if the government truly wanted agriculture to progress, it needed to reduce cultivators' tax burden and waive land registration fees.[38]

To bolster their arguments for greater leniency and support, local agronomists cited alternative measures that other countries had taken to ease the tax burden on farmers and assist them in accessing capital. For instance, they claimed that in France smaller farmers with incomes of less than 2,000 francs were not required to pay taxes, those making more than 4,000 francs paid only half the codified tax, and the "masters of large resources" were charged only 8% interest on their net profit. Yet even with such concessions, al-Ahdab marveled, farmers still used agricultural journals and their government representatives to complain about high taxes![39] Farmers in Switzerland, meanwhile, had recourse to cooperative societies that would loan them money at no more than 4% interest.[40] In Lebanon the journal of the Order of Agricultural Engineers, *The Agricultural Life*, noted how Turkey had shifted primarily to a consumption tax with most agricultural taxes abolished as of 1932.[41]

As agronomists and technocrats debated the pros and cons of the *terbiʿ* and suggested alternatives, the work of the mandate's cadastral service, which would establish the basis for the land tax envisioned to eventually replace the *terbiʿ*, was already under way. Early French reports indicated that French officials saw this work not as a break from Ottoman initiatives but as a continuation of them. Immediately after occupying Syria in 1920, they portrayed this "special service" as "resum[ing]" the Ottoman "reform projects of the registration of lands," implementing a system that "respect[ed] the fundamental principles" of "Ottoman legislation." They claimed that legislative, administrative, and technical actions would ensure "modern" property registration, making it legible to new land legislation and providing a "better basis" for tax collection.[42] The director appointed to lead the service, Camille Duraffourd, highlighted in his application for the position his expertise in Ottoman approaches to the cadastre, acquired during a *stage* in Istanbul at the General Direction of the Cadastre in late 1919, insisting that it made him exceptionally qualified for the job.[43] This experience, he declared, "permitted [him] to expand [his] knowledge relative to this service in general, and more particularly to that which concerns the property regime in Turkey and its relative laws."[44] Those who supported his application clearly considered such knowledge valuable, citing in his favor his "thorough knowledge of the Ottoman legislation concerning questions of property, the laws and rules of the Ottoman cadastre, [and] the geographic services of the Ottoman army."[45]

Two processes were fundamental to the cadastral service's work: *remembrement*, which involved consolidating small landholdings; and *démembrement*, which consisted of dividing state land, large estates, "collective property" (presumably *mushaᶜ*), and "undivided domain" into plots for small property owners. Edouard Achard, the French agricultural counselor, recommended prioritizing the division of collective properties and undivided domains, as he deemed this approach more cost-effective.[46] It was also less likely to antagonize large landowners, whose existence Achard deemed necessary despite idealizing small property owners.[47] Official reports maintained this small property ideal as essential to the region's development (*mise en valeur*) because it would become the basis for an "equitable" tax, exemplifying the "progress" they claimed to bring.[48] Yet despite posing as exemplars of these practices of "progress," *remembrement* was not much more advanced in the metropole. In fact, the geographer Albert Demangeon, writing in 1920, the year of the cadastral service's establishment, insisted that mechanized farming (motoculture) had not fulfilled its promise in France because of the lack of widespread *remembrement*.[49] It would take the World War II–era Vichy regime to realize its broader implementation.[50]

The practice of *mushaᶜ*, land held in common by villagers and redistributed periodically, was a particular object of criticism from both local and

French officials, even though it proved remarkably resilient to technocratic efforts to dismantle it. In critiques that echoed those of the Ottoman officials discussed in chapter 1, French reports denounced *musha*ʿ as inimical to "the progress of agriculture" and spoke of "the hindrance caused by this mode of tenure to agricultural credit" and "to the free exercise of right of property."[51] Local technocrats claimed that *musha*ʿ resulted in agriculture's underdevelopment and "paralysis" and led "the peasant to inertia and idleness."[52] ʿAtallah noted how "Prussia, Westphalia, Luxembourg, Alsace, Bavaria, Switzerland, Hungary, France, and others" had reformed comparable land-tenure arrangements, bypassing "special interests in order to secure the general welfare."[53] Some of the historiography has replicated this technocratic discourse, dismissing and dehistoricizing the practice as "unproductive," "difficult to exploit," or "traditional."[54] Such dismissals obscure for whom this form of tenure was so problematic. For cultivators, especially those working rain-fed lands more conducive to monoculture yields that could vary substantially from year to year, *musha*ʿ afforded protection from powerful large landowners and environmental misfortunes.[55] On the other hand, for sources of agrarian capital, especially foreign banks, *musha*ʿ was a major headache; it was for their loans and coffers that this practice proved particularly "unproductive" and "difficult to exploit."

In an effort to pave the way for French banks to freely invest in lands under the mandate, one of the first laws passed by the High Commission established "a modern mortgage regime."[56] Issued on 20 March 1922, the law essentially amended the series of Ottoman laws passed in February and March 1913 to suit the demands of French banks. As one French report explained, the new law "respect[ed] the fundamental principles that are at the base of the Ottoman legislation," merely adding "order and cohesion that it previously lacked."[57] In practice, this "order and cohesion" primarily strengthened the hand of creditors and allowed for the creation of mortgage banks.[58]

As French officials sought to satisfy the demands of metropole capital, local technocrats also embraced land reform, but they warned against pursuing approaches that were too expensive, exposed farmers to greater risk, or failed to account for local dynamics. In making their case, they stressed continuities with and the accomplishments of Ottoman precedents while also drawing on examples from around the globe. Al-Jazaʾiri hailed the Tanzimat reforms for enacting measures to alleviate some forms of exploitation that caused small property owners to sell their land.[59] In a series of articles the lawyer Ibrahim Shishakli compared the 1875 French Rural Code and its precedents in Roman law with the 1858 Ottoman land law's basis in Islamic law. He concluded that, after some initial issues created by the 1858 law, the Ottoman laws of 1913 had essentially removed distinctions between what usufruct rights holders in *miri* land and owners of private lands (*mulk*) could do with their property. As he saw it, the main problem with the original 1858 law was the power it invested in the land office official (*tamlik mamur*), whose permission had to be obtained for any modifications. The 1913 amendments allowed usufruct rights holders greater freedom in managing their property. The kinds of taxes they paid remained the only effective difference between them and owners of private property.[60]

Alongside these Ottoman precedents, local technocrats highlighted projects undertaken by other states to break up large landownership or lands held in common to create small property owners. The 1891 Purchase of Land Act in Ireland, Stolypin's efforts to break up communally held property in Russia between 1906 and 1912, and efforts in the United States and Australia to limit the amount of land farmers could purchase represented reforms that secured "justice and freedom" and led to agricultural "progress."[61] They looked to Germany, Bosnia, Romania, Bulgaria, Belgium, and France as examples of countries where land had become successfully concentrated in the hands of middling or peasant farmers.[62] Meanwhile, Syria was not the only country still contending with vast lands held by a few; al-Shihabi noted that England, Ireland, and Scotland had a similar problem.[63]

Local technocrats eyed state lands and the property of large landowners as prime targets for their land reform program but expressed a number of caveats about how such a program should proceed. Al-Shihabi, for one, distinguished between large landowners who had acquired their land "by right" and those who had not. It was the lands of the latter to which the questions should apply of whether to transfer those lands to someone who would improve their exploitation and how that transfer might occur.[64] In addition, as the government facilitated small property creation, it needed to improve protections for newly created landowners. Both Tarmanini and al-Jazaʾiri supported legislation like the five-*feddan* law in Egypt, which would prevent the sale or seizure of lots smaller than 100 *donums*, or 250 *donums* if the land was rain-fed.[65] Al-Jazaʾiri also advocated legal measures that would protect the peasant and enable him "to defend . . . his interests from landowners as a peer from a peer," citing "a well-known proverb of the Arabs" that "the nation does not rise unless her peasant is uplifted."[66] Anxious to minimize disruptions to peasant-landlord relations while also creating small property owners and defending their interests, local technocrats underscored the need to pursue reforms, as various European governments had done, that were in line "with the disposition of the people and spirit of [the government's] laws."[67] Inspiration could be drawn from the past and other countries, certainly not just France, but ultimately Syria had to pursue its own unique path.

ʿAtallah expressed doubt about the government's capacity to undertake a "true cadastre" because of the major expenditure and long timeframe involved, proposing instead an approach that combined elements of the Torrens methods with Ottoman precedents. He noted that the Torrens method, a form of land registration first used in Australia in 1858 that relied on transfer of title, had been adopted by a number of countries after adapting it to "their traditions, laws, and economies."[68] Because the current system, in his opinion, was unsustainable and needed a replacement that responded to farmers' desires, he proposed the Torrens system as an alternative to estimation and tax farming that would still ensure a just and stable revenue source for the treasury.[69]

ʿAtallah's plan centered on fulfilling three basic conditions. First, a law would require all landowners (*irbab al-ʿaqarat*) to partition (*ifraz*) their shares by an appointed time. Second, by the end of this period, if someone refused to partition his or her share, "then his property was considered at large [*mahlulan*] and the government received and transferred it . . . to the interests of the owner without consulting him." Finally, scattered shares needed to be exchanged with a neighbor or transferred or ceded (*faragh*), and if the owner could not do this in the allotted time, then the government would do it for him or her.[70] ʿAtallah acknowledged that Germany and Australia had faced opposition in the beginning when carrying out similar reforms, but, like those "sophisticated countries" (*al-bilad al-raqiya*), "in our country" it could also be made compulsory given the benefits.[71]

After establishing these conditions, the state would set up offices of land registration that included agricultural and public works engineers in the center of each county (*liwa*). The office's administrators would register names alphabetically based on testimony, presentation of an identity card (*tadhkirat nufus*), and papers establishing the ownership of a sorted piece of land. Each owner would then submit an application requesting a technical commission to survey and estimate his land. Fees would be collected, and income credited to the treasury against the costs involved. The committee, composed of an agricultural engineer and a public works engineer (and some servants to carry their tools), would survey the land, create a map, and study the lot to estimate its price and productive strength. Notably, ʿAtallah did not associate this map-drawing process with foreign methods but rather compared it with the methods used by Sultan Abdulhamid II to map his property in Syria. The result would be checked and registered in the central office and a copy registered like an identity card. This copy would have the same value as the security, and the owner would have absolute right to mortgage a portion of his or her property, endorsing the copy on the back like a promissory note (*havale*).[72]

For ʿAtallah, the benefits of registering land according to this method lay not just in the taxation system it would enable but also in the detailed knowledge it would provide about each piece of land: its climate, the typical crops planted, new crops that might be introduced, harvest yields, and "the aptitude of its residents and their degree of progress."[73] He suggested dividing land into twelve different categories and, after announcing them to villages, imposing a fixed tax (*rusum maktuʿa*) that, due to production's susceptibility to natural factors, would not exceed five years. At the end of that period, another fixed tax (*rasm thabit*) would be established based on the land's value.[74] Al-Jazaʾiri concurred that a fixed tax based on such a classification system was "the most just," but he stressed the necessity of taking into account even more fully the amount of rain a parcel of land received.[75]

Like French officials, local technocrats favored the creation of small property owners using a map-based registration system as a means to both facilitate inflows of capital and encourage initiative. They agreed that stopgap measures were necessary until a new land tax based on the assessed land's value could be put into effect. However, in contrast to French officials, they expressed far more concern about the effects of this transition on both the state treasury and cultivators' finances if costs were not carefully managed, environmental factors were not given due consideration, and the process became drawn out. And drawn out it was. In 1929 officials first applied the land tax in the *sanjak* of Alexandretta to forty villages; in 1930 they expanded it to ten more. Although the land tax was "instituted" in Syria in 1927, the details are murky as to when and how widely its collection first started.[76] Assessing this rental value on which the land tax was based was complicated because of usufruct rights or tenant farming arrangements and because of annual fluctuations in agricultural income resulting from harvest size and changing crop prices.[77] A new land law that further addressed issues of land registration and mortgage credit would not be passed until 12 November 1930.[78] By 1933—already three years beyond the five-year limit proposed by ʿAtallah once the fixed tax came into effect—only 1,399,464 hectares had been surveyed and registered.[79]

This delay meant that for most of the interwar period many farmers continued to be subject to the *terbiʿ* with all its attendant issues. Despite claiming to protect farmers from "oppression and dishonesty," the *terbiʿ* perpetuated all the inequities of the original tithe distribution and the tax on gross revenue.[80] It also made few allowances for environmental fluctuations, allowing crop re-estimation only if losses amounted to a reduction of 25% or more because of "exceptional circumstances, such as partial or complete destruction of village crops by floods, fire by an unknown hand, locusts, war or revolt."[81] Relatively good harvests and high market prices marked the period from 1921 to 1924; after 1924 the effects of drought and pests intensified, devastating many farmers year after year.[82]

As for market prices, in Syria, the impact of the *terbiʿ* was substantially exacerbated by the 1926 fall of the French franc, which was pegged to Syria's pound.[83] In response, mandate administrators created the Syrian gold pound, which became the currency basis for taxation. In 1926 they converted the base of the *terbiʿ* from the Syrian paper pound to the gold pound using a rate of exchange of 2.7 to 1. As a result, the four-year assessment was equal to the real money burden of those years despite the paper pound's substantial depreciation.[84] This adjustment increased the *terbiʿ* by 97%, even though it should only have increased 25% if assessed on the basis of the unstable Syrian paper pound. This exaggerated rate remained in effect until 1933.[85] In contrast, the Lebanese Parliament managed to overrule the government and set the rate of exchange at 5 to 1, which substantially reduced the relative tax burden on cultivators in Greater Lebanon.[86]

A French report published several years after the *terbiʿ* had been in effect insisted that farmers welcomed this system because it freed them from the abuses involved in collecting the tithe and encouraged initiative—they could expand the areas they farmed, take better care of their crops to increase yields, or plant more profitable crops. The tax was fixed, so anything cultivators produced that exceeded it was theirs to keep![87] Such naïve and condescending expectations suggested willful ignorance. Many farmers likely did not have access to additional land, nor was switching to more lucrative crops always a feasible proposition for both subsistence and ecological reasons. Initiative was unlikely to compensate for lack of rain or the devastation of locusts. Rather, the tax's primary purpose was to streamline collection and ensure a steady annual revenue to the treasury.[88] As illustrated in the next section, insisting on a set revenue from a source still very much subject to environmental, political, and economic instability meant that the ensuing years would lead to accumulating devastation for cultivators and the agricultural production both they and the treasury depended on.

The "Fruits" of Mandate Rule: Revolt, Tenacious Pests, and Accumulating Debt

As the late 1920s approached, almost a decade after the end of World War I, technocrats and farmers alike increasingly expressed frustration with the state of the region's agriculture. Agricultural production is cyclical, its rhythms determined by the succession of seasons and the unique combination of challenges that each of those cycles brings. Over the course of the 1920s, farmers faced a series of accumulating disruptions to these cycles. Some were the usual challenges—uneven or insufficient rainfall, harsh dry winds, locusts, voles—but some were new. These ranged from the aftereffects of World War I, which included decreases in local labor availability, to the global phenomenon of dumping by countries that had overproduced during the war, the novel Sunn bug pest, the new exigencies of the mandate's tax regime, and the 1925–1927 Great Syrian Revolt that started in the Hawran and spread through much of the region. In contrast to instances of resistance during the Ottoman period, the revolt did not remain a localized event to protest new tax policies or encroachments on local autonomy or elite exactions; it was an anticolonial uprising that mobilized a substantial cross-section of society in common cause to overthrow mandate rule.[89] Its suppression was brutal and highly disruptive to the agricultural cycles that ensured both sustenance and revenue. As the revolt's reverberations echoed through the countryside, the region's agronomists focused their efforts on trying to combat the animals that also ravaged it. Meanwhile, mandate officials doubled down not only on suppressing the revolt but also on implementing fiscal policies. The accumulating effects of both struggles over the course of multiple agricultural cycles meant that the plight of many cultivators throughout the region grew increasingly bleak by the end of the 1920s.

In 1924 harvests in rain-fed areas east and south of Aleppo, around Hama, and in parts of the Jabal Druze suffered from drought, locusts, voles, and the Sunn bug. The first three were familiar concerns, but the Sunn bug, according to one French report, was "from the region of Baghdad" and "unknown."[90] In contrast, local agronomists noted that the Sunn bug was not in fact unknown; it had destroyed crops in the region in 1911, a drier, hotter year when it had affected most of the same villages as in 1924. One report suggested that the bug's impact had been less severe and that between 1911 and 1924 it had rarely appeared. Some farmers maintained that the insect had inflicted similar damage in the past, but such incidents were once-a-decade occurrences.[91] This time the Sunn bug appeared northwest of Hama and southwest of Maʿarat al-Nuʿman on 650 km² (65,000 hectares, or 800,000 *donums*), leading to a loss of about 182,500 gold Ottoman liras.[92] The situation in Hama was so bad that farmers could not pay their taxes. Loans from the Agricultural Bank were requested to ensure seeds for the next season and to prevent cultivators from deserting their villages even as, in some eastern areas, the insect was already causing villagers to migrate west.[93]

Mandate officials seized on the moment to promote their preferred crop, suggesting that farmers around Aleppo interplant their cereals with cotton, which the Sunn bug did not attack. They also welcomed westward migration as a way to provide additional labor for cotton-cultivating areas. Their efforts to address the Sunn bug itself focused on destroying its eggs and collecting samples and sending them to Algeria, Tunisia, France, and Iraq to study the insect's life cycle.[94] In the interim, local agronomists undertook their own studies of the insect's life cycle and gathered information based on experiences and observations from farmers and villagers in affected areas to offer advice before the next harvest.[95] One village had eradicated the insect by flooding fields. If such a tactic was not possible, the agronomist Hilmi Barudi recommended burning any stubble in the fields or plowing the fallow in an effort to eradicate grasses that might sustain the pests. Barudi proposed legumes, such as lentils, grass peas, different vetch varieties, and fava beans—notably, unlike cotton, food crops for

FIGURE 21. A farmer feeds his crops to a ravenous dog representing "taxes and the tithe." Source: *al-Zira'a al-Haditha* (*Modern Agriculture*), January 1925, Bibliothèque Orientale.

people or animals—as potential substitutes, but he acknowledged that local farmers could not easily replace wheat and barley. Until the discovery of more effective treatments, he suggested that farmers attempt a strategy that some had found at least partly successful the previous year: planting a wheat variety that matured early, such as *himariya* (the wheat commonly grown in the Homs and Hama areas), and harvesting the wheat before it fully matured.[96]

As central Syria grappled with Sunn bugs, in Jabal al-Druze the situation deteriorated even further because of "extraordinary drought." There was a disastrous 25–100% loss of grain crops in 1925—ten villages in the north had "*nulle*" harvests. Peasants deserted their villages; in an area where there had been sixty families, only five remained. Summer crops did slightly better, but dry pastures led to a 15–40% loss in animals.[97] Simultaneously, around Aleppo and Hama, Sunn bugs struck again in force, attacking a zone of 1,200 km^2 (120,000 hectares).[98] They increased their spread to the east and north, but the damage was somewhat mitigated by precautions taken in response to suggestions from the Agriculture Office based on Barudi's studies.[99] Meanwhile, in the Ghuta of Damascus, a frost in early April devastated the city's orchard crops.[100] As the situation escalated, the editor of *al-Zira^ca al-Haditha* accused the government of neglecting peasants and demanding more than they could pay, insisting on their right to complain.[101]

Opposition to French policies, particularly those intended to facilitate inflows of French capital through creating small property ownership, also mounted. In Jabal al-Druze the French governor of the statelet, Captain Gabriel Carbillet, had primed discontent in part because of his attempt to create small private property by making villagers plant a million grapevines on land they first cleared of stones, from which they built fences around the vine-planted fields. These fields were then deemed their personal property (*un titre de possession définitive*). A rather understated mandate report to the League of Nations acknowledged that this project, not to mention forcing the peasants to help build roads and waterworks through *corvée* labor instead of paying taxes, "could have caused some discontent among the masses."[102] Meanwhile, Druze shaykhs were angered by attempts to undermine their authority. Instead of driving a wedge between different groups in Druze society, these measures were opposed by most Druze peasants and shaykhs, and, when the High Commission refused to even listen to their grievances, they revolted during the summer of 1925.[103]

Resistance to such policies was not limited to the Jabal al-Druze. Greater Lebanon, the state of Syria, and the Alawite State had all promulgated laws in the late spring and early summer of 1925 that modified the 18 February 1328 Ottoman law regarding property registration in order to allow for surveys that would determine the boundaries and surface areas of each piece of land to be registered.[104] In Greater Lebanon Duraffourd noted that many villagers refused to show up to demonstrate their claims.[105] As the revolt quickly spread from the Hawran to Damascus and areas farther north, in those areas where the work of the cadastre was under way, discontent notably manifested in the destruction of cadastral records.[106] By October, the revolt had reached Hama, where rebels attacked and burned the archives of the Sérail, which contained the offices of both the cadastral registry and taxation.[107] In November another group murdered three French cadastral workers and burned the archives of the regional cadastral office in the town of Kusayr near Homs.[108] The British consul attributed the action to landlords upset by "a cadastral restriction of their land usurpations."[109] Rebel operations reached Hasbaya and Rashaya on the southwestern slopes of the Anti-Lebanon Mountains in Greater Lebanon by November.[110] In January 1926 an election boycott in Aleppo led to arrests and protests.[111] In each instance the French response was ruthless, involving machine gun fire and aerial shelling in most cases.[112]

The expanding revolt and the destruction that accompanied it paralleled farmers' ongoing struggles with Sunn bugs, voles, locusts, and drought. By 1926 Sunn bugs had spread to the Biqaᶜ Valley and southern Lebanon, and that, along with other weather conditions, including drought, reduced harvests in some areas by 20–50%.[113] In Hama farmers fearing the Sunn bugs' return switched almost entirely to barley.[114] At the Salamiya agricultural school, local agronomists had deduced that Sunn bugs inflicted the most damage on wheat because their emergence from overwintering coincided with wheat's ripening. Because barley ripened earlier, it was less susceptible.[115] Wheat, however, was more remunerative, so local agronomists sought a variety that matured at the same time as barley, meanwhile urging

FIGURE 22. An aerial view of the village of Kusayr and surrounding farmland. Such images assisted in mapping the cadastre (Sarrage, *Nécessité*, 40), 1930. Source: Institut Français du Proche-Orient, Armée du Levant, https://hal.archives-ouvertes.fr/hal-02510824v1.

farmers to switch out wheat and divide and plant their fields according to the following rotation: barley; sorghum and chickpeas; and melons and legumes.[116] Whether based on this advice or farmers' own observations, by 1927 cultivation had substantially shifted to barley in areas that had been hard hit by Sunn bugs in 1926.[117]

Suggestions for grappling with the bugs involved not only observations obtained from the school's experiments but also those made by farmers throughout the region, all of which *al-Zira'a al-Haditha* conveyed to its readership. In May 1927, following two years of experiments with wheats from "hot lands," al-Ahdab announced to the journal's readers that the wheat variety *hindiye* from the Algerian Agricultural Institute proved promising.[118] This wheat reached maturity by 23 May, and Sunn bugs did their worst damage starting in early June.[119] However, farmers with lands near the Sunn bugs' overwintering sites needed to be cautious about planting early-maturing wheat because the emerging bugs could wreak havoc between 20 March and 10 April before they moved on to other fields. In these areas the journal reported that farmers found planting late-maturing wheat helpful, although this option needed soil that retained moisture well. In addition to detailing the results from the school's experiments, al-Ahdab encouraged readers to undertake their own trials in Sunn-bug-afflicted areas.[120]

By the end of 1927, five years of relentless attacks by Sunn bugs led to poverty among both peasants and landowners in Hama, where insufficient loans from the Agricultural Bank prevented them from fully sowing their land. Many landowners stopped planting not only wheat but also barley and switched to sorghum, broad beans, and lentils.[121] Even as farmers around Hama found ways to cope with Sunn bugs, the bugs moved on, ravaging wheat fields to the northwest in Idlib, Maara, and Harim.[122] In 1928 they spread to the northeast, appearing for the first time east of Aleppo in Bab, Jarablus, and Azaz.[123] Voles were also on the move from field to field; their presence intensified in areas near Aleppo because the Quwayq River flowing through the region had not recently submerged fields as in past years. The rodents, already a problem west of the ʿAsi River in 1924, had multiplied, spreading to Idlib, Harim, Azaz, and Jabal Samaan, where they appeared in early February 1927 in "deep red lands."[124]

Just as these animals spread easily from field to field, with no regard for mandate statelets' political boundaries—suggesting the mandate's fragmented and uncoordinated administration may have facilitated their

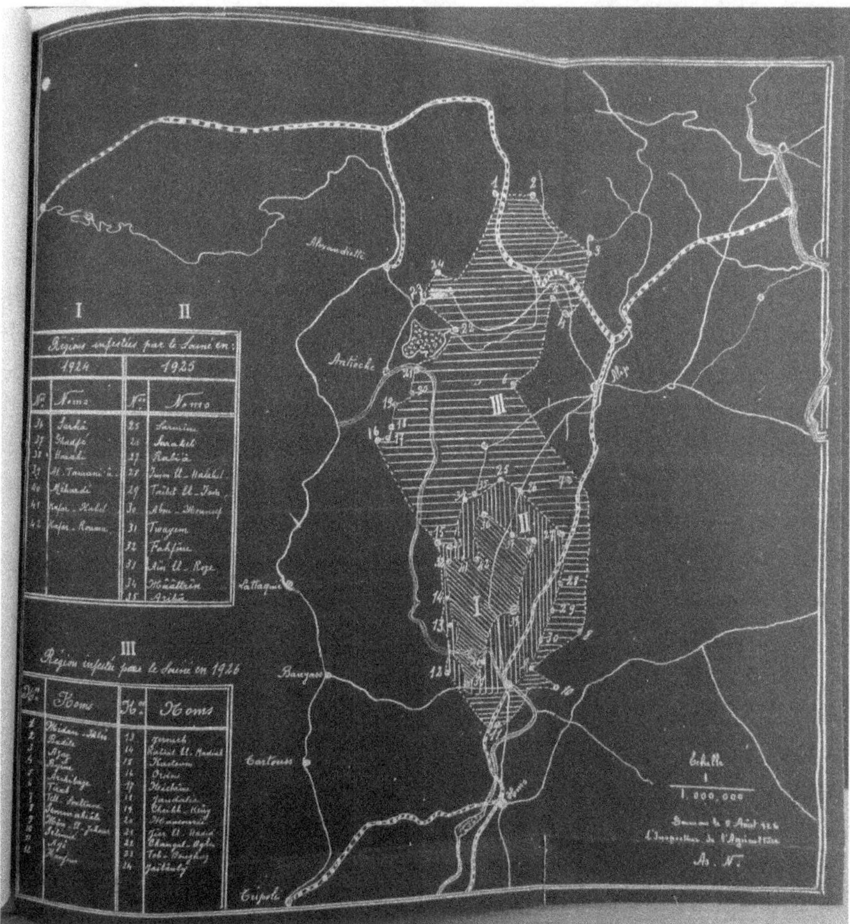

FIGURE 23. Map of Sunn bug spread from 1924 to 1926 sent to the League of Nations. Reproduced with permission of the United Nations Archives at Geneva, R28/1/4284, map accompanying report by E. Achard titled "Le 'Souné' dans l'état de Syrie: Campagne 1926," 15 September 1926.

spread—locusts were also undeterred by political borders.[125] Albeit a well-known insect in the region, thwarting its effects on crops called for coordination across international borders. Before, such efforts had primarily occurred within the confines of Ottoman imperial boundaries; the agricultural inspector discussed in chapter 2 who had moved with ease to Aleppo after dealing with locusts in Urfa would have had to cross an international border. Local agronomists held an international locust conference and established the International Locust School to determine how best to combat the insects, and the Agriculture Ministry paid students from the Salamiya school, in the absence of sufficient "technical" employees, to travel to areas from Syria's southern border to Dayr al-Zor to participate in the fight.[126]

French officials encouraged the use of chemical insecticides and rodenticides, which had become a major industry in France by the interwar period.[127] Among those they imported and/or distributed were Paris green, sodium arsenate, pyrethrum, calcium cyanide, and arsenic acid. In some cases, such as with the arsenic acid, they provided the chemicals to villagers for free.[128] But farmers were skeptical of using sodium arsenate and copper arsenate on voles—the rodents just moved to other fields. Besides some villagers feared the effects of arsenic on their own animals.[129]

Local farmers and agronomists tended to prioritize other, less poisonous strategies. One approach focused on collecting and disposing of the rodents to prevent their spread. In Jabal Samaan they devised a trap that, according to one report, was "very ingenious and rustic," a model of which was sent to Damascus.[130] Muhammad Hibrawi, the agricultural employee for Jabal Samaan, found blowing red pepper–laced smoke into their dens most effective, noting that a skilled worker could collect fifty to sixty voles a day. He also urged farmers not to kill the voles' natural predators, namely, snakes, ticks, and large birds.[131] As for the Sunn bug, collecting the adult insects, protecting their predators, such as partridges and quail, and intense cold were among the most successful means of control.[132] Such methods eschewed the synthetic chemicals imported from France and relied on natural predators and physical labor to effect control, although the additional labor required was not particularly amenable to farmers because it was needed at the same time as the barley harvest and the sowing of summer crops. Some experiments using sodium arsenate and gas also apparently worked, although one French report warned that it was "not conscientious to deploy . . . planes of asphyxiating gas on a territory densely populated with animals, and of an expanse such that the costs of destruction would not equal the property value of lands to be liberated."[133]

Complaints escalated as the decade wore on, with many suggesting that the challenges facing agriculture had become uniquely severe under the mandate. In Hama, when rains returned in 1927 after successive dismal harvests, farmers declared them to be "gold pounds sent by the sky, not of Napoleons, but of Ottoman pounds," because, according to one intelligence report, they were convinced that "as long as the French were in

Syria, harvests would be bad."[134] Comparing measures taken to combat locusts in Algeria with those afforded to farmers in Syria, *al-Ziraʿa al-Haditha* highlighted local efforts and decried the mandate's failure to support them with "scientific" means such as those used in Algeria.[135] The journal *Wakt* also complained about the lack of scientific methods and adequate funds to combat insects and impede their reproduction in subsequent years, claiming the government fought harmful insects "with the slowness of the turtle." It added, "If the locusts . . . were not sufficient, God permitted, that other insects, like the Sunn pest, . . . the olive tree fly and others, make their appearance. Most of these insects were unknown before the war and the people believe that they appeared, for the most part, after the occupation."[136] French intelligence reports admitted that locust eradication efforts had been insufficient in some areas, focusing on the impossibility of fully plowing under all affected land in al-Hasaka, given the means available to farmers. On the other hand, they had thrice-plowed lands in other parts of Aleppo and reported success in eradicating locusts from Jarablus, Manbij, and Jabal Samaan.[137] Insecticides were of course also on offer.[138]

As Sunn bugs, voles, and locusts munched their way through the regions' fields, the fallout from the revolt and the new tax burden intensified farmers' hardships. In 1927 French officials admitted that farmers in Hama were in a "precarious position," but they could not secure reductions in payments.[139] In Aleppo a 20% reduction in the *terbiʿ* granted only for a set period did not provide adequate time for farmers to sell their harvests to settle their debts.[140] In 1928 the governments allowed a 35% reduction in the *terbiʿ* for Hama.[141] Meanwhile, farmers in Homs grappled with a 50% decrease in wheat and barley from the previous year.[142] In Aleppo peasants were in such a "miserable" state as a result of a combination of Agricultural Bank loans and taxes that some were forced to sell their unharvested cotton at 10–15% below market price.[143] In the face of consecutive deficient harvests and insufficient measures to address them, the exponential increase of an already onerous tax burden added fuel to the fire of opposition to mandate rule. Some farmers (*agriculteurs*) with means even sent a telegram to Paris to convey their incapacity to pay the tithe.[144]

Local technocrats and agronomists excoriated the mandate's response to these compounding crises, underscoring the lack of investment despite the government's reliance on agriculture for a substantial portion of its budget. *Al-Ziraʿa al-Haditha* cited Achard's observation that agricultural

FIGURE 24. A baby lamb labeled "Syrian Agriculture" confronts a ferocious lion labeled "Usurers [interest]." Source: *al-Ziraʿa al-Haditha (Modern Agriculture)*, January 1928, Bibliothèque Orientale.

taxes accounted for more than 50% of the budget, querying whether agriculture did not therefore deserve at least 50% of the government's care.[145] Al-Ahdab criticized the *terbiʿ* for not being applied in the spirit in which it had been created.[146] To demonstrate the weight of existing taxes on the cultivator, especially those in rain-fed areas where production varied greatly from year to year, al-Ahdab ran the numbers, detailing the expenses involved in farming 500 *donums*, the returns expected, and the taxes excised thereof.[147] Based on his calculations, the current system left the farmer with 4 gold gurush per person per day. How, he demanded, was the farmer supposed to feed himself on such a paltry sum?[148] He contrasted the situation with France, where, despite agriculture's greater "degree of development," farmers paid less tax than in Syria![149]

The government responded by insisting it could not lower the *terbiʿ*, offering instead an estimation to village owners who requested it.[150] As provided for in the *terbiʿ* legislation, the estimation had to yield a loss of more than 25%. In addition, the request for estimation had to be made in April and had to pertain to all crops in the village.[151] But this decision also elicited complaints. One "large farmer" penned an article in which he lambasted the government for basing the *terbiʿ* on the new Syrian gold pound, noting that despite protests over the exorbitant rate, the government refused to budge and enforced collection "with the might of the gendarme, seizures of farmers' provisions, and landowners' capital."[152] However, he was also critical of reverting to estimation, insisting that the tithe, being levied on gross and not net production, was "incompatible with modern financial methods."[153] He attributed these decisions, which affected hundreds of thousands of farmers, to the government's failure to consult specialists in the agriculture ministry, urging it to do so and to treat Syria with the same compassion it had reserved for its "brother" Lebanon.[154] Despite this technocratic critique, many villagers were happy to take the government up on its offer; in 1932, 50% of villages would request estimation.[155]

The operations of the region's agricultural banks further added to farmers' woes. Mandatory authorities had reorganized the centralized Ottoman Agricultural Bank and its branches into five separate, autonomous banks—one each for Syria, Greater Lebanon, Latakia, Jabal al-Druze, and Alexandretta—between 1923 and 1928.[156] Despite mandate officials' insistence that the banks would help farmers improve their lands, the banks' terms meant that it was feasible to use their loans only for basic necessities, such as tools, seeds, livestock, wages, and fertilizer.[157] With the accumulation of bad harvests, farmers frequently found their most pressing need to be seed, although the banks' resources were at times insufficient to provide even this, forcing farmers to seek assistance from private moneylenders instead.[158]

French banks were eager to channel their capital into Syria, but only on terms that minimized their risk, namely, with high interest rates and the statelets as guarantors.[159] The Crédit Foncier de Syrie and the Crédit Foncier d'Algérie et de Tunisie (CFAT) each insisted that they were not in a position to undertake loans to small cultivators unless made through the intermediary of the statelets' agricultural banks, in which case they "would strongly encourage them," because, as the president of CFAT put it, the way that "would contribute the most fully to increase the economic wealth of the country would be credit easily distributed to small indigenous property owners for the amelioration of their agricultural installations."[160] CFAT began lending against mortgages as collateral only in April 1928, once such assurances had been established.[161] The Banque de Syrie et du Grand Liban also expressed interest but claimed it could not itself make the loans because it only negotiated titles of credit for less than three months and "the advances required by the work of the soil" generally needed nine months. The rhythms of the agricultural cycle were not conducive to its short-term lending practices. Nonetheless, it was willing to give the agricultural banks "capital of a significance" on the condition that these funds would be "judiciously employed."[162] Although seeking to infuse the countryside with their capital, these banks, whose operations were largely opaque to scrutiny, because they were not required to publicly disclose their accounts, also attempted to establish substantial distance between themselves and cultivators through the intermediary of the state-guaranteed agricultural bank.[163]

Local agronomists and technocrats were critical of the foreign land-credit banks, insisting that they needed to operate on terms more suitable to the returns of agricultural production, such as longer repayment periods and lower interests rates.[164] Tarmanini compared the "treatments" of credit offered at 9–11% interest, compared with the 6–7% interest of foreign banks, to an "anesthetic drug" that strained the peasant with extreme demands.[165] They were joined in their criticism by the Aleppo Chamber of Agriculture, which condemned mandate policies toward agrarian credit for disregarding agriculture's vulnerability to inevitable and annual fluctuations. The bank had failed to fulfill its purpose, especially given the previous four years of bad harvests resulting from Sunn bugs, locusts, and uncooperative weather. Not only was the bank undercapitalized and using "the most extreme rigor in recovering its debts," but it also had committed an "economic error" by putting up for sale simultaneously a large number of villages, which led to a depreciation in agricultural land values. Farmers, they continued, should not be treated as bankers or merchants because harvest yields, which fluctuated greatly from year to year, determined their ability to pay. The fact that cultivators still used the bank despite its "draconian conditions"—11% interest rate, short terms for repayment, and the risk of losing their property—indicated their desperation. Contrasting the situation with France, where, they claimed, banks granted loans for longer and easily renewable terms, they urged the mandate government to increase the bank's capital and reduce its rates to no more than 9% and halt the selling of property.[166]

Even French intelligence officials admitted that the bank's operations had had "disastrous consequences." Their practice of lending only on mortgages, but against property undervalued at 40%, exacerbated the difficulties the banks were supposed to alleviate. Year after year, debtors were perpetually unable to pay back their debts, which resulted in the bank selling their land, animals, and tools, and increasing its own unpopularity.[167] In 1928 the general direction in Aleppo granted a brief respite, postponing collection and spreading out repayment over five years after assessing Sunn bug damage.[168] In Lebanon, on the other hand, the second trimester of 1928 saw a number of bankruptcies.[169] Instead of reassessing or altering the banks' policies, however, French officials tended to blame local practices and ecological conditions, such as the "exhausted" soil, insufficient water, and crop rotations "that will not address the economic and climatological conditions of the country." Despite the funds' limited nature, officials insisted that they should be used to underwrite a "progressive development plan of agricultural and hydraulic resources."[170]

Local technocrats and agronomists, taking stock of how agriculture had fared after a decade of mandate rule, also critiqued the failure to develop and adhere to a comprehensive economic plan backed by substantial flows of capital. Despite the eagerness to find outlets for French capital through mortgage lending, al-Shihabi questioned the reluctance to invest in larger-scale projects, such as irrigation works or agricultural companies, both of which he saw as crucial to agricultural development.[171] Al-Jazaʾiri renewed calls for an overarching government plan because, despite "important, small, individual, personal undertakings" for agricultural reform, "economic success always depends on a complete general plan applied with fundamentals and durability and continuity."[172]

Al-Ziraʿa al-Haditha was incensed that, despite the latest developments in agricultural technologies and practice, the funding allotted to agriculture aimed to accomplish only the most mundane tasks instead of supporting new initiatives. Out of no less than 20 million gold dinars spent in a land of 3 million people, only 500,000 gold lira had been allotted to agriculture. These funds had primarily paid employees' salaries and helped farmers deal with pests—that is, "negative" works, the things the government was expected to do just to keep farmers from suffering major losses, not to substantially increase their yields.[173]

These critiques urged the government to proactively adopt and apply scientific and technical knowledge as the basis of its agricultural administration, relying on "the masters of opinion and science in the agriculture of the country and its economy."[174] One critic observed that even autocracies relied on the opinions of scientific experts. Thus a "government from the spirit of the represented people" should rely even more on local and representative councils for plans, laws, and organization regarding "scientific matters."[175] Tarmanini contrasted the government's neglect of agriculture for ten years with the "governments of the West and diligent governments of the East." He exhorted it to examine "the economic laws that governments of the West are pursuing in dealings with their people and adapt from them what helps it to undertake its obligations to rescue the country from this abyss that reached it because of [its] negligence."[176] The refusal by those responsible for mandate governance to allow technocrats to call the shots had been fundamental to the deterioration in agriculture and the economy.

Other articles in the press echoed these appeals for more proactive technocratic policies. Blaming Achard and the director of the service, but not al-Kaylani, the minister of agriculture and a champion of scientific agriculture, *Les Échos de Damas* demanded to know the ministry's response to farmers' "just demands for tax relief," not to mention plans for irrigation, protection against foreign competition, statistics collection, and recording of atmospheric conditions. Even the common practices of collecting and killing locusts, which were basic duties of the Agriculture Ministry, had been carried out by peasants at their own expense while the ministry "rested."[177] *Wakt*, with perhaps a touch of sarcasm, concurred, highlighting the disconnect between French claims to superior knowledge and the increasing desperation of local farmers.

> We received with joy the mandate government hoping that it would help us with serious technical advice. It sent us counselors and inspectors who claim to possess a vast science and great experience. . . . Why then do these insects make us suffer for some years, and why is science powerless at combatting them? . . . The locusts, the Sunn bugs, the lack of water, the halting of commerce for customs and political reasons, the heavy taxes, all this creates a general discontent among the people.[178]

In addition to pressure from inflation, falling land values, animal-induced crop damage, drought, and high interest rates, the inflexibility of the *terbiᶜ* led to various absurd circumstances at the village level. Not only did it perpetuate the fraud and inequitable distribution that characterized existing tithe assessments—the very problems French officials claimed they were trying to eradicate—but it was also incapable of accommodating basic fluctuations in village life, such as planting different crops, adding trees, removing trees, or changes in landownership.

Complaints to the high commissioner's office illustrated the resulting conundrums. A petition from Idlib with 157 seals and 68 signatures detailed how over the years individual wealth and land values changed as some villagers sold land and others acquired it and as some villagers planted olive trees and others removed trees. Yet, the *terbiᶜ* continued to tax each person and plot as though everything was frozen in 1925. The unequal distribution had become so disconnected from reality that in 1932 authorities agreed to an estimation, assessing the tithe at 8,000 Syrian pounds. When the government demanded 13,000 Syrian pounds the following year, the petitioners requested that its apportionment follow the distribution of the tithe determined in 1932.[179] Another complaint from Ras Baᶜalbak in Lebanon suggested that a lack of protection from influential local leaders had resulted in an increased tax burden that became enshrined in the *terbiᶜ* and was impossible to pay, especially with deficient harvests. Furthermore, despite no longer raising silkworms since 1929, as of 1934 the government still assessed a tax of 35,000 piastres for the cocoon harvest.[180]

Meanwhile, the process of creating small private property from state lands revealed disagreements between local technocrats and rural communities over assessing and administering these marginal regions. Arrêté 275, issued on 5 May 1926, aimed to regulate these sales, enabling the director of state lands to block the sale, rent, or mortgaging of these lands for a number of years in order to protect new small property owners. As director of state lands, al-Shihabi oversaw sales of five villages in the Hawran and two each in Homs and Hama in 1927, followed by forty more—half in Homs and Hama and half in Aleppo—in 1928. Ultimately, the state planned to sell 90% of the land to peasants or middling farmers.[181]

A complaint from seven villages in the district of Manbij near Aleppo, however, expressed concern about the process of registration itself. Following the Ottoman withdrawal and arrival of the mandate, the villagers asserted that "their ancient traditions were no longer respected and their legal rights were trampled" as a result of "inexplicable despotism."[182]

In particular, they complained about heavy taxes imposed by estimators who had surveyed and registered the land at the inflated price of 10 Syrian pounds per *shumbul*. This amount exceeded that paid by neighboring villages with irrigated fields, pastures, and summer and winter harvests. They threatened to abandon the lands if the disparity remained unaddressed.[183]

One of the targets of their ire was Wasfi Zakariya, the inspector of state domains and a frequent contributor to *al-Ziraʿa al-Haditha*, who had agreed to the overestimation, which they attributed to their absence when it was made. In support of their claim regarding the land's actual value, they submitted a statement signed by a number of local mukhtars and imams who attested that, on the basis of their "knowledge, observation, erudition, and expertise," the villages' land were rain-fed, the soil rocky, and that three *donums* of it were not valued at more than 1 Syrian pound.[184] Aware of the environmental challenges their lands posed, they insisted on deferring to local expertise about the environment when determining the value of their lands to ensure a fair and just tax bill. Their idea of what constituted legitimate expertise differed from that of local technocrats.

When, shortly after this clash, the land law, enshrined in Arrêté 3339, passed on 12 November 1930, it established a new set of regulations governing land transactions based on the cadastre's registration.[185] It is unclear just how immediately or widely officials applied or enacted the law's dictates in the years that followed, but reactions suggest that its implementation also involved bypassing the usual reliance on local expertise in addition to favoring those in positions of power. One petition expressed alarm at the abolition of representative counsels and their replacement with one judge for adjudicating matters related to cadastral disputes. Signed with sixty-two signatures, the letter writers insisted that "most of the judges designated as presidents of the Commissions [for the work of the cadastre] have neither the experience nor the competence desired to judge the affairs of the cadastre and of delimitation, especially given that the older registers are obscure and demand, in order to be understood, much reflection and capacity."[186] In another instance, villagers feared that the actions of a local notable, who had requested that the cadastral service delimit an area of land that had been in litigation between two villages, would hurt their claims in the case.[187]

In addition, as discussed earlier, costs continued to be a concern, especially in the wake of the financial and environmental crises of the 1920s and early 1930s. *Al-Zira^ca al-Haditha* urged the government to take on more if not all of the cost burden, noting that it was unacceptable to expect the local community to bear it.[188] In Homs, where the cadastre concentrated most of its initial work, the introduction of a new tax for cadastral fees led several large landowners to express outrage. One of them declared that he was inclined to just sell the land for half the amount instead.[189]

In Deir Baʿalba, just northeast of Homs, a series of petitions captured the cadastre's myriad adverse effects on village life. About a hundred villagers, who redistributed their land "once every ten years . . . by the drawing of lots," wrote to the high commissioner to demand his immediate intervention, as their lands were about to be divided and they wanted to "maintain the former state of things."[190] They insisted that their current practices enabled "cultivators to profit, during this time, from the fruits of their labor, different plots to be improved one after the other, and the poor to be helped and assisted by the rich" because their lands "are not of the same value. Some are good and close and some are mediocre and remote by nearly 10 km."[191] Appealing to the government's concern for treasury revenues, they asserted that the partition would cause the abandonment of inferior lands, as they were far from villagers' homes and difficult to protect from Bedouin, among others, not to mention that the severely indebted village would have to bear the costs, which already exceeded the value of its lands.[192]

In 1937 and 1938 the villagers wrote again to complain that the mukhtar was using the cadastre to have lands registered in his name.[193] The petitioners cited a tradition in which lands were recorded in the name of the oldest son but worked by all. They noted that when the cadastral commission carried out their operations, they did not consult with the council of elders and they had, as a result, registered all lands worked by multiple brothers under one name. Consequently, mortgages taken out on what should have been a portion of the property were taken out on all of it.[194] Despite imploring the French high commissioner to protect their claims to these lands that had been theirs "for more than 500 years without contest" and on which they had paid all taxes and usage fees, the delegate of the High Commission wrote that it was not possible to respond.[195]

The Crises of the 1930s: The Ecological Limits of Extraction

During the summer of 1930, French intelligence reported the emergence of a civil disobedience campaign spearheaded by Fakhri al-Barudi and fed by mounting discontent over the accumulating fallout from the mandate's agricultural policies, which was increasingly compounded by the reverberations of the global economic crisis following the 1929 stock market crash.[196] As strikes spiked in urban areas to protest the deteriorating economic situation, mandate officials feared that al-Barudi's campaign had the potential to turn rural communities, which they viewed as less prone to organized resistance than urban agitators, against them as well.[197] Even though the 1929 and 1930 harvests had generally been good, that had not substantially improved matters. On the contrary, it had precipitated a fall in prices, which a glut of grain on the world market and the importation of Australian and Russian wheat further exacerbated, making it difficult for farmers to cover seed and labor costs. Such conditions would have weighed heavily in any case, but when combined with a fixed tax based on higher market prices and a less debased currency, they made the taxes a "terrible burden."[198] Concern was particularly acute for areas where monocultures prevailed, such as the Hawran, which almost exclusively grew grains. Facilities to store grain until prices improved would have provided one means of relief, but these were lacking.[199] Around Aleppo reports suggested that landlords suffered more than farmers, which had led some near Idlib to sell their unharvested crops to local pastoralists rather than pay for the costs of harvesting and threshing them.[200] This ominous beginning to the 1930s foreshadowed the more dire situation to come, as mandate policies pushed many of the region's farmers to the brink, fomenting increasingly coordinated nationalist mobilization around agricultural and rural concerns. Nationalists and mandate officials sparred over how to respond to the crisis as each group attempted to turn rural discontent to their advantage and position themselves as the effective mediators.

Early in the 1930s these compounding crises contributed to the growing popularity of undertaking a civil disobedience campaign inspired by "the method of Gandhi 'the Satyagraha' or 'non-violent resistance.' "[201] After meeting in open fields in the Ghuta, where, one intelligence report recounted, National Bloc members "violently attacked the government and moderate parties and disapproved the negotiations on the subject of an entente with the latter," they decided that if they could not get a favorable response to their demands from the high commissioner, they would indeed pursue noncooperation and, "if needed," civil disobedience.[202] One report admitted that "the situation of the gentlemen farmers [*agriculteurs*] was in truth not bright and their lot worthy of interest," but it also accused nationalists of "exploiting" the economic crisis.[203] Even "pro-mandate" farmers had approached mandate officials to complain about the exorbitant taxes.[204]

Worried that al-Barudi's civil disobedience campaign might appeal to peasants, French officials pursued various measures to thwart political organization. They decreased the tithe throughout much of Syria by 30% for 1930 and 20% for 1929 as a "rather adroit political action" to stifle dissent. They were satisfied to report that any traction al-Barudi's "economic pact," which bound supporters to buy local products, might have gained had no real impact on markets.[205] Seeking other sources of exploitable discontent, the officials suggested capitalizing on frustration over taxes paid by the Hawran but spent primarily on Damascus's priorities. The Hawran population, they claimed, was "easy to direct" and "fundamentally attached to the mandate power" and therefore "merit that some efforts be made to improve the Sanjak's administrative and economic situation."[206] Manipulating rural discontent continued to be essential to their divide-and-rule strategy.

Throughout 1931 and 1932 the crisis worsened. Although the agricultural banks offered loans to help farmers defray their obligations to the state, in some areas peasants had become so indebted that the capital advanced to them exceeded the value of their land.[207] Even though banks in the region reduced their rates from 9% to 5% in 1930, the accumulation of overlapping natural and financial crises meant that the proceeds from an entire year's work was sufficient to pay off only some interest. The debt continued to pile up. Even selling land would not discharge it. Bankruptcies rose.[208] In response, the government lowered the *terbiʿ* on grains by 33.33% in Syria and Alexandretta, 65% in Lebanon, and 45% in the ʿAlawite State.[209]

The crisis was so dire that *al-Ziraʿa al-Haditha* ceased publication from December 1929 to November 1931 because fees from its beleaguered subscribers dwindled.[210] Upon resuming, it harshly criticized the government's policies, stating that if the region "had enjoyed prudent, insightful governments" since the war, it would have suffered fewer "catastrophes and blights."[211] Farmers, in particular, had suffered more than others, being condemned to live as though it was the Middle Ages. To defend and lobby for their interests, the journal urged them to form unions or societies, which would, among other things, allow them to secure granaries for storage. Lacking facilities to store their crops forced farmers to sell when prices were low, exacerbating their already dire situation and benefiting only a minuscule number of wealthy farmers in each town who had the means to speculate in the low-priced grains, which they would sell later when prices rose.[212] The journal welcomed a law, passed "a bit late" in September 1931, that allowed farmers to take out loans against their crops and thus required the Agricultural Bank to establish granaries to store the mortgaged harvests, helping alleviate the problem. Still, it urged farmers to pursue cooperation and solidarity as the surest means of protecting their interests.[213] Matters would further improve if the bank made installments payable for at least twenty-five years and collected the tithe in accordance with Ottoman-era practices, namely, in markets based on the sale price and not directly through the *terbiᶜ* or the *tahmis*, which were "full of injustice and stupidity," depriving the farmer of seed, sustenance, or fodder.[214]

To better assess the nature of farmers' latest complaints, Saᶜid Tarmanini, the editor of *al-Ziraᶜa al-Haditha*, set out to tour the countryside just as new elections in Syria were getting under way.[215] These elections, which would bring a slate of moderate National Bloc candidates to power, occurred during the spring and summer of 1932 and coincided with one of the worst agricultural seasons in decades.[216] In Hama a group of *agriculteurs* telegrammed the high commissioner to present their case. Complaining of drought and insect damage combined with the global economic crisis, they requested postponing arrears payments, only collecting the interest on agricultural bank payments, and a return to the *terbiᶜ* of 1924 along with estimation, noting the inequitable treatment that Syria received compared with Lebanon, where the *terbiᶜ* had been lowered substantially.[217] *Al-Ziraᶜa al-Haditha* also criticized the government for not immediately granting a reduction, noting that estimation would incur expenses beyond farmers' capacity. It suggested that employees of the agricultural and finance ministries could visit villages to verify the state of the harvest, and if farmers still needed an estimation after an initial reduction, they could request one, but only those whose harvests were found to be better than what they claimed should pay. The government could thus demonstrate its "equity" and "justice" by relieving farmers of additional financial burdens.[218]

Alarmed by the growing crisis, a number of "experts" (*ahl al-khibra wa al-ma*ʿ*rifa*) responded to the journal's call to provide an assessment of the situation and offer solutions.[219] The responses from Tawfiq al-Ahdab, the general agricultural inspector for the northern area, Mustafa al-Shihabi, the director of state lands, and ʿAbd al-Qadir al-Kaylani, the former commerce and agriculture minister and one of the signatories of the Hama letter, echoed a common theme: Farmers' hardships derived from the mandate government's harsh taxation and lending policies and were exacerbated by postwar changes in global commodity circulation.[220] For al-Ahdab agricultural borrowing policies exemplified the mandate's deleterious impact. Farmers borrowed what they could to keep on doing their work, hoping for good harvests and prices that would enable them to repay their debts either in installments or all at once. Since 1920, however, their situation had become increasingly precarious, a process that al-Ahdab divided into three stages of increasing severity: From 1920 to 1926, farmers lost what they had earned during the war; from 1926 to 1929, various misfortunes deprived them of what they had before the war; and then in 1930 even the "strongest farmers," hoping for a good season, mortgaged what remained of their wealth and were disappointed.[221] Still, the effects had been unevenly distributed. Despite pitiful harvests, large farmers could still pay off small loans, although interest continued to accumulate on larger ones. Small and middling farmers, however, had been piling on debt since 1926 and could not even pay the interest, resulting in the loss of their entire wealth.[222] In part, this was due to the overproduction of certain crops precipitated by the war. Citing statistics from the International Institute of Agriculture, al-Shihabi noted that during the war cultivated areas in such countries as Argentina, Australia, Canada, and the United States had expanded. This expansion led to overproduction and stockpiling that after the war had driven down seed prices with ongoing repercussions for Syria.[223] Al-Kaylani highlighted the intersection of this decrease in prices with the soaring increase in taxes over a ten-year span and the destruction caused by field mice and Sunn bugs, culminating in the crisis.[224]

Their solutions emphasized the need for an agricultural politics involving more government intervention, investment, and protection. Not only was a more "just" tax assessment and the postponement of arrears collection necessary, but also the government should offer free seeds and fodder to those whose crops had been destroyed by drought and provide basic sustenance to get them through the 1933 season as well as adequate capital to fend off the predations of moneylenders.[225] Similar to French government practice in the metropole, Syria needed its government to impose effective tariffs to protect domestic production in addition to finding more foreign markets for local products.[226] In particular, the new constitutional government had a duty to ameliorate the corruption of the past ten years by allotting resources to immediate needs, such as buying new tools "to distribute to farmers in installments of five to ten years."[227]

For al-Kaylani, such policies would represent a reversal from the government's wasteful spending on projects that were supposedly in support of agriculture but really served other interests. For example, in the name of increasing irrigation, substantial money had been spent on implements and technical employees under a French director. Despite these measures, al-Kaylani insisted that the country had not seen even partial benefits from their work. All they had done was dig a few wells in the Syrian desert (*badiya*) for the benefit of oil companies. He summed up this issue and hundreds of others like it as follows: "The government sucked the blood of the people not to mention their money for its own sake and led them to the abyss of bankruptcy."[228] Each of these "experts" emphasized a central role for the government in subsidizing and protecting agriculture and criticized policies that treated it primarily as a revenue-generating cash cow. In contrast to some representations of National Bloc politics, these nationalist technocrats clearly had a plan for economic development, particularly as it related to agricultural concerns. Actions taken in the ensuing months suggested that even more moderate National Bloc members were on board, in large part because for many of them the state of the country's agricultural production was intimately bound up with their "own interests."[229]

Whether they had an economic development plan or not, nationalist leaders clearly saw the crisis as an opportunity to seize the initiative from mandate officials and make an appeal for broader support among rural communities. In August the finance and agriculture minister Jamil Mardam Bey toured rural areas to assess the situation, which would have been particularly striking east of Aleppo, where more than 600 villages lay desolate. *Al-Ziraʿa al-Haditha* urged the government to take responsibility for providing seeds and subsidies, suggesting that if existing resources were inadequate, because of the inherited deficit of almost 12 million francs, then it should approach the High Commission to obtain funds from the common interests.[230] Following the trip, Jamil Mardam Bey and Muhammad Ali Bey al-ʿAbid, the Syrian president, traveled to Beirut to wrangle with the Bank of Syria and Greater Lebanon to secure a loan for seeds for farmers in northern Syria.[231] On 7 November 1932 the government debated borrowing 10 million francs at 5% interest, eventually promulgating a law for the loan on 30 November 1932. The discussion was of particular interest, according to the high commissioner, because large landowners insisted that "they were ruining and indebting themselves to come to the aid of their farmers" and because others, such as the Damascene lawyer Faʾiz Khuri, emerged as "eloquent defenders of small cultivators."[232]

Such sentiments suggest that years of predominantly bad harvests combined with elevated taxes and high-interest loans had severely strained landlords' capacity to fulfill the obligations that characterized their relationships with the farmers who worked their land. Typically expected to provide seed, housing, and/or livestock and pay a portion or all of the tax in return for a percentage of the crop, depending on the arrangement, landlords also loaned at exorbitant rates to farmers to defray their expenses. But lacking liquid capital themselves, the landlords relied on funds borrowed from the Agricultural Bank, private banks, or grain merchants at rates of 10%, 15–24%, or 24–30%, respectively.[233] Successive cycles of inadequate harvests to repay these debts meant that the landlords themselves were reaching the point of insolvency, especially in areas around Hama and Aleppo, where, as discussed in chapter 1, the precarity of dry-farming cultivation had initially facilitated their capacity to thwart Ottoman attempts to create small property owners.

Meanwhile, the environmental conditions for farmers continued to deteriorate. Despite some early abundant autumn rains around Salamiya and Hama as farmers waited for seeds, by January 1933 *al-Qabas* reported that the oldest people in Hama could not remember a drier or colder year.[234] In Dayr al-Zor farmers planted what seeds they had, but large areas remained unsown because of a lack of government assistance and difficulty in obtaining additional seeds or money for seeds from local merchants.[235] Reports poured in of people dying of hunger in northern Syria, some after watching their flocks perish before them. Five hundred villagers had reportedly taken refuge in the city, and others headed for Beirut and Tripoli. In Jabal al-Druze, Latakia, and Lebanon seeds lay in drought-stricken fields. In Latakia and the Hawran birds ate insufficiently buried seeds, further exacerbating the situation.[236] Increasingly, it became clear that the farmers of northern Syria were not the only ones who would be desperate for seeds.

The anxiously awaited improvement in environmental conditions proved just as vain as the desired amelioration in government policy. As farmers anxiously watched the sky, accusations flew in the press about the lateness and paucity of government assistance. The Council of Ministers unanimously adopted a reform plan drawn up by the director of economic services, Yusuf ʿAtallah, which the Parliament's agricultural commission then defeated in a 9 to 3 vote, using budgetary reasons as a pretext.[237] The nationalists had managed to get only one member on the commission, but Fakhri al-Barudi's resignation in mid-December suggested that they soon lost even that voice.[238] The press jumped on the vote, attributing it to the "instigation 'of a foreign government officer,'" a not-too-subtle reference to Achard, who it accused of having "rendered to the country no service worthy of mention" and who, due to his age, "deserved to be retired." The press also took the commission to task for its decision, which saved a mere 50,000 Syrian pounds while the country's primary source of wealth, agriculture, suffered.[239]

As anxious cultivators awaited the bank's decision on the loan, al-Barudi, Jamil Mardam Bey, and Jamil Ibrahim Pasha, a large landowner and National Bloc leader from Aleppo, traveled to Homs, Hama, and Aleppo in late December to personally distribute loans to farmers.[240] Meanwhile, the Bank of Syria and Greater Lebanon, which was initially reluctant to grant the requested loan, finally agreed in early January but declared that it would not undertake another.[241] Its hand was likely forced by a stack of reports detailing the severity of the crisis that the High Commission's delegate for the Syrian Republic passed along with assurances that they "emanate exclusively from French services" and thus "no preoccupation of an internal political order or demagoguery taints the[ir] sincerity and objectivity."[242] Despite this internal acknowledgment, based on sources that French officials considered objective, that cultivators' desperation was legitimate, officials continued to push back on demands for more concessions and assistance.

The bank's paltry loan of 250,000 Syrian pounds was insufficient to meet farmers' needs.[243] The government distribution plan allotted 79,294 Syrian pounds to the Aleppo region, 75,745 to Damascus, and 20,000 for the Jazira and Dayr al-Zor, with the remaining 60,000 and 14,961 going to farmers in the state lands of Aleppo and Damascus, respectively, but the press insisted it was too little too late.[244] In some cases the aid amounted to 25, 40, or 50 piastres per person—insufficient funds it claimed to feed one family a meal.[245] According to *Les Échos*, in one instance, an entire village was allotted only 179 piastres. Some farmers did not even receive enough to cover their transportation costs to the center of the district, presumably where many of them had to go to receive the promised aid.[246] In the region of Jarablus near Aleppo, one of the worst hit areas, where 104 villages out of 430 had been deserted, both villagers and pastoralists rejected the government's allotment of 10,000 pounds as insufficient.[247]

The direness of the situation prompted a critique of budgetary priorities. Members of "the syndicate of the graduates of the agricultural schools" published multiple articles in both the nationalist *al-Qabas* and the French-language *Les Échos de Damas* newspapers, lambasting Achard and urging the government to undertake the project outlined by ʿAtallah. If the government needed to cut the budget, they suggested it should do so by "eliminating the supplementary credits to ministers and firing the government employees who do nothing but read the newspapers and take their salaries at the end of each month."[248] They claimed that rejection of the proposed plan, the fundamentals of which had already been applied in such places as Turkey, Palestine, and even Transjordan, exposed Syrian farmers to increasing unevenness within a global sphere where foreign agriculture had widely adopted and adapted "modern" techniques. Not only were Syrian farmers exposed to this competition, but they were also simultaneously expected to contribute 75% to the state's revenues. The country, they concluded, desperately needed an "agricultural politics."[249] *Al-Qabas* critiqued the divided treasuries of the various states, asserting that if the country had one united treasury, it would have a reserve to deal with such a desperate state of affairs. It contrasted the situation with that of the Ottoman era, which it considered exemplary of responsible fiscal administration, as the region of 3 million inhabitants "had been administered . . . in such a way that its expenses did not exceed those necessary for two Ottoman provinces."[250] Ultimately, in Syria at least, the government approved an average reduction of 51% for 1932 taxes, which the Parliament increased to 61%, based on observations from commissions sent to districts to assess the severity of the damage.[251]

By the spring of 1933, fruitless negotiations over a treaty between French officials and moderate members of the National Bloc who championed a policy of "honorable cooperation" had exhausted the patience of the Bloc's more radical members. Led by the venerable Ibrahim Hananu from Aleppo, this radical contingent forced the resignation of moderate National Bloc leaders Jamil Mardam Bey and Mazhar Raslan in April 1933.[252] The following June a Parliament boycotted by nationalists annulled arrears prior to 1928 and gave extensions for those due between 1928 and 1932.[253] That summer High Commissioner Henri Ponsot was transferred to Morocco.[254] Meanwhile, nearly 15,000 peasants fled their villages for Aleppo, and 300 villages to the east of the city were reportedly deserted.[255] The culmination of successive cycles of poor harvests, low market prices, and heavy taxes also likely explains the massive debts accumulated by the al-Yusuf family between 1926 and 1933 that would lead them to consider selling some of their lands to the Jewish National Fund in 1934, as discussed in chapter 4.[256] In October 1933 Comte Damien de Martel, the new high commissioner, arrived, purportedly intent on overseeing an economic recovery after the devastation wrought by the global depression; he was immediately met with clamoring for a moratorium on mortgage debt.[257]

Shortly after de Martel's arrival, a group of Aleppan elites sought to hold him to his word, dispatching a telegram that expressed their frustrations with the increasingly aggressive tax collection tactics of the financial services. Instead of providing seed and provisions to farmers beset by three years of miserable harvests, soldiers accompanied the collectors and, with "methods used in the Middle Ages and contrary to justice," seized work animals, seeds, and supplies. If the new high commissioner truly wanted to revive the country's economy, these methods had to cease.[258] Seeking a French opinion on the matter, de Martel wrote to Lavastre, the mandate's delegate in Aleppo, who thrived on thwarting nationalist demands and thus brusquely dismissed the telegram as a political publicity stunt.[259] De Martel's selection in March 1934 of Taj al-Din, widely regarded as a quisling for his willingness to acquiescent to French demands, to resume leadership of the government did not bode well for local frustration with the government's lack of action on farmers' behalf.[260] In response, over the next year farmers and landowners would channel this frustration into increasing political organization that would bring together groups from around the region.[261]

One initial salvo from Aleppo in this escalating dispute, a petition signed by about 140 farmers, underscored their increasing desperation as they faced yet another year of ruinous environmental conditions. Sent in May

1934, when the disappointing yields of the imminent harvest would have been distressingly clear, they explained that they had anticipated a better 1933–1934 season but insufficient rain during a crucial period in April and March had dashed those hopes, further compounding the struggles of previous years. Their demands struck a familiar refrain: decrease the Agricultural Bank's interest rate—this time to 3%—and base it on simple interest; increase as of 1935 to thirty years the time allotted to repay debts of more than 500 pounds dinars (*livres dinars*); reduce back taxes from 1928–1932; postpone for a year suffering farmers' repayment of advances made for seed purchases; renew previous orders, such as a moratorium, related to debt given the "uncontestable fact" of their inability to pay; and take measures to protect the harvest from foreign competition.[262] De Martel initially appeared predisposed to consider their demands, noting that they seemed characterized by "moderation and objectivity," but upon seeking an opinion from the interior, the French delegate in Damascus tersely disabused him of this impression.[263] The delegate insisted that the harvest had been relatively decent except for a few places in the Hawran and denied any basis for their requests, dismissing them as the opposition's "economic" program. Reducing tax arrears was "nothing less than to compensate a deficient taxpayer." Any favors shown by the Agricultural Bank should go to small property owners. There was no reason to delay payment for seed advances or to adopt a moratorium on debt. Finally, "all useful steps" had been taken to protect wheat and flour from foreign competition.[264]

Complaints from Lebanon also stressed the excessiveness of taxation, the violence of recovery methods, and the lack of investment despite these exactions.[265] The residents of Jubayl, in a petition laced with flattery for "our dear France," decided to bypass mandate authorities and requested a 75% reduction in their tax rate from the French minister of foreign affairs himself, but de Martel rejected it on the basis that "such a measure would . . . destroy the very structure of the Lebanese budget."[266] Other petitions pointed out the injustice of excessive tax collection while not attending to basic infrastructure. The villagers of Sir al-Duniya in northern Lebanon insisted that they did not even know they were government subjects until tax collectors showed up and "sold the jewelry of the widow and orphan to collect taxes that are spent in other happy regions."[267] The inhabitants of Tyre demanded the cancellation of the combined tithe and land tax as well as back taxes, or at least the permission to pay the latter in ten annual installments. They also requested that the government "open an agricultural bank like that under the Ottomans," provide funds for irrigation projects as the previous regime had, build roads, and clean up swamps.[268] The local delegate passed along their petition to de Martel with a dismissive cover letter.[269] In Ras Baᶜalbak the inhabitants, unable to pay the exorbitant sums demanded by tax collectors, complained about the seizure of their flocks, buildings, and entire maize harvest, the subsistence crop of poor villagers who would starve without it.[270] The head of the Services Spéciaux in Baᶜalbak, Captaine Desfarges, suggested it could be interesting to investigate, but in his opinion Ras Baᶜalbak was not being taxed out of proportion with the rest of the Bekaa.[271]

Such refusals to make concessions to struggling farmers fueled increasingly organized resistance. Powerful landowners from Damascus and surrounding towns held a conference in late June 1934 to coordinate their demands, electing an executive committee as well as various local subcommittees that would keep the executive committee abreast of local conditions.[272] In July another group in Aleppo formed "to defend farmers [*agriculteurs*] from the seizure of their assets."[273] Authorized by statements (*mazbatas*) to represent the farmers of Aleppo's districts and heavily surveilled by French intelligence services, this Committee for the Defense of the Rights of Farmers joined forces with its counterpart in Damascus for a second conference in September, where attendees elected an executive committee representing Damascus, Aleppo, Homs, Hama, Dayr al-Zor, and the Hawran.[274] After sending a delegation to meet with Lavastre and lay before him examples, such as a 7-*donum* plot of land producing a net yield of 17 gold piastres but assessed 1,700 gold piastres in taxes, they received only evasive responses. They then regrouped to discuss their next course of action.[275] Of diverse political leanings—members of the National Bloc, the League of National Action, and the Nationalist Youth were all present—they vigorously debated their options. Some proposed civil disobedience; ᶜAbd al-Razzaq al-Dandashi, of the League of National Action, suggested that the only way to achieve real results was just to refuse to pay taxes. Others preferred asking the government to take out a loan to assist them.[276]

As this resistance became increasingly organized over the summer, de Martel, noting a midsummer intensification in complaints about the "extreme harshness" of tax collection methods concurrent with villagers placing crops on threshing floors for assessment, demanded an "accurate and objective report" from the mandate's regional delegates.[277] By and large, the delegates insisted that tax collection was proceeding without too much trouble, although one acknowledged that tax collectors in Aleppo visited local villages accompanied by mobile guards and gendarmes, and another admitted that in the Euphrates and Jazira region, the government placed "sizable military escorts" at their disposal.[278] In Lebanon as well, gendarmes accompanied the tax collectors.[279] One official deflected criticisms of such methods, insisting not only that they were exaggerated but also that "without a doubt the remarks and gestures of these rather unsophisticated people [i.e., the soldiers] lack finesse and nuance, but they correspond on the whole with the mentality [*mentalité*] of the Syrian peasant."[280] Justifying the disproportionality of mandate taxation and its violent enforcement necessitated depicting peasants as simple and accustomed to such treatment as *longue durée* victims of violence.

De Martel observed that mandate authorities' countenancing of such methods, which were "arbitrary with respect to [taxpayers'] fortune or rank," risked nurturing resistance. Instead, he suggested that the aggression be more targeted and requested the names of "big capitalists, large landowners, parliamentarians, and high-level civil servants" who were behind in their payments.[281] His delegates obliged, providing detailed lists of taxpayers from the "notability," defined in at least one set of lists by all those who owed more than 100 livres libano-syriennes to the treasury, hardly the upper echelon of society usually denoted by the "politics of notables" but rather a combination of wealthy landowners and more middling taxpayers.[282] Such strategies challenge assertions that the High Commission "abandoned its rural strategy of undercutting the material base of the absentee landowning class" following the 1925–1927 Syrian Revolt.[283] The reports acknowledged that these grievances were not without foundation but simultaneously insisted that they were ultimately political and therefore should not encourage leniency in collecting the sums due. Although couched in terms of saving the budget, such divide-and-rule policies suggested that the insistence on collecting taxes was intended primarily as punishment.

By the time conference delegates decided to insist on a personal meeting with the high commissioner himself, de Martel had received these stacks of confidential reports detailing the names and amounts owed by "recalcitrant taxpayers." If their intent was to bypass Lavastre's evasiveness, Lavastre cut them off at the pass. Writing the high commissioner just before the delegates' arrival, Lavastre explained that their situation was indeed "critical" but that it was their own fault as well as the result of a general decrease in land values. Accusing them of lacking interest in the cultivation of their properties, he claimed that they relied on peasant farmers (*fallah*) and were happy with "a modest revenue burdened with few expenses and taxes." Reducing their taxes would threaten the equilibrium of the budget. Even though concessions might be made on a case-by-case basis, the lists he had just sent contained the names of those who had to pay.[284] In essence, despite a global economic crisis and historic drought, Lavastre insisted that the main reason these landowners were suffering was because they had not invested more in their properties.

The delegation of representatives from Damascus, Aleppo, and Antioche, which was also accompanied by Fakhri al-Barudi, presented two rather modest requests to the high commissioner from their broader complaints: readjust the basis for assessing taxes and suspend collection for some months.[285] To their first point, the high commissioner assured them he was already aware of the issue and would study it further after returning from an imminent trip to France. As for their second request, de Martel, primed by Lavastre's letter, informed the delegation that he considered their demands to suspend tax collection for even a few months "revolutionary" and "after a long and tiresome discussion" could only promise the exercise of moderation in the fulfillment of Agricultural Bank debts and the collection of back taxes.[286]

The press assailed mandate officials for their continued insistence that these complaints were just political in nature and were not reflective of real hardship. In advance of the delegation's visit to Beirut, *al-Ayyam* urged the high commissioner "to listen to . . . 'the language of numbers not the language of politics.' "[287] *Al-Qabas* invoked the government's intransigence to call into question its legitimacy. In "bitter terms" it mocked the "prosperity" that mandate governance claimed to be bringing to the region, insisting that, on the contrary, its methods were "the most prodigious and the most modern way to pressure the people and to condemn to death the economic life in general and agriculture in particular." Speculating that a landowning cabinet minister had perhaps received special treatment instead of paying his arrears, it concluded that "the government that does not think about the future of the people who nourish its Treasury is not worthy to remain in power."[288]

Meanwhile, tensions emerged between different levels of the bureaucracy, as those on the ground in the worst affected areas insisted that complaints were not exaggerated and that enacting seizures in the absence of compliance would be detrimental not just to farmers but to the treasury as well. A tax collector who witnessed the incapacity of one of the north's biggest farmers to pay suggested that only 1934 taxes be collected, but the director of finance and the treasury official (*mudir mal*) insisted on collecting 1933 back taxes as well.[289] In Hama an officer of the *Services Spéciaux* warned that the current system was "neither in the interest of the landowners nor the government," and he urged mandate authorities to adopt an approach that would not predominantly result in "forced sale at a low price."[290] The assistant delegate in Alexandretta insisted on the need for a "particularly equitable" tax base "if we do not want to provoke at a later stage vehement protests."[291] Nonetheless, officials at the top largely begrudged concessions.

In Aleppo the Committee for the Defense of the Rights of Farmers urged the high commissioner to pay attention to "the fact that farmers and peasants [*cultivateurs et paysans*] do not cease to be victims of oppressions and abuses and that their situation always goes from bad to worse," imploring him to consider the delegation's requests.[292] They threatened to refuse to pay taxes and invited the authorities to seize their lands if the government did not agree to postpone collection and provide assistance with fall sowing.[293] Although they appreciated the High Commission's economic projects, their "very critical situation" precluded them from anticipating any means to achieve them. Rather, they demanded elimination of the tithe and the institution of a tax on revenue.[294] A joint appeal to the government by delegates from Damascus and Aleppo in late November met only assurances that their case was being studied.[295] In response to such platitudes, the executive committee of the Agricultural Congress of northern Syria attempted to turn up the heat on mandate authorities in March 1935 by sending a petition to the Permanent Mandates Commission and Paris, with copies going to foreign representatives as well.[296] Demanding justice and referencing the "precise data figures demonstrating agricultural taxes exceed half gross revenue leading to [farmers'] general ruin," they alleged in telegram-speak that "persistence this attitude demonstrates evident goal to ruin agriculture only resource of country."[297]

These protesters were not the only ones insisting that the numbers did not add up. Even as these elites positioned themselves as interlocutors on both the local and international levels, throughout the region villagers launched their own protest campaigns, sending petitions directly to the high commissioner's office that detailed the dire straits in which they found themselves. Their misfortunes ranged from drought, Sunn bugs, and a "plague from the skies" to, in one instance, flood.[298] The petitions also stressed the disproportionate nature of the taxes assessed, explaining that the sums demanded were exorbitant and offering to pay something more in line with current harvests and market prices.[299] Many confirmed the allegations of illegally confiscated land, livestock, and harvests that were then put up for auction, despite Aleppo's director of finances "categorically deny[ing]" the deployment of such measures.[300] The Maronite archbishop of Damascus described "numerous" tax collectors seizing "plowing implements, products of the harvest, cattle, kitchen utensils, and even . . . a goat, a sewing machine, etc."[301]

Many petition writers threatened to abandon their lands.[302] Like the villagers in Aleppo several years before, some made good on such threats. In Jabal al-Druze the delegate noted the "exceptional scale of emigration in 1934," reporting that in total 6,230 Druze had left their villages for Lebanon, Palestine, Transjordan, and Syria. Although he expected many to eventually return, he indicated that it depended on the Agricultural Bank's willingness to provide the assistance they needed to sow their lands.[303] In southern Lebanon the delegate observed that the exodus from countryside to town had increased "in a disturbing way since our arrival in the country," attributing peasant flight primarily to the burden of taxes.[304] The government's plan to reinstate the *terbiʿ* in 1935 and to collect back taxes further fueled discontent.[305]

While French officials disparaged Ottoman land and tax policies as defective and lacking in "order and cohesion" in contrast to their own, villagers, landowners, and economic elites contrasted mandate policies unfavorably with Ottoman ones.[306] Mandate policies, they protested, were disproportionate, irrational, and abstract, with the extraction demanded from agriculture completely detached from the realities of the land's production. Some petitioners insisted on a return to the prior system with assessors determining taxes based on the year's harvest yields or reducing the rate to one that villagers could pay while still ensuring their subsistence.[307] In Alexandretta the recent introduction of the land tax (*contribution foncier*) was "for [farmers] a disagreeable surprise since it brought very significant disturbances to agricultural methods practiced *ab antique* by the uniform taxation of all the lands, cultivated or not," while increasingly outdated assessments for the fixed tax led to extreme cases of disproportionate taxation in relation to actual revenues.[308] The use of tax collectors from outside the village was also a source of discontent. The Maronite archbishop of Damascus suggested a return to tax collection by local village leaders (*mukhtars*), who "living locally, know the inhabitants and can collect the taxes at an opportune time; whereas the tax collectors, strangers to the region, do not make but short and rare appearances. . . . Furthermore the method of collecting taxes by the mukhtars would economize nine-tenths of the budget of the tax collectors."[309]

In Hama, a region of "bad payers," according to the assistant delegate, a letter signed by almost 250 signatories insisted that Ottoman policies were fair and rational compared with mandate methods.

> We were hoping that our condition during the time of the mandate of the esteemed French government would be closer to justice and logic than during the Turkish government; rather, the reality of the situation is we see our condition in a wreck. Instead of continual progress [we] confront unceasing decline. Now we pay three times as much as we paid during the time of the Turkish government in taxes, despite the greater support of circumstances for agriculture at that time from the present, considering the proportionality of the expenses of production and its value and the lack of encountering pests like those which have stricken the farmer for ten years until now from the Sunn bug, lack of water, and others. The tithe [*dariba al-ʿushriya*] and the property tax [*dariba al-amlakiya*] on land, even though they existed during the time of the Turkish government, they were nominal more than real, and what was levied on the taxpayers [was] in a manner realistic to circumstances, and that which was levied was taken with justice, i.e., the tithe was taken in kind [*ʿaynan*] or by its actual, true price. In current conditions it is taken with a price greater than its actual price by a lot.[310]

Adopting the discourse of progress, the petition writers expressed their appreciation for the concept and then proceeded to argue point by point how Ottoman policies were actually more just and logical than those of the mandate.[311] They also insisted on the illegality of collection methods, which "seek to recover [agricultural taxes] without observance of the law that

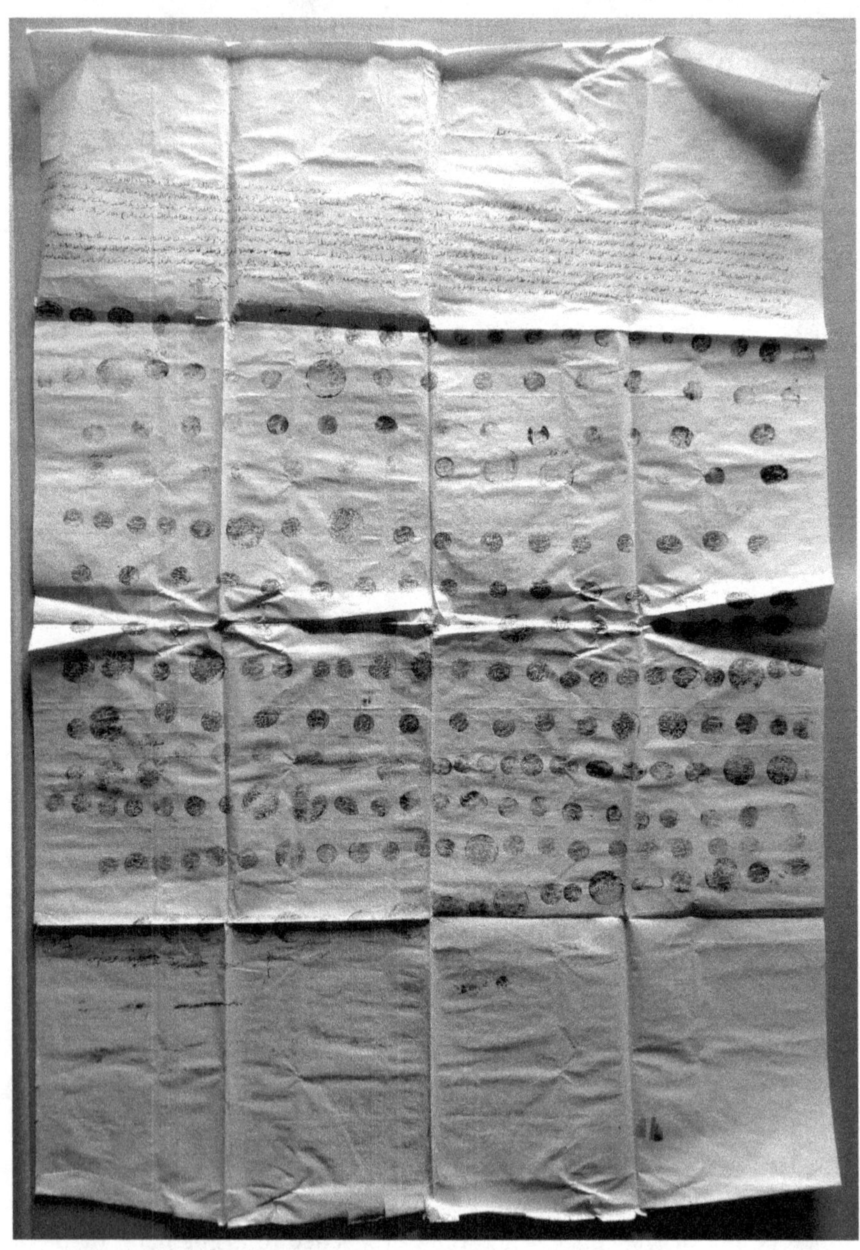

FIGURE 25. Petition from Hama cultivators protesting tax collection, 1935. Reproduced with permission of the Centre des Archives Diplomatiques de Nantes, Syrie-Liban/1, 867.

exempts seeds and provisions."[312] The High Commission's delegate to the Syrian Republic dismissed their claims, writing de Martel that both he and the minister of finance agreed that it was necessary "to react vigorously in this *sanjak* against fiscal laziness," resorting to the same platitude that a response to certain demands was under study by the ministry for 1936.[313] Cultivators anxious about their seed supplies and subsistence for 1935 were unlikely to be mollified by such assurances.

During the summer of 1935 the plight of cultivators became front-page news in the nationalist press. The National Bloc newspaper *al-Qabas* recounted harrowing tales of farmers forbidden from extracting their grain until they paid all their back taxes. Officials were sent to villages to prevent the harvest from being moved to threshing floors in addition to searching markets and requisitioning crops "as if [they were] drugs or weapons."[314] Farmers resisted, contending that paying all the demanded taxes would take their entire crop, if not more, and would leave them with nothing to eat or to sow. In Homs a group of farmers demanded that the tithe be reduced at least by half or they would leave their "crops to fate."[315] One reporter described a scene he witnessed in which a group of farmers begged the local financial official "to permit them to take out what will barely keep them and their families alive" because they did not even have food for one day, but the official was uncompromising in his refusal.[316] Another writer, identified as a *fallah* from Homs, scorned the government's offer to lower the tithe by only 30% and lambasted the ban on removing the crops from storehouses, which left them at the mercy of rats and the elements. He contrasted the government's uncompromising position with a farmer who milked his cows only to the extent that he had fed them, insisting that "this [approach] does not appeal to our government because it does not give anything yet wants to milk in a manner that God has not permitted."[317] He suggested that the government could learn from the farmer who had to strike a balance between feeding and milking his animals.

Nationalist leaders continued to position themselves as defenders of the oppressed peasant. In the midst of the crisis, citing the government's ongoing lack of response to their demands, the Damascus, Homs, and Hama Chambers of Agriculture resigned and "delegations of *agriculteurs*" from throughout Syria arranged a meeting in Damascus. As one large-landowning attendee summarized their conclusions, the rate of taxation "had taken a real form of dispossession, driving the peasants to misery.

Today they can no longer pay anything."[318] To ameliorate the situation, the meeting's attendees demanded a new estimation to establish a revised fixed tithe based on net revenues, assessed after taking into account deductions for expenses and grain prices. Despite the government touting the formation of a commission to help peasants after studying the Chamber of Agriculture's proposals, the commission had not proceeded to any practical plans of action. If the government persisted in its "negligence," large landowners throughout Syria threatened to leave their lands uncultivated.[319]

Some farmers seem to have taken these elites at their word as mediators. In one instance a group of villagers appealed to Fakhri al-Barudi to intervene on their behalf against their *mudir* and his violent tax collection methods. Al-Barudi reportedly sent them to the high commissioner along with an open letter excoriating the administration and its employees but also congratulating them on pursuing policies that would encourage civil disobedience.[320] Meanwhile, in Homs, the Financial Services, seemingly intent on sending a message to obstinate and obstreperous elites, broke into the homes of three notables who had not paid their taxes to seize their movable assets.[321]

When French officials made promises about looking into reforms for 1936, an article in the nationalist press rejected any reform that did not come from Parliament and attacked French officials' competence, questioning in particular the French finance counselor's capacity "to pronounce upon the commercial, financial, and agricultural politic to adopt in the country."[322] Another article by an author who identified himself as a farmer from Homs lamented how the government's current policies made taxation rank alongside the Sunn bug and field mice as a major pest of agriculture.[323] In the summer of 1936 the government formed estimation commissions to reevaluate the tithe, and although one report suggested that this measure had lessened discontent, as the summer drew to a close other reports surfaced of acts of resistance.[324] Some villagers repulsed one tax collector's efforts because they stated "unanimously and directly" that a new government more favorable to their interests would soon be in power, an apparent reference to the ongoing treaty negotiations in Paris (news it had been signed reached Syria on 10 September).[325] Nonetheless, the summer of 1936 saw "some of the worst bankruptcies since the great world depression . . . aggravated by unusually poor harvests in the Hawran," indicating that such measures were too little too late.[326]

Eventually French officials had to admit that the harvest "dominated" the finances of the government: "If the harvest is abundant, the tax is easily collected and the budget balances. Drought produces scarcity and the deficit; no savings, no bank resources to assure the wealth of the treasury."[327] Duraffourd continued to churn out his annual cadastral progress reports, but in the absence of the cadastre's completion and perhaps also in response to the furor taxation methods had provoked under the mandate, in 1938 he also produced an analysis that compared Ottoman and mandate taxation methods with the system French administrators had used in Tunisia and Morocco, the *tertib*.[328] The *tertib*, which had initially been proposed for Syria, was a proportional tax assessed on the gross production of the harvest, but only at 5%.[329] His assessment acknowledged the concerns of Syrian landowners and peasants regarding the difficulties of assessing a fixed tax given the fluctuations in climatic conditions prevailing in the region. However, he also insisted that they were being stubborn, even irrational, out of habit, underlining (literally) that "it is nearly impossible to make them understand that they benefit in the system of a set tax at a rate that is, in the majority of cases, less than that which would result from the strict application of the texts determining in the past the tithe."[330]

Such an assessment did not acknowledge farmers' and local technocrats' main complaint about the fixed tax: its basis in an average of four relatively good years made increasingly disproportionate by currency depreciation, falling market prices, and changes in cultivation practices. Local technocrats and agronomists had generally been skeptical of the fixed tax, well aware of its ignominious past during the short-lived implementation attempts by Ottoman governors, and instead promoted a tax based on net revenues that accounted for and encouraged investment. As for Syrian farmers, until there were reserves that would allow them to make up the difference in a year of deficient harvests, they preferred to pay a proportional tax.[331] The mandate policies that had ravaged agriculture for almost two decades—inadequate responses to insects, rodents, and drought, lack of investment, and unrelenting tax collection—combined with the fallout from the global economic depression had made building such reserves practically impossible. In addition, the disproportionate tax burden led to "many lands . . . being left uncultivated because of the lack of working capital," discouraging investment and employment in agriculture.[332]

Duraffourd, after evaluating a number of options for assessing agricultural taxes, eventually concluded that, although the *tertib* would actually be the best option for Syria, it required "a suitable organization and specialized personnel," which were not available. He thus suggested the fixed tax used in Palestine,[333] which required classifying lands but not evaluating them, and an *impôt foncier* derived from the value of land sales like that used by Switzerland and Turkey.[334] The fixed-tax option sounded suspiciously similar to what ʿAtallah had urged back in 1924. Almost two decades after bleeding the country dry of its agricultural wealth, or as Syrian farmers liked to put it, milking it beyond what it had been fed, at least one French official finally admitted that maybe the mandate's approach to taxation had not been so rational after all.

As for nationalist leaders, when the new Syrian Parliament convened to debate and craft policy following post-treaty elections and the installation of a National Bloc government at the end of 1936, supporting agriculture was a top priority. The elections had indicated widespread support for the National Bloc, including in rural districts where the Bloc refrained from running candidates and instead allowed local community leaders to run as "nationalists."[335] During the ensuing year, the government passed multiple decrees for a moratorium on debt and a law that "completely reworked" the statutes regulating the Agricultural Bank.[336] Representatives reportedly outdid themselves declaiming against the neglect agriculture had suffered under the mandate, leading to what currently afflicted it "from underdevelopment and deterioration and from stagnation and ruin."[337] Plans were afoot to increase the ministry's budget by 80% from the previous year, such an increase being necessitated by the budget's previous paucity, although it would still make up only 2.78% of the general budget. Even at that rate, the increased budget would not exceed 35,000 Egyptian pounds for all of Syria, which was similar to east Jordan's agricultural budget, even though east Jordan was comparable to only one Syrian *muhafaza*.[338] "Only after the production wheel turned its natural rotation" had the peasant and the farmer finally begun to feel some measure of "ease and prosperity after that suffocating distress and that trouble [i.e., during the years 1929–1935]."[339] The cycles of agricultural production needed time to recover from years of insufficient inputs and the devastation of both human and environmental disruptions. It was during these debates that al-Hakim had expressed his desire to see agriculture properly funded so long as it was based on a well-planned program with "stringent, effective oversight."[340] With such a program, the parliament's "respected representatives" (i.e., the country's elites) could demonstrate their "dedication to the health of the countryside's inhabitants and its social and economic life" and "the enlightenment of its children in practical agricultural education." The *Syrian Agricultural Journal* (essentially a restoration of *Modern Agriculture* under a different name but with the same editor and supported by the government) thanked the representatives for their noble intentions, insisting that "first the rain fell in drops, then it pours."[341]

Conclusion

The 6 April 1937 issue of *al-Qabas* lamented the decline of the condition of the *fallah* since the war, accusing "the responsible powers" of "contempt and negligence . . . until the *fallah* has become like the milk cow that benefits with her milk and good things her owner who neglects to care for her and is not interested in ensuring the continuity of her milk."[342] The unrelenting quest of mandate officials to premise a stable budget on agricultural production ran smack into the unpredictability of yields from ecologies well-known for their annual variability. Their decision to raise custom fees to make up the gap between expected and actual tax revenues only furthered the region's economic travails. Echoing the criticisms leveled at mandate taxation policies and their impact on agriculture, the all-Syrian Chamber of Commerce Congress decried these customs policies as having for their "primary goal . . . to maximize income not the future of commerce."[343] Local officials also complained about the lack, "strange as it seems," of "any organization of permanent coordination and collaboration between the Directorates of Agriculture of our different states."[344]

As French officials revamped Ottoman policies to create a colonial state space that served the priorities of a French imperial sphere—that is, making investment in land more attractive to foreign, particularly French, capital and prioritizing a cadastre that would ensure that land's legibility to the same, all within a fragmented political landscape created to facilitate their rule—local officials pushed back. Local officials' proposals prioritized investment but focused on its central role in establishing the institutions of an economically integrated national state space that would facilitate coordination and the creation of an environment that encouraged, and even rewarded, the risk taking necessary to stay competitive in global markets.

Such aspirations ran counter to French goals. Instead, under the mandate, assistance to farmers, when it occurred, largely consisted of the basic resources they needed to start each season and was often calculated as a political gesture to thwart nationalist ambitions.[345] The cumulative effect of these policies was to produce ongoing cycles of increasing debt as farmers struggled with the escalating demands of tax and debt collection alongside old and new environmental factors whose effects were not limited by political boundaries. The nature of the agricultural cycle meant that the negative impacts of these events grew over time, resulting in spiraling "unevenness" both between different communities in Syria and Lebanon and between the region and the global sphere.

The escalating outcry from villagers and nationalist elites alike met dismissal from French officials. Despite internal correspondence acknowledging that the complaints were legitimate, official responses insisted that the grievances were primarily politically motivated, especially when they came from elites. As for peasant farmers, reports and analyses tended to depict them as perpetually oppressed, resistant to change, and inured to violence, not as having legitimate concerns.[346] Jacques Weulersse, a member of the Institute Français de Damas from 1932–1938, protégé of Albert Demangeon, and the author of an often-cited book about the Syrian peasantry, insisted that mandate efforts at land distribution had intended to create small peasant property owners.[347] Statistics from the end of the mandate suggest that its implementation had the opposite effect, increasing land consolidation.[348] But Weulersse was dismissive of the mandate's role in this process, attributing it to peasants' inability to defend their "new rights" because of their "ignorance" or "suspicion" in an "anti-peasant society."[349]

Mandate officials' insistence on assessing an abstract, increasingly arbitrary tax on agricultural production detached from the realities of production and markets left farmers increasingly indebted, desperate, and exposed as the mandate progressed. As a result, this situation intensified pressure on elite landowners, who struggled to fulfill their obligations to the peasants who worked their land. Meanwhile, local agronomists and technocrats scrambled to propose solutions to the environmental challenges and alternatives to the administrative ones. In doing so, their demands referenced a broader international context in which like-minded officials elsewhere were grappling with similar problems. They advocated comprehensive state infrastructure and interstate coordination that would simultaneously mediate rural communities' exposure to international markets, support scientific experimentation, and ensure a secure environment for investment, all aimed at trying to counter the unevenness that colonial state space had wrought. Mandate officials' understanding of local dynamics as primarily composed of antagonism between rapacious landlords and oppressed peasants left no space to acknowledge these technocrats' aspirations or contributions or how an emphasis on cultivator welfare and productivity was fundamental to their vision for the nation's economic prosperity.

With the region's agricultural production and their own interests at stake, landowning nationalist elites organized in their defense around the issue of agrarian reform, arrogating to themselves the roles of mediator and defender of the oppressed peasant and cultivator. Their critiques as well as those of villagers contradicted French discursive representations of "progress" and "justice," stressing instead the arbitrary and abstract nature of mandate rule that had resulted in desperation and loss. This state of affairs tended to reinforce elites' position as intermediaries, leading them to claim as their fundamental duty and responsibility under a new nationalist government the shielding and protection of the nation's peasants from the effects of colonial rule.

EPILOGUE

As World War II raged, a group of technocrats and agronomists from Syria and Lebanon met in Beirut on April 19–26, 1942, for a third *semaine sociale* to discuss and reflect on the topic of "l'Agriculture Richesse Nationale."[1] Expounding on their version of agricultural *mise en valeur* for Syria and Lebanon, they emphasized "the social and moral significance of these reforms" in a manner that was decidedly secular in its assessment.[2] Their evaluation was also overwhelmingly critical, despite the fact that these men represented some of the most privileged under the mandate's administration. The themes were familiar, repeating the same refrain that had characterized technocrats' proposals since the mandate's inception: irrigation, education, markets, land-tenure reform, credit, and the paradox of a rural to urban exodus alongside an enthusiasm among elites for a "return to the land."[3] Ultimately, they concluded, mandate policies had had a deleterious effect on local agricultural infrastructure.

Fouad Saadé, in his overarching assessment of "le problème agricole," was unstinting in his scathing appraisal of the mandate government's record, with its emphasis on proposals over action. He cited the continuing dominance of large landownership, the "lack of a master plan and perseverance" for disseminating "modern" technical methods, the nonexistence of agricultural schools, farm schools, research stations, and model fields, and even the failure to pursue a "rational test of dry farming."[4] Like many of his Syrian and Lebanese colleagues during the mandate, Saadé was just as qualified, if not more so, within French networks of expertise, not to mention Syrian and Lebanese ones, than many of the French officials he likely had to deal with. He was a Lebanese agronomist who had received his agricultural engineering (*ingénieur agricole*) diploma from the National School of Agriculture in Montpellier in 1924, and, out of the forty-four students in his class, he had received the silver medal.[5]

Saadé's solution echoed that of his colleagues from decades before: more state support for agriculture. To be competitive, Syrian-Lebanese agriculture needed "under directive of the state, to discipline itself with a view to exploiting at best the cultures perfectly adapted to our climate and our soil."[6] "Anemic agricultural budgets" had led "a skeletal administration to vegetate miserably." Funds and an agricultural politics realized by "rational application" were urgently required.[7] Egypt, Palestine, and Cyprus offered examples that Syria and Lebanon could emulate in building these agricultural institutions, including agricultural cooperatives.[8] From the collaborative efforts for building infrastructure that had characterized the initiatives of elites and state officials in the late Ottoman period, the centrality of "state-directed planning" to implementing "modern" agriculture had emerged as a fully articulated concept.

However, mandate rule had injected its particular politics into this trajectory, disrupting these infrastructure-building initiatives with its own priorities. Mandate officials had divided the region into statelets, whose maintenance or expansion of this infrastructure operated primarily according to the dictates of political expediency and relationships cultivated between cooperative elites and mandate officials. In the early days of World War II this state of affairs posed a challenge to officials seeking to mobilize the region's resources for the war effort. As Charles Pavie explained, when the Service Agricole of the Economic Office of War was created, it confronted a situation in which,

> during the mandate period, no comprehensive action, no coordination of scattered efforts had been done. . . . The counselors of each state or *sanjak* working as they pleased. . . . No comprehensive guidelines, no technical centralization to the Delegation of the information that constituted the archives and documents of the local agricultural services. No inventory of the means of implementation that these same services

> had at their disposition, especially when these were the result of personal activity deployed by the counselors.[9]

During wartime, the lack of coordination and centralization that mandate officials had considered an essential component of their divide-and-rule tactics for maintaining control and thwarting nationalist ambitions became a substantial liability.

In April 1941 the British government formed the Cairo-headquartered Middle East Supply Center (MESC) with the immediate aim of curtailing civilian imports into the region and facilitating the movement of war supplies.[10] Following the fall of the Vichy regime in Syria and Lebanon in July 1941, the MESC extended its operations into the area, taking steps to intervene in this decentralized administration through the Spears Mission.[11] A year later—the same year as the agriculture-focused *semaine sociale*—it became a joint agency with the United States. A key consequence of the center's activities was an attempt at broad regional coordination of economic activity, particularly that involving agriculture, in an effort to reshape the region's "economic geographies."[12] To reduce reliance on imports, the MESC prioritized increasing essential food supplies through local production.[13] It boosted production by importing large quantities of machinery and fertilizers, encouraging a substantial expansion in land under cultivation, especially in the Jazira.[14] Aerial grain surveys sought to monitor the extent of crop production, while censuses, centralized grain collection directly from farmers, distribution controlled through the newly established Bread Grains Office (Office des céréales panifiables), and a rationing regime aimed to ensure more uniform access.[15] As inflation soared and some benefited, including speculators and merchants, others' purchasing power plummeted.[16] To address the increased currency supply, the MESC proposed assessing more direct taxes. This proposition found little traction in a government filled with landowners for whom memories of contestations over the mandate's direct taxation policies were likely still fresh.[17] In 1942 the government finally replaced the tithe and land tax with a tax on agriculture that affected "the commercial part of this production" and instituted a new tax on revenue deemed more "in harmony with the principle of the capacity to contribute."[18] Even though the tax rate was only 3–4%, it provoked outrage in urban areas.[19]

Previous assessments of the MESC's role have credited it with being instrumental in shaping key "institutional mechanisms" in the independent nation-states that emerged in the region postwar and precipitating a shift from market-based liberalism to statist development strategies. Such assessments have suggested that local elites' participation in MESC operations was fundamental to developing their administrative acumen.[20] Indeed, some post-independence institutions, such as MIRA, the government grain collection agency that managed distribution between Syria and Lebanon, clearly had roots in the MESC's operations.[21] Other scholars have traced the Syrian state's emphasis on agricultural self-sufficiency, state control, and centralized planning back to the late 1950s.[22] A perspective of over a century, however, demonstrates that local technocrats and bureaucrats, many of whom were eminently well qualified within the networks of expertise in which they circulated, had prioritized a state-centered approach to economic planning, particularly in relation to agriculture, since the beginning of the mandate and before. What the MESC did accomplish was to largely supplant French authority and influence over economic policy in the region, creating a space in which local technocrats could begin to enact their vision, although they would have to wait until the end of World War II to fully gain independent administrative control.

But the world in which newly independent Syria and Lebanon found themselves was very different from that of the post–World War I era. Instead of Colonial Party members scheming to devise a system that would make their imperial ambitions palatable within the League of Nations framework, the United Nations emerged in a world teeming with development economists, engineers, and other such specialists jockeying to bolster their respective national interests as much as their universalizing vision of development. There was even an International Bank for Reconstruction and Development, founded in 1944, ready to disperse, with conditions, the infusions of capital that elites had desired for decades. The Syrian and Lebanese governments were keen to avail themselves of these resources, but on their own nationalist terms. Whereas in 1917 and 1922 local technocrats and agronomists such as Hüseyin Kâzım and Mustafa al-Shihabi had crafted recommendations for agricultural development at the behest of Ottoman and national governments, respectively, in 1946 the Syrian government commissioned a London-based consulting firm to survey the country's resources and provide advice.[23] Just under a decade later it requested another report from the International Bank for Reconstruction and Development. Foreign experts made up both teams. The Lebanese government quickly availed itself of a loan from the bank for electrical power and irrigation projects.[24]

Meanwhile, other foreign experts, many of whom had worked with the MESC, began to compile their own independent assessments of what they understood as the region's "possibilities of development."[25] As French mandate power waned, they were quick to offer their visions regarding what they perceived to be the region's need for expertise and technical assistance. The Scientific Advisory Mission established under the auspices of the MESC had initially provided advice on issues of production and supply, but, more long term, its remit included the goal of identifying "the main scientific and technical problems facing the Middle East region."[26] Following a conference in Cairo in February 1944 attended by foreign and local agronomists and technocrats, one of the mission's members, B. A. Keen, compiled a report and presented its recommendations to the MESC's director general in May 1945.[27] In a similar vein, the development economist Doreen Warriner, who had also worked with the MESC, wrote a series of reports for the Royal Institute of International Affairs in London; these reports were largely based on the work of French mandate scholars and the studies of Paul Klat, a scholar at the American University of Beirut, whom she had enlisted during the war to compile studies about three villages in the region.[28]

The representation of the region that emerged from these reports was one that largely parroted the rhetorical frameworks and stock explanations of mandate officials. In this analysis rural Syria was ridden with poverty primarily because of its lack of small peasant proprietors. Vast stretches of fallow, indicative of extensive cultivation practices by farmers who had not yet adopted "modern" methods, or fertile but uncultivated land demonstrated "a great waste of land resources" driven by the dominance of oppressive landlords who were uninterested in improving their lands and oppressed peasants who had no incentive to invest. Lebanon fared somewhat better in this narrative as thoroughly cultivated, much of it intensively so, by peasants with a higher standard of living because they were primarily landowners.[29] Still "development" of its fruit industry had been "chaotic," and farmers had not yet "adopted simple poultry improvements methods."[30]

The essence of these reports' recommendations for development, however, paralleled those that local technocrats had been making for the past half century, if not longer. They urged finishing the cadastral survey and eliminating *musha*ʿ and "strip" farming. Cooperative societies and more accessible credit, especially from an agricultural bank focused on small cultivators, would break farmers' reliance on merchants and moneylenders. Setting up multiple dry-farming experimental communities, building infrastructure for machinery maintenance and training in its use, decreasing the precarity of water resources, and improving pest- and disease-control methods and coordination were all priorities.[31] Because the tithe had been abolished, agricultural production was taxed at 7% when products were brought to market. One report suggested that this tax should be augmented with a land tax levied in proportion to the land's production but at a low enough rate that "detailed, complex classification of land" would be unnecessary; it would also exclude smallholdings.[32] In sum, it was a program for a host of state-directed institutions and initiatives that would reduce risk, facilitate experimentation, make resources more legible for capital investment, and allow for a degree of extraction, but not to the detriment of small farmers.

Echoing the critiques of local technocrats, the reports cast Syria and Lebanon's lack of facilities for agricultural training and education as a major impediment to their development prospects. Despite the "obvious need," Keen noted that there was no "full-scale agricultural experiment station in the Lebanon or in Syria." Furthermore, he was doubtful that qualified personnel could be found to run such as station, noting, "There is little provision for agricultural education or the training of candidates for posts in the agricultural service" and that "the few agricultural assistants and advisors have mostly been trained in French schools, e.g., Algiers, to not a very high standard."[33] The course at the Beirut International College, he noted, was insufficient for teacher training, especially because it lacked an experimental farm. As a result, "help" needed to "be sought abroad, either by sending students to study abroad or by the temporary employment of foreign teachers," with the latter deemed more desirable.[34] Keen's assessment reflected the deterioration of the region's agricultural educational infrastructure after decades of mandate rule and reiterated the criticisms that local technocrats had been making about its condition for almost as long.

Reports prepared for the Syrian government also underscored the need to expand agricultural education and training. Recommendations included recruiting foreign experts or sending Syrian employees abroad for training;

that is, policies pursued to further the region's dependence on French metropole institutions produced results that justified perpetuating foreign intervention or dependence by another means.[35] This training would ensure staff for extension-service-like programs who would work closely with farmers or for a network of demonstration farms that would determine the best crops for each locality, teach farmers how to plant them, and distribute seeds and advice. Rural education would work to maintain children in their villages, and expanded intermediate and secondary education would prepare students for government positions. The government would maintain ongoing exchanges of information with other regional states.[36] It was a plan that could have been taken straight from an Ottoman technocrat's playbook for imperial agricultural development or from reforms pursued by the Faysali government; however, nowhere in these assessments was there an acknowledgment of the Ottoman legacy or frustrated local technocratic attempts to pursue these very goals for well over two decades.

Also largely absent from these reports was any discussion of how mandate policies had shaped the region's "special problems" that they identified.[37] Warriner, for example, emphasized how French officials had tried to pursue various measures, only to be defeated by the intransigence of "village custom," local "confusion," or their ill-advised collaboration with "the landowners."[38] Local technocratic efforts to establish cooperatives, reform the Agricultural Bank, lobby for irrigation works, and extend village-level education received passive voice recognition—for example, "efforts were made" but failed to "raise the standard of the peasant" because of "the framework of the existing system."[39] Such sweeping generalizations and lack of actors obscured local technocrats' activities and the resistance they had faced from mandate policies. It also led to seeming non sequiturs, such as Warriner's insistence that Duraffourd's cadastral office had been "successful" but that there still had been "no fundamental reforms in the land system."[40] Meanwhile, she understood the Syrian government's decision to discontinue this work post-mandate as a victory for "large landowners," despite the government's insistence that it was for lack of funds.[41]

Such an ahistorical understanding of the changes that had affected agriculture over the preceding century perhaps goes a long way in explaining Warriner's surprise, expressed in a follow-up report written almost a decade later, about agriculture's rapid expansion in the region. Warriner expressed amazement at the rapidity with which mechanization had taken off since the "inertia" of ten years prior, "completely confut[ing] some current doctrines." According to these doctrines, economic development required "foreign capital, foreign experts, good public services, long-term planning, agrarian reform, plus, for good measure, a revolution." According to Warriner, "Syria has had none of these things," and its "governments have done almost nothing to promote agricultural development," the exception being the establishment of a cotton bureau.[42]

Instead, Warriner attributed one of the main sources of this sudden expansion to what she termed the merchant-tractorists. These were merchants who had amassed substantial wartime profits, which they then invested in cultivating lands located along the desert line east of Aleppo, by the Euphrates, and into the Jazira. They rented these lands from shaykhs who had been granted them by French authorities in 1940 and 1941.[43] In contrast to landowners in the "old regions," by which she meant Homs, Hama, the Hawran, and Jabal al-Druze, who were "not much interested in long-term improvement," she characterized the merchant-tractorists as enterprising "risk-takers, gamblers in grain and investors in irrigation" who were "self-made men, with no inherited wealth."[44] The fact that the government had come to the immediate aid of distressed farmers after a drought in 1955 by distributing seed, while the agricultural and state banks had imposed an immediate moratorium, does not seem to have registered as crucial to sustaining their success, despite her acknowledgment that without the banks' assistance they would have gone bankrupt.[45] As this book has demonstrated, interest in such technologies had been palpable in the region since World War I, if not before, but landowners and farmers had found their ambitions thwarted by mandate trade policies and the insecurity of their income and investments under mandate rule.

This dehistoricized account of agricultural development facilitated the production of a narrative that characterized the region as behind in the process of modernization, at a stage resembling that of western Europe a century or more before. In contrast to the Beirut *semaine sociale* presentations, where speakers decried the actively detrimental impact of mandate policies, in these development reports, if they mentioned mandate policies at all, it was primarily to highlight their incapacity to imprint on a fundamentally "static" society. According to this logic, the issues identified represented endemic problems characteristic of a phase of development that "western Europe and Great Britain" had passed through centuries before, whereas the Middle East was just on the verge of this shift.[46] "Syrian society [was] no longer static," Warriner proclaimed, now that its "rapid upward and outward expansion resemble[d] that of Western Europe during the nineteenth century; or perhaps the Middle West would be a better comparison." Notably, she did not attribute this state of affairs to state involvement, which she claimed had "played little part in economic life"; rather, it was the "rise of new liberal entrepreneurs," operating in the vein of "Victorian business men," who were responsible for this shift.[47] There was no place in these narratives to acknowledge more than a century of technocratic efforts by Ottoman, Syrian, and Lebanese state officials to create, refine, and refashion multiple institutions that would have enabled them to intervene in rural communities, increasing their legibility to administrators and their productive capacity for the treasury.

Rather, within a broader discussion of "Middle East agricultural development," Syria and Lebanon's agricultural sector was rapidly becoming a clearly defined "object of development" with its own distinct parameters.[48] These observations did not go unnoticed by local authorities and technocrats, who were not uninterested in the insights these reports might provide. Nonetheless, when the Cultural Department of the League of Arab States commissioned an Arabic translation of Keen's *Agricultural Development of the Middle East*, they called on one of their own, the Syrian agronomist Mustafa al-Shihabi, to provide commentary for it. Al-Shihabi corrected, expounded on, and added context to the report's exaggerations, overgeneralizations, and quickly out-of-date assessments regarding the region's infrastructure, with emphasis on Syria in particular.[49] Yet his commentary was unlikely to reach a wide audience beyond the Arabic-speaking world, whereas the English-language development reports and their representations of the region were likely to be widely read.[50]

Al-Shihabi, meanwhile, would not mince words in criticizing the mandate's impact. In a series of essays titled "Lectures in Colonialism" ("Muhadarat fi al-Istiʿmar"), which he published in 1956 and 1957 and presented to the Institute of Advanced Arabic Studies, he covered a wide range of topics related to both the history of colonialism and the recent experience of its effects on Syria under the mandate. He devoted an especially critical section to the Agriculture Ministry, contrasting in no uncertain terms the agriculture politics of mandate rule unfavorably with what had preceded it.[51] He complained of the government's inability to combat pests, its failure to open depots for distributing useful agricultural implements as the Ottoman and Faysali governments had done, and its closure of the Salamiya school while opening the Bouka one for "political not agricultural" reasons.[52]

Al-Shihabi lambasted the French counselor of agriculture for maintaining a rather cozy relationship with senior large landowners, spending much of his time offering them coffee and cigarettes when they came to visit him while neglecting the practical work required of the government to support agriculture. Despite the trope of the unscrupulous landlord being a fixture in French justifications for their land and tax policies, in practice, those willing to cooperate with mandate rule found that their interests were largely not threatened. As for the counselor, the main evidence of his activities, according to al-Shihabi, was copious "theoretical reports" from which "the agriculture of the country does not advance."[53] Progress, he suggested, was a product of applied practice and experimentation and coordinated government support—that is, the technocratic approaches that he and his colleagues had urged for decades and that they considered essential to facilitating intervention in rural areas. In contrast to French narratives about the progress and rational approaches their rule was supposed to impart to the region, for al-Shihabi state-directed local technocratic intervention constituted the path to a "modern" and "rational" agricultural infrastructure that the region required for its agricultural development.

This technocratic vision was one with roots in the reforms pursued by Ottoman officials from over a century before. This book has traced the permutations of these reforms during the intervening century to illuminate the continuities with these origins even as local technocrats grappled with technological change and imperial transition. One constant throughout was the friction between the ever-mounting demands of capital and the ecological limits of extraction. In contrast to industrial production, attempts to increase the output of agricultural production ran into the constraints of the seasonal cycles of biotic resources and the unpredictability of nature.[54] Facing the challenges and risks of these unpredictable cultivation cycles but also desiring to streamline and make revenue extraction more efficient to meet mounting financial pressures, Ottoman bureaucrats undertook a series of intersecting reforms to make the empire's main source of revenue—its rural agrarian countryside—more legible to government officials. From new land legislation to the Agricultural Bank, provincial reorganization to frequently revised tax collection policies, these reforms aimed to create the administrative structures of a more homogenized and intrusive state space across the empire's provincial hinterlands. They also represented new "way[s] of organizing nature" to respond to the empire's increasingly dire fiscal situation.[55]

At the same time that these reforms enabled a degree of greater homogenization of institutions and levels of oversight, they also created new opportunities for redirecting flows of capital through the countryside. Despite these measures' professed goal of creating and protecting small farmer usufruct holders, local elites often co-opted them in order to consolidate power and pursue their own interests. In Hama, for example, this led to greater land consolidation, not because farmers were afraid to register their land but because local elites took advantage of adverse environmental conditions, namely, drought, coupled with the higher taxes imposed by recent reforms to dispossess peasants who had tried and failed to access the resources of the Agricultural Bank. State officials anxious to uphold the small farmer usufruct holder ideal enshrined in the Land Code struggled with how to thwart such machinations. Yet the institutions of Ottoman state space often depended on the participation of elites to function, which could lead to tensions between them and government officials.

As the empire's financial woes mounted in the wake of the 1870s financial crisis and rising debt, merely streamlining extraction and increasing the possibilities for investment proved insufficient. Ottoman technocrats became increasingly focused on boosting the land's productive capacity as well. Like the students sent abroad to agricultural schools and Reşid Bey during his jaunt to Chicago, they networked with colleagues around the globe, observing new technologies and learning new methods. However, successful implementation required local expertise. To this end, the infrastructure of Ottoman scientific agriculture brought together these internationally networked technocrats and the expertise of local farmers, such as Farmer Ahmet, to experiment with and assess these technologies' suitability to Ottoman ecologies.

Despite these initiatives, many elites were frustrated by their slow pace, demanding greater government investment, better support for risk-taking farmers, especially those with substantial landholdings, and projects focused on the protection and welfare of peasant farmers. Some of their most vocal proponents would occupy prominent positions in the post-1908 CUP government under which this infrastructure's expansion accelerated. Over time, the knowledge produced, deemed "scientific" and therefore distinct from the existing local knowledge that was nonetheless involved in its production, circulated among the empire's model farms and fields, its myriad agricultural schools, and its institutes for regional specialties, such as silk or dairy production. Landowning elites with capital to spare and the security to take on the risks involved were eager consumers of the knowledge that these institutions had to offer. For the vast majority of farmers, however, the practices that these institutions promoted were incompatible with their economic means and land-tenure arrangements.

In the aftermath of World War I, as the region transitioned from Ottoman provinces to French mandate states, local technocrats continued to promote these approaches to rural administration and scientific agriculture but were sidelined by French colonial officials and their policies, offering a stark contrast to the privilege they had enjoyed within the Ottoman bureaucracy. Despite speaking a common technocratic language with French officials, Syrian and Lebanese technocrats found themselves battling to defend their expertise and forge a role as intermediaries between rural communities and a national state space. French officials intent on realigning the region's agricultural infrastructure to respond to the postwar demands of metropole commercial and political interests disregarded their proposals for comprehensive national economic planning. Far from supporting a comprehensive plan, colonial authorities divided the region into statelets and realigned its infrastructure in an effort to create dependency on the metropole and to incorporate the region into a colonial state space.

The tension produced by the opposing goals of these two visions for the region's agriculture came at a pivotal moment globally for technocratic intervention in the rural sphere. World War I had allowed some countries, such as the United States, to greatly expand and mechanize production, whereas other countries found their farmland turned into battlefields. Technocrats around the world, grappling with these consequences, sought new strategies to stay competitive in a world of fluctuating crop prices, where commodities, even highly perishable ones such as frozen meat, could be easily transported and threaten local production.[56] Their strategies took multiple forms: encouraging the use of new technologies, building additional infrastructure, imposing protective tariffs, changing tax policies, ramping up statistics collection. In the United States, for instance, this was the critical period when efforts escalated to make, as Deborah Fitzgerald put it, "every farm a factory."[57]

Syrian and Lebanese technocrats, meanwhile, found their proposals in this vein sidelined by the priorities of mandate officials. The onset of the Great Depression a decade later further exacerbated economic woes in the countryside, spurring even more technocratic action and mobilization across the political spectrum in response to the resulting discontent.[58] In Syria and Lebanon, however, colonial officials spurned local initiatives to respond to the crisis and refused to acknowledge, even despite warnings from their own lower-level administrators, that escalating protest was first and foremost a product of the present moment and the colonial state's administrative policies. As farmers coped with challenges ranging from Sunn bugs to devastating drought, the colonial state demanded increasingly higher taxes that mired farmers in successively deeper piles of debt. The violent disruptions, environmental challenges, and financial uncertainty of the mandate years meant few were willing or had the means to invest in risky new technologies.

Instead of recognizing these dynamics, colonial officials dismissed this discontent and the reluctance to invest as the product of an age-old animosity between negligent, powerful landlords and oppressed peasants who lacked initiative because they did not own their land, with some even comparing the situation to that of *ancien régime* France.[59] Mandate reports highlighted how French officials were maintaining Ottoman policies with modifications to make them more "modern"—modifications such as those involving the Land Law and the Agricultural Bank's statutes that conveniently made them more exploitable within a French imperial space and removed the limited protections they had originally offered cultivators. According to influential French officials, farmers who complained were beholden to a *mentalité* that failed to embrace the improvements that could have relieved their distress. In any event, these accounts insisted, big landowners were a class whose demise was inevitable. Such explanations could not acknowledge the historically contingent circumstances that spurred local landowners', farmers', and technocrats' protests and demands. Neither could they account for the strain that mandate policies had placed on obligations and practices developed in response to meeting the fiscal burden imposed on agriculture in environments that were not always so amenable to carrying these burdens. Finally, a tractor was not just a tractor. Adopting new technologies and methods would entail a number of new obligations—the more elaborate the technology, the more potentially diverse those relationships.[60] The restructuring of local space to suit French imperial ambitions in an increasingly uneven global sphere did not lend itself to taking on these risks or obligations.

Local technocrats were keenly aware of this spiraling unevenness, manifested in increasing rural indebtedness and unfavorable trade balances. They sought to address it by acting as interlocutors using the institutions of national state space to intervene in rural areas while also claiming to protect vulnerable peasants from these escalating global inequalities. Their proposals and projects underscored the centrality of the region's agricultural management to its economic independence, which was inexorably bound up with obtaining its political independence. Steeped in late Ottoman reform programs, they insisted that more radical changes were necessary to meet the unprecedented challenges of their current global reality. They drew inspiration from around the globe as they grappled with the dynamics of a global economy characterized by increasingly fierce competition and uneven economies of scale driven by farmers with access to resources that were less and less beholden to the limits of the "somatic energy regime" and the states who supported them.[61] In contrast to French representations of the region that characterized it as temporally behind, local agronomists and technocrats asserted the immediacy of their ideas to the dictates of their contemporaneous political and geographic context. They drew from their counterparts elsewhere who were also struggling with this transition but crafted proposals that responded to what they understood as their region's particular needs, positioning themselves as those best equipped to manage the material and structural changes that these proposals entailed. Yet their claims to be acting in accordance with "modernity" and "science" clashed with French officials' insistence that they were the sole purveyors of such notions. Furthermore, mandate administrators' insistence on maintaining "Ottoman" practices, albeit tweaked to serve French interests, stymied these technocrats' efforts to innovate.

The region's agricultural space in the aftermath of World War II and independence from mandate control represented an amalgam of the mandate legacy, recent efforts by local elites to reassert control, and the hasty attempt to reorder the region's economic resources under the auspices of the MESC. This situation, coupled with mandate representations of the region as temporally behind, provided fodder for development reports that stressed the region's lack of experts, antiquated land regime, insufficient infrastructure, and lack of credit facilities. But these critiques were nothing new. A perspective of more than 100 years illustrates their deep historical roots among technocrats in the region and their decades-old efforts to address them. It also underscores the challenges posed by local dynamics and the recent obstacles imposed by colonial rule that had reorganized the region's agricultural space and its relations on various scales: global, imperial, and local.

ACKNOWLEDGMENTS

The writing of this book has been a journey of many years and would not have been possible without the support, encouragement, and generosity of many.

I have been lucky to benefit from the kindness and wisdom of many mentors and the support of a number of institutions over the years. The Georgetown History Department is where this project first germinated. Judith Tucker has been unfailing in her encouragement and gentle guidance from the very beginning. Her passion remains a constant inspiration. John McNeill first drew me into the world of environmental history. I have greatly benefited from his support and generosity with his time over the years. James Collins's enthusiasm and thoughtful mentoring never fails to enlighten. I am grateful for his continued good humor. Others who provided guidance or support at key moments include Osama Abi-Mershed, Aparna Vaidik, Alison Games, Mustafa Aksakal, Kathryn Olesko, and Sylvia Önder. At New York University, Zachary Lockman, Ilana Feldman, and Timothy Mitchell each challenged me to consider new perspectives that continue to influence how I approach the writing of history. At the College of William and Mary, Julie Galambush and Tamara Sonn first inspired me and gave me the confidence to embark on this path many years ago.

The research and writing for this project has received support from a number of sources over the years, including a Kluge Fellowship from the

Library of Congress, the Fulbright Institute of International Education, the American Research Institute in Turkey, the Institute for Turkish Studies, a Cosmos Scholars Grant, the Georgetown University Graduate School, the Georgetown University History Department, the US Department of Education Foreign Language and Area Studies Program, the Critical Language Scholarship Program, and the Center for Arabic Study Abroad.

A Postdoctoral Fellowship at the Watson Institute for International and Public Affairs at Brown University gave me crucial time to think and expand on the initial project. At Brown, Beshara Doumani provided encouragement and incisive commentary that pushed me to explore new dimensions in my work. I also would like to thank the faculty of the Brown History Department and the Watson Institute as well as the other postdoctoral fellows who took the time to provide helpful and constructive feedback on the project. I have completed the work on this manuscript as a faculty member in the Department of History at the University of Massachusetts, Lowell, where I have been surrounded by an exceedingly supportive and friendly group of colleagues. For their good-humored encouragement and sage advice, I would like to thank dann j. Broyld, Chris Carlsmith, Abby Chandler, Shehong Chen, Andrew Drenas, Lisa Edwards, Lauren Fogle, Bob Forrant, Elizabeth Herbin-Triant, Paul Keen, Chad Montrie, Michael Pierson, Jane Sancinito, Christoph Strobel, and Patrick Young.

The dedication and enthusiasm of archivists and librarians in countless institutions across three continents were crucial to accessing the materials on which this book is based. I am especially grateful to the staffs of the Ottoman Archives, Atatürk Kitaplığı, the Bibliothèque Orientale in Beirut, the American University of Beirut, the Corm Archive, the Centre des Archives Diplomatiques de Nantes, the Ministère des Affaires Ètrangères archives in Paris, the Marseille Chamber of Commerce archives, and the Library of Congress for their assistance and patience. I would also like to thank the interlibrary loan staff at multiple institutions who have ensured access to otherwise inaccessible sources. In particular, Rose Paton has been indefatigable in her efforts to track down even the most obscure works that I have sought. I am grateful to Meredith Sadler for creating the wonderful, detailed maps. Some of the material in Chapter 5 first appeared in the chapter "Mapping the Cadastre, Producing the *Fellah*: Technologies and Discourses of Rule in French Mandate Syria and Lebanon," in *The Routledge Handbook of the History of the Middle East Mandates*, 1st ed., edited by

Cyrus Schayegh and Andrew Arsan, pp. 170–82 (Routledge, 2015). It is reproduced by permission of Taylor & Francis Group.

At Stanford University Press, I am thankful to Kate Wahl for supporting this project and for her patience and insightful advice throughout the process of bringing this book to fruition. Cat Ng Pavel and Tiffany Mok were assiduous in their efforts to see this book through production, and Mimi Braverman was a diligent copyeditor. I would also like to thank the two anonymous peer reviewers for their insightful and thoughtful comments and enthusiasm for the project.

I thank the participants in the Agrarian Studies Colloquium at Yale University, especially K. Sivaramakrishnan and Basil Bastaki, for their feedback on a portion of the manuscript. I am also grateful to Nora Barakat, Camille Cole, and Peter Hill and the other members of the Ottoman Political Economies Workshop, namely Herman Adney, Önder Akgül, Nader Atassi, Murat Bozluolcay, Lâle Can, Tolga Cora, Aviv Derri, Zoe Griffith, Antonis Hadjikyriacou, Vladimir Hamed-Troyansky, Joanna Innes, Ceyda Karamürsel, Chihab El-Khachab, Anaïs Massot, Nada Moumtaz, Ellen Nye, Daniel Stoltz, Stefan Winter, and Naz Yücel.

Over the course of this project, other friends and colleagues around the world have provided insights, encouragement, and sources; been generous with their erudition; and/or shared memorable adventures and good times. Those who have thereby made this journey all the better include Elena Abbott, Soha El-Achi, Oscar Aguirre-Mandujano, Zeynep Akçakaya, Charles Anderson, Elizabeth Angell, Allen Bailey, Sahar Bazzaz, James Benton, Mary Berkmen, Dominique Blonz, Quentin Brosseau, Allison Brown, Megan Brown, Palmira Brummett, Josh Carney, M. Talha Çiçek, Craig Daigle, Nick Danforth, Yorgos Dedes, Jenn De Vries, Susanna Ferguson, Zach Foster, Aimee Genell, Maïté George, Matthew Ghazarian, Benan Grams, Chris Gratien, Selim Güngörüler, Zerene Haddad, Kelly Hammond, Timur Hammond, Betsy Herbin-Triant, Amy Hsieh, Onur Inal, Simon Jackson, Nancy Jacobs, Aaron Jakes, Jennifer Johnson, Michelle Jurkovich, Anjali Kamat, Rachel Kantrowitz, Sarah Al-Kazaz, Hikmet Kocamaner, Selim Kuru, Avital Livny, Fredrik Meiton, Gabe Michael, Lindsay Michael, Madoka Morita, Duff Morton, Sylvia Mullins, Martha Mundy, Emily Neumeier, Fatma Öncel, Aurelie Perrier, Jackson Perry, Graham Auman Pitts, Nova Robinson, Riad Saadé, Safa Saraçoğlu, Richard Saumarez Smith, Nadya Sbaiti, Danielle V. Schoon, Sherene Seikaly, Nir Shafir, Ali Sipahi, Jordan Smith, Dale Stahl, Kirsten Swenson, Michael

Talbot, Salim Tamari, Steve Tamari, Özge Tekin, Yücel Terzibaşoğlu, Lucy Thiboutot, Meltem Toksöz, Alp Eren Topal, Özlem Unsal, Larisa Veloz, and Murat Cihan Yıldız. I also owe an immense debt of gratitude to friends and colleagues who, in addition to the support mentioned above, read portions of the manuscript and provided critical and incisive feedback, namely, Camille Cole, Muriam Haleh Davis, Aviv Derri, Sam Dolbee, Laura Goffman, Faisal Husain, Hilary Falb Kalisman, Thomas Kuehn, and Naz Yücel. In addition to reading parts of the manuscript, Nora Barakat has provided encouragement, good humor, and insights since this project's earliest days. I am immensely grateful for her friendship and that we had the opportunity to go through the process of publishing our first books together.

Many long conversations with Diane North sustained me over the stages of writing this book. For her continued curiosity and encouragement I am most grateful. Evan A. North did not live to see this book take shape due to his untimely death, but his enthusiasm and care in its early stages was a gift. I would also like to thank Pam Williams and Jack Allen for their hospitality in ensuring I had a home away from home while working in the Library of Congress. Thank you to Catherine Hanor for always being there with a listening ear. Finally, my parents, Alan and Blanche Williams, have been a part of this journey since the beginning with unfailing support for my curiosity and passion for history. This project would not have been possible without them. I dedicate this book to them.

NOTES

Introduction

1. *Türk Ansiklopedisi*, 420; TNA, FO 195.2337, Fontana to Lowther, 15 November 1910. "École Agronome de Paris" is the term used by the British Consul. It is unclear whether he is referring to the Grignon Agricultural School, located in Thiverval-Grignon, or l'Institut national agronomique, located in Versailles, both of which were a short distance from Paris.

2. Kâzım Kadri, *Meşrutiyetten*, 68–69.

3. *Türk Ansiklopedisi*, 420.

4. See Kâzım Kadri, *Meşrutiyetten*, 136–39.

5. Refik and Behcet, *Beyrut Vilayeti*, 1: 58. He moved to Beirut eight months before the start of World War I (Kâzım Kadri, *Meşrutiyetten*, 139).

6. Refik and Behcet, *Beyrut Vilayeti*, vol. 1, frontmatter, 58.

7. Haqqi Bey, *Lubnan*, 2: 367–79. Mount Lebanon's special status had been revoked in 1915, which meant that the Ottoman Interior Ministry appointed its governors (Akarlı, *Long Peace*, 199).

8. Refik and Behcet, *Beyrut Vilayeti*, vol. 1, frontmatter; Kâzım, "Dibajat al-Kitab," 1, 2.

9. Given the administrative divisions of the region into the provinces of Beirut, Syria, and Aleppo, Kâzım's proposal does not refer to Aleppo specifically.

10. Kâzım, "Suriye Ziraatına," 58, 59–60.

11. Kâzım, "Suriye Ziraatına," 59.

12. Kâzım, "Suriye Ziraatına," 59.

13. Kâzım, "Suriye Ziraatına," 61.

14. Kâzım, "Suriye Ziraatına," 63.

15. Kâzım, "Suriye Ziraatına," 60–61.

16. Kâzım, "Suriye Ziraatına," 62, 63.

17. Kâzım, "Lamha," 378.

18. CCM, MQ.5.4/35, "Lettre." See chapter 3 for more details.

19. Roederer and Roederer, *Syrie*.

20. See Shiva, *Violence*; and Worster, *Dust Bowl*, 89–90.

21. For these efforts in France, the United States, Russia, and Japan, see Moulin, *Peasantry*; Paxton, *French Peasant Fascism*; Gilbert, *Planning Democracy*; Fullilove, *Profit of the Earth*; Fitzgerald, *Every Farm a Factory*; Moon, *Plough*; Sunderland, *Taming the Wild Field*; Kotsonis, *Making Peasants Backwards*; Kotsonis, *States of Obligation*; Fernández et al., *Agriculture*; Waswo, "Transformation"; Smethurst, *Agricultural Development*; K. Smith, *Time of Crisis*; and Wigen, *Making of a Japanese Periphery*.

22. During the first decades of the Tanzimat, the region was divided into *eyalets*. Following the promulgation of the first provincial regulation in 1864, the region was redivided between the provinces (*vilayets*) of Syria and Aleppo. Following the events of 1860 in Mount Lebanon, the special district (*mutasarrifiyya*) of Mount Lebanon was created in 1861 and, in 1888, the Ottoman administration carved out the province of Beirut. During the latter decades of the Ottoman Empire, the eastern Mediterranean encompassed the provinces of Syria, Beirut, and Aleppo and the special districts of Mount Lebanon, Zor, and Jerusalem.

23. Several scholars have traced elements of continuity from the late Ottoman period through the mandate, although they all ultimately focus more on the post-Ottoman period. See, for example, Watenpaugh, *Being Modern*; Provence, *Last Ottoman Generation*; Schayegh, *Middle East*; and Norris, *Land of Progress*.

24. Several recent works have underscored the value of tracing continuities and divergences in rural institutions or resource management over time periods distinguished by changes in political regimes. See, for example, Rosenthal, *Fruits of Revolution*; Matteson, *Forests in Revolutionary France*; and Peterson, *Pipe Dreams*.

25. For other recent works in this vein, see Yaycıoğlu, *Partners of the Empire*; Duffy, *Nomad's Land*; and Minawi, *Ottoman Scramble*.

26. Goswami, *Producing India*.

27. Makdisi, "Ottoman Orientalism," esp. 770; Deringil, " 'They Live' "; Norris, *Land of Progress*.

28. Minawi, *Ottoman Scramble*; Kuehn, *Empire*; Minawi, "Beyond Rhetoric"; Kuehn, "Shaping." For a critique of the assumptions underlying this perspective on Ottoman governance, see Cole, "Empire on Edge," 28–29. On institution building even in the Syrian interior, see Barakat, *Bedouin Bureaucrats*.

29. Saraçoğlu, *Nineteenth Century Local Governance*; Aymes, *Grand progrès*.

30. See "French Mandate for Syria and the Lebanon."

31. On the environment influencing human intentions, see Nash, "Agency."

32. For several recent examples, see Mikhail, *Nature and Empire*, 273–74; Jakes, "Boom, Bugs, Bust"; Derr, *Lived Nile*; and Peterson, *Pipe Dreams*.

33. J. W. Moore, *Capitalism*, 2.

34. Robbins, *Political Ecology*, 3. See also Peet et al., *Global Political Ecology*.

35. For works more focused on environmental management, see Mikhail, *Nature and Empire*; S. White, *Climate of Rebellion*; Husain, *Rivers of the Sultan*; and Gratien, *Unsettled*

Plain. For those dealing more specifically with capital accumulation and expertise production, see Jakes, *Egypt's Occupation*; and Derr, *Lived Nile*, respectively.

36. See, for example, Gelvin, *Divided Loyalties*; Khoury, *Urban Notables*; Khoury, *Syria*; Thompson, *Colonial Citizens*; Watenpaugh, *Being Modern*; Dueck, *Claims of Culture*; Hanssen, *Fin de Siècle Beirut*; and Kayalı, *Arabs and Young Turks*. Some scholars have focused on specific aspects of urban-rural relations, such as the Syrian Revolt, instances of peasant resistance, and violent strategies of colonial control. See Provence, *Great Syrian Revolt*; Batatu, *Syria's Peasantry*; Hanna, *al-Qadiya (1820–1920)*; Hanna, *al-Qadiya (1920–1945)*; and Neep, *Occupying Syria*. For one of the only accounts focused on more general change in rural areas, see Lewis, *Nomads*.

37. For the broader repercussions of ideas about technological and scientific superiority in colonial contexts, see Adas, *Machines*.

38. On this shift, see Wrigley, *Energy*; and Mitchell, *Carbon Democracy*.

39. On time-space compression and the forms of control and connection that this facilitated, see Harvey, *Condition of Postmodernity*, 240–83; Headrick, *Tentacles of Progress*; Ross, *Ecology and Power*, 15; Gelvin and Green, *Global Muslims*; and Barak, *Powering Empire*.

40. See Ross, *Ecology and Power*; and Ax et al., *Cultivating the Colonies*.

41. See, for example, Hodge, *Triumph of the Expert*; Ludden, *Agricultural Production*; Ludden, *Early Capitalism*; Ludden, *Agrarian History*; Whitcombe, *Agrarian Conditions*; M. Davis, *Late Victorian Holocausts*; Arnold and Guha, *Nature*; and Beinart and Hughes, *Environment and Empire*. For work on an earlier period, see Grove, *Green Imperialism*.

42. See Burbank and Cooper, *Empires*, 16–17.

43. See Richards, *Egypt's Agricultural Development*, 53–110; and Tucker, *Women*, 36.

44. Owen, *Middle East*, 245.

45. Khater, *Inventing Home*; Labaki, *Introduction*; Ducousso, *Industrie*.

46. On the eastern Mediterranean's diversity and its impact on social spaces, see Doumani, *Family Life*, 16, 39.

47. Most of these areas remained marshlands throughout the period covered in this book, although they would later be drained, especially starting in the 1940s and 1950s. See Métral, "Land Tenure"; and Vedat, "Human-Induced Wetland Degradation."

48. Ashton, "Geography of Syria," 170.

49. Eddé, *Géographie*, 14.

50. Al-Shihabi, *Zira*ʿ*a*, 47–48.

51. Sarrage, *Nécessité*, 113–24; al-Shihabi, *Zira*ʿ*a*, 589–603.

52. Sarrage, *Nécessité*, 115; Ministère des affaires étrangères, *Rapport (1937)*, 64.

53. Al-Shihabi, *Zira*ʿ*a*, 47; Eddé, *Géographie*, 19–20; Ashton, "Geography of Syria," 167–68.

54. See, for example, al-Shihabi, *Zira*ʿ*a*.

55. Burbank and Cooper, *Empires*, 14–15.

56. Raj, *Relocating Modern Science*; DelBourgo and Dew, *Science and Empire*; Bennett and Hodge, *Science and Empire*; Beattie et al., *Eco-Cultural Networks*; Drayton, *Nature's Government*; Boomgaard, *Empire and Science*; Kirchberger and Bennett, *Environments of Empire*. For another perspective on networks, see Arsan, *Interlopers of Empire*.

57. Khoury, *Syria*, 55–57, 89; Burke, "Comparative View"; Mizrahi, *Genèse*. These works tend to focus on officials involved in the early years of the mandate.

58. One exception is Provence, *Last Ottoman Generation*, which examines the impact of the Ottoman legacy through circulations of military officers.

59. Khoury, *Syria*; Khoury, *Urban Notables*. Khoury provides background details on major nationalist and pro-mandate politicians, which he breaks down by religion, education, occupation, and class origin. He then explains their response to mandate rule by how they acted on the "interests" implied by these categories (Khoury, *Syria*, 252–61). Delving into broader political or economic ideas that shaped their approach is beyond the scope of his project.

60. On methodological considerations involved in focusing on individuals, see Cole, "Empire on Edge," 40–42.

61. Omar, "Arabic Thought," 45.

62. See, for example, Thompson, "Akram al-Hourani"; and Ajl, "Political Economy."

63. Seikaly, *Men of Capital*; Jakes, *Egypt's Occupation*.

64. See Jakes, *Egypt's Occupation*, 10.

65. For discussions about the Ottoman "technocratic gaze," see Gratien, "Ottoman Quagmire," 585; and Low, *Imperial Mecca*, 33–34.

66. Many of these men, who for the most part were educated and well-off, were quite influential in the technocratic circles in which they circulated, even though they were not the most wealthy or influential politically, resulting in their relative absence in the literature. Recent work on Egypt has begun to explore the role of some of these elites. See Derr, *Lived Nile*; and Gasper, *Power of Representation*. For the more substantial literature on urban notables, see, for example, Khoury, *Urban Notables*; and Schilcher, *Families in Politics*.

67. For Istanbul elites, see Quataert, "Ottoman Reform."

68. Lefebvre, "Space and the State," 227, 243–44.

69. Goswami, *Producing India*, 32; emphasis in original.

70. Mitchell, "Society," 77.

71. For instance, Ottoman officials, in an effort to reduce the power and influence of certain "imperial intermediaries," implemented policies that expanded the array of intermediaries on whom they relied, diffusing power in the process, and increasingly prioritized the employment of officials trained in the empire's expanding school system. See Fortna, *Imperial Classroom*; Rogan, "Aşiret Mektebi"; Provence, *Last Ottoman Generation*; and Burbank and Cooper, *Empires*, 13–14.

72. Goswami, *Producing India*, 27.

73. Hodge, *Triumph of the Expert*, 7–8.

74. See, for example, Mundy and Saumarez Smith, *Governing Property*; Rogan, *Frontiers of the State*; Fischbach, *State, Society, and Land*; Özbek, "Tax Farming"; Özbek, *İmparatorluğun Bedeli*; Quataert, "Dilemma of Development"; and Schaebler, "Practicing *Mushaʿ*." Martin Bunton discusses aspects of these reforms' continued legacy and incorporation into British mandate policies in Palestine (Bunton, *Colonial Land Policies*).

75. See Hinnebusch, *Peasant and Bureaucracy*. For their legacies, see Hinnebusch, *Authoritarian Power*.

76. See, for example, Bourdieu, *Distinction*. On expertise as a performance, see Derr, *Lived Nile*. For a broader look at expertise production in the mandates, see Bourmand et al., *Experts*.

77. On boundary-work, see Gieryn, "Boundary-Work." Boundary-work functioned similarly in colonial contexts; see Prakash, *Another Reason*.

78. Mitchell, "Stage of Modernity," 26.

79. Cooper, *Colonialism*, 146.

80. For example, Michael Gasper argues that the Egyptian intelligentsia incorporated scientific agriculture into representations of "the peasant" in order to articulate "a vision of Egypt's future while positioning themselves socially and politically in Egypt's present" (Gasper, *Power of Representation*, 3). See in particular Gasper, *Power of Representation*, ch. 4 ("Scientific Agriculture: Cultivators, Agriculturalists, or Peasants?").

81. Mitchell, *Rule of Experts*, 37. On the production of scientific knowledge, see, for example, Latour, *Reassembling the Social*.

82. El Shakry, *Great Social Laboratory*, 5–10. For example, see Kâzım's introduction to his translation of an agricultural book written by Eugène Leroux, a French author (Kâzım, *İlm-i Ziraat*; Leroux, *Cours d'agriculture*). Kâzım indicated that he was unable to translate the book directly into Ottoman; rather, he had to alter it to suit "our agriculture methods" (Kâzım, *İlm-i Ziraat*, 4).

83. Relying on local knowledge was not new, as Alan Mikhail has demonstrated for an earlier period (Mikhail, *Nature and Empire*), but the increasing insistence on using the language of science to demarcate between this knowledge and that produced at the nexus of local knowledge and new technologies was more pronounced by the late nineteenth century. For the importance of local sources to the production of Ottoman knowledge about Yemen, see also Kuehn, "We Know Nothing About Yemen."

84. Stolz, *Lighthouse*; Elshakry, *Reading Darwin*; El Shakry, *Great Social Laboratory*.

85. Yalçınkaya, *Learned Patriots*.

86. Meiton, *Electrical Palestine*.

87. Swearingen, *Moroccan Mirages*; D. K. Davis, *Resurrecting the Granary*, esp. 174; Peterson, *Pipe Dreams*.

88. Quataert, "Ottoman Reform"; Whitaker, "Union"; Keyder and Tabak, *Landholding*; Hanna, *al-Qadiya (1820–1920)*; Hanna, *al-Qadiya (1920–1945)*; Lewis, *Nomads*; Ouahes, "French Mandate Syria and Lebanon."

89. In a number of files, the original petition, sometimes in Arabic and sometimes in Ottoman Turkish, was preserved alongside the translation. In others, however, it was not. Whenever possible, I have used the original petition.

Chapter One

1. BOA, BEO 210/15701, Representative of the Governor Finance Director Zühdü to Agriculture Ministry, 1 Mayıs 1309 [13 May 1893]; BOA, Y.A.HUS 278/4, Foreign Office to Sublime Porte, 1 Temmuz 1309 [13 July 1893].

2. BOA, HR.SYS 72/58, translation (into Ottoman) of correspondence from the Washington Embassy, 27 Haziran 1893 [27 June 1893]; BOA, Y.A.HUS 278/4, Foreign Office to Sublime Porte, 1 Temmuz 1309 [13 July 1893].

3. BOA, İ.HUS 17/1311-R-23, letter from Chicago exhibition commissioner, 29 Haziran 1309 [11 July 1893].

4. BOA, BEO 308/23052, letter from Forest, Mines, and Agriculture Minister, 16 Teşrinievvel 1309 [28 October 1893]; BOA, BEO 317/23738, letter from Forest, Mines, and Agriculture Minister, 7 Teşrinisani 1309 [19 November 1893].

5. Quataert, "Ottoman Reform," 72–79.

6. See, for example, Özbek, "Tax Farming," 231–33; and Saraçoğlu, *Nineteenth Century Local Governance*.

7. Derri, "Imperial Creditors," 1074. See also Saraçoğlu, *Nineteenth Century Local Governance*, 2; and S. Çelik, "Science."

8. Saraçoğlu, *Nineteenth Century Local Governance*, 14–22; Shaw, "Nineteenth-Century Ottoman Tax Reforms," 422; Hanioğlu, *Brief History*, 45–47.

9. Quataert suggests that agriculture was the source of 56% of " 'national' income" by 1914 (Quataert, "Age of Reforms," 845).

10. Birinci Köy ve Ziraat Kalkınma Kongresi, *Türk Ziraat Tarihine Bir Bakış*, 76. The council's mission was to form a cadre of internal and external experts to study matters pertaining to land and nature and propose ways to encourage agriculture, trade, and industry.

11. Birinci Köy ve Ziraat Kalkınma Kongresi, *Türk Ziraat Tarihine Bir Bakış*, 77; Güran, *19. Yüzyıl*, 45. The Commerce Ministry had just been established in May of that year.

12. *Düstur: I. Tertib*, 1: 5. The other two areas were enhanced security for the empire's subjects and standardizing conscription.

13. *Düstur: I. Tertib*, 1: 5.

14. Özbek, "Tax Farming," 231; Gross, "Ottoman Rule," 15. On the implementation of this reform in the eastern Mediterranean, see Maʿoz, *Ottoman Reform*, 78–79.

15. Özbek, "Tax Farming," 231, 233. On tax revolts during the Tanzimat, see Aytekin, "Tax Revolts."

16. Özbek, "Tax Farming," 233.

17. İslamoğlu, "Politics," 304.

18. Özbek, "Tax Farming," 233; İslamoğlu, "Politics," 303–4; Shaw, "Nineteenth-Century Ottoman Tax Reforms," 422. Shaw notes that, as a result of the new system, tax revenues dropped noticeably in 1840 (422). According to Maʿoz, in the eastern Mediterranean, by the end of 1841, the *muhassıl* system had largely reverted back to *iltizam*, although some taxes continued to be collected by *muhassıls* as well as by military governors (Maʿoz, *Ottoman Reform*, 79).

19. Özbek, "Tax Farming," 234.

20. Birinci Köy ve Ziraat Kalkınma Kongresi, *Türk Ziraat Tarihine Bir Bakış*, 81; Güran, *19. Yüzyıl*, 45.

21. Güran, *19. Yüzyıl*, 48.

22. Birinci Köy ve Ziraat Kalkınma Kongresi, *Türk Ziraat Tarihine Bir Bakış*, 82. This survey was conducted during the same period as the initial *temettuat* registration, although it appears to have been a distinct inquiry; see Mundy and Saumarez Smith, *Governing Property*, 42; and İslamoğlu, "Politics," 296–97.

23. Güran, *19. Yüzyıl*, 46; Ubicini, *Letters on Turkey*, 330–31. It is unclear what kind of farmers might have benefited from these funds.

24. See, for example, Gueslin, *Origines*, 34. In the German states, individuals, not a centralized state, initiated these efforts. One mayor, Friedrich-Wilhelm Raiffeisen,

established a fund to aid farmers in acquiring animals in 1849 (49–50). Meanwhile, in France, government officials looked to German experiments for their initial inquiry into the matter in the 1840s before expanding their investigation to England and other countries a decade later. They did not actually establish the short-lived Crédit Agricole until 1860 (72, 75).

25. Mundy and Saumarez Smith, *Governing Property*, 43.

26. Maʿoz, *Ottoman Reform*, 95; Birinci Köy ve Ziraat Kalkınma Kongresi, *Türk Ziraat Tarihine Bir Bakış*, 83. For the text of the ordinance (*talimatname*), see Lutfî, *Tarih-i Lutfî*, 120–23.

27. Lutfî, *Tarih-i Lutfî*, 120–23; Birinci Köy ve Ziraat Kalkınma Kongresi, *Türk Ziraat Tarihine Bir Bakış*, 83–84. The *talimatname* emphasized the injunction not to sell with the phrase "zinhar ve zinhar," or "Beware!" For these officials' presence in the eastern Mediterranean, see Maʿoz, *Ottoman Reform*, 163.

28. Şener, *Tanzimat Dönemi*, 133–34.

29. Güran, *19. Yüzyıl*, 49; Ubicini, *Letters on Turkey*, 321–22. Based on responses from the provincial surveys, the Agriculture Council had narrowed its focus to improving road and river transportation, providing credit for agriculture and trade, and easing the tax burden through more equitable distribution (Güran, *19. Yüzyıl*, 48–49).

30. Güran, *19. Yüzyıl*, 49; Kaya, "Searching," 76–78; Ubicini, *Letters on Turkey*, 322.

31. Güran, *19. Yüzyıl*, 46; Ubicini, *Letters on Turkey*, 331. Ubicini refers to a sum of 20 million piastres that was disbursed annually from the Public Works Treasury starting in 1845. In 1846 an agricultural ministry was briefly established before being incorporated into the Commerce Ministry and then coming under the Public Works Council in the 1850s (Quataert, "Ottoman Reform," 76).

32. Güran, *19. Yüzyıl*, 47; Yıldırım, "Osmanlı'da İlk Çağdaş." Quote from Güran.

33. Ubicini, *Letters on Turkey*, 324–25.

34. See, for example, Ubicini, *Letters on Turkey*, 323–24.

35. Yıldırım, "Osmanlı'da İlk Çağdaş," 234.

36. Güran, *19. Yüzyıl*, 136–38; Doumani, *Rediscovering Palestine*, 135–36; Derri, "Bonds of Obligation," 127–29. For the roots of *selem* contracts in Islamic law, see Cuno, "Contrat *salam*"; and on their function as investments more so than as contracts of sale, see Doumani, "Contrat *salam*"; and Johansen, "Le contrat *salam*." The term is transliterated as *selem* in Ottoman and *salam* in Arabic.

37. Doumani, *Rediscovering Palestine*, 138, 140–42.

38. Doumani, *Rediscovering Palestine*, 142–43.

39. Doumani, for instance, traces how such contracts on the olive harvest were used by soap manufacturers to ensure a supply of raw materials. See Doumani, *Rediscovering Palestine*, 142–49.

40. According to M. Safa Saraçoğlu, in Bulgaria the government deemed such contracts "illegal" in an effort to push peasants instead to borrow from funds overseen by institutions of the central government. See Saraçoğlu, *Nineteenth Century Local Governance*, 29–30, 119–20.

41. Lutfî, *Tarih-i Lutfî*, 121.

42. For discussion of a similar process in Egypt, see Cuno, *Pasha's Peasants*, 81–84, 194–97. Cuno explains how privately held property could be "pawned," in contrast to land

held through usufruct rights, which technically could not be, although peasants still "pawned" it in village-level transactions largely opaque to the central administration (82).

43. "Tapu nizamnamesi (5 Cemaziyülahir 1263 [21 May 1847])," Art. 2, in Karakoç, *Tahşiyeli Kavanin*, 2: 307.

44. Doumani, *Rediscovering Palestine*, 154; Mundy and Saumarez Smith, *Governing Property*, 44.

45. Mundy and Saumarez Smith, *Governing Property*, 44–45, 255n39. Notably, this reform meant that daughters did not have to pay the *tapu* fee to acquire the land. Keiko Kiyotaki indicates that there was a commission fee on transfer by inheritance; see Kiyotaki, *Ottoman Land Reform*, 145.

46. Mundy and Saumarez Smith, *Governing Property*, 44–45. The *tapu* regulation also included tax exemptions for purchases of land that required additional preparation before cultivation and outlined a process whereby the Istanbul-based Office of Land Registry issued new title deeds to replace the handwritten ones that had been issued by local officials or tax farmers. See Kiyotaki, *Ottoman Land Reform*, 145–46; and Mundy and Saumarez Smith, *Governing Property*, 45.

47. Doumani, *Rediscovering Palestine*, 153–55.

48. "Tapu nizamname," Art. 10, 310. The recommendation of Aleppo's agricultural director, Ahmet Ağa, received due attention. BOA, HR.MKT. 66/69, 9 Safer 1270 [11 November 1853].

49. "Eyalet meclislerine verilen talimat-ı seniyye," in *Mecmua-yi Kavanin*, 56–75.

50. "Eyalet meclislerine," Arts. 27, 43, 44, 46, in *Mecmua-yi Kavanin*, 64, 68–69.

51. Özbek, "Tax Farming," 234–35.

52. For a translation of the report about the petition and a thoughtful in-depth examination of its broader implications, see Doumani, *Rediscovering Palestine*, 146–49, quotes from 146. The report reassured the governor that the villagers had been encouraged to resolve their differences and that the shaykhs had cautioned against drawing up future contracts without the villagers' knowledge. See Doumani, *Rediscovering Palestine*, 147.

53. Taylor, "Fragrant Gardens," 39–69.

54. Reilly, *Small Town in Syria*, 103–4. Reilly notes that these cases were a "reoccurring pattern in the mid-nineteenth century" (103). However, his research covers cases from 1727–1734, 1788–1800, and 1849–1852, the last set of which almost exactly parallels the timeframe during which this new tax policy was in effect. Additional research in these court records for ensuing years would help ascertain to what extent, if any, this "reoccurring pattern" represents an anomaly in response to the new tax policy.

55. Özbek, "Tax Farming," 235. The government attempted to enforce this approach from 1850 to 1853. During this same period in Nablus, subdistrict heads (*shaykh al-nahiya*) took on the role of *muhassıl* and the governor of Sidon issued a decree to be proclaimed in 213 villages warning the 13 *muhassıl*s of Nablus and Jenin to cease and desist from "their practice of extorting money and crops from peasants under the pretext of being unsalaried government employees who were merely covering their expenses" (Doumani, *Rediscovering Palestine*, 170, 176;, quote from p. 176). The *tahmis* also does not appear to have been implemented everywhere because, as discussed later in this

chapter, it was introduced and quickly rescinded in Syria some years after this initial policy went into effect. Such evidence suggests that several approaches to taxation were in use at any given time, despite the edicts issued from Istanbul.

56. Özbek, "Tax Farming," 235–36. According to Özbek, in some more distant areas of the empire, the government was willing to use the rental contracts at fixed prices (236).

57. Özbek, "Tax Farming," 236–37. For the terms of this lending, see Autheman, *Imperial Ottoman Bank*, 20–21.

58. *Düstur: I. Tertib*, 1: 12–13.

59. *Düstur: I. Tertib*, 1: 13.

60. Autheman, *Imperial Ottoman Bank*, 28–29; Eldem, *History of the Ottoman Bank*, 52–53.

61. Eldem, *History of the Ottoman Bank*, 56.

62. Autheman, *Imperial Ottoman Bank*, 29.

63. Owen, *Middle East*, 167, 168.

64. Shaw, "Nineteenth-Century Ottoman Tax Reforms," 426–27; Kaya and Terzibaşoğlu, "Tahrir'den Kadastro'ya," 20.

65. İslamoğlu, "Politics," 291.

66. Moulin, *Peasantry*, 39–40; İslamoğlu, "Politics," 292.

67. İslamoğlu, "Politics," 292.

68. For the text of the law, see *Düstur: I. Tertib*, 1: 165–99; for Art. 8, see *Düstur: I. Tertib*, 1: 167. It should be noted that there were some exceptions. For example, Article 25 specified that if fruit trees or vines were left to grow on *miri* land for three years and reached fruit-bearing capacity, then that land came under full ownership of the usufruct rights holder, but it would still be subject to the tithe and not a fixed rent (1: 170).

69. *Düstur: I. Tertib*, 1: 166, Art. 3. Before tax farmers and *muhassıls* the law characterized the position as belonging to owners of large landholdings, such as *timars* and *ziamets*.

70. For this criticism, see Sluglett and Farouk-Sluglett, "Application," 413. Other scholars agree that the law facilitated the consolidation of large lands, attributing it to such factors as "preexisting patterns of human geography," but they do not offer more precise explanations for how consolidation resulted from the Land Code's implementation. See, for example, Gerber, *Social Origins*, 72–73; and Batatu, *Syria's Peasantry*, 109, 125. For a discussion of the interpretations of the law's significance, see Quataert, "Age of Reforms," 856–61.

71. Mundy and Saumarez Smith, *Governing Property*. For a more general perspective on the negotiated nature of the rights obtained in relation to the law, see İslamoğlu, "Property as a Contested Domain."

72. *Düstur: I. Tertib*, 1: 200, Art. 1.

73. Mundy and Saumarez Smith, *Governing Property*, 55.

74. *Düstur: I. Tertib*, 1: 200, Art. 2.

75. Shaw, "Nineteenth-Century Ottoman Tax Reforms," 426–27; İslamoğlu, "Politics," 297–98, 305–7; Kaya and Terzibaşoğlu, "Tahrir'den Kadastro'ya," 23. To refine their technique, in 1858 commissions undertook initial survey work in Bursa and Yanya before moving on to Beirut in 1862 and then expanding to other areas of the empire (Kaya and Terzibaşoğlu, "Tahrir'den Kadastro'ya," 21).

76. İslamoğlu, "Politics," 305.

77. "Tahrîr-i nüfus ve emlâke dair nizâmnâme," *Düstûr-i atîk* (1282 [1866]), 891, Art. 4. For the English translation, see Ongley, *Ottoman Land Code*, 115.

78. For a critical discussion of the historiography about villagers refusing to register their land, see mcelrone, "From the Pages of the *Defter*," 5–27. Of course, the government may have focused on elite attempts at evasion because they were more likely to deprive the treasury of substantial resources.

79. "Tahrîr-i nüfus," 892, Art. 7; Ongley, *Ottoman Land Code*, 116–17.

80. Shaw, "Nineteenth-Century Ottoman Tax Reforms," 427.

81. Gross, "Ottoman Rule," 140.

82. For additional details, see Mundy and Saumarez Smith, *Governing Property*, 47. For the original, see *Düstur: I. Tertib*, 1: 244; and for the English translation of the Rabiulevvel 1279 [August–September 1862] law outlining these provisions, see Ongley, *Ottoman Land Code*, 136–37.

83. Mundy and Saumarez Smith, *Governing Property*, 47.

84. Özbek, "Tax Farming," 237.

85. Özbek, "Tax Farming," 238. The evidence for this outcry comes primarily from the Balkans. More case studies are needed to understand how the implementation of fixed-price farms played out elsewhere. Özbek contrasts this approach with that taken in Russia, where, following the emancipation of the serfs several months after this reform went into effect in the Ottoman Empire, emancipated peasants found that they were not granted "the status of personhood" (237).

86. *Al-Jinan* (1870), 423–25. Despite this enthusiasm, the journal's editor raised various issues with the process, opining that he hoped the government would "transform the tithe into fixed funds, the amount to be adjusted based on the net income of the treasury in past years," which he had heard it had planned to do in three years' time. He suggested that Syrian peasants would benefit from the "ease" provided by the tax system recently implemented in Mount Lebanon (425). Following the establishment of the special district (*mutasarrifiyya*) in Mount Lebanon in 1861, the government established a fixed property tax (*emlak vergisi*) on assessed land values and rental revenue (Akarlı, "Taxation," 32–33).

87. BOA, MVL 767/89, report dated 14 Rabiulahir 1280 [28 September 1863]. Foreign merchants also continued to defy the government's efforts to limit interest rates to 12%. For a discussion of this confrontation over the empire's Usury Regulations, see Derri, "Bonds of Obligation," 135–38, 143–51.

88. Autheman, *Imperial Ottoman Bank*, 35.

89. Autheman, *Imperial Ottoman Bank*, 33.

90. Kiyotaki, "Ottoman State Finance," 2–3; Autheman, *Imperial Ottoman Bank*, 35; Great Britain, *Foreign Office List*, 97.

91. Autheman, *Imperial Ottoman Bank*, 35-36.

92. Autheman, *Imperial Ottoman Bank*, 40–41. After retiring from the Treasury, Foster would serve as the bank's governor in Istanbul (Great Britain, *Foreign Office List*, 97).

93. Mundy and Saumarez Smith, *Governing Property*; Barakat, "Underwriting"; Kiyotaki, *Ottoman Land Reform*; Saliba, "Wilayat Suriyya"; Çetinsaya, *Ottoman Administration*, 8–9; Saraçoğlu, *Nineteenth Century Local Governance*; Gross, "Ottoman Rule."

94. *Düstur: I. Tertib*, 1: 609–10. See "Ziraat müdirlerinin vezaif memuriyetlerine dair tâlimattir," 17 Şaban 1280 [27 January 1864], *Düstur: I. Tertib*, 2: 434–36.

95. *Düstur: I. Tertib*, 1: 612–13.

96. See, for example, *Salname-yi Vilâyet-i Halep*, first published in 1867, which contained these details, whereas the early volumes of the *Salname-yi Vilâyet-i Suriye*, first published in 1868, did not. The first provincial yearbook that appeared in 1866 was for Bosna. In 1867 coverage expanded to include Aleppo province, and in 1868 yearbooks for the provinces of Syria, Konya, and Tuna joined them (Duman, *Osmanlı Yıllıkları*, 112).

97. *Düstur: I. Tertib*, 1: 610, 614, 617, 619.

98. *Düstur: I. Tertib*, 1: 623.

99. *Düstur: I. Tertib*, 1: 618–19.

100. Autheman, *Imperial Ottoman Bank*, 229–30; Thobie, *Intérêts*, 468–69; Owen, *Middle East*, 103. The bank did have investments in real estate outside the empire (Autheman, *Imperial Ottoman Bank*, 254).

101. Quataert, "Dilemma," 212.

102. *Düstur: I. Tertib*, 2: 387, 389–90, Arts. 1, 10–11.

103. Güran, *19. Yüzyıl*, 150; Saraçoğlu, *Nineteenth Century Local Governance*, 28–29; Quataert, "Dilemma of Development," 212; Du Velay, *Essai sur l'histoire*, 205–6. For the full text of the law, see *Düstur: I. Tertib*, 2: 387–98.

104. *Düstur: I. Tertib*, 2: 388, Art. 6; Du Velay, *Essai sur l'histoire*, 206–7. Du Velay notes that the committee members were unsalaried. State yearbooks (*Salname-yi Devlet-i Âliye-yi Osmaniye*) maintained a record of the funds' capital by province.

105. Gueslin, *Origines*, 49–50, 57.

106. Kotsonis, *Making Peasants Backwards*, 15–18. In 1850 a magistrate, Hermann Schulze-Delitzsch, started the first of a number of cooperative advance associations with capital stock, although these were less concerned with the plight of farmers, for whom their terms were more unfavorable. Among the unfavorable terms were high rates of interest on loans (7–13%) and terms that did not take into consideration the time period necessary for agricultural production (Gueslin, *Origines*, 59–63).

107. Gueslin, *Origines*, 56; Kotsonis, *Making Peasants Backwards*, 15–18.

108. Gueslin, *Origines*, 75, 108–9

109. Gueslin, *Origines*, 26, 75, 76–77.

110. Gueslin, *Origines*, 114.

111. Gueslin, *Origines*, 77. Apparently, the Crédit Agricole became "lost in non-agricultural operations" and collapsed in 1876, in no small part because of loans totaling 168 million francs that the organization made to Khedive Ismail in Egypt, who, in the midst of the financial crisis of the early 1870s, was unable to repay even the arrears on the debt (Gueslin, *Origines*, 112–13; Souchon, *Agricultural Credit*, 2). Efforts in other parts of Europe started even later, with the establishment of an individually initiated rural fund in the Province of Padua in 1883 and a law issued by the Belgium state in 1884 for the formation of a general fund that could be used for agricultural loans (Gueslin, *Origines*, 67, 69). Popular banks had started earlier in the 1860s (Gueslin, *Origines*, 66–67).

112. Kaya and Terzibaşoğlu, "Tahrir'den Kadastro'ya," 20–24. See the table of the areas with registered towns (25).

113. Kaya and Terzibaşoğlu, "Tahrir'den Kadastro'ya," 23.

114. Mundy and Saumarez Smith, *Governing Property*, 66; al-Tabbakh, *I'lam al-Nubala'*, 3: 458. See, for example, the seven-member Tahrir Commission in the *Salname-yi Vilâyet-i Halep* (1871), 51.

115. Al-Tabbakh, *I'lam al-Nubala'*, 3: 458.

116. Birinci Köy ve Ziraat Kalkınma Kongresi, *Türk Ziraat Tarihine Bir Bakış*, 198–200; *Salname-yi Devlet-i Âliye-yi Osmaniye* (1869), 37.

117. Owen, *Middle East*, 101–2, 167–68, 171; Lewis, *Nomads*, 46–49; Gross, "Ottoman Rule."

118. Owen, *Middle East*, 170; Lewis, *Nomads*, 42–46, 60–62.

119. Gross, "Ottoman Rule," 147–48, 165, quote from 147; Owen, *Middle East*, 170; Schilcher, "Hauran Conflicts," 174; Schilcher, "Great Depression," 171; Barakat, *Bedouin Bureaucrats*.

120. Gross, "Ottoman Rule," 136–38; Kuneralp, *Son Dönem*, 38. According to Gross, the evidence suggests that in the province of Syria, the Hawran was the main area where the land law had not yet been applied. Gross also indicates that the reform program was primarily crafted by Reşid Paşa, although the council's suggestions were incorporated.

121. Great Britain, "Circular," 1–4.

122. Notably, the views of W. Gifford Palgrave, based in Trabzon, diverged from those of other British officials who submitted reports. For instance, the report from Richard Wilkinson in Salonica was relatively complimentary of the effects that small property had on the cultivator, whereas his colleague in Istanbul, the senior second secretary Lionel Moore, sent an upbeat assessment of the state of land tenure in the surrounding province. Such contrasts suggest that Palgrave's blanket criticisms might be more reflective of his particular prejudices and idiosyncrasies than the actual state of affairs in all the regions he claimed to cover. Several scholars have used his report to assess the impacts of the Land Code, albeit with caveats (Great Britain, "Report by Consul Palgrave," 276–92; Great Britain, "Report by Consul Wilkinson," 303–5; Great Britain, "Report by Mr. Moore," 273–76; Kiyotaki, *Ottoman Land Reform*, 150–52; Pamuk, *Ottoman Empire, 90–95*).

123. Great Britain, "Report by Consul Palgrave," 276–77, 283–85.

124. Great Britain, "Report by Consul Palgrave," 282. As one Syrian agronomist would note over half a century later, the British Isles had still not implemented reforms to break up large-property ownership, which he considered to its detriment (al-Shihabi, "Aham Adwa'na al-Iqtisadiya wa Talafiha 2" (January 1928 [1929?]), 29). See chapter 5 for more details. On nineteenth-century land law in England, see Spring, "Landowners."

125. Great Britain, "Report by Consul Palgrave," 283.

126. *Düstur: I. Tertib*, 1: 625, Arts. 1 and 3.

127. *Düstur: I. Tertib*, 1: 637, Art. 56.

128. *Düstur: I. Tertib*, 1: 631, Art. 23, and 1: 632–33, Arts. 29–31. According to Young, the director of agriculture and commerce post was abolished in 1872, so it is unclear what impact these directors ultimately had (Young, *Corps*, 1: 53).

129. On how this implementation played out in Bulgaria, see Saraçoğlu, *Nineteenth Century Local Governance*.

130. Mundy and Saumarez Smith, *Governing Property*, 51.

131. Mundy and Saumarez Smith, *Governing Property*, 70; mcelrone, "From the Pages of the *Defter*," 59–60.

132. Reilly, "Status Groups," 529.

133. Özbek, "Tax Farming," 239.

134. Gross, "Ottoman Rule," 114, 164; Owen, *Middle East*, 171. Owen states that the bad harvests lasted from 1869 to 1879; Gross claims that they continued for five to six years after the initial drought of 1869–1870.

135. Owen, *Middle East*, 109.

136. Masters, "Aleppo," 75.

137. Pehlivan, "El Niño," 342–43.

138. Özbek, "Tax Farming," 239; Owen, *Middle East*, 109.

139. Autheman, *Imperial Ottoman Bank*, 85–86; Arrighi, *Long Twentieth Century*, 167–69; Kasaba, *Ottoman Empire*, 107–8. Duties had been set at 8% (Autheman, *Imperial Ottoman Bank*, 85). In the empire, 1840–1873 were boom years (Quataert, "Age of Reforms," 829).

140. In France the tithe had been abolished, but instead of another comparable tax levied on peasants, the burden of taxation shifted to urban areas, where customs dues from 1804 constituted a key source of indirect taxation (Moulin, *Peasantry*, 44). By the eve of World War I, taxes on the peasantry were still relatively light, as the government tried to encourage "small family farms" (Moulin, *Peasantry*, 142).

141. Autheman, *Imperial Ottoman Bank*, 86.

142. Autheman, *Imperial Ottoman Bank*, 80–81; Eldem, "Imperial Ottoman Bank," 50; Hanioğlu, *Brief History*, 91.

143. Autheman, *Imperial Ottoman Bank*, 87; Owen, *Middle East*, 108–9; Hanioğlu, *Brief History*, 92.

144. Winkler, *Foreign Bonds*, 34–35; Quataert, "Age of Reforms," 773.

145. Birinci Köy ve Ziraat Kalkınma Kongresi, *Türk Ziraat Tarihine Bir Bakış*, 198–200; *Salname-yi Devlet-i Âliye-yi Osmaniye* (1869), 37. Although "agriculture" had originally been in the council's name in the late 1860s, it disappeared for a few years, reappearing in the mid-1870s.

146. *Düstur: I. Tertib*, 3: 570–71.

147. BOA, A}MKT.MHM 480/13, draft dated 7 Receb 1293 [29 July 1876].

148. Hanioğlu, *Brief History*, 111. For the 13 Haziran 1292 [25 June 1876] *kararname* spelling out the duties of the Commerce and Agriculture Council, see *Düstur: I. Tertib*, 3: 473–77.

149. Birinci Köy ve Ziraat Kalkınma Kongresi, *Türk Ziraat Tarihine Bir Bakış*, 199–200; *Düstur: I. Tertib*, 3: 473–77. Presumably these unhealthy areas consisted of marshy lands.

150. Shaw, "Nineteenth-Century Ottoman Tax Reforms," 429.

151. Özbek, "Tax Farming," 240; Özbek, *İmparatorluğun Bedeli*, 59.

152. Hanioğlu, *Brief History*, 120.

153. Quataert, "Age of Reforms," 843–48.

154. Quataert, "Age of Reforms," 843; Lewis, *Nomads*, 42–46, 60–62. See chapter 2.

155. Quataert, "Age of Reforms," 872, 875.

156. Akarlı, "Problems," 169–70, 172–74; Quataert, "Age of Reforms," 798.

157. Barakat, *Bedouin Bureaucrats*; Özbek, "Tax Farming," 239–43.

158. Akarlı, "Problems," 157–58, 159–60, 162. Among the forms of knowledge considered necessary to implement the land tax were productive capacity of the land, levels of initial investment required, methods used, market prices, and land-tenure arrangements as well as allowances for damage caused by insects, floods, etc. or higher levels of extraction in the event of a particularly good year (161). The detailed fine-tuning necessary for assessing and collecting this tax meant that, even in areas where it was applied, it proved difficult to maintain and within a decade or so many areas had reverted to a fixed-rate tax assessed collectively on the village (165). According to Özbek, peasants approved this shift to a land tax, whereas large landlords resisted it and tried to use their local authority to evade its mandates (Özbek, "Tax Farming," 240; Özbek, *İmparatorluğun Bedeli*, 59). In the Hawran during this period, Schilcher notes that the well-known Tanzimat reformer Midhat Pasha, who was governor of Syria from 1878 to 1880, resisted the government's attempts to impose a fixed land tax. Instead, he bypassed existing tax farming elites and found new tax farmers, among whom were village shaykhs. This approach enabled him to extract increased revenues despite a year of poorer harvests, much to the previous tax farmers' chagrin. Schilcher positions this as background to the outbreak of clashes in the Hawran during the early 1880s, although it is unclear exactly how these conflicts are related to the changing approaches to taxation (Schilcher, "Violence," 58–60).

159. Akarlı, "Problems," 160. This concern became more pressing as officials sought to encourage farmers to invest in more capital intensive inputs.

160. Özbek, "Tax Farming," 241.

161. Saliba, "Wilayat Suriyya," 224.

162. Özbek, "Tax Farming," 241.

163. Saliba, "Wilayat Suriyya," 225; Gross, "Ottoman Rule," 369.

164. BOA, ŞD 301/32, telegram sent to the Grand Vizier's office with twenty-seven signatures, 3 Haziran 1300 [15 June 1884]; BOA, ŞD 301/32, telegram from Ahmet Hamdi to Finance Ministry, 16 Haziran 1300 [28 June 1884]. According to the correspondence, the governor had attempted to ensure that the base of the *tahmis* was in line with the productive capacity of the land, calling in the villages' elders and headmen to detail "each village lands' conditions, *feddan* quantity, degree of prosperity, and harvest yields" (BOA, ŞD 301/32, response dated 30 Haziran 1300 [12 July 1884]).

165. Özbek, "Tax Farming," 232, 242; Akarlı, "Problems," 164.

166. Birdal, *Political Economy*, 52–54. The negotiations lasted from September through December.

167. Quataert, "Age of Reforms," 773–74, 856, 871; Aricanli, "Agrarian Relations," 34; Blaisdell, *European Financial Control*, 92. Only the silk tithes of Bursa, Edirne, and Samsun were still collected by Ottoman agents (Morawitz, *Finances de la Turquie*, 321).

168. Blaisdell, *European Financial Control*, 127–28.

169. Quataert, "Ottoman Reform," 130–31. Although a local administrative council still continued to manage the funds, it had to report quarterly to the Commerce and Public Works Ministry.

170. Somel, *Modernization*, 146; Quataert, "Dilemma," 213. An additional 0.5% surtax was added in 1897 and 0.63% in 1900 for military supplies (Young, *Corps*, 5: 303).

171. Quataert, "Ottoman Reform," 131–32.

172. Du Velay, *Essai sur l'histoire*, 207; *Düstur: I. Tertib*, 6: 136, 137. The French translation of the law can be found in Young, *Corps*, 5: 342–54. In addition to the 1% raised as capital for the bank from the tithe, the bank's resources would consist of the amounts that had been collected for the public utility funds and their debts as well as any interest accruing once the bank was operational. The bank was supposed to stop accruing capital from the tithe once it achieved a capital of 10 million Ottoman pounds and would pay an interest rate of 4%. Funds had to be deposited for a fixed amount of time and for no less than three months (*Düstur: I. Tertib*, 6: 137).

173. *Düstur: I. Tertib*, 6: 142. The Agricultural Bank was also to be a source of funding for the state's co-emerging scientific agriculture programs, discussed in more detail in chapter 2. One-third of the bank's annual profits would go to the bank's capital, one-third to the agricultural institutions in each province with a bank branch, and one-third to the minister of commerce for combating epizootics, improving cattle breeding, and acquiring better seeds (*Düstur: I. Tertib*, 6: 142, Art. 39). However, Quataert indicates that the distinction between one-third allocated locally and one-third going to the center quickly disappeared and that, except for one year after 1892, two-thirds went to the center (Quataert, "Dilemma," 220).

174. *Düstur: I. Tertib*, 6: 140–141, Arts. 24, 29; mcelrone, "From the Pages of the *Defter*," 233–36. Loans with a different repayment format could be taken for three months to one year (Art. 24). According to one source, the law capped the interest rate charged by private individuals at 3%, but even "the most honest demanded 12%" (Médawar, *Syrie agricole*, 28). In 1890 the British consul claimed that the rate could be as much as 20–30% in Aleppo, whereas an agronomist from Syria writing about Latakia in 1905 indicated that the rate could be 10%, 12%, or even 15% (Issawi, *Fertile Crescent*, 76; T. Saadé, *Essai*, 42). This meant that most peasants still preferred the higher interest rates of private lenders.

175. *Düstur: I. Tertib*, 6: 140–41, Arts. 25, 32. Some years later, this period of delay was extended to 10 years for those suffering damages or living in extreme poverty who had originally borrowed for much shorter terms (Young, *Corps*, 5: 348).

176. *Düstur: I. Tertib*, 6: 140, Art. 26; 6: 141–42, Art. 36; 6: 742, Arts. 1, 2; and 6: 742–43, Arts. 3–5; Young, *Corps*, 5: 350–51.

177. *Düstur: I. Tertib*, 6: 138. The board consisted of a director, the inspector of agriculture in the province, and two delegates chosen by the Chambers of Agriculture and Commerce as well as the local municipality. On accusations of corruption against branches of the bank by the Syria and Beirut agricultural inspector, see later discussion in this section.

178. Khoury, *Urban Notables*, 30–44.

179. Autheman, *Imperial Ottoman Bank*; Hanioğlu, *Brief History*, 136–37. Hanioğlu describes the Agricultural Bank as an "embryonic, unofficial national bank" (136).

180. Quataert, "Dilemma," 223–25. Quataert uses "nonagricultural functions" to suggest that the bank's involvement in this array of activities undercuts official claims that it was devoted primarily to agricultural development.

181. Issawi, *Fertile Crescent*, 76.

182. Derri, "Bonds of Obligation," 169–71.

183. Issawi, *Fertile Crescent*, 76.

184. Issawi, *Fertile Crescent*, 76; Médawar, *Syrie agricole*, 28, İslamoğlu, "Property as a Contested Domain," 31–32; Derri, "Bonds of Obligation," 169–71.

185. Quataert, "Dilemma," 216.

186. BOA, DH.MKT 1665/45, draft dated 26 Eylül 1305 [8 October 1889].

187. Barakat, "Underwriting," 387–88, 389; *Düstur: I. Tertib*, 6: 370–71, Art. 24.

188. Barakat, "Underwriting"; Özbek, "Tax Farming."

189. *Salname-yi Devlet-i Âliye-yi Osmaniye* (1875), 71; *Salname-yi Devlet-i Âliye-yi Osmaniye* (1878), 141; Quataert, "Ottoman Reform," 77–78.

190. BOA, A}MKT.MHM 727/31, report of Aram Efendi, 10 Şaban 1310 [27 February 1893]. At least two of the students studying in France, Çeras Efendi and Torkomyan Efendi, had been sent to the agricultural school in Montpellier. After completing their studies, Torkomyan was to return to take up a ministry post as inspector of the imperial estates (*emlâk-i hümayun*), and Çeras Efendi and Nuri Efendi, who was also studying in France, were to be sent to Algeria for further education (BOA, İ.DH 880/70216, 19 Mart 1299 [31 March 1883]; Quataert, "Ottoman Reform," 87). However, it is unclear whether their continuation in Algeria actually transpired, as they were appointed agricultural inspectors of Adana and Aydın, respectively, in 1883 (Quataert, "Ottoman Reform," 85).

191. *Salname-yi Devlet-i Âliye-yi Osmaniye* (1885), 466; *Salname-yi Devlet-i Âliye-yi Osmaniye* (1890), 474.

192. Quataert, "Ottoman Reform," 94.

193. Quataert, "Ottoman Reform," 72. Other countries were creating similar ministries during this period. In 1882 France formed an agricultural ministry under Gambetta—a move considered "a first tentative step towards an efficient administrative structure" (Moulin, *Peasantry*, 108). In 1893 Russia also established a new Ministry of Agriculture and State Domains (Sunderland, *Taming the Wild Field*, 191).

194. It is unclear whether Reşid Bey was among the government-sponsored students who studied abroad, but it seems likely, given his education in France and at the Mekteb-i Sultani, one of the high schools from which the students were chosen to send to France. According to the *Salname-yi Devlet-i Âliye-yi Osmaniye*, he was the agricultural inspector for Syria from 1892 through 1895 (*Salname-yi Devlet-i Âliye-yi Osmaniye* [1892], 520; [1894], 568; [1895], 600).

195. BOA, Y.PRK.TKM. 24/15, letter from J. Delbet, 13 February 1892.

196. BOA, BEO 159/11880, Beirut governor to Sublime Porte, 21 Kanunuevvel 1308 [2 January 1893]. See Hanssen, *Fin de Siècle Beirut*.

197. BOA, BEO 18/1349, Reşid Bey to the Grand Vizier, 5 Mart 1309 [17 March 1893].

198. BOA, BEO 210/15701, Representative of the Governor Finance Director Zühdü to Agriculture Ministry, 1 Mayıs 1309 [13 May 1893].

199. BOA, HR.SYS 72/58, translation (into Ottoman) of correspondence from the Washington Embassy, 27 Haziran 1893 [27 June 1893]; BOA, Y.A.HUS 278/4, Foreign Office to Sublime Porte, 1 Temmuz 1309 [13 July 1893].

200. BOA, BEO 18/1349, Reşid Bey's report, n.d.

201. BOA, İ.HUS 17/1311-R-23, Chicago exhibition commissioner to Ministry, 29 Haziran 1309 [11 July 1893].

202. BOA, BEO 296/22193, draft to Commerce and Public Works Ministry, 7 Teşrinievvel 1309 [19 October 1893]; BOA, Y.A.HUS 278/65, Grand Vizier office's decision, 13

Temmuz 1309 [25 July 1893]; BOA, İ.HUS 17/1311-R-23, Correspondence from chief clerk of Yıldız Palace, 5 Teşrinievvel 1309 [17 October 1893]. The document indicates 50–60 lira.

203. BOA, BEO 307/23023, Reşid Bey to Sublime Porte, 10 Teşrinievvel 1309 [22 October 1893]. This folder contains a letter indicating that Reşid Bey is sending the report; folder BEO 18/1349 contains the undated report.

204. BOA, BEO 18/1349, Reşid Bey's report, n.d.

205. BOA, BEO 18/1349, Reşid Bey's report, n.d.; *Levant Herald*, 4 September 1893, quoted in Z. Çelik, *Displaying the Orient*, 142. The entire quote is as follows: "show to the native industrialists and agriculturists such foreign methods, models, and types of production as might enlarge their ideas of their own work and enable them to improve it as to render Turkey in an economic sense less and less tributary to foreign countries."

206. BOA, BEO 18/1349, letter from the Forest, Mines, and Agriculture Minister, 27 Teşrinisani 1309 [9 December 1893]; BOA, BEO 307/23023, draft dated 25 Teşrinievvel 1309 [6 November 1893].

207. Z. Çelik, *Displaying the Orient*, 139.

208. BOA, BEO 308/23052, letter from Forest, Mines, and Agriculture Minister, 16 Teşrinievvel 1309 [28 October 1893]; BOA, BEO 317/23738, letter from Forest, Mines, and Agriculture Minister, 7 Teşrinisani 1309 [19 November 1893]. It is unclear whether the minister followed through on the threat to temporarily deprive Reşid Bey of work.

209. Pierce, *Photographic History*, 315.

210. Z. Çelik, *Displaying the Orient*, 80–88; Deringil, *Well-Protected Domains*, 155–61, quote from p. 160.

211. BOA, BEO 473/35410, note from Education Minister, 9 Kanunusani 1310 [21 January 1895]; BOA, BEO 476/35635, draft to the Finance Ministry, 3 Eylül 1310 [15 September 1894].

212. BOA, BEO 391/29304, draft to the Commerce and Public Works Ministry, 13 Nisan 1310 [25 April 1894].

213. I base this assumption on references, in documents from the fall of 1895, to a man of the same name and identified as from among the (presumably former) agricultural inspectors of the imperial domains who had started publishing a journal in Cairo that was censored in the empire (BOA, MF.MKT 288/38, MF.MKT 291/28, MF.MKT 301/17).

214. BOA, Y.PRK.TKM. 24/15, letter from J. Delbet, 13 February 1892. It is possible that Reşid Bey and Ahmet Rıza met in Paris, where they both studied agriculture. They both also attended the 1889 Exposition Universelle in Paris (Rıza, *Meclis-i Mebusan*, 10).

215. Turnaoğlu, *Formation*, 94, 99; *Basirüşşark*, 24 October 1895. This is the only issue of *Basirüşşark* that I have been able to find.

216. Zürcher, "Ottoman Sources," 14–27; Turnaoğlu, *Formation*, 86–114.

217. *Basirüşşark*, 24 October 1895.

218. Mardin, *Religion*, 166; Rıza, *Meclis-i Mebusan*, 9.

219. Özbek, "Tax Farming," 242–43.

220. Schilcher, "Violence," 71–73.

221. See, for example, *Salname-yi Vilâyet-i Suriye* (1888), 216; (1892), 168; (1893), 233; (1896), 245; and (1897), 233. The 1888 yearbook specifies the amounts collected by *sancak*. In that year, the *emaneten idare* method was used only in Latakia, Beirut, Hama, Hawran, and the Balqa, but not in Trablus, ʿAkka, and Şam. Although the amounts collected in

most of these *sancaks* by this method were relatively minor, compared with the amount collected by fixed-price auctions, in the Hawran almost half of the tithe (48%) was collected by *emaneten idare*. In Basra, despite increasing efforts at oversight, tax farmers continued to work the system to their advantage and still managed to use it to amass substantial wealth and power (Cole, "Empire on Edge," 122–191).

222. Thobie, *Intérêts*, 503.

223. Schilcher "Violence," 65, 68.

224. Provence, "Ottoman and French Mandate Land Registers," 36, 38. To my knowledge, Provence is the only scholar of Syrian history who has examined these ledgers and written about them. He identifies them as "registrations by survey of land under cultivation for tax purposes" (38). He describes the process of surveying by government agents thus: "The registrations did not include revenue stamps and there were rarely witnesses listed. They record agricultural land within each village, and notations define borders by adjoining holdings and almost always some village *mushaʿ*, or communally held land, comprised at least one border" (38). This sounds similar to the process Mundy and Saumarez Smith describe in ʿAjlun for the *yoklama* and the follow-up tours by the *yoklama* scribes to ascertain deaths or still undeclared properties in a campaign that, in ʿAjlun at least, lasted from 1889 to 1899 (Mundy and Saumarez Smith, *Governing Property*, 70–71, 98).

225. Young, *Corps*, 6: 90.

226. E. Saadé, *Agriculture*, 17; T. Saadé, *Essai*, 41; Gross, "Ottoman Rule," 140; Médawar, *Syrie agricole*, 25–26. Médawar claimed that officials registered lands at ten to fifteen times more than their real value, whereas T. Saade estimated that it was two to three times. Médawar's estimate is supported by a 1905 petition from Hama (BOA, DH.MKT 1142/20, copy of a petition to the province, 26 Kanunuevvel 1320 [8 January 1905]).

227. Barakat, "Underwriting," 386. According to T. Saadé, by 1905 in Latakia the amount taken for the agricultural bank had reached 1.75% (T. Saadé, *Essai*, 39).

228. BOA, Y.PRK.TNF 4/81.

229. The 1890 amendment allowed for property to be auctioned even if it was necessary for the maintenance of the debtor's or guarantor's household. An amendment in 1894 specified that if no one was willing to buy the property or if bids were insufficient to cover the debt, then the bank could outbid them, transfer the title to itself, and put the assets up for auction once a year had passed. If the former rights holder could pay off their debt during the year, the property would be returned to them (*Düstur: I. Tertib*, 6: 744, 1555–56; Young, *Corps*, 5: 352–53). An additional amendment in 1900 specified that if the land was put back up for auction at the end of one year and fetched a price higher than that which the bank had originally paid, the funds would be given to the owner of the sold land rather than being registered as bank revenue, which was the process in the 1894 law (*Düstur: I. Tertib*, 7: 452).

230. Quataert, "Ottoman Reform," 135–36; Güran, *19. Yüzyıl*, 153; Young, *Corps*, 5: 351. Young claims that the exceptional use of such guarantees for loans of up to 300 piastres started in 1900, whereas Quataert dates it to 1895. According to Quataert, by 1901, only 1.7 million of the 55 million piastres lent by the bank used nonproperty security (Quataert, "Ottoman Reform," 439n23).

231. On extensive agriculture as the norm, see Quataert, "Age of Reforms," 777–78.

232. I borrow the phrase "people of capital" from Seikaly, *Men of Capital.*

233. BOA, DH.MKT 618/68, copy of a report from the Council of State's civil office, 7 Teşrinievvel 1318 [20 October 1902]. French scholars during the mandate would identify this arrangement as one of four timeless tenant farming relationships (*métayage*) in the region: (1) *murabi*ʿ (landowner paid all expenses and tax; farmer kept one-fourth of harvest); (2) *hamawiya* partnership (landowner provided land and housing; farmer provided labor; all other expenses were split 50–50, as were profits after paying all taxes and expenses); (3) *halabiya* partnership (landowner provided housing and seed and paid tax; farmer provided livestock and labor; they shared equally in expenses and losses and, after subtracting the tithe, the harvest); and (4) *khoms* (landowner provided land and housing and paid tax; farmer contributed labor, livestock, and seed; after the tithe was subtracted from the harvest, the landowner took one-fifth of what remained and the farmer took the rest). By 1933, 70% of the land in Hama was worked according to this arrangement. See [Gaulmier], "Notes sur la propriété foncière," 135.

234. BOA, DH.MKT 618/68, copy of a report from the Council of State's civil office, 7 Teşrinievvel 1318 [20 October 1902].

235. BOA, DH.MKT 1142/20, copy of a petition to the province, 26 Kanunuevvel 1320 [8 January 1905].

236. See, for example, Gerber, *Social Origins*, 83–84.

237. For example, Batatu notes that ninety-eight villages in the region belonged to three families: the Barazis (forty-nine), the ʿAzms (twenty-five), and the al-Kaylanis (twenty-four) (Batatu, *Syria's Peasantry*, 124–25). His numbers are drawn from a work published in 1940 by Jacques Weulersse (Weulersse, *Pays des Alaouites*, 1: 363). For more on Weulersse, see chapter 5. According to Gaulmier, a French scholar writing in 1933, Hama consisted of 114 villages, 90 of which were either completely or partly owned by the Barazis, ʿAzms, al-Kaylanis, or Tayfurs ([Gaulmier], "Notes sur la propriété foncière," 131, 132). Muhammad Kurd ʿAli, writing in 1926, put the number of villages in Hama at 124, with 80%, or about 99, owned by large landowners (Kurd ʿAli, *Kitab Khitat al-Sham* 4: 214).

238. For an example of this claim, see Khoury, *Urban Notables*, 27. For a discussion of these reasons, see Gerber, *Social Origins*, 72–73; Quataert, "Age of Reforms," 856–57; and Reilly, "Status Groups," 528–29.

239. Reilly ("Status Groups," 529–30) makes a distinction between "debt" and "the workings of the land code" as understood by scholars who claim that the code facilitated the emergence of "absentee landlords" because peasants did not want to register land in their names (see Warriner, "Land Tenure," 76.) Reilly's careful and incisive analysis of the Damascus court records meticulously refutes this claim. How the "debt" is acquired is not explicitly stated, but the implication is that it is not connected to the Land Code.

240. BOA, DH.MKT 1142/20, draft response from the Interior Ministry to the province of Syria, 21 Kanunuevvel 1322 [3 January 1907]. In the province of Syria the issue of inflated land values in the registers was apparently a problem in Hama, Hawran, and Karak.

241. BOA, DH.MKT 1142/20, draft response from the Interior Ministry to the province of Syria, 21 Kanunuevvel 1322 [3 January 1907]. The report makes explicit a difference between these two ways of gaining loans used by the villagers, suggesting that some of

the land was held as *mülk* and thus could be literally mortgaged (*terhin*), whereas other land was held as *miri* and thus the usufruct was transferred (*ferağ*).

242. BOA, DH.MKT 1142/20, copy of a petition to the province, 26 Kanunuevvel 1320 [8 January 1905]; BOA, DH.MKT 1142/20, draft response from the Interior Ministry to the province of Syria, 21 Kanunuevvel 1322 [3 January 1907]. The report and petition do not give any explanation for why the villagers' initial appeals to the bank were turned down. In June 1905 the tithe law was amended once again, although it is unclear to what degree machinations like those in Syria were behind the revisions.

243. Rıza, *Meclis-i Mebusan*, 9.

244. T. Saadé, *Essai*, 3; E. Saadé, *Agriculture*, 38–39; Médawar, *Syrie agricole*, 19. On the accessibility of this kind of option only to those with resources, see Médawar, *Syrie agricole*, 29–30. I have not been able to trace the backgrounds of Wady Médawar and Toufik Saadé.

245. E. Saadé, *Agriculture*, 23–24; Médawar, *Syrie agricole*.

246. The school was established in 1855 by the "Frères de la Doctrine Chrétienne" with the intent of providing "scientific and technical" training to students "on top of classical studies to those who work in the countryside so that agriculture would be prosperous" (Quéméré et al., "Evolutions pédagogiques," 401; Riley, *Reports*). Students, who defended their theses before the Société des Agriculteurs de France from 1883 to 1939, were expected to continue pursuing practical agriculture work after graduation. These Syrian students attended the school during a period when it welcomed a number of foreign students; this lasted until 1905, after which the school was forced to secularize and almost closed (Quéméré et al., "Evolutions pédagogiques," 401–2). One report noted that, although the school operated much like one of the state's practical agricultural schools, it charged about four times as much in fees for room and board and instruction. The report characterized it as "a private agricultural school of a high class, receiving, however, a subvention from the State" (Jenkins, *Report on Agricultural Education*, 117–18). In France, the school catered to "conservative agrarian notables" and encouraged the "dissemination of agrarian corporatism and social paternalism" (Paxton, *French Peasant Fascism*, 31).

247. Toufik Saadé had been educated by Latakia's Frères des Ecoles chrétiennes and the Pères Lazaristes of Antoura (T. Saadé, *Essai*, 226).

248. See Hakim, *Suriya wa al-ʿAhd al-ʿUthmani*, 95; E. Saadé, *Agriculture*, vii.

249. Médawar, *Syrie agricole*, 24, 31.

250. T. Saadé, *Essai*, 40; Médawar, *Syrie agricole*, 24–25.

251. Médawar, *Syrie agricole*, 24; E. Saadé, *Agriculture*, 18. As discussed, the government had attempted to use village shaykhs previously with lackluster results.

252. Médawar, *Syrie agricole*, 25–26.

253. Médawar, *Syrie agricole*, 27–28; E. Saadé, *Agriculture*, 21; T. Saadé, *Essai*, 42. This reflects the approach used in *salam* contracts. E. Saadé suggested an interest rate of 3–4%.

254. Médawar, *Syrie agricole*, 19.

255. Médawar, *Syrie agricole*, 27, 33.

256. E. Saadé, *Agriculture*, 20; Médawar, *Syrie agricole*, 28–30; T. Saadé, *Essai*, 10. The term used was Rumelia.

257. Médawar, *Syrie agricole*, 35–36; E. Saadé, *Agriculture*, 13. "Capitalists" is the term Médawar uses. He appears to include at least some large landowners in this group.

258. E. Saadé, *Agriculture*, 13–14. Saadé likened this role to that of syndicates or cooperatives in France, which had been legalized in 1884 and were grouped into federations run by competing rural elites (Moulin, *Peasantry*, 104–5).

259. Médawar, *Syrie agricole*, 39–40.

260. Médawar, *Syrie agricole*, 34–35.

261. Médawar, *Syrie agricole*, 34–35; E. Saadé, *Agriculture*, 20.

262. Médawar, *Syrie agricole*, 42–43.

263. *Düstur: I. Tertib*, 8: 277–78, Art. 42. Compare *Düstur: I. Tertib*, 6: 376–77, Art. 39.

264. In 1905 the administration also suggested that agents collect the kilometric guarantees for the railroads in cash using the five-year average, but this met with "strenuous objections" from PDA officials (Blaisdell, *European Financial Control*, 143–44). Clearly they had doubts about the reliability of this method for ensuring they received their financing.

265. Pan-Montojo and Mignemi, "International Organizations," 241–42.

266. On Ottoman attendance at these conferences, see *VIIe Congrés International d'Agriculture*, vol. II, première partie, xiv, lx; *VIII Internationaler landwirtschaftlicher Kongress*, vol. I, 64, 147; and "Müsahaba," *Osmanlı Ziraat ve Ticaret Gazetesi*, 20 Mayıs 1323 [2 June 1907]. For Méline's full speech in French, see *VIII Internationaler landwirtschaftlicher Kongress*, 175–82.

267. FAO, International Institute of Agriculture Archives, A-1, "Convention Internationale de 7 Juin 1905."

268. Lubin, "International Institute"; FAO, International Institute of Agriculture Archives, A-4c, "Conférence Agricole Internationale de Rome, 1905." The institute's organizers considered the statistical reports an essential step to maintaining a degree of stability in global market prices.

269. FAO, International Institute of Agriculture Archives, A-1, "Convention créant l'IIA, Rome, 1905"; see also BOA, Y.PRK.HR 34/58.

270. BOA, DH.MKT 1098/37, copy of a telegraph from the Interior Ministry, 24 Haziran 1322 [7 July 1906].

271. Williams, "'The Agriculture Ministry of the Whole World'."

272. See Hanioğlu, *Brief History*, 145.

273. *Türk Ansiklopedisi*, 420; Kâzım Kadri, *Meşrutiyetten*, 68–69; Kayalı, *Arabs and Young Turks*, 54.

274. "Osmanlı Ziraat Cemiyeti," *Çiftçi* 1, no. 1 (12 April 1909): 2; İhsanoğlu, "Genesis of Learned Societies," 176. Graduates of the agriculture and forestry schools formed the other societies.

275. "Osmanlı Ziraat Cemiyeti," *Çiftçi* 1, no. 1 (12 April 1909): 2, 3.

276. Kâzım, "Bir Ziraat," 7.

277. Kâzım, "Bir Ziraat," 7–8.

278. Kâzım, "Bir Ziraat," 8.

279. BOA, DH.MUİ 94-2/15, Ottoman Agricultural Society to the Interior Ministry, 28 Nisan 1326 [11 May 1910].

280. BOA, DH.MUİ 732/25, Governor of Syria to the Interior Ministry, 4 Mart 1326 [17 March 1910].

281. The CUP apparently considered halving the tithe but deemed it not practicable (Ahmad, "Agrarian Policies," 278–79).

282. BOA, DH.MUİ 732/25, Governor of Syria to the Interior Ministry, 4 Mart 1326 [17 March 1910].

283. BOA, DH.MUİ 732/25, Governor of Beirut to the Interior Ministry, 10 Mart 1326 [23 March 1910].

284. See Orman ve Maadin ve Ziraat Nezareti Kalem-i Mahsus Müdüriyet Istatistik Şubesi, *1325 senesi*; Orman ve Maâdin ve Ziraat Nezareti İstatistik İdaresi, *1323 senesi*. These compilations were followed in 1917 by a set of "Industrial Statistics for 1913 and 1915" (Ticaret ve Ziraat Nezareti, *Sanayi istatistiği*) and agricultural ones for 1916/1917 (Ticaret ve Ziraat Nezareti, *Memalik-i Osmaniye'nin 1329 senesine mahsus ziraat istatistiğidir*).

285. See map from Atatürk Kitaplığı Collection titled "Ticaret ve Ziraat Nezareti Devlet-i Osmaniye'nin 1329 senesi ahval-i ziraiyesine mahsus istatistikleri," Hrt_000219.

286. For more on these statistical compilations, see Williams, "'The Agriculture Ministry of the Whole World'."

287. See, for example, *Meclis-i Mebusan zabıt ceridesi*, İ:88, C:1, 18 Nisan 1327 [1 May 1911], 55–67; and *Meclis-i Mebusan zabıt ceridesi*, İ:88, C:2, 18 Nisan 1327 [1 May 1911], 61–94.

288. Pamuk, "Ottoman Economy," 114; Conte and Sabatini, "Ottoman External Debt," 87–89.

289. Thobie, *Intérêts*, 468–75; Médawar, *Syrie agricole*, 35.

290. See Karakoç, *Tahşiyeli Kavanin*, 1: 473; "Loi provisoire sur la délimitation et l'enregistrement de la propriété immobilière," 18 February 1913, in Ottoman Empire, *Code Foncier Ottoman* ([Istanbul]: Imp. Française L. Mourkidès, [1913?], 7–26. The French translation of this stipulation is "à titre definitive."

291. BOA, DH.İD 2/29, General Director of the Agricultural Bank to the Interior Ministry, 24 Mayis 1330 [6 June 1914]. He defines the practice as "within the borders of a village having lands without distinction tied to a land deed in that village name, one year one farmer cultivates a field, the next year that field he leaves and sows another field."

292. Mundy and Saumarez Smith, *Governing Property*; Firestone, "Land-Equalizing *Musha*ʿ Village." Firestone argues that this form of landholding evolved as a way to protect rural communities from the uncertainty and pressures that accompanied incorporation into an increasingly globalized agricultural commodity market over the course of the nineteenth century. For a critique of Firestone, see Mundy, "La propriété dite *mushâ*'."

293. BOA, DH.İD 2/29, Council of State decision, 8 Nisan 1328 [21 April 1912].

294. BOA, DH.İD 2/29, General Director of the Agricultural Bank to the Interior Ministry, 24 Mayis 1330 [6 June 1914]; BOA, DH.İD 2/29, Syria's governor Mehmet Akif to the Interior Ministry, 9 Temmuz 1330 [22 July 1914]. The phrase translates as "the necessity to procure and facilitate the farmers' use and borrowing in general from the Agriculture Bank by attaching people's names individually to imperial land deeds with the detachment and division of the land of every village."

295. BOA, DH.İD 2/29, Syria's governor Mehmet Akif to the Interior Ministry, 9 Temmuz 1330 [22 July 1914].

296. BOA, DH.İD 2/29, General Director of the Agricultural Bank to the Interior Ministry, 24 Mayis 1330 [6 June 1914].

297. BOA, DH.İD 2/29, Syria's governor Mehmet Akif to the Interior Ministry, 9 Temmuz 1330 [22 July 1914].

298. Mitchell, "Society," 77.

299. BOA, DH.ID 44-2/3, Hüseyin Kâzım, governor of Aleppo, to the Interior Ministry, 15 Kanunusani 1326 [28 January 1911].

300. See Watenpaugh, *Being Modern*, 95–119. For the rabble-rousing governor description, see Lewis, *Nomads*, 52.

301. See, for instance, Klein, *Margins of Empire*, 128–69; and Özok-Gündoğan, "Peripheral Approach," 179–215.

302. Yücel Terzibaşoğlu, quoted in Özok-Gündoğan, "Peripheral Approach," 202.

303. Klein, *Margins of Empire*, 147–49. For another perspective, see Mundy and Saumarez Smith, *Governing Property*. Although there were clearly some flagrant abuses of power, more research is necessary to determine to what extent these were representative. Mundy and Saumarez Smith demonstrate that in parts of the province of Syria, property ownership continued to be divided and inherited in shares throughout this period. One of Kâzım's dispatches also suggests that fair division and registration of land followed the reform and that instances of fraud were endemic but exceptional (BOA, DH.ID 44-2/3, Hüseyin Kâzım, governor of Aleppo, to the Interior Ministry, 19 Mart 1327 [1 April 1911]).

304. Nonetheless, it appears that at least in some areas—Bitlis province, for example—"energetic" governors were able to obtain some relief for deprived villagers. See Klein, *Margins of Empire*, 155.

305. Mitchell, "Society, 77.

306. Ironically, during Kâzım's time in Aleppo, his agricultural expertise would be called into question because of his handling of a locust invasion. See BOA, DH.H 25/35; and BOA, DH.İD 104-1/6, Dürrizade to the Sublime Porte, 26 Şubat 1326 [11 March 1911]. In this letter Dürrizade does not mince words in expressing his frustration with Kâzım for not taking into account the opinions of local experts on how to handle the locusts. See also Dolbee, *Locusts of Power*.

307. TNA, FO 195.2337, Fontana to Lowther, 15 November 1910.

308. MAE, Syrie-Liban 114, French consul to Pichon, 29 August 1910.

309. The tipping point for the recall of the previous governor, Fakhri Pasha, was his order for the arrest of a critical journalist, Mustafa Azim. See Watenpaugh, *Being Modern*, 68–94.

310. MAE, Syrie-Liban 114, French consul to Pichon, 29 August 1910.

311. For the French translation, see MAE, Syrie-Liban 114, addendum following French consul to Pichon, 29 August, 1910; and for excerpts translated into English from Arabic, see Watenpaugh, *Being Modern*, 99–100.

312. MAE, Syrie-Liban 114, addendum following French consul to Pichon, 5 November 1910.

313. Kayalı, *Arabs and Young Turks*, 67, 26, 27.

314. TNA, FO 195.2272, Longworth to O'Conor, 10 January 1908.

315. BOA, DH.ID 44–2/3, Hüseyin Kâzım, governor of Aleppo, to the Interior Ministry, 15 Kanunusani 1326 [28 January 1911].

316. MAE, Syrie-Liban 114, French consul to Pichon, 24 December 1910.

317. BOA, DH.ID 44–1/30, Hüseyin Kâzım, governor of Aleppo, to the Interior Ministry, 26 Kanunuevvel 1326 [8 January 1911].

318. MAE, Syrie-Liban 115, French consul to Pichon, 1 and 7 February 1911; TNA, FO 195.2366, Fontana to Lowther, 20 March 1911. According to this report, of 270,000 sheep ordered from Mosul, only 30,000 arrived after traveling across the Euphrates.

319. BOA, DH.ID 44–2/3, Hüseyin Kâzım, governor of Aleppo, to the Interior Ministry, 15 Kanunusani 1326 [28 January 1911]. On the issue of ensuring that land values were properly evaluated so that loans could be taken out that were commensurate with the land's value, see BOA, DH.İD 44–1/28.

320. BOA, DH.ID 44–2/3, Hüseyin Kâzım, governor of Aleppo, to the Interior Ministry, 15 Kanunusani 1326 [28 January 1911]. See also the accompanying photo of the disabled man that Kazîm submitted as evidence. On the history of "holy folly," see Scalenghe, *Disability*, 102–17.

321. BOA, DH.ID 44–2/3, Hüseyin Kâzım, governor of Aleppo, to the Interior Ministry, 15 Kanunusani 1326 [28 January 1911]. The Celali brigands referred to a series of late-sixteenth- and early-seventeenth-century rebellions against Ottoman authority in Anatolia.

322. BOA, DH.ID 44–2/3, Hüseyin Kâzım, governor of Aleppo, to the Interior Ministry, 15 Kanunusani 1326 [28 January 1911].

323. BOA, DH.ID 44–2/3, Hüseyin Kâzım, governor of Aleppo, to the Interior Ministry, 15 Kanunusani 1326 [28 January 1911].

324. See Watenpaugh, *Being Modern*, 95–119; and BOA, DH.MTV 18/20.

325. TNA, FO 195.2366, Fontana to Lowther, 3 June 1911.

326. See TNA, FO 195.2366, note sent 21 July 1911; and MAE, Syrie-Liban 115, French consul to de Selves, 22 July 1911.

327. MAE, Syrie-Liban 114, French consul to Pichon, 12 October 1910. See also TNA, FO 195.2337, Fontana to Lowther, 15 November 1910.

328. Özbek, "Tax Farming," 243.

329. E. Saadé, *Agriculture*, 10, 11.

Chapter Two

1. BOA, DH.İD 99/32, report from the agricultural inspector for Beirut, Syria, and Aleppo provinces, 26 Teşrinievvel 1326 [8 November 1910].

2. BOA, DH.İD 99/32, report from the agricultural inspector for Beirut, Syria, and Aleppo provinces, 26 Teşrinievvel 1326 [8 November 1910].

3. See Douwes and Lewis, "Trials." Their analysis does not include any Ottoman documents.

4. BOA, BEO 3884/291293, testimony of the mukhtar of the western neighborhood, n.d., p. 12.

5. Cuinet, *Syrie*, 339–40. Combine harvesters were also touted as more economical than hiring harvest workers, saving 20 francs 70 per hectare, according to Cuinet's estimate.

6. Cuinet, *Syrie*, 340. To respond to this need for spare parts and repair facilities, government officials concerned with agricultural experimentation were often preoccupied with establishing and operating *demirhaneler* (forges). See, for example, BOA, DH.İD 99/32, Forest, Mines, and Agriculture Ministry to the Interior Ministry, 28 Eylul 1326 [11 October 1910]; and BOA, ŞD 2246/2, Aleppo Governor to the Interior Ministry, 16 Şubat 1325 [1 March 1910].

7. Strohmeier, "Abd al-Rahman Pasha al-Yusuf," 360. Strohmeier quotes from Khoury (*Syria*, 446) and expresses surprise at the "remarkable exception to that rule"—that is, that landowners did not want to invest in their lands—represented by a letter from the protagonist of his chapter, Abd al-Rahman Pasha al-Yusuf. The letter, from September 1918, meticulously details al-Yusuf's plans for agriculturally developing his lands.

8. Behar, "Dairy Industry," 186.

9. For information about schools in France, Germany, the United States, and Russia, see Boulet, *Enjeux de la formation*; Harwood, *Technology's Dilemma*; G. E. Moore, "Involvement"; and Moon, *Plough*, 270. Moon identifies 1893–1913 as years of major growth in agricultural education infrastructure in Russia, a period that coincided with a similar phenomenon in the Ottoman context (270).

10. For a full list of the institutions in operation and those planned for future expansion, see "Ziraat Nezaretince şimdiye kadar vücuda getirilen ve getirilmesi mutasavver olan müessesat ziraiye," *Orman ve Maadin ve Ziraat ve Baytar Mecmuası [Forest, Mines, Agriculture, and Veterinarian Review]* 4 (28 Şubat 1326 [13 March 1911]): 337–45.

11. Médawar, *Syrie agricole*, 47–48. For land acquisition in the late nineteenth century, see Khoury, *Urban Notables*; Doumani, *Rediscovering Palestine*, 155–65; Alff, "Levantine Joint-Stock Companies," 156–58; Schilcher, "Great Depression," 171–72; Schilcher, "Hauran Conflicts," 174; Gross, "Ottoman Rule"; Lewis, *Nomads*, 46–53; and Masters, "Political Economy," 309–11.

12. On the role of science in producing subjectivities among Istanbul elites more broadly in the late Ottoman Empire, see Yalçınkaya, *Learned Patriots*.

13. On boundary-work, see Gieryn, "Boundary-Work."

14. On the exclusions inherent in the production of a discourse of modernity, see Scott, *Seeing*, 335; and Latour, *We Have Never Been Modern*.

15. See, for example, BOA, DH.İD 99/32, report from the agricultural inspector for Beirut, Syria, and Aleppo provinces, 8 November 1910; and BOA, T.ZTİ 3056/62, report signed by the agricultural school's director Abdussettar, 23 Şubat 1327 [4 March 1912].

16. Jasanoff, "Idiom of Co-Production," 3.

17. Güran, *19. Yüzyıl*, 47; Yıldırım, "Osmanlı'da İlk Çağdaş"; Demirel and Doğanay, "Osmanlı'da Ziraat Eğitimi." Before this school was established, an Ottoman natural history museum and herbarium had provided a place for the production of scientific agricultural knowledge, but it was destroyed by fire in 1848 (S. Çelik, "Science").

18. BOA, A}MKT.MHM 727/31, report of Aram Efendi, 10 Şaban 1310 [27 February 1893]. The Scientific Agriculture Committee was formed in 1892 to coordinate the central government's agricultural reform program. It consisted of five departments: general reform; phylloxera; administration of scientific agricultural institutions, such as model farms and fields as well as agricultural schools; industrial agriculture; and veterinary medicine (Quataert, "Ottoman Reform," 78–79).

19. BOA, A}MKT.MHM 727/31, report of Aram Efendi, 10 Şaban 1310 [27 February 1893]. For Nuri Bey's posting to Aydın and the elimination of the agricultural director position, see Quataert, "Ottoman Reform," 85, 78.

20. BOA, I.MMS 117/5047, letter from Nuri Bey Efendi, 3 Teşrinievvel 1306 [15 October 1890].

21. BOA, I.MMS 117/5047, list of proposed destinations. The provincial breakdown was as follows: Syria, Beirut, Baghdad, Diyarbekir, Adana, Aleppo (hot-climate agriculture); Aydın, Hüdavendigar, Salonica, Edirne, Trabzon (irrigation, with two students destined for each province except Trabzon); Konya, Ankara, Sivas, Mamurat al-Aziz, Monastir (cold-climate agriculture); and Aleppo, Trabzon, Monastir (viticulture and cheese making).

22. BOA, I.MMS 117/5047, letter from Nuri Bey Efendi, 3 Teşrinievvel 1306 [15 October 1890].

23. BOA, I.MMS 117/5047, Commerce Minister to the Grand Vizier, 26 Teşrinisani 1306 [8 December 1890]; BOA, I.MMS 117/5047, document signed by the Grand Vizier, 19 Kanunuevvel 1306 [31 December 1890], and accompanying note, 20 Kanunuevvel 1306 [1 January 1891]. Quataert chronicles the outcome of this decision. See Quataert, "Ottoman Reform," 89–90. Initially one student would have gone to Marmirolle to learn about viticulture and cheese making for Aleppo; three to the Merchines school to learn about cold-climate agriculture for Sivas, Ankara, and Konya; four to Avignon for education in irrigation for use in Edirne, Salonica, Hüdavendigar, and Aydin; and two to the Rouïba school, after which they would have been employed in Adana and Syria (BOA, I.MMS 117/5047, Commerce Minister to the Grand Vizier, 26 Teşrinisani 1306 [8 December 1890]). On their return, those who obtained a diploma would commit to working for five years in the model fields or agricultural schools with a monthly salary of no less than 800 gurush or else repay the costs spent on their education (BOA, I.MMS 117/5047, Meclis-i Mahsus decision, 19 Kanunuevvel 1306 [31 December 1890]).

24. See Ediger and Bowlus, "Greasing the Wheels," 193.

25. BOA, Y.A.HUS 244/46, letter from Commerce Minister, 12 Subat 1306 [24 February 1891].

26. BOA, BEO 91/6803, draft to Commerce and Public Works Ministry, 6 Teşrinievvel 1308 [18 October 1892]; Charmasson et al., *Enseignement agricole*, 40.

27. BOA, MV 36/31, Meclis-i Vükela's decision, 15 Eylül 1304 [7 October 1888]. An imperial decree (*irade*) affirming this decision was subsequently issued (Quataert, "Ottoman Reform," 110–11). According to the decision, efforts to establish agricultural schools and model farms had been started in Edirne, Izmir, Salonica, and the area around Istanbul—presumably a reference to the Halkalı Agricultural School. On the 1887 Hatch Act, see G. E. Moore, "Involvement."

28. BOA, Y.PRK.ŞD 2/9. See also Quataert, "Ottoman Reform," 113. The 1303 [1887/1888] Public Works budget would provide initial funding to the tune of 108,700 gurush with ongoing yearly maintenance funds of 31,200 gurush to be deducted from the fields' produce (BOA, MV 36/31, Meclis-i Vükela's decision, 15 Eylül 1304 [7 October 1888]). Further financial encouragement was forthcoming in 1892, when the Council of State urged that the production of these model fields be exempted from the tithe and that their buildings

not be subject to the land tax (*vergi*) (BOA, İ.TNF 1/19, 1 Cemaziyülevvel 1310 [21 November 1892]. This was confirmed by another imperial decree (*irade*). See Quataert, "Ottoman Reform," 113. Quataert insists that these fields "primarily directed their efforts towards the average cultivator and stressed on the spot training available to all regardless of age or financial status" (113). It is difficult to evaluate how true this statement was in practice, although there does seem to have been an official intent to make these institutions as accessible as possible.

29. BOA, A}MKT.MHM 727/31, report of Aram Efendi, 10 Şaban 1310 [27 February 1893].

30. Quataert claims that the Halkalı Agricultural School, which was established to train staff and teachers for model fields and agriculture schools, "was unable to draw upon any indigenous tradition of agricultural science and borrowed extensively from the achievements of the West" (Quataert, "Ottoman Reform," 103). Although a number of the early employees of the school might have been trained in European schools, looking at how this knowledge was applied in the empire's institutions of scientific agriculture suggests that "indigenous traditions" were indeed an integral part of their operations.

31. Kuneralp, *Son Dönem*, 9; Quataert, "Ottoman Reform," 72.

32. BOA, A}MKT.MHM 727/31, 10 Şaban 1310 [27 February 1893]. The chart that indicates cultivation is under way is undated, but it seems fair to assume that it was produced around the same time as Aram Efendi's report dated 15 Şubat 1308 [27 February 1893], which it accompanies. BOA, BEO 1167/87481, Council of State, 15 Haziran 1314 [27 June 1898].

33. BOA, A}MKT.MHM 727/31, 10 Şaban 1310 [27 February 1893]. See undated chart.

34. Water resources were also an issue in Konya, for example. See BOA, BEO 1167/87481, report from the Council of State, 15 Haziran 1314 [27 June 1898]. The realization that the land of Syria's model field was not ideal and the conclusion that a model field was not a necessity in the province prompted a request to sell the field's land and transfer the funds received to the model farm in Edirne (BOA, A}MKT.MHM 727/31, 10 Şaban 1310 [27 February 1893], see undated chart). The explanation in the document is rather opaque. For more details, see BOA, A.}MKT.MHM 727/3, letter from Forest, Mines, and Agriculture Minister, 21 Nisan 1309 [3 May 1893].

35. Quataert, "Ottoman Reform," 115–21.

36. BOA, A}MKT.MHM 727/31, 10 Şaban 1310 [27 February 1893], undated chart; BOA, İ.OM 1/2, decision from Council of State, 15 Mayıs 1309 [27 May 1893]. By May 1893, of the 30,000 gurush allotted for the field's construction, almost 27,000 had already been spent on construction expenses, but at least 20,000 gurush were still needed for the pump.

37. BOA, İ.OM 1/2, decision from Council of State, 15 Mayıs 1309 [27 May 1893]. For further details on the amounts allotted for the field, see also BOA, BEO 244/18275, draft dated 12 Temmuz 1309 [24 July 1893]. Two other documents also detail how these funds were available to make up the 9,500 gurush needed for the Aleppo model field to purchase two pairs of oxen: BOA, ŞD 519/15, letter from the Forest, Mines, and Agriculture Minister, 1 Şubat 1310 [13 February 1895]; and BOA, Y.PRK.ŞD 2/9, Council of State note, 2 Mart 1310 [14 March 1894].

38. BOA, ŞD 521/39, letter from the Forest, Mines, and Agriculture Minister, 15 Teşrinisani 1311 [27 Kasım 1895]. The sum was 29,780 gurush 17 para.

39. *Düstur: I. Tertib*, 6: 142, Art. 39.

40. BOA, ŞD 518/8, letter from the Forest, Mines and Agriculture Minister, 11 Eylül 1310 [23 September 1894].

41. BOA, BEO 509/38170, letter from the Forest, Mines, and Agriculture Minister, 15 Teşrinievvel 1310 [27 October 1894].

42. BOA, Y.PRK.TNF 4/81. The bank also held a net total of 171,178 gurush 33 para allocated for scientific employees, of which 116,217 gurush 35 para amounted to their actual salaries and expenses. Despite this reliance on the bank's funds, animosity between Selim Bey and the Agricultural Bank's director and head of the Council of State's finance office, Cemaleddin Pasha, possibly imperiled his ability to secure the requested sums. Quataert suggests that internal intrigues provoked by Selim's antagonistic approach to politics—although a favorite of the sultan's, he was despised by other officials, such as the Agricultural Bank director and the grand vizier, whose authority he bypassed in appealing directly to the sultan with requests—could have been responsible for delays in funding for various agricultural projects (Quataert, "Ottoman Reform," 73–75, 433n44).

43. Young, *Corps*, 349.

44. BOA, ŞD 519/2, letter from the Forest, Mines, and Agriculture Minister, 10 Kanunusani 1310 [22 January 1895].

45. BOA, ŞD 524/5, letter from the Forest, Mines, and Agriculture Minister, 30 Nisan 1313 [12 May 1897]; BOA, İ.RSM 7/26, 26 Muharrem 1315 [27 June 1987]. See also Quataert, "Ottoman Reform," 113. It should be noted that the customs exemptions list was continuously updated to include only equipment still deemed "modern" (Quataert, "Ottoman Reform," 162).

46. Melkon submitted a spirited statement (*layiha-i itiraziye*) protesting the charges against him. See BOA, ŞD 2232/6, "Protest Statement to the Council of State Final Court of Appeals," 2 Teşrinievvel 1314 [15 October 1898]. Oddly, even though Melkon Efendi is listed in the Aleppo *salname* for 1894–1896 as the "province agricultural inspector consolidated with the model farm director," in the *Salname-yi Devlet-i Âliye-yi Osmaniye*, Vahan Efendi continues to be listed as the agricultural inspector for Aleppo from 1891 to 1895, after which the position is no longer listed until 1903, when it appears consolidated with the model field director and is held by Hamdi Efendi (*Salname-yi Devlet-i Âliye-yi Osmaniye* [1903], 586; *Salname-yi Vilâyet-i Halep* [1894], 141; *Salname-yi Vilâyet-i Halep* [1895], 121; *Salname-yi Vilâyet-i Halep* [1896], 122). The two positions were originally consolidated in 1891 (Quataert, "Ottoman Reform," 114).

47. BOA, ŞD 2232/6, "Head farmer Ahmed's testimony," 28 Kanunuevvel 1312 [28 January 1897]. Ahmet Bey indicates that 1 mecidiye equals 19 gurush. Ahmed signed his testimony with a signet seal, perhaps indicating a certain social status in the community. (In the court proceedings regarding the Selimiye agricultural school, the poorest farmers and other local community members tended to sign with a thumbprint.)

48. BOA, I.MMS 117/5047, Meclis-i Mahsus decision, 19 Kanunuevvel 1306 [31 December 1890]; BOA, ŞD 2232/6, field work log from June 1896 to early January 1897.

49. See BOA, ŞD 2232/6, inspector's report, 29 Teşrinisani 1313 [11 December 1897]. During the period described in the documents, Melkon was under investigation for

allegedly embezzling from the field. The model fields appear to have been somewhat prone to this. Quataert mentions embezzlement was also a problem in the Ankara model field (Quataert, "Ottoman Reform," 115).

50. BOA, ŞD 2232/6, information gathered from various testimonies, 28 Kanunuevvel 1312 [28 January 1897]; and field work log from June 1896 to early January 1897. The oxen were named Sarı and Maviru. It is unclear whether these are their names, types, or color—*sarı*, for example, can mean "yellow." The horses were named Zeytuna and Bebe. Zeytuna may have died, as her name disappears from the records around September 14 and Kamer, or Moon, appears.

51. *Salname-yi Vilâyet-i Halep* (1894), 141; *Salname-yi Vilâyet-i Halep* (1895), 121; *Salname-yi Vilâyet-i Halep*, (1896), 122. That the field's guard was an ağa may reflect the role this powerful social group had played in providing rural security since at least the eighteenth century (Reilly, *Small Town in Syria*, 97).

52. Even though the knowledge applied in the field was local, Melkon Efendi pursued contacts with larger imperial and international networks of those invested in the spread of scientific agriculture. See, for example, BOA, ŞD 2231/6, copy of the Aleppo model field director Melkon Efendi's testimony, 24 Şubat 1312 [8 March 1897]. In fact, Melkon Efendi appears to have exchanged a series of letters with Amasyan Efendi, the minister of agriculture, Aram Efendi, the president of the scientific agriculture association (*ziraat heyet-i fenniye*), and Nubar Pasha, the Egyptian minister—letters that in part got him into trouble. I have been unable to confirm his educational background, although it seems he might have had some training in Europe.

53. BOA, ŞD 2232/6, field work log from June 1896 to early January 1897.

54. *Salname-yi Vilâyet-i Halep* (1897), 122; BOA, T.ZTİ 3056/48, chart signed by Agop Oscan, 1 Kanunusani 1327 [14 January 1912]. It is possible that Ahmet's son eventually joined him in the model field, as the 1912 chart listed another farmer also from Tal Jabin with a father named Ahmet. See chapter 3 for more details.

55. Work on the Salonica school started in 1889, and it accepted its first twenty students in 1890 (BOA, A}MKT.MHM 727/31, report of Aram Efendi, 10 Şaban 1310 [27 February 1893]). For additional information on the Salonica school, see Küçükceran, *Agrarian Economy*, 133–38.

56. Quataert, "Ottoman Reform," 98–99.

57. Soydan, *120 yıllık eğitim*, 255; Quataert, "Ottoman Reform," 94. Quataert adds that the applicants also had to be knowledgeable in Turkish and French.

58. Quataert, "Ottoman Reform," 101.

59. On schools, see Somel, *Modernization*; see also Quataert, "Ottoman Reform," 107.

60. Quataert, "Ottoman Reform," 97–98. For a fuller discussion of which officials attended specific German or French agricultural schools, see Quataert, "Ottoman Reform," 64–91 (ch. 3, "The Development of the Agrarian Bureaucracy").

61. Quataert, "Ottoman Reform," 103.

62. On the students' obligation to work ten years for the government or else reimburse a set amount for their education, see Quataert, "Ottoman Reform," 107.

63. Quataert, "Ottoman Reform," 433n44.

64. BOA, BEO 1167/87481, Council of State report, 15 Haziran 1314 [27 June 1898].

65. BOA, BEO 1167/87481, Council of State report, 15 Haziran 1314 [27 June 1898]. Securing additional land was not possible so long as the losses of the original owners was not made good.

66. BOA, BEO 1167/87481, Council of State report, 15 Haziran 1314 [27 June 1898].

67. BOA, BEO 1167/87481, Council of State report, 15 Haziran 1314 [27 June 1898].

68. BOA, BEO 1167/87481, Council of State report, 15 Haziran 1314 [27 June 1898].

69. See, for example, Harwood, *Technology's Dilemma*; and Forclaz, "Shaping the Future."

70. BOA, MF.İBT 211/34, grade chart for the 1907–1908 school year.

71. BOA, MF.MKT 677/57, Aleppo education director's deputy Mehmet to the Education Ministry, 14 Kanunuevvel 1318 [27 December 1902].

72. *Salname-yi Vilâyet-i Halep* (1900), 135; BOA, MF.MKT 694/33, Aleppo Education Director Celaluddin to the Education Ministry, 4 Kanunusani 1318 [17 January 1903].

73. *Salname-yi Vilâyet-i Halep* (1899–1903); BOA, MF.MKT 694/33, Aleppo Education Director Celaluddin to the Education Ministry, 4 Kanunusani 1318 [17 January 1903]. The telegram uses the term *neş'et* to refer to Ahmet Hamdi's graduation from the Salonica school. His proposed replacements, however, are always identified as "graduates" (*mezun*) of the Halkalı Ziraat Mektebi. Among the fourteen students sent abroad to study agriculture in the early 1890s is an Ahmet Hamdi Efendi, who graduated from the Dar al-Şafaqa and excelled in the knowledge of arithmetic and geometry (BOA, Y.A.HUS 244/46). It is unclear if this is the same person.

74. BOA, MF.MKT 694/33, see table from 11 Şubat 1318 [24 February 1903]. For the classes they were each assigned to teach, see *Salname-yi Vilâyet-i Halep* (1903), 140.

75. BOA, MF.MKT 681/39, Ahmet Hamdi Efendi to the governor of Aleppo, 24 Teşrinievvel 1318 [6 November 1902].

76. The governor and, initially, the administration of the preparatory schools suggested that, in light of Hamdi Efendi's good service, he should be allowed to teach with the appointed salary the courses for which he was qualified—the preparatory schools administration even requested that he be asked what courses he would be interested in and capable of teaching for the agricultural branch. BOA, MF.MKT 681/39, Aleppo governor to the Education Ministry, 28 Teşrinievvel 1318 [10 November 1902]; BOA, MF.MKT 681/39, note from the preparatory schools administration, 12 Kanunuevvel 1318 [25 December 1902]; BOA, MF.MKT 677/57, *idadi* schools office's response, dated 24 Kanunuevvel 1318 [6 January 1903], to a telegram sent by the Aleppo education director's deputy Mehmet to the Education Ministry, 14 Kanunuevvel 1318 [27 December 1902]. The main issue seems to have been the advanced lessons of the third year, which Hamdi Efendi was not considered qualified to teach by either the local education directorship or the preparatory schools administration (BOA, MF.MKT 677/57, Aleppo education director's deputy Mehmet to the Education Ministry, 14 Kanunuevvel 1318 [27 December 1902]). According to Mehmet, "Here there is no teacher from the masters of expert knowledge"; BOA, MF.MKT 683/3, note from preparatory schools' administration, 16 Kanunusani [29 January 1903]).

77. BOA, MF.MKT 683/3, note from preparatory schools' administration, 16 Kanunusani [29 January 1903]. Because Hamdi Efendi had started the program in the fall

of 1900, the 1902–1903 school year was the first time the third year would have been offered.

78. BOA, MF.MKT 721/17, Ahmet Hamdi Efendi to the Education Ministry, 28 Mart 1319 [10 April 1903]. Although Ahmet Hamdi studied at the Salonica agricultural school, his Ottoman grammar suggests that he was not a native Turkish speaker.

79. BOA, MF.MKT 721/17, Ahmet Hamdi Efendi to the Education Ministry, 28 Mart 1319 [10 April 1903]; BOA, MF.MKT 709.53, Ahmet Hamdi to the Aleppo Education Directorship, 13 Mart 1319 [26 March 1903]. On the distance of the school from the city center, see BOA, MF.MKT 694.33, Aleppo Education Director to the Education Ministry, 11 Şubat 1318 [24 February 1903].

80. BOA, MF.MKT 709/53, Ahmet Hamdi to the Aleppo Education Directorship, 13 Mart 1319 [26 March 1903]. Although his earlier petition indicated that he had not been invited to teach during the first two months of the 1902–1903 school year, this petition suggests that Hamdi Efendi was teaching again by the winter semester.

81. Hamdi Efendi had been promised a 200-gurush monthly salary (BOA, MF.MKT 721/17, Ahmet Hamdi Efendi to the Education Ministry, 28 Mart 1319 [10 April 1903]). The courses to be taught as part of the program were *mevalid-i selase* (which referred to minerals, strata of the earth, plants, and animals), agricultural operations, agricultural methods notebook, agricultural geography, practical agricultural geometry, application to agriculture of science and chemistry, science (*ʿilm*) of weather conditions, agricultural animals, agricultural plants, agricultural lessons, agricultural machines, industrial agriculture, science (*fenn*) of [illegible], and the knowledge (*ʿilm*) of abundance's application to agriculture (BOA, MF.MKT 683/3, see enclosed chart from the Education Ministry, n.d.). On the specifics of *mevalid-i selase*, see al-Barudi, *Mudhakkirat*, 44.

82. On the 1904 reforms, see Somel, *Modernization*, 178–79, 184–85; and *Salname-yi Vilâyet-i Halep* (1904), 144.

83. BOA, MF.MKT 694/33. Abdussettar's records specify that he was one-eyed. See copy of birth certificate copied on the same page as his diploma in the file.

84. With qualifications such as these, unlike Hamdi Efendi, Abdussettar Efendi and Nureddin Efendi made it clear that they would not work without pay. This stance prompted the Aleppo education director to assert, when it seemed likely that their salaries would be delayed for two months, that he would pay them out of necessity from the education fund (*maarif sandığı*) to ensure continuity in agricultural lessons. BOA, MF.MKT 692/13, Aleppo Education Director to the Education Ministry, 17 Şubat 1318 [2 March 1903]. Hamdi died soon after these events from cholera, but his children would petition to have his salary of 280 gurush/month transferred to them (BOA, MF.MKT 1002/43, Aleppo Education Director to the Ministry of Education, 28 Nisan 1323 [11 May 1907]). See also BOA, BEO 2774/208050, Financial Minister, 4 Şubat 1321 [17 February 1906]; BOA, BEO 2617/196237; and BOA, BEO 2766/207398.

85. El-Husrî, *Malumat-ı ziraiye*. Over the ensuing years, Satiʿ al-Husri would publish a number of other books on agriculture. See, for example, el-Husrî, *Mebadî-i Ulum-ı Tabiiyeden Hikmet ve Kimya*; and el-Husrî, *Mebadî-i Ulum-ı Tabiiyeden Tatbikat-ı Ziraiye*. For more on al-Husri's Ottoman background, see Cleveland, *Making of an Arab Nationalist*, 3–46.

86. BOA, MF.MKT 694/33.

87. BOA, MF.MKT 736/57, Aleppo Education Director to the Education Ministry, 30 Haziran 1319 [13 July 1903].

88. BOA, MF.MKT 810/43, Abdussettar to the Education Ministry, 12 Eylül 1320 [25 September 1904].

89. *Salname-yi Vilâyet-i Halep* (1905), 151.

90. BOA, BEO 553/41443, Governor of Syria to the Sublime Porte, 7 Kanunuevvel 1310 [19 December 1894]; BOA, BEO 553/41443, statement signed by thirteen members of the Council, 19 Kanunusani 1310 [31 January 1895].

91. BOA, MF.MKT 248/52, Syrian Education Minister to the Education Ministry, 4 Şubat 1310 [16 February 1895].

92. BOA, MF.MKT 248/52, Syrian Education Minister to the Education Ministry, 4 Şubat 1310 [16 February 1895]. Indeed, the Halkalı school did end up drawing its students from the *idadi* schools as well as the Bursa and Salonica practical agricultural schools, although students from the Bursa school had to pass an entrance exam, whereas those from the Salonica school did not (Quataert, "Ottoman Reform," 102).

93. BOA, MF.MKT 697/29, chart dated 15 Teşrinievvel 1318 [28 October 1902].

94. BOA, MF.MKT 697/29, chart dated 15 Teşrinievvel 1318 [28 October 1902]; and draft addressed to the Province of Syria Education Directorship, 24 Mayıs (?) 1319 [6 June (?) 1903]. A petition from Karak requested a graduate of the agricultural school to teach classes in that region as well, citing the tax revenues of Karak, Tafila, and Maᶜan to justify the added expense (BOA, DH.MKT 2310/84, draft addressed to the Education Ministry and the Forest, Minerals, and Agriculture Ministry, 25 Şevval 1317 [26 February 1900]).

95. BOA, MF.MKT 636/49, Syria Education Director to Ministry of Education, 7 Mayıs 1318 [20 May 1902]. On Maktab ᶜAnbar, see Rogan, "Political Significance"; and Deguilhem, "State Civil Education." Maktab ᶜAnbar has also been the subject of a number of memoirs. See, for example, Qasimi, *Maktab ʿAnbar.*

96. It is unclear whether this Melkon is the same as the Melkon who was the director of the Aleppo model field. BOA, MF.MKT 697/29, Syria Education Director to Education Ministry, 1 Teşrinievvel 1319 [14 October 1903]. Melkon was threatening to resign if he was not paid in full. BOA, MF.MKT 823/58, Syria Governor Nazim to the Education Ministry, 9 Eylül 1320 [22 September 1904].

97. BOA, MF.MKT 814/78, Syria Education Director to Ministry of Education, 24 Haziran 1320 [6 July 1904].

98. BOA, MF.MKT 636/49; the imperial order is dated 24 Temmuz 1320 [6 August 1904]. On Beirut, see BOA, MF.MKT 730/30, Beirut Education Minister to the Education Ministry, 11 Haziran 1319 [24 June 1903].

99. BOA, MF.MKT 636/49, telegraph draft from the Education Ministry to the Syria Education Directorship, 11 Eylül 1320 [24 September 1904].

100. Khoury, *Syria*, 274–75; Khoury, *Urban Notables*, 43. Duma is a major village in the Ghuta, the rich agricultural lands around Damascus.

101. Al-Barudi, *Mudhakkirat*, 7, 44.

102. Al-Barudi, *Mudhakkirat*, 175; Khoury, *Urban Notables*, 33–34.

103. Al-Barudi, *Mudhakkirat*, 176.

104. Al-Barudi, *Mudhakkirat*, 172.

105. Al-Barudi, *Mudhakkirat*, 172–73.

106. Al-Barudi, *Mudhakkirat*, 191.

107. Al-Barudi, *Mudhakkirat*, 192; al-Khatib, *Amir Mustafa al-Shihabi*, 11, 12; Faris, *Min Huwa*, 113. It is unclear whether al-Shihabi studied at the agricultural school in Chalon-sur-Saône, which al-Barudi discusses in his memoirs. Al-Shihabi's biographer indicates that after one year in Chalon-sur-Saône, he received a certificate of high-level primary studies from the school there (al-Khatib, *Amir Mustafa al-Shihabi*, 11). He had already studied in the French preparatory school in Istanbul for two years and at Maktab al-ʿAnbar for one (al-Khatib, *Amir Mustafa al-Shihabi*, 10–11).

108. Al-Barudi, *Mudhakkirat*, 193. Al-Barudi received word in Paris that his father was not going to send him "one gurush."

109. Médawar, *Syrie agricole*, 30–31; E. Saadé, *Agriculture*, 11.

110. E. Saadé, *Agriculture*, 11, 9.

111. Quataert, "Ottoman Reform," 72–75; Hanssen, "Malhamé-Malfamé."

112. BOA, I.OM 1326Z-1; Quataert, "Ottoman Reform," 98. By 1910, the Halkalı school was to become a university *(darülfünun)*.

113. BOA, BEO 2106/157904, draft prepared for the Forest, Mines, and Agriculture Ministry concerning the province of Syria, 12 Haziran 1319 [25 June 1903]; BOA, T.ZTI 3047/40, Forest, Mines and Agriculture Ministry to the Aleppo Model Field Director's representative, 2 May 1907; BOA, T.ZTI 3047/44, Forest, Mines and Agriculture Ministry to the Province of Syria's Agriculture Inspectorship, 2 May 1907.

114. BOA, DH.MKT 2721/3, Governor of Syria's office to the Interior Ministry, 16 Kanunuevvel 1324 [29 December 1908]. The unit referred to in the document is *atik dönüm*, which referred to an older *dönüm* measure.

115. BOA, DH.MKT 2721/3, Governor of Syria's office to the Interior Ministry, 16 Kanunuevvel 1324 [29 December 1908].

116. BOA, DH.MKT 1258/14, draft to the Forest, Mines, and Agriculture Ministry, 15/19 Mayıs 1324 [28 May 1908/1 June 1908] The Ghuta was its own subdistrict.

117. BOA, DH.MKT 1258/14, draft to the Forest, Mines, and Agriculture Ministry, 15/19 Mayıs 1324 [28 May 1908/1 June 1908].

118. BOA, ŞD 2243/12, Zor governor et al. to the Interior Ministry, 4 Şubat 1323 [17 February 1908].

119. BOA, ŞD 2243/12, Zor governor et al. to the Interior Ministry, 4 Şubat 1323 [17 February 1908].

120. BOA, DH.MKT 1241/82, copy of the Council of State's financial office's minutes, 19 Nisan 1324 [2 May 1908].

121. BOA, DH.İD 99/32, Forest, Mines, and Agriculture Ministry to the Interior Ministry, 18 Ağustos 1326 [31 August 1910].

122. BOA, ŞD 2307/7, Beirut general committee to the Interior Ministry, 9 Mart 1325 [22 March 1909]. The benefits included tax exemptions on crops and trees planted.

123. BOA, ŞD 2307/7, Forest, Mines, and Agriculture Minister to the Council of State, 22 Eylül 1325 [5 October 1909].

124. BOA, DH.MUİ 732/25, Governor of Beirut to the Interior Ministry, 10 Mart 1326 [23 March 1910].

125. BOA, DH.MUİ 732/25, Governor of Aleppo to the Interior Ministry, 9 Mart 1326 [22 March 1910].

126. BOA, DH.MUİ 732/25, Governor of Syria to the Interior Ministry, 4 Mart 1326 [17 March 1910].

127. "The Need of the Hawran for an Agricultural School," *Al-Ittihad al-Osmani*, 29 April 1913.

128. BOA, DH.MKT 2721/3, Governor of Syria's office to the Interior Ministry, 16 Kanunuevvel 1324 [29 December 1908]. The letter indicates that there was a petition to turn the old field into just a model nursery, although there had still been no answer regarding this request.

129. BOA, DH.MKT 2721/3, Governor of Syria's office to the Interior Ministry, 16 Kanunuevvel 1324 [29 December 1908].

130. BOA, DH.MKT 2721/3, Governor of Syria's office to the Interior Ministry, 16 Kanunuevvel 1324 [29 December 1908].

131. BOA, DH.MKT 2832/89, Forest, Mines, and Agriculture Minister to the Interior Ministry, 19 Mayıs 1325 [1 June 1909]. The minister also urged the establishment of chambers of agriculture.

132. The Selimiye agricultural school still exists in Selimiye today as a Faculty of Agriculture.

133. BOA, DH.İD 99/32, report from the agricultural inspector for Beirut, Syria, and Aleppo provinces, 26 Teşrinievvel 1326 [8 November 1910].

134. Lewis, *Nomads*, 60–61.

135. Lewis, "Malaria," 280, 278; Lewis, *Nomads*, 61–62.

136. Lewis, "Malaria," 284–85. Lewis traced the canals' construction back to the Roman and pre-Ottoman period, citing an inscription from as late as March 1496 on a mosque in Hama that indicates that a major *foqqara*, another term for *qanat* primarily used in North Africa, that brought water from Selimiye to Hama (the clear water of Selimiye was considered superior to the murkier waters of the ʿAsi River that runs through Hama) had a specially designated fund from which no money was allowed to be diverted (285). With the extension of the Ottoman Empire into the region in 1516, settlement tended to recede westward (285).

137. Lewis, *Nomads*, 62; Lewis, "Malaria," 286.

138. BOA, DH.MUİ 732/25, Governor of Syria to the Interior Ministry, 4 Mart 1326 [17 March 1910].

139. Kurd ʿAli, *Kitab Khitat al-Sham*, 4: 214.

140. BOA, DH.MUİ 732/25, Governor of Syria to the Interior Ministry, 4 Mart 1326 [17 March 1910].

141. BOA, DH. İD 99/32, report from the agricultural inspector for Beirut, Syria, and Aleppo provinces, 26 Teşrinievvel 1326 [8 November 1910]; BOA, BEO 3884/291293.

142. Douwes and Lewis, "Trials," 215, 228. The expansion of educational institutions into the Selimiye region had started several years earlier with a plan to build five elementary schools. The agricultural school would continue this process. (BOA, BEO 3352/251358, Governor of Syria to Interior Ministry, 26 Mayıs 1324 [8 June 1908]). This document does not trace the process but discusses the initial plan to establish the elementary schools. One interviewee speculated that at least 9,000 people had contributed to the sum (BOA, BEO 3884/291293, testimony of Ahmet bin Mahfuz al-Haj, n.d. [although given the dates of other papers in the file, this document is probably from the spring of 1911]), p. 4.

143. BOA, BEO 3884/291293, Interior Ministry Investigative Commission to Interior Ministry, 29 (?) Mart 1327 [11 (?) April 1911].

144. In the transcript interviews take place in both Arabic and Turkish with questions sometimes being asked in one language and answered in the other. See BOA, BEO 3884/291293.

145. BOA, BEO 3884/291293, testimony of Ahmet bin Mahfuz al-Haj, n.d., p. 5.

146. BOA, BEO 3884/291293, testimony of Muhammad bin Ali Zahra of the people of Selimiye and Muhammad bin Ahmet al-Hamvi of the people of Selimiye, n.d., pp. 1–3.

147. BOA, BEO 3884/291293, testimony of the headman of the eastern and northern neighborhoods, Hüseyin ʿAli Mahfuz, n.d., p. 9. The exact phrase he used was "the owners of property and lands and the owners of wealth" (*ashab al-amlak wa al-arazi wa ashab al-tharwa).*

148. BOA, BEO 3884/291293, testimony of the headman of the Qabile neighborhood, n.d., p. 11; and testimony of the headman of the western neighborhood, n.d., p. 12.

149. BOA, BEO 3884/291293, testimony of the headman of the western neighborhood, n.d., p. 12.

150. BOA, BEO 3884/291293, testimony of the headman of the eastern and northern neighborhoods, Hüseyin ʿAli Mahfuz, n.d., p. 9.

151. BOA, BEO 3884/291293, report of the province's civil inspector's assistant to the Interior Ministry, 13 Mart 1327 [26 March 1911].

152. BOA, BEO 3884/291293, list appended to the end of the inquiry, 27 Şubat 1326 [12 March 1911]. In addition to discontent over the confiscated funds, there also appears to have been concerns about how the land for the school would be set aside and divided. See BOA, BEO 3884/291293, report of the province's civil inspector's assistant to the Interior Ministry, 13 Mart 1327 [26 March 1911].

153. BOA, DH.ID 99/32, Governor of Syria to the Interior Ministry, 9 Kanunusani 1327 [22 January 1912].

154. *Osmanlı Ziraat ve Ticaret Gazetesi*, 1 Teşrinisani 1326 [14 November 1910], inside front cover; BOA, MF.MKT 694/33.

155. BOA, T.ZTİ 3056/62. Activities mentioned in the report included artificial and natural pastures, bird raising, animal breeding, natural versus artificial fertilizers, orchard planting, dairying, beekeeping, and silkworm raising.

156. BOA, T.ZTİ 3056/62, report signed by the agricultural school's director, Abdussettar, 23 Şubat 1327 [4 March 1912].

157. BOA, T.ZTİ 3056/62, report signed by the agricultural school's director, Abdussettar, 23 Şubat 1327 [4 March 1912].

158. BOA, T.ZTİ 3056/62, report signed by the agricultural school's director, Abdussettar, 23 Şubat 1327 [4 March 1912]; BOA, BEO 3884/291293, testimony of the headman of the eastern and northern neighborhoods, Hüseyin ʿAli Mahfuz, n.d., pp. 8–10.

159. BOA, T.ZTİ 3056/62, report signed by the agricultural school's director, Abdussettar, 23 Şubat 1327 [4 March 1912].

160. BOA, T.ZTİ 3056/62, report signed by the agricultural school's director, Abdussettar, 23 Şubat 1327 [4 March 1912].

161. See chapters 4 and 5 for more details.

162. "Şeyden Evvel Ziraat Lazımdır," *Ekinci* 1, no. 6 (20 Haziran 1329 [3 July 1913]): 41.

163. BOA, BEO 1167/87481, Council of State, 15 Haziran 1314 [27 June 1898]. See *Ticaret ve Ziraat Nezareti Mecmuası*; the seventeenth issue was published in April 1912 and publication would continue at least until June 1918. A fourth issue had been published in March 1911 under the title *Orman ve Maadin ve Ziraat ve Baytar Mecmuası*. Previous versions of this review had appeared earlier, such as the *Orman ve Maadin ve Ziraat Mecmuası*, which had been published at least since the 1880s. See chapter 3 for more details.

164. "Bir Mektub Münasibetiyle," *Ekinci* 1, no. 11 (26 Tesrinievvel 1329 [8 November 1913]): 87.

165. "Bir Mektub Münasibetiyle," *Ekinci* 1, no. 11 (26 Tesrinievvel 1329 [8 November 1913]): 87–88.

166. BOA, DH.İD 79/34, Society for National Defense to the Interior Ministry, 13 Temmuz 1329 [26 July 1913].

167. Louisides, "Commercial Letter," 228.

168. Louisides, "Commercial Letter," 228. Interestingly, according to Louisides' assessment, the Germans had the most favorable banking terms in the region as they "allow . . . six to nine months credits without charging any interests with the exception of a few lines." He also noted that no American banks were represented in the region and that the British had to change their methods to stay competitive (226).

169. Manachy, "Report from Aleppo," 292. It seems likely that this exhibition coincided with the governorship in Aleppo of Hüseyin Kâzım, a fervent advocate of scientific agriculture, as discussed earlier. Manachy urged American manufacturers to take greater interest in this market, suggesting that once another brand became popular with the local population, other companies would have more trouble getting theirs accepted. According to one estimate, as of 30 June 1911 Great Britain, Germany, and Belgium were the chief exporters of machinery to the Ottoman Empire with the United States providing $133,639 worth of trade, composed primary of "reapers, steam plows, and thrashing machines" ("Share of United States in the Machinery and Ironware Trade," *Levant Trade Review*, 2, no. 3 [December 1912]: 232). Although it is unclear what percentage of this pertains to machinery sold in the Levant, clearly some machines were in use in the region. Another page from the same issue contains a photo captioned "An American Threshing Machine at Work in Syria" (212).

170. *Al-Iqtisad*, issue 7, 193. Unfortunately only the first issue of those preserved still contains the date, 15 October 1910. Because the journal indicates that it was supposed to be published twice a month, issue 7 probably appeared sometime early in 1911. The journal contained a number of articles comparing agricultural developments in Europe and the United States with those in the Ottoman Empire. It also offered local farmers advice on the best way to pursue agricultural improvements in the Ottoman Empire in articles with such titles as "Agriculture, Agriculture—O Syrians—'Teach, for Teaching Benefits,'" 129; "The Agricultural Plan," 167; "The Future of Wheat," 175; and "How to Advance Syrian Agriculture: 'We Are in a Valley and Scientific Agriculture Is in a Valley,'" 289. This last phrase draws on common Arabic expression to express a vast difference between two opinions or ideas.

171. NARA, RG 84, Box 6, Aleppo Syria, General Correspondence 1914. On Fuad Mudarris Zade, see Watenpaugh, *Being Modern*, 103.

172. Strohmeier, "Abd al-Rahman Pasha al-Yusuf," 364.

173. This would seem to be in the same vicinity as the sultan's estates.

174. NARA, RG 84, Box 6, Aleppo Syria, General Correspondence 1914, Jackson to Youngblood and Shaw, 5 March 1914.

175. "Haleb Çiftlik Mektebinin İcraat ve Islahat-ı Ziraiyesi," *Ticaret ve Ziraat Nezareti Mecmuası*, 3, no. 19 (31 May 1328 [13 June 1912]): 439.

176. NARA, RG 84, Box 6, Aleppo Syria, General Correspondence 1914, Morse to Jackson, 12 January 1914; Shaw to Jackson, 31 January 1914; Widtsoe to Jackson, 11 February 1914; and Youngblood to Jackson, 26 January 1914.

177. NARA, RG 84, Box 6, Aleppo Syria, General Correspondence 1914, Shaw to Jackson, 31 January 1914; Widtsoe to Jackson, 11 February 1914; and Youngblood to Jackson, 26 January 1914.

178. NARA, RG 84, Box 6, Aleppo Syria, General Correspondence 1914, Jackson to Youngblood and Shaw, 5 March 1914. A *shumbul* is a measure of wheat equivalent to one camel load, that is, in Jackson's estimation about 220 pounds. This seems to refer to the small *shumbul*, estimated at 100–150 kilograms. The large *shumbul* was 200–260 kilograms. See Latron, *Vie rurale*, 10, 25.

179. Kurd ʿAli, *Kitab Khitat al-Sham*, 4: 216.

180. It is unclear how much the additional 4 *shumbuls* subtracted from the initial harvest would affect the amount remaining to apportion.

181. NARA, RG 84, Box 6, Aleppo Syria, General Correspondence 1914, Widtsoe to Jackson, 11 February 1914; and Youngblood to Jackson, 15 April 1914.

182. See translation of document in Strohmeier, "Abd al-Rahman Pasha al-Yusuf," 362–64. In the final months of the war, sometime before 10 September 1918, a German official sought to convince Abd al-Rahman to allow a German company and German farmers to help him pursue these plans that had been put on hold. The official was enthusiastic about the possibilities for massive investment in German machines and expertise as well as the influence Abd al-Rahman's use of them would exert and the example it would set for other large landowners in Syria (363, 264).

183. NARA, RG 84, Box 6, Aleppo Syria, General Correspondence 1914, Jackson to the Department of State, 9 April 1914.

184. NARA, RG 84, Box 6, Aleppo Syria, General Correspondence 1914, Walter A. Wood, Export Department, to Jackson, 25 February 1914.

185. Khuri, "Agriculture," 78. These figures for wheat are much higher than anything that would be achieved during the mandate up until 1933 and on the whole higher for barley as well within the same time period. The question of how "Syria" is defined in these statistics is unclear.

Chapter Three

1. As cited by al-Shihabi, "Aham Adwaʾna al-Iqtisadiya wa Talafiha" (November 1928): 7.

2. CA, Box 001, Ref SC/13, Correspondances Alep 1922, Depolla to Charles Corm, 9 August 1922. *Agriculteurs* is a difficult word to translate. Technically it means "farmer," particularly a farmer of means, but in the context of the mandate it often seems to be applied to large landowners with substantial investment in agricultural production.

3. Aleppo's governor, Kamil Pasha al-Qudsi, was 75 years old, from a major landowning family, and had directed Aleppo's "secret service" under Abdulhamid. Chosen by

French general Lamothe as governor for his acquiescence to French rule, al-Qudsi's high opinion of his own influence is ironic, because, apparently "in Aleppo . . . [it] was virtually nil" (Khoury, *Syria*, 99).

4. CA, Box 001, Ref SC/13, Correspondances Alep 1922, Depolla to Charles Corm, 9 August 1922.

5. CA, Box 001, Ref SC/13, Correspondances Alep 1922, Depolla to Charles Corm, 1 September 1922.

6. Worster, *Dust Bowl*, 89–90; Fitzgerald, *Every Farm a Factory*, 17–18, 100.

7. Worster, *Dust Bowl*, 90.

8. Worster, *Dust Bowl*.

9. The challenges that limited tractor use in the eastern Mediterranean were not exclusive to that region. In France, Switzerland, and elsewhere, tractors remained a hard sell for a variety of reasons, including the prevalence of small scattered plots, the expense of and debt incurred in buying one, the difficulties in repairing them, and their lack of adaptability compared with draft animals or human labor. See Fitzgerald, *Every Farm a Factory*, 93–103; Bivar, *Organic Resistance*, 25, 38; Auderset and Moser, "Mechanisation"; and Herment, "Tractorisation."

10. CA, Box 001, Ref SC/13, Correspondances Alep 1922, Depolla to Charles Corm, 14 July 1922.

11. See, for example, al-Shihabi, *Ziraʿa*, 127–32.

12. Here I draw on the work of Harvey, *Spaces of Global Capitalism*; and Lefebvre, *Production of Space*.

13. Khoury, "Syrian Independence Movement"; Khoury, *Syria*, 50–52.

14. On improved extraction, see Özbek, "Tax Farming," 225.

15. See Barakat, "Underwriting"; and Derri, "Bonds of Obligation."

16. Özbek, "Tax Farming," 227.

17. For the Ottoman laws with commentary, see Karakoç, *Tahşiyeli Kavanin*, vol. 1. For the French translation, see *Code Foncier Ottoman*, 7–26, 38–41.

18. See chapter 2.

19. This list does not include those teaching agriculture in the local schools, a position for which certified training was also desirable, as discussed in chapter 2.

20. BOA, T.ZTİ 3056/48, chart signed and dated 1 Kanunusani 1327 [14 January 1912] by Agop Oscan. The chart suggests that the total number of employees should have been eighteen—a post listed as depot employee was left blank. The chart also notes that there were plans to establish a dairy school but that this had not yet been achieved.

21. BOA, T.ZTİ 3056/48, chart signed and dated 1 Kanunusani 1327 [14 January 1912] by Agop Oscan. The eighth civil servant had graduated from the Aleppo *idadi* school.

22. BOA, T.ZTİ 3056/48, chart signed and dated 1 Kanunusani 1327 [14 January 1912] by Agop Oscan.

23. BOA, T.ZTİ 3056/48, chart signed and dated 1 Kanunusani 1327 [14 January 1912] by Agop Oscan; BOA, T.ZTİ 3056/24, table from 1326 [1910/1911]. Emin Zihni Efendi was in the position for only about a year, from 16 August 1326 [29 August 1910] to September 1911. See CADN, Syrie-Liban/1, 2173, "État de Service," 6 January 1928.

24. BOA, T.ZTİ 3056/48, chart signed and dated 1 Kanunusani 1327 [14 January 1912] by Agop Oscan. One notable exception is the employee Mardirus Efendi, who was identified

as holding the field's "farmer chieftainship" and came from Sivas. He was possibly the same Mardirus who worked in the field in the 1890s as a guard. See BOA, ŞD 2232/6. How he moved from one position to the other is unclear.

25. BOA, T.ZTİ 3056/60, Emin Zihni Efendi to the Forest, Mines, and Agriculture Ministry, 23 Nisan 1327 [6 May 1911], and the accompanying chart. Looking toward future projects, Emin Zihni Efendi noted that the climate was well suited to orange growing but that better water resources were needed for production to expand beyond Antakya, İskenderun, and parts of Aleppo.

26. BOA, T.ZTİ 3056/48, chart signed and dated 1 Kanunusani 1327 [14 January 1912] by Agop Oscan; CADN, Syrie-Liban/1, 2173, "État de Service," 6 January 1928.

27. Even this degree of dispersal around the eastern Mediterranean was not enough for some agriculture enthusiasts. See Dolbee and Hazkani, "Impossible Is not Ottoman," 252.

28. BOA, T.ZTİ 3057/52. The unsold implements amounted to 9,786 gurush 10 para.

29. BOA, T.ZTİ 3057/52. One Deering Ideal reaper sold for 9,786.10 gurush, five Izmir plows for 114 gurush, four Eckert plows (*saban*) made for light soils for 99.30 gurush, and four Rud. Sack plows (*pulluk*) for 230.35 gurush. The Alfa Viola cream separators each sold for 712.20 gurush. The Deering reaper was the only award-winning reaper at the Chicago Exhibition in 1893 (*Deering Harvesters*, 16). The Izmir plow is likely a plow that had been produced since at least the early twentieth century and had won a medal in 1904 at an exposition in Athens (Quataert, "Ottoman Reform," 160).

30. BOA, T.ZTİ 3057/52, chart signed by Agop, 29 Haziran 1330 [12 July 1914]. In 1329 [1913/1914] funds were sent to the central administration in May, August, September, and January. The highest sales occurred in May, June, August, December, and February, which seems to roughly correspond to some of the busiest times in the annual agricultural calendar, although because the chart does not indicate what implements were sold when, it is not possible to trace a direct correlation. The high amounts sold in June and August could also reflect the use of income from the harvest to purchase new equipment. See BOA, T.ZTİ 3057/52, chart signed by Agop, the depot director, and the agriculture clerk, 29 Haziran 1330 [12 July 1914]).

31. BOA, T.ZTİ 3057/52, exports and imports chart signed by Agop, the depot director, and the agriculture clerk, 29 Haziran 1330 [12 July 1914].

32. BOA, T.ZTİ 3057/52, charts for Damascus depot dated 1326, 1327, 1328, and 1329; BOA, T.ZTİ 3057/59, chart for Damascus depot indicating numbers of implements present at beginning of 1330; BOA, T.ZTİ 3057/52, chart for 1329 signed by Theologos, 18 Haziran 1330 [1 July 1914]; BOA, T.ZTİ 3057/52, chart for 1325 signed by Theologos, 18 Haziran 1330 [1 July 1914]. The Beirut depot increased its imports from 33,460 francs worth in 1909/1910 [1325] to 11,065 gurush and 53,908 francs in 1913/1914 [1329]. The machines imported in francs and those imported in gurush represent two different groups of implements. Most of the instruments imported for ʿAkka, Nablus, Haifa, and Beirut were denominated in francs, whereas those destined for Trablus and Latakia were primarily denominated in gurush. The bulk of the imports through Beirut were destined for Nablus and ʿAkka, but machinery had also been ordered for Tripoli, Latakia, Haifa, the *sancak* of Beirut, and Beirut itself.

33. BOA, T.ZTİ 3057/52, chart of "Agricultural tools and implements that arrived in 1327 to the Hawran agricultural implement depot" and chart of "Agricultural implements that arrived in 1328 to the Hawran depot," 20 Nisan 1330 [3 May 1914].

34. BOA, T.ZTİ 3057/52, chart of "Agricultural tools and implements that arrived in 1327 to the Hawran agricultural implement depot" and chart of "Agricultural implements that arrived in 1328 to the Hawran depot," 20 Nisan 1330 [3 May 1914].

35. "Implement Exhibits at the Columbian Exposition," *Farm Implement News*, 14, no. 18 (4 May 1893): 22.

36. Cuinet, *Syrie*, 340.

37. See, for example, Syracuse Chilled Plow Company, *Catalogue of Farm Implements*, 33, 39; and Ardrey, "Plow," n.p. The process was invented and patented in the United States and involved a slower cooling process for the interior, which strengthened the metal.

38. BOA, T.ZTİ 3057/52, chart of "Agricultural tools and implements that arrived in 1329 to the Hawran agricultural implement depot," 20 Nisan 1330 [3 May 1914]. The Izmir plows were still slightly more expensive than the Syracuse plows, which were priced at 70.24 gurush (no. 0) and 99.74 gurush (no. 00) each in 1328 [1912/1913].

39. BOA, T.ZTİ 3057/52, Homs chart for 1329; BOA, T.ZTİ 3057/60, Homs chart for 1330.

40. BOA, T.ZTİ 3057/57, Aleppo agriculture director Agop to the Commerce and Agricultural Ministry, 10 Haziran 1330 [23 June 1914]; and copy of Aleppo Province Agricultural Directorship's 8 Temmuz 1330 addendum, 13 Temmuz 1330 [26 July 1914].

41. BOA, T.ZTİ 3057/57, Aleppo agriculture director Agop to the Commerce and Agricultural Ministry, 10 Haziran 1330 [23 June 1914]. For an example of an insurance contract, see BOA, T.ZTİ 3057/44.

42. For example, the province of Beirut had a "useful plant" budget of 7,000 gurush for the year 1327. See "Beyrut Vilayetin Ahval-i Umumiye-i Ziraiyesi," *Ticaret ve Ziraat Nezareti Mecmuası* 3, no. 19 (13 June 1912): 408. See also "Haleb Çiftlik Mektebinin İcraat ve Islahat-ı Ziraiyesi," *Ticaret ve Ziraat Nezareti Mecmuası* 3, no. 19 (13 June 1912); "Suriye Vilayetinde Tecarib Ziraiye," *Ticaret ve Ziraat Nezareti Mecmuası* 3, no. 21 (13 August 1912); and "Haleb Ziraat Mektebinde Tecarib Ziraiye," *Ticaret ve Ziraat Nezareti Mecmuası* 4, nos. 29–30 (13 September 1913).

43. "Haleb Çiftlik Mektebinin," 431–32.

44. "Suriye Vilayetinde Tecarib Ziraiye," 752–56.

45. "Haleb Çiftlik Mektebinin," 429.

46. "Suriye Vilayetinde Tecarib Ziraiye," 753.

47. "Suriye Vilayetinde Tecarib Ziraiye," 754–55.

48. "Haleb Çiftlik Mektebinin"; "Suriye Vilayetinde Tecarib Ziraiye." On the differences between local (*yerli*) cotton varieties and American or Egyptian cotton, see Gratien, *Unsettled Plain*, 104–5.

49. Toprak, *Türkiye'de "Milli İktisat"*; Hanioğlu, *Brief History*, 188–92; Ahmad, "Agrarian Policies." On previous attempts by the Ottomans to increase custom dues and the ensuing vociferous objections by the "capitulatory powers," see Thobie, *Intérêts*, 503–5.

50. Pitts, "Fallow Fields; Williams, "Economy"; Schilcher, "Famine of 1915–1918"; *Al-ʿAsima*, 15 April 1920; Çiçek, *War and State Formation*, 232–57.

51. *Al-ʿAsima*, 15 April 1920.

52. BOA, DH.UMVM 132/35, Governor Hulusi to the Interior Ministry, 27 Mayıs 1331 [9 June 1915].

53. BOA, DH.UMVM 137/22, Agriculture director of the province of Syria, "Report on the Province of Syria's Agricultural Affairs Concerning the 1331 Annual Budget," 22 Kanunuevvel 1332 [4 January 1917].

54. BOA, DH.UMVM 137/22, "Report on the Province of Syria's Agricultural Affairs"; BOA, DH.UMVM 147.80, Agriculture director of the province of Syria, "Report on the Operations of the Agricultural Budget for the Year 1332," 8 Nisan 1333 [8 April 1917].

55. BOA, DH.UMVM 137/22, Commerce and Agriculture Minister Mustafa to the Interior Ministry, 12 Şubat 1332 [25 February 1917]; BOA, DH.UMVM 145.41, Interior Ministry draft to the Grand Vizier, 16 Kanunusani 1332 [29 January 1917].

56. BOA, DH.UMVM 147/80, "Report on the Operations," 8 Nisan 1333 [8 April 1917]; BOA, DH.UMVM 147.103, Finance director in the name of the Syrian governor to the Interior Ministry, 9 Nisan 1333 [9 April 1917]; BOA, DH.UMVM 147.103, draft to the Commerce and Agriculture Ministry, 5 Mayıs 1332 [18 May 1916].

57. BOA, DH.UMVM 147/80, "Report on the Operations," 8 Nisan 1333 [8 April 1917], and chart "Damascus model field 331–332 agricultural year crop table," 8 Nisan 1333 [8 April 1917].

58. BOA, DH.İ.UM 11–5.9/26, Zor mutasarrıf to the Interior Ministry, 29 Kanunusani 1334 [29 January 1918], and chart of land to be taken by eminent domain, 27 Haziran 1333 [27 June 1917].

59. BOA, DH.İ.UM 11–5.9/26, Zor mutasarrıf to Interior Ministry, 29 Kanunusani 1334 [29 January 1918]. It is not clear whether Zor was subject to the same extent of famine deprivation that affected areas farther west.

60. This presents a stark contrast to the United States, where the war fueled capital investment in agriculture, which in turn encouraged purchases of new machinery. See Worster, *Dust Bowl*, 89–97.

61. Kâzım, "Suriye Ziraatına," 63.

62. BOA, DH.ŞFR 597/49, Abdülhalık to the Interior Ministry, 4 Teşrinievvel 1334 [4 October 1918].

63. Himadeh, "Monetary and Banking System," 313. Because the Lausanne Treaty did not require repayment of these amounts, the portion of the banks' business that derived from deposit transactions was adversely affected. However, Himadeh notes that the banks inherited the assets, but not the liabilities, of the Ottoman Agricultural Bank, suggesting that some assets must have been left behind (313).

64. Schilcher, " Famine of 1915–1918," 250, 254.

65. Khoury, *Syria*, 37. For a detailed account of this government's political activities, see Thompson, *How the West Stole Democracy*.

66. Y. Hakim, *Suriya wa al-ʿAhd al-Faysali*, 144, 159; Faris, *Min Huwa*, 125–26. See also Y. Hakim, *Suriya wa al-Intidab al-Faransi*; Y. Hakim, *Bayrut*; and Y. Hakim, *Suriya wa al-ʿAhd al-ʿUthmani*.

67. Y. Hakim, *Suriya wa al-ʿAhd al-Faysali*, 145. Hakim notes that al-Shihabi's appointment was part of the ministry's "great fortune."

68. *Al-ʿAsima*, 19 June 1919; Qasimiya, *Hukuma al-ʿArabiya*, 224.

69. *Al-ʿAsima*, 19 June 1919. These "detailed maps" would seem to be a form of cadastral survey.

70. *Al-ʿAsima*, 24 April 1919.

71. *Al-ʿAsima*, 17 June 1920.

72. Qasimiya, *Hukuma al-ʿArabiya*, 226–27; CADN, Syrie-Liban/1, Cabinet Politique 2371, M. M. Florimond to the High Commissioner, 19 October 1920.

73. *Al-ʿAsima*, 10 March 1919.

74. Al-Shihabi, *Ziraʿa*, 11; Achard, "Notes," 103–4. The school appears to have been located in the environs of Hawsh Balas. Achard's article refers to it being in "Blass."

75. Al-Shihabi, *Ziraʿa*, 11; *al-ʿAsima*, 18 September 1919.

76. *Al-ʿAsima*, 17 April 1919.

77. *Al-ʿAsima*, 24 April 1919.

78. *Al-ʿAsima*, 2 June 1919.

79. *Al-ʿAsima*, 18 September 1919.

80. *Al-ʿAsima*, 6 October 1919.

81. *Al-ʿAsima*, 27 June 1919.

82. For these members, see "Çiftçiler Derneği Aza-i Asliyesinden," *Çiftçiler Derneği Mecmuası*, 14 Teşrinisani 1334 [25 November 1918].

83. Ferid, "Ateşli Pulluklar," 433–34. Ferid published his article in the May 1919 issue of the *Çiftçiler Derneği Mecmuası* [*Farmers Association Journal*], noting the lack of access to knowledge about new agricultural developments in England, France, and the United States for four years since the outbreak of war. He aimed to help make up for this lack of information by sharing his tractor competition experience (433).

84. Ferid, "Ateşli Pulluklar," 435.

85. MAE, Syrie-Liban 75, Secretary of the delegation of the Hedaz [*sic*] to the Minister [of Agriculture], 25 March 1920. When the minister of agriculture requested the opinion of the minister of foreign affairs on the matter, he was informed that he should not respond because the delegation should have addressed their request to the minister of foreign affairs. See MAE, Syrie-Liban 75, Minister of Agriculture to the Minister of Foreign Affairs, 1 April 1920; and draft about "Exposition de Damas," 9 April 1920.

86. Al-Shihabi, *Ziraʿa*, 2.

87. Al-Shihabi, *Ziraʿa*, 11.

88. Al-Shihabi, *Ziraʿa*. For soil types and regional divisions, see al-Shihabi, *Ziraʿa*, 42–76.

89. See Gelvin, *Divided Loyalties*, 151–60. Gelvin discusses how this representation grew in popularity over the course of the Faysali period.

90. Al-Shihabi, *Ziraʿa*, 41. Al-Shihabi noted that such a division had not been attempted elsewhere, at least as far as he was aware. His book served as the reference for Muhammad Kurd ʿAli's better-known work *Khitat al-Sham*, in which Kurd ʿAli used al-Shihabi's accounts of the region's divisions and flora almost verbatim in his description. See Kurd ʿAli, *Kitab Khitat al-Sham*, 4: 156–57.

91. Al-Shihabi, *Ziraʿa*, 42–43.

92. Al-Shihabi, *Ziraʿa*, 43.

93. Al-Shihabi, *Ziraʿa*, 44.

94. Al-Shihabi, *Ziraʿa*, 44, 45.

95. Al-Shihabi, *Zira*ʿ*a*, 45.

96. Al-Shihabi, *Zira*ʿ*a*, 47; Cuinet, *Syria*, 345–47. See the introduction to this book for more details.

97. Al-Shihabi, *Zira*ʿ*a*, 47–48.

98. Al-Shihabi, *Zira*ʿ*a*, 47.

99. Al-Shihabi, *Zira*ʿ*a*, 48.

100. Al-Shihabi, *Zira*ʿ*a*, 49. Al-Shihabi does not address how one would know in advance which years would have adequate rain.

101. Al-Shihabi, *Zira*ʿ*a*, 41–49.

102. C. Hakim, *Origins*, 219–21, 239–44; quote from 244.

103. A. Naccache, "Notre avenir économique," 7, 8; Kaufman, *Reviving Phoenicia*, 89. This was not always Corm's position. In fact, up until at least the spring of 1919, Corm was also advocating for a united independent Syria, though from a perspective that insisted on "disregarding all consideration of ritual or religion" (Kaufman, *Reviving Phoenicia*, 88–89). The change in his position to calling for an independent Lebanon seems to have followed that of the Administrative Council. Hakim suggests that this shift was a response to fears that Faysal would reach an agreement with French officials to establish a Greater Syria that would not allow for an autonomous Lebanon (C. Hakim, *Origins*, 243).

104. The contributors discussed here would go on to become the chief engineer of the Lebanese government and its first director of public works (Albert Naccache), the inspector of finances and inspector general of services fonciers (Amin Mouchahwar), the general prosecutor (Paul Noujaim), and the director of agriculture (Assad Younes). See Kaufman, *Reviving Phoenicia*, 46, 90; P. Naccache, *Autre Liban*, 11; "Cedars in Lebanon," *The Forest Worker* (November 1925): 27; Mouchawar, *Notice*; and Haut-Commissariat, *Syrie et le Liban en 1921*, 232–33. Corm would become the region's Ford dealer (Kaufman, *Reviving Phoenicia*, 96). During the war, both Naccache and Noujaim contributed to the volume compiled by the Ottoman governor of Beirut, Ismail Hakkı Bey, about Mount Lebanon. See Haqqi Bey, *Lubnan*.

105. A. Naccache, "Notre avenir économique," 2–10; Noujaim, "Question du Liban."

106. A. Naccache, "Notre avenir économique," 3–4. For the context in which this arrangement arose, see Makdisi, *Culture of Sectarianism*.

107. A. Naccache, "Notre avenir économique," 4; Younes, "Agriculture au Liban," 259.

108. A. Naccache, "Notre avenir économique," 2. Naccache insisted that "natural" Lebanon's geographic integrity was evident based on the nature of the slopes of Mount Lebanon and the Anti-Lebanon Mountains. The two ranges had once been one, he claimed, but the tallest peaks had collapsed, forming the Biqaʿ Valley. Thus Lebanon's natural boundaries included the Biqaʿ Valley (A. Naccache, "Notre avenir économique," 3).

109. A. Naccache, "Notre avenir économique," 4.

110. See Cuinet, *Syrie*.

111. Noujaim, "Question du Liban," 77–81; A. Naccache, "Notre avenir économique," 5. Despite the fact that adding these territories would ensure greater parity between Christian and non-Christian populations in the envisioned Greater Lebanon, proponents of Greater Lebanon reassured their audience that Christians would still be a majority. The imperative for agricultural self-sufficiency, including the natural resources to support it, took precedence. See A. Naccache, "Notre avenir économique," 5 and tables on 8–10. According to his calculations, the population of "administrative Lebanon" in

1913 was 79% Christian and 21% non-Christian. In 1919, "natural Lebanon" encompassed 54.2% Christians and 45.8% non-Christians.

112. Younes, "Agriculture au Liban," 261–64; Mouchahwar, "Nos ressources," 25. Interestingly, Mouchahwar addresses the question of agricultural development in "Syria" but appears to take as his frame of reference only those areas that would come under French mandate rule, in contrast to al-Shihabi, who included the areas that would come under British mandate as well.

113. C. Hakim, *Origins*, 253–54, 260.

114. Froidevaux, "L'indépendance du Grand-Liban," 300.

115. Khoury, *Syria*, 57.

116. Noujaim, "Question du Liban," 79; A. Naccache, "Notre avenir économique," 5.

117. Ironically, although *La Revue Phénicienne*'s contributors were largely successful in achieving their vision of natural Lebanon, this did not in fact make them self-sufficient in grain. In fact, in the aftermath of independence one of the most acrimonious issues between Lebanon and Syria would be Lebanon's reliance on Syria for grain supplies and Syria's political use of this reliance, charging what the Lebanese decried as exorbitant prices (Chaitani, *Post-Colonial Syria and Lebanon*, 88–89).

118. See Chevallier, "Lyon et la Syrie en 1919"; Khoury, *Syria*, 38; and Jackson, "What Is Syria Worth?"

119. Thobie, *Intérêts*; MAE, Syrie-Liban 62, "La Syrie," 24 January 1919, p. 201; Roederer and Roederer, *Syrie*, 53–54; Khoury, *Syria*, 31. On the political role and strategies of the Colonial Party before the war, see Andrew and Kanya-Forstner, "French Colonial Party."

120. Roederer and Roederer, *Syrie*, 56. French officials were annoyed when the Ottoman government chose a German company to build the trans-Anatolia railroad that would eventually reach Baghdad (Shorrock, *French Imperialism*, 140). But it was not just foreign concerns that they felt threatened their interests. When the Ottoman government decided to build the Hijaz railway, a section of which from Damascus to Deraʿa (in the Hawran) would compete with the French line from Damascus to Muzerib (also in the Hawran), they demanded compensation and, after "acrimonious" negotiations, managed to extract a concession to extend the Damascus-Hama line as far as Aleppo as well as compensation for any losses to the competing line (Shorrock, *French Imperialism*, 147–48).

121. MAE, Syrie-Liban 62, "La Syrie," 24 January 1919, pp. 206–7. By way of the ports of Beirut in 1913 and Alexandretta in 1912, exports to France totaled 16,405,383 francs versus imports that totaled only 6,623,705 francs. The United Kingdom was the chief source of the region's imports at 40,031,403 francs. Austria-Hungary was next with 7,483,732 francs. In contrast to France's balance of trade with the region, these countries' balance of trade was decidedly in their favor, with only 833,344 francs and 400,871 francs in exports from the region to the United Kingdom and Austria-Hungary, respectively. Exports to France included silk cocoons, cotton, cereals, leather, legumes, eggs, licorice, olive oil, and dried fruits. Imports from it included silks, cochineal, lead, tin, steel, jewelry, clothes, pharmaceutical products, glass, lingerie, preserves, cement, alcohol, sugar, and soap.

122. MAE, Syrie-Liban 62, "La Syrie," 24 January 1919, pp. 217–18.

123. Jackson, "What Is Syria Worth?"

124. CCM, MQ.5.4/35, Baron d'Anthouard to President of the CCM, 6 May 1915.

125. CCM, MQ.5.4/35, "Note sur la Syrie," 11 May 1915.

126. CCM, MQ.5.4/35, "Note sur la Syrie," 11 May 1915.

127. CCM, MQ.5.4/35, "Lettre à Monsieur le Ministre des Affaires Étrangères sur la Question de la Syrie suive d'une note sur la valeur économique de ce pays," 1915.

128. CCM, MQ.5.4/35, "Lettre," 7; emphasis in original.

129. CCM, MQ.5.4/35, "Lettre," 13–24 (quotes from pp. 13 and 24); emphasis in original. The pamphlet contrasted this French administration with the "disorder," "ignorance," and "embezzlement of the Turks" (24).

130. CCM, MQ.5.4/35, "Lettre," 24.

131. See, for example, CCM, MQ.5.4/35, President of the CCM to Baron d'Authouard, 27 July 1915; President of the CCM to Director of the Société Lyonnaise Sericicole and Soie d'Extrême-Orient, 27 July 1915; President of the CCM to the President of the Lyon Chamber of Commerce, 27 July 1915; and President of the CCM to Émile Senart, President of the Comité de l'Asie Française, 28 July 1915.

132. CCM, MQ.5.4/35, President of Paris Chamber of Commerce to President of Marseille Chamber of Commerce, 18 March 1916.

133. For additional efforts in this vein, see Jackson, "What Is Syria Worth?" 91–92.

134. Roederer and Roederer, *Syrie*, xix.

135. Thobie, *Intérêts*, 473, 513; Roederer and Roederer, *Syrie*, xxv. The Society of Economic Initiative in Syria was formed in Paris in 1910 (Thobie, *Intérêts*, 512). Paul Roederer and H. Terrail, the Lyonnais silk merchant, also sat together on the Council of the Bank of Lebanon, which was formed in Paris in December 1913 (Thobie, *Intérêts*, 473). Paul was killed in May 1915 (Roederer and Roederer, *Syrie*, xxvi).

136. Roederer and Roederer, *Syrie*, 121.

137. Roederer and Roederer, *Syrie*, 116, 98–99, 123.

138. Roederer and Roederer, *Syrie*, 99.

139. Roederer and Roederer, *Syrie*, 90.

140. Roederer and Roederer, *Syrie*, 91. It was an ironic conclusion, given the financial travails of the mandate years and frequent complaints about bloated budgets.

141. Roederer and Roederer, *Syrie*, 132.

142. Roederer and Roederer, *Syrie*, xix. The sentiment is most explicitly addressed in the book's preface by M. Pierre-Alype, the man to whom, under the mandate, the high commissioner, Jouvenel, would give the task of imposing direct rule over the Syrian state during the Great Revolt of 1925–1927, which precipitated the crushing of the revolt with major military force (Khoury, *Syria*, 189–90).

143. CCM, MQ.5.4/35, booklets pertaining to Congrès Français de la Syrie (3, 4, and 5 January 1919).

144. Huvelin, *Que vaut la Syrie*, 6; H. F., "Mission Française en Syrie," 311. For an in-depth analysis of the conference and the resulting mission's overall aims and analytical framework based on a wartime-derived emphasis on economic development and the ideologies of Lyonnaise and Marseillaise interests in the region that predated the war, see Jackson, "What Is Syria Worth?"

145. See also Khoury, *Syria*, 51.

146. CADN, Syrie-Liban/3, Direction du Personnel 5, "Achard, Edouard," Dossier Individuel. Although technically the Institut national agronomique was conceived of as

l'école normale supérieure d'agriculture—that is, the highest institution for agricultural education in France—its graduates, known as *ingénieurs agronomes*, lost out on a bid to have their degrees recognized as superior to that of the graduates of the national agricultural schools (Grignon, Montpellier, and Rennes), known as *ingénieurs agricoles*, in a government decree issued in August 1918 (Trocmé, "Titre d'ingénieur agricole," 370). For more on the distinctions between these schools, see also Charmasson et al., *Enseignement agricole*, 74).

147. CADN, Syrie-Liban/3, Direction du Personnel 5, "Achard, Edouard," Dossier Individuel.

148. Huvelin, *Que vaut la Syrie*, 6; Roche and Vernus, *Dictionnaire biographique*, 366; "Paul Évariste Parmentier," *Racines Comtoises: Patrimoine et photographies de Franche-Comté*, http://www.racinescomtoises.net/index?/category/5640-paul_evariste_parmentier_1860_1941.

149. H. F., "Mission Française en Syrie," 309–10.

150. H. F., "Mission Française en Syrie," 310. On the French presence in Cilicia, see Gratien, *Unsettled Plain*, 165–75.

151. See Khoury, *Syria*, 31, 34, 38, 51.

152. Khoury, *Syria*, 39. De Caix would hold this position until 1924.

153. H. F., "Mission Française en Syrie," 311.

154. MAE, Syrie-Liban 60, "Valeur Économique de la Syrie," Note de M. Berthelot, 5 June 1920. See also "La Syrie au Sénat et la discussion des douzièmes provisoires," *L'Asie Française* 21, no. 188 (January 1921): 30.

155. CADN, Syrie-Liban/3, Direction du Personnel 5, "Achard, Edouard"; MAE, Syrie-Liban 60, "Valeur Agricole de la Partie Septentrionale de la Syrie," note from Achard, 17 April 1920, p. 13. It is not clear what map Achard is referring to exactly, but it seems to be something officials were using in Paris to get a sense of the areas under cultivation in the region. This area would seem to reference, at least in part, cultivation on farms that had been part of the sultan's estates and had become state lands held by the treasury after the 1908 revolution (al-Shihabi, "Aham Adwaʾna al-Iqtisadiya wa Talafiha 2" (December 1928): 30; Lewis, *Nomads*, 54).

156. See Lewis, *Nomads*, 41–57. Various British and German travelers to the region made frequent observations to this effect in the late nineteenth and early twentieth centuries (55–56).

157. MAE, Syrie-Liban 60, "Valeur Agricole de la Partie Septentrionale de la Syrie," note from Achard, 17 April 1920, pp. 13, 14.

158. Khoury, *Syria*, 39; MAE, Syrie-Liban 60, "Valeur économique de la Syrie," Note de M. Berthelot, 5 June 1920.

159. MAE, Syrie-Liban 60, "Valeur Économique de la Syrie," Note de M. Berthelot, 5 June 1920. France's eventual withdrawal from Cilicia, which they estimated contained 300,000 hectares suitable for cotton cultivation, would be a major blow to these ambitions.

160. MAE, Syrie-Liban 60, "Valeur Économique de la Syrie," Note de M. Berthelot, 5 June 1920.

161. "Les affaires d'Orient à la Chambre des députés," *L'Asie Française* 20, no. 181 (April 1920): 122.

162. "Covenant of the League of Nations," 28 July 1919, https://avalon.law.yale.edu/20th_century/leagcov.asp.

163. See "La discussion du budget des Affaires étrangères et les affaires du Levant à la Chambre des députés," *L'Asie Française* 20, no. 184 (July-August 1920): 257–59, 268. As of 4 April 1922, however, mandate authorities would find their credits for Syria gradually reduced (Khoury, *Syria*, 47).

164. Gelvin, *Divided Loyalties*, 3–4; Khoury, *Syria*, 99–110; Watenpaugh, *Being Modern*, 174–82.

165. See, for example, "La Syrie au Sénat et la discussion des douzièmes provisoires," *L'Asie Française* 21, no. 188 (January 1921): 31; "Le Sénat et les questions du Levant," *L'Asie Française* 21, no. 192 (May 1921): 195; and "Les crédits de l'armée du Levant à la Chambre des Députés," *L'Asie Française* 22, no. 204 (July-August 1922): 313.

166. "Bérard, Victor," https://www.senat.fr/senateur-3eme-republique/berard_victor0445r3.html.

167. "Les affaires du Levant au Sénat," *L'Asie Française* 20, no. 184 (July-August 1920): 274. Bérard cites the mission's report as it appeared in *La Géographie* 33, no. 5 (May 1920): 424–27. A more extended version was later included in *L'Asie Française* (H. F., "Mission Française en Syrie").

168. "La discussion du budget," 260.

169. "Exposé verbal du général Gouraud," *L'Asie Française* 21, no. 188 (January 1921): 11. The territorial expanse referred to is that of Lebanon and the region controlled by Faysal, including Damascus, Homs, and Aleppo (11).

170. Huvelin, *Que vaut la Syrie*, 10.

171. Huvelin, *Que vaut la Syrie*, 11.

172. Gouraud even wrote to the president of the CCM to thank him for writing to the minister of commerce and industry in support of his request for additional funds at a crucial moment, noting that "it is particularly agreeable to me to feel on this occasion how our common action can be fertile" (CCM, MQ.5.4/35, Gouraud to President of CCM, 4 January 1922). See CCM, MQ.5.4/35, Gouraud to President of the CCM, 18 December 1921; President of CCM to Minister of Commerce and Industry, 27 December 1921; and Gouraud to President of CCM, 4 January 1922. According to Khoury, as of April 1922, funds allotted for Syria were being reduced, although this did not mean the end of the occupation (Khoury, *Syria*, 47).

173. Thus the areas that had once composed parts of the Ottoman provinces of Syria, Beirut, and Aleppo as well as the special district (*mutasarrifiyya*) of Mount Lebanon became gradually incorporated into the French imperial sphere.

174. Burns, *Tariff*, 132. Despite not being a League of Nations member, the United States would also benefit from the same tariff rates as League members due to a special arrangement (41–42).

175. Khoury, *Syria*, 71. That did not stop some aspiring settlers from writing to the ministry to request a concession of land to work. See MAE, Syrie-Liban 75, Lucien Chambon to M. le Ministre, 18 June 1919, p. 85; Lucien Lemoine to M. le Chef du Service des concessions, 23 June 1919, p. 89; Lucien Chambon to M. le Deputé, 19 July 1919, p. 93; and M. Bertrand to the Minister of Agriculture, 9 (?) August 1919, p. 106.

176. Khoury, *Syria*, 58, 78.

177. CADN, Syrie-Liban/1, 1842, Rapport trimestriel du 4o trimestre 1920 (État d'Alep).

178. MAE, Syrie-Liban 61, "Motoculture," 68. Ironically, given their enthusiasm, motoculture was still not widespread in France itself. In 1920, Albert Demangeon, a scholar of human geography at the Sorbonne, wrote that "progress [in France] . . . had proceeded slowly, but happily motoculture seems to have won its case" (Demangeon, *Déclin*, 299; de Martonne, "Nécrologie"). Still, he declared that it was not widespread enough in the metropole, urging the country to take inspiration from the success of machines in the United States and more recently Britain (Demangeon, *Déclin*, 299).

179. MAE, Syrie-Liban 60, Berthelot to the High Commission, 6 January 1921.

180. Haut-Commissariat, *Syrie et le Liban en 1921*, 315–32. Fourteen pages were devoted to listing the French participants in the exhibition, two to Syrian products (including cheese from the Salamiya school), and two to listing all the foreign participants.

181. Haut-Commissariat, *Syrie et le Liban en 1921*, xviii. See also *La Géographie* 34, no. 1 (June 1920): 92, which highlighted that "a large place will be reserved for implements of motoculture" at the upcoming fair. Harking back to the granary of Rome was a common refrain in French colonial discourse to suggest local incapacity to realize the full productivity of their land. For a discussion of this in North Africa, see D. K. Davis, *Resurrecting the Granary.*

182. Haut-Commissariat, *Syrie et le Liban en 1921*, 325–26, 331.

183. MAE, Syrie-Liban 75, de Caix to Kammerer, 5 November 1920; Khoury, *Syrie*, 73–74. De Caix insisted that the promise of the market was "very big"—Achard estimated that although a fifth of Aleppo was under cultivation, three-fourths of it could be. In another communication, de Caix stated even more explicitly, "French industry must be able to provide the necessary agricultural material for Syria and I would not be disposed to favor the introduction of machines from foreign brand" (MAE, Syrie-Liban 75, de Caix to Beirut, 24 December 1920).

184. MAE, Syrie-Liban 61, "Bulletin économique no. 8," February 1921, p. 69.

185. CADN, Syrie-Liban/2, 7, "Enseignement technique," "L'enseignement professionnel des garçons et le développement économique de la Syrie," 7 November 1921.

186. Khoury notes that "neglect" from investors would become characteristic of mandate rule. See Khoury, *Syria*, 45.

187. MAE, Syrie-Liban 61, "Bulletin économique no. 8," February 1921, pp. 68–69.

188. TNA, FO 861.72, "Report on the Situation in Aleppo and District," 15 February 1921.

189. NARA, RG 166, FAS Box 473, "Market for Tractors, Tractor Attachments and Implements," Aleppo Consulate to the Department of State, 1 November 1924, p. 15. This report from the U.S. Foreign Agricultural Service indicates that "with reference to tractors and farm machinery, the French authorities entered the country, it appears, with the intention to follow the most exclusive policy" (15).

190. MAE, Syrie-Liban 61, "Bulletin économique no. 8," February 1921, pp. 68–69.

191. TNA, FO 861.72, "Report on the Situation in Aleppo and District," 15 February 1921.

192. MAE, Syrie-Liban 75, de Caix for Gouraud, 24 December 1920. De Caix thought that ʿAkkar might be the closest to approximate it.

193. At the time of the Foire-Exhibition in April and May of 1921, Ibrahim Hananu's revolt was still under way in the Aleppan hinterland. This resistance to French rule

continued through the fall of 1921. See Khoury, *Syria*, 105–10; and Watenpaugh, *Being Modern*, 174–81. On Aleppo and Alexandretta's centrality to French economic ambitions, see Jackson, "What Is Syria Worth?" 98–99.

194. NARA, RG 166, FAS Box 473, "Market for Tractors, Tractor Attachments and Implements," Aleppo Consulate to the Department of State, 1 November 1924, pp. 15, 16. The Americans clearly understood that this was a sensitive issue—the document in which these numbers were reported was marked "strictly confidential" (15–16). A mandate report from 1922 even acknowledged that this skepticism resulted from the majority of the imported machines being unsuited to local conditions. See Haut-Commissariat, *Syrie et le Liban en 1922*, 211.

195. Parmentier, "L'Agriculture en Syria," 213–14.

196. Parmentier, *Manuel d'agriculture*. The manual took the form of an "agricultural catechism" (Mizrahi, *Genèse*, 234).

197. Achard, "Notes," 97.

198. Achard, "Notes," 100.

199. Achard, "Notes," 100.

200. Achard, "Notes," 100. Measuring distance by the time it took to ride a horse from point A to point B was a common practice in the late Ottoman period.

201. Achard, "Notes," 100–101.

202. Achard had not been quite so adamant about this position in his essay for the Foire-Exposition's booklet, stating that "in a land of extensive culture like the east of Syria, large property is necessary" (Achard, "Syrie pays d'agriculture," 164).

203. Achard, "Notes," 101–2.

204. MAE, Syrie-Liban 62, M. N. Négib (?) Moussalli, "Mémoire sur la création d'un Crédit Foncier Syrien," August 1917. Moussalli cited the soil's fertility, the region's diverse crops, and the profits this entailed, especially because its crops ripened earlier, ensuring no lack of markets. Yet in his conception of how the organization would operate, "the indigenous Syrian element," though supported by the French, would know best how to organize matters because of "its contact with the rural class," suggesting an intermediary role that does not appear to have been on the French agenda.

205. For example, the Imperial Ottoman Bank became la Banque de Syrie, capitalized at 10 million francs with a statute deposited in Paris on 26 December 1918 (MAE, Syrie-Liban 62, "La Syrie," 24 January 1919, pp. 21–22).

206. When the Société Générale expressed an interest in investing in Syria, its director general suggested it could receive support from the Beirut branch of the Banque de Salonique and be capitalized with 5 million francs (MAE, Syrie-Liban 71, M. Homberg to the Minister of Foreign Affairs, 6 December 1918). The bank was duly constituted by April 1919 and by October Le Crédit Foncier d'Algérie et de Tunisie (CFAT) was supporting it financially and controlling its operations (MAE, Syrie-Liban 71, President of the Counsel to the Minister of Foreign Affairs, 19 [?] October 1919). Not long afterward, the Banque Française d'Egypte, which had worked closely with the Marseille Chamber of Commerce to ensure government support for French influence in the region postwar, established an affiliate Société Foncier de Syrie with the intent of the "acquisition and *mise en valeur* of lands." Its initial capital was 10 million francs, but in November 1919 it requested permission to increase this to 20 million because, even though it had no intention of

going public, it had received the adherence of an important Syrian group and to satisfy them it needed to increase its capital (MAE, Syrie-Liban 71, Banque Française d'Egypt to the Minister of Foreign Affairs, 11 November 1919; CCM, MQ.5.4/35, Comte Cressaty, Director of the French Bank of Egypt, to President of the CCM, 16 December 1915; this latter letter makes reference to secret, ongoing negotiations—that is, those that would result in the Sykes-Picot Agreement—and the need to ensure that the French position remained strong on a claim to *la Syrie Intégrale*). Interestingly, the Crédit Lyonnais does not seem to have been among the banks vying for access under the mandate. In the Levant it had branches only in Jaffa and Jerusalem, both of which came under British mandate (Issawi, *Fertile Crescent*, 410).

207. MAE, Syrie-Liban 72, Director of the Counsel of CFAT to the Minister of Foreign Affairs, 19 January 1921.

208. Bonin, *Outre-mer bancaire*, 195.

209. MAE, Syrie-Liban 72, CFAT to the High Commissioner, 24 June 1921.

210. Al-Shihabi, "Ma Jad min al-Sinaʿat al-Shamiya baʿd al-Harb al-Kubra," 244.

211. Khoury, *Syria*, 58–59. On the production of "minorities" as a category during this period, see also B. T. White, *Emergence*.

212. Gieryn, "Boundary-Work." For a discussion of how boundary-work operated in the building of the electrical grid in mandate Palestine, see Meiton, *Electrical Palestine*.

213. The journal originally had a publishing run from 1924 to 1932. The same editor started publishing a similar journal under the title *al-Majalla al-Ziraʿiya al-Suriya* in late 1938 (the second issue appeared in January 1939). See chapters 4 and 5 for additional details. Although it is not possible to know the exact breadth of the journal's circulation, it does seem to have been read throughout the region. According to the journal *al-Marʾa*, *al-Ziraʿa al-Haditha* "does not lack praise and commendation because what it has regarding the relationship with the agricultural wealth of the country, which farmers cannot do without, ensures its spread and progress" ("Al-Suhuf wa al-Majallat," *Al-Marʾa* 2, no. 2 [February 1932]: 24). *Al-Marʾa* was another journal published out of Hama by Nadima al-Sabuni with the proclaimed goal of "raising the level of the woman" (al-Sabuni, "Taqdim al-Majalla," 2). *Al-Ziraʿa al-Haditha* also had a relatively active "Barid al-Qurra" (post of the readers, or letters to the editor) section where people could write in with questions or observations, which the journal would publish. The well-established journal *al-ʿIrfan*, which was based in Saida in southern Lebanon and published on a variety of topics, included cartoons excerpted from *al-Ziraʿa al-Haditha* to accompany its own articles about agriculture; see, for example, al-Zayn, "al-Ziraʿa wa al-Sinaʿa." On *al-ʿIrfan*, see Weiss, *In the Shadow*. Although it seems to have been the only journal of such quality and longevity in the region exclusively devoted to agriculture, at least one other agricultural journal, *al-Hayat al-Ziraʿiya*, was circulating. *Al-Ziraʿa al-Haditha* included at least one excerpt from it, but I have been unable to locate copies of it; see "al-Muqtataf," *al-Ziraʿa al-Haditha* 5, no. 5 (March 1932): 332, which includes an excerpt from volume 1, issue 3, of the journal. *Al-ʿAsima* also mentions a journal titled *al-Fallah*, although it is unclear how long it was in print (*al-ʿAsima* 32 [5 June 1919]). For a translated excerpt of Wilhelm's cotton report, see Wilhelm, "Ziraʿat al-Qutn fi Suriye"; and Wilhelm, "Ziraʿat al-Qutn fi Suriye 2." For Arabic translations of Achard's reports on cotton, see Achard, "al-Qutn fi

Suriye" (February 1924); Achard, "al-Qutn fi Suriye" (March 1924); and Achard, "Zira'at al-Qutn fi Suriye 2."

214. See, for example, Parmentier, "al-Zira'a fi Suriya"; Parmentier, "al-Zira'a fi Suriya 2"; Parmentier, "al-Zira'a fi Suriye 7"; and Parmentier, "al-Zira'a fi Suriye 9."

215. See, for example, al-Jabri, "Zira'at al-Qutn al-Baladi"; and "Anwa' al-Qutn al-Amrikiya," *al-Zira'a al-Haditha* 2, no. 1 (January 1925): 34–35. Notably, when the journal translated Parmentier's articles, it omitted his preference for "European" specialists and references to only French-specific projects. Where Parmentier urged "creation of a Direction of agricultural services and the nomination of special professors of agriculture," *al-Zira'a al-Haditha* merely translated the suggestion as "appoint agriculture teachers in most agricultural districts (*kazas*) and subdistricts (*nahiyas*)" (Parmentier, "L'Agriculture en Syria," 213–14; Parmentier, "al-Zira'a fi Suriye 9," 92).

216. "Al-Zira'a fi Suriya 4: T'amim al-'Ilm al-Zira'i," *al-Zira'a al-Haditha*, 2, no. 10 (December 1925): 583.

217. CCM, MQ.5.4/35, CCM to Chamber of Commerce of Tripoli, 7 November 1922; CCM to Chamber of Commerce of Aleppo, 7 November 1922; and CCM to Chamber of Commerce of Damascus, 7 November 1922.

218. CCM, MQ.5.4/35, Chamber of Commerce of Damascus to CCM, 4 March 1923; Chamber of Commerce of Aleppo to CCM, 27 January 1923.

219. See *al-Majalla al-Iqtisadiya / La Revue Économique*. The *Economic Journal*'s owner was Na'im Janbart and featured photos of prominent directors and inspectors in the local Aleppan and Syrian administration, including an opening photo of Salim Janbart, a well-off merchant and the president of the Aleppo Chamber of Commerce who was known for his more moderate positions toward mandate politics (Khoury, *Syria*, 379–80).

220. "L'agriculture," *al-Majalla al-Iqtisadiya / La Revue Économique* 1, no. 1 (July-August 1925): 17.

221. "L'agriculture," 17, 18.

222. CADN, Syrie-Liban/3, Direction du Personnel 131, "Pavie, Charles," Bulletin Individuel de Notes. Pavie held the post of counselor for economic and agricultural affairs for Aleppo in 1922 and then was the agricultural and economic affairs inspector from January 1923 until May 1925. He was reassigned to the "Alawite Territory" as the director of agricultural and economic services in June 1925, shortly before the first issue of *La Revue Économique* came out in July-August 1925.

223. CADN, Syrie-Liban/3, Direction du Personnel 131, "Pavie, Charles."

224. "Les machines agricoles," *al-Majalla al-Iqtisadiya / La Revue Économique* 1, no. 1 (July-August 1925): 21.

225. Worster, *Dust Bowl*, 89–90; Herment, "Tractorisation," 186; Fitzgerald, "Blinded by Technology," 462–64.

226. Al-Ahdab, "Nafaqat," 161.

227. Al-Shihabi, *Zira'a*, 130–31.

228. Al-Shihabi, *Zira'a*, 132.

229. Al-Shihabi, *Zira'a*, 128. French officials agreed with him, noting in a confidential report that "farmers would not seem otherwise hostile to the use of these machines, but the big pitfall is the lack of a special repair shop" (CADN, Syrie-Liban/1, 1845, "Rapport Trimestriel Hama, 1927," 25 July 1927).

230. CADN, Syrie-Liban/1, 1845, "Rapport Trimestriel Hama, 1927," 25 July 1927.

231. CA, Box 001, Ref SC/13, Correspondances Alep 1922, telegram from Depolla to Corm, 26 June 1922; and telegram from Depolla to Corm, 4 July 1922.

232. CA, Box 001, Ref SC/13, Correspondances Alep 1922, Aleppo branch to Direction Générale in Beirut, 12 July 1922.

233. CA, Box 001, Ref SC/13, Correspondances Alep 1922, Aleppo branch to Direction Générale in Beirut, 20 June 1922.

234. "Les machines agricoles," 21–22.

235. CA, Box 001, Ref SC/13, Correspondances Alep 1922, Aleppo branch to Direction Générale in Beirut, 20 June 1922. The reference appears to be to *najil*, a term that can refer to either couch grass or orchard grass (Wehr, *Arabic-English Dictionary*, 1109). In 1927 *al-Zira*ʿ*a al-Haditha* devoted an entire article to the challenges posed by this grass (al-Barudi, "Najil").

236. "Les machines agricoles," 22.

237. Al-Shihabi, *Zira*ʿ*a*, 127–29.

238. Al-Khatib, *Amir Mustafa al-Shihabi*, 12.

239. Faris, *Min Huwa*, 16.

240. Faris, *Min Huwa*, 16. After independence al-Ahdab would go on to become the *wikala* of the Directorate of National Economy, and in 1948 he would be appointed the general director for agricultural matters in the Ministry of the National Economy.

241. Faris, *Min Huwa*, 298–99.

242. See al-Jazaʾiri, "al-Islah al-Ziraʿi fi Suriya," 426. On the Berlin school, see Harwood, *Technology's Dilemma*, 112–26.

243. ʿAtallah, "al-Hala al-Ziraʿiya wa al-Iqtisadiya fi Biladna," 317. It is unclear whether he includes Lebanon in this unified Syria.

244. See, for example, ʿAtallah, "al-Hala al-Ziraʿiya wa al-Iqtisadiya fi Suriya," 130, 134; and ʿAtallah, "al-Hala al-Ziraʿiya wa al-Iqtisadiya fi Biladna," 317.

245. For a similar phenomenon in early-twentieth-century Russia, see Kotsonis, *Making Peasants Backwards*, 97–115.

246. Al-Ahdab, "al-Hala al-Ziraʿiya fi Suriya," 11–12. Ironically, by 1935 this period would later be recalled as one of relative prosperity given agriculture's dire economic straits as the mandate proceeded ("Que veut l'Agriculture?" *Les Échos*, 9 August 1935; CADN, Syrie-Liban/1, 863, "Étude sur la situation de l'agriculture au Liban," 23 April 1935, p. 15).

247. Al-Ahdab, "al-Hala al-Ziraʿiya fi Suriya," 11.

248. Al-Ahdab, "al-Hala al-Ziraʿiya fi Suriya," 15; al-Ahdab, "Daraʾib al-Ziraʿa fi Suriya 2," 466; ʿAtallah, "al-Hala al-Ziraʿiya wa al-Iqtisadiya fi Suriya," 131–32, 132–34; "al-Ziraʿa fi Suriya 4: Tʿamim al-ʿIlm al-Ziraʿi," *al-Zira*ʿ*a al-Haditha*, 2, no. 10 (December 1925): 583–84; [al-Ahdab], "al-Hala al-Ziraʿiya fi Suriya 2," 250; al-Jazaʾiri, "al-Islah al-Ziraʿi fi Suriya 3," 43–46.

249. For one of his speeches, see, for example, al-Shihabi, "Aham Adwaʾna al-Iqtisadiya wa Talafiha" (November 1928). This article and the others that followed it were transcripts from a series of lectures given in 1928 and 1929 to the Arab Academy of Damascus.

250. Al-Shihabi, "Ma Jad min al-Sinaʿat al-Shamiya baʿd al-Harb al-Kubra," 245.

251. Al-Shihabi, "Ma Jad min al-Sinaʿat al-Shamiya baʿd al-Harb al-Kubra," 247.

252. Burns, *Tariff*, 45–49, 134–42. French imports rose from 9.3% before the war to an average of 15.3% between 1921 and 1932 (133).

253. Burns, *Tariff*, 53. By 1932 only a third of Syria's trade was with neighboring countries, compared with half before the war, when those countries had been Ottoman provinces. See also Khoury, "Syrian Independence Movement." Burns notes that immediately after the war Syria had a greater degree of local industry than Turkey did; however, Turkish authorities would not negotiate a tariff agreement until the frontier was settled, which did not happen until 1930, by which point Turkey had started its own industrialization program (54).

254. Al-Shihabi, "Ma Jad min al-Sinaʿat al-Shamiya baʿd al-Harb al-Kubra," 249–50.

255. Al-Shihabi, "Ma Jad min al-Sinaʿat al-Shamiya baʿd al-Harb al-Kubra 2," 297.

256. Khoury, *Syria*, 31, 38.

257. Al-Shihabi, "Aham Adwaʾna al-Iqtisadiya wa Talafiha 2" (December 1928), 12.

258. Al-Shihabi, "Aham Adwaʾna al-Iqtisadiya wa Talafiha" (November 1928), 14.

259. CADN, Syrie-Liban/1, 861, Services Économiques—Sanjak de Homs (1925?), "École d'Agriculture de Salamieh," n.d. Al-Ahdab's award was at the rank of knight (Faris, *Min Huwa*, 17).

260. Faris, *Min Huwa*, 241; CADN, Syrie-Liban/1, 953, "Nationalistes Damas Information," Collet, 20 March 1928, in which Mustafa al-Shihabi is listed as a "Francophobe." The "medal of agricultural merit" appears to refer to the Ordre du Mérite agricole of the officer rank.

261. Faris, *Min Huwa*, 299. This debate is covered in chapter 5. Presumably this medal was an Ordre du Mérite agricole.

262. Khoury, *Syria*, 45.

263. Khoury, *Syria*, 50, 82–83; Safieddine, *Banking on the State*, 15–42.

264. This will be explored more fully in the following chapters and the epilogue.

Chapter Four

1. Zakariya, *Qura*, 11. Wasfi Zakariya graduated with an agricultural engineering degree from the Halkalı Agricultural School, taught at the Salamiya agricultural school, and then became headmaster of the school until 1914. In 1914 he went to work in the "House of Silk" directorship in Beirut and then taught in the Latrun school between Yafa and Jerusalem before being drafted into the army during World War I. After the war he headed the Salamiya agricultural school again until 1924, when he became an inspector for state lands. Following the dissolution of the Syrian Agricultural Stock Company, he left Syria in 1936 for Yemen and then Iraq, where his agricultural expertise was in demand (Zakariya, *Qura*, 10–11).

2. Zakariya, "Kif yajab," 423. According to Hans Wehr, *murabiʿ* refers to a partner "sharing one quarter of the gains or losses" in an agricultural exploitation (Wehr, *Arabic-English Dictionary*, 374). In Syria specifically, it indicated an arrangement in which the landlord fronted all the expenses and the farmer contributed labor. The farmer received one-fourth or one-fifth of the harvest after taxes (Kurd ʿAli, *Kitab Khitat al-Sham* 4: 216).

3. Zakariya, "Kif Yajab," 423.

4. Zakariya, "Kif Yajab," 423–24.

5. Zakariya, "Kif Yajab," 424.

6. Zakariya, "Kif Yajab," 425.

7. Zakariya, "Kif Yajab," 423.

8. Auderset and Moser, "Mechanisation."

9. For this characterization of peasants, see Khoury, *Syria*, 64. This skepticism did not mean that they were not receptive. According to one assessment, the "peasant population . . . is not rebellious to technical progress"; rather, it wanted to learn, "provided that one instructs it and that one furnishes to it the means to adopt [the procedures]" (Mounayer, *Régime*, 203). For a similar argument about agricultural change in Europe, see Auderset and Moser, "Mechanisation."

10. "L'agriculture," *al-Majalla al-Iqtisadiya / La Revue Économique* 1, no. 1 (July-August 1925): 19.

11. See Burns, *Tariff*. New tariff regimes on agricultural products often exacerbated matters.

12. See Forclaz, "Shaping the Future."

13. Forclaz, "Shaping the Future," 335. For instances of these interventions in Egypt and Iraq, see El Shakry, *Great Social Laboratory*, 89–142; and Pursley, "Education for Real Life," respectively.

14. Thompson, *Colonial Citizens*, 65; Longrigg, *Syria and Lebanon*, 259–83.

15. Achard, "Syrie pays d'agriculture," 166.

16. Haut-Commissariat, *Syrie et le Liban en 1922*, 236–37. The curriculum of the Salamiya school, however, was faulted for being too book-oriented and not practical enough.

17. CADN, Syrie-Liban/1, 1847, "Alep—Rapport trimestriel, 1er Trimestre, 1928," transmitted with a note dated 1 May 1928.

18. Haut-Commissariat, *Syrie et le Liban en 1922, 20, 217, 237;* Ministère des affaires étrangères, *Rapport (1924)*, 55.

19. Headrick, *Tentacles of Progress*, 13; Hodge, *Triumph of the Expert*.

20. Ministère des affaires étrangères, *Rapport (Juillet 1922–Juillet 1923)*, 28; Ministère des affaires étrangères, *Rapport (Juillet 1923–Juillet 1924)*, 37–38.

21. Khoury, *Syria*, 521.

22. Khoury, *Syria*, 58–60.

23. Haut-Commissariat, *Syrie et le Liban sous l'occupation*, 113. CADN, Syrie-Liban/1, 1842, "État des Alaouites Rapport Trimestriel—Octobre, Novembre, Décembre 1922."

24. CADN, Syrie-Liban/1, 1844, État des Alaouites, "Rapport pour le deuxième trimestre 1925," 30 July 1925.

25. Ministère des affaires étrangères, *Rapport (Juillet 1922–Juillet 1923)*, 28.

26. CADN, Syrie-Liban/1, 1843, État des Alaouites, "Rapport pour le quatrième trimestre 1924," 20 January 1925.

27. CADN, Syrie-Liban/1, 1844, "Rapport Trimestriel Alaouites 1925," 15 October 1925; CADN, Syrie-Liban/1, 1847, "Rapport pour le deuxième trimestre 1928," 25 July 1928; CADN, Syrie-Liban/1, 1848, "Rapport pour le deuxième trimestre 1929," 31 August 1929. In other areas, local chambers of agriculture took the initiative. For example, in the mountain town of Haffe the municipality took out an agricultural bank loan after its chamber of agriculture acquired some land to establish its own nursery (CADN,

Syrie-Liban/1, 1850, Government of Latakia, "Rapport pour le première trimestre 1930," 6 May 1930; CADN, Syrie-Liban/1, 1851, Government of Latakia, "Rapport Trimestriel," 21 October 1932).

28. Ministère des affaires étrangères, *Rapport (1924)*, 55.

29. CADN, Syrie-Liban/1, 1842, "État des Alaouites Rapport Trimestriel—Octobre, Novembre, Décembre 1923."

30. CADN, Syrie-Liban/1, 1848, "Rapport pour le deuxième trimestre 1929," 31 August 1929; CADN, Syrie-Liban/1, 1851, Government of Latakia, "Rapport Trimestriel," 21 October 1932.

31. CADN, Syrie-Liban/1, 1844, "Rapport Trimestriel Alaouites 1925," 15 October 1925; CADN, Syrie-Liban/1, 1845, "Rapport Trimestriel Alaouites 1926," 4 November 1926; CADN, Syrie-Liban/1, 1845, "Rapport Trimestriel Alaouites 1927," 2 August 1927.

32. CADN, Syrie-Liban/1, 1845, "Rapport Trimestriel Alaouites 1926," 4 November 1926; CADN, Syrie-Liban/1, 1847, Government of Latakia, "Rapport pour le 1er trimestre 1928," 30 April 1928; Ministère des affaires étrangères, *Rapport (1930)*, 126. This approach seems similar to the Ottoman method of farming out experiments to local producers, discussed in chapter 2.

33. Ministère des affaires étrangères, *Rapport (1924)*, 55; Haut-Commissariat, *Syrie et le Liban en 1921*, 233; Haut-Commissariat, *Syrie et le Liban en 1922*, 237; Ministère des affaires étrangères, *Rapport (Juillet 1922–Juillet 1923)*, 52.

34. CADN, Syrie-Liban/1, 1844, "Rapport Trimestriel Grand Liban 1926," 22 October 1926; Ministère des affaires étrangères, *Rapport (1926)*, 133.

35. CADN, Syrie-Liban/1, 1844, "Liban Rapport Trimestriel politique et administratif," 20 August 1926.

36. CADN, Syrie-Liban/1, 1844, "Liban Rapport Trimestriel politique et administratif," 20 August 1926; CADN, Syrie-Liban/1, 1844, "Rapport Trimestriel Grand Liban 1926," 22 October 1926.

37. CADN, Syrie-Liban/1, 1844, "Rapport Trimestriel Grand Liban 1926," 22 October 1926.

38. Ministère des affaires étrangères, *Rapport (1929)*, 111; CADN, Syrie-Liban/1, 1847, "Grand Liban," 23 January 1929; CADN, Syrie-Liban/1, 1848, "Rapport Trimestriel Juillet-Août-Septembre 1929," 22 October 1929. The center was initially established for seven years.

39. CADN, Syrie-Liban/1, 1845, "Rapport Trimestriel Janvier-Février-Mars 1927," 2 May 1927; Ministère des affaires étrangères, *Rapport (1929)*, 111.

40. CADN, Syrie-Liban/1, 1845, "Rapport Trimestriel Janvier-Février-Mars 1927," 2 May 1927. The moldboard plows (*charrue à versoir*) were the plows that Achard had dismissed as inappropriate for use in areas such as Aleppo, although he noted that the Blass agricultural school set up under the Faysal government had two *araires à versoir*. *Araire*, sometimes translated as "scratch plow," designates a lighter plow than a *charrue* (Wallerstein, *Modern World-System*, 88n91; Achard, "Notes," 97, 99).

41. Ministère des affaires étrangères, *Rapport (1924)*, 55.

42. CADN, Syrie-Liban/1, 1847, "Rapport Trimestriel Janvier-Février-Mars 1928," 1 May 1928.

43. CADN, Syrie-Liban/1, 1848, "Rapport Trimestriel Juillet-Août-Septembre 1929," 22 October 1929.

44. The station opened in July 1930 and repaired other equipment as well. CADN, Syrie-Liban/1, 1850, "Rapport sur la situation de la République Libanaise (3ème Trimestre 1930)," 27 October 1930; CADN, Syrie-Liban/1, 1850, "Rapport Trimestriel sur la situation de la République Libanaise (4ème Trimestre 1930)," 28 January 1931; CADN, Syrie-Liban/1, 1848, "Rapport Trimestriel Juillet-Août-Septembre 1929," 22 October 1929.

45. CADN, Syrie-Liban/1, 1851, "Rapport Trimestriel Janvier-Février-Mars 1932," 25 April 1932.

46. Haut-Commissariat, *Syrie et le Liban en 1922*, 237; CADN, Syrie-Liban/1, 1843, "Rapport Trimestriel 1er trimestre 1924," 15 April 1924.

47. Achard, "Syrie pays d'agriculture," 165–66; Haut-Commissariat, *Syrie et le Liban en 1922*, 237. One of the earliest reports by mandate authorities to the League of Nations envisioned the school as an institution that would serve all the federated statelets (Ministère des affaires étrangères, *Rapport [Juillet 1922–Juillet 1923]*, 6).

48. CADN, Syrie-Liban/1, 1844, "Rapport Trimestriel État de Syrie 1925," 1 August 1925; CADN, Syrie-Liban/1, 1844, "Rapport Trimestriel (1ère trimestre 1925) Région Nord," 6 May 1925; CADN, Syrie-Liban/1, 1845, "Rapport Trimestriel Hama 1926," 15 January 1927; Ministère des affaires étrangères, *Rapport (1928)*, 54.

49. See the next section, "Elite Expertise and Rural Education: The Local Politics of Agricultural Knowledge Production."

50. CADN, Syrie-Liban/1, 1842, "Bulletin Trimestrial no. 2," n.d. (The previous document, which is also marked "Bulletin Trimestrial no. 2," is dated 31 March 1921.)

51. CADN, Syrie-Liban/1, 1843, "Rapport Trimestriel 3ème trimestre 1924," 28 October 1924.

52. Ministère des affaires étrangères, *Rapport (1931)*, 90.

53. "ʿAwda 'al-Ziraʿa al-Haditha,'" *al-Ziraʿa al-Haditha* 5, no. 1 (November 1931): 1.

54. Ministère des affaires étrangères, *Rapport (Juillet 1923–Juillet 1924)*, 37; CADN, Syrie-Liban/1, 1842, "Rapport Trimestriel du 4° trimestre 1920," n.d.

55. Ministère des affaires étrangères, *Rapport (Juillet 1922–Juillet 1923)*, 52; Haut-Commissariat, *Syrie et le Liban en 1922*, 237. On the orphanage, see Sarrage, *Nécessité*, 145; and CADN, Syrie-Liban/2, 168, "Note," 19 May 1941.

56. For a discussion of developments concerning the Muslimiya school, see the section "Influence in the Countryside: The Politics of Educating the *Fallah*."

57. CADN, Syrie-Liban/1, 1843, "Rapport Trimestriel 3° trimestre 1924," n.d.

58. CADN, Syrie-Liban/1, 1843, "Rapport Trimestriel 3° trimestre 1924," n.d.; CADN, Syrie-Liban/1, 1847, "Rapport Trimestriel 1° trimestre 1928," 1 May 1928; CADN, Syrie-Liban/1, 1846, "Rapport Trimestriel 1° trimestre 1927," 29 April 1927.

59. CADN, Syrie-Liban/1, 1847, "Rapport Trimestriel 1° trimestre 1928," 1 May 1928. Where the trial took place is not stated.

60. CADN, Syrie-Liban/1, 1846, "Rapport Trimestriel 2° trimestre 1927," n.d.; CADN, Syrie-Liban/1, 1847, "Rapport Trimestriel 2° trimestre 1928," n.d.; CADN, Syrie-Liban/1, 2109, "Rapport Trimestriel 2ème trimestre 1929," 22 August 1929.

61. CADN, Syrie-Liban/2, 109, "Note sur l'enseignement et la vulgarisation agricoles dans la Syrie du Nord, " 11 July 1934.

62. CADN, Syrie-Liban/1, 1847, "Rapport Trimestriel 1° trimestre 1928," 1 May 1928; CADN, Syrie-Liban/1, 2109, "Rapport Trimestriel 2ème trimestre 1929," 22 August 1929. In 1931 an attempt "by amateurs" to raise silkworms in Zor produced less than "brilliant" results (CADN, Syrie-Liban/1, 1849, "Rapport Trimestriel du 4° trimestre 1931," 10 January 1932).

63. CADN, Syrie-Liban/1, 1849, "Bulletin d'Informations Trimestriel Quatrième Trimestre 1931," 23 January 1932; Ministère des affaires étrangères, *Rapport (1932)*, 107; Ministère des affaires étrangères, *Rapport (1934)*, 114.

64. Ministère des affaires étrangères, *Rapport (1934)*, 114; CADN, Syrie-Liban/1, 1851, "Bulletin d'Informations Trimestriel Premier Trimestre 1933," 12 May 1933.

65. Ministère des affaires étrangères, *Rapport (1929)*, 87; Ministère des affaires étrangères, *Rapport (1931)*, 115; Ministère des affaires étrangères, *Rapport (1934)*, 124.

66. Goswami, *Producing India*, 132. Here, I borrow the concept of socializing from Goswami's discussion of it in colonial India.

67. "Ziraat Nezaretince"; CADN, Syrie-Liban/2, 36, "Enseignement officiel," "Organisation du Personnel de l'Enseignement Primaire et Secondaire," in folder dated 1925. For the purpose of a teaching qualification, mandate authorities recognized the Halkalı degree and a *diplôme d'ingénieur agronome*.

68. Ministère des affaires étrangères, *Rapport (1925)*, 96.

69. CADN, Syrie-Liban/3, Direction du personnel 5, "Achard, Edouard," High Commissionner to Soubhi Bey Barakat, 4 November 1922; CADN, Syrie-Liban/2, 27, "Enseignement technique et professionnel," "Esquisse d'un Programme d'Enseignement Professional pour la Syrie et Le Liban." The report was circulated between the high commissioner and the counselor for public instruction (CADN, Syrie-Liban/2, 27, correspondence).

70. For more details on Bériel's prior experience in Tunisia and his expectations based on that, see CADN, Syrie-Liban/2, 111, "Réunion des conseillers," 3rd session, 3 May 1934.

71. CADN, Syrie-Liban/2, 92, "Esquisse d'un Programme," 20.

72. CADN, Syrie-Liban/2, 92, "Formation Professionnelle," 2, 3; CADN, Syrie-Liban/2, 92, "Esquisse d'un Programme," 6.

73. CADN, Syrie-Liban/2, 92, "Esquisse d'un Programme," 10.

74. CADN, Syrie-Liban/2, 92, "Esquisse d'un Programme," 24.

75. CADN, Syrie-Liban/2, 92, "Esquisse d'un Programme," 24.

76. CADN, Syrie-Liban/2, 92, "Esquisse d'un Programme," 21; CADN, Syrie-Liban/2, 36, "Programme d'Enseignement professionnel au Liban," n.d. but attached to correspondence marked 11 February 1924.

77. CADN, Syrie-Liban/2, 92, "Esquisse d'un Programme," 21.

78. CADN, Syrie-Liban/2, 92, "Esquisse d'un Programme," 20, 27.

79. CADN, Syrie-Liban/2, 92, "Esquisse d'un Programme," 4.

80. CADN, Syrie-Liban/2, 92, "Esquisse d'un Programme," 4.

81. CADN, Syrie-Liban/2, 92, "Esquisse d'un Programme," 27–28. Even Parmentier's book on Syrian agriculture was too advanced.

82. See, for example, al-Shihabi, *Zira*ʿ*a*, based on experiments during the Faysali period; and Zakariya, *Durus*. Hüseyin Kazım's *Çiftçi Çocuğu* had also recently been published in Ottoman.

83. CADN, Syrie-Liban/2, 92, "Esquisse d'un Programme," 20, 27. This process would be highly mediated by political and economic concerns. Bériel also suggested that eventually students could be trained through a *stage* in farm schools that had become *écoles normales professionelles* or in the School of Arts et Métiers for more industrially inclined pursuits.

84. CADN, Syrie-Liban/2, 92, "Esquisse d'un Programme," 20.

85. CADN, Syrie-Liban/2, 36, "Programme d'Enseignement professionnel au Liban."

86. CADN, Syrie-Liban/2, 36, "Programme d'Enseignement professionnel au Liban."

87. CADN, Syrie-Liban/2, 36, "Programme d'Enseignement professionnel au Liban."

88. CADN, Syrie-Liban/2, 36, "Programme d'Enseignement professionnel au Liban."

89. CADN, Syrie-Liban/2, 36, High Commissioner to the Governor of Greater Lebanon, 11 February 1924.

90. In a seemingly unironic reference to the impacts of such a policy in North Africa, while marveling at the existence of French institutions of higher education in the Levant, which Bériel attributed to the "persevering and dedicated actions of our missions, supported by our government," he noted that the large cities of North Africa, except for Algiers, "remain deprived of institutions of higher education" (CADN, Syrie-Liban/2, 92, "Esquisse d'un Programme," 5).

91. See Boulet, *Enjeux de la formation*; and Charmasson et al., *Enseignement agricole*, 44. Even as Bériel insisted on France's tutelary position in relation to technical education in Syria, he admitted that France itself had been a latecomer to such education compared with other countries and had pursued it at great cost for the past fifteen years in order to catch up (CADN, Syrie-Liban/2, 92, "Formation Professionnelle," 5).

92. Achard, "Syrie pays d'agriculture," 165–66. As discussed in chapter 3, Achard considered such education pointless without first implementing widespread property reform (164).

93. CADN, Syrie-Liban/2, 101, Assistant Counselor for Public Instruction in the Syrian Republic to the Counselor of the High Commission Delegate of the High Commission for the Syrian Republic, 5 September 1933.

94. CADN, Syrie-Liban/2, 92, "Esquisse d'un Programme," 28.

95. As discussed later, this possibility concerned French officials. For a comparable tension between agricultural education and bureaucratic aspirations in the British mandates of Iraq, Jordan, and Palestine, see Kalisman, "Next Generation of Cultivators."

96. Al-Shihabi was the director of agriculture and forestry from 1918 to 1923 and director of state lands from 1923 to 1934 (al-Khatib, *Amir Mustafa al-Shihabi*, 12).

97. Al-Shihabi, *Zira'a*, title page. By 1937 al-Shihabi would be recognized as among a group of local experts capable of explaining the "adaptation of Arabic to scientific needs and modern techniques" at the 1937 International Exposition in Paris (CADN, Syrie-Liban/2, 135, Counselor for Public Instruction to the Syrian Republic to Counselor for Public Instruction to the High Commission, 19 December 1936). He would eventually also write several dictionaries of technical terms detailing their translation from French to Arabic to English. See, for example, al-Shihabi, *Chihabi's Dictionary*; and al-Shihabi, *Dictionnaire français-arabe*.

98. Al-Shihabi, *Ziraʿa*, 5; Wehr, *Arabic-English Dictionary*, 873. Al-Shihabi defines the Nabateans as Arab. For more on these circulations of agricultural expertise, see Watson, *Agricultural Innovation*.

99. Al-Shihabi, *Ziraʿa*, 5. Al-Shihabi himself was able to peruse the book at the Beyazit Library in Istanbul.

100. Al-Shihabi, *Ziraʿa*, 5–8. See also the preface to Ibn al-Awam, *Le livre de l'agriculture*, 3–100.

101. Al-Shihabi, *Ziraʿa*, 8.

102. Al-Shihabi, *Ziraʿa*, 8.

103. See Ebn el-Awam, *Libro de Agricultura*; and al-ʿAwam, *Livre de l'agriculture*, 98.

104. Al-Shihabi, *Ziraʿa*, 8.

105. Al-Shihabi, *Ziraʿa*, 589. For the more widespread appeal of developments in dry farming elsewhere in the region and internationally, see Tesdell, "Planting Roots"; and Tesdell, "Shadow Spaces."

106. Al-Shihabi, *Ziraʿa*, 590. See also Widtsoe, *Dry-Framing*.

107. Al-Shihabi, *Ziraʿa*, 590. *Tilawa* can also mean "recitation" (Wehr, *Arabic-English Dictionary*, 117).

108. El-Awam, *Libro de agricultura*, front matter.

109. Al-ʿAwam, *Livre de l'agriculture*, 98.

110. Al-ʿAwam, *Livre de l'agriculture*, 98–99.

111. This section is based primarily on sources whose frame of reference is Syria, particularly the areas that made up the statelets of Aleppo and Damascus, which were combined under a common administration in 1924, ending the Syrian Federation (Khoury, *Syria*, 138).

112. See, for example, "al-Ziraʿa fi Suriye 4," *al-Ziraʿa al-Haditha* 2, no. 10 (December 1925): 582.

113. "Al-Ziraʿa fi Suriye 4," 582–83.

114. "1700 Madrasa Ziraʿiya," *al-Ziraʿa al-Haditha* 5, no. 4 (February 1932), 212–13. The statistics the journal provided were as follows: Germany, 1,700 agricultural schools and 70,000 students; France, 70 schools and 2,500 students; Belgium, 8,000 centers for seasonal agricultural lessons with more than 35,000 attendees; and Denmark, 95 schools and 10,000 students as well as 130 centers and 11,000 attendees.

115. "1700 Madrasa Ziraʿiya," 213.

116. Achard, "Syrie pays d'agriculture," 166.

117. For example, in 1930 and 1931 the Salamiya school graduated students from Hama, Damascus, Aleppo, Rakka, Homs, Salamiya, Idlib, Dayr al-Zor, and Jayrud in Syria; Tulkarim in Palestine; and Beirut, Sawfar, and Jadayda Marjʿayun in Lebanon ("al-ʿAlam al-Ziraʿi," *al-Ziraʿa al-Haditha* 5, no. 1 [November 1931]: 64; and "al-ʿAlam al-Ziraʿi," *al-Ziraʿa al-Haditha* 5, no. 2 [December 1931]: 135–36).

118. "Al-Suhuf wa al-Majallat," *Al-Marʾa* 2, no. 2 (February 1932): 24. As a "former rebel," Saʿid Tarmanini had been condemned to death by the mandate administration but was pardoned. He was considered a "notorious extremist" and was known for encouraging assaults on voting bureaus in 1931. According to French intelligence reports, he would later become the commander of the Hama Iron Shirts. See CADN, Syrie-Liban/1,

473, "Renseignements sur les Signataires de la Pétition de Hama du 7 décembre 1933"; and CADN, Syrie-Liban/1, 1934, Bulletin d'Information Hebdomadaire, Homs, 26 January 1937.

119. Haut-Commissariat, *Syrie et le Liban sous l'occupation*, 112.

120. Haut-Commissariat, *Syrie et le Liban sous l'occupation*, 113.

121. See CADN, Syrie-Liban/1, 864, "École d'Agriculture de Selemieh," "Information" from Berthelot, 18 November 1937; and "Tasmid al-Hinta Nauʿ al-Asmida wa Miqdariha," *al-Ziraʿa al-Haditha* 3, nos. 6–7 (September-October 1927): 435, which featured a photo of a *fallah* working in the school's fields. Despite mandate reports from the late 1920s insisting that the students received a practical education, Berthelot claimed their training was "almost purely theoretical education" because they aimed to be *ingénieurs agricoles.* Another mandate report noted that some sons of cultivators who had been admitted in 1930 did not follow any courses and worked only in the fields (CADN, Syrie-Liban/1, 1850, "Rapport Trimestriel Homs-Hama," 27 December 1930).

122. Sarrage, *Nécessité*, 118; Traboulsi, *Agriculture syrienne*, 93. By the early 1930s, 360 canals had been restored in the region.

123. CADN, Syrie-Liban/1, 864, "École d'Agriculture de Selemieh," "Information" from Berthelot, 18 November 1937.

124. Debbané, *L'Expérimentation Agricole*, 41.

125. "Khirriju al-Ziraʿa wa al-Hukuma," *al-Ziraʿa al-Haditha* 4, no. 5 (March 1929): 228.

126. See Dodge, "Institute of Rural Life," 211, 214. Dodge implied that students with large landholdings were generally more content to return to work them (214).

127. CADN, Syrie-Liban/2, 68, "Inventaire économique des États sur Mandat," "Enseignement technique," 1929.

128. Al-Jazaʾiri, "al-Islah al-Ziraʿi fi Suriye 3," 44.

129. CADN, Syrie-Liban/2, 62, "Enseignement officiel," Hissam al-Din al-Kuzbari, President to the Committee of the Defense on the Graduates of the Agriculture School to the High Commission, n.d.

130. CADN, Syrie-Liban/2, 62, "Enseignement officiel," Deputy Delegate of the High Commission to the High Commissioner, December 1928. The request seems to have gone unheeded.

131. "Khirriju al-Ziraʿa," 228; Sarrage, *Nécessité*, 146; Haut-Commissariat, *Syrie et le Liban sous l'occupation*, 243–44.

132. "Khirriju al-Ziraʿa," 228.

133. CADN, Syrie-Liban/1, 953, "Grève a l'École d'Agriculture de Selemieh," 18 November 1929; and "Information no. 2814," 12 November 1929.

134. CADN, Syrie-Liban/1, 953, "Grève a l'École d'Agriculture de Selemieh," 18 November 1929. Nawras al-Kaylani was the leader of the local union movement and had an influential "grip on nationalist political life in Hama," but the National Bloc wanted to reduce his influence because he was not aligned with them (Khoury, *Syria*, 368–70). Tawfiq Shishakli was both a mentee of Nawras al-Kaylani and the preferred candidate of the National Bloc for Hama (Faris, *Min Huwa*, 247; Khoury, *Syria*, 370–71).

135. CADN, Syrie-Liban/1, 953, "Grève à l'École d'Agriculture de Selemieh," 18 November 1929.

136. CADN, Syrie-Liban/1, 953, Information no. 2933, 3 December 1929. In addition to the three students named in the text, the others were Wassal al-Hawrani, Sabit Tayfur,

and Muhammad, son of Abdallah Khuri. The Tayfur and al-Kaylani families were two of the four biggest landowners in Hama (Khoury, *Syria*, 172).

137. CADN, Syrie-Liban/1, 954, "École d'Agriculture de Selemieh," Information no. 32, 18 September 1930. One report noted that during the summer of 1930 Salamiya was much calmer because the primarily nationalist employees of the school were on vacation (CADN, Syrie-Liban/1, 1850, Rapport Trimestriel Homs-Hama, 27 September 1930).

138. CADN, Syrie-Liban/2, 68, "Inventaire économique des États sur Mandat," "Enseignement technique," 1929; CADN, Syrie-Liban/2, 76, "Enseignement technique and agricole," students of the second and third year of the Practical Agricultural School of Salamiya to the High Commissioner, 26 August 1930. The Salamiya school admitted students following a *concours* (competitive exam), which they could take only after completing the sixth class of secondary studies (CADN, Syrie-Liban/2, 85, "Équivalences de baccalauréat," Collet to the Inspector General, 8 July 1931). *Al-Qabas* characterized the transformation as one from a technical or scientific school (*madrasa fanniya*) to a practical school (*madrasa ʿamaliya*) ("Madrasat Salamiya al-Ziraʿiya," *al-Qabas*, 27 July 1930).

139. See Bourdieu, *Distinction*, 133.

140. "Madrasat Salamiya al-Ziraʿiya," *Al-Qabas*, 27 July 1930; "Ilghaʾ Madrasat Salamiya al-Ziraʿiya: Jinaya ʿala Ziraʿat al-Bilad," *al-Qabas*, 28 (31?) July 1930. *Al-Qabas* noted in the school's defense that its operations were actually run more economically than those of the nursery in Damascus ("Ilghaʾ Madrasat Salamiya al-Ziraʿiya: Jinaya ʿala Ziraʿat al-Bilad," *al-Qabas*, 10 August 1930).

141. CADN, Syrie-Liban/2, 85, "Équivalences de baccalauréat," Helleu to MAE (Section des Écoles), 22 July 1931; and Collet to the Inspector General, 8 July 1930. For comparison, other high schools granted diplomas after six years of study with a weekly average of seven hours of French, whereas Salamiya's three-year course of study included only four hours per week until 1930 (CADN, Syrie-Liban/2, 85, "Équivalences de baccalauréat," Collet to the Inspector General, 8 July 1931). However, given that Salamiya's students had already completed the sixth class of secondary studies, they presumably had had a substantial amount of French before starting at Salamiya.

142. Tarmanini questioned the usefulness of French instruction for village children when their schools should have been focused on applying practical elementary agriculture knowledge in accompanying fields ("Madaris al-Qura wa al-Ziraʿa," *al-Ziraʿa al-Haditha* 5, no. 3 [January 1932]: 147).

143. CADN, Syrie-Liban/2, 85, "Équivalences de baccalauréat," Collet to the Inspector General, 11 July 1931.

144. CADN, Syrie-Liban/2, 76, "Enseignement technique and agricole," students of the second and third year of the Practical Agricultural School of Salamiya to the High Commissioner, 26 August 1930. The drama around the schools seems to have inflamed passions in more than one department. On 4 December 1929 the Instruction Publique (IP) Counselor for Syria wrote to the IP Counselor of the High Commission, "You have asked me for an account of the incidents of the agricultural school at Salamiya. I have the honor to let you know that this costly institution is the responsibility of the Minister of Agriculture to which I am not accredited" (CADN, Syrie-Liban/2, 76, "Enseignement officiel"). The amount requested for the school by the state of Syria in the 1929–1930 budget was 14,000 livres syriennes papier (CADN, Syrie-Liban/1, 954, "Budget

de l'Instruction Publique," "Liste des Travaux Demandés par les Divers Services de l'État de Syrie"), although the minister of public works noted that these amounts were subject to revision (CADN, Syrie-Liban/1, 954, "Budget de l'Instruction Publique," Minister of Public Works of the State of Syria to Hoppenot, 23 December 1929).

145. Even those students who managed to study abroad were not necessarily guaranteed the certification they sought. See, for example, ANF, F.10.2477, which documents the struggle of Syrian students attending the Montpellier National School of Agriculture to obtain the title of *ingénieur agricole*.

146. See "al-Muqtatafat," *al-Zira*ʿ*a al-Haditha* 3, nos. 6–7 (September-October 1927); 3, nos. 9–10 (December-January 1927); 3, no. 3 (April 1927); and 4, no. 1 (November 1928).

147. "1700 Madrasa Ziraʿiya," 212; "Rihla Ziraʿiya fi Filistin," *al-Zira*ʿ*a al-Haditha* 3, nos. 6–7 (September-October 1927): 445. The journal also closely followed developments in such neighboring countries as Turkey, for example, comparing the fact that three women in Turkey were able to pursue advanced agricultural studies at the same time that a decision had been taken to shut down the Salamiya school. See "al-Ziraʿa wa al-Jins al-Latif fi Turkiya," *al-Zira*ʿ*a al-Haditha* 5, nos. 9–10 (August-September 1932): 624.

148. See the author's remarks prefacing the second article in which he thanks readers for their compliments ("Hadith al-Fallah," *al-Zira*ʿ*a al-Haditha* 3, no. 4 [May 1927]: 242).

149. "Hadith al-Fallah," *al-Zira*ʿ*a al-Haditha* 3, no. 4 (May 1927): 242.

150. "L'agriculture," 19. Part of the problem was that this extraction would take some time to materialize as the agronomist needed several years to become acquainted with the local environment and assess how it responded to new experiments, yet he would expect to be paid, presumably from the start, more than a "simple supervisor [*wakil*]" (Debbané, *L'expérimentation agricole*," 41–42).

151. For this suggestion of refusal to invest, see Khoury, *Syria*, 446, 447. Khoury claims that "rarely did [landowning] families reinvest in the agricultural productivity of their lands or in agricultural-based industries," which he attributed to their preference for "exceedingly expensive pleasures" and proclivity for "conspicuous consumption." In fact, this tension between enthusiasm and reluctance may even reflect a generational divide among landowning elites. According to J. Gaulmier, in 1933 "it happens often that the notable is equipped with a scientific title obtained in a European agriculture school or has a diploma from the National School of Salamiya," which would indicate an initial investment even if they were not able/allowed to apply this knowledge in practice ([Gaulmier], "Notes sur la propriété foncière," 136). Médawar suggested that such a divide was already apparent in the early twentieth century (Médawar, *Syrie agricole*, 29–30). For more on financial insecurity, see chapter 5.

152. CADN, Syrie-Liban/1, 1571, "Mémoire de la Chambre d'Agriculture d'Alep sur la situation agricole," February 1928. The Aleppo Chamber of Agriculture also urged the high commissioner to combat pests more effectively with "skillful and active persons."

153. Dodge, "Institute of Rural Life," 214.

154. "Hadith al-Fallah," *al-Zira*ʿ*a al-Haditha* 3, no. 2 (March 1927): 122–26; "Hadith al-Fallah," *al-Zira*ʿ*a al-Haditha* 3, no. 4 (May 1927): 242–46.

155. "Hadith al-Fallah," *al-Zira*ʿ*a al-Haditha* 3, no. 4 (May 1927): 243.

156. "Hadith al-Fallah," *al-Zira*ʿ*a al-Haditha* 3, no. 4 (May 1927): 243.

157. "Hadith al-Fallah," *al-Zira*ʿ*a al-Haditha* 3, no. 4 (May 1927): 244–45.

158. "Hadith al-Fallah," *al-Ziraʿa al-Haditha* 3, no. 4 (May 1927): 244–45.

159. "Hadith al-Fallah," *al-Ziraʿa al-Haditha* 3, no. 4 (May 1927): 245–46.

160. "Hadith al-Fallah," *al-Ziraʿa al-Haditha* 3, no. 2 (March 1927): 122–26.

161. "Hadith al-Fallah," *al-Ziraʿa al-Haditha* 3, no. 2 (March 1927): 123.

162. "Hadith al-Fallah," *al-Ziraʿa al-Haditha* 3, no. 2 (March 1927): 124.

163. See chapter 3.

164. "Al-Muqtatafat," *al-Ziraʿa al-Haditha*, 4, no. 2 (December 1928): 32–33. Najjar would later become the director of agriculture for Lebanon.

165. ʿAtallah, "al-Hala al-Ziraʿiya wa al-Iqtisadiya fi Suriya," 132–34; "al-Taʿlim fi al-Barriya," *al-Ziraʿa al-Haditha* 5, no. 2 (December 1931): 75–78; "Madaris al-Qura wa al-Ziraʿa," *al-Ziraʿa al-Haditha* 5, no. 3 (January 1932): 147–48.

166. CADN, Syrie-Liban/2, 2, "Réforms fondamentales de l'Instruction Publique en Syrie," n.d. but contained in folder marked 1919–1920, p. 7.

167. Haut-Commissariat, *Syrie et le Liban sous l'occupation*, 103.

168. "Al-Taʿlim fi al-Barriya," 77–78.

169. CADN, Syrie-Liban/1, 863, "Étude sur la situation de l'agriculture au Liban," 23 April 1935. The committee seems to be referring to all schools, not just ones in villages.

170. Ministère des affaires étrangères, *Rapport (1929)*, 186.

171. CADN, Syrie-Liban/2, 67, "Requête des jeunes gens de Deir Zor," 16 November 1929.

172. "Al-Taʿlim fi al-Barriya," 75–78.

173. "Al-Taʿlim fi al-Barriya," 77.

174. "Al-ʿAlam al-Ziraʿi," *al-Ziraʿa al-Haditha* 5, no. 1 (November 1931): 65. On the Kadoorie school, see Kalisman, "Next Generation of Cultivators," 161–64.

175. "Al-Fallahun wa al-Batala," *al-Ziraʿa al-Haditha* 5, no. 1 (November 1931): 2–3.

176. "Al-Ziraʿa fi Suriya," *al-Ziraʿa al-Haditha* 2, nos. 6–7 (July-August 1925): 360–61.

177. "Khirriju al-Ziraʿa," 227.

178. "Khirriju al-Ziraʿa," 227. "Boldly" is how the writer characterized the article—"*al-kalima al-jariʾa*" (226).

179. "Khirriju al-Ziraʿa," 227. Inspectors from the Ottoman Civil Service School had commonly been called in to arbitrate disputes in rural areas.

180. A disagreement between Muhammad Kurd ʿAli, the minister of public instruction for Syria, and the High Commission further underscored concerns about oversight. In 1929 Kurd ʿAli lodged a complaint with the High Commission's secretary general about the elimination of inspector positions for Damascus and Hawran and their replacement with a post of inspector general (CADN, Syrie-Liban/1, 954, "Budget de l'Instruction Publique," Kurd ʿAli to the Inspector General, 31 December 1929). Stressing the suitability of those who held these posts, Kurd ʿAli highlighted both their close relation to those they inspected and their administrative training and acumen. Mustafa Bey Tamir, the inspector for Damascus, had twenty years of experience in teaching and administration and had taught most of the professors in the Faculty of Medicine and Law. Awad Bey Amiri, the inspector for the Hawran, not only hailed from the Hawran but also had studied in Europe, and as a Hawrani representative of the Syrian government he demonstrated the government's concern for the interests of the Hawran. Alluding to the inadequacy of mandate educational efforts, Kurd ʿAli added that the people of

the Hawran "did not cease to demand from the Syrian government the creation of new primary schools" (CADN, Syrie-Liban/1, 954, "Budget de l'Instruction Publique," Explications, 31 December 1929). An attached table of the budget proposed by the French counselor versus that proposed by the Syrian minister of public instruction indicated distinct priorities. The minister aimed to allot more to the salaries of the staff of the central administration, high schools, and primary schools as well as to scholarly materials, whereas the counselor proposed more for subsidies and repair work on the ruins of Palmyra. (The minister did not allot any funds for Palmyra, which he indicated should come out of the public works budget.) The issue of Damascus's concern for the Hawran was politically fraught; as discussed in chapter 5, French officials liked to highlight how the population of the Hawran felt neglected by Damascus despite being a major source of tax revenue, a disgruntlement readily exploited by French officials as part of their divide-and-rule strategy.

181. Lack of qualifications was an issue for both local and French officials (Khoury, *Syria*, 75–76, 116–17). The exiled Syro-Palestinian Congress was particularly scathing in its critique of French technicians working under the mandate; see CADN, Syrie-Liban/1, 960, "Rapport du Comité Exécutif du Congrès Syro-Palestinien d'Egypte à la S.D.N.," 20 June 1933.

182. CADN, Syrie-Liban/2, 36, "Programme d'enseignement professionnel au Liban," n.d. but attached to correspondence marked 11 February 1924; "Khirriju al-Zira^ca," 228–29.

183. "Khirriju al-Ziraʿa," 228–29.

184. Haut-Commissariat, *Syrie et le Liban sous l'occupation*, 113; "Madaris al-Qura wa al-Ziraʿa," *al-Ziraʿa al-Haditha* 5, no. 3 (January 1932): 147–48.

185. For more on the countryside versus city, see Khoury, *Syria*, 60–66.

186. UNAG, Session 22, 1932 Pétitions, 809, "Étudiants de l'École d'Agriculture de Selimie" to the High Commissioner, 2 January 1932. On the circumstances surrounding the elections, see Khoury, *Syria*, 365–74.

187. "Al-ʿAlam al-Ziraʿi," *al-Ziraʿa al-Haditha* 5, nos. 9–10 (August-September 1932): 622–23.

188. Khuri, "Agriculture," 100; Sarrage, *Nécessité*, 145.

189. "Al-ʿAlam al-Ziraʿi," 622. Khoury notes that the National Bloc "never stretched so far as to include problems of internal social and economic development, which they perceived to be inimical to their own interests" (Khoury, *Syria*, 264).

190. "Bilad Ziraʿiya bila Madrasa Ziraʿiya wa 200 Alf Lira Tunfiq ʿala Madrasat al-Tibb?!" *al-Qabas*, 30 August 1932; Najib al-Rayyis, "Tatlubu Tʿaliman Ibtidaʾiyan wa Ziraʿiyan ama Madrasat al-Tibb fayajab Ilghauʾha," *al-Qabas*, 31 August 1932. *Al-Qabas* was particularly incensed because the medical school received 200,000 lira a year while the agricultural school was being shut down.

191. "Al-ʿAlam al-Ziraʿi," 622.

192. "Hawla Ilghaʾ al-Madrasa al-Ziraʿiya," *al-Ziraʿa al-Haditha* 5, nos. 9–10 (August-September 1932): 523–24.

193. "Hawla Ilghaʾ al-Madrasa," 523–24. The journal had already made the point earlier that, although the school could graduate 100 students a year, if the government

was not going to provide posts for the school's graduates, then it might as well turn the school into an elementary one for the children of *fallahin*, citing the waste of spending 40,000 Syrian lira a year on ten graduates who go "knocking on government doors in vain" ("Khirriju al-Zira'a," 229).

194. CADN, Syrie-Liban/2, 100, "Enseignement officiel," "Loi de 6 juillet 1933."

195. CADN, Syrie-Liban/2, 100, "Enseignement officiel," Exposé des motifs, 1 October 1933. Although the government represented this as an imperfect solution to social conditions, internal meetings between French counselors continued to stress the difference between Syria and "the Occident," urging the examination of primary programs to ensure that they were not "too academic or too directly inspired by the Occident" (CADN, Syrie-Liban/2, 111, "Réunion des conseillers," 3rd session, 3 May 1934).

196. For a similar approach in Iraq, see Pursley, "Education for Real Life."

197. CADN, Syrie-Liban/2, 100, "Enseignement officiel," Exposé des motifs, 1 October 1933; and "Loi de 6 juillet 1933."

198. CADN, Syrie-Liban/1, 109, "Note sur l'enseignement," 11 July 1934.

199. CADN, Syrie-Liban/2, 168, "Note," 19 May 1941.

200. CADN, Syrie-Liban/2, 152, "Enseignement technique, professionnel, et agricole," "L'Enseignement Technique en Syrie et au Liban durant l'Année scolaire 1938–39."

201. CADN, Syrie-Liban/2, 152, "Enseignement technique, professionnel, et agricole," "L'Enseignement technique en Syrie et au Liban durant l'année scolaire 1938–39"; Dodge, "Institute of Rural Life," 214.

202. CADN, Syrie-Liban/2, 152, "Enseignement technique, professionnel, et agricole," "Note" from Bounoure to the Secretary General, 28 March 1939.

203. Who authorized this farming out is unclear.

204. CADN, Syrie-Liban/1, 864, "École d'Agriculture de Selemieh," "Information" signed by Berthelot, 18 November 1937. Tawfiq's brother is likely Khadir Shishakli, who had attended the school.

205. CADN, Syrie-Liban/2, 152, "Enseignement technique, professionnel, et agricole," Mirza Moustapha to Berthelot, 8 March 1939; "Note" from Bounoure to the Secretary General, 28 March 1939. Bounoure emphasized that he did not know de Fleurac and could not vouch for his capabilities.

206. See, for example, CADN, Syrie-Liban/1, 862, "État de Syria—La sécheresse et la situation agricole," "Le Conseiller pour l'Agriculture," 6 January 1933; and "La situation agricole," 29 December 1932 (this article is attributed to the "students with diplomas from the agricultural schools"; it does not make clear which schools are meant, but presumably the students of Salamiya would be among those writing). For more details, see also "Autour du rapport du Director de l'agriculture," *Les Échos de Damas*, 5 January 1933; and chapter 5.

207. CADN, Syrie-Liban/1, 862, "État de Syria—La sécheresse et la situation agricole," "La réforme agricole," 1, 2, 3 January 1933.

208. "Al-Madrasa al-Zira'iya," *Al-Qabas*, 27 April 1935.

209. The inspector was most likely Tawfiq Ahdab, who had been the director of the Salamiya agricultural school in the 1920s. See chapter 5 for more details.

210. CADN, Syrie-Liban/1, 109, "Note sur l'enseignement," 11 July 1934.

211. CADN, Syrie-Liban/1, 109, "Note sur l'enseignement," 11 July 1934.

212. Khoury, *Syria*, 445. The al-Yusuf family patriarch's interest in developing his lands is discussed in chapter 2.

213. Khoury, *Syria*, 448.

214. Khoury, *Syria*, 445–47; *Taqrir Ziraʿi ʿan Qura al-Btayha wa al-Julan*, 7–8, 28. This was exactly the approach to nationalist agricultural development suggested by al-Shihabi over a decade before.

215. *Taqrir Ziraʿi ʿan Qura al-Btayha wa al-Julan, ha-wa*, 40–41. The committee identified themselves as "farmers and landowners in Ghuta Damascus." It included two agricultural engineers, one of whom was Wasfi Zakariya, whose anecdote opened this chapter. The other was Nuri Ibish, who had received his degree from the "Agricultural College" in England and would become one of the biggest landowners in Damascus by the mandate's end, as well as Tawfiq and Shamsi al-Malki and Amin al-Dalati (Faris, *Min Huwa*, 47).

216. *Taqrir Ziraʿi ʿan Qura al-Btayha wa al-Julan*; Khoury, *Syria*, 449. See chapter 5 for a discussion of these taxation and agricultural bank policies.

217. CADN, Syrie-Liban/1, 863, "Étude sur la situation de l'agriculture au Liban," 23 April 1935; Johnson, *Class and Client in Beirut*, 65–67. Johnson notes that Daʿuq served on the Advisory Council established by French authorities in 1920 and, although nationalists boycotted elections in 1922, he was elected in 1925 to the Beirut Representative Council, from which position he engaged in vocal opposition to mandate policies. He was especially critical of the annexation of lands to create Greater Lebanon but was nonetheless willing to negotiate with mandate officials and act as intermediary between them and more hardline nationalists.

218. CADN, Syrie-Liban/1, 863, "Étude sur la situation de l'agriculture au Liban," 23 April 1935.

219. "Al-Ziraʿa fi al-Majlis al-Niyabi," *Al-Majallah al-ziraʿiya al-Suriya* 1, no. 2 (January 1939): 198–99.

220. CADN, Syrie-Liban/2, 67, "Exposition de la paix et de la Société de Nations," Schoeffler (?) to the High Commissionner, 6 November 1929.

221. CADN, Syrie-Liban/2, 62, "Rapport."

222. Haut-Commissariat, *Syrie et le Liban sous l'occupation*, 114–15.

223. CADN, Syrie-Liban/2, 89, "Centre agricole de Bouka," "Procès-verbal," 5 May 1930.

224. On the relative powerlessness of Representative Councils and reliance on the French, see Khoury, *Syria*, 134.

225. CADN, Syrie-Liban/2, 89, "Centre agricole de Bouka," "Procès-verbal," 5 May 1930. The Center cost 20,000 livres syriennes to run annually.

226. Haut-Commissariat, *Syrie et le Liban sous l'occupation*, 113; Sarrage, *Nécessité*, 146; CADN, Syrie-Liban/2, 87, "Subventions scolaires," Bounoure to Peyrton, June 1931. There was considerable correspondence about how to ensure that, should the agreement between the ʿAlawite State and the school be terminated before the 25 years of the contract were up, the funds invested by the Oeuvres françaises would not revert back to the ʿAlawite State. See CADN, Syrie-Liban/2, 89, "Centre agricole de Bouka." In 1935 the center also received a subsidy from the High Commission to facilitate the installation of

two looms. CADN, Syrie-Liban/1, 977, "École de Bouka," Lagarde to Schoeffler, 9 October 1935.

227. CADN, Syrie-Liban/2, 94, "Mandate français"; CADN, Syrie-Liban/2, 101, "Enseignement technique," "L'Enseignement professional." The school had twenty-eight students in 1932 and 1933. Most students were from Latakia, although some came from Palestine and Lebanon. Students from Jabal al-Druze and Alexandretta received scholarships to attend. In August 1934, thirty-one candidates had presented for admission, but only fourteen were accepted. (Ministère des affaires étrangères, *Rapport (1929)*, 81, 86; Ministère des affaires étrangères, *Rapport (1930)*, 114; Ministère des affaires étrangères, *Rapport (1931)*, 103; CADN, Syrie-Liban/2, 110, "Mandat français").

228. CADN, Syrie-Liban/1, 976, "Procès verbale du Conseil Représentatif du Gouvernement de Lattaquié," 12 December 1934; CADN, Syrie-Liban/2, 134, "Centre agricole de Bouka," Deputy Delegate for Latakia to Meyrier, 21 May 1937.

229. CADN, Syrie-Liban/1, 976, "Propaganda antimandataire," "Avant Propos à Monsieur le Gouverneur du Gouvernement de Lattaquié," n.d. but cover letter dated 30 September 1935.

230. Haut-Commissariat, *Syrie et le Liban sous l'occupation*, 113. CADN, Syrie-Liban/2, 134, "Centre agricole de Bouka," note from the Counselor for Public Instruction, 8 March 1937. This seems to have been a not uncommon issue with mandate agricultural institutions; the Maydan station in Aleppo had a similar problem.

231. The agriculture minister in 1932 used "second Ghuta" to refer to the area, an allusion to the oasis around Damascus. "Al-ʿAlam al-Ziraʿi," *al-Ziraʿa al-Haditha*, 5, nos. 9–10 (August-September 1932): 622. For Bériel's take, see CADN, Syrie-Liban/2, 109, "Note sur l'enseignement," 11 July 1934.

232. Haut-Commissariat, *Syrie et le Liban sous l'occupation*, 112.

233. "Madrasat al-Ziraʿa wa Abniyatiha," *al-Ziraʿa al-Haditha* 4, no. 6 (April 1929): 285–86. According to Tarmanini, the Salamiya school only had the buildings from the Ottoman era, despite hopes for advancing agriculture. He accused the government of being stingy in providing funds for even basic amenities, such as laboratories and stables. He insisted he was not aiming to make Salamiya similar to "agricultural schools of the West."

234. See Khoury, *Syria*, 457–81, 524.

235. CADN, Syrie-Liban/2, 134, "Centre agricole de Bouka," Peyrton to the Delegate General," 17 December 1935.

236. CADN, Syrie-Liban/2, 134, "Centre agricole de Bouka," Peyrton to the Delegate General," 17 December 1935; Delegate of the High Commissioner to the Alaouite State to Martel, 15 October 1936; "Note for the Secretary General," 4 May 1937.

237. CADN, Syrie-Liban/2, 134, "Centre agricole de Bouka," Kayali to the Governor of Latakia, 10 July 1937. In 1941 Peyrton requested over 700,000 francs from French administrators to start a secondary agricultural program at Bouka, but his request was denied for budgetary reasons. See CADN, Syrie-Liban/2, 167, "Enseignement technique et agricole," Peyrton to Bounoure (?), 29 January 1941; and Bounoure to Peyrton, 17 February 1941. Bounoure noted that he did not "renounce" the idea but that they would have to wait for "better days."

238. Al-Shihabi had noted the lack of "agricultural schools of all degrees" in a memorandum circulated in 1936. He also argued that peasants should be obligated to send their children to village schools (CADN, Syrie-Liban/2, 136, "Enseignement Officiel," circular from the Minister of Public Education, Mustafa Chehabi, 19 December 1936).

239. CADN, Syrie-Liban/2, 109, "Note sur l'enseignement," 11 July 1934; CADN, Syrie-Liban/1, 2173, "Orphelinat Foch," Lavastre, Assistant Delegate of Aleppo, to the High Commissioner, 19 October 1929, and High Commissioner to the Damascus Delegate, 26 March 1928; Sarrage, *Nécessité*, 145. Another mandate report dated the founding of the orphanage to the beginning of 1919 with 300 boys, most of whom were Armenian (CADN, Syrie-Liban/2, 68, "Inventaire économique des États sur Mandat," "Enseignement technique," 1929).

240. CADN, Syrie-Liban/2, 68, "Inventaire économique des États sur Mandat," "Enseignement technique," 1929; CADN, Syrie-Liban/1, 2173, "Orphelinat Foch," Damascus Delegate to the High Commissioner, 25 October 1927. The Oeuvres françaises allotted a 40,000 franc subsidy until 1930, and the state of Syria was prevailed on to contribute 32,500 francs, which it did until January 1934 (CADN, Syrie-Liban/2, 109, "Note sur l'enseignement," 11 July 1934).

241. CADN, Syrie-Liban/1, 2173, "Orphelinat Foch," Damascus Delegate to the High Commissioner, 1 March 1928; and Reclus to Delhumeau, 25 February 1928.

242. CADN, Syrie-Liban/1, 2173, "Orphelinat Foch," Damascus Delegate to the High Commissioner, 23 April 1928; CADN, Syrie-Liban/1, 2173, "Orphelinat Foch," "État de Service," 6 January 1928. After being fired from his post as agricultural director of Aleppo because he was Armenian, Oscan oversaw the fuel service at Aleppo's Baghdad railroad station with the same salary until the fall of Aleppo, after which he "was reappointed to government service in recognition of his prior services and decorated with a war medal." From September to April 1921 he was based in Adana, first as director of the French orphanage for Armenians and then as inspector for French orphanages, a post he left for personal reasons. During the mandate he had served as the agricultural agent for Jabal Samaan and Maara and as the under-inspector of agriculture and forests of the Agricultural Service of Aleppo and had been named director of the locust struggle in late 1923. He eventually had to retire from fighting locusts because it required frequent trips and, because of an illness, he found it too burdensome. Illness eventually put him in hospitals for thirteen and a half months.

243. CADN, Syrie-Liban/1, 2173, "Orphelinat Foch," Damascus Delegate to the High Commissioner, 23 April 1928.

244. CADN, Syrie-Liban/3, Direction du personnel 128, "Oscan," Oscan to Lavastre, 23 December 1930. Since 16 January 1928, Oscan had spent 20,500 francs on building construction and repair, 18,000 francs on materials, 5,000 francs on buying and repairing bed linens, and 5,000 francs on clothing and shoes. It should be noted that a series of contradictory reports dating from 1928 and 1929 (i.e., the first years in which Oscan would have served as director) suggest at first that the orphanage was well run in the third trimester of 1928 and the first trimester of 1929; then, suddenly, following an inspection in the second trimester of 1929, it was declared "unkept" and the supervisor was asked to resign. See CADN, Syrie-Liban/1, 2109,"Rapport Trimestriel [Alep], 2ème trimestre, 1929" and "Rapport Trimestriel [Alep], 3ème trimestre, 1929"; and CADN,

Syrie-Liban/1, 1848, "[Alep] Rapport Trimestriel, 1er trimestre, 1929." The same was also suggested for Oscan, although he was still running the orphanage in December 1930, and on the basis of his accomplishments since his arrival, Lavastre, the assistant delegate for Aleppo, suggested that he be rewarded with a 500 franc bonus at the end of the year. See CADN, Syrie-Liban/3, Direction du personnel 128, "Oscan," Lavastre to the High Commissioner, 27 December 1930.

245. CADN, Syrie-Liban/2, 109, "Note sur l'enseignement," 11 July 1934.

246. CADN, Syrie-Liban/2, 109, "Note sur l'enseignement," 11 July 1934.

247. CADN, Syrie-Liban/2, 109, "Note sur l'enseignement," 11 July 1934.

248. Bériel did not mention Oscan by name, indicating only that Muslimiya was being run by Armenians. I have found no evidence that Oscan was replaced or passed away during this period, so I assume it was still under his direction.

249. CADN, Syrie-Liban/2, 109, "Enseignement technique et professionnel," Abbé Gariador and Abbé de la Lajudie to Lagarde, 18 April 1934; CADN, Syrie-Liban/2, 85, "Étudiants orientaux en France." Obeid studied in France during the 1930–1931 school year.

250. CADN, Syrie-Liban/2, 109, "Enseignement technique et professionnel," Abbé Gariador and Abbé de la Lajudie to Lagarde, 18 April 1934.

251. CADN, Syrie-Liban/2, 109, "Enseignement technique et professionnel," Abbé Gariador and Abbé de la Lajudie to Lagarde, 18 April 1934; Bounoure to Lagarde, 13 September 1934. Bounoure noted that in the well-watered lands of the convent the monks primarily tended mulberries, fruit trees, and vegetables, which was not appropriate for an agricultural school. The dairy, which treated the milk of 10 cows and 300 goats, was, he contended, dilapidated, despite Abbot Gariador's insistence that over the past year the community had invested "significant capital" in transforming it into a "modern agricultural enterprise," although the crisis prevented them from expanding as much as they would have liked. Despite this effort to demonstrate the community's own investment in the project before asking for additional funds, Bounoure contended that if public Lebanese funds were used for the project—Gariador had requested 80,000 francs the first year and 30,000 francs for each following year—every other Greek and Maronite convent would claim to be starting an agricultural school and the rule of dividing subsidies among religious communities would "squander the allotted credit and make it completely ineffective." Despite these excuses, he may have considered the proposition worthwhile earlier on, as he mentioned a Greek Catholic project to Bériel that could be a possibility for agricultural education in the May 1934 counselors meeting (see CADN, Syrie-Liban/2, 111, "Réunion des conseillers," 3rd session, 3 May 1934).

252. CADN, Syrie-Liban/2, 109, "Enseignement technique et professionnel," Bounoure to Lagarde, 13 September 1934.

253. CADN, Syrie-Liban/2, 144, "Enseignement technique, agricole, et professionnel," ʿArida to Bounoure, 2 September 1938. Mandate officials considered the School of Arts and Métiers "the most important establishment of technical education" in the mandates. It had a French director until 1928, when a Lebanese director took over (CADN, Syrie-Liban/2, 68, "Inventaire économique des États sur Mandat," "Enseignement technique," 1929).

254. CADN, Syrie-Liban/2, 144, "Enseignement technique, agricole, et professionnel," Bounoure to ʿArida, 8 September 1938; Abisaab, "Warmed or Burnt"; Thompson, *Colonial Citizens*, 204.

255. CADN, Syrie-Liban/2, 152, "Enseignement technique, professionnel, et agricole," most of the residents of Bsharri to the High Commissioner, 2 July 1939; and most of the residents of Bsharri to the Counselor for Public Instruction, 2 July 1939.

256. CADN, Syrie-Liban/2, 77, "Institut de la Vie Rurale," Delegate in Latakia to the High Commission, 10 July 1930.

257. CADN, Syrie-Liban/2, 77, "Institut de la Vie Rurale," Bayard Dodge to the High Commissioner, 22 July 1930. For broader context about the American-French rivalry over education in the latter years of the mandate, see Dueck, *Claims of Culture, 164–80.*

258. CADN, Syrie-Liban/2, 77, "Institut de la Vie Rurale," agreement between the Near East Foundation and the American University of Beirut, 1 April 1930.

259. See also, for example, Ludden, "Introduction," in which he notes the way development and educational institutions used the language of science to transcend political divides (10).

260. CADN, Syrie-Liban/2, 77, "Institut de la Vie Rurale," "Note au sujet de la création d'un 'Institut de Vie Rurale,'" 22 July 1930.

261. CADN, Syrie-Liban/2, 77, "Institut de la Vie Rurale," "Note au sujet de la création d'un 'Institut de Vie Rurale,'" 22 July 1930.

262. CADN, Syrie-Liban/2, 85, "Institut de la Vie Rurale," "Note regarding 'The Near East Foundation,'" 15 May 1931.

263. CADN, Syrie-Liban/2, 85, "Institut de la Vie Rurale," "Note," 15 May 1931.

264. CADN, Syrie-Liban/2, 85, "Institut de la Vie Rurale," "Note," 15 May 1931.

265. CADN, Syrie-Liban/2, 85, "Institut de la Vie Rurale," "Note for the Secretary General," n.d.

266. CADN, Syrie-Liban/2, 85, "Institut de la Vie Rurale," note by Bounoure to the Secretary General, May 1931.

267. CADN, Syrie-Liban/2, 95, "Rapports," "Université Américaine de Beyrouth pendant l'année 1932"; Dodge, "Institute of Rural Life," 211. Dodge indicates that the institute trained seventy-five boys.

268. CADN, Syrie-Liban/2, 109, "Enseignement technique et professionnel," "Note . . . Inspections dans la Bekaa," 13 September 1934.

269. CADN, Syrie-Liban/2, 136, "Écoles étrangères," "Note pour M. Kieffer," 12 February 1937; AUB, Students, 1930s, Box 4, "Village Welfare Service Yearbook 1939–1940," "The Village Welfare Service," Halim Najjar, n.d.

270. AUB, Students, 1930s, Box 3, Village Welfare Service Yearbook 1938–1939, Harry G. Dorman Jr. to Halim Najjar, 9 June 1938; AUB, Students, 1930s, Box 4, "Village Welfare Service Yearbook 1939–1940," "The Village Welfare Service," Halim Najjar, n.d.

271. AUB, Students, 1930s, Box 4, "Village Welfare Service Yearbook 1939–1940," "The Village Welfare Service," Halim Najjar, n.d.; Dodge, "Institute of Rural Life," 215–16.

272. AUB, Students, 1930s, Box 3, Village Welfare Service Yearbook 1938–1939, "Report of the Committee on Agricultural Work." See also, for example, "Mashruʿ Inʿash al-Qariya," *al-Qabas*, 2 February 1937.

273. AUB, Students, 1930s, Box 4, Village Welfare Service Yearbook 1939–1940, "General Report for July, August, September, 1939."

274. CADN, Syrie-Liban/2, 152, "Enseignement technique, professionnel, et agricole," "L'Enseignement technique en Syrie et au Liban durant l'année scolaire 1938–39"; Dodge, "Institute of Rural Life," 214.

275. AUB, Students, 1930s, Box 4, Village Welfare Service Yearbook 1939–1940, Institute of Rural Life, "General Report for July, August, September, 1939."

276. AUB, Students, 1930s, Box 4, Village Welfare Service Yearbook 1939–1940, Institute of Rural Life, "Annual Narrative Report, 1 July 1938–30 June 1939."

277. AUB, Students, 1930s, Box 4, Village Welfare Service Yearbook 1939–1940, Institute of Rural Life, "Monthly report, January 1940." For a discussion of the acquisition of the al-ʿAbid and Quwwatli holdings, see Khoury, *Urban Notables*, 37–39, 41–42; for litigation involving the al-ʿAbid lands a few years after this course, see MWT, Sijil 257, [missing] to the Judge Commissioner, 15 April 1943.

278. CADN, Syrie-Liban/2, 102, "Mandat français," appended to a note dated 27 September 1933; Khoury, *Syria*, 137.

279. CADN, Syrie-Liban/2, 102, "Mandat français," appended to a note dated 27 September 1933.

Chapter Five

1. "Al-Ziraʿa fi al-Majlis al-Niyabi," *Al-Majalla al-Ziraʿiya al-Suriya* 1, nos. 3–4 (February-March 1939): 334–35. Al-Hakim would go on to serve as the works minister in at least two cabinets in 1945 (Longrigg, *Syria and Lebanon*, 345, 350) and as minister of economy in 1947 (Chaitani, *Post-Colonial Syria and Lebanon*, 81).

2. "Al-Ziraʿa fi al-Majlis al-Niyabi," 331–32, 337–39.

3. See N. Smith, *Uneven Development*; and Cooper, *Colonialism*, 91. Both of these scholars draw on the work of Henri Lefebvre in conceptualizing "unevenness." For an application of these concepts to colonial India, see Goswami, *Producing India*, esp. 36–37.

4. For an overview of the financial impacts of mandate policy on Syria, see al-Saleh, "Évaluation." For contestation regarding the linkage of the pound to the franc over the course of the mandate, see Khoury, *Syria*, 85–86, 480–81.

5. For a brief overview of these crises in the early 1930s, see Khoury, *Syria*, 398–99. However, environmental challenges started much earlier, as will be demonstrated in this chapter.

6. Williams, "Mapping the Cadastre."

7. See, for example, CADN, Syrie-Liban/1, 870, "Projet de moratoire pour les dettes foncières," Lavastre to the High Commissioner, 21 December 1933.

8. See, for example, Weulersse, *Paysans*, 173–209. On the pervasiveness of the discourse of progress, see Achard, "Syrie pays d'agriculture," 154, 168.

9. Khoury, *Syria*, 61, 65, 399; Batatu, *Syria's Peasantry*, 115–17; Provence, *Great Syrian Revolt*. Quote is from Khoury, *Syria*, 61. On the mandate regime's friendliness to peasants, see, in addition to Khoury, Schaebler, "Practicing *Mushaʿ*," 286; and Hanna, "Attitude."

10. Thompson, *Colonial Citizens*, 31, 80; Khoury, *Syria*, 399.

11. Ferguson, *Anti-Politics Machine*.

12. Ferguson, *Anti-Politics Machine*, 9. The original quote is, "What it does, how it does it, and why."

13. According to one local, mid-1930s assessment, "Syrian legislation appears to have been guided by financial and administrative requirements, rather than by the desire to effect an equitable distribution of the tax burden" (G. Hakim, "Fiscal System," 397).

14. This discourse would also be adopted by future historians. For example, Khoury claimed that peasants' "conservative" and "suspicious" reaction and resistance to mandate policies resulted from their insistence on maintaining their "traditional way of life" (Khoury, *Syria*, 64, 156, 157). An alternative assessment might recognize that this reaction reflected their awareness that these changes would make them less secure and more exposed to risk and exploitation.

15. Khoury, *Syria*, 62; Schaebler, "Practicing *Mushaʿ*," 280–82; Whitaker, "Union," 86–90.

16. Ministère des affaires étrangères, *Rapport (Juillet 1922–Juillet 1923)*, 53.

17. Himadeh, *Monetary and Banking System of Syria*, 220–21. ; Thobie, *Intérêts*, 468-472.

18. Haut-Commissariat, *Syrie et le Liban en 1922*, 225–26. Indeed the first application of the new tax in the *sanjak* of Alexandretta in 1929 did lead to higher returns (G. Hakim, "Fiscal System," 356).

19. See, for example, al-Ahdab, "al-Hala al-Ziraʿiya fi Suriya," 12.

20. G. Hakim, "Fiscal System," 345. See chapter 1 for more details. The land tax (*werko* or *vergi*) of 0.5% on *miri* land and 1.6% on *mülk* land, which was not tithed, also continued to be in effect but, according to one assessment, was relatively minor in comparison, although it still constituted another tax burden on agriculture (G. Hakim, "Fiscal System," 353–54).

21. Haut-Commissariat, *Syrie et le Liban sous l'occupation*, 236; G. Hakim, "Fiscal System," 347. See also Batatu, *Syria's Peasantry*, 61; and al-Shihabi, "Aham Adwaʾna al-Iqtisadiya wa Talafiha" (November 1928), 11.

22. Haut-Commissariat, *Syrie et le Liban sous l'occupation*, 236.

23. Al-Shihabi, "Aham Adwaʾna al-Iqtisadiya wa Talafiha" (November 1928), 10–11.

24. G. Hakim, "Fiscal System," 348–49; al-Shihabi, "Aham Adwaʾna al-Iqtisadiya wa Talafiha" (November 1928), 11.

25. Al-Shihabi, "Aham Adwaʾna al-Iqtisadiya wa Talafiha" (November 1928), 9.

26. Al-Shihabi, "Aham Adwaʾna al-Iqtisadiya wa Talafiha"(November 1928), 9–10. It is interesting that at this point in the speech al-Shihabi switches from referring to the *fallah*, which had been the primary actor in his narrative, to the *irbab al-ziraʿa*, which literally means "masters of agriculture" but seems to have been primarily used when referring to large landowners.

27. "Al-Ziraʿa fi Suriya 2: al-Daraʾib wa al-ʿAshar," *al-Ziraʿa al-Haditha* 2, no. 8 (October 1925): 446–47.

28. "Al-Ziraʿa fi Suriya 2: al-Daraʾib wa al-ʿAshar," 448.

29. Al-Shihabi, "Aham Adwaʾna al-Iqtisadiya wa Talafiha" (November 1928), 12. Al-Shihabi noted that the new tax was supposed to be suitable for local environmental conditions, such as years of drought, that could befall eastern regions or the losses caused by locusts, Sunn bugs (*souné*), or other pests, although he admitted that Arrêté 339 of 23 March 1927, which established the parameters of the tax, did not deal with how this would be accomplished and suggested that the government would have to study it (12).

30. ʿAtallah, "al-Hala al-Ziraʿiya wa al-Iqtisadiya fi Suriya," 132.

31. Haut-Commissariat, *Syrie et le Liban en 1922*, 226; Haut-Commissariat, *Syrie et le Liban en 1921*, 168; Haut-Commissariat, *Syrie et le Liban sous l'occupation*, 236. The *tertib* involved a calculation based on the surface area cultivated, the land's productive capacity, and the value of its produce.

32. G. Hakim, "Fiscal System," 347; Haut-Commissariat, *Syrie et le Liban sous l'occupation*, 236.

33. G. Hakim, "Fiscal System," 347; Sadir, *Majmuʿat*, 3: 20–21. Notably, the law did not refer to a more equitable distribution of the tax burden.

34. Al-Jazaʾiri, "al-Islah al-Ziraʿi fi Suriya 2," 523. The intent, al-Jazaʾiri explained, had been to "impose a set tax on the land and save the *fallah* from control of the oppressors/usurpers [*al-mutighalliba*] and large landowners [*iktaʿiyin*]," but ultimately "these approaches did not benefit the government at that time so it returned to the tithe." Al-Jazaʾiri noted that the government had similarly instituted the *tasdis*, an average of six years, in Macedonia.

35. Al-Shihabi, "Aham Adwaʾna al-Iqtisadiya wa Talafiha" (November 1928), 11.

36. Al-Ahdab, "al-Hala al-Ziraʿiya fi Suriya," 15; al-Ahdab, "Daraʾib al-Ziraʿa fi Suriya," 360; al-Ahdab, "Daraʾib al-Ziraʿiya fi Suriya 2," 465.

37. Al-Ahdab, "Daraʾib al-Ziraʿiya fi Suriya 2," 462, 466.

38. Al-Ahdab, "Daraʾib al-Ziraʿiya fi Suriya 2," 465–66. In particular, al-Ahdab criticized road, entrance, and poll taxes.

39. Al-Ahdab, "al-Hala al-Ziraʿiya fi Suriya," 13. Government policies in France around the time of World War I had indeed sought to shore up the security of small rural property owners. These policies included lighter taxes (by 1929, French peasants contributed only 5% of the country's revenue from income tax) and 25-year loans from the Crédit Agricole at 1% interest or, following the war, 2% interest for former soldiers—a far cry from the lending policies enacted by mandate officials in Syria (Moulin, *Peasantry*, 141–42).

40. Al-Ahdab, "al-Hala al-Ziraʿiya fi Suriya," 14–15.

41. "Muqtatafat—al-Daraʾib al-Ziraʿiya," *al-Ziraʿa al-Haditha* 5, no. 5 (March 1932): 332, which is a reprinted excerpt from *al-Hayat al-Ziraʿiya* 1, no. 3.

42. Ministère des affaires étrangères, *Rapport (Juillet 1922–Juillet 1923)*, 29–30, 53.

43. CADN, Syrie-Liban/3, Direction du personnel 59, "Duraffourd," Duraffourd to Gouraud, 24 September 1920.

44. CADN, Syrie-Liban/3, Direction du personnel 59, "Duraffourd," Duraffourd to Gouraud, 24 September 1920.

45. CADN, Syrie-Liban/3, Direction du personnel 59, "Duraffourd," note added to Duraffourd letter to Gouraud, 30 September 1920.

46. CADN, Syrie-Liban/1, 1571, "Agriculture 1927–1928," "Notes Achard—Le Problème de l'Agriculture Syrienne: Le problème agraire," 19 December 1925. As discussed in chapter 3, French-capitalized banks were anxious to establish legislation that would protect their interests (MAE, Syrie-Liban 72, "Note Jointe," 24 June 1921, pp. 155–59). According to a cadastral report from 1922, "It is not without interest to note that the French establishments of credit, previously or newly created, were the principal beneficiaries of loan operations on mortgages, of which the country had a pressing need to improve its commercial and agricultural situation" (CADN, Syrie-Liban/1, 388, "Notice sur

les Services Fonciers de Syrie," 1922, p. 5). The laws governing the property created by these efforts would ensure that these lands were legible to the capital of foreign banks.

47. Achard, "Syrie pays d'agriculture," 164.

48. Haut-Commissariat, *Syrie et le Liban en 1922*, 226, 321. See also Achard, "Syrie pays d'agriculture," 164, 168.

49. Demangeon, *Déclin*, 299, 300.

50. Bivar, *Organic Resistance*, 16, 28–29; Jones, "Challenge of Land Reform," 120, 136, 140.

51. CADN, Syrie-Liban/1, 1571, "Agriculture 1927–1928," "Notes Achard—Le Problème de l'Agriculture Syrienne: Le problème agraire," 19 December 1925, p. 7; CADN, Syrie-Liban/1, 870, "Notice sur le démembrement et l'aménagement des terres "mouchaa" possédées dans l'indivision collective," 1935, p. 3.

52. ʿAtallah, "al-Hala al-Ziraʿiya wa al-Iqtisadiya fi Suriya 3," 237; "Al-Ziraʿa fi Suriya. 3: al-mushaʿ," *al-Ziraʿa al-Haditha* 2, no. 9 (November 1925): 513.

53. ʿAtallah, "al-Hala al-Ziraʿiya wa al-Iqtisadiya fi Suriya," 131.

54. See, for example, Khoury, *Syria*, 61–62, 64, 157. As discussed in chapter 1, scholars have argued that the practice of *mushaʿ* was a relatively recent development.

55. Even French officials, when it suited their purposes, recognized the benefits of *mushaʿ*. One noted that it "permitted fellahs to resist the influence of large urban landowners" (Weulersse, *L'Oronte*, 71). Doreen Warriner, writing in the aftermath of Syrian independence, claimed that Duraffourd himself "considered that the *mushaa* custom had a real basis in the social life of the country and should not be abolished," although I have yet to find a statement to this effect from Duraffourd himself and a study he produced in 1935 is highly critical of the practice (Warriner, *Land and Poverty*, 91; CADN, Syrie-Liban/1, 870, "Notice sur le démembrement," 1935).

56. Himadeh, *Monetary and Banking System of Syria*, 220.

57. Ministère des affaires étrangères, *Rapport (Juillet 1922–Juillet 1923)*, 30.

58. Himadeh, *Monetary and Banking System of Syria*, 220.

59. Al-Jazaʾiri, "al-Islah al-Ziraʿi fi Suriya," 429–30.

60. Shishakli, "Bahith fi al-Tashriʿ al-Ziraʿi"; Shishakli, "Bahith fi al-Tashriʿ al-Ziraʿi 2"; Shishakli, "Bahith fi al-Tashriʿ al-Ziraʿi [3]"; Shishakli, "al-Tashriʿ al-Ziraʿi."

61. Al-Jazaʾiri, "al-Islah al-Ziraʿi fi Suriya," 428–29; "Purchase of Land (Ireland) Act, 1891," http://www.irishstatutebook.ie/eli/1891/act/48/enacted/en/print.html.

62. Al-Jazaʾiri, "al-Islah al-Ziraʿi fi Suriya," 428–29; al-Shihabi, "Aham Adwaʾna al-Iqtisadiya wa Talafiha 2" (January 1928 [1929?]), 29.

63. Al-Shihabi, "Aham Adwaʾna al-Iqtisadiya wa Talafiha 2" (January 1928 [1929?]), 29.

64. Al-Shihabi, "Aham Adwaʾna al-Iqtisadiya wa Talafiha 2" (January 1928 [1929?]), 34. Although al-Shihabi did not expound on what would constitute an acquisition that was not "by right," it seems possible that some of the shenanigans discussed in chapter 1 might qualify.

65. Al-Jazaʾiri, "al-Islah al-Ziraʿi fi Suriya," 430–31; "Al-Ziraʿa fi Suriya 2: al-Malakun," *al-Ziraʿa al-Haditha* 2, no. 8 (October 1925): 444. Of course, such a law could lead to other problems; see Jakes, *Egypt's Occupation*, 214–15.

66. Al-Jazaʾiri, "al-Islah al-Ziraʿi fi Suriya 2," 524–25. Among the measures al-Jazaʾiri proposed were to set limits on the period of tenancy or guarantee a cultivator had to stay in particular village, give cultivators the freedom to sow as they desired, and

restrict the land rent or the guarantee so as to enable an owner to improve his or her land.

67. Al-Shihabi, "Aham Adwaʾna al-Iqtisadiya wa Talafiha 3" (February 1929),174.

68. ʿAtallah, "al-Hala al-Ziraʿiya wa al-Iqtisadiya fi Suriya 3," 237.

69. ʿAtallah, "al-Hala al-Ziraʿiya wa al-Iqtisadiya fi Biladna 4," 315.

70. On the declaration of boundaries, expanses, place, and name, see ʿAtallah, "al-Hala al-Ziraʿiya wa al-Iqtisadiya fi Suriya 3," 238.

71. ʿAtallah, "al-Hala al-Ziraʿiya wa al-Iqtisadiya fi Suriya 3," 238.

72. ʿAtallah, "al-Hala al-Ziraʿiya wa al-Iqtisadiya fi Suriya 3," 239–40. Abdulhamid II's lands, or *Emlak-ı Hümayun*, had provided the sultan with his own substantial personal income during the late Ottoman period until they were transferred to the state after the 1908 CUP revolution. Under the mandate, they became incorporated into state "domaines" land. On the Sultan's lands, see Yücel, "Sustaining the Empire."

73. ʿAtallah, "al-Hala al-Ziraʿiya wa al-Iqtisadiya fi Biladna 4," 316.

74. ʿAtallah, "al-Hala al-Ziraʿiya wa al-Iqtisadiya fi Biladna 4," 316–17. ʿAtallah suggested dividing land into mountainous and plains regions, and within these two basic divisions dividing it into six more categories: good irrigated land without trees, good rain-fed land without trees, average rain-fed land without trees, poor rain-fed land without trees, irrigated land with trees, and rain-fed land with trees.

75. Al-Jazaʾiri, "al-Islah al-Ziraʿi fi Suriya 2," 524.

76. G. Hakim, "Fiscal System," 355, 356.

77. CADN, Syrie-Liban/1, 971, "Étude relative à la dime et au Wirgho en vigueur en Syrie, et au Tertib en vigueur au Maroc et en Tunisie," 20 October 1938, p. 46.

78. Himadeh, *Monetary and Banking System of Syria*, 221.

79. Khuri, "Land Tenure," 64–65, 69; Sarrage, *Nécessité*, 42–43. Roger Owen and Şevket Pamuk suggest that this figure was less than half the land under cultivation by 1938 (*History*, 65), although another estimate from 1936 put the cultivated area at 1 million hectares, or one-fourth of the total cultivatable area (Khuri, "Agriculture," 73). The discrepancy could in part be due to whether fallow was included. Khuri noted that 2 million hectares were "used" for agriculture, but half of that was allowed to lie fallow, so only 1 million was cultivated. Fallow is an essential part of the cycle that maintains soil fertility and would have been counted among a farmers' shares and included in the cadastral survey, suggesting the land to be surveyed and registered was closer to at least 2 million hectares. Ultimately 4 million hectares were estimated to be cultivatable, including marshlands, lands lacking irrigation, lands too close to the desert and therefore subject to incursions by pastoralists, or areas cultivatable only with "modern methods" (Khuri, "Land Tenure," 73–75). By the end of 1940, one report indicated that 3 million hectares in Syria and 380,000 hectares in Lebanon had been mapped by the cadastre (F. Saadé, "Problème," 20), which would be about three-fourths of this cultivatable land, although another report from 1944 suggested that only 40% of Syria's "inhabited lands" had been mapped (Republic of Syria, *Economic Development of Syria*, 8). At the beginning of 1953, another report put the figure at 45% (International Bank for Reconstruction and Development, *Economic Development of Syria*).

80. G. Hakim, "Fiscal System," 348–49, 397–98; Sarrage, *Nécessité*, 128; Sadir, *Majmuʿat*, 3: 20–21.

81. G. Hakim, "Fiscal System," 349. The *arrêté* only explicitly referred to flood and locusts; it did not mention drought.

82. Sarrage, *Nécessité*, 125.

83. The exchange rate of the American dollar fluctuated between 54.7 Syrian piastres in April 1922 to 202.8 piastres in July 1926 (Himadeh, "Monetary and Banking System," 265).

84. G. Hakim, "Fiscal System," 351–52. Hakim indicates that this conversion happened in 1927, but several French intelligence reports suggest that it had already gone into effect in 1926 (CADN, Syrie-Liban/1, 1845, "État des Alaouites Rapport Trimestriel, Avril-Mai-Juin 1926," 15 August 1926; CADN, Syrie-Liban/1, 1845, "Rapport trimestriel Hama, 4ème trimestre, 1926," 15 January 1927).

85. Sarrage, *Nécessité*, 127. An article in *al-Ziraʿa al-Haditha* placed this increase at 100% (Muzariʿ Kabir [a large farmer], "Maslaha al-Khazina wa Maslaha al-Zarraʿ," *al-Ziraʿa al-Haditha* 4, nos. 9–10 (November-December 1929): 456). A British estimate cited by Khoury places it at 87.5%, although the chronology appears off, as he suggests French unwillingness "to adjust land taxes [*impôt foncier*?] to the prevailing rate of exchange" was "a catalyst for the revolt" (Khoury, *Syria*, 213). Because this increase did not go into effect until 1927 (or 1926), when the revolt was in its final days (or at least well underway), it could hardly have been a catalyst, although it may have increased discontent toward the end. A French report from Latakia put the increase there in 1926 at 86% (CADN, Syrie-Liban/1, 1845, "État des Alaouites Rapport Trimestriel, Avril-Mai-Juin 1926," 15 August 1926). On pegging the French franc to the Syrian pound, see Khoury, *Syria*, 86, 137, 213.

86. The government had proposed a 3 to 1 rate. The application of the *terbiʿ* in Greater Lebanon differed from Syria on several points. Notably, it was applied only in those areas that were not part of the former *mutasarrifiyya* of Mount Lebanon and farmers did not have the option to ask for an assessment of their crops (G. Hakim, "Fiscal System," 352).

87. Haut-Commissariat, *Syrie et le Liban sous l'occupation*, 236.

88. G. Hakim, "Fiscal System," 397.

89. See Provence, *Great Syrian Revolt*; Khoury, *Syria*, 205.

90. CADN, Syrie-Liban/1, 1843, "Rapport Trimestriel [Aleppo], 4° trimestre, 1924."

91. Barudi, "Hasharat al-Suna," 38; Hallaj, "Hasharat al-Suna fi Suriya," 287. The 1911 Sunn bug attack had spared some villages near the ʿAsi River where land was more humid.

92. Hallaj, "Hasharat al-Suna fi Suriya," 287; CADN, Syrie-Liban/1, 1843, "Rapport Trimestriel [Aleppo], 4° trimestre, 1924."

93. CADN, Syrie-Liban/1, 1843, "Rapport Trimestriel [Aleppo], 4° trimestre, 1924."; CADN, Syrie-Liban/1, 1843, "Rapport Trimestriel, 3ème trimestre 1924, Damas, 28 October 1924." In 1924 the Sunn pest also appeared in areas of Tartus and at the Bouka farm in Latakia. In 1925 it returned to Bouka and was found around Tyre in southern Lebanon. More broadly, it appeared in Mosul, Iran, southern Russia, Greece, and Italy (Hallaj, "Hasharat al-Suna fi Suriya," 288).

94. CADN, Syrie-Liban/1, 1843, "Rapport Trimestriel [Aleppo], 4° trimestre, 1924."

95. Among the observations obtained from villagers and reported by *al-Ziraʿa al-Haditha* to its readership were the following: Peasants who were carrying out winter plowing of a field stumbled upon a bunch of Sunn bugs, buried 30 cm deep under a rock,

that had survived the intense cold. The bugs started to emerge from the ground in early March, appearing first on land exposed to heat and spreading as the temperature warmed. Villagers had seen eggs in the soil on the roots of plants, not just on plant leaves, and eggs were produced at different times depending on the village; mating observed in early May indicated that the bugs mated more than once (Hallaj, "Hasharat al-Suna fi Suriya," 288–91).

96. Barudi, "Hasharat al-Suna," 39–40; Kurd ʿAli, *Kitab Khitat al-Sham*, 4: 194–95. Barudi also challenged what he deemed some farmers' misconceptions about the insect, claiming that the idea that it did not perish for three years after it first appeared was "nonsense" (*haraʾ*), that leaving a field fallow for two to three years did not deter it, and that it was incorrect to believe that two kinds of Sunn bug existed—a white variety and a black variety—and that it was the black one that was destructive. Rather, he countered with his own observations that these varieties were actually the same insect, just at different stages of the life cycle (Barudi, "Hasharat al-Suna," 39–40).

97. CADN, Syrie-Liban/1, 1844, "Rapport trimestriel, 2ème trimestre 1925, État du Djebel Druze 1925." Other reports offered conflicting assessments of the damage caused by drought in the Hauran (CADN, Syrie-Liban/1, 1844, "Rapport Trimestriel Damas, 2ème trimestre, 1925"; CADN, Syrie-Liban/1, 1844, "Rapport Trimestriel, État de Syrie, 2ème trimestre, 1925").

98. CADN, Syrie-Liban/1, 1844, "Rapport Trimestriel, Étate de Syrie, 2ème trimestre, 1925."

99. Hallaj, "Hasharat al-Suna fi Suriya," 288.

100. Khoury, *Syria*, 168.

101. "Al-Ziraʿa fi Suriya: al-Fallah wa al-Hukuma," *al-Ziraʿa al-Haditha* 2, nos. 6–7 (July 1925): 361.

102. Ministère des affaires étrangères, *Rapport (1925)*, 17–18. See also Provence, *Great Syrian Revolt*, 51–52; and Khoury, *Syria*, 156–57. According to the MAE report, vines were chosen because "the raisin is an important element of Druze food" (17). The details of the situation suggest that this project did not intend to "transform" communally held property that was already under cultivation in Jabal al-Druze (Khoury, *Syria*, 156). The fact that peasants had to clear the fields of stones before planting the grapevines suggests that these were not the same lands held according to *mushaʿ* arrangements, where they planted their grains; rather, the implication seems to be that they would hold these vineyards privately alongside their communally held grain fields.

103. Khoury, *Syria*, 156–60; Provence, *Great Syrian Revolt*, 51–62.

104. Ministère des affaires étrangères, *Rapport (1925)*, 110. Greater Lebanon's law was passed on 16 May 1925, Syria's on 29 June 1925, and the Alawite State's on 23 April 1925.

105. CADN, Syrie-Liban/1, 2432 bis, report titled "État du Grand-Liban: Travaux du cadastre et d'amélioration agricole," 31 May 1925, p. 17.

106. Khoury, *Syria*, 160–61. The spread of the revolt from the Hawran to Damascus followed networks of relationships long established through the grain trade between Druze farmers and Damascene merchants and moneylenders, particularly in the city's southern Maydan quarter.

107. Khoury, *Syria*, 172–73.

108. CADN, AE 217, Duraffourd to the Delegate of the High Commission for the State of Syria, 5 December 1925.

109. TNA, FO 406.56, "Further Correspondence Respecting Eastern Affairs, Part XVII," July–December 1925.

110. Khoury, *Syria*, 180–81.

111. Khoury, *Syria*, 185–87.

112. See, for example, Khoury, *Syria*, 173, 177, 181, 187; and CADN, AE 217, Duraffourd to the Delegate of the High Commission for the State of Syria, 5 December 1925.

113. CADN, Syrie-Liban/1, 1844, "Rapport Trimestriel Grand Liban (Octobre, Novembre, et Décembre 1926)," 12 February 1927.

114. CADN, Syrie-Liban/1, 1845, "Rapport Trimestriel Hama, 4ème trimestre, 1926," 15 January 1927.

115. Al-Ahdab, "Ziraʿat al-Hinta" (May 1927), 228.

116. Al-Ahdab, "Ziraʿat al-Hinta" (May 1927), 228. Barudi, "Hasharat al-Suna," 28. The Sunn bug did not affect sorghum or chickpeas.

117. CADN, Syrie-Liban/1, 1571, "Agriculture 1927–1928," report by Achard titled "Les emblavures de Blé et d'Orge de la campagne agricole 1926–1927," 15 February 1927.

118. Al-Ahdab, "Ziraʿat al-Hinta" (May 1927), 228. A French report seemed unaware of these efforts, noting in January 1927 that "it does not seem that anywhere had one done trials of early-maturing wheat recommended by the inspector of Agriculture" (CADN, Syrie-Liban/1, 1845, "Rapport Trimestriel Hama 1926," 15 January 1927). The journal ceased publication for 1926 as a result of financial losses from meager subscriptions ("al-Ziraʿa al-Haditha fi ʿAmha al-Rabaʿ" *al-Ziraʿa al-Haditha* 3, no. 1 (February 1927): 1).

119. Al-Ahdab, "Ziraʿat al-Hinta" (May 1927), 229–30.

120. Al-Ahdab, "Ziraʿat al-Hinta" (September-October 1927), 456–61.

121. CADN, Syrie-Liban/1, 1845, "Rapport Trimestriel Hama, 4ème trimestre, 1927," 13 January 1928.

122. CADN, Syrie-Liban/1, 1846, "Alep Rapport Trimestriel, 2ème trimestre, 1927."

123. CADN, Syrie-Liban/1, 1847, "Alep Rapport Trimestriel, 2ème trimestre, 1928."

124. Hibrawi, "Faʾr al-Haql," 231–32; Barudi, "al-Faʾr al-Barri wa Adraruh," 152; CADN, Syrie-Liban/1, 1846, "Alep Rapport Trimestriel, 2ème trimestre, 1927."

125. Hilmi Barudi, for example, noted that, for eradication methods to be effective, they needed to be generally applied in all lands affected by voles and it was the government's responsibility to organize this work (Barudi, "al-Faʾr al-Barri wa Adraruh," 156).

126. "Al-ʿAlam al-Ziraʿi—Muʾtamar al-Jarad al-Dawli," *al-Ziraʿa al-Haditha* 4, no. 3 (December 1928): 51; "al-ʿAlam al-Ziraʿi—al-Jarad fi Suriya," *al-Ziraʿa al-Haditha* 4, nos. 9–10 (November-December 1929): 523–24. On the broader locust fight, see Dolbee, *Locusts of Power.*

127. Jas, "Public Health," 372. In France doctors and pharmacists fiercely opposed the increasing use of these poisons, particularly those containing arsenic, but they faced pushback from others who insisted on the pesticides' economic importance, leading to relatively lax enforcement of regulations to protect public health (371–74).

128. CADN, Syrie-Liban/1, 1846, "[Alep] Rapport Trimestriel, 1er trimestre, 1927"; CADN, Syrie-Liban/1, 1846, "Alep Rapport Trimestriel, 2ème trimestre, 1927"; CADN, Syrie-Liban/1, 1845, "Rapport trimestriel Grand Liban, 2ème trimestre, 1927"; CADN, Syrie-Liban/1, 1847, "Vilayet d'Alep Rapport Trimestriel, 1er trimestre, 1928"; CADN, Syrie-Liban/1, 1848, "[Alep] Rapport Trimestriel, 1er trimestre, 1929."

129. CADN, Syrie-Liban/1, 1846, "Sandjak Autonome d'Alexandrette, Rapport pour le 2ème trimestre de l'année 1928"; CADN, Syrie-Liban/1, 1846, "Alep Rapport Trimestriel, 2ème trimestre, 1927"; CADN, Syrie-Liban/1, 1846, "[Alep] Rapport Trimestriel, 1er trimestre, 1927."

130. CADN, Syrie-Liban/1, 1846, "[Alep] Rapport Trimestriel, 1er trimestre, 1927."

131. Hibrawi, "Fa'r al-Haql," 231–32.

132. CADN, Syrie-Liban/1, 1846, "[Alep] Rapport Trimestriel, 1er trimestre, 1927"; CADN, Syrie-Liban/1, 1847, "Vilayet d'Alep Rapport Trimestriel, 2ème trimestre, 1928"; CADN, Syrie-Liban/1, 1847, "Rapport Trimestriel Grand Liban, 2ème trimestre, 1928"; CADN, Syrie-Liban/1, 1847, "Rapport Trimestriel Grand Liban, 1er trimestre, 1928"; CADN, Syrie-Liban/1, 1847, "Vilayet d'Alep Rapport Trimestriel, 1er trimestre, 1928."

133. "Al-ʿAlam al-Ziraʿi—Faʾr al-Haql," *al-Ziraʿa al-Haditha* 4, no. 3 (December 1928): 53; "Faʾr al-Haql," *al-Ziraʿa al-Haditha* 5, no. 4 (February 1932): 234; CADN, Syrie-Liban/1, 1846, "Alep Rapport Trimestriel, 2ème trimestre, 1927."

134. CADN, Syrie-Liban/1, 1845, "Rapport Trimestriel Hama 1927," 25 July 1927.

135. "Al-ʿAlam al-Ziraʿi—Mukafaha al-Jarad fi al-Jazaʾir Ghayrha fi Suriya," *al-Ziraʿa al-Haditha* 4, nos. 9–10 (November-December 1929): 519–20. The people and supplies mobilized in Algeria involved "60,000 workers, 4,000 soldiers, 200,000 zinc plates, 2,658 pieces of cloth, 1,696 mechanical sprayers, 764 flame bellows, 65 flamethrowers, 494 air bottles, 549 barrels, 951 hoes, 1,011 shovels, 353 normal sprayers, 73 [?] and 538 gloves, and 252 masks" as well as "300,380 liters of Karzil (?), 21,337 kilograms of heavy oil, and 190,000 grams of molasses, and 78,680 kilograms of arseniate soda." The journal *Doğru Yol* also urged the government to use zinc plates (CADN, Syrie-Liban/1, 1846, "[Alep] Rapport Trimestriel, 1er trimestre, 1927"). For a description of other methods used to fight the insects, see Dolbee, *Locusts of Power.*

136. CADN, Syrie-Liban/1, 1847, "Vilayet d'Alep Rapport Trimestriel, 2ème trimestre, 1928."

137. CADN, Syrie-Liban/1, 1846, "[Alep] Rapport Trimestriel, 1er trimestre, 1927."

138. CADN, Syrie-Liban/1, 1847, "Vilayet d'Alep Rapport Trimestriel, 1er trimestre, 1928."

139. CADN, Syrie-Liban/1, 1845, "Rapport Trimestriel Hama, 3ème trimestre, 1927," 26 October 1927.

140. CADN, Syrie-Liban/1, 1846, "Vilayet d'Alep Rapport Trimestriel, 3ème trimestre, 1927," 9 November 1927.

141. CADN, Syrie-Liban/1, 1846, "Rapport Trimestriel Hama, 2ème trimestre, 1928," 30 June 1928.

142. CADN, Syrie-Liban/1, 1846, "Rapport Trimestriel Homs, 2° trimestre, 1928."

143. CADN, Syrie-Liban/1, 1846, "Vilayet d'Alep Rapport Trimestriel, 3ème trimestre, 1927," 9 November 1927."

144. MAE, Syrie-Liban 566, telegram from Aleppo, 18 July 1930, p. 12.

145. "Al-Ziraʿa wa al-Daraʾib," *al-Ziraʿa al-Haditha* 4, nos. 7–8 (May-June 1929): 346.

146. Al-Ahdab, "al-Daraʾib wa al-Ziraʿa," 14–15.

147. Al-Ahdab, "al-Daraʾib ʿala al-Ziraʿa fi Suriya," 362–64.

148. Al-Ahdab, "al-Daraʾib ʿala al-Ziraʿa fi Suriya," 365.

149. Al-Ahdab, "al-Daraʾib ʿala al-Ziraʿa fi Suriya," 366–68.

150. "ʿAlam al-Ziraʿa—Qarar al-aʿshar," *al-Ziraʿa al-Haditha* 4, nos. 7–8 (May-June 1929): 425–26; Sarrage, *Nécessité*, 128.

151. "ʿAlam al-Ziraʿa—Qarar al-aʿshar," *al-Ziraʿa al-Haditha* 4, nos. 7–8 (May-June 1929): 425–26.

152. Muzariʿ Kabir, "Maslaha al-Khazina," 457.

153. Muzariʿ Kabir, "Maslaha al-Khazina," 458–59.

154. Muzariʿ Kabir, "Maslaha al-Khazina," 457, 461.

155. G. Hakim, "Fiscal System," 350; Sarrage, *Nécessité*, 128.

156. Himadeh, "Monetary and Banking System," 313.

157. Himadeh, "Monetary and Banking System," 311, 317–18.

158. See, for example, CADN, Syrie-Liban/1, 1845, "Rapport trimestriel, Hama, 4ème trimestre, 1927," 13 January 1928; and Himadeh, "Monetary and Banking System," 317.

159. Himadeh, "Monetary and Banking System," 310–11. This was one of the primary aims of the 20 March 1922 Arrêté 1329 establishing a "modern mortgage regime," which "regulate[d] more definitely the rights of the privileged creditors in mortgage, lien, and sale with power of redemption" (Himadeh, *Monetary and Banking System of Syria*, 220).

160. MAE, Syrie-Liban 330, President of CFAT to Minister of Foreign Affairs, 10 February 1928. The letter notes that there was an *arrêté* issued just before this policy was created that the president felt would "permit the resumption and intensification of our operations in Syria" regarding mortgages, in which the bank planned to engage.

161. Himadeh, "Monetary and Banking System," 310.

162. MAE, Syrie-Liban 331, Banque de Syrie et du Grand Libran to the Minister of Foreign Affairs, 29 December 1927. The bank considered that the agricultural banks' current mode of operation "left much to be desired."

163. MAE, Syrie-Liban 331, Banque de Syrie et du Grand Libran to the Minister of Foreign Affairs, 29 December 1927; Himadeh, *Monetary and Banking System of Syria*, 225. Himadeh noted that companies offering mortgage credit were required to provide a full report of their accounts only if their head offices were in the mandate states. Because all the companies offering these credits under the mandate were foreign, they were not subject to this stipulation. As one disgruntled technocrat put it, their numbers just did not add up ("Al-Masraf al-Ziraʿi fi Suriya," *al-Ziraʿa al-Haditha* 3, nos. 9–10 (November-December 1927): 506).

164. Al-Shihabi, "Aham Adwaʾna al-Iqtisadiya wa Talafiha 3" (February 1929), 177; al-Jazaʾiri, "al-Islah al-Ziraʿi fi Suriya," 430–31.

165. "Al-Ziraʿa fi al-Gharb wa al-Ziraʿa fi Suriya," *al-Ziraʿa al-Haditha* 4, no. 3 (December 1928): 3.

166. CADN, Syrie-Liban/1, 1571, "Mémoire de la Chambre d'Agriculture d'Alep sur la situation agricole," February 1928.

167. CADN, Syrie-Liban/1, 1846, "Alep Rapport Trimestriel, 2ème trimestre, 1927."

168. CADN, Syrie-Liban/1, 1847, "Vilayet d'Alep Rapport Trimestriel, 2ème trimestre, 1928."

169. CADN, Syrie-Liban/1, 1848, "Rapport Trimestriel [Grand Liban], Avril-May-June 1929," 25 July 1929.

170. CADN, Syrie-Liban/1, 1846, "Alep Rapport Trimestriel, 2ème trimestre, 1927."

171. Al-Shihabi, "Aham Adwaʾna al-Iqtisadiya wa Talafiha 3" (February 1929), 176.

172. Al-Jazaʾiri, "Islah al-Ziraʿi fi Suriya," 426, 427. Supposedly, mandate officials had devised a comprehensive economic program in 1921, but it had still not been put into practice as of 1929 (Burns, *Tariff*, 32).

173. "Siyasatna al-Ziraʿiya," *al-Ziraʿa al-Haditha* 4, no. 2 (April 1928): 2.

174. "Siyasatna al-Ziraʿiya," *al-Ziraʿa al-Haditha* 4, no. 2 (April 1928): 4.

175. "Siyasatna al-Ziraʿiya," *al-Ziraʿa al-Haditha* 4, no. 2 (April 1928): 2.

176. "Al-Ziraʿa fi al-Gharb wa al-Ziraʿa fi Suriya," *al-Ziraʿa al-Haditha* 4, no. 3 (December 1928): 3.

177. G. Pharès, "Dans le Ministère de l'Agriculture et l'Économie on ne fait rien," *Les Échos de Damas*, 28 August 1930. According to Khoury, Shaykh ʿAbd al-Qadir al-Kaylani was "the only committed nationalist to join the [Taj al-Din] government" in February 1928 (Khoury, *Syria*, 329). French reports agreed that al-Kaylani had been a thorn in their side, noting that his "attitude towards the Constituent Assembly is the most reprehensible" after Shaykh Taj replaced him with the more compliant Badiʿ Bey in October 1930 (CADN, Syrie-Liban/1, 1848, "Bulletin d'Information Trimestriel (Octobre-Décembre 1930)," 27 December 1930). *Les Échos* suggested that during al-Kaylani's tenure as minister, he had little influence over agricultural policy.

178. CADN, Syrie-Liban/1, 1847, "Vilayet d'Alep Rapport Trimestriel, 2ème trimestre, 1928."

179. CADN, Syrie-Liban/1, 867, "Plainte des habitants d'Idlib a/s des impôts," 20 December 1933. The situation was exacerbated by the fact that when the *terbiʿ* was initially calculated, local officials had reduced the amount owed by some farmers and increased it for others to make up the difference, not to mention that they had added nonexistent taxpayers to the registry. One official had already been sentenced to 10 years in prison for these offenses, and two others were under investigation.

180. CADN, Syrie-Liban/1, 867, "Requête de Mgr Abou Assaly relative à la perception des impôts," 13 October 1934.

181. Sadir, *Majmuʿat*, 4: 5–25; al-Shihabi, "Aham Adwaʾna al-Iqtisadiya wa Talafiha 2" (January 1928 [1929?]), 33.

182. CADN, Syrie-Liban/1, 831, "Réclamations des habitants," Villagers to the High Commissioner, 9 August 1930. This is based on the French translation; the file did not include the Arabic original.

183. CADN, Syrie-Liban/1, 831, "Réclamations des habitants," Villagers to the High Commissioner, 9 August 1930; Villagers to the High Commissioner, 21 July 1930.

184. CADN, Syrie-Liban/1, 831, "Réclamations des habitants," Villagers to the High Commissioner, 21 July 1930; Mukhtars, Imams, and Villagers to the High Commissioner, 26 July 1930. I did not find a reply to this petition in the archives.

185. Himadeh, *Monetary and Banking System of Syria*, 221–22.

186. CADN, Syrie-Liban/1, 955, "Demande de maintien des functions des membres des conseils administratifs," 10 February 1932. The letter writers noted that if mandate authorities were concerned about making economies in the budget, they would do better to "abolish many other functions that are useless and the holders of which do not furnish any work."

187. CADN, Syrie-Liban/1, 979, "Requête des habitants de Taldo," 15 October 1940. The French deputy delegate to the region insisted that there was no need to respond as "the operations were legitimate."

188. "Al-Shiyuaᶜ fi al-Barriya," *al-Ziraᶜa al-Haditha* 5, nos. 7–8 (May-June 1932): 404.

189. CADN, Syrie-Liban/1, 870, "Nouvelle taxe pour frais cadastraux imposé[s] par le Gouvernement Syrien," Sûreté Générale report, 24 April 1934. See, for example, CADN, Syrie-Liban/1, 254, "Rapport Général sur les Travaux de Cadastre," 1933; and Ministère des affaires étrangères, *Rapport (Juillet 1922–Juillet 1923)*, 31.

190. CADN, Syrie-Liban/1, 979, "Requête des villageois de Deir Baalba," 13 November 1934.

191. CADN, Syrie-Liban/1, 979, "Requête des villageois de Deir Baalba," 13 November 1934.

192. CADN, Syrie-Liban/1, 979, "Requête des villageois de Deir Baalba," 13 November 1934.

193. CADN, Syrie-Liban/1, 979, "Requête des villageois de Deir Baalba," Villagers to the High Commissioner, 18 September 1937.

194. CADN, Syrie-Liban/1, 979, "Requête des villageois de Deir Baalba," Villagers to the High Commissioner, 18 September 1937.

195. CADN, Syrie-Liban/1, 979, "Requête des villageois de Deir Baalba," Villagers to the High Commissioner, 15 March 1938; Delegate of the High Commission for the Syrian Republic to de Martel, 13 May 1938.

196. CADN, Syrie-Liban/1, 1848, "Bulletin d'Information Trimestriel Damas, Julliet–Septembre 1930," 27 September 1930.

197. On urban resistance, which has received more attention in the literature, see Khoury, *Syria*, 347–49; and Thompson, *Colonial Citizens*. Among the causes for urban discontent were new taxes, falling wages, and increasingly unemployment.

198. CADN, Syrie-Liban/1, 1848, "Bulletin d'Information Trimestriel Damas, Julliet–Septembre 1930," 27 September 1930; "Bulletin d'Information Trimestriel Damas, Avril-Mai-Juin 1930," 27 June 1930; "Bulletin d'Information Trimestriel Damas, Janvier–Mars 1930," 25 (?) March 1930; and "Rapport Trimestriel [Grand Liban], Julliet-Août-Septembre 1929," 22 October 1929; CADN, Syrie-Liban/1, 2109, "Rapport Trimestriel [Alep], 2ème trimestre, 1929"; CADN, Syrie-Liban/1, 1850, "Bulletin d'Information Trimestriel Aleppo, 2éme trimestre, 1930," 7 July 1930; "Bulletin d'Information Trimestriel Homs and Hama, 2ème trimestre," 26 June 1930; and "Bulletin d'Information Trimestriel Damas, Janvier–Mars 1930," 25 March 1930 (in folder labeled as Hawran trimester reports). Between these pressures and the usual pest suspects, Bosra and the area around Deraᶜa were in especially dire straits (CADN, Syrie-Liban/1, 1849, "Bulletin Trimestriel Hawran, 4ème trimestre, 1930," 3 January 1931). Because of locusts and wheat rust from damp soil, Latakia's harvest was also not stellar (CADN, Syrie-Liban/1, 1850, "Rapport pour le 2ème trimestre [Latakia], 1930," 28 July 1930).

199. CADN, Syrie-Liban/1, 1849, "Bulletin Trimestriel Hawran, 4ème trimestre, 1930," 3 January 1931.

200. CADN, Syrie-Liban/1, 1850, "Bulletin d'Information Trimestriel Alep, 2ème trimestre, 1930," 7 July 1930.

201. CADN, Syrie-Liban/1, 1850, "Bulletin d'Information Trimestriel Damas, Janvier–Mars 1930," 25 March 1930.

202. CADN, Syrie-Liban/1, 1850, "Bulletin d'Information Trimestriel Damas, Janvier–Mars 1930," 25 March 1930. According to reports from Latakia, this movement was not gaining any traction there (CADN, Syrie-Liban/1, 1850, "Bulletin d'Information Trimestriel [Latakia], de 1er Juillet au 30 Septembre 1930," 4 October 1930). For more on Barudi's economic-oriented activism, see Khoury, *Syria*, 275–77.

203. CADN, Syrie-Liban/1, 1848, "Bulletin d'Information Trimestriel Damas, Julliet–Septembre 1930," 27 September 1930.

204. CADN, Syrie-Liban/1, 1848, "Bulletin d'Information Trimestriel Damas, Julliet–Septembre 1930," 27 September 1930.

205. CADN, Syrie-Liban/1, 1848, "Bulletin d'Information Trimestriel Damas, Julliet–Septembre 1930," 27 September 1930; CADN, Syrie-Liban/1, 1850, "Bulletin d'Information Trimestriel Aleppo, 2éme trimestre, 1930," 7 July 1930.

206. CADN, Syrie-Liban/1, 1850, "Bulletin Trimestriel du Hauran [2nd trimester]," 27 June 1930; "Bulletin Trimestriel Hauran, 3ème trimestre, 1930," [?] September 1930 (in folder labeled Jabal al-Druze).

207. CADN, Syrie-Liban/1, 1849, "Bulletin Trimestriel Hauran, 4ème trimestre, 1930," 3 January 1931.

208. CADN, Syrie-Liban/1, 1848, "Bulletin d'Information Trimestriel Damas, October-Décembre 1930," 27 December 1930; "Hatha al-Riba," *al-Ziraʿa al-Haditha* 5, no. 1 (November 1931): 4. The continuing importation of cheap foreign grain was of particular concern. *Al-Ziraʿa al-Haditha* noted that some of the main culprits, such as Canada, the United States, the South American republics, and Australia, could produce enormous amounts of grain because they had access to "the most modern agricultural tools and the most abundant means of production. . . . It is impossible for our farmers to compete in his own house [soil?] and in the markets of his fathers and grandfathers" ("Asʿar al-Hubub wa Wajab al-Hukuma," *al-Ziraʿa al-Haditha* 5, no. 4 [February 1932]: 210).

209. MAE, Syrie-Liban 549, High Commissioner to the President of the Counsel, 19 February 1932, pp. 26–27.

210. "ʿAwda "Al-Ziraʿa al-Hadith"," *al-Ziraʿa al-Haditha* 5, no. 1 (November 1931): 1. The editor noted that, because the journal lacked advertisements, all expenses came out of his own pocket.

211. "Bahith fi al-Iqtisad al-Ziraʿi: Wajib al-Hukuma Hiyal al-Azma al-Iqtisadiya," *al-Ziraʿa al-Haditha* 5, no. 4 (February 1932): 242.

212. "Al-Naqabat al-Ziraʿiya," *al-Ziraʿa al-Haditha* 5, no. 4 (February 1932): 207; "al-Azma al-Iqtisadiya," *al-Ziraʿa al-Haditha* 5, no. 2 (December 1931): 78–79.

213. "Al-Azma al-Iqtisadiya," *al-Ziraʿa al-Haditha* 5, no. 2 (December 1931): 79; "al-Istiqrad bi-Mukabil al-Mahsulat al-Ziraʿiya," *al-Ziraʿa al-Haditha* 5, nos. 7–8 (May-June 1932): 407–8. The amount was not to exceed 50% of the crop value.

214. "Bahith fi al-Iqtisad al-Ziraʿi: Wajib al-Hukuma Hiyal al-Azma al-Iqtisadiya," *al-Ziraʿa al-Haditha* 5, no. 4 (February 1932): 244–45.

215. "Mudir al-majalla," *al-Ziraʿa al-Haditha* 5, no. 4 (February 1932): 274.

216. "Daribat al-Aᶜshar," *al-Ziraᶜa al-Haditha* 5, nos. 7–8 (May-June 1932): 406; Khoury, *Syria*, 374, 379.

217. CADN, Syrie-Liban/1, 978, "Requête des habitants de Hama a/s des impôts," 29 May 1932.

218. "Daribat al-Aᶜshar," *al-Ziraᶜa al-Haditha* 5, nos. 7–8 (May-June 1932): 406–7. For a text of the new estimation regulation, see "Nizam al-Takhmin al-Jadid," *al-Ziraᶜa al-Haditha* 5, nos. 7–8 (May-June 1932): 507–9.

219. "Al-Azma al-Ziraᶜiya fi Suriya," *al-Zira'a al-Haditha* 5, nos. 7-8 (May-June 1932): 439.

220. "Al-Azma al-Ziraᶜiya fi Suriya," *al-Zira'a al-Haditha* 5, nos. 9–10 (August-September 1932): 592. The journal especially commended al-Kaylani's solidarity for preventing the French representative Bruére from closing the Salamiya agricultural school. The journal was especially appreciative of this stance, given that the first national constitutional government had decided to turn the school into a practical agricultural center, a move the journal condemned as a "huge scientific mistake" (592).

221. Al-Ahdab, "al-Azma al-Ziraᶜiya fi Suriya," 440–41.

222. Al-Ahdab, "al-Azma al-Ziraᶜiya fi Suriya," 441.

223. Al-Shihabi, "al-Azma al-Ziraᶜiya fi Suriya," 444–47.

224. Al-Kaylani, "al-Azma al-Ziraᶜiya fi Suriya," 592–93. This perhaps reflects his connection to Hama, situated in an agricultural region that had been hard hit by the Sunn bug in particular.

225. Al-Ahdab, "al-Azma al-Ziraᶜiya fi Suriya," 441–42; al-Shihabi, "al-Azma al-Ziraᶜiya fi Suriya," 447–50.

226. Al-Shihabi, "al-Azma al-Ziraᶜiya fi Suriya," 447–50. Al-Shihabi noted that the French government increased tariffs when the harvest was good and reduced them when it was poor.

227. Al-Kaylani, "al-Azma al-Ziraᶜiya fi Suriya," 595.

228. Al-Kaylani, "al-Azma al-Ziraᶜiya fi Suriya," 594.

229. Khoury, *Syria*, 264, 268. Khoury claims that "the 'nationalism of the *pashas*' never stretched so far as to include problems of internal social and economic development, which they perceived to be inimical to their own interests" (264).

230. "Buʾs al-Ziraᶜa wa al-Zarraᶜ," *al-Ziraᶜa al-Haditha* 5, nos. 9–10 (August-September 1932): 525; CADN, Syrie-Liban/1, 862, "État de Syrie La Sécheresse et la Situation Agricole Correspondance," High Commission to the President of the Council, MAE, 28 October 1932. The High Commission noted that even the most rigorous collection of arrears would not make up the difference. For more on Mardam Bey's position, see Khoury, *Syria*, 374, 379–80.

231. CADN, Syrie-Liban/1, 862, "État de Syrie La Sécheresse et la Situation Agricole Correspondance," Delegate General of the High Commission to the President of the Council, MAE, 16 September 1932. They initially requested 15 million francs, but when the bank's director asked the High Commission for its opinion, the delegate informed him that the requested amount was too high. Particularly because he judged that these nationalists' effort to aid farmers in a region with "moderate delegates in the Syrian Parliament [was] not exclusively humanitarian," he suggested half that amount would suffice and should be disbursed through an institution such as the Agricultural Bank.

232. CADN, Syrie-Liban/1, 862, "État de Syrie La Sécheresse et la Situation Agricole Correspondance," High Commissioner to the President of the Council, MAE, 18 November 1932; CADN, Syrie-Liban/1, 862, "Emprunt de L.L.S. 250,000. Par le Gouvernement Syrien à la Banque de Syrie et du Grand Liban," President of the Council of Ministers to the High Commission's delegate for the Syrian Republic, 13 December 1932; Ministère des affaires étrangères, *Rapport (1932)*, 90.

233. Mounayer, *Régime*, 202; [Gaulmier], "Notes sur la propriété foncière," 135.

234. See CADN, Syrie-Liban/1, 862, "État de Syrie La Sécheresse et la Situation Agricole," "La famine à Hama," 10 January 1933; "Information sur la Situation Économique & Agricole," 2 December 1932; "Information sur la Situation Économique & Agricole," 26 November 1932; and "Situation Économique," 5 December 1932.

235. CADN, Syrie-Liban/1, 862, "État de Syrie La Sécheresse et la Situation Agricole," "A/s. Ensemencements," 19 November 1932.

236. See CADN, Syrie-Liban/1, 862, "État de Syrie La Sécheresse et la Situation Agricole," "Extrait de la revue de la presse arabe de Damas," 23 December 1932; "Information sur la situation économique," 25 December 1932; "Grand Liban La Sécheresse et la Situation Agricole," A/s. La pluie, 28 December 1932; Gouvernement des Alaouites La Sécheresse et la Situation Agricole," "Situation Agricole et Économique," 31 December 1932; and "Gouvernement de Djebel Druze La Sécheresse et la Situation Agricole," "Affairs Économiques et Agricoles, 15 and 23 December 1932.

237. "La Nécessité d'une Politique Agricole," *Les Échos de Damas*, 30 December 1932; CADN, Syrie-Liban/1, 862, "État de Syrie La Sécheresse et la Situation Agricole," "Extrait de la revue de la presse arabe de Damas—la réforme agricole," 1, 2, and 3 January 1933.

238. CADN, Syrie-Liban/1, 862, "État de Syrie La Sécheresse et la Situation Agricole Correspondance," High Commissioner to the President of the Council, MAE, 18 November 1932; "Fakhri el Baroudi se rétire de la commission agricole" *Les Échos de Damas*, 14 Décembre 1932. Al-Barudi had resigned in protest over the commission's allocation of additional funds for drilling artesian wells.

239. CADN, Syrie-Liban/1, 862, "État de Syrie La Sécheresse et la Situation Agricole," "Extrait de la revue de la presse arabe de Damas—la réforme agricole," 1, 2, and 3 January 1933; "Extrait de la revue de la presse arabe de Damas," 5 January 1933; "Le Conseiller pour l'Agriculture," 6 January 1933.

240. CADN, Syrie-Liban/1, 862, "État de Syrie La Sécheresse et la Situation Agricole," "A/s. des Prêts aux agriculteurs," 28 December 1932; "Au secours des agriculteurs," 29 December 1932. On Jamil Ibrahim Pasha's background, see Khoury, *Syria*, 107, 186, 270–71.

241. CADN, Syrie-Liban/1, 862, "Emprunt de L.L.S. 250,000. Par le Gouvernement Syrien à la Banque de Syrie et du Grand Liban," secret response from Diplomatie Paris to the General Delegate Beirut, 6 January 1933.

242. CADN, Syrie-Liban/1, 862, "Emprunt de L.L.S. 250,000. Par le Gouvernement Syrien à la Banque de Syrie et du Grand Liban," High Commmision's delegate for the Syrian Republic to the General Delegate of the High Commission, 28 December 1932.

243. "Les Distributions des Secours aux Cultivateurs," *Les Échos de Damas*, 6 January 1933; "L'emprunt . . . agricole," *Les Échos de Damas*, 13 January 1933.

244. "Les Distributions des Secours aux Cultivateurs," *Les Échos de Damas*, 6 January 1933.

245. CADN, Syrie-Liban/1, 862, "État de Syrie La Sécheresse et la Situation Agricole," "Extrait de la revue de la presse arabe de Damas—les prêts aux cultivateurs," 1, 2, and 3 January 1933; "L'emprunt . . . agricole," *Les Échos de Damas*, 13 January 1933.

246. "L'emprunt . . . agricole," *Les Échoes de Damas*, 13 January 1933.

247. CADN, Syrie-Liban/1, 862, "État de Syrie La Sécheresse et la Situation Agricole," "Distribution de Secours aux Agriculteurs," 9 January 1933; "Extrait de la revue de la presse arabe de Damas—les secours aux cultivateurs," 6 January 1933; and "A/s. Distribution de Secours aux Agriculteurs Eprouvés," 3 January 1933.

248. CADN, Syrie-Liban/1, 862, "État de Syrie La Sécheresse et la Situation Agricole," "Revue de la Presse arabe de Damas—la situation agricole," 29 December 1932; "Le Conseiller pour l'Agriculture," 6 January 1933; "La Nécessité d'une Politique Agricole," *Les Échos de Damas*, 30 December 1932; "Autour du rapport du Director de l'agriculture," *Les Échos de Damas*, 5 January 1933. *Les Échos* explained that the "union of agriculture school graduates" was a group of about 200 young people who had graduated from French and foreign agricultural schools as well as the Salamiya agricultural school. Staying "on the fringes of politics," they aimed "to encourage agriculture in Syria and agricultural education, notably in initiating cultivators in modern methods, in defending their rights and in helping them" ("La nécessité d'une politique agricole," *Les Échos de Damas*, 30 December 1932).

249. "La nécessité d'une politique agricole," *Les Échos de Damas*, 30 December 1932. The fundamentals included the establishment of experimental fields, nurseries, and farm schools; reforestation; and a collective fight against insects and diseases that affected plants and animals.

250. CADN, Syrie-Liban/1, 862, "État de Syrie La Sécheresse et la Situation Agricole," "Extrait de la revue de la presse arabe de Damas—les finances de l'État de Syrie," 5 January 1933.

251. Ministère des affaires étrangères, *Rapport (1932)*, 90.

252. Khoury, *Syria*, 380–88.

253. On the nationalist boycott of Parliament, see Khoury, *Syria*, 389. CADN, Syrie-Liban/1, 867, "Perception des impôts," deputy delegate in Aleppo to the High Commissioner, 18 August 1934.

254. Khoury, *Syria*, 390.

255. Sarrage, *Nécessité*, 126.

256. Khoury, *Syria*, 445–46. Khoury attributes the al-Yusuf family's troubles to losses in land rent as a result of falling crop prices from the global economic crisis and extravagant living. Losses in land rent were certainly an issue but should be understood in the broader context of losses in agriculture that preceded and continued through the crisis, leading to widespread bankruptcies and therefore falling land prices.

257. See Khoury, *Syria*, 390–92, 442–43; CADN, Syrie-Liban/1, 870, Information No. 7568, "Au sujet des agriculteurs," 7 December 1933; and CADN, Syrie-Liban/1, 870, Petition from the people of Dayr al-Zor, 16 December 1933. The petitioners complained that "the situation has become intolerable and it has reached the point where there is no demand and no desire for anything displayed in the market and no one buys the properties except mortgagers and creditors with cheap prices that range between a ten and a fourth [of their value]," or, as the French translation put it, "the only commerce that is still practiced, it is the sale of lands to creditors who by the way do not buy them except at a low price, fluctuating between a tenth and a quarter of the real price."

258. CADN, Syrie-Liban/1, 867, "Requête des agriculteurs syriens," telegram sent 25 December 1933. Similar practices—that is, a gendarme accompanying a government official in order to seize a peasant's belongings to pay off debts—were not uncommon in France itself during the Great Depression and resistance to these sales fomented political organization there as well (Paxton, *French Peasant Fascism*, 78).

259. CADN, Syrie-Liban/1, 867, "Requête des agriculteurs syriens," Lavastre to de Martel, 15 February 1934.

260. See Khoury, *Syria*, 189, 442. Taj al-Din had originally headed the government from 1928 to 1931 (Khoury, *Syria*, 259).

261. Khoury, *Syria*, 443; CADN, Syrie-Liban/1, 867, "Requête des agriculteurs syriens," Source Sûreté Alep Information no. 3835, 15 November 1934; Information no. 166/S, 19 December 1934.

262. CADN, Syrie-Liban/1, 867, "Requête des agriculteurs syriens," Aleppo farmers to High Commissioner, 17 May 1934. Out of the approximately 140 individuals who signed the letter, many explicitly identified themselves as farmers (*muzariʿ*). Not all signatories indicated the villages or regions to which they belonged, but among the places mentioned in the signatures were ʿAssan, al-Safira, Tal Shagib, and al-Hadir—all localities to the south and southeast of Aleppo—and the district of Azaz to its north. Notably, in addition to signatures from farmers, the imams of ʿAssan, al-Safira, and Tal Shagib and the mukhtar of ʿAssan and the mukhtar's representative from al-Safira all signed with their official seals. Among the finer points made by the petitioners was that the tithe reductions in effect until 1927 had not benefited them because the original tithe was based on the price of the 1925 dollar, inflating its value. They were then expected to pay the full inflated tithe until 1933, when it was finally reduced by 50% to account for this previous inflation. Thus, in essence, from 1928 to 1932 they had paid "double [its] real value." Their critique of the Agricultural Bank's policy extended to its method of calculating interest payments. According to their complaint, the bank added to the initial capital due "exorbitant, already overdue interests and requir[ed] in addition an interest of 6% on the amount obtained in order to renew a loan." They claimed that the bank's rules scarcely allowed them to take compound interest and had essentially been formulated to put farmers at the mercy of usurers. In fact, they suggested that usurers were actually charging less interest than the bank at a time when creditors were discounting the debt owed them and were even going so far as to drop the interest due no matter the amount. Similarly, farmers indebted in cash to the government hoped for the same kind of treatment that such private creditors were extending to their own debtors.

263. CADN, Syrie-Liban/1, 867, "Requête des agriculteurs syriens," Form 972, 11 June 1934.

264. CADN, Syrie-Liban/1, 867, "Requête des agriculteurs syriens," Delegate to Syrian Republic to de Martel, 27 June 1934.

265. In August 1933 the Lebanese government abolished the tithe and land tax (as well as the *miri* land tax, which had applied only in the former Ottoman special district of Mount Lebanon) and replaced them with a "unified land tax," which might in part explain this sudden flurry of petitions in 1934 (G. Hakim, "Fiscal System," 357–58).

266. CADN, Syrie-Liban/1, 867, "Liban," Inhabitants of Jubayl to MAE, 4 April 1934; de Martel to MAE, 13 July 1934.

267. CADN, Syrie-Liban/1, 867, "Requête des habitants de Sir a/s des impôts," 13 September 1934.

268. CADN, Syrie-Liban/1, 867, "Desiderata exprimés par les habitants du Caza de Tyr," 2 July 1934. Tyre inhabitants were also apparently paying an increased land tax that had been imposed during the war, the maintenance of which they deemed inequitable.

269. CADN, Syrie-Liban/1, 867, "Desiderata exprimés par les habitants du Caza de Tyr," 7 August 1934.

270. CADN, Syrie-Liban/1, 867, "Requête de Mgr Abou Assaly relative à la perception des impôts," 13 October 1934. The sums included two years of back taxes.

271. CADN, Syrie-Liban/1, 867, "Doléances des habitants de Ras Baʿalbak a/s des impôts," Desfarges to the delegate of the High Commission for the Lebanese Republic, 24 October 1934.

272. "Les décisions du Congrés des agriculteurs," *Les Échos de Damas*, 29 June 1934. The localities represented on the executive committee included Damascus, Homs, Hama, Qalamun, Hawran, Wadi al-ʿAjam, Zabadani, and Duma. The committee also sought Aleppo's participation.

273. CADN, Syrie-Liban/1, 867, "Requête d'agriculteurs syriens," Information no. 2445, 9 July 1934.

274. CADN, Syrie-Liban/1, 867, "Requête d'agriculteurs syriens," Information no. 3039, 4 September 1934; Information no. 55/SS, 15 September 1934.

275. CADN, Syrie-Liban/1, 867, "Requête d'agriculteurs syriens," "Questions locales," 15 September 1934; "Clôture du 'Congrès' des Agriculteurs," *Les Échos de Damas*, 14 September 1934.

276. "Clôture du 'Congrès' des Agriculteurs," *Les Échos de Damas*, 14 September 1934; CADN, Syrie-Liban/1, 867, "Requête d'agriculteurs syriens," Information no. 55/SS, 15 September 1934.

277. CADN, Syrie-Liban/1, 867, "Perception des impôts," de Martel to Beirut, Damascus, Homs, Aleppo, Alexandretta, Dayr al-Zor, Latakia, Soueida, 2 August 1934.

278. See, for example, CADN, Syrie-Liban/1, 867, "Perception des impôts," deputy delegate of the High Commission for Aleppo to the High Commissioner, 18 August 1934; and Colonel Jacquot, deputy delegate of the High Commission for the Territories of the Euphrate, to the High Commissioner, 10 August 1934.

279. CADN, Syrie-Liban/1, 867, "Liban," "Note pour Monsieur Lagarde," 30 July 1934.

280. CADN, Syrie-Liban/1, 867, "Perception des impôts," deputy delegate in Aleppo to the High Commissioner, 18 August 1934.

281. CADN, Syrie-Liban/1, 867, "Perception des impôts," de Martel to Beirut, Aleppo, Antioch, Dayr al-Zor, Soueida, Latakia, Damascus, 18 August 1934.

282. CADN, Syrie-Liban/1, 867, "Perception des impôts." On the "politics of notables," see Hourani, "Ottoman Reform." For a critique, see Gelvin, "Politics of Notables."

283. Khoury, *Syria*, 262.

284. CADN, Syrie-Liban/1, 867, "Requête d'agriculteurs syriens," Lavastre to de Martel, 13 September 1934. The lists referred to were those detailing who owed more than 100 livres libano-syriennes. The delegate from Alexandretta offered a similar explanation, noting that "a certain number of rich local farmers, not being resolved until this day to substitute the tractor for the archaic plow, have not obtained the returns

assumed by the tax authorities" (CADN, Syrie-Liban/1, 867, "Perception des impôts," Alexandrette delegate to de Martel, 2 [?] September 1934).

285. "Clôture du 'Congrès' des Agriculteurs," *Les Échos de Damas*, 14 September 1934.

286. CADN, Syrie-Liban/1, 867, "Requête d'agriculteurs syriens," LaGarde to the delegate of the High Commission in the state of Syria and attached compte-rendu, 20 September 1934.

287. CADN, Syrie-Liban/1, 867, "Requête d'agriculteurs syriens," "Questions locales," 15 September 1934.

288. CADN, Syrie-Liban/1, 867, "Liban," "Questions Locales," 2 October 1934.

289. CADN, Syrie-Liban/1, 867, "Liban," "Questions Locales," 2 October 1934.

290. CADN, Syrie-Liban/1, 867, "Perception des impôts," 3 July 1934. Lieutenant de Visme, officer of the Special Services and head of post in Hama, suggested that unless the government allowed landowners to take the portion needed for their subsistence from the fourth of the harvest due them, they would lose interest in cultivating their lands. Furthermore, to avoid making both peasants and landowners wait to sell, usually at lower prices, he proposed consigning the portion to be seized for taxes to a solvent third party or the landowner if appropriate guarantees could be provided.

291. CADN, Syrie-Liban/1, 867, "Perception des impôts," Assistant Delegate for Alexandretta to de Martel, 22 August 1934.

292. CADN, Syrie-Liban/1, 867, "Requête des agriculteurs syriens," Sadek Rifai to the High Commissioner, 25 October 1934.

293. CADN, Syrie-Liban/1, 867, "Requête des agriculteurs syriens," Source Sûreté Alep Information no. 3635, 29 October 1934.

294. CADN, Syrie-Liban/1, 867, "Requête des agriculteurs syriens," Source Sûreté Alep Information no. 3835, 15 November 1934. This suggestion followed de Martel's 2 November suspension of Parliament (Khoury, *Syria*, 443).

295. CADN, Syrie-Liban/1, 867, "Requête des agriculteurs syriens," Source Sûreté Alep Information no. 4084, 7 December 1934.

296. CADN, Syrie-Liban/1, 867, "Requête des agriculteurs syriens," telegram to the High Commission signed by Rashid Rustum (secretary) and Ahmed al-Mudarris (president), 3 March 1935; Source Sûreté Alep Information no. 3635, 29 October 1934. Rustum was a key leader among students in Aleppo, and al-Mudarris was a big landowner (Khoury, *Syria*, 272, 574; Faris, *Min Huwa*, 406).

297. CADN, Syrie-Liban/1, 867, "Requête des agriculteurs syriens," telegram to the High Commission signed by Rashid Rustum and Ahmed al-Mudarris, 3 March 1935. A report from southern Lebanon detailed a comparable situation there, noting that the market prices from 1924 that had served as the base of the *terbi*ʿ had, as of 1932, dropped by as much as 50%, meaning that farmers were paying more than 50% of their harvests as tax (CADN, Syrie-Liban/1, 867, "Étude sommaire sur les impôts fonciérs," report from the Administrative Counselor of South Lebanon, 15 June 1935, p. 2).

298. See, for example, CADN, Syrie-Liban/1, 867, "Requête d'un group d'habitants d'Idlib," 7 December 1935 (drought, Sunn bugs); "Requête du Conseil des Anciens-Zebdani," 11 July 1935 (plague from the sky); "Requête des propriétaires de Tal al Akhdar, Tal Sinnein, Moucheirfé et Sayadé (Békaa)," 12 July 1935 (flood); and "Requête des habitants de Kafr Chouwaya," 3 August 1935; CADN, Syrie-Liban/1, 868, "Plainte des

cultivateurs du sandjak d'Alexandrette contre les impôts," 17 November 1935 (Sunn bugs); and "Requête des habitants d'El Hermel a/s paiement des impôts," 24 April 1936.

299. CADN, Syrie-Liban/1, 867, "Requête d'agriculteurs de la région d'Alep," 1 September 1935; "Tal al Akhdar"; and "Kafr Chouwaya"; CADN, Syrie-Liban/1, 868, "El Hermel." In particular, the residents of El Hermel stated that they could not pay the "Tarbi," which was based on years of good harvests and high prices.

300. This description of mandate taxation methods is taken from Sarrage, *Nécessité*, 125–26. See also "Taqdi ʿala mawsim al-fallah al-khasib," *al-Qabas*, 25 June 1935, in which the author expresses shock and dismay at how officials went into a village and illegally confiscated the farmers' animals and basic tools. See also CADN, Syrie-Liban/1, 867, "Requête de Mgr Jean el Hage archevêque de Damas," December 1934; "Kafr Chouwaya"; "Requête d'un group d'habitants d'Idlib"; and "Plainte des cultivateurs du sandjak d'Alexandrette." For this denial, see CADN, Syrie-Liban/1, 867, "Requête des agriculteurs syriens," Djaouhari to Assistant Delegate of Aleppo, 5 November 1934; and Assistant Delegate of Aleppo to Counselor Delegate for the Syrian Republic, 6 November 1934.

301. CADN, Syrie-Liban/1, 867, "Requête de Mgr Jean," pp. 2–3.

302. See CADN, Syrie-Liban/1, 867, "Zebdani"; "Kafr Chouwaya"; "Requête d'un group d'habitants d'Idlib"; "Plainte des cultivateurs du sandjak d'Alexandrette"; and "Requête d'agriculteurs syriens," letter from Hama cultivators to the High Commissioner, 9 July 1935.

303. CADN, Syrie-Liban/1, 867, "Perception des impôts," Colonel Devic to de Martel, 24 August 1934.

304. CADN, Syrie-Liban/1, 867, "Étude sommaire sur les impôts foncièrs," report from the Administrative Counselor of South Lebanon, 15 June 1935, p. 5.

305. Sarrage, *Nécessité*, 128.

306. Ministère des affaires étrangères, *Rapport (Juillet 1922–Juillet 1923)*, 29–30.

307. See, for example, CADN, Syrie-Liban/1, 976, "Requête des habitants du village de Mecheirefet Samouk (Lattaquié) a/s des impôts," 20 October 1933. This is based on the French translation of the petition, as the original Arabic was not preserved in the file.

308. CADN, Syrie-Liban/1, 867, "Perception des impôts," Assistant Delegate for Alexandretta to the General Delegate of the High Commissioner, 25 (?) September 1934; CADN, Syrie-Liban/1, 863, "Étude sur la situation de l'agriculture au Liban," 23 April 1935. See also CADN, Syrie-Liban/1, 867, "Perception des impôts," petition from Alexandretta to de Martel, July 1934, where the petitioners express indignation that taxpayers would be compelled to pay "even in the absence of revenues." Much of the uncultivated land may have been composed of fallow in a rotational cycle, although it is also plausible that it remained uncultivated because of a lack of seed or labor.

309. CADN, Syrie-Liban/1, 867, "Requête de Mgr Jean," pp. 2–3. French officials noted in the margins this "curious apology of mukhtars" (1). The high salaries commanded by government employees, including tax collectors, repeatedly came up as a major grievance.

310. CADN, Syrie-Liban/1, 867, "Perception des impôts," deputy delegate to Hama and Homs to Comte Martel, 8 August 1934; and "Requête d'agriculteurs syriens," letter from Hama cultivators, 9 July 1935. Translated from the original in Arabic. *ʿAynan* can also mean "by the eye."

311. CADN, Syrie-Liban/1, 867, "Requête d'agriculteurs syriens," letter from Hama cultivators.

312. CADN, Syrie-Liban/1, 867, "Requête d'agriculteurs syriens," letter from Hama cultivators. Interestingly, the French translation of this sentence in their petition refers to "the abstraction made of agricultural taxes."

313. CADN, Syrie-Liban/1, 867, "Requête d'agriculteurs syriens," Delegate of the High Commission to Martel, 25 October 1935. The finance minister at this point was Henri Hindiya, identified by Khoury as a "moderate or pro-French" bureaucrat (Khoury, *Syria*, 260). One such demand was still a new estimation based on current prices.

314. "Taqdi ʿala mawsim al-fallah al-khasib," *al-Qabas*, 25 June 1935; "Saihat al-Muzariʿin fi Kull Makan," *al-Qabas*, 13 August 1935.

315. "Al-Ghurfa al-Ziraʿiya fi Homs Tastaqil," *al-Qabas*, 11 August 1935.

316. "Taqdi ʿala mawsim al-fallah al-khasib," *al-Qabas*, 25 June 1935.

317. "Saihat al-Muzariʿin fi Kull Makan," *al-Qabas*, 13 August 1935.

318. "Que veut l'agriculture?" *Les Échos de Damas*, 9 August 1935.

319. "Que veut l'agriculture?" *Les Échos de Damas*, 9 August 1935. The insistence on taxing net revenues echoes other reform proposals from the mid-1930s, maintaining the position held by local technocrats since the early years of the mandate. See, for example, Sarrage, *Nécessité*, 128, who suggested a 12.5% tax on net revenues in 1935 and that peasants should not be compelled to pay unless they realized a profit.

320. CADN, Syrie-Liban/1, 867, "Damas," Source Sûreté Damas no. 3031, 30 October 1935.

321. CADN, Syrie-Liban/1, 868, "La Question des impôts," Information no. 131, 15 January 1936.

322. CADN, Syrie-Liban/1, 868, "La Question des Impôts," Letter to the Department no. 1282, 27 December 1935.

323. Salah al-Din al-Husayni, "al-Hasharat allati Taftuku bi-l-Mawsim al-Ziraʿi," *al-Qabas*, 26 July 1936.

324. CADN, Syrie-Liban/1, 868, "La Question des Impôts," Arrêté no. 162, 8 August 1936; and Arrêté no. 163, 8 August 1936; "Note" from the High Commission's delegate to Syria, 31 July 1936; Deputy Delegate for Aleppo to High Commission's delegate to Syria, 31 August 1936.

325. CADN, Syrie-Liban/1, 868, "La Question des Impôts," Deputy Delegate for Aleppo to High Commission's delegate to Syria, 31 August 1936; Khoury, *Syria*, 468.

326. Khoury, *Syria*, 480.

327. CADN, Syrie-Liban/1, 868, "Situation politique et financière de la Syrie et au Liban," 29 January 1937.

328. CADN, Syrie-Liban/1, 971, "Étude relative à la dîme et au Wirgho en vigueur en Syrie, et au Tertib en vigueur au Maroc et en Tunisie."

329. CADN, Syrie-Liban/1, 971, "Étude relative à la dîme et au Wirgho en vigueur en Syrie, et au Tertib en vigueur au Maroc et en Tunisie," 20 October 1938, pp. 19, 53–54. Duraffourd contrasts this with the *impôt foncier* in France, which was assessed on net revenue and which he traced back to the influence of the Physiocrats (16–17).

330. CADN, Syrie-Liban/1, 971, "Étude relative à la dîme et au Wirgho en vigueur en Syrie, et au Tertib en vigueur au Maroc et en Tunisie," p. 12.

331. CADN, Syrie-Liban/1, 971, "Étude relative à la dîme et au Wirgho en vigueur en Syrie, et au Tertib en vigueur au Maroc et en Tunisie," p. 12. It is interesting to recall in this discussion the origins of the 12.5% rate at which the tithe was assessed in the late Ottoman period and which for Duraffourd indicated its contrasting heaviness for farmers (13). The additional 2.5% was intended to raise money for schools and capital for the agricultural bank and so theoretically was a means of providing to some extent those reserves that farmers insisted were necessary for implementing a fixed tax.

332. G. Hakim, "Fiscal System," 401.

333. For an example of the calculations involved, see CADN, Syrie-Liban/1, 971, "Caza de Homs—Village de Gajar Emir," 25 October 1938, p. 15. But even this tax would be heavier than the land tax and tithe together. The estimated tax for the village of Gajar Emir near Homs, for example, amounted to 72,488 piastres syriennes, compared with a total tax from land tax and tithe (*terbi*ᶜ) of 60,316 piastres syriennes. On the Palestine tax, see Bunton, *Colonial Land Policies*, 150–55.

334. CADN, Syrie-Liban/1, 971, "Étude relative à la dîme et au Wirgho en vigueur en Syrie, et au Tertib en vigueur au Maroc et en Tunisie," p. 59. In Turkey a consumption tax had also replaced the tithe in 1925.

335. Khoury, *Syria*, 470–71.

336. Ministère des affaires étrangères, *Rapport (1937)*, 75.

337. Al-Tarmanini, "Aqwal al-Nawab Kalima al-Majalla Hawlha," 107.

338. Al-Tarmanini, "Awqal al-Nawab Kalima al-Majalla Hawlha," 108–9. The journal indicated that, based on the statistics available to it, Palestine had an agricultural budget of not less than 1 million Syrian lira and east Jordan's was more than 300,000 Syrian lira, whereas Egypt's ranged between 1.25 and 1.5 million Egyptian pounds (109).

339. Al-Tarmanini, "Awqal al-Nawab Kalima al-Majalla Hawlha," 109–10.

340. "Al-Ziraᶜa fi al-Majlis al-Niyabi," *al-Majalla al-Ziraᶜiya al-Suriya* 1, no. 2 (January 1939): 199.

341. Al-Tarmanini, "Awqal al-Nawab Kalima al-Majalla Hawlha," 110. ᶜUmar Tarmanini was not only the director of the journal but also the inspector in the Ministry of National Economy "Agriculture."

342. "Bayan min al-Jamᶜiya al-Ziraᶜiya al-Suriya," *al-Qabas*, 6 April 1937.

343. Burns, *Tariff*, 28. See chapter 3 for more details.

344. CADN, Syrie-Liban/1, 863, "Étude sur la situation de l'agriculture au Liban," 23 April 1935.

345. As Stephen Longrigg put it in 1958, seed and cash loans were offered as "famine relief rather than as a step in progressive economics" (Longrigg, *Syria and Lebanon*, 281).

346. See, for example, Weulersse, *Paysans*.

347. Colin, "Notes et comptes rendus," 53; Weulersse, *Paysans*, 196.

348. Khoury, *Syria*, 64–65; Zakarya, "Syria," 250–51. Zakarya estimates that small landholdings fell from 25% to 15% during the mandate based on the research of al-Sibaᶜi. See al-Sibaᶜi, *Adwa*ʾ. The events covered in this chapter raise the question of whether those who successfully consolidated landownership during the mandate were the same as those who had consolidated landownership during the late Ottoman period. Ramez Tomeh's work, based on files from the Expropriation Department of the Directorate of State Domain Lands in the Ministry of Agriculture and Agrarian Reform, compiled

during the land reforms of 1958 and 1963, suggests that although the big landowners from the late Ottoman period did retain substantial holdings, they were dwarfed by those acquired during the mandate by the brothers Husayn and Nuri Ibish, whose family had not been big landowners before the mandate. Their holdings in the Damascus *muhafaza*, as recorded in the files, were almost twelve times greater than those of any of the other big landowning families. The major exception was the al-Yusuf family, one of whose siblings was married to Husayn Ibish (Tomeh, "Landownership"; Khoury, *Syria*, 446). Further research is necessary to better understand these dynamics.

349. Weulersse, *Paysans*, 196–97.

Epilogue

1. The *semaine sociale* was an occasional meeting among certain Christian elites to debate and reflect on a pressing issue of the moment. Among those presenting were Fouad Saadé, Soubhi Mazloum, Jean Debbané, Léon Mourad, Bichara Tabbah, and Michel Gillet, SJ. Aleppan Soubhi Mazloum had studied in French schools in Beirut and Paris, including the Sorbonne, and had received his doctorate in engineering from the Paris Faculty of Sciences in 1939. Starting in 1928, he oversaw the hydraulic studies service of northern Syria. He would go on to become the general director of irrigation and hydraulic forces (1948–1958), director of large public works (1959–1960), and secretary general of the Ministry of the Plan (1961–1963) (Pardé, "Nécrologie," 447–48). Mourad also hailed from Aleppo, where he had overseen the Office of National Economy (1927–1934); he then transferred to Beirut to work in the High Commission's office supervising tariffs and trade agreements (1934–1938), followed by positions with the customs bureau in Alexandretta (1938–1939), the Rationing Office (1939–1942), and the Provisioning Office (1942–1944). He held prominent positions in the Syrian government post-mandate, such as working for MIRA, the government's grain-collecting agency (Faris, *Min Huwa*, 411; for more on Mourad's career, see Schad, "Figure of the Native Expert"). Tabbah ran a newspaper, *Le Réveil*, and obtained his law degree from the faculty in Lyon in 1935. He would go on to serve in various legal posts in the Lebanese administration post-independence (Chavanne, "Nécrologie"). Michel Gillet, a Jesuit father, worked in a mission in the ʿAlawite mountains during the 1930s and early 1940s before being expelled following Syrian independence. His photographs demonstrate a keen interest in rural life (see Verdeil, "P. Michel Gillet," 313, 322). Jean Debbané came from a prominent family in Sidon, had graduated from the Jesuit Collège de Jamhour, and was a former student of the École des Sciences politique de Paris and an engineer from the École colonial d'Agriculture de Tunis. He had undertaken experiments with his brother Georges Debbané in Sidon between 1933 and 1938 to establish the "best method of disinfecting our citrus plantations," and the brothers would go on to found Debbané Agri in 1952 with an initial focus of spraying citrus orchards by contract (Möller, "'We do not Learn,'" 275–76; Debbané, *L'Expérimentation Agricole*, 22; "Our History," https://www.debbaneagri.com/en/who-we-are/our-history). Fouad Saadé had worked in Lebanon's Agriculture Ministry from 1924-1932 and at the time of the *semaine sociale* was a member of the Beirut municipal council. After a 1931 visit to the Chilean desert, he would become the exclusive purveyor of Chilean fertilizers in the region. In later years, he would serve as one of Lebanon's delegates to the Food and Agriculture Organization (Roberto Khatlab, "Fouad Saadé,

pionnier des relations économiques et diplomatiques entre Chili et le Moyen-Orient," *L'Orient-Le Jour*, 18 January 2010).

2. F. Saadé, "Problème," 14.

3. See *Troisième Semaine Sociale de Beyrouth*, "Table de Matières."

4. F. Saadé, "Problème," 22, 23. The one area in which Saadé did think substantial progress had been made was the work of the cadastre and the application of the *impôt foncier* it facilitated. Despite this, he was critical of the cadastre administration's failure to better tailor its application to local conditions. In Lebanon, for instance, he noted that the current system needed modifying for fruit trees because the *impôt foncier* taxed the number of trees planted and was not based on the harvest and its vicissitudes (F. Saadé, "Problème," 19–21).

5. ANF, F.10.2477–8, "ENA Montpellier Années 1923–24: Examens de Sortie," Minister of Agriculture to the Director of the National School of Agriculture of Montpellier, 22 August 1924; and acknowledgment of receipt by Fouad Saadé, 20 September 1924.

6. F. Saadé, "Problème," 25.

7. F. Saadé, "Problème," 28.

8. F. Saadé, "Problème," 22, 24.

9. SHAT, 4H329, "Note au sujet des travaux du Service Agricole de l'Office Économique de Guerre," from Pavie, 10 January 1946. During the war, Pavie had been promoted to head the agricultural service in the Economic Office of War (see CADN, Syrie-Liban/3, Direction du Personnel 131, "Pavie, Charles," "Relevé des services de M. Pavie").

10. Keen, *Agricultural Development*, iii; Vitalis and Heydemann, "War," 117–18. On the use and significance of the recently coined term *Middle East* in the center's name, see Seikaly, *Men of Capital*, 83–84.

11. Thompson, *Colonial Citizens*, 231; Seikaly, *Men of Capital*, 83.

12. Seikaly, *Men of Capital*, 84; Owen and Pamuk, *History*, 70; Keen, *Agricultural Development*, iii.

13. Keen, *Agricultural Development*, iii.

14. Petran, *Syria*, 82; TNA, FO 922.209, K. A. H. Murray, Director of Food, to the General Secretary, Spears Mission, 23 December 1944.

15. TNA, FO 922.196; Vitalis and Heydemann, "War," 119, 120, 121–22.

16. Petran, *Syria*, 82; Khoury, *Syria*, 596; Owen and Pamuk, *History*, 71. According to some accounts, these conditions also enabled peasants to finally pay off years of debt, although the evidence for this comes from Palestine and has been contested by recent scholarship (see Owen and Pamuk, *History*, 71; and Seikaly, *Men of Capital*, 156–62). According to one report from Syria and Lebanon, despite a belief that high prices were helping peasants pay off their debts, this was not in fact true, because the debts had been contracted in gold and therefore higher prices did not reduce their weight (TNA, FO922.264, "Report on Visit to Syria—July 14th–22nd," 25 July 1944).

17. Vitalis and Heydemann, "War," 129–30.

18. Al-Saleh, "Évaluation," 396.

19. Vitalis and Heydemann, "War," 130; Khoury, *Syria*, 596.

20. Vitalis and Heydemann, "War," 105, 121, 126.

21. Chaitani, *Post-Colonial Syria and Lebanon*; Republic of Syria, *Economic Development of Syria*, 28.

22. See, for example, Ajl, "Political Economy."

23. Republic of Syria, *Economic Development of Syria*. I use "national" here to refer to the Faysali government's brief period in Damascus. Although al-Shihabi's book was not published until after the French occupation, the geographic space in which he locates his program for development is clearly the state claimed by the Faysali government, and the work he undertook to write it was in its service.

24. See "Guarantee Agreement (Electric Power and Irrigation Projects) Between Republic of Lebanon and International Bank for Reconstruction and Development," 25 August 1955 (Washington, DC: World Bank, 1955); and "Loan Agreement (Electric Power and Irrigation Projects) Between International Bank for Reconstruction and Development and Litani River Authority," 25 August 1955 (Washington, DC: World Bank, 1955). Notably the Lebanese government does not appear to have commissioned a study like the Syrian one.

25. Warriner, *Land and Poverty*, 94–98.

26. Keen, *Agricultural Development*, iii.

27. See Keen, *Agricultural Development*.

28. Oldfield, "Warriner," 506. Warriner mentions that the reports were prepared for the MESC, but not by whom, although she does include a citation in her bibliography (Warriner, *Land and Poverty*, 86).

29. Warriner, *Land and Poverty*, 81–86. This emphasis on creating small cultivating proprietors was a common one in the development literature. For an analysis of the disastrous consequences of a project undertaken with this purpose in neighboring Iraq in the 1940s, see Pursley, *Familiar Futures*, 125–50.

30. Keen, *Agricultural Development*, 83.

31. Republic of Syria, *Economic Development of Syria*, 19–25, 175; International Bank for Reconstruction and Development, *Economic Development of Syria*, 35–103. The Gibb report did not specifically reference *mushaʿ*, but it referred to land passing to another farmer after a year or two and use of "strip" farming, both of which it deemed inimical to "farm[ing] in an economical manner" (Republic of Syria, *Economic Development of Syria*, 19). Regarding pests, despite the report recommending increased use of poison to control pests, it noted that with respect to locusts, for example, farmers preferred the "iron sheet method" to deploying poisoned bait (24–25). Zinc plating placed along the edge of ditches in which farmers would trap and kills locusts had been a common method of eradicating them in the region since at least World War I (see Dolbee, *Locusts of Power*).

32. International Bank for Reconstruction and Development, *Economic Development of Syria*, 68–69.

33. Keen, *Agricultural Development*, 84.

34. Republic of Syria, *Economic Development of Syria*, 19.

35. International Bank for Reconstruction and Development, *Economic Development of Syria*, 322.

36. Republic of Syria, *Economic Development of Syria*, 19; International Bank for Reconstruction and Development, *Economic Development of Syria*, 95–99.

37. The phrase "special problems" is taken from Keen, *Agricultural Development*, 79.

38. Warriner, *Land and Poverty*, 91, 92, 94.

39. Warriner, *Land and Poverty*, 94.

40. Warriner, *Land and Poverty*, 92, 94.

41. Warriner, *Land Reform*, 101.

42. Warriner, *Land Reform*, 74.

43. Warriner, *Land Reform*, 88–89, 105.

44. Warriner, *Land Reform*, 75, 81, 88. Ironically, one of the few landowners in the "old regions" that Warriner found "remarkable" was Husayn Ibish, whom she characterized as "not a rich man" but one who had managed to snap up some low-priced marshy land during the war, which he had drained and turned into a thriving estate. She contrasted his British-like demeanor—"in character and appearance [he] recalls the English or Scottish landowners of a generation ago, a tall, gaunt old man in tweeds, who would look right in Banbury market or on the Warwickshire County Council"—with the French-like behavior of the "old landowner families" who had the "mentality . . . of the *grand seigneur*," despite their use of tractors, canals, and pumps (95–96). Of course, Ibish was not quite as self-made as Warriner implied. The son of a well-off livestock merchant, he had married Wajiha al-Yusuf, the daughter of ʿAbd al-Rahman Pasha al-Yusuf, whose family's land had been the desired site for the Syrian Agricultural Stock Company discussed in chapter 4. During the mandate, when many large landowners had become heavily indebted, Ibish managed to maintain his credit, even borrowing money for his indebted in-laws, and eventually became the biggest landowner in Damascus (Khoury, *Syria*, 446).

45. Warriner, *Land Reform*, 89.

46. Middle East Supply Center, *Proceedings*; Keen, *Agricultural Development*, viii.

47. Warriner, *Land Reform*, 110–11.

48. Warriner, *Land and Poverty*; Warriner, *Land Reform*; International Bank for Reconstruction and Development, *Economic Development of Syria*. I borrow the phrase from Mitchell, *Rule of Experts*.

49. Keen, *Taṭawwur*. They had originally wanted al-Shihabi to translate the book, but he had demurred because he insisted he knew only the basics of English (1).

50. For a similar phenomenon in Egypt, see Derr, *Lived Nile*. Testament to the ongoing legacy of the relative accessibility of these two texts, a survey of WorldCat reveals that 2 libraries hold the Arabic text and that more than 250 hold some form of the English one.

51. Al-Shihabi, *Muhadarat*.

52. Al-Shihabi, *Muhadarat*, 168.

53. Al-Shihabi, *Muhadarat*, 167–68. Certainly there are a number of quite lengthy theoretical reports authored by the counselor in the archives. For a sample, see CADN, Syrie-Liban/1, 1571, Agriculture 1927–1928, "Notes Achard."

54. Auderset and Moser, "Mechanisation," 147; Goodman et al., *From Farming to Biotechnology*, 1, 2.

55. J. W. Moore, *Capitalism*, 2.

56. See, for example, Paxton, *French Peasant Fascism*, 22–23; Waswo, "Transformation," 583; and Fitzgerald, *Every Farm a Factory*.

57. Fitzgerald, *Every Farm a Factory*.

58. Waswo, "Transformation," 598; Gilbert, *Planning Democracy*; Bulaitis, *Communism in Rural France*; Paxton, *French Peasant Fascism*.

59. See Latron, *Vie rurale*, 242.

60. Fitzgerald, *Every Farm a Factory*, 5.

61. On the "somatic energy regime," see McNeill, *Something New*, 11–13.

BIBLIOGRAPHY

Archival Sources

FRANCE

Centre des Archives Diplomatiques de Nantes (CADN), Nantes

Syrie-Liban/1

Syrie-Liban/2

Syrie-Liban/3

Acquisitions Extraordinaires (AE)

Ministère des Affaires étrangères (MAE), La Courneuve, Paris

Levant 1918–1929, Syrie-Liban

Levant 1930–1940, Syrie-Liban

Archives Nationales de France (ANF), Pierrefitte-sur-Seine, Paris

Sous-série F/10

Chambre de Commerce de Marseille archives (CCM), Marseille

MQ.5.4/35

Service historique de l'armée de la terre (SHAT), Vincennes

4H (1917–1946)

ITALY

Food and Agriculture Organization Archives (FAO), Rome

International Institute of Agriculture archives (IIA)

LEBANON

American University of Beirut Archives and Special Collections (AUB), Beirut

Village Welfare Service Yearbooks

Corm Archive (CA), Beirut

SWITZERLAND
United Nations Archives at Geneva (UNAG)
League of Nations Pétitions
R28

SYRIA
Markaz al-watha'iq al-ta'rikhiya (MWT), Damascus
Mandate Era Court Registers

TURKEY
Devlet Arşivleri Başkanlığı Osmanlı Arşivi (BOA), Istanbul
A.}MKT.MHM Sadaret Mektubi Mühimme Kalemi Evrakı
BEO Bab-ı Ali Evrak Odası Evrakı
DH.H Dahiliye Nezareti Hukuk Evrakı
DH.İ.UM Dahiliye Nezareti İdare-i Umumiye Evrakı
DH.İD Dahiliye Nezareti İdare Evrakı
DH.MKT Dahiliye Nezareti Mektubi Kalemi
DH.MUİ Dahiliye Muhaberat-ı Umumiye İdaresi Evrakı
DH.ŞFR Dahiliye Nezareti Şifre Evrakı
DH.UMVM Dahiliye Nezareti Umur-ı Mahalliye ve Vilayat Müdürlüğü Evrakı
HR.MKT Hariciye Nezareti Mektubi Kalemi Evrakı
HR.SYS Hariciye Nezareti Siyasi
İ.DH İrade Dahiliye
İ.HUS İrade Hususi
İ.MMS İrade Meclis-i Mahsus
İ.OM İrade Orman ve Maadin
İ.RSM İrade Rüsumat
İ.TNF İrade Ticaret ve Nafia
MF.İBT Maarif Nezareti Tedrisat-ı İbtidaiye Kalemi
MF.MKT Maarif Nezareti Mektubi Kalemi
MV Meclis-i Vükela Mazbataları
ŞD Şura-yı Devlet Evrakı
T.ZTİ Ticaret-Nafia-Ziraat-Orman-Meâdin Nezaretleri Defterleri
Y.A.HUS Yıldız Sadaret Hususi Maruzat Evrakı
Y.PRK.HR Yıldız Perakende Evrakı Hariciye Nezareti Maruzatı
Y.PRK.ŞD Yıldız Perakende Evrakı Şura-yı Devlet Maruzatı
Y.PRK.TKM Yıldız Perakende Evrakı Tahrirat-ı Ecnebiye ve Mabeyn Mütercimliği
Y.PRK.TNF Yıldız Perakende Evrakı Ticaret ve Nafia Nezareti Maruzatı

UNITED KINGDOM
The National Archives (TNA), Kew
Foreign Office Papers

UNITED STATES
National Archives and Records Administration (NARA), College Park, Maryland
Record Group 84
Record Group 166, Foreign Agricultural Service

Newspapers and Periodicals

AMERICAN UNIVERSITY OF BEIRUT LIBRARY, BEIRUT

Al-Ittihad al-ʿUthmani

ATATÜRK KITAPLIĞI, ISTANBUL

Çiftçi

Çiftçiler Derneği Mecmuası

Ekinci

Orman ve Maadin ve Ziraat ve Baytar Mecmuası

Osmanlı ve Ticaret Gazetesi

Ticaret ve Ziraat Nezareti Mecmuası

BIBLIOTHÈQUE NATIONALE DE FRANCE, PARIS

Les Échos de Damas

BIBLIOTHÈQUE ORIENTALE, BEIRUT

Al-Iqtisad

Al-Majalla al-Ziraʿiye al-Suriya

Al-Ziraʿa al-Haditha

HARVARD COLLEGE LIBRARY, CAMBRIDGE, MASSACHUSETTS

Al-Marʾa

LEBANESE NATIONAL ARCHIVES, BEIRUT

Al-ʿIrfan

LIBRARY OF CONGRESS, WASHINGTON, DC

Al-Qabas

MILLI KÜTÜPHANESI, ANKARA

Basirüşşark

OTHER PERIODICALS

Annales de Géographie

L'Asie Française

Al-ʿAsima

Farm Implement News

The Forest Worker

La Géographie

Al-Jinan

Levant Trade Review

al-Majalla al-Iqtisadiya / La Revue Économique

Meclis-i Mebusan zabıt ceridesi

L'Orient-Le Jour

La Revue Phénicienne

Salname-yi Devlet-i Âliye-yi Osmaniye, vols. 1–66

Salname-yi Vilâyet-i Halep, vols. 1–34

Salname-yi Vilâyet-i Suriye, vols. 1–31

Published Sources

Abisaab, Malek. “Warmed or Burnt by Fire? The Lebanese Maronite Church Navigates French Colonial Policies, 1935.” *Arab Studies Quarterly* 36, no. 4 (2014): 292–312.

Achard, E.-C. “Notes sur la Syrie.” *L’Asie Française*, suppl. (July-August 1922): 94–113.

Achard, E. “al-Qutn fi Suriye.” *al-Ziraʿa al-Haditha* 1, no. 2 (February 1924): 58–63.

Achard, E. “al-Qutn fi Suriye.” *al-Ziraʿa al-Haditha* 1, no. 3 (March 1924): 145–48.

Achard, E. “La Syrie pays d’agriculture.” In *La Syrie et le Liban en 1921: La Foire-Exposition de Beyrouth, conférences, liste des récompenses*, ed. Haut-Commissariat de la République Française en Syrie et au Liban, 149–69. Paris: Emile Larose, 1922.

Achard, E. “Ziraʿat al-Qutn fi Suriye 2.” *al-Ziraʿa al-Haditha* 1, nos. 7–8 (July-August 1924): 409–13.

Adas, Michael. *Machines as the Measure of Man: Science, Technology, and Ideologies of Western Dominance*. Ithaca, NY: Cornell University Press, 1989.

al-Ahdab, Tawfiq. “al-Azma al-Ziraʿiya fi Suriya.” *al-Ziraʿa al-Haditha* 5, nos. 7–8 (May-June): 439–44.

al-Ahdab, Tawfiq. “al-Daraʾib ʿala al-Ziraʿa fi Suriya.” *al-Ziraʿa al-Haditha* 4, nos. 7–8 (May-June 1929): 362–68.

al-Ahdab, Tawfiq. “Daraʾib al-Ziraʿa fi Suriya.” *Al-Ziraʿa al-Haditha* 1, nos. 7–8 (July-August 1924): 357–61.

al-Ahdab, Tawfiq. “Daraʾib al-Ziraʿa fi Suriya 2.” *Al-Ziraʿa al-Haditha* 1, no. 9 (September 1924): 461–66.

al-Ahdab, Tawfiq. “al-Daraʾib wa al-Ziraʿa.” *al-Ziraʿa al-Haditha* 3, no. 1 (February 1927): 13–17.

al-Ahdab, Tawfiq. “al-Hala al-Ziraʿiya fi Suriya.” *Al-Ziraʿa al-Haditha* 1, no. 1 (January 1924): 11–16.

[al-Ahdab, Tawfiq]. “al-Hala al-Ziraʿiya fi Suriya 2.” *Al-Ziraʿa al-Haditha* 1, no. 5 (May 1924): 250–54.

al-Ahdab, Tawfiq. “Nafaqat al-Hasad wa al-Alat al-Haditha: Intaj Kathir ba-Masraf Qalil.” *Al-Ziraʿa al-Haditha* 3, no. 3 (April 1927): 159–65.

al-Ahdab, Tawfiq. “Ziraʿat al-Hinta fi Munatiq al-Suna.” *al-Ziraʿa al-Haditha* 3, no. 4 (May 1927): 228–30.

al-Ahdab, Tawfiq. “Ziraʿat al-Hinta fi Munatiq al-Suna.” *al-Ziraʿa al-Haditha* 3, nos. 6–7 (September-October 1927): 459–61.

Ahmad, Feroz. “The Agrarian Policies of the Young Turks, 1908–1918.” In *Économie et sociétés dans l’Empire Ottoman*, ed. Jean-Louis Bacqué-Grammont and Paul Dumont, 275–88. Paris: Éditions du Centre National de la Recherche Scientifique, 1983.

Ajl, Max. “The Political Economy of Thermidor in Syria: National and International Dimensions.” In *Syria: From Independence to Proxy War*, ed. Linda Matar and Ali Kadri, 209–45. Cham, Switzerland: Palgrave Macmillan, 2019.

Akarlı, Engin. *The Long Peace: Ottoman Lebanon, 1961–1920*. Berkeley: University of California Press, 1993.

Akarlı, Engin Deniz. “The Problems of External Pressures, Power Struggles, and Budgetary Deficits in Ottoman Politics Under Abdulhamid II (1876–1909): Origins and Solutions.” PhD diss., Princeton University, 1976.

Akarlı, Engin Deniz. "Taxation in Ottoman Lebanon, 1861–1915." *al-Abhath* 34 (1987): 32–33.

Alff, Kristen. "Levantine Joint-Stock Companies, Trans-Mediterranean Partnerships, and Nineteenth-Century Capitalist Development." *Comparative Studies in History and Society* 60, no. 1 (2018): 150–77.

Andrew, C. M., and A. S. Kanya-Forstner. "The French 'Colonial Party': Its Composition, Aims, and Influence, 1885–1914." *The Historical Journal* 14, no. 1 (1971): 99–128.

Ardrey, R. L. "Plow." In *The Americana: A Universal Reference Library, Comprising the Arts and Sciences, Literature, History, Biography, Geography, Commerce, etc., of the World*, ed. Frederick Converse Beach, 16. New York: Scientific American Compiling Department, 1912.

Aricanli, Tosun. "Agrarian Relations in Turkey: A Historical Sketch." In *Food, States, and Peasants: Analyses of the Agrarian Question in the Middle East*, ed. Alan Richards. Boulder, CO: Westview Press, 1986.

Arnold, David, and Ramachandra Guha, eds. *Nature, Culture, Imperialism: Essays on the Environmental History of South Asia*. Delhi: Oxford University Press, 1995.

Arrighi, Giovanni. *The Long Twentieth Century: Money, Power, and the Origins of Our Times*. London: Verso, 2010.

Arsan, Andrew. *Interlopers of Empire: The Lebanese Diaspora in Colonial French West Africa*. New York: Oxford University Press, 2014.

Ashton, Bessie L. "The Geography of Syria." *Journal of Geography* 27, no. 5 (1928): 167–80.

ʿAtallah, Yusuf. "al-Hala al-Ziraʿiya wa al-Iqtisadiya fi Biladna 4." *al-Ziraʿa al-Haditha* 1, no. 6 (June 1924): 315–18.

ʿAtallah, Yusuf. "al-Hala al-Ziraʿiya wa al-Iqtisadiya fi Suriya." *al-Ziraʿa al-Haditha* 1, no. 3 (March 1924): 130–34.

ʿAtallah, Yusuf. "al-Hala al-Ziraʿiya wa al-Iqtisadiya fi Suriya 3." *al-Ziraʿa al-Haditha* 1, no. 5 (May 1924): 237–40.

Auderset, Juri, and Peter Moser. "Mechanisation and Motorisation: Natural Resources, Knowledge, Politics, and Technology in 19th- and 20th-Century Agriculture." In *Agriculture in Capitalist Europe, 1945–1960: From Food Shortages to Food Surpluses*, ed. Carin Martiin, Juan Pan-Montojo, and Paul Brassley, 145–64. London: Routledge, 2016.

Autheman, André. *The Imperial Ottoman Bank*, trans. J. A. Underwood. Istanbul: Ottoman Bank Archives and Research Center, 2002.

Ebn el-Awam, Abu Zacaria Iahia Aben Mohamed Ben Ahmed. *Libro de Agricultura*, trans. Don Josef Antonio Banqueri. Madrid: La Imprenta Real, 1802.

Ibn al-Awam. *Le livre de l'agriculture*, trans. J.-J. Clément-Mullet. Paris: Librairie A. Franck, 1864.

Ax, Christina Folke, Niels Brimnes, Niklas Thode Jensen, and Karen Oslund, eds. *Cultivating the Colonies: Colonial States and Their Environmental Legacies*. Athens: Ohio University Press, 2011.

Aymes, Marc. *Un grand progrès, sur le papier: histoire provinciale des réformes ottomanes à Chypre au XIXe siècle*. Leuven: Peeters, 2010.

Aytekin, E. Attila. "Tax Revolts During the Tanzimat Period (1839–1876) and Before the Young Turk Revolution (1904–1908): Popular Protest and State Formation in the Late Ottoman Empire." *Journal of Policy History* 25, no. 3 (2013): 308–33.

Barak, On. *Powering Empire: How Coal Made the Middle East and Sparked Global Carbonization.* Oakland: University of California Press, 2020.

Barakat, Nora Elizabeth. *Bedouin Bureaucrats: Mobility and Property in the Ottoman Empire.* Stanford, CA: Stanford University Press, 2023.

Barakat, Nora. "Underwriting the Empire: Nizamiye Courts, Tax Farming, and the Public Debt Administration in Ottoman Syria." *Islamic Law and Society* 26 (2019): 374–404.

al-Barudi, Fakhri. *Awraq wa Mudhakkirat Fakhri al-Barudi, 1887-1966: khamsun ʿaman min hayat al-watan.* Damascus: Wizara al-Thaqafa, 1999.

al-Barudi, Hilmi. "Najil." *al-Ziraʿa al-Haditha* 3, no. 3 (April 1927): 145–49.

Barudi, Hilmi. "al-Faʾr al-Barri wa Adraruh." *al-Ziraʿa al-Haditha* 1, no. 3 (March 1924): 152–56.

Barudi, Hilmi. "Hasharat al-Suna." *al-Ziraʿa al-Haditha* 2, no. 1 (January 1925): 36–40.

Barudi, Hilmi. "Hasharat al-Suna wa Tanawub al-Zuruʿ." *al-Ziraʿa al-Haditha* 3, no. 1 (February 1927): 26–30.

Batatu, Hanna. *Syria's Peasantry, the Descendants of Its Lesser Rural Notables, and Their Politics.* Princeton, NJ: Princeton University Press, 1999.

Beattie, James, Edward Melilo, and Emily O'Gorman, eds. *Eco-Cultural Networks and the British Empire: New Views on Environmental History.* London: Bloomsbury Academic, 2015.

Behar, J. "Dairy Industry in the Turkish Empire." *Levant Trade Review* 6, no. 1 (1916): 182–87.

Beinart, William, and Lotte Hughes. *Environment and Empire.* Oxford, UK: Oxford University Press, 2007.

Bennett, Brett M., and Joseph M. Hodge. *Science and Empire: Knowledge and Networks of Science Across the British Empire, 1800–1970.* New York: Palgrave Macmillan, 2011.

Birdal, Murat. *The Political Economy of Ottoman Public Debt: Insolvency and European Financial Control in the Late Nineteenth Century.* London: I. B. Tauris, 2010.

Birinci Köy ve Ziraat Kalkınma Kongresi. *Türk Ziraat Tarihine Bir Bakış.* İstanbul: Devlet Basımevi, 1938.

Bivar, Venus. *Organic Resistance: The Struggle over Industrial Farming in Postwar France.* Chapel Hill: University of North Carolina Press, 2018.

Blaisdell, Donald C. *European Financial Control in the Ottoman Empire: A Study of the Establishment, Activities, and Significance of the Administration of the Ottoman Public Debt.* New York: AMS Press, 1966.

Bonin, Hubert. *Un outre-mer bancaire méditerranéen: histoire du Crédit Foncier d'Algérie et de Tunisie.* Paris: Publications de la Société Française d'Histoire d'Outre-Mer, 2004.

Boomgaard, Peter, ed. *Empire and Science in the Making: Dutch Colonial Scholarship in Comparative Global Perspective, 1760–1830.* New York: Palgrave Macmillan, 2013.

Boulet, Michel, ed. *Les enjeux de la formation des acteurs de l'agriculture, 1760–1945: acts du colloque—ENESAD 19–21 janvier 1999.* Dijon: Educagri, 2000.

Bourdieu, Pierre. *Distinction: A Social Critique of the Judgement of Taste.* Cambridge, MA: Harvard University Press, 1979.

Bourmand, Philippe, Norig Neveu, and Chantal Verdeil, eds. *Experts et expertise dans les mandats de la Société des Nations: figures, champs et outils.* Paris: Presses de l'Inalco, 2020.

Bulaitis, John. *Communism in Rural France: French Agricultural Workers and the Popular Front.* London: I. B. Tauris, 2008.

Bunton, Martin. *Colonial Land Policies in Palestine, 1917–1936*. New York: Oxford University Press, 2007.

Burbank, Jane, and Frederick Cooper. *Empires in World History: Power and the Politics of Difference*. Princeton, NJ: Princeton University Press, 2010.

Burke, Edmund, III. "A Comparative View of French Native Policy in Morocco and Syria, 1912–1925." *Middle Eastern Studies* 9, no. 2 (1973): 175–86.

Burns, Norman. *The Tariff of Syria, 1919–1932*. Beirut: American Press, 1933.

Çelik, Semih. "Science, to Understand the Abundance of Plants and Trees: The First Ottoman Natural History Museum and Herbarium, 1836–1848." In *Environments of Empire: Networks and Agents of Ecological Change*, ed. Ulrike Kirchberger and Brett M. Bennett, 85–102. Chapel Hill: University of North Carolina Press, 2020.

Çelik, Zeynep. *Displaying the Orient: Architecture of Islam at Nineteenth-Century World's Fairs*. Berkeley: University of California Press, 1992.

Çetinsaya, Gökhan. *Ottoman Administration of Iraq, 1890–1908*. London: Routledge, 2006.

Chaitani, Youssef. *Post-Colonial Syria and Lebanon: The Decline of Arab Nationalism and the Triumph of the State*. London: I. B. Tauris, 2007.

Charmasson, Thérèse, Michel Duvigneau, Anne-Marie Lelorrain, and Henri Le Naou. *L'enseignement agricole: 150 ans d'histoire*. Lyon: Educagri, 1999.

Chavanne, Albert. "Nécrologie: Bichara Tabbah." *Revue International de Droit Comparé* 24, no. 4 (1972): 879–81.

Chevallier, Dominique. "Lyon et la Syrie en 1919: les bases d'une intervention." *Revue Historique* 224, no. 2 (1960): 275–320.

Çiçek, M. Talha. *War and State Formation in Syria*. London: Routledge, 2014.

Cleveland, William L. *The Making of an Arab Nationalist: Ottomanism and Arabism in the Life and Thought of Sati*ʿ *al-Husri*. Princeton, NJ: Princeton University Press, 1972.

Code Foncier Ottoman. Istanbul: Imp. Française L. Mourkidès, 1913.

Cole, Camille Lyans. "Empire on Edge: Law, Land, and Capital in Gilded Age Basra." PhD diss., Yale University, 2020.

Colin, Élicio. "Notes et comptes rendus: Jacques Weulersse (1905–1946)." *Annales de Géographie* 56, no. 301 (1947): 53–54.

Conte, Giampaolo, and Gaetano Sabatini. "The Ottoman External Debt and Its Features Under European Financial Control (1881–1914)." *Journal of European Economic History* 3 (2014): 69–96.

Cooper, Frederick. *Colonialism in Question: Theory, Knowledge, History*. Berkeley: University of California Press, 2005.

Cuinet, Vital. *Syrie, Liban et Palestine, géographie administrative, statistique, descriptive et raisonnée*. Paris: E. Leroux, 1896.

Cuno, Kenneth M. "Contrat *salam* et transformations agricoles en basse Égypte à l'époque ottoman." *Annales: Histoire, Sciences Sociales* 61, no. 4 (2006): 925–40.

Cuno, Kenneth M. *The Pasha's Peasants: Land, Society, and Economy in Lower Egypt, 1740–1858*. Cambridge, UK: Cambridge University Press, 1992.

Davis, Diana K. *Resurrecting the Granary of Rome: Environmental History and French Colonial Expansion in North Africa*. Athens: Ohio University Press, 2007.

Davis, Mike. *Late Victorian Holocausts: El Niño Famines and the Making of the Third World*. New York: Verso, 2001.

Debbané, Jean. *L'Expérimentation agricole et l'enseignement rurale: Comment les organiser au Liban et en Syrie.* Beirut: Éditions Les Lettres Orientales, 1942.

Deering Harvesters for 1900. Chicago: Deering Harvester Co., 1900. https://archive.org/details/deeringharvester00deer.

Deguilhem, Randi. "State Civil Education in Late Ottoman Damascus: A Unifying or a Separating Force?" In *The Syrian Land: Processes of Integration and Fragmentation—Bilād al-Shām from the 18th to the 20th Century*, ed. Thomas Philipp and Birgit Schäbler, 221–50. Stuttgart: F. Steiner, 1998.

DelBourgo, James, and Nicholas Dew. *Science and Empire in the Atlantic World.* New York: Routledge, 2008.

Demangeon, Albert. *Le déclin de l'Europe.* Paris: Payot, 1920.

de Martonne, Emm. "Nécrologie: Albert Demangeon." *Annales de Géographie* 49, no. 280 (1940): 161–69.

Demirel, Muammer, and Fatma Kaya Doğanay. "Osmanlı'da Ziraat Eğitimi: Halkalı Ziraat Mektebi." *U.Ü. Fen-Edebiyat Fakültesi Sosyal Bilimler Dergisi* 12, no. 21 (2011/2012): 183–99.

Deringil, Selim. " 'They Live in a State of Nomadism and Savagery': The Late Ottoman Empire and the Post-Colonial Debate." *Comparative Studies in Society and History* 45, no. 2 (2003): 311–42.

Deringil, Selim. *The Well-Protected Domains: Ideology and the Legitimation of Power in the Ottoman Empire, 1876–1909.* London: I. B. Tauris, 2011.

Derr, Jennifer L. *The Lived Nile: Environment, Disease, and Material Economy in Egypt.* Stanford, CA: Stanford University Press, 2019.

Derri, Aviv. "Bonds of Obligation, Precarious Fortunes: Empire, Non-Muslim Bankers, and Peasants in Late Ottoman Damascus, 1820s–1890s." PhD diss., New York University, 2021.

Derri, Aviv. "Imperial Creditors, 'Doubtful' Nationalities, and Financial Obligations in Late Ottoman Syria: Rethinking Ottoman Subjecthood and Consular Protection." *International History Review 43, no. 5* (2021): 1060–79.

Dodge, Bayard. "The Institute of Rural Life at Beirut." In *The Proceedings of the Conference on Middle East Agricultural Development*, ed. Conference on Middle East Agricultural Development and Middle East Supply Center, 211–17. Cairo, n.p., 1944.

Dolbee, Samuel. *Locusts of Power: Borders, Empire, and Environment in the Modern Middle East, 1858–1939.* Cambridge, UK: Cambridge University Press, 2023.

Dolbee, Samuel, and Shay Hazkani. " 'Impossible Is not Ottoman': Menashe Meirovitch, ʿIsa al-ʿIsa, and Imperial Citizenship in Palestine." *International Journal of Middle East Studies* 47, no. 2 (May 2015): 241–262.

Doumani, Beshara. "Le contrat *salam* et les relations ville-campagne dans la Palestine ottomane." *Annales: Histoire, Sciences Sociales* 61, no. 4 (2006): 901–24.

Doumani, Beshara. *Family Life in the Ottoman Mediterranean: A Social History.* Cambridge, UK: Cambridge University Press, 2017.

Doumani, Beshara. *Rediscovering Palestine: Merchants and Peasants in Jabal Nablus, 1700–1900.* Berkeley: University of California Press, 1995.

Douwes, Dick, and Norman N. Lewis. "The Trials of Syrian Ismailis in the First Decade of the 20th Century." *International Journal of Middle East Studies* 21, no. 2 (1989): 215–32.

Drayton, Richard. *Nature's Government: Science, Imperial Britain, and the "Improvement" of the World*. New Haven, CT: Yale University Press, 2000.

Ducousso, Gaston. *L'industrie de la soie en Syrie et au Liban*. Beyrouth: Imprimerie Catholique, 1913.

Dueck, Jennifer M. *The Claims of Culture at Empire's End: Syria and Lebanon Under French Rule*. Oxford, UK: Oxford University Press, 2010.

Duffy, Andrea E. *Nomad's Land: Pastoralism and French Environmental Policy in the Nineteenth-Century Mediterranean World*. Lincoln: University of Nebraska Press, 2019.

Duman, Hasan. *Osmanlı yıllıkları (salnameler ve nevsaller): Bibliyografya ve bazı İstanbul kütüphanelerine göre bir katolog denemesi*. İstanbul: İslâm Tarih, Sanat ve Kültürü Araştırma Merkezi, 1982.

Düstur: I. Tertib, vol. 1. İstanbul: Matbaa-yi Amire, 1289 [1872].

Düstur: I. Tertib, vol. 2. İstanbul: Matbaa-yi Amire, 1289 [1872].

Düstur: I. Tertib, vol. 3. İstanbul: Matbaa-yi Amire, 1293 [1876].

Düstur: I. Tertib, vol. 6. Ankara; Devlet Matbaası, 1939.

Düstur: I. Tertib, vol. 8. Ankara: Devlet Matbaası, 1943.

Du Velay, A. *Essai sur l'histoire financière de la Turquie depuis le règne du sultan Mahmoud II jusqu'à nos jours*. Paris: Arthur Rousseau, 1903.

Eddé, Jacques. *Géographie de la Syrie et du Liban*. Beyrouth: Imprimerie Catholique, 1931.

Ediger, Volkan Ş., and John V. Bowlus. "Greasing the Wheels: The Berlin-Baghdad Railway and Ottoman Oil, 1888–1907." *Middle Eastern Studies* 56, no. 2 (2020): 193–206.

Eldem, Edhem. *A History of the Ottoman Bank*. Istanbul: Ottoman Bank Historical Research Center, 1999.

Eldem, Edhem. "The Imperial Ottoman Bank: Actor or Instrument of Ottoman Modernization." In *Modern Banking in the Balkans and West-European Capital in the Nineteenth and Twentieth Centuries*, ed. Kostas P. Kostis, 50–60. Aldershot, UK: Ashgate, 1999.

Elshakry, Marwa. *Reading Darwin in Arabic, 1860–1950*. Chicago: University of Chicago Press, 2013.

El Shakry, Omnia. *The Great Social Laboratory: Subjects of Knowledge in Colonial and Postcolonial Egypt*. Stanford, CA: Stanford University Press, 2007.

Faris, George. *Min Huwa fi Suriya 1949*. Damascus: al-Matbʾa al-Ahaliya, 1950.

Ferguson, James. *The Anti-Politics Machine: "Development," Depoliticization, and Bureaucratic Power in Lesotho*. Cambridge, UK: Cambridge University Press, 1994.

Ferid, Osman. "Ateşli Pulluklar." *Çiftçiler Derneği Mecmuası* 3, no. 5 (1 May 1335 [1 May 1919]): 432–36.

Fernández, Lourenzo, Juan Pan-Montojo, and Miguel Cabo, eds. *Agriculture in the Age of Fascism: Authoritarian Technocracy and Rural Modernization, 1922–1945*. Turnhout, Belgium: Brepols, 2014.

Firestone, Yaʿakov. "The Land-Equalizing *Mushaʿ* Village: A Reassessment." In *Ottoman Palestine, 1800–1914: Studies in Economic and Social History*, ed. Gad G. Gilbar, 91–129. Leiden: Brill, 1990.

Fischbach, Michael R. *State, Society, and Land in Jordan*. Leiden: Brill, 2000.

Fitzgerald, Deborah. "Blinded by Technology: American Agriculture in the Soviet Union, 1928–1932." *Agricultural History* 70, no. 3 (1996): 459–86.

Fitzgerald, Deborah. *Every Farm a Factory: The Industrial Ideal in American Agriculture*. New Haven, CT: Yale University Press, 2003.

Forclaz, Amalia Ribi. "Shaping the Future of Farming: The International Labor Organization and Agricultural Education, 1920s to 1950s." *Agricultural History Review* 65, no. 2 (2017): 320–39.

Fortna, Benjamin C. *Imperial Classroom: Islam, the State, and Education in the Late Ottoman Empire*. Oxford, UK: Oxford University Press, 2002.

"French Mandate for Syria and the Lebanon." *American Journal of International Law* 17, no. 3, suppl. (July 1923): 177–82.

Froidevaux, Henri. "L'indépendance du Grand-Liban." *L'Asie Française* 20, no. 185 (September-October 1920): 298–300.

Fullilove, Courtney. *The Profit of the Earth: The Global Seeds of American Agriculture*. Chicago: University of Chicago Press, 2017.

Gasper, Michael. *The Power of Representation: Publics, Peasants, and Islam in Egypt*. Stanford, CA: Stanford University Press, 2009.

[Gaulmier, J.] "Notes sur la propriété foncière dans la Syrie Centrale." *L'Asie Française* 309 (April 1933): 130–37.

Gelvin, James L. *Divided Loyalties: Nationalism and Mass Politics in Syria at the Close of Empire*. Berkeley: University of California Press, 1998.

Gelvin, James L. "The 'Politics of Notables' Forty Years After." *Middle East Studies Association Bulletin* 40, no. 1 (June 2006): 19–29.

Gelvin, James L., and Nile Green, eds. *Global Muslims in the Age of Steam and Print*. Berkeley: University of California Press, 2014.

Gerber, Haim. *The Social Origins of the Modern Middle East*. Boulder: Lynne Reinner, 1987.

Gieryn, Thomas F. "Boundary-Work and the Demarcation of Science from Non-Science: Strains and Interests in Professional Ideologies of Scientists." *American Sociological Review* 48, no. 6 (1983): 781–95.

Gilbert, Jess. *Planning Democracy: Agrarian Intellectuals and the Intended New Deal*. New Haven, CT: Yale University Press, 2015.

Goodman, David, Bernardo Sorj, and John Wilkinson. *From Farming to Biotechnology: A Theory of Agro-Industrial Development*. Oxford, UK: Basil Blackwell, 1987.

Goswami, Manu. *Producing India: From Colonial Economy to National Space*. Chicago: University of Chicago Press, 2004.

Gratien, Chris. "The Ottoman Quagmire: Malaria, Swamps, and Settlement in the Late Ottoman Mediterranean." *International Journal of Middle East Studies* 49 (2017): 583–604.

Gratien, Chris. *The Unsettled Plain: An Environmental History of the Late Ottoman Frontier*. Stanford, CA: Stanford University Press, 2022.

Great Britain. "Circular Addressed to Her Majesty's Representatives Abroad, 26 August 1869." In *Reports from Her Majesty's Representatives Respecting the Tenure of Land in the Several Countries of Europe: 1869–70*, Part I, 1–4. London: Harrison & Sons, 1870–1871.

Great Britain. *Foreign Office List, Forming a Complete British Diplomatic and Consular Handbook, January 1878*. London: Harrison, 1878.

Great Britain. "Report by Consul Palgrave Respecting Land Tenure in Eastern Turkey, 30 December 1869." In *Reports from Her Majesty's Representatives Respecting the Tenure of Land in the Several Countries of Europe: 1869–70*, Part II, 276–92. London: Harrison & Sons, 1870–1871.

Great Britain. "Report by Consul Wilkinson Representing Tenure of Land in the Consular District of Salonica, 14 December 1869." In *Reports from Her Majesty's Representatives Respecting the Tenure of Land in the Several Countries of Europe: 1869–70*, Part II, 303-05. London: Harrison and Sons, 1870–1871.

Great Britain. "Report by Mr. Moore Respecting Tenure of Land in Turkey, 25 January 1870." In *Reports from Her Majesty's Representatives Respecting the Tenure of Land in the Several Countries of Europe: 1869–70*, Part II, 273–76. London: Harrison & Sons, 1870–1871.

Gross, Max L. "Ottoman Rule in the Province of Damascus, 1860–1909." PhD diss., Georgetown University, 1979.

Grove, Richard H. *Green Imperialism: Colonial Expansion, Tropical Forest Edens, and the Origins of Environmentalism, 1600–1860*. Cambridge, UK: Cambridge University Press, 1996.

Gueslin, André. *Les origines du crédit agricole (1840–1914)*. Nancy: Université de Nancy II, 1978.

Güran, Tevfik. *19. Yüzyıl Osmanlı Tarımı*. İstanbul: Eren Yayıncılık, 1998.

Hakim, Carol. *The Origins of the Lebanese Nationalist Idea, 1840–1920*. Berkeley: University of California Press, 2013.

Hakim, George. "Fiscal System." In *The Economic Organization of Syria*, ed. Saʿid B. Himadeh, 333–402. Beirut: American Press, 1936.

Hakim, Yusuf. *Bayrut wa Lubnan fi ʿAhd al-ʿUthman*. Bayrut: Dar al-Nahar, 1980.

Hakim, Yusuf. *Suriya wa al-ʿAhd al-Faysali*. Beirut: Dar al-Nahar, 1986.

Hakim, Yusuf. *Suriya wa al-ʿAhd al-ʿUthmani*. Bayrut: Dar al-Nahar, 1980.

Hakim, Yusuf. *Suriya wa al-Intidab al-Faransi*. Bayrut: Dar al-Nahar, 1983.

Hallaj, Rufaʾil. "Hasharat al-Suna fi Suriya." *al-Ziraʿa al-Haditha* 2, no. 5 (June 1925): 287–91.

Hanioğlu, M. Şükrü. *A Brief History of the Late Ottoman Empire*. Princeton, NJ: Princeton University Press, 2008.

Hanna, Abdullah. "The Attitude of the French Mandatory Authorities Towards Land Ownership in Syria." In *The British and French Mandates in Comparative Perspectives*, ed. Nadine Méouchy and Peter Sluglett, 457–75. Leiden: Brill, 2004.

Hanna, Abdullah. *al-Qadiya al-ziraʿiya wa-al-harakat al-fallahiya fi Suriya wa-Lubnan (1820–1920)*, vol. 1. Bayrut: Dar al-Farabi, 1975.

Hanna, Abdullah. *al-Qadiya al-ziraʿiya wa-al-harakat al-fallahiya fī Suriya wa-Lubnan (1920–1945)*, vol. 2. Bayrut: Dar al-Farabi, 1978.

Hanssen, Jens. *Fin de Siècle Beirut: The Making of an Ottoman Provincial Capital*. Oxford, UK: Oxford University Press, 2005.

Hanssen, Jens. " 'Malhamé-Malfamé': Levantine Elites and Transimperial Networks on the Eve of the Young Turk Revolution." *International Journal of Middle East Studies* 43, no. 1 (2011): 25–48.

Haqqi Bey, Ismaʿil, comp. *Lubnan, Mabahith ʿilmiya wa-ijtimaʿiya*, 2 vols. Beirut: Publications de l'Université Libanaise, 1969–1970 [1918].

Harvey, David. *The Condition of Postmodernity: An Enquiry into the Origins of Cultural Change*. Oxford: Blackwell, 1992.

Harvey, David. *Spaces of Global Capitalism: Towards a Theory of Uneven Geographical Development*. London: Verso, 2006.

Harwood, Jonathan. *Technology's Dilemma: Agricultural Colleges Between Science and Practice in Germany, 1860–1934*. Oxford, UK: Peter Lang, 2005.

Haut-Commissariat de la République Française en Syrie et au Liban. *La Syrie et le Liban en 1921: La Foire-Exposition de Beyrouth, conférences, liste des récompenses*. Paris: Emile Larose, 1922.

Haut-Commissariat de la République Française en Syrie et au Liban. *La Syrie et le Liban en 1922*. Paris: Emile Larose, 1922.

Haut-Commissariat de la République Française en Syrie et au Liban. *La Syrie et le Liban sous l'occupation et le mandat français, 1919–1927*. Nancy: Berger-Levrault, 1929.

Headrick, Daniel R. *The Tentacles of Progress: Technology Transfer in the Age of Imperialism, 1850–1940*. New York: Oxford University Press, 1988.

Herment, Laurent. "Tractorisation: France, 1946–1955." In *Agriculture in Capitalist Europe, 1945–1960: From Food Shortages to Food Surpluses*, ed. Carin Martiin, Juan Pan-Montojo, and Paul Brassley, 185–205. London: Routledge, 2016.

H. F. [Henri Froidevaux?]. "Une mission française en Syrie." *L'Asie Française* 20, no. 185 (September-October 1920): 309–12.

Hibrawi, Muhammad. "Faʾr al-Haql." *al-Ziraʿa al-Haditha* 3, no. 4 (May 1927): 231–32.

Himadeh, Saʿid B. "Monetary and Banking System." In *Economic Organization of Syria*, ed. Saʿid B. Himadeh, 263–329. Beirut: American Press, 1936.

Himadeh, Saʿid B. *Monetary and Banking System of Syria*. Beirut: American Press, 1935.

Hinnebusch, Raymond A. *Authoritarian Power and State Formation in Baʿthist Syria: Army, Party, and Peasant*. Boulder, CO: Westview Press, 1990.

Hinnebusch, Raymond. *Peasant and Bureaucracy in Baʿthist Syria: The Political Economy of Rural Development*. Boulder, CO: Westview Press, 1989.

Hodge, Joseph Morgan. *Triumph of the Expert: Agrarian Doctrines of Development and the Legacies of British Colonialism*. Athens: Ohio University Press, 2007.

Hourani, Albert. "Ottoman Reform and the Politics of Notables." In *The Modern Middle East: A Reader*, ed. Albert Hourani, Philip Khoury, and Mary C. Wilson, 83–109. London: I. B. Tauris, 2005.

Husain, Faisal H. *Rivers of the Sultan: The Tigris and Euphrates in the Ottoman Empire*. Oxford, UK: Oxford University Press, 2021.

el-Husrî, Mustafa Satı. *Malumat-ı ziraiye*. İstanbul: Karabet Matbaası, 1321 [1904].

el-Husrî, Mustafa Satı. *Mebadî-i ulum-ı tabiiyeden hikmet ve kimya: tatbikat-ı ziraiye, sınaiye, sıhhiye ve beytiyeleri*. İstanbul: Matbaa-i Hayriye ve Şürekâsı, 1327 [1911].

el-Husrî, Mustafa Satı. *Mebadî-i ulum-ı tabiiyeden tatbikat-ı ziraiye*. İstanbul: Matbaa-i Hayriye ve Şürekâsı, 1328 [1912].

Huvelin, Paul. *Que vaut la Syrie?* Paris: Comité de l'Asie Française, 1921.

İhsanoğlu, Ekmeleddin. "Genesis of Learned Societies and Professional Associations in Ottoman Turkey." *Archivum Ottomanicum* 14 (1995): 161–89.

International Bank for Reconstruction and Development. *The Economic Development of Syria*. Baltimore: John Hopkins University Press, 1955.

İslamoğlu, Huri. "Politics of Administering Property: Law and Statistics in the Nineteenth-Century Ottoman Empire." In *Constituting Property: Private Property in the East and West*, ed. Huri İslamoğlu, 276–320. London: I. B. Tauris, 2004.

İslamoğlu, Huri. "Property as a Contested Domain: A Reevaluation of the Ottoman Land Code of 1858." In *New Perspectives on Property and Land in the Middle East*, ed. Roger Owen, 3–61. Cambridge, MA: Center for Middle Eastern Studies and Harvard University Press, 2000.

Issawi, Charles. *The Fertile Crescent, 1800–1914: A Documentary Economic History*. New York: Oxford University Press, 1988.

al-Jabri, Makin. "Zira^cat al-Qutn al-Baladi." *al-Zira^ca al-Haditha* 1, no. 4 (April 1924): 204–7.

Jackson, Simon. "What Is Syria Worth? The Huvelin Mission, Economic Expertise, and the French Project in the Eastern Mediterranean, 1918–1922." *Monde(s)* 2, no. 4 (2013): 83–103.

Jakes, Aaron. "Boom, Bugs, Bust: Egypt's Ecology of Interest, 1882–1914." *Antipode* 49, no. 4 (2017): 1035–59.

Jakes, Aaron G. *Egypt's Occupation: Colonial Economism and the Crises of Capitalism*. Stanford, CA: Stanford University Press, 2020.

Jas, Nathalie. "Public Health and Pesticide Regulation in France Before and After *Silent Spring*." *History and Technology* 23, no. 4 (2007): 369–88.

Jasanoff, Sheila. "The Idiom of Co-Production." In *States of Knowledge: The Co-Production of Science and the Social Order*, ed. Sheila Jasanoff, 1–12. London: Routledge, 2004.

al-Jaza'iri, Muhammad ʿAli ʿAbd al-ʿAziz. "al-Islah al-Ziraʿi fi Suriya." *al-Ziraʿa al-Haditha* 3, nos. 6–7 (September-October 1927): 426–31.

al-Jaza'iri, Muhammad ʿAli ʿAbd al-ʿAziz. "al-Islah al-Ziraʿi fi Suriya 2." *al-Ziraʿa al-Haditha* 3, nos. 9–10 (November-December 1927): 523–27.

al-Jaza'iri, Muhammad ʿAli ʿAbd al-ʿAziz. "al-Islah al-Ziraʿi fi Suriye 3." *al-Ziraʿa al-Haditha* 4, no. 1 (November 1928): 43–46.

Jenkins, H. M. *Report on Agricultural Education in North Germany, France, Denmark, Belgium, Holland, and the United Kingdom*. London: Eyre & Spottiswoode, 1884.

Johansen, Baber. "Le contrat *salam*: Droit et formation du capital dans l'Empire abbasside (XIe–XIIe siècles)." *Annales: Histoire, Sciences Sociales* 61, no. 4 (2006): 863–99.

Johnson, Michael. *Class and Client in Beirut: The Sunni Muslim Community and the Lebanese State, 1840–1985*. London: Atlantic Highlands, 1986.

Jones, Peter M. "The Challenge of Land Reform in Eighteenth- and Nineteenth-Century France." *Past and Present* 216 (August 2012): 107–42.

Kalisman, Hilary Falb. "'The Next Generation of Cultivators': Teaching Agriculture in Iraq, Palestine, and Transjordan (1920–1960)." *Histoire de l'Éducation* 148, no. 2 (2017): 143–64.

Karakoç, Serkiz. *Tahşiyeli Kavanin*, vol. 1. İstanbul: Kütüphane-yi Cihan, 1341–1343 [1925–1927].

Karakoç Serkiz. *Tahşiyeli Kavanin*, vol. 2, *Arazi kanunu, tapu nizamnamesi*. İstanbul: Kütüphane-yi Cihan, 1340–1342 [1924–1926].

Kasaba, Reşat. *The Ottoman Empire and the World Economy: The Nineteenth Century*. Albany: State University of New York Press, 1988.

Kaufman, Asher. *Reviving Phoenicia: The Search for Identity in Lebanon*. London: I. B. Tauris, 2014.

Kaya, Alp Yücel. "Searching for Economic and Administrative Reforms: The Enquiry of 1863 in the Ottoman Empire." In *The Golden Age of State Enquiries: Rural Enquiries in the Nineteenth Century*, ed. Nadine Vivier, 75–89. Turnhout, Belgium: Brepols, 2014.

Kaya, Alp Yücel, and Yücel Terzibaşoğlu. "Tahrir'den Kadastro'ya: 1874 İstanbul Emlak Tahriri ve Vergisi 'Kadastro tabir olunur tahrir-i emlak.'" *Tarih ve Toplum: Yeni Yaklaşımlar* 9 (Fall 2009): 7–56.

Kayalı, Hasan. *Arabs and Young Turks: Ottomanism, Arabism, and Islamism in the Ottoman Empire, 1908–1918*. Berkeley: University of California Press, 1997.

al-Kaylani, ʿAbd al-Qadir. "al-Azma al-Ziraʿiya fi Suriya." *al-Ziraʿa al-Haditha* 5, no. 9–10 (August-September 1932): 592–96.

Kâzım, Hüseyin. "Bir Ziraat Gazetesinin Vazifesi." *Çiftçi* 1, no. 1 (April 12, 1909): 5–8.

Kâzım, Hüseyin. *Çiftçi Çocuğu* [Farmer Child]. İstanbul: Matbaʿa-i Hayiriya Şirkası, 1329–1331 [1913/1914–1915/1916].

Kâzım, Hüseyin. "Dibajat al-Kitab." In *Lubnan, Mabahith ʿilmiya wa-ijtimaʿiya*, comp. Ismaʿil Haqqi Bey, 1: 1–2. Beirut: Publications de l'Université Libanaise, 1969 [1918].

Kâzım, Hüseyin. "Suriye Ziraatına Müteallik Bir İki Söz." In *Beyrut Vilayeti*, comp. Mehmet Refik and Mehmet Behcet, 1: 58–65. Beirut: Vilayet Matbaası, 1333 [1917].

Kâzım, Hüseyin. *İlm-i Ziraat*. İstanbul: Tanin Matbaası, 1327 [1911/1912].

Kâzım, Hüseyin. "Lamha Nazariya fi al-Ziraʿa." In *Lubnan, Mabahith ʿilmiya wa-ijtimaʿiya*, comp. Ismaʿil Haqqi Bey, 2: 367–79. Beirut: Publications de l'Université Libanaise, 1970 [1918].

Kâzım Kadri, Hüseyin. *Meşrutiyetten Cumhuriyete Hatıralarim*. İstanbul: Dergah Yayınları, 2000.

Keen, B. A. *The Agricultural Development of the Middle East*. London: His Majesty's Stationery Office, 1946.

Keen, Bernard. *Tatawwur al-ziraʿa fi al-Sharq al-Awsat*, trans. al-Sayyid Amin Nazif. Cairo: Maktabat al-Nahdah al-Misriya, 1950.

Keyder, Çağlar, and Faruk Tabak, eds. *Landholding and Commercial Agriculture in the Middle East*. Albany: State University of New York Press, 1991.

Khater, Akram Fouad. *Inventing Home: Emigration, Gender, and the Middle Class in Lebanon, 1870–1920*. Berkeley: University of California Press, 2001.

al-Khatib, Adnan. *al-Amir Mustafa al-Shihabi, 1893–1968*. Damascus: Matbaʿat al-Taraqqi, 1968.

Khoury, Philip. *Syria and the French Mandate: The Politics of Arab Nationalism, 1920–1945*. Princeton, NJ: Princeton University Press, 1987.

Khoury, Philip S. "The Syrian Independence Movement and the Growth of Economic Nationalism in Damascus." *Bulletin of the British Society for Middle Eastern Studies* 14, no. 1 (1987): 25–36.

Khoury, Philip S. *Urban Notables and Arab Nationalism: The Politics of Damascus, 1860–1920*. Cambridge, UK: Cambridge University Press, 1983.

Khuri, Albert. "Agriculture." In *Economic Organization of Syria*, ed. Saʿid B. Himadeh, 73–115. Beirut: American Press, 1936.

Khuri, Albert. "Land Tenure." In *Economic Organization of Syria*, ed. Saʿid B. Himadeh, 51–69. Beirut: American Press, 1936.

Kirchberger, Ulrike, and Brett M. Bennett, eds. *Environments of Empire: Networks and Agents of Ecological Change*. Chapel Hill: University of North Carolina Press, 2020.

Kiyotaki, Keiko. *Ottoman Land Reform in the Province of Baghdad*. Leiden: Brill, 2019.

Kiyotaki, Keiko. "Ottoman State Finance: A Study of Fiscal Deficits and Internal Debt in 1859–63." Working Paper no. 90/05, London School of Economics (April 2005).

Klein, Janet. *The Margins of Empire: Kurdish Militias in the Ottoman Tribal Zone*. Stanford, CA: Stanford University Press, 2011.

Kotsonis, Yanni. *Making Peasants Backwards: Agricultural Cooperatives and the Agrarian Question in Russia, 1861–1914*. New York: St. Martin's Press, 1999.

Kotsonis, Yanni. *States of Obligation: Taxes and Citizenship in the Russian Empire and Early Soviet Republic*. Toronto: University of Toronto Press, 2014.

Küçükceran, Zeynep. *The Agrarian Economy and Primary Education in the Salonican Countryside in the Hamidian Period (1876–1908)*. Istanbul: Libra Kitapçılık ve Yayıncılık Ticaret, 2014.

Kuehn, Thomas. *Empire, Islam, and Politics of Difference: Ottoman Rule in Yemen, 1849–1919*. Leiden: Brill, 2011.

Kuehn, Thomas. "Shaping and Re-Shaping Colonial Ottomanism: Contesting Boundaries of Difference and Integration in Ottoman Yemen, 1872–1919." *Comparative Studies of South Asia, Africa, and the Middle East* 27, no. 2 (2007): 315–31.

Kuehn, Thomas. " 'We Know Nothing About Yemen!' Ottoman Imperial Governance in Southwest Arabia and the Politics of Knowledge Production, 1871–1914." *Journal of Arabian Studies* 8, no. 1 (2018): 5–24.

Kuneralp, Sinan. *Son Dönem Osmanlı Erkân ve Ricali (1839–1922)*. İstanbul: İsis, 1999.

Kurd ʿAli, Muhammad. *Kitab Khitat al-Sham*, vol. 4. Damascus: Matba'at al-Taraqqi, 1345 [1926].

Labaki, Boutros. *Introduction á l'histoire économique de Liban: soie et commerce extérieur en fin de période Ottomane (1840–1914)*. Beirut: Librairie Orientale, 1984.

Latour, Bruno. *Reassembling the Social: An Introduction to Actor-Network-Theory*. Oxford, UK: Oxford University Press, 2005.

Latour, Bruno. *We Have Never Been Modern*. Cambridge, MA: Harvard University Press, 1993.

Latron, André. *La vie rurale en Syrie et au Liban: étude d'économie sociale*. Beirut: Imprimerie catholique, 1936.

Lefebvre, Henri. *The Production of Space*. Malden, MA: Blackwell, 1991.

Lefebvre, Henri. "Space and the State." In *State, Space, World: Selected Essays*, ed. Neil Brenner and Stuart Elden, 223–53. Minneapolis: University of Minnesota Press, 2009.

Leroux, Eugène. *Cours d'agriculture*, 3rd ed. Paris: G. Masson, 1906.

Lewis, Norman N. "Malaria, Irrigation, and Soil Erosion in Central Syria." *Geographical Review* 39, no. 2 (1949): 278–90.

Lewis, Norman N. *Nomads and Settlers in Syria and Jordan, 1800–1980*. Cambridge, UK: Cambridge University Press, 1987.

Longrigg, Stephen Helmsley. *Syria and Lebanon Under French Mandate*. London: Oxford University Press, 1958.

Louisides, P. J. "Commercial Letter from Cyprus." *Levant Trade Review* 1, no. 2 (November 1911): 226–28.

Low, Michael Christopher. *Imperial Mecca: Ottoman Arabia and the Indian Ocean Hajj*. New York: Columbia University Press, 2020.

Lubin, David. "The International Institute of Agriculture and Its Influence on Economic Welfare: Reply to Some Comments Made by the Minister of Agriculture of France." [Rome: International Institute of Agriculture], 1911. https://archive.org/details/internationalins01lubi4.

Ludden, David. *An Agrarian History of South Asia*. Cambridge, UK: Cambridge University Press, 1999.

Ludden, David, ed. *Agricultural Production and South Asian History*. New Delhi: Oxford University Press, 2005.

Ludden, David. *Early Capitalism and Local History in South India*. Oxford, UK: Oxford University Press, 2005.

Ludden, David. "Introduction." In *Agricultural Production and Indian History*, ed. David Ludden, 1–35. Delhi: Oxford University Press, 1994.

Lutfî, Ahmet. *Tarih-i Lutfî*, vol. 7. Dersaadet [Istanbul]: Mahmut Bey Matbaası, 1306 [1890/1891].

Makdisi, Ussama. *The Culture of Sectarianism: Community, History, and Violence in Nineteenth-Century Lebanon*. Berkeley: University of California Press, 2000.

Makdisi, Ussama. "Ottoman Orientalism." *American Historical Review* 107, no. 3 (2002): 768–96.

Manachy, Lorenzo Y. "Report from Aleppo." *Levant Trade Review*, 1, no. 3 (December 1911): 292–96.

Maʿoz, Moshe. *Ottoman Reform in Syria and Palestine, 1840–1861: The Impact of the Tanzimat on Politics and Society*. Oxford, UK: Clarendon Press, 1968.

Mardin, Şerif. *Religion, Society, and Modernity in Turkey*. Syracuse, NY: Syracuse University Press, 2006.

Masters, Bruce. "Aleppo: The Ottoman Empire's Caravan City." In *The Ottoman City Between East and West: Aleppo, Izmir, and Istanbul*, by Edhem Eldem, Daniel Goffman, and Bruce Masters, 17–78. Cambridge, UK: Cambridge University Press, 1999.

Masters, Bruce. "The Political Economy of Aleppo in an Age of Ottoman Reform." *Journal of the Economic and Social History of the Orient* 53 (2010): 309–11.

Matteson, Kieko. *Forests in Revolutionary France: Conservation, Community, and Conflict, 1669–1848*. New York: Cambridge University Press, 2015.

mcelrone, susynne. "From the Pages of the *Defter*: A Social History of Rural Property Tenure and the Implementation of the Tanzimat Land Reform in Hebron, Palestine (1858–1900)." PhD diss., New York University, 2016.

McNeill, J. R. *Something New Under the Sun: An Environmental History of the Twentieth-Century World*. New York: Norton, 2001.

Mecmua-yi Kavanin. İstanbul: Takvimhane-i Amire, 1851.

Médawar, Wady. *La Syrie agricole*. Beauvais: Imprimerie A. Dumontier, 1903.

Meiton, Fredrik. *Electrical Palestine: Capital and Technology from Empire to Nation*. Oakland: University of California Press, 2019.

Métral, Françoise. "Land Tenure and Irrigation Projects in Syria: 1948–1982." In *Land Tenure and Social Transformation in the Middle East*, ed. Tarif Khalidi, 465–81. Beirut: American University of Beirut, 1984.

Middle East Supply Center. *The Proceedings of the Conference on Middle East Agricultural Development*. Cairo: Middle East Supply Center, 1944.

Mikhail, Alan. *Nature and Empire in Ottoman Egypt*. Cambridge, UK: Cambridge University Press, 2011.

Minawi, Mostafa. "Beyond Rhetoric: Reassessing Bedouin-Ottoman Relations Along the Route of the Hijaz Telegraph Line at the End of the Nineteenth Century." *Journal of the Economic and Social History of the Orient* 58, nos. 1–2 (2015): 75–104.

Minawi, Mostafa. *The Ottoman Scramble for Africa: Empire and Diplomacy in the Sahara and the Hijaz*. Stanford, CA: Stanford University Press, 2016.

Ministère des affaires étrangères. *Rapport à la Société des Nations sur la situation de la Syrie et du Liban (année 1925)*. Paris: Imprimerie nationale, 1926.

Ministère des affaires étrangères. *Rapport à la Société des Nations sur la situation de la Syrie et du Liban (année 1926)*. Paris: Imprimerie nationale, 1927.

Ministère des affaires étrangères. *Rapport à la Société des Nations sur la situation de la Syrie et du Liban (année 1928)*. Paris: Imprimerie nationale, 1929.

Ministère des affaires étrangères. *Rapport à la Société des Nations sur la situation de la Syrie et du Liban (année 1929)*. Paris: Imprimerie nationale, 1930.

Ministère des affaires étrangères. *Rapport à la Société des Nations sur la situation de la Syrie et du Liban (année 1930)*. Paris: Imprimerie nationale, 1931.

Ministère des affaires étrangères. *Rapport à la Société des Nations sur la situation de la Syrie et du Liban (année 1931)*. Paris: Imprimerie nationale, 1932.

Ministère des affaires étrangères. *Rapport à la Société des Nations sur la situation de la Syrie et du Liban (année 1932)*. Paris: Imprimerie nationale, 1933.

Ministère des affaires étrangères. *Rapport à la Société des Nations sur la situation de la Syrie et du Liban (année 1934)*. Paris: Imprimerie nationale, 1935.

Ministère des affaires étrangères. *Rapport à la Société des Nations sur la situation de la Syrie et du Liban (année 1937)*. Paris: Imprimerie nationale, 1938.

Ministère des affaires étrangères. *Rapport sur la situation de la Syrie et du Liban (Juillet 1922–Juillet 1923)*. Paris: Imprimerie nationale, 1923.

Ministère des affaires étrangères. *Rapport sur la situation de la Syrie et du Liban (Juillet 1923–Juillet 1924)*. Paris: Imprimerie nationale, 1924.

Ministère des affaires étrangères. *Rapport sur la situation de la Syrie et du Liban (année 1924)*. Geneva: League of Nations, 1925.

Mitchell, Timothy. *Carbon Democracy: Political Power in the Age of Oil*. London: Verso, 2013.

Mitchell, Timothy. *Rule of Experts: Egypt, Techno-Politics, Modernity*. Berkeley: University of California Press, 2002.

Mitchell, Timothy. "Society, Economy, and the State Effect." In *State/Culture: State-Formation After the Cultural Turn*, ed. George Steinmetz, 76–97. Ithaca, NY: Cornell University Press, 1999.

Mitchell, Timothy. "The Stage of Modernity." In *Questions of Modernity*, ed. Timothy Mitchell, 1–34. Minneapolis: University of Minnesota Press, 2000.

Mizrahi, Jean-David. *Genèse de l'état mandatoire: service des renseignements et bandes armees en Syrie et au Liban dans les années 1920*. Paris: Publications de la Sorbonne, 2003.

Möller, Esther. "'We Do not Learn for School, but for Life': Alumni Associations at French Schools in Lebanon in the 1930s and 1940s as Privileged Spaces of Sociability." In

Entangled Education: Foreign and Local Schools in Ottoman Syria and Mandate Lebanon (19th–20th Centuries), ed. Julia Hauser, Christine B. Linder, and Esther Möller, 265–82. Beirut: Ergon Verlag Würzburg in Kommission, 2016.

Moon, David. *The Plough That Broke the Steppes: Agriculture and Environment in Russia's Grasslands, 1700–1914*. Oxford, UK: Oxford University Press, 2013.

Moore, Gary E. "The Involvement of Experimental Stations in Secondary Agricultural Education, 1887–1917." *Agricultural History* 62, no. 2 (1988): 164–76.

Moore, Jason W. *Capitalism in the Web of Life: Ecology and the Accumulation of Capital*. London: Verso, 2015.

Morawitz, Charles. *Les finances de la Turquie*. Paris: Guillaumin, 1902.

Mouchahwar, Amin. "Nos ressources agricoles, industrielles, minières et commerciales." *La Revue Phénicienne* (July 1919): 21–26.

Mouchawar, Amin. *Notice sur les impôts et les taxes au Liban*. Harissa, Lebanon: Imprimerie de Saint Paul, 1934.

Moulin, Annie. *Peasantry and Society in France Since 1789*. Cambridge, UK: Cambridge University Press, 1991.

Mounayer, Nassib. *La régime de la terre en Syrie: études historiques juridiques, et économiques*. Paris: Librairie Générale de Droit et de Jurisprudence, 1929.

Mundy, Martha. "La propriété dite mushâ' en Syrie: à propos des travaux de Yaʿakov Firestone." *Revue du Monde Musulman et de la Méditerranée* 79–80 (1996): 273–87.

Mundy, Martha, and Richard Saumarez Smith. *Governing Property, Making the Modern State: Law, Administration, and Production in Ottoman Syria*. London: I. B. Tauris, 2007.

Naccache, Albert. "Notre avenir économique." *La Revue Phénicienne* (July 1919): 2–10.

Naccache, Pierre, ed. *Un autre Liban: les écrits d'Albert Naccache, 1917–1951*. Paris: Geuthner, 2018.

Nash, Linda. "The Agency of Nature or the Nature of Agency." *Environmental History* 10, no. 1 (2005): 67–69.

Neep, Daniel. *Occupying Syria Under the French Mandate: Insurgency, Space, and State Formation*. Cambridge, UK: Cambridge University Press, 2012.

Norris, Jacob. *Land of Progress: Palestine in the Age of Colonial Development, 1905–1948*. Oxford, UK: Oxford University Press, 2013.

Noujaim, Paul. "La question du Liban: étude de politique économique et de statistique descriptive." *La Revue Phénicienne* (August 1919): 66–81.

Oldfield, Sybil. "Warriner, Doreen Agnes Rosemary Julia." In *The Oxford Dictionary of National Biography, ed. H. C. G. Matthew and Brian Harrison, 506–8*. Oxford, UK: Oxford University Press, 2004.

Omar, Hussein. "Arabic Thought in the Liberal Cage." In *Islam After Liberalism*, ed. Faisal Devji and Zaheer Kazmi, 17–45. London: Oxford University Press, 2017.

Ongley, F., trans. *The Ottoman Land Code*. London: W. Clowes & Sons, 1892.

Orman ve Maâdin ve Ziraat Nezareti İstatistik İdaresi. *1323 senesi Avrupa-yi Osmanî ziraat istatistiği*. İstanbul: Mahmut Bey Matbaası, 1326 [1910/1911].

Orman ve Maadin ve Ziraat Nezareti Kalem-i Mahsus Müdüriyet Istatistik Şubesi. *1325 senesi Asya ve Afrika-i Osmanî ziraat istatistiği*. Dersaadet: Matbaa-i Osmaniye, 1327 [1911/1912].

Ouahes, Idir. "French Mandate Syria and Lebanon: Land, Ecological Interventions, and the 'Modern' State." In *Environments of Empire: Networks and Agents of Ecological Change*, ed. Ulrike Kirchberger and Brett M. Bennett, 61–82. Chapel Hill: University of North Carolina Press, 2020.

Owen, Roger. *The Middle East in the World Economy, 1800–1914*. London: I. B. Tauris, 2009 [1981].

Owen, Roger, and Şevket Pamuk. *A History of Middle East Economies in the Twentieth Century*. Cambridge, MA: Harvard University Press, 1999.

Özbek, Nadir. *İmparatorluğun Bedeli: Osmanlı'da Vergi, Siyaset ve Toplumsal Adalet (1839–1908)*. İstanbul: Boğaziçi Üniversitesi Yayınevi, 2015.

Özbek, Nadir. "Tax Farming in the Nineteenth-Century Ottoman Empire: Institutional Backwardness or the Emergence of Modern Public Finance?" *Journal of Interdisciplinary History* 49, no. 2 (2018): 219–45.

Özok-Gündoğan, Nilay. "A Peripheral Approach to the 1908 Revolution in the Ottoman Empire: Land Disputes in Peasant Petitions in Post-Revolutionary Diyarbekir." In *Social Relations in Ottoman Diyarbekir, 1870–1915*, ed. Joost Jongerden and Jelle Verheij, 179–215. Leiden: Brill, 2012.

Pamuk, Şevket. "The Ottoman Economy in World War I." In *The Economics of World War I*, ed. Stephen Broadberry and Mark Harrison, 112–36. Cambridge, UK: Cambridge University Press, 2005.

Pamuk, Şevket. *The Ottoman Empire and European Capitalism, 1820–1913: Trade, Investment, and Production*. Cambridge, UK: Cambridge University Press, 1987.

Pan-Montojo, Juan, and Niccolò Mignemi. "International Organizations and Agriculture, 1905–1945." *Agricultural Historical Review* 65, no. 2 (2017): 237–76.

Pardé, Maurice. "Nécrologie: sur un hydrologue disparu de haute distinction: Soubhi Mazloum." *Annales de Géographie* 404 (1965): 447–48.

Parmentier, Paul. "L'Agriculture en Syria: IV." *Revue de Botanique Appliquée et d'Agriculture Colonial* 2, no. 9 (May 31, 1922): 208–14.

Parmentier, Paul. *Manuel d'agriculture, par demandes et par réponses, à l'usage des cultivateurs syriens et des élèves des écoles*. Lyon: M. Audin, 1922.

Parmentier, Paul. "al-Ziraʿa fi Suriya." *al-Ziraʿa al-Haditha* 1, no. 1 (January 1924): 25–36.

Parmentier, Paul. "al-Ziraʿa fi Suriya 2." *al-Ziraʿa al-Haditha* 1, no. 2 (February 1924): 64–81.

Parmentier, Paul. "al-Ziraʿa fi Suriye 7." *al-Ziraʿa al-Haditha* 1, nos. 7–8 (July-August 1924): 380–88.

Parmentier, Paul. "al-Ziraʿa fi Suriye 9." *al-Ziraʿa al-Haditha* 2, no. 2 (March 1925): 88–92.

Paxton, Robert O. *French Peasant Fascism: Henry Dorgère's Greenshirts and the Crises of French Agriculture, 1929–1939*. New York: Oxford University Press, 1997.

Peet, Richard, Paul Robbins, and Michael Watts, eds. *Global Political Ecology*. New York: Routledge, 2011.

Pehlivan, Zozan. "El Niño and the Nomads: Global Climate, Local Environment, and the Crisis of Pastoralism in Late Ottoman Kurdistan." *Journal of the Economic and Social History of the Orient* 63 (2020): 316–56.

Peterson, Maya. *Pipe Dreams: Water and Empire in Central Asia's Aral Sea Basin*. Cambridge, UK: Cambridge University Press, 2019.

Petran, Tabitha. *Syria*. New York: Praeger, 1972.

Pierce, James Wilson. *Photographic History of the World's Fair and Sketch of the City of Chicago: Also a Guide to the World's Fair and Chicago*. Baltimore: R. H. Woodward, 1893.

Pitts, Graham. "Fallow Fields: Famine and the Making of Lebanon." PhD diss., Georgetown University, 2016.

Prakash, Gyan. *Another Reason: Science and the Imagination of Modern India*. Princeton, NJ: Princeton University Press, 1999.

Provence, Michael. *The Great Syrian Revolt and the Rise of Arab Nationalism*. Austin, TX: University of Austin Press, 2005.

Provence, Michael. *The Last Ottoman Generation and the Making of the Modern Middle East*. Cambridge, UK: Cambridge University Press, 2017.

Provence, Michael. "Ottoman and French Mandate Land Registers for the Region of Damascus." *Middle East Studies Association Bulletin* 39, no. 1 (2005): 32–43.

Pursley, Sara. " 'Education for Real Life': Pragmatist Pedagogies and American Interwar Expansion in Iraq." In *The Routledge Handbook of the History of the Middle East Mandates*, ed. Cyrus Schayegh and Andrew Arsan, 88–105. London: Routledge 2015.

Pursley, Sara. *Familiar Futures: Time, Selfhood, and Sovereignty in Iraq*. Stanford, CA: Stanford University Press, 2019.

Qasimi, Zafir. *Maktab ʿAnbar: suwar wa-dhikrayat min hayatina al-thaqafiya wa-al-siyasiya wa-al-ijtimaʿiya*. Beirut: Dar al-Mashriq, 1964.

Qasimiya, Khayriyah. *Al-Hukuma al-ʿArabiya fi Dimashq bayna 1918–1920*. Cairo: Dar al-Maʿarif bi-Misr, 1971.

Quataert, Donald. "The Age of Reforms, 1812–1914." In *An Economic and Social History of the Ottoman Empire, 1300–1914*, ed. Halil İnalcik and Donald Quataert, 761–933. Cambridge, UK: Cambridge University Press, 1994.

Quataert, Donald. "Dilemma of Development: The Agricultural Bank and Agricultural Reform in Ottoman Turkey, 1888–1908." *International Journal of Middle East Studies* 6, no. 2 (1975): 210–27.

Quataert, Donald. "Ottoman Reform and Agriculture in Anatolia, 1876–1908." PhD diss., University of California, Los Angeles, 1973.

Quéméré, Pierre, Arnaud Taillefer, and Olivier Perru. "Les evolutions pédagogiques à l'Institut de Beauvais de 1855 à 1945." In *Les enjeux de la formation des acteurs de l'agriculture, 1760–1945: acts du colloque, ENESAD, 19–21 janvier 1999*, ed. Michel Boulet, 401–7. Dijon: Educagri, 2000.

Raj, Kapil. *Relocating Modern Science: Circulation and the Construction of Knowledge in South Asia and Europe, 1650–1900*. New York: Palgrave Macmillan, 2007.

Refik, Mehmet, and Mehmet Behcet, comps. *Beyrut Vilayeti*. Beirut: Vilayet Matbaası, 1333 [1917].

Reilly, James A. *A Small Town in Syria: Ottoman Hama in the Eighteenth and Nineteenth Centuries*. Oxford, UK: Peter Lang, 2002.

Reilly, James A. "Status Groups and Propertyholding in the Damascus Hinterland, 1828–1880." *International Journal of Middle East Studies* 21, no. 4 (1989): 517–39.

Republic of Syria (Sir Alexander Gibb & Partners). *The Economic Development of Syria*. London: Queen Anne's Lodge, 1947.

Richards, Alan. *Egypt's Agricultural Development, 1800–1980: Technical and Social Change*. Boulder, CO: Westview Press, 1982.

Riley, C. V., ed. *Reports of the United States Commissioners to the Universal Exposition of 1889 at Paris*, Vol. 5, *Agriculture*. Washington, DC: US Government Printing Office, 1891.

Rıza, Ahmet. *Meclis-i Mebusan ve Ayân resisi Ahmed Rıza Bey'in Anıları*. İstanbul: Arba, 1988.

Robbins, Paul. *Political Ecology: A Critical Introduction*. Chichester, UK: Wiley, 2012.

Roche, Max, and Michel Vernus. *Dictionnaire biographique du département du Doubs*. Lons-le-Saunier: Arts et Littérature, 1996.

Roederer, Carl, and Paul Roederer. *La Syrie et la France*. Paris: Berger-Levrault, 1917.

Rogan, Eugene L. "Aşiret Mektebi: Abdülhamid II's School for Tribes (1892–1907)." *International Journal of Middle East Studies* 28, no. 1 (1996): 83–107.

Rogan, Eugene. *Frontiers of the State in the Late Ottoman Empire: Transjordan, 1850–1921*. Cambridge, UK: Cambridge University Press, 1999.

Rogan, Eugene L. "The Political Significance of an Ottoman Education: Maktab ʿAnbar Revisited." In *From the Syrian Land to the States of Syria and Lebanon*, ed. Thomas Philipp and Christoph Schumann, 77–94. Beirut: Orient-Institut, 2004.

Rosenthal, Jean-Laurent. *The Fruits of Revolution: Property Rights, Litigation, and French Agriculture, 1700–1860*. Cambridge, UK: Cambridge University Press, 1992.

Ross, Corey. *Ecology and Power in the Age of Empire: Europe and the Transformation of the Tropical World*. Oxford, UK: Oxford University Press, 2017.

Saadé, Edouard. *L'agriculture à lattaquié*. Beauvais: Imprimerie Départmentale de l'Oise, 1905.

Saadé, Fouad. "Le problème agricole au Liban et en Syrie." In *Troisième semaine sociale de Beyrouth: l'agriculture richesse nationale, 19–26 April 1942*, 13–32. Beirut: Éditions Le Lettres Orientales, 1942.

Saadé, Toufik. *Essai sur l'agriculture a l'Attaquié [sic] (Syrie)*. Beauvais: Imprimerie A. Dumontier, 1905.

al-Sabuni, Nadima. "Taqdim al-Majalla." *Al-Marʾa* 1, no. 1 (October 1930): 2.

Sadir, Yusuf Ibrahim. *Majmuʿat Muqarrarat Hukumat Suriya*. Beirut: Matbaʿat Sadir, 1934.

Safieddine, Hicham. *Banking on the State: The Financial Foundations of Lebanon*. Stanford, CA: Stanford University Press, 2019.

al-Saleh, Mohammed Ali. "Une évaluation de la gestion mandataire de l'économie syrienne." In *The British and French Mandates in Comparative Perspective / Les mandats français et anglaise dans une perspective comparative*, ed. Nadine Méouchy and Peter Sluglett, 385–413. Leiden: Brill, 2004.

Saliba, Najib Elias. "Wilayat Suriyya: 1876–1909." PhD diss., University of Michigan, 1971.

Saraçoğlu, M. Safa. *Nineteenth Century Local Governance in Ottoman Bulgaria: Politics in Provincial Councils*. Edinburgh: Edinburgh University Press, 2018.

Sarrage, Mohammed. *La nécessité d'une réforme agraire en Syrie*. Toulouse: Imprimerie du Sud-Ouest, 1935.

Scalenghe, Sara. *Disability in the Ottoman Arab World, 1500–1800*. New York: Cambridge University Press, 2014.

Schad, Geoffrey D. "The Figure of the Native Expert: Léon Mourad in the Service of the High Commission for Syria and Lebanon." In *Experts et expertise dans les mandats de la Société des Nations: figures, champs et outils*, ed. Philippe Bourmand, Norig Neveu, and Chantal Verdeil, 103–19. Paris: Presses de l'Inalco, 2020.

Schaebler, Birgit. "Practicing *Mushaʿ*: Common Lands and the Common Good in Southern Syria Under the Ottomans and the French." In *New Perspectives on Property and Land in the Middle East*, ed. Roger Owen, 241–307. Cambridge, MA: Harvard University Press, 2000.

Schayegh, Cyrus. *The Middle East and the Making of the Modern World*. Cambridge, MA: Harvard University Press, 2017.

Schilcher, Linda Schatkowski. *Families in Politics: Damascene Factions and Estates of the 18th and 19th Centuries*. Wiesbaden: F. Steiner, 1985.

Schilcher, Linda Schatkowski. "The Famine of 1915–1918 in Greater Syria." In *Problems of the Modern Middle East in Historical Perspective*, ed. John P. Spagnolo, 231–58. Reading, UK: Ithaca Press, 1992.

Schilcher, L. Schatkowski. "The Great Depression (1873–1896) and the Rise of Syrian Arab Nationalism." *New Perspectives on Turkey* 5–6 (Fall 1991): 167–89.

Schilcher, L. Schatkowski. "The Hauran Conflicts of the 1860s: A Chapter in the Rural History of Modern Syria." *International Journal of Middle East Studies* 13, no. 2 (1981): 159–79.

Schilcher, Linda Schatkowski. "Violence in Rural Syria in the 1880s and 1890s: State Centralization, Rural Integration, and the World Market." In *Peasants and Politics in the Modern Middle East*, ed. Farhad Kazemi and John Waterbury, 50–84. Miami: Florida University International Press, 1991.

Scott, James C. *Seeing Like a State: How Certain Schemes to Improve the Human Condition Have Failed*. New Haven, CT: Yale University Press, 1998.

Seikaly, Sherene. *Men of Capital: Scarcity and Economy in Mandate Palestine*. Stanford, CA: Stanford University Press, 2016.

Şener, Abdüllatif. *Tanzimat Dönemi Osmanlı Vergi Sistemi*. İstanbul: İşaret, 1990.

Shaw, Stanford J. "The Nineteenth-Century Ottoman Tax Reforms and Revenue System." *International Journal of Middle East Studies* 6, no. 4 (1975): 421–59.

al-Shihabi, Mustafa. "Aham Adwaʾna al-Iqtisadiya wa Talafiha." *al-Ziraʿa al-Haditha* 4, no. 1 (November 1928): 7–14.

al-Shihabi, Mustafa. "Aham Adwaʾna al-Iqtisadiya wa Talafiha 2." *al-Ziraʿa al-Haditha* 4, no. 2 (December 1928): 5–12.

al-Shihabi, Mustafa. "Aham Adwaʾna al-Iqtisadiya wa Talafiha 2." *al-Ziraʿa al-Haditha* 4, no. 3 (January 1928 [1929?]): 26–34.

al-Shihabi, Mustafa. "Aham Adwaʾna al-Iqtisadiya wa Talafiha 3." *al-Ziraʿa al-Haditha* 4, no. 4 (February 1929): 173–79.

al-Shihabi, Mustafa. "al-Azma al-Ziraʿiya fi Suriya." *al-Ziraʿa al-Haditha* 5, nos. 7–8 (May/June 1932): 444–51.

al-Shihabi, Mustafa. *Chihabi's Dictionary of Agricultural and Allied Terminology: English-Arabic, with an Arabic English Glossary*. Beirut: Librairie du Liban, 1978.

al-Shihabi, Mustafa. *Dictionnaire français-arabe des termes agricoles*. Cairo: Imprimerie Misr, 1957.

al-Shihabi, Mustafa. "Ma Jad min al-Sinaʿat al-Shamiya baʿd al-Harb al-Kubra 1." *al-Ziraʿa al-Haditha* 4, no. 5 (March 1929): 244–53.

al-Shihabi, Mustafa. "Ma Jad min al-Sinaʿat al-Shamiya baʿd al-Harb al-Kubra 2." *al-Ziraʿa al-Haditha* 4, no. 6 (April 1929): 294–301.

al-Shihabi, Mustafa. *Muhadarat fi al-Istiʿmar*. Cairo: Jamiʿat al-Duwal al-ʿArabiyah, Maʿhad al-Dirasa, 1957.

al-Shihabi, Mustafa. *al-Ziraʿa al-ʿAmaliya al-Haditha* [Modern Practical Agriculture]. Damascus: Matbaʿa al-Hukuma, 1340 [1922].

Shishakli, Ibrahim. "Bahith fi al-Tashriʿ al-Ziraʿi." *al-Ziraʿa al-Haditha* 1, nos. 7–8 (July-August 1924): 398–402.

Shishakli, Ibrahim. "Bahith fi al-Tashriʿ al-Ziraʿi 2." *al-Ziraʿa al-Haditha* 1, no. 9 (September 1924): 491–93.

Shishakli, Ibrahim. "Bahith fi al-Tashriʿ al-Ziraʿi [3]." *al-Ziraʿa al-Haditha* 1, no. 12 (December 1924): 686–91.

Shishakli, Ibrahim. "al-Tashriʿ al-Ziraʿi: al-Tasarruf bil-Arazi al-Amiriya." *al-Ziraʿa al-Haditha* 2, no. 3 (April 1925): 158–61.

Shiva, Vandana. *The Violence of the Green Revolution: Third World Agriculture, Ecology, and Politics*. London: Zed Books, 1991.

Shorrock, William I. *French Imperialism in the Middle East: The Failure of Policy in Syria and Lebanon, 1900–1914*. Madison: University of Wisconsin Press, 1976.

al-Sibaʾi, Badr al-Din. *Adwaʾ ʿala al-Raʾsmal al-Ajnabi fi Suriya, 1850–1958*. Damascus: Dar al-Jamahir, 1968.

Sluglett, Peter, and Marion Farouk-Sluglett. "The Application of the 1858 Land Code in Greater Syria: Some Preliminary Observations." In *Land Tenure and Social Transformation in the Middle East*, ed. Tarif Khalidi, 409–21. Beirut: American University of Beirut, 1984.

Smethurst, Richard J. *Agricultural Development and Tenancy Disputes in Japan, 1870–1940*. Princeton, NJ: Princeton University Press, 1986.

Smith, Kerry. *A Time of Crisis: Japan, the Great Depression, and Rural Revitalization*. Cambridge, MA: Harvard University Asia Center, 2001.

Smith, Neil. *Uneven Development: Nature, Capital, and the Production of Space*. Athens: University of Georgia Press, 2008.

Somel, Selçuk Akşın. *The Modernization of Public Education in the Ottoman Empire, 1839–1908: Islamization, Autocracy, and Discipline*. Leiden: Brill, 2001.

Souchon, A. *Agricultural Credit in France*. Exposition Universelle de San Francisco. Évreux: C. Hérissey, 1915.

Soydan, Hasan, ed. *120 yıllık eğitim çınarı Halkalı Ziraat Mekteb-i Âlisi*. Ankara: Gıda Tarım ve Hayvancılık Bakanlığı, 2011.

Spring, Eileen. "Landowners, Lawyers, and Land Law Reform in Nineteenth-Century England." *American Journal of Legal History* 21, no. 1 (1977): 40–59.

Stolz, Daniel A. *The Lighthouse and the Observatory: Islam, Science, and Empire in Late Ottoman Egypt*. Cambridge, UK: Cambridge University Press, 2018.

Strohmeier, Martin. "Abd al-Rahman Pasha al-Yusuf, a Notable in Damascus (1873/74–1920)." In *Provincial Elites in the Ottoman Empire*, ed. Antonis Anastasopoulos, 349–67. Rethymno: Crete University Press, 2005.

Sunderland, Willard. *Taming the Wild Field: Colonization on the Russian Steppe*. Ithaca, NY: Cornell University Press, 2004.

Swearingen, Will. *Moroccan Mirages: Agrarian Dreams and Deceptions, 1912–1986*. London: I. B. Tauris, 1987.

Syracuse Chilled Plow Company. *Catalogue of Farm Implements*. Syracuse, NY: Syracuse Chilled Plow Co., 1900. http://catalog.hathitrust.org/Record/012323198.

al-Tabbakh, Muhammad Raghib. *Iʿlam al-Nubalaʾ bi-Tarikh Halab al-Shahbaʾ*, vol. 3. Haleb: al-Matbaʿa al-ʿIlmiya, 1925.

"Tahrîr-i nüfus ve emlâke dair nizâmnâme." *Düstûr-i atîk*. [İstanbul]: Matbaa-yi Amire, 1282 [1866].

*Taqrir Zira*ʿ*i* ʿ*an Qura al-Btayha wa al-Julan*. Damascus: Matbaʿat Babil Akhwan, 1934 [?].

al-Tarmanini, ʿUmar. "Aqwal al-Nawab Kalima al-Majalla Hawlha." *al-Majalla al-Zira*ʿ*iya al-Suriya* 1, no. 2 (January 1939): 107–10.

Taylor, Malissa Anne. "Fragrant Gardens and Converging Waters: Ottoman Governance in Seventeenth-Century Damascus." PhD diss., University of California, Berkeley, 2011.

Tesdell, Omar Imseeh. "Planting Roots, Claiming Space." *NACLA: Report on the Americas* 50, no. 1 (2018): 68–73.

Tesdell, Omar Imseeh. "Shadow Spaces: Territory, Sovereignty, and the Question of Palestinian Cultivation." PhD diss., University of Minnesota, 2013.

Thobie, Jacques. *Intérêts et impérialisme dans l'empire ottoman (1895–1914)*. Paris: Imprimerie Nationale, 1977.

Thompson, Elizabeth F. "Akram al-Hourani and the Baath Party in Syria: Bringing Peasants into Politics." In *Justice Interrupted: The Struggle for Constitutional Government in the Middle East*, by Elizabeth F. Thompson, 207–35. Cambridge, MA: Harvard University Press, 2013.

Thompson, Elizabeth. *Colonial Citizens: Republican Rights, Paternal Privilege, and Gender in French Syria and Lebanon*. New York: Columbia University Press, 2000.

Thompson, Elizabeth F. *How the West Stole Democracy from the Arabs: The Syrian Congress of 1920 and the Destruction of Its Historic Liberal-Islamic Alliance*. New York: Grove Press, 2021.

Ticaret ve Ziraat Nezareti. *Memalik-i Osmaniye'nin 1329 senesine mahsus ziraat istatistiğidir*. İstanbul: Matbaa-yi Osmaniye, 1332 [1916/1917].

Ticaret ve Ziraat Nezareti. *Sanayi istatistiği: 1329 ve 1331 seneleri*. İstanbul: Matbaa-yi Amire, 1917.

Tomeh, Ramez George. "Landownership and Political Power in Damascus: 1858–1958." MA thesis, American University of Beirut, 1977.

Toprak, Zafer. *Türkiye'de "Milli İktisat" (1908–1918)*. Ankara: Yurt Yayinlari, 1982.

Traboulsi, Izzat. *L'agriculture syrienne entre les deux guerres*. Beirut: Imprimerie Nassar, 1948.

Trocmé, Marie Benedict. "Le titre d'ingénieur agricole." In *Les enjeux de la formation des acteurs de l'agriculture, 1760–1945: acts du colloque, ENESAD, 19–21 janvier 1999*, ed. Michel Boulet, 367–71. Dijon: Educagri, 2000.

Troisième Semaine Sociale de Beyrouth: L'agriculture richesse nationale, 19–26 April 1942. Beirut: Éditions Les Lettres Orientales, 1942.

Tucker, Judith E. *Women in Nineteenth-Century Egypt*. Cambridge, MA: Cambridge University Press, 1985.

Türk Ansiklopedisi. İstanbul: Milli Eğitim Bakanlığı, 1943.

Turnaoğlu, Banu. *The Formation of Turkish Republicanism*. Princeton, NJ: Princeton University Press, 2017.

Ubicini, M. A. *Letters on Turkey: An Account of the Religious, Political, Social, and Commercial Condition of the Ottoman Empire, the Reformed Institutions, Army, Navy, etc.*, trans. Lady Easthope. London: John Murray, 1856.

Vedat, Çalışkan. "Human-Induced Wetland Degradation: A Case Study of Lake Amik (Southern Turkey)." Ohrid, Macedonia: BALWOIS, 2008. https://balwois.com/wp-content/uploads/old_proc/ffp-1144.pdf.

Verdeil, Chantal. "Le P. Michel Gillet, dans la Montagne Alaouite en Syrie (1934–1945)." *Tempora: Annales d'Histoire et d'Archéologie* 22 (2013–2017): 311–42.

VIIe Congrés International d'Agriculture, Rome, Avril-Mai 1903, vol. 2, *première partie*. Rome: Imprimerie de l'Unione Cooperativa Editrice, 1904.

VIII Internationaler landwirtschaftlicher Kongress, Wien, 21-25 Mai 1907, vol. 1. Vienna: Druckerei Johann N. Vernay, 1907.

Vitalis, Robert, and Steven Heydemann. "War, Keynesianism, and Colonialism: Explaining State-Market Relations in the Postwar Middle East." In *War, Institutions, and Social Change in the Middle East*, ed. Steven Heydemann, 100–145. Berkeley: University of California Press, 2000.

Wallerstein, Immanuel. *The Modern World-System II: Mercantilism and the Consolidation of the European World-Economy, 1600–1750*. Berkeley: University of California Press, 2011.

Warriner, Doreen. *Land and Poverty in the Middle East*. London: Royal Institute of International Affairs, 1948.

Warriner, Doreen. *Land Reform and Development in the Middle East*. London: Royal Institute of International Affairs, 1957.

Warriner, Doreen. "Land Tenure in the Fertile Crescent." In *The Economic History of the Middle East, 1800–1914*, ed. Charles Issawi, 72–78. Chicago: University of Chicago Press, 1966.

Waswo, Ann. "The Transformation of Rural Society, 1900–1950." In *The Cambridge History of Japan*, vol. 6, *The Twentieth Century*, ed. Peter Duus, 541–605. Cambridge, UK: Cambridge University Press, 1988.

Watenpaugh, Keith David. *Being Modern in the Middle East: Revolution, Nationalism, Colonialism, and the Arab Middle Class*. Princeton, NJ: Princeton University Press, 2006.

Watson, Andrew M. *Agricultural Innovation in the Early Islamic World*. Cambridge, UK: Cambridge University Press, 1983.

Wehr, Hans. *Arabic-English Dictionary*. Ithaca, NY: Spoken Languages Services, 1994.

Weiss, Max. *In the Shadow of Sectarianism: Law, Shiʿism, and the Making of Modern Lebanon*. Cambridge, MA: Harvard University Press, 2010.

Weulersse, Jacques. *L'Oronte, étude de fleuve*. Tours: Arrault, 1940.

Weulersse, Jacques. *Le pays des Alaouites*, vol. 1. Tours: Arrault, 1940.

Weulersse, Jacques. *Paysans de Syrie et du Proche-Orient*. Paris: Gallimard, 1946.

Whitaker, James Long. "The Union of Demeter with Zeus: Agriculture and Politics in Modern Syria." PhD diss., Durham University, 1996.

Whitcombe, Elizabeth. *Agrarian Conditions in Northern India: The United Provinces Under British Rule, 1860–1900*, vol. 1. Berkeley: University of California Press, 1972.

White, Benjamin Thomas. *The Emergence of Minorities in the Middle East: The Politics of Community in French Mandate Syria*. Edinburgh: Edinburgh University Press, 2011.

White, Sam. *The Climate of Rebellion in the Early Modern Ottoman Empire*. Cambridge, UK: Cambridge University Press, 2011.

Widtsoe, John A. *Dry-Farming: A System of Agriculture for Countries Under a Low Rainfall*. New York: Macmillan, 1912.

Wigen, Kären. *The Making of a Japanese Periphery, 1750–1920*. Berkeley: University of California Press, 1995.

Wilhelm, Ivan. "Zira^cat al-Qutn fi Suriye." *al-Zira^ca al-Haditha* 2, no. 4 (May 1925): 198–202.

Wilhelm, Ivan. "Zira^cat al-Qutn fi Suriye 2: Sahel al-^cAmik." *al-Zira^ca al-Haditha* 2, no. 5 (June 1925): 271–77.

Williams, Elizabeth. "Economy, Environment, and Famine: World War I from the Perspective of the Syrian Interior." In *Syria in World War I: Politics, Economy, and Society*, ed. M. Talha Çiçek, 150–68. London: Routledge, 2016.

Williams, Elizabeth R. " 'The Agriculture Ministry of the Whole World': The International Institute of Agriculture and the Politics of Ottoman Statistics Collection." *Comparative Studies of South Asia, Africa and the Middle East* (forthcoming).

Williams, Elizabeth. "Mapping the Cadastre, Producing the *Fellah*: Technologies and Discourses of Rule in French Mandate Syria and Lebanon." In *The Routledge Handbook of the History of the Middle East Mandates*, ed. Cyrus Schayegh and Andrew Arsan, 170–82. New York: Routledge, 2015.

Winkler, Max. *Foreign Bonds: An Autopsy*. Washington, DC: Beard Books, 1999 [1933].

Worster, Donald. *Dust Bowl: The Southern Plains in the 1930s*. Oxford, UK: Oxford University Press, 2004 [1979].

Wrigley, E. A. *Energy and the English Revolution*. Cambridge, UK: Cambridge University Press, 2010.

Yalçınkaya, M. Alper. *Learned Patriots: Debating Science, State, and Society in the Nineteenth-Century Ottoman Empire*. Chicago: University of Chicago Press, 2015.

Yaycıoğlu, Ali. *Partners of the Empire: The Crisis of the Ottoman Order in the Age of Revolutions*. Stanford, CA: Stanford University Press, 2016.

Yıldırım, Mehmet Ali. "Osmanlı'da İlk Çağdaş Zirai Eğitim Kurumu: Ziraat Mektebi (1847–1851)." *OTAM* 24 (2010): 223–38.

Younes, Assad Bey. "L'agriculture au Liban." *La Revue Phénicienne* 1, nos. 4–6 (1919): 259–64.

Young, George. *Corps de droit ottoman: recueil des codes, lois, règlements, ordonnances et actes les plus importants du droit intérieur, et d'études sur le droit coutumier de l'Empire ottoman*, vol. 1. Oxford, UK: Clarendon Press, 1905.

Young, George. *Corps de droit ottoman: recueil des codes, lois, règlements, ordonnances et actes les plus importants du droit intérieur, et d'études sur le droit coutumier de l'Empire ottoman*, vol. 5. Oxford, UK: Clarendon Press, 1906.

Young, George. *Corps de droit ottoman: recueil des codes, lois, règlements, ordonnances et actes les plus importants du droit intérieur, et d'études sur le droit coutumier de l'Empire ottoman*, vol. 6. Oxford, UK: Clarendon Press, 1906.

Yücel, Naz. "Sustaining the Empire: Transformation of Property Regime in the Late Ottoman Empire, 1876–1913." PhD diss., George Washington University, 2022.

Zakariya, Ahmad Wasfi. "Kif Yajab an Yakun al-Zira^ca." *al-Zira^ca al-Haditha* 3, nos. 6–7 (September-October 1927): 419–25.

Zakariya, Ahmad Wasfi. *al-Qura wa al-Baldat fi Janub Bilad al-Sham*. Damascus: Dar wa-Mu'assasat Raslan, 2008.

Zakariya, [Ahmad] Wasfi. *al-Durus al-Zira'iya*. Damascus: Matba'at al-Taraqqi, 1343 [1925].

Zakarya, Khuder. "Syria." In *Commoners, Climbers and Notables*, ed. C. van Nieuwenhuijze, 248–67. Leiden: Brill, 1977.
al-Zayn, Muhammad Adib. "al-Zira^ca wa al-Sina^ca." *al-^cIrfan* 13, no. 7 (March 1927): 804–15.
Zürcher, Erik-Jan. "Ottoman Sources of Kemalist Thought." In *Late Ottoman Society: The Intellectual Legacy*, ed. Elisabeth Özdalga, 14–27. London: Routledge Curzon, 2005.

Websites

http://www.racinescomtoises.net/index?/category/5640-paul_evariste_parmentier_1860_1941
http://www.irishstatutebook.ie/eli/1891/act/48/enacted/en/print.html
https://www.senat.fr/senateur-3eme-republique/berard_victor0445r3.html
https://www.debbaneagri.com/en/who-we-are/our-history

INDEX

Page number in *italic* indicate maps, tables, or images.

Abdulaziz (Sultan), 36
Abdulhamid II (Sultan): ascent of, 43–44; lands of, 221, 357n72. *See also* state space and agrarian networks, Hamidian era; tax policies, Hamidian era
Abdullah Efendi, 92
Abdulmecid I (Sultan), 36
Abdussettar Efendi, 93–94, 106–7, 313nn83–84
al-ᶜAbid, Muhammad Ali Bey, 245
al-ᶜAbid, Nazik, 204
Achard, Edouard: agricultural assessments, 144, 145, 147, 328n155, 330n183; on agricultural education, 166; criticism of, 191–92, 246, 247; education, 144, 328n146; experimental stations, 169; journal reports by, 154; land reform, 217, 340n92, 355n46; land tax proposals, 151–52, 331n202; technology recommendations, 150–51, 337n40
Adana, 82–83
Adana Practical Agricultural School, *76*
Ağa Khan, 104
Agop Efendi, 49, 124
agrarian credit: in other countries, 38, 216, 288n24, 293n106, 293n111, 355n39. *See also* Agricultural Bank; state space and agrarian networks
— OTTOMAN ERA: debt payment, 300n229; inflated land values and debt, 55–56, 301nn240–241; interest rates, 297nn174–175; interest-free loans, 27, 288n23; loan securities, 48, 300n230; on *mushaᶜ* (collectively held) land, 62, 63, 65, 121, 304nn291–292, 304n294; needs assessment, 27, 288n22; regional funds, 38, 293n104; *selem* contracts, 29, 31, 289n36, 289nn39–40, 290n52; Tanzimat reforms, 38–39
— MANDATE ERA: creation of mortgage banks, 218; and economic crisis of 1930s, 241–43; interest rates, 245; loan operations, 355n46; loan terms, 233–35, 362nn159–160, 362nn162–163; moratorium on debt, 260; moratorium on mortgage debt sought, 248, 368n257
agriculteurs, 117, 319n2

Agricultural Bank. *See also* agrarian credit; state space and agrarian networks
— OTTOMAN ERA: agricultural exhibition, 111, 318n169; corruption accusations, 47, 297n177; credit, 54, 297nn174–175, 300n230; criticism of, 58, 70–71; distribution through region, 121; establishment, 46–47, 297n172; expansion, 62; financing of equipment, 123; financing of model fields, 84, 310n42; funding of agricultural schools, 101, 103; interest rates, 58, 369n262; lending practices, 63, 65, 70–71, 304nn291–292, 304n294; loan denials, 56, 302n242; monetary resources taken from, 128, 323n63; as protection against monopolists, 55; scope of activities, 47–48, 297n173, 297nn179–180
— MANDATE ERA: establishment of graneries, 242; interest rates, 249; loan requests following Sunn bug invasion, 224; reorganization, 233
Agricultural Congress of northern Syria, 253
Agricultural Development of the Middle East (Keen), 272, 378nn49–50
agricultural education: in other countries, 178, 341n114. *See also* experimental stations; Halkalı Agricultural School (Halkalı Ziraat Mektebi); Salamiya (Selimiye) Agricultural School; scientific agriculture in Ottoman era
— OTTOMAN ERA: elite education and nature of expertise, 91–97; expansion of homegrown schools, 86–90, 311n57; farm school near Istanbul (1847), 28, 80, 307n17; map of institutions, *103*; statistics, *76*; before World War I, 121; during World War I, 126–27
— FAYSAL ERA, 130–31
— MANDATE ERA: influence and educating the *fallah*, 194–97; influence and locally managed projects, 199–204; and political ties, 164–65; proposals for, 150; proposed farm school in Biqaʿ Valley, 199, 351n251; proposed school in Bsharri, 200, 351n253; rural primary education, 185–88, 189–90, 345n180, 346n181, 347n195; training in France, 174–75, 340n83, 340nn90–92
— POST-MANDATE ERA, 269–70
agricultural exploitation and French frustrations, 147–53
agricultural exploitation and politics of empire, 139–47, *141*, 328n155
agricultural extension workers, 203–4
The Agricultural Life (journal), 169, 216
agricultural organizations: international, 59–60, 72–73; local, 58–59, 61–62, 303n258, 303n274
agricultural self-sufficiency and national space: in Faysal era, 128–35; and Greater Lebanon, 135–39
agricultural technologies: overview, 3–4, 117–21, 160–61; networks and knowledge production, 12–14, 286n59; and state space, 14–16. *See also* agricultural education; agronomists; experimental stations; scientific agriculture in Ottoman era; state space and agrarian networks; technocrats
— OTTOMAN ERA: challenges to implementation, 76–77, 306n5, 307n6; scientific agriculture before and during World War I, 121–28; work animals, *113*, 319n178
— POST–WORLD WAR I ERA: agricultural self-sufficiency and national space, Faysal era, 128–35; agricultural self-sufficiency and national space, Greater Lebanon, 135–39
— MANDATE ERA: agricultural exploitation and French frustrations, 147–53; agricultural exploitation and politics of empire, 139–47, *141*, 328n155; assessment of impact, 163; networks and knowledge production, 164, 188–89; plow demonstrations, 169, 337n40; technocrats and reform negotiations

in early mandate, 153–60; tractor use, 168
agricultural technology (motoculture) in France, 330n178
agriculture, state building, and imperial politics, 4–8
Agriculture and Commerce Ministry maps, *xv*
agriculture and industry council (Ottoman), 25, 288n10
Agriculture Council (Ottoman), 26–27, 289n27, 289n29
Agriculture Ministry, risk assessments, 77
agriculture school graduates, union of, 247, 368n248
agronomists. *See also* elites; technocrats
— OTTOMAN ERA: agricultural education, 97; criticism of administration, 56–59; education of, 81–82, 302nn246–247; and knowledge networks, 90
— FAYSAL ERA, 129
— MANDATE ERA: criticism of foreign land-credit banks, 234; criticism of government, 231–32, 235–36, 363n172; criticism of tax system, 216; reform proposals in early Mandate, 153–54, 157; *semaine sociale*, 264–65, 271, 375n1
al-Ahdab, Tawfiq: awards, 160; career summary, 334n240; criticism of tax system, 216, 232, 355n38; on economic crisis, 243; education, 157; on goal of Salamiya School, 179; as inspector, 347n209; reform proposals, 158, 334n246; Sunn bug invasion, 228, 360n118
Ahmet Bey, 310n47
Aintab, 100, 121
Ajlun, 101, 126, 135
ʿAkka, 45–46
ʿAkkar, 150, 167–68, 173, 202–3
ʿAlawite resistance to French rule, 146
ʿAlawite State, 139, 153, 167–68, 171, 226–27, 241
Aleppan Agricultural Company, 129–30
Aleppo: ecological zones, 134–35
— OTTOMAN ERA: administrative provinces and districts, 284n22; agricultural administration employees, 121–22, 320nn19–20, 320n24; agricultural demonstrations, 111; agricultural education, 91–94; agricultural infrastructure, 121–24; agricultural infrastructure integrated with other provinces, 79; agricultural planning, 99; bank loans, 48; cadastral survey, 39; conflicting interests and clashes, 25; experimental stations, 82–83, 84–86, *85*, 89, 98, 125, 312n65; food shortages, 42; implement depots, 122–23, 126; investment in agricultural technologies, 111–13, 114; limits of reform, 25, 65–72, 305n303, 306n321; maps, *xii*; provincial yearbooks, 37
— MANDATE ERA: administrative division, 139; agricultural education, 170–71, 203; agricultural resources assessment, 144, 145; agricultural technologies, 149, 150, 155–56, 331n194; credit relief, 235; economic crisis, 244; emigration from villages, 248; government loans to farmers, 246; harvests, 224–25, 231, 240; land reform, 237; locusts, 231; petition from farmers, 248–49, 369n262; Quwayq River, 11; resistance to mandate rule/government, 146, 250, 253, 330n193; revolt, 227; Sunn bug invasion, 225–26; tax collection tactics, 248–49, 251; *terbiʿ* tax, 231; Village Welfare Service, 203; voles, 228
Aleppo Chamber of Agriculture, 183, 234, 344n152
Alexandretta: administrative division, 139; Agricultural Bank, 233; experimental stations, 171, 194; French influence, 171; tax policies and resistance, 253, 370n284; tax returns from, 354n18; taxes, land tax, 221–22, 254–55, 372n308; *terbiʿ* tax, 241

Algeria, 18, 142, 361n135
Amasyan Efendi, 49, 80–81, 311n52
American University of Beirut, 187, 190, 200–204, 352n267
Amik Valley (marsh), 9, 126
Amiri, Awad Bey, 345n180
Anatolia, 42
Ankara, 82–83
Ankara Practical Agricultural School, *76*
Arab government (Faysal era), 4, 128–35, *133*, 138, 148, 209, 324n85, 377n23
Arab Revolt. *See* Arab government (Faysal era)
Aram Efendi, 49, 81, 311n52
ʿArida (Maronite patriarch), 200
Armenians, 122
ʿAsi River, 11, *11*
al-ʿAsima, 332n213
ʿAssan, 369n262
ʿAtallah, Yusuf: awards, 160; criticism of tax system, 215; during economic crisis, 246, 247; education, 157; reform proposals, 158, 192, 220–21, 357n74
Australia, 220, 365n208
Austria-Hungary, 139, 326n121
al-ʿAwwam, Yahya bin Muhammad bin, 176, 177
al-Ayyam, 252
Azaz, 228, 369n262
Azim, Mustafa, 305n309
ʿAzm family, 301n237
al-ʿAzma, Yusuf, 146
Azmi Bey, 2

Baʿalbak, 36, 45–46, 53
Bab, 228
Badiʿ Bey, 363n177
Balkans, tax policies, 292n85
Bani Sakhr Bedouin, 39–40
Bank of Syria and Greater Lebanon, 234–35, 245, 246–47, 362n162, 366n231
banks and banking in Mandate, 152–53, 331nn204–206. *See also* agrarian credit
Banque de Syrie, 331n205
Banque Française d'Egypte, 331n206
Barazi family, 301n237
al-Barudi, Fakhri: civil disobedience campaign, 240–41; education, 95–97, 315n108; resignation from agricultural commission, 246, 367n238; resistance to government and intervention for peasants, 246, 252, 258; support for agricultural education, 130
Barudi, Hilmi, 224–25, 359n96, 360n125
al-Barudi family, 156
Batatu, Hanna, 301n237
Baʿthist reformers, roots of, 67
Behcet, Mehmet, 2
Beirut
— OTTOMAN ERA: administrative provinces and districts, 284n22; agricultural assessments (Kâzım), 2; agricultural education, 99; agricultural infrastructure integrated with other provinces, 79; implement depots, 123, 126; maps, *xiv*; tax collection, 45–46; tax system, 63
— MANDATE ERA: agricultural education, 171; agricultural technologies, 149–50; emigration from villages to, 245; experimental stations, 169
Beirut International College, 269
Belgium, 219, 293n111, 341n114
Bérard, Victor, 140, 146
Bériel, Monsieur: on Foch Orphanage, 198–99, 351n248; Institute of Rural Life, 202; knowledge production and technical education, 172–74, 178, 340n83, 340nn90–91; proposals for rural schools, 190; on Salamiya School, 182, 197; on Tal Tuqan enterprise, 192
Berthelot, Philippe, 145, 148, 342n121
Berthelot, Pierre, 191
Billotte, General, 167–68
Biqaʿ Valley: ecological zones, 134–35; geography, 9
— OTTOMAN ERA: administrative provinces and districts, 138; sale of *miri* lands to urban investors, 39–40; *selem* contracts, 36; tax collection, 45–46

— MANDATE ERA: agricultural education, 199, 202–3; agricultural resources assessment, 144; agricultural technology, 150, 168; and creation of Greater Lebanon, 136, 138; experimental stations, 168–69; Sunn bug invasion, 227; Village Welfare Service, 203
Birket Zade Rifat Ağa, 69
Book of Agriculture (kitab al-falaha) (al-ʿAwwam), 177
Book of Nabatean Agriculture (Ibn Wahshiyya), 176, 340nn97–98
Bosra, 364n198
Bouka, 168
Bouka school (Centre Agricole de Bouka), 195–97, *195*, 200, 348–49nn225–227, 349n230, 358n93
boundary-work, 16, 17, 18, 153–54, 201
Bounoure, Gabriel: Bouka school, 349n237; Institute of Rural Life, 202–3; proposed farm school in Biqaʿ Valley, 199, 351n251; proposed school in Bsharri, 200; Salamiya School, 190–91, 347n205
Bread Grains Office (Office des céréales panifiables), 266
Bsharri village, 200, 351n253
al-Btayha enterprise, 192–93, 348n215
Bulgaria, 219, 289n40
Burbank, Jane, 8
Bursa Practical Agricultural School, 87

cadastral service (Mandate era), 216–17, 226, *227*, 357n79
cadastral survey (Ottoman era), 62–63, *64*
Canada, 365n208
Case manufacturer, 149
Cemaleddin Pasha, 310n42
Centre Agricole de Bouka, 195–97, *195*, 200, 348–49nn225–227, 349n230, 358n93
Çerasi Efendi, 298n190
Cevdet Efendi, 92
CFAT (Crédit Foncier d'Algérie et de Tunisie), 152, 233–34, 331n206, 362nn159–160
Chamber of Commerce Congress, 261
Chambers of Commerce and Agriculture (Aleppo), 155
Chicago Columbian Exposition (1893), 22, 50–52, 123, 299n208, 321n29
Chtaura, 169
Cilicia, 128, 145, 147, 328n159
civil disobedience campaign, 240–41
Clemenceau, Georges, 138
Clément-Mullet, J. J., 177
Colonial Party (France), 145–47
colonial state space, 14–15. *See also* agricultural exploitation and politics of empire
Columbian Exposition (Chicago; 1893), 22, 50–52, 123, 299n208, 321n29
Comité de l'Asie Française, 140, 144–45
Commerce and Agriculture Council, 43, 49–50, 295n149
Commerce and Agriculture Ministry, 39, 63, *64*, 99
Commerce and Public Works Ministry, 50, 84
Commerce Ministry, 25, 288n11
Commission Internationale d'Agriculture, 60, 164–65
Committee for the Defense of the Rights of Farmers, 250, 253
Committee of Economic Recovery, 194
Committee of Union and Progress (CUP). *See* CUP (Committee of Union and Progress)
continuities from Ottoman period, 4–5, 158–60, 211, 273–74
Cooper, Frederick, 8
Corm, Charles, 136, 325n103
Crawford, J. Forrest, 201, 202
cream separators, 123, 321n29
Crédit Agricole, 38–39, 288n24, 293n111, 355n39
Crédit Foncier, 39
Crédit Foncier d'Algérie et de Tunisie (CFAT), 152, 233–34, 331n206, 362nn159–160

Crédit Foncier de Syrie, 152, 233–34, 362nn159–160
Crédit Lyonnais, 331n206
Crimean War (1853–1856), 31–32
crises of 1930s. *See* Mandate rural administration, crises of 1930s
Cuinet, Vital, 306n5, 307n6
Cultivator (*Ekinci*) (journal), 108, 109–10
CUP (Committee of Union and Progress): agricultural change, 78, 97–101; publications, 1, 52; scientific agriculture, 121–28; technocrats, 24–25
currencies, 222, 358nn83–86
customs duties and tariffs
— CUSTOMS: on dyed silk, 159; exemptions list, 84, 310n45; rates, 42, 53, 261, 295n139
— TARIFFS: and "dumping" of agricultural products, 210; proposed, 244; rates, 329n174, 366n226

al-Dalati, Amin, 348n215
Damascus
— OTTOMAN ERA: agricultural education, 94–95; agricultural technologies, 111, 114; elite influence on banks, 47; experimental stations, 84; implement depots, 122–23, 126, 127
— FAYSAL ERA, 128–29
— MANDATE ERA: administrative division, 139; agricultural education, 203, 345n180; agricultural technologies, 149; government loans to farmers, 246; harvests, 226; resistance to government, 250, 370n272; revolt, 226–27, 359n106; Village Welfare Service, 203
Damascus Chamber of Agriculture, 257–58
al-Dandashi, ʿAbd al-Razzaq, 250
Dannevig, Valentine, 204–5
Danube Province, 38
Daʿuq, ʿUmar, 194, 348n217
Dayr Baʿalba, 239
Dayr al-Zor, 127, 171, 186, 230, 245, 246
De Caix, Robert, 144, 148, 204–5, 328n152, 330n183, 330n192
De Fleurac, Bonniot, 191, 347n205
De Lajudie, Abbot, 199
De Martel, Damien (Comte), 248–49, 250–52, 370n284
De Serres, Olivier, 176
De Visme, Lieutenant, 371n290
Debbané, Georges, 375n1
Debbané, Jean, 375n1
Delhumeau, Monsieur, 198
Demangeon, Albert, 217, 330n178
Demirjian, Mr., 114
Denmark, 341n114
Depolla, Mr. (Fordson tractor dealer), 117–18, 156
Deraʿa (Hawran), 127, 130, 364n198
Derri, Aviv, 48
Desfarges, Captaine, 250
development literature, 20, 267–72, 377nn28–29, 377n31
Dodge, Bayard, 201, 202, 342n126, 352n267
drought: Ottoman era, 42, 56, 126, 295n134; Mandate era, 225–26, 245–46, 359n97
Dry-Farming (Widtsoe), 177
Duma, 125
Duraffourd, Camille: appointment of, 217; assessment of taxation methods, 259–60, 373n329, 374n331, 374n333; on *mushaʿ* (collectively held) land, 356n55; on revolt, 226; Warriner's assessment of, 270

east Jordan, 260, 374n338
eastern Mediterranean: ecological zones, 134–35; geography of region, 9, 11–12, 285n47; map of botanical regions, *10*; Ottoman administrative provinces and districts, 284n22
Les Echoes de Damas, 191, 236, 247, 363n177, 368nn248–249
École Agronome de Paris, 1, 283n1
ecological limits of extraction. *See* Mandate rural administration, crises of 1930s

ecologies of extraction and provincial legibility. *See* state space and agrarian networks
Egypt, 9, 17, 287n80, 289n42, 293n111, 374n338
elite education and nature of expertise, 91–97
elite expertise and rural education: nationalist or international influence in rural schools, 188–94; rural primary education, 185–88, 189–90, 345n180, 346n181, 347n195; Salamiya School and criticism of government, 179–83; work opportunities for foreign-trained agronomists, 183–85
elites. *See also* agronomists; technocrats
— OTTOMAN ERA: in administration, 23, 37, 39; in Agricultural Bank administration, 47, 297n177; capital accumulation, 8; cooperation in agricultural infrastructure, 127; elite education and nature of expertise, 91–97; in regional councils, 27–28, 39–40; and scientific agriculture, 63, 76–79, 111–15, 319n182; scientific agriculture and local knowledge, 274–75; tax collection, 37, 45; tax collection and extortion, 30–31, 54–56, 290n52, 290nn54–55; tensions with imperial government, 24–25, 46, 65–72, 305n303, 306n321
— MANDATE ERA: as mediators between mandate authorities and cultivators, 20; reinvestment in land, 183, 344n151; resistance to government, 250–52, 257–58, 370n272
environmental management and agricultural resources, 6–8
Erzurum, 84
Euphrates region, 251, 271
experimental stations. *See* agricultural education; agricultural technologies; nurseries; Salamiya (Selimiye) Agricultural School; scientific agriculture in Ottoman era
— OTTOMAN ERA: under CUP government, 98–101, 315n116; customs exemptions for, 84, 310n45; directors, 310n46; embezzlement accusations, 310n49; establishment and funding, 82–86, 308nn27–28, 309n36, 309n38, 310n42; field staff, 84–86, *85*, 311n51, 311n54; improvements to crop varieties, 124–26, 322n42; livestock, 311n50; local specialization and model fields, 80–86; shortcomings, 88–89, 309n34; during World War I, 126–27
— MANDATE ERA: decrease in, 163; imperial interests and hierarchies of expertise, 166–71; nurseries, 167–68, 171, 194–95, 336n27; purpose, 166–71, 172–74

Fakhri Pasha, 305n309
al-Fallah, 332n213
Farmer Ahmet (head farmer), 84–85, 311n54
Faysal era (Arab government), 4, 128–35, *133*, 138, 148, 209, 324n85, 377n23
Ferguson, James, 211, 353n12
Ferid, Osman, 131, 324n83
Fikret, Tevfik, 1
Finance Ministry (Ottoman), 26–27, 123
Firestone, Yaʿakov, 304n292
Fitzgerald, Deborah, 276
Foch Orphanage, 170, 197–99, 350nn239–240, 350n244, 351n248
Foire-Exhibition trade fair (Beirut; 1921), 148–50, 330nn180–181
foreign merchants, corruption by, 36, 292n87
Forest, Mines, and Agriculture Ministry, 22–23, 50, 108
France: agrarian credit, 38–39, 288n24, 355n39; agricultural education, 341n114; agricultural ministry, 298n193; campaigners for colonialism, 3–4; currency exchange rates, 222; customs duties, 295n140; elite resistance, 38–39; land reforms, 219;

France (*continued*)
motoculture, 330n178; tax collection tactics, 369n258; tax policies, 295n140, 355n39; tractor use, 320n9; trade, 139–40, 326n121. *See also* Mandate for Syria and Lebanon
Franco-Syrian Treaty of Independence (1936), 197
French companies, 149, 330n186, 330n189
French Mandate. *See* Mandate for Syria and Lebanon
French North Africa, 18
Fuad Pasha, 36
Furn al-Showbak, 169

Gabert, Monsieur, 202
Gajar Emir, 374n333
Gariador, Abbot, 199, 351n251
Gasper, Michael, 17, 287n80
Gaulmier, J., 301n237, 344n151
Germany: agrarian credit, 38, 288n24, 293n106; agricultural education, 341n114; elite co-optation, 38; investment attempts in Syria, 319n182; land reforms, 219, 220
Ghab Valley, 9
Ghuta: agricultural assessments, 159; agricultural education, 130; attacks by National Bloc members in, 240–41; ecological zones, 134–35; experimental stations, 98, 126, 169; harvests, 226
Gibb report, 377n31
Gillet, Michel, SJ, 375n1
Goswami, Manu, 15
Gouraud, Henri, 144, 147, 148, 329n172
Great Britain, 40, 294n122, 294n124
Greater Lebanon: Agricultural Bank, 233; agricultural education, 174–75; Christians, 325n111; creation of, 135–39; currency exchange rates, 222; experimental stations, 167, 168–69, 194; revolt, 226–27; "socialization" to French priorities, 171; *terbiʿ* tax application, 358n86. *See also* Lebanon; Mandate for Syria and Lebanon
Greece, Sunn bug invasion, 358n93
Gross, Max L., 294n120
Gülhane, Edict of (1839), 25

al-Hadir, 369n262
"Hadith al-Fallah" (series of articles), 182–85
Haifa, 45–46, 48
Hakim, Carol, 325n103
Hakim, George, 358n83
al-Hakim, Hikmat, 195, 207–8, 353n1
al-Hakim, Yusuf, 129
Hakkı Pasha, 22, 50
Halkalı Agricultural School (Halkalı Ziraat Mektebi): under CUP government, 98, 315n112; establishment, 50, 87, *88*; and local knowledge, 309n30; ranking of, 91; statistics, 75–76, *76*; student body, 94, 314n92
Hama: ecological zones, 134–35; irrigation, 11, *11*
— OTTOMAN ERA: agricultural education, 94; experimental stations, 126; land distribution, 55–56, 62, 274, 301n237; "*tahmis*" method and corruption, 54–56
— MANDATE ERA: agricultural technologies, 149, 271; cotton industry, 170; economic crisis, 242–43; environmental conditions, 245; harvests, 230–31; land reform, 237; resistance to government, 253, 255, *256*, 257, 371n290, 373nn312–313; revolt, 226–27; Sunn bug invasion, 224, 225–26, 227, 228; *terbiʿ* tax, 231
Hama Chamber of Agriculture, 257–58
Hamdi Efendi, Ahmet: agricultural inspector, 91–93, 312n73; education, 313n78; model field director, 310n46; teacher, 312n73, 312nn76–77, 313nn80–81, 313n84
Hamdi Pasha, 45–46, 215
Hamidiye district, 55
Hananu, Ibrahim, 248, 330n193
Hanioğlu, M. Şükrü, 297n179

Haqqi Bey, Isma^cil, 2
Harim, 171, 228
harvests of 1870s, 42, 295n134
harvests of 1930s, 240, 364n198
al-Hasaka, 231
Hasbaya, 226–27
al-Hasibi, Subhi Bey, 96
Hawran: ecological zones, 134–35
— OTTOMAN ERA: agricultural education, 99–100; agricultural projects under CUP, 99–100, *100*; agricultural technologies, *100*, 123; experimental stations, 126; implement depots, 122–23, 126, 127; *musha^c* (collectively held) lands, 62; sale of *miri* lands to urban investors, 39–40; tax resistance, 53; wells, 99
— MANDATE ERA: agricultural education, 345n180; agricultural technologies, 271; drought, 359n97; environmental conditions, 245–46; harvests, 240, 258; revolt, 226–27, 359n106; rural discontent, 241
al-Hawrani, Wassal, 342n136
al-Hayat al-Zirai^cya, 332n213
Himadeh, Sa^cid B., 362n163
Hindiya, Henri, 373n313
Homs: ecological zones, 134–35
— OTTOMAN ERA, 122–23, 124, 126, 127
— MANDATE ERA: agricultural education, 170, 190; agricultural technologies, 149, 271; cotton industry, 170; harvests, 231; land reform, 237; resistance to government, 257; tax collection tactics, 258; tax policies, 239; water infrastructure, 12
Homs Chamber of Agriculture, 257–58
Hüdavendigar model farm, 84
Hüdavendigar Practical Agricultural School, *76*
al-Husri, Sati^c, 93, 313n85
Huvelin, Paul (mission of), 143–47

Ibish, Husayn, 374n348, 378n44
Ibish, Nuri, 348n215, 374n348
Ibn Wahshiyya, 176
Ibrahim Pasha, Jamil, 246
Idlib, 91, 207–8, 228, 237, 240
Idlib *rüşdiye* school, 91–94
^cIlm al-Din, Izzeldin, 96
imperial interests and hierarchies of expertise: Arab science of agriculture, 176–78; experimental stations, 166–71; "socialization" to French priorities, 171–76
imperial networks and private initiatives, 108–15, *109*, 318n169
Imperial Ottoman Bank, 36–37, 38, 42, 47, 293n100, 331n205
implement depots
— OTTOMAN ERA: under CUP government, 99–100; interest in, 115, 121–24, 321n27; local dynamics and state prerogatives, 77–78; prices and sales, 321nn29–30, 321n32; during World War I, 126, 127
— MANDATE ERA: failure to open, 273; sales, 170
inheritance: of land by women, 30, 290n45; of usufruct rights, 33
Institut Agricole de Beauvais, 57, 302n246
Institut national agronomique (France), 328n146
Institute of Rural Life, 200–203, 352n267
International Bank for Reconstruction and Development, 267–68
International Congresses of Agriculture, 59–60
international influence in rural schools, 188–94
International Institute of Agriculture, 60, 164–65, 303n268
International Labor Organization, 164–65
International Locust School, 229–30
Iran, Sunn bug invasion, 358n93
al-^cIrfan (journal), 332n213
irrigation: Hama, 11, *11*; Salamiya (Selimiye) area, 102, 179, 316n136
Islahat Fermanı (Reform Edict) (1856), 31–32

İslamoğlu, Huri, 32, 34
Ismail, Khedive, 293n111
Ismailis, 102, 103, 104, 191
Istanbul. *See* Halkalı Agricultural School
Italy, Sunn bug invasion, 358n93

Jabal al-Druze: administrative division, 139; Agricultural Bank, 233; agricultural education, 100; agricultural technologies, 271; drought, 225, 245, 359n97; emigration from, 254; harvests, 224, 225; land distribution, 226, 359n102; nurseries, 171; pro-French sentiment, 153; revolt, 226; Sunn bug invasion, 224
Jabal Samaan, 125, 126, 228, 231
Jabal al-Shaykh, 135
Jabla, 168
Jackson, Jesse B., 111, 112, 319n178
Janbart, Naʿim, 333n219
Janbart, Salim, 154, 333n219
Jarablus, 228, 231, 247
al-Jazaʾiri, Muhammad ʿAli: criticism of government, 157–58, 235, 363n172; on land reform, 218–20, 356n66; on tax system, 215–16, 221, 355n34
Jazira, 246, 251, 271
Jenin, 134, 290n55
Jerusalem district, *xiv*, 284n22
Johnson, Michael, 348n217
Jordan Valley (al-Ghor), 126, 134
Jubayl, 249

Karak, 62, 99, 134–35
Kaspar Bey, Nafliyan, 74, 75
al-Kayali, Abdul Rahman, 197
al-Kaylani, ʿAbd al-Qadir, 236, 243–44, 363n177, 366n220, 366n224
al-Kaylani, Nawras, 181, 189, 342n134
al-Kaylani, Nazim, 181
al-Kaylani family, 301n237, 342n136
Kâzım Kadri Bey, Hüseyin: agricultural assessments, 2–3, 128; career summary, 1–3, 283n1, 283n5; and limitations of reform, 65–72, 305n303, 305n306, 306n321, 318n169; locust invasion, 305n306; in Ottoman Agricultural Society, 61; publications, 110–111; "translation" of modernity, 287n82
Keen, B. A., 268, 269
Kemal Efendi, 92
Kevork Efendi, 49
Khankan, Yahya, 191
Khoury, Philip S., 286n59, 329n172, 344n151, 346n189, 358n85, 363n177, 368n229, 368n256, 373n313
Khuri, Faʾiz, 208, 245, 357n79
Khuri, Mohammad Abdallah, 342n136
Kiyotaki, Keiko, 290n45
Klat, Paul, 268
Konya, 82–83, 84
Kurd ʿAli, Muhammad, 301n237, 345n180
Kusayr, 226, *227*

Lagarde, 199
land laws and reforms. *See also* large landownership/owners; tax policies
— OTTOMAN ERA: and debt incursion, 55–56, 301n237, 301n239; registration and land values, 54, 300n226, 301n240; registration and surveying process, 291n75, 300n224; registration by roll-call (*yoklama*), 41, 300n224; Tanzimat reforms, 32–35, 39–41, 292n78, 294n120; *tapu* (title deed) regulations, 28–30, 33–34, 290n46, 291n70
— MANDATE ERA: cadastral service and land distribution, 216–23; goals of, 211–12, 354n18; land distribution, 226, 262, 374n348; land reform, 216–23, 226, 237–39, 262, 363–64nn186–187, 374n348; registration, 222, 357n79
land reforms in other countries, 219, 220
land tax. *See* tax policies
large landownership/owners: *agriculteurs*, 117, 319n2; debt and "workings of the land code", 55–56, 301n237, 301n239; responses to scientific agriculture, 78–79, 111–15, 319n182; as target of

Mandate reforms, 219–20, 356n64. *See also* land laws and reforms
Latakia: Agricultural Bank, 233; Bouka school, 195–97, *195*, 200, 348–49nn225–227, 349n230, 358n93; civil disobedience campaign, 365n202; currency exchange rates, 358n85; drought, 245–46; experimental stations and nurseries, 167–68, 194; harvests, 364n198; Sunn bug invasion, 358n93
Lausanne Treaty, 323n63
Lavastre, 248, 250, 251–52, 350n244
League of National Action, 250
League of Nations, 146–47, 171–72, 186, 201
Lebanon: "natural" Lebanon, 136, *137*, 138–39, 325n108. *See also* Greater Lebanon; Mandate for Syria and Lebanon
— MANDATE ERA: agricultural education, 204–6; bankruptcies, 235; debt payment, 376n16; drought, 245; economic crisis of 1930s, 249–50, 371n297; emigration from villages, 254; map, *xvi*; nurseries, 194; tax collection tactics, 251; tax policies, 369n265, 370n268; *terbiʿ* tax, 241, 242
— POST-MANDATE ERA: bank loans, 267–68, 377n24; reliance on Syrian grain, 326n117; world conditions, 267
"Lectures in Colonialism" (al-Shihabi), 272–73
Levant Trade Review, 77
Lewis, Norman N., 316n136
local knowledge: and cadastral survey, 62–63, *64*; gathered by Ottoman Agricultural Society, 61–62; at Halkalı Agricultural School, 309n30; and language of science, 17–18, 287n83; local specialization and model fields, 80–86; and science of agriculture, 78–80, 90, 125; and scientific agriculture, 274–75; tension with institutionally derived knowledge, 163–64, 172–74. *See also* agricultural education; scientific agriculture in Ottoman era; technocrats
locusts, 126, 229–30, 231, 236, 305n306, 364n198
Longrigg, Stephen, 374n345
Lyon, France, 140–42

Maara, 126, 228
Macedonia, 355n34
mahlul (uncultivated or abandoned) land, 30, 41, 102, 220
al-Majalla al-Ziraʿiya al-Suriya, 332n213
Maktab ʿAnbar school, 94–95
al-Malki, Tawfiq and Shamsi, 348n215
Manachy, Lorenzo Y., 318n169
Manbij, 231, 237–38
Mandate for Palestine and Mesopotamia, 145
Mandate for Syria and Lebanon: continuities from Ottoman period, 4–5, 158–60, 211, 273–74; currency exchange rates, 222, 358nn83–86; establishment, 5–6, 146–47, 329n173; maps, *xvi*. *See also* agrarian credit; agricultural education; agricultural technologies; Greater Lebanon; Lebanon, Mandate era; Mandate rural administration; politics of agricultural expertise; Syria, Mandate era; tax policies; technocrats
Mandate rural administration, 207–63; overview, 207–12, 261–63, 275–77, 374n345; criticism by *semaine sociale*, 264–65, 375n1, 376n4; criticism of government, 235–36, 363n172; criticism of, post-mandate, 272–73; debt crisis, 231–35, *232*; drought, 225–26, 245–46, 359n97; land reform, 216–23, 226, 237–39, 262, 363–64nn186–187, 374n348; land reform and taxation, 212–16, 354n26, 354n29; pests, 224–25, 228–31, 236, 360n125, 360n127, 361n135; revolt, 223–24, 226–27, 358n85. *See also* Sunn bug invasion
— CRISES OF 1930S: economic crisis causes, 241–43; environmental conditions, 245–46; harvests, 240, 364n198;

— CRISES OF 1930S (*continued*)
National Bloc and relief, 260–61; proposed solutions, 243–45, 366nn230–231; resistance to government, 250–61, 370n272, 370n284; Syrian government policy, 246–49, 369n262
Manuk Efendi, 49–50
Maʿoz, Moshe, 288n18
maps: agricultural institutions, *103*; and agricultural statistics, *xv*; Aleppo Province, *xii*; Beirut Province, *xiv*; eastern Mediterranean, *10*; Jerusalem district, *xiv*; mandate government of Latakia, *xvi*; mandate Sanjak of Alexandretta, *xvi*; mandate state of Jabal al-Druze, *xvi*; mandate state of Lebanon, *xvi*; mandate state of Syria, *xvi*; Mount Lebanon district, *xiv*; "natural" Lebanon, *137*; Ottoman agricultural statistics, 63, *64*; Sunn bug spread, *229*; Syria as envisioned by Faysal's government, *133*; Syria as envisioned by supporters of French expansion, *141*; Syria Expedition (Lebanon), *137*; Syria Province, *xiv*; Syria's botanical regions, *10*; Zor District, *xiii*
al-Marʾa (journal), 332n213
Mardam Bey, Jamil, 189, 244–45, 246, 248
Mardirus Efendi, 320n24
Marj Ibn ʿAmir, 134
Maronite archbishop of Damascus, 254, 255, 372n309
Marseille, France, 140–42, 154
Marseille Chamber of Commerce, 140–42, 143, 154, 327n129
marsh lands, 9, 285n47
Maysalun, Battle of, 138, 146
Mazloum, Soubhi, 375n1
Médawar, Wady, 57, 58, 59, 300n226, 303n257, 344n151
medical education, 189, 346n190
Mehmet (deputy to Aleppo education director), 312n76
Melhamé Bey, Selim, 51, 84, 97, 310n42
Méline, Jules, 60
Melkon Efendi: allegations against, 84–86, 310n46, 310n49; networks, 311n52
Melkon Efendi (provincial agricultural inspector and teacher), 95, 314n96
merchant-tractorists, 271, 378n44
MESC (Middle East Supply Center), 266–68, 277–78, 377n28
methodology and sources, 18–21
Midhat Pasha, 38
Mikhail, Alan, 287n83
Millerand, Alexandre, 138, 144–45
Ministry of the Cadastre (Tahrir-i Emlak Nezareti), 32, 39
MIRA (government grain collection agency), 267, 375n1
miri (state-owned) land: and 1858 Land Code, 32–35; sale to urban investors, 39–40, 294n120; usufruct rights in, 29–30, 289n42
Mitchell, Timothy, 16, 17
model and experimental fields. *See* experimental stations
Modern Agriculture (*al-Ziraʿa al-Haditha*). See *al-Ziraʿa al-Haditha* (*Modern Agriculture*)
Modern Practical Agriculture (al-Shihabi), 132, 134–35, 176, 177, 324n90, 377n23
modernity, science, and expertise, 16–18. *See also* elite expertise and rural education; local knowledge; politics of agricultural expertise
Monastir, 82–83
Moon, David, 307n9
Moore, Lionel, 294n122
Morocco, 18
Morse, Stanley, 112
Mosul, 358n93
Mouchahwar, Amin, 325n104, 326n112
Mount Lebanon: ecological zones, 135; maps, *xiv*
— OTTOMAN ERA: agricultural assessments (Kâzım), 2, 3; silkworm production, 9; special status, 283n7, 284n22; tax policies, 292n86
— POST–WORLD WAR I ERA, 135–36

— MANDATE ERA: agricultural resources assessment, 144; tax policies, 369n265
Mourad, Léon, 375n1
Moussalli, N., 152, 331n204
al-Mudarris, Ahmed, 371n296
Mudarris Zade, Fuad, 111–14
Mudarris Zade Zeki Paşa, 69
Muhammad bin Ahmet, 104
Muhammad bin ʿAli, 104
Mundy, Martha, 35, 300n224, 305n303
murabiʿ (type of sharecropping), 162, 335n2
Murad V (Sultan), 43
mushaʿ (collectively held) land: benefits of, 218, 304n292, 356n55; definition, 304n291; as impediment to progress, 62, 217–18; and lending practices, 63, 65, 121, 304n294
Muslimiya: experimental stations, 167, 170, 173; Foch Orphanage, 170, 197–99, 350nn239–240, 350n244, 351n248
Mustapha (Mirza) (Ismaili leader), 191

Nabateans, 176, 341n98
Nablus, 290n55
Naccache, Albert, 136, 325n104, 325n108, 325n111
Nafiʿ Pasha, 69–71
Najjar, Halim, 185, 201, 202, 345n164
Nasih Efendi, 92
National Bloc: attacks by members, 240–41; elections (1932), 242; elections (1936), 260–61; at head of government, 189, 346n189; and al-Kaylani, 342n134; moderate members forced out, 247–48; resistance to government, 250
nationalism: limits of, 368n229; as threat in rural schools, 175, 188–94, 340n95
Nationalist Youth, 250
nationalists: crisis as opportunity, 244–45, 366n231; as mediators between mandate authorities and cultivators, 20; resistance to government, 257–58
"natural" Lebanon. *See* Greater Lebanon
Nazareth, 48
Nazim Bey, 74, 75
Near East Foundation, 187, 200–201
Nebk, 126
networks: agricultural organizations, international, 59–60, 72–73; agricultural organizations, local, 58–59, 61–62, 303n258, 303n274; and knowledge production, 12–14, 286n59; and knowledge production, Ottoman era, 90; and knowledge production, Mandate era, 164, 188–89; and private initiatives, Ottoman era, 108–15, *109*, 318n169. *See also* agronomists; local knowledge; state space and agrarian networks; technocrats
1930s crises. *See* Mandate rural administration, crises of 1930s
North Africa, 340n90
Noujaim, Paul, 325n104
Nour, Risqallah, 199
Nubar Pasha, 311n52
Nureddin Efendi, 93–94, 313n84
Nuri Bey Efendi, 81, 298n190
nurseries, 167–68, 171, 191, 194–95, 336n27, 347n203. *See also* experimental stations

Obeid, Antoine Issa, 199
Office of Tithe and Livestock Tax, 44, 45
Oscan, Agop, 122, 198, 350n242, 350n244, 351n248
Ottoman Agricultural and Industrial Exhibition, 51, 299n205
Ottoman Agricultural Society, 61–62
Ottoman Agriculture and Commerce Journal, 60
Ottoman Bank, 32, 36
Ottoman Civil Service School, 187, 345n179
Ottoman empire: administrative provinces and districts, 284n22; agriculture as primary revenue source, 25, 288n9; debt, 24, 36–37; financial crisis, 42–43; fiscal exigencies of Crimean War, 31–32; state space and rural

Ottoman empire (*continued*)
communities, 14–16, 286n71. *See also* agrarian credit; agricultural education; agricultural technologies; agronomists; elites; scientific agriculture in Ottoman era; state space and agrarian networks; tax policies; technocrats
Owen, Roger, 357n79
Özbek, Nadir, 53, 72, 291n56, 292n85

Padua, 293n111
Palestine: agricultural budget, 374n338; debt payment, 376n16; ecological zones, 134–35; fixed tax, 260, 374n333; rural education, 187; summer camps, 203
Palgrave, W. Gifford, 40, 294n122
Pamuk, Şevket, 357n79
Panic of 1857 (USA), 32
Paris Chamber of Commerce, 142
Paris Peace Conference (1919), 135–36
Parmentier, Paul, 144, 150, 154, 328n146, 333n215
Pavie, Charles, 155, 265–66, 333n222, 376n9
PDA (Public Debt Administration), 24, 46, 296nn166–167, 303n264
people of capital, 54–55. *See also* elites
pesticides, 230, 360n127
pests: in development reports, 269, 377n31; locusts, 126, 229–30, 236, 305n306, 364n198; strategies against, 230–31, 360n125, 360n127, 361n135; various, 126; voles, 228–29, 360n125. *See also* Sunn bug invasion
Peyrton, Monsieur, 197, 199, 349n237
Pierre-Alype, M., 327n142
plows: demonstrations, 169, 337n40; designs, 114–15, 123; prices, 321n29, 322n38; sales, 123–24, 170
politics of agricultural expertise: overview, 162–66, 204–6; elite expertise and criticism of government, 178–83; elite expertise and political influence in rural schools, 188–94; elite expertise and rural primary education, 185–88, 189–90, 345n180, 346n181, 347n195; elite expertise and work opportunities, 183–85; imperial interests and Arab science of agriculture, 176–78; imperial interests and experimental stations, 166–71; imperial interests and "socialization" to French priorities, 171–76; influence and educating the *fallah*, 194–97; influence and Foch Orphanage, 170, 197–99, 350nn239–240, 350n244, 351n248; influence and locally managed projects, 199–204
politics of empire and agricultural exploitation, 139–47, *141*, 328n155
Ponsot, Henri, 248
post–World War II agrarian policies, 277–78
Provence, Michael, 300n224
provincial regulations: administrative restructuring, 30–31; councils, 26–28, 36–37, 43, 289n27; thwarting of reforms, 65–66; yearbooks, 37, 53, 293n96, 299n221. *See also* state space and agrarian networks; tax policies
Public Debt Administration (PDA), 24, 46, 296nn166–167, 303n264
public works capital, 28, 46, 289n31, 296nn169–170

al-Qabas (newspaper): criticism of government, 247; criticism of mandate policies, 191–92; on economic crisis, 261; on resistance to government, 252; on Salamiya School, 181–82, 189, 343n140, 346n190; on tax collection tactics, 257
Qabile neighborhood, 105
Qadari, Ahmad, 96
Qalamun, 135
Qalavas Efendi, 49
qanats (irrigation tunnels), 102, 316n136. *See also* irrigation

Quataert, Donald, 297n173, 297n180, 300n230, 308n28, 309n30, 310n42, 311n57
al-Qudsi, Kamil Pasha, 117–18, 319n3
Quwayq River, 11, 198, 228
al-Quwwatli, Shukri, 204

Raiffeisen, Friedrich-Wilhelm, 288n24
railroads, 139, 303n264, 326n120
Raqqa, 126
Ras al-ʿAyn, 169
Ras Baʿalbak, 236, 237, 250
Rashaya, 226–27
Rashid (brother of Maronite patriarch ʿArida), 200
Raslan, Mazhar, 248
reapers, 123, 321n29
Reclus, Monsieur, 202
Reform Edict (Islahat Fermanı) (1856), 31–32
Reilly, James A., 290n54, 301n239
relief efforts, 69, 305n304, 306n318
repertoires of power, 8
Reşid Bey, Ahmet, 22, 50–52, 298n194, 299n208, 299n214
Reşid Pasha, 39, 294n120
Revue de botanique appliquée et d'agriculture colonial, 154
La Revue Économique, 155, 157, 333n219
Ringelmann, Max, 176
Rıza Bey, Ahmet, 52–53, 61–62, 299n214
Roederer, Carl, 142, 327n142
Roederer, Paul, 142
rural primary education, 185–88, 345n180, 346n181
Russia: agrarian credit, 38; agricultural education infrastructure, 307n9; agricultural ministry, 298n193; Sunn bug invasion, 358n93; tax policies, 292n85
Russo-Ottoman War (1877–1878), 42, 44, 46
Rustum, Rashid, 371n296

Saadé, Edouard, 57, 303n258
Saadé, Fouad, 264–65, 375n1, 376n4
Saadé, Toufik, 57, 300n226, 302n247
al-Sabuni, Nadima, 332n213
Sadiq Bey, Yusuf, 61–62
Safad, 48
al-Safira, 369n262
Safita, 138
Saida, 36, 149
Salamiya (Selimiye) Agricultural School. *See also* agricultural education; Salamiya (Selimiye) district; Tarmanini, ʿUmar
— OTTOMAN ERA: activities, 106, 317n155; building of, 74–75; funding, 103–4, 316n142, 317n144, 317n152; rural resistance to, 75–76, 101, 102–8; statistics, *76*
— FAYSAL ERA, 130–31
— MANDATE ERA: Bériel's assessment of, 173; closure, 169, 346n190, 346n193, 366n220; conflicts with officials, 178–83, 342n136, 343nn140–142, 343–44nn144–145; curriculum, 179, 336n16, 342n121, 343n141; efforts to reopen, 190–91; experimental stations, 167; funding, 191, 343n144, 349n233; goals, 179–80, 338n47; graduates in rural administration, 187–88; lands and nurseries, 190–91, 347n203; student body, 166, *180*, 341n117, 342n126, 343n138; students in fight against locusts, 230; Sunn bug invasion, 227–28
—, POST-MANDATE ERA, 316n132
Salamiya (Selimiye) district, 55, 102–3, 179, 245, 316n136. *See also* Salamiya (Selimiye) Agricultural School
Salonica Practical Agricultural School, 87, 311n55
Salt, 126, 135
San Remo conference, 138, 146
Saumarez Smith, Richard, 35, 300n224, 305n303
Schulze-Delitzsch, Hermann, 293n106
Science Fairy, 78–79
Scientific Advisory Mission, 268
Scientific Agriculture Committee, 80–81, 307n18

scientific agriculture in Ottoman era: overview, 23–24, 74–80, 115–16, 306n5, 307n6; agricultural change under CUP, 97–101; agricultural education expansion, 86–90, 311n57; elite agronomists, 56–59; elite education and nature of expertise, 91–97; imperial networks and private initiatives, 108–15, *109*, 318n169; local specialization and model fields, 80–86; map of institutions, *103*; Salamiya Agricultural School and rural reaction, 102–8; before and during World War I, 121–28. *See also* agricultural education; agricultural technologies; agronomists; elites; experimental stations; technocrats

Selim Bey. *See* Melhamé Bey, Selim

Selimiye Agricultural School. *See* Salamiya (Selimiye) Agricultural School

semaine sociale, 264–65, 271, 375n1

Service Agricole of the Economic Office of War, 265–66

al-Shabandar, ʿAbd al-Ghani, 96

Shakib Efendi, 92

Shaw, George W., 112

Shaw, Stanford J., 288n18

al-Shihabi, al-Amir Mustafa: agricultural assessments, 326n112; appointment as director of agricultural division, 129; on Arab agricultural knowledge, 176–78; awards, 160; career summary, 340nn96–97; criticism of government, 235, 243; criticism of mandate's impact, 272–73; criticism of tax system, 213–14, 215–16, 354n26, 354n29; education, 96, 315n107; and Keen's *Agricultural Development*, 272, 378nn49–50; large landownership, 219, 356n64; *Modern Practical Agriculture*, 132, 134–35, 324n90, 377n23; nationalist agricultural development, 348n214; proponent of tractor use, 156, 157, 333n229; proponent of village schools, 350n238; reform proposals for self-sufficiency, 158–61; regional self-sufficiency and national space, 132–35; on tariff rates, 366n226

Shishakli, Ibrahim, 219

Shishakli, Khadir Abdul Rahman, 181, 191, 347n204

Shishakli, Tawfiq, 181, 342n134

shumbul, 113, *113*, 319n178

silk industry, 99, 159, 167, 168, 169

Sir al-Duniya, 249

Sivas, 82–83, 84

social differentiation and scientific agriculture, 77–80, 87–89, 94–97, 105–6, 107–8, 311n57

"socialization" to French priorities, 171–76

Société Foncier de Syrie, 331n206

Société Générale, 331n206

South American republics, 365n208

Spears Mission, 266

state space and agrarian networks: overview, 14–16, 22–25, 72–73, 273–75. *See also* agrarian credit; Agricultural Bank; agronomists; provincial regulations; tax policies; technocrats

—TANZIMAT ERA: administrative restructuring, 30–31; aims of, 23; land law, 28–30, 32–35, 39–41; needs assessment and investment, 26–28; other areas of reform, 288n12; provincial regulations, 26–28, 36–37, 43, 289n27

—HAMIDIAN ERA: overview, 43–44; agricultural organizations, international, 59–60; agricultural organizations, local, 58–59, 61–62, 303n258, 303n274; bureaucracy, 49–50, 53, 62–63, *64*, *65*; criticism of government, 50–53, 56–59; Hüseyin Kâzım and the limits of reform in Aleppo, 65–72, 305n303, 306n321; land ownership, 53–56; land registration, 48–49, 53; scientific agriculture, 56–59

Sukas, 168

Suleiman (Emir) (Ismaili deputy), 191

Sunn bug invasion: Agriculture Ministry response to, 207–8; changes in crops, 227–28, 360n118; observations, 358–59nn95–96; in other countries, 358n93; spread of, 224–26, *229*, 358n91, 358n93. *See also* pests
Supreme Council of Judicial Ordinances (Meclis-i Vala-yı Ahkam-ı Adliye), 26–27
Sur district, 36
Switzerland, 260, 320n9
Sykes-Picot Agreement, 119, 143, 331n206
Syria: botanical regions, *10*; maps, *xiv*, *xvi*, *133*, *141*. *See also* Salamiya (Selimiye) Agricultural School
— OTTOMAN ERA: administrative provinces and districts, 284n22; agricultural assessments (Kâzım), 2–3, 283n9; Agricultural Bank branches, 62; agricultural education, 91, 94–95, 126–28, 314n94; agricultural infrastructure integrated with other provinces, 79; agricultural pests, 126; agricultural projects under CUP, 99–101, 316n128; agricultural technologies, 111–12; botanical regions, *10*; harvests in 1870s, 42; harvests of wheat, 115, 319n185; land registration, 41, 53, 300n224; land registration and overvaluations, 35, 301n240; maps, *xiv*; model and experimental fields, 82–83, 88, 89, 98, 100–101, 125–26, 127, 315n116, 316n128; *musha*ᶜ (collectively held) lands, 63, 65; provincial yearbooks, 37, 53, 299n221; sale of *miri* lands to urban investors, 39–40, 294n120; "*tahmis*" method and corruption, 54–56; tax collection, 36, 45–46; tax system, 62–63
— FAYSAL ERA: agricultural education, 131; agricultural technology, 132, 324n85; maps, *133*; regional self-sufficiency and national space, 138
— MANDATE ERA: Agricultural Bank, 233; agricultural budget, 260; agricultural education, 197, 204–6; agricultural resources assessment, 143–45, 147; agricultural technologies, 150–51, *214*; cotton industry, 170; crises of 1930s, 246–49; currency exchange rates, 222; debt payment, 376n16; experimental stations, 169–71; maps, *xvi*; nationalists win elections, 242; nurseries, 194–95; resistance to government, 250–61; revolt, 226–27, 358n85; Sunn bug invasion, 207–8; *terbi*ᶜ tax, 222–23, 241, 242; tithes, 241. *See also* elite expertise and rural education; Mandate for Syria and Lebanon
— POST-MANDATE ERA: development, 267–68, 269–70, 377n31; Lebanon's reliance on Syrian grain, 326n117; world conditions, 267
Syrian Agricultural Stock Company, 193
Syrian Chambers of Agriculture, 257–58
Syrian Chambers of Commerce, 154
Syrian Revolt (1925–1927), 211–12, 354n13, 358n85
Syro-Palestinian Congress, 346n181

Taanayel, 127
Tabbah, Bichara, 375n1
Taj al-Din government, 248, 363n177, 369n260
Tal Shagib, 369n262
Tal Tuqan enterprise, 192
Talabaya, 202–3
Tamimi, Rafiq, 2
Tamir, Mustafa Bey, 345n180
Tanin newspaper, 1, 61
tapu (title deed) regulations. *See* land laws and reforms
tariffs. *See* customs duties and tariffs
Tarmanini, Saᶜid, 179, 341n118
Tarmanini, ᶜUmar: awards, 160; career summary, 374n341; criticism of foreign land-credit banks, 234; criticism of government, 236; on French instruction, 182, 343n142; on land reform, 219; on Salamiya agricultural school, 197–98, 349n233; on tax

Tarmanini, ʿUmar (*continued*)
system, 214–15; and *al-Ziraʿa al-Haditha (Modern Agriculture)*, 154, 179. See also *al-Ziraʿa al-Haditha (Modern Agriculture)*; Salamiya (Selimiye) Agricultural School

Tartus, 168, 358n93

tax policies: in other countries, 355n39. *See also* state space and agrarian networks

— OTTOMAN TANZIMAT ERA: *muhassıl* system, 26, 288n18, 290n55; *tahmis* tax, 31, 290n55; tax farming (*iltizam*), 25–26, 31, 41–42, 288n18, 291n56; tithes, 28, 30–31, 35–36, 292nn85–86

— OTTOMAN HAMIDIAN ERA: collection experiments, 44–46; critiques, 57–58; land registration and property values, 53–54; *tahmis*, 215–16; *tahmis* tax, 45–46, 53, 296n164; *tasdis*, 355n34; tax farming (*iltizam*), 44, 46, 48–49; tithes, 46, 48–49, 53, 59, 62–63, 299n221, 302n242

— MANDATE ERA: criticism of, 231–33; goals of, 354n18; *impôt foncier*, 260, 358n85, 373n329, 376n4; land reform and taxes, 212–16, 354n26, 354n29; land tax, 151–52, 331n202, 354n20, 370n268; petition for tax reduction, 249–50; political cartoon, *225*; reform proposals, 257–58, 373n319; replacement of tithe and land tax, 266; resistance to government, 250–61, 370n284, 371n290, 371nn296–297, 372nn299–300; tax collection tactics, 248–50, 251, 254–55, 257, 372n300, 372n309; *terbiʿ* tax, 215–16, 222–23, 231, 232–33, 236–37, 355n33, 355n38, 358n86, 363n179; *terbiʿ* tax and market prices, 371n297; *terbiʿ* tax reduction, 241, 242; *tertib* tax, 215, 259, 373n329; tithes, 213–14, 369n262; unified land tax, 369n265

Tayfur, Sabit, 342n136

Tayfur family, 301n237, 342n136

technicians, French, 346n181

technocratic ideas, continuity of, 4–5, 158–60, 211, 273–74

technocrats: overview, 4, 12–18, 272–78, 286n66. *See also* agricultural education; agricultural technologies; agronomists; elites; scientific agriculture in Ottoman era

— OTTOMAN ERA: in administration, 49–52; agricultural institutions, 76–77; in agricultural organizations, 59–62; critique of administration, 50–53, 57–59; education of, 56–57, 298n190, 298n193, 308n21, 308n23; influence of, 286n66; and local knowledge, 17, 80–81, 287nn82–83; local knowledge and new methods, 90; relationships with rural areas, 15–17, 286n71, 287n80; support for scientific agriculture, 73

— POST-WORLD WAR I ERA, 135–39

— MANDATE ERA: advocacy for agricultural training, 178–83; criticism of foreign land-credit banks, 234; criticism of government, 235–36; criticism of land laws, 218, 219; criticism of response to crises, 231–32; criticism of tax system, 215–16, 219–22, 259, 357n74, 374n331; economic planning, 267; and local knowledge, 163–64; nationalism and economic plan, 244; reform negotiations in early mandate, 153–60; *semaine sociale*, 264–65, 271, 375n1; support for scientific agriculture and tractor use, 119, 320n9; tensions with mandate officials, 120–21, 163–66, 209–10; work opportunities, 183–85, 344nn150–151

— POST-MANDATE ERA, 272–78

technologies. *See* agricultural technologies

tenant farming and corruption, 54–55, 301n233

Terrail, Henri, 140

The Theatre of Agriculture and the Administration of Fields (de Serres), 176
threshing, *214*
Tomeh, Ramez, 374n348
Torkomyan Efendi, 298n190
Torrens system, 220–21
tractors: challenges to use of, 155–56, 320n9, 333n229, 334n235; support for, 131–32, 168, 324n83, 324n85. *See also* agricultural technologies
trade: Ottoman era, 139–40; Mandate era, 158–59, 334n246. *See also* customs duties and tariffs
Transjordan, 203
"translation" of modernity, 17, 287n82
Tripoli, Lebanon, 149, 245
Tunisia, 142
Turkey, 260, 344n147, 374n334
Tyre, 168–69, 249–50, 358n93, 370n268

United Kingdom, 139, 326n121
United Nations, vision of development, 267
United States, 266–68, 323n60, 329n174, 331n194, 365n208
United States dollar, 358n83
urban resistance, 240, 364n197
usufruct rights, 29–30, 33, 35, 219, 289n42, 291n68

Vahan Efendi, 83, 310n46
Varbedian, T. R., 114
Village Welfare Service, 203
voles, 228–29, 360n125

Wadi al-Ajam, 125
Wakt (journal), 231, 236
Walter A. Wood company, 114
Warriner, Doreen, 268, 270–71, 272, 356n55, 378n28, 378n44
water resources, 9, 11–12, 83, 150, 309n34, 321n25
Wehr, Hans, 335n2
Weulersse, Jacques, 262
Widtsoe, John A., 112, 177
Wilhelm, Ivan, 154
Wilkinson, Richard, 294n122
women: in advanced agricultural studies, 344n147; in extension courses, 204; land inheritance, 30, 290n45
World War I, 126–27, 223, 275–76
World War II, 265–67

Yanya, 82–83
Younes, Assad, 325n104
Young, George, 300n230
Youngblood, B., 112–13
al-Yusuf, ʿAbd al-Rahman Pasha, 112, 114, 319n182, 378n44
al-Yusuf, Wajiha, 378n44
al-Yusuf family, 193, 248, 368n256

Zabadani, 53, 125
Zakariya, (Ahmad) Wasfi, 162–63, 193, 238, 335n1, 348n215
Zakarya, Khuder, 374n348
Zihni Efendi, Emin, 122, 321n25
al-Ziraʿa al-Haditha (*Modern Agriculture*): cessation of publication, 241–42, 360n118, 365n210; circulation, 332n213; on closure of Salamiya School, 189, 346n193; currency exchange rates and taxes, 358n85; dissemination of knowledge, 182–83, 344n147; on financial crisis, 231–32, *232*, 239, 242–43, 366n220; funding of, 170; on grain imports, 365n208; on locusts, 231; on need for schools, 178, 181; on pitfalls of book-derived knowledge, 162–63; reports by French officials, 154, 333n215; on rural primary education, 186; on Sunn bug invasion, 228; on taxes, 242, 365n213. *See also* Tarmanini, ʿUmar
Zor District: administrative provinces and districts, 284n22; maps, *xiii*; model and experimental fields, 98–99, 127, 323n59

STANFORD **OTTOMAN WORLD** SERIES

Critical Studies in Empire, Nature, and Knowledge

Nükhet Varlık and Ali Yaycioğlu, editors

The Stanford Ottoman World Series showcases cutting-edge interdisciplinary scholarship in Ottoman history from the thirteenth century to the nineteenth century. Books in the series are concerned with three major themes—empire, nature, and knowledge—and the connections among them. The books in this series foster ambitious and innovative scholarship and open new paths in Ottoman studies and beyond.

CPSIA information can be obtained
at www.ICGtesting.com
Printed in the USA
JSHW020510200623
43278JS00001BA/1

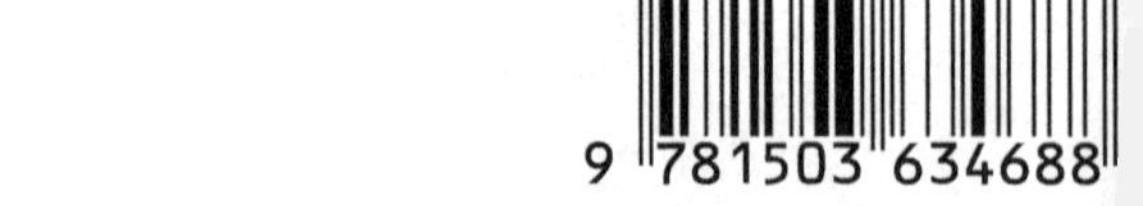